Brookings Papers
ON ECONOMIC ACTIVITY

50ᵀᴴ Anniversary

SUMMER 2020 Special Edition

COVID-19 AND THE ECONOMY
PART ONE

JANICE EBERLY

JAMES H. STOCK

Editors

DAVID H. ROMER

JUSTIN WOLFERS

Guest Editors

BROOKINGS INSTITUTION PRESS
Washington, D.C.

Copyright © 2021 by
THE BROOKINGS INSTITUTION
1775 Massachusetts Avenue, N.W., Washington, D.C. 20036

ISSN 0007-2303
ISBN: Print 978-0-8157-3904-3; ebook: 978-0-8157-3905-0

Brookings Papers
ON ECONOMIC ACTIVITY

50ᵀᴴ Anniversary

SUMMER 2020 Special Edition

COVID-19 AND THE ECONOMY
PART ONE

SESSION ONE: Labor Markets and Consumer Spending   1

TOMAZ CAJNER, LELAND D. CRANE, RYAN A. DECKER, JOHN GRIGSBY,
ADRIAN HAMINS-PUERTOLAS, ERIK HURST, CHRISTOPHER KURZ,
and AHU YILDIRMAZ
The US Labor Market during the Beginning of the Pandemic Recession   3

NATALIE COX, PETER GANONG, PASCAL NOEL, JOSEPH VAVRA,
ARLENE WONG, DIANA FARRELL, FIONA GREIG, and ERICA DEADMAN
*Initial Impacts of the Pandemic on Consumer Behavior: Evidence from
Linked Income, Spending, and Savings Data*   35

Comment by Jonathan A. Parker   70
General Discussion   78

SESSION TWO: Safety Net Programs and Poverty   83

JEEHOON HAN, BRUCE D. MEYER, and JAMES X. SULLIVAN
Income and Poverty in the COVID-19 Pandemic   85

MARIANNE P. BITLER, HILARY W. HOYNES,
and DIANE WHITMORE SCHANZENBACH
The Social Safety Net in the Wake of COVID-19   119

Comment by Abigail Wozniak   146
General Discussion   156

SESSION THREE: Emerging Market and Developing Economies 159

PINELOPI KOUJIANOU GOLDBERG and TRISTAN REED
The Effects of the Coronavirus Pandemic in Emerging Market and Developing Economies: An Optimistic Preliminary Account 161
Comments by Şebnem Kalemli-Özcan and Michael Kremer 212
General Discussion 232

SESSION FOUR: Labor Markets and the Economics
of Non-pharmaceutical Interventions 237

ALEXANDER W. BARTIK, MARIANNE BERTRAND, FENG LIN,
JESSE ROTHSTEIN, and MATTHEW UNRATH
Measuring the Labor Market at the Onset of the COVID-19 Crisis 239

SUMEDHA GUPTA, KOSALI SIMON, and COADY WING
Mandated and Voluntary Social Distancing during the COVID-19 Epidemic 269

Comments by Victor Chernozhukov and Caroline Buckee 316
General Discussion 322

SESSION FIVE: Macroeconomics and Epidemiology 327

JOSE MARIA BARRERO, NICHOLAS BLOOM, and STEVEN J. DAVIS
COVID-19 Is Also a Reallocation Shock 329
Comment by Katharine Abraham 372
General Discussion 380

DAVID BAQAEE, EMMANUEL FARHI, MICHAEL MINA,
and JAMES H. STOCK
Policies for a Second Wave 385
Comment by Daron Acemoglu 432
General Discussion 442

SESSION SIX: Federal Reserve Programs 445

MARKUS BRUNNERMEIER and ARVIND KRISHNAMURTHY
Corporate Debt Overhang and Credit Policy 447
Comment by Ben S. Bernanke 489
General Discussion 499

BPEA 50th ANNIVERSARY Special Edition

The year 2020 marks the 50th anniversary of the *Brookings Papers on Economic Activity* (*BPEA*). Since its founding in 1970, *BPEA* has published high-quality independent research on timely economic challenges using state-of-the-art empirical methods and conceptual approaches. Currently led by coeditors Janice Eberly and James Stock, *BPEA* is widely recognized as a premier economics journal with a long-standing reputation for rigorous analysis and real-world application and relevance.

As the COVID-19 pandemic ravaged the world in 2020, policymakers faced unprecedented challenges in developing adequate responses to alleviate its adverse impact on the global economy. Under this exceptional circumstance, *BPEA* immediately convened two conferences uniquely devoted to exploring the pandemic's impact on the economic activity, financial markets, and individual lives. The papers included in this volume, which were presented in June 2020 at the first of these two conferences, represents the best thinking of economists early in the pandemic. They also highlight the ability of research teams to come together in difficult times to inform public policymaking moving forward.

Ideas launched at *BPEA* often become policy soon afterward. In recent years, major findings have changed how we think about the student loan crisis, the high cost of health care, and long-term unemployment among American workers. *BPEA* research has also informed several of the Federal Reserve's most discussed tools and processes, including quantitative easing, forward guidance, and the current review of its monetary policy framework. *BPEA* addresses policy issues as they are emerging, such as the financial crisis in 2008, Brexit in 2016, and COVID-19 in 2020. It was a *BPEA* paper that identified the deepening mortality crisis due to "deaths of despair" in 2017.

For nearly half a century, *BPEA* has attracted top talent to serve as editors, authors, discussants, and advisers, including more than twenty Nobel laureates, Federal Reserve chairs, members of the President's Council of Economic Advisers, and chief economists from both public and private financial institutions. *BPEA* conferences have convened these distinguished economic experts and acted as a trusted platform for lively intellectual debate and discussion. The platform that the *Brookings Papers* creates for generating and debating policy-relevant research is as great now as it was fifty years ago, and we are committed to ensuring the continued success of this enterprise for the next fifty years.

PURPOSE The *Brookings Papers on Economic Activity* publishes research on current issues in macroeconomics, broadly defined. The journal emphasizes rigorous analysis that has an empirical orientation, takes real-world institutions seriously, and is relevant to economic policy. Papers are presented and discussed at conferences held twice each year, and the papers and discussant remarks from each conference are published in the journal several months later. Research findings are described in a clear and accessible style to maximize their impact on economic understanding and economic policymaking; the intended audience includes analysts from universities, governments, and businesses. Topics covered by the journal include fiscal and monetary policy, consumption and saving behavior, business investment, housing, asset pricing, labor markets, wage and price setting, business cycles, long-run economic growth, the distribution of income and wealth, international capital flows and exchange rates, international trade and development, and the macroeconomic implications of health care costs, energy supply and demand, environmental issues, and the education system.

We would like to thank the supporters of the Brookings Papers on Economic Activity conference and journal, including the Alfred P. Sloan Foundation; BlackRock Global Fixed Income; Brevan Howard Research Services Limited; General Motors Company; the National Science Foundation, under grant no. 1756544; and State Farm Mutual Automobile Insurance Company.

The papers and discussant remarks reflect the views of the authors and not necessarily the views of the funding organizations or the staff members, officers, or trustees of the Brookings Institution.

CALL FOR PAPERS Most papers that appear in the *Brookings Papers on Economic Activity* are solicited by the editors, but the editors also consider submitted proposals. Editorial decisions are generally made about a year in advance of each conference. Therefore, proposals should be received by December 1 for the following fall conference and by June 1 for the following spring conference. Proposals can be submitted at http://connect.brookings.edu/submit-your-paper-to-bpea.

ACCESSING THE JOURNAL All past editions of the *Brookings Papers on Economic Activity*, including versions of the figures in color—along with appendix materials, data, and programs used to generate results—are made freely available for download at www.brookings.edu/bpea/search. To purchase subscriptions or single copies, visit www.brookings.edu/press, or contact the Brookings Institution Press at (866) 698-0010 or P.O. Box 465, Hanover, PA 17331-0465. Brookings periodicals are available online through both the Online Computer Library Center (contact the OCLC subscription department at (800) 848-5878) and Project Muse (http://muse.jhu.edu). Archived issues of the *Brookings Papers on Economic Activity* are also available through JSTOR (www.jstor.org).

Janice Eberly *Northwestern University*
Wendy Edelberg *Brookings Institution*
Barry Eichengreen *University of California, Berkeley*
Eduardo Engel *University of Chile*
William B. English *Yale University*
Emmanuel Farhi *Harvard University*
Diana Farrell *JPMorgan Chase Institute*
John G. Fernald *Federal Reserve Bank of San Francisco*
Raquel Fernández *New York University*
Michael Feroli *J.P. Morgan*
James Feyrer *Dartmouth College*
Martin Fleming *IBM*
Christopher L. Foote *Federal Reserve Bank of Boston*
Kristin J. Forbes *Massachusetts Institute of Technology*
Benjamin M. Friedman *Harvard University*
John N. Friedman *Brown University*
Jason Furman *Harvard University*
William Gale *Brookings Institution*
Jordi Galí *Center for Research in International Economics*
Peter Ganong *University of Chicago*
Amy Ganz *The Aspen Institute*
Domenico Giannone *Amazon Inc.*
Karen Glenn *Social Security Administration*
Pinelopi Koujianou Goldberg *Yale University*
Austan D. Goolsbee *University of Chicago*
Robert J. Gordon *Northwestern University*
Tracy Gordon *Urban Institute*
Egor Gornostay *Peterson Institute for International Economics*
Stephen C. Goss *Social Security Administration*
Josh Gotbaum *Brookings Institution*
Carol Graham *Brookings Institution*
Megan Greene *Harvard University*
Fiona Greig *JPMorgan Chase Institute*
John Grigsby *Northwestern University*
Erica L. Groshen *Cornell University*
Jonathan H. Gruber *Massachusetts Institute of Technology*
Krishna Guha *Evercore ISI*
Sumedha Gupta *Indiana University*
Robert E. Hall *Stanford University*
James D. Hamilton *University of California, Davis*
Adrian Hamins-Puertolas *Federal Reserve Board*
Jeehoon Han *University of Chicago*
Samuel G. Hanson *Harvard University*
Joshua K. Hausman *University of Michigan*
Zhiguo He *University of Chicago*
Bart Hobijn *Arizona State University*
Douglas Holtz-Eakin *American Action Forum*
Harry Holzer *Georgetown University*
Julie L. Hotchkiss *Federal Reserve Bank of Atlanta*
Jessica S. Howell *The College Board*
Caroline Hoxby *Stanford University*
Hilary W. Hoynes *University of California, Berkeley*
Erik Hurst *University of Chicago*
Yannis M. Ioannides *Tufts University*

Charles I. Jones *Stanford University*
Lisa B. Kahn *University of Rochester*
Şebnem Kalemli-Özcan *University of Maryland*
Zeynal Karaca *Agency for Healthcare Research and Quality*
Lawrence Katz *Harvard University*
Melissa Kearney *University of Maryland*
Amit Khandelwal *Columbia University*
Anupam Khanna *NASSCOM*
Michael T. Kiley *Federal Reserve Board*
Aaron Klein *Brookings Institution*
Jeffrey Kling *Congressional Budget Office*
Amanda Kowalski *University of Michigan*
Spencer D. Krane *Federal Reserve Bank of Chicago*
Michael Kremer *Harvard University*
Arvind Krishnamurthy *Stanford University*
Sarah Kroeger *University of Notre Dame*
Randall S. Kroszner *University of Chicago*
Dirk Krueger *University of Pennsylvania*
Adriana Kugler *Georgetown University*
Christopher Kurz *Federal Reserve Board*
Greg Leiserson *Washington Center for Equitable Growth*
Nellie Liang *Brookings Institution*
Feng Lin *University of Chicago*
Deborah J. Lucas *Massachusetts Institute of Technology*
Nancy Lutz *National Science Foundation*
Dean Maki *Barclays*
Christos Makridis *Massachusetts Institute of Technology*
N. Gregory Mankiw *Harvard University*
Victoria Marone *Northwestern University*
Donald Marron *Urban Institute*
Mark Mazur *Urban-Brookings Tax Policy Center*
Warwick J. McKibbin *Australian National University*
Karel Mertens *Federal Reserve Bank of Dallas*
Bruce D. Meyer *University of Chicago*
Laurence Meyer *Monetary Policy Analytics*
Michael Miller *Social Security Administration*
Michael Mina *Harvard University*
Jeffrey Miron *Harvard University*
Robert A. Moffitt *Johns Hopkins University*
Rakesh Mohan *Yale University*
Simon Mongey *University of Chicago*
Giuseppe Moscarini *Yale University*
Jud Murchie *Wells Fargo & Company*
Emi Nakamura *University of California, Berkeley*
Vikram Nehru *Johns Hopkins University*
Christopher J. Nekarda *Federal Reserve Board*
Serena Ng *Columbia University*
Pascal Noel *University of Chicago*
Giovanni P. Olivei *Federal Reserve Bank of Boston*
Kevin O'Rourke *New York University*
Peter R. Orszag *Lazard Freres & Co. LLC*
Çağlar Özden *World Bank*
Jonathan A. Parker *Massachusetts Institute of Technology*
Evgenia Passari *Université Paris, Dauphine*

Joseph Vavra *University of Chicago*
Stan A. Veuger *American Enterprise Institute*
Alan D. Viard *American Enterprise Institute*
Gianluca Violante *Princeton University*
Annette Vissing-Jørgensen *University of California, Berkeley*
Polina Vlasenko *Social Security Association*
William L. Wascher *Federal Reserve Board*
Mark W. Watson *Princeton University*
Tara Watson *Williams College*
Beatrice Weder di Mauro *Centre for Economic Policy Research*
David Wessel *Brookings Institution*
Johannes Wieland *University of California, San Diego*
David Wilcox *Peterson Institute for International Economics*
Amy Williamson *University of Wisconsin-Madison*
Jon Willis *Federal Reserve Bank of Atlanta*
Coady Wing *Indiana University*
Sarah Wolfe *Morgan Stanley*
Justin Wolfers *University of Michigan*
Arlene Wong *Princeton University*
Abigail Wozniak *Federal Reserve Bank of Minneapolis*
Constantine Yannelis *University of Chicago*
Haocheng Ye *Massachusetts Institute of Technology*
Janet Yellen *Brookings Institution*
Ahu Yildirmaz *Automatic Data Processing Research Institute*
Ellen Zentner *Morgan Stanley*
Yulia Zhestkova *University of Chicago*

Francisca P. Alba *Brookings Institution*
Zachary Babat *Brookings Institution*
Cayli Baker *Brookings Institution*
Siobhan Drummond *Brookings Institution*
Grace Edna *Brookings Institution*
Claire Haldeman *Brookings Institution*
Stephanie K. Holzbauer *Brookings Institution*
Mary E. King *Brookings Institution*
Payce Madden *Brookings Institution*
Jimmy O'Donnell *Brookings Institution*
Tyler Powell *Brookings Institution*
David Skidmore *Brookings Institution*

SESSION ONE
Labor Markets and Consumer Spending

TOMAZ CAJNER
Federal Reserve Board

LELAND D. CRANE
Federal Reserve Board

RYAN A. DECKER
Federal Reserve Board

JOHN GRIGSBY
University of Chicago

ADRIAN HAMINS-PUERTOLAS
Federal Reserve Board

ERIK HURST
University of Chicago

CHRISTOPHER KURZ
Federal Reserve Board

AHU YILDIRMAZ
Automatic Data Processing, Inc.

The US Labor Market during the Beginning of the Pandemic Recession

ABSTRACT Using weekly administrative payroll data from the largest US payroll processing company, we measure the evolution of the US labor market during the first four months of the global COVID-19 pandemic. After aggregate employment fell by 21 percent through late April, employment rebounded somewhat through late June. The reopening of temporarily shuttered businesses contributed significantly to the employment rebound, particularly for smaller businesses. We show that worker recall has been an important component of recent employment gains for both reopening and continuing businesses. Employment losses have been concentrated disproportionately among lower wage workers; as of late June employment for workers in the lowest wage quintile was still 20 percent lower relative to mid-February levels. As a result, average base wages increased between February and June, though this increase arose entirely through a composition effect. Finally, we document that businesses have cut nominal wages for almost 7 million workers while forgoing regularly scheduled wage increases for many others.

Conflict of Interest Disclosure: The authors and discussant did not receive financial support from any firm or person for this paper or from any firm or person with a financial or political interest in this paper. They are currently not officers, directors, or board members of any organization with an interest in this paper. Automatic Data Processing, Inc. (ADP) reviewed the paper to ensure privacy protection of its clients and to ensure it did not contain proprietary information. The views expressed in this paper are those of the authors and do not necessarily reflect those of ADP, the Federal Reserve Board, or the University of Chicago.

3

W e use administrative data from Automatic Data Processing, Inc. (ADP)—one of the world's largest providers of cloud-based human resources management solutions—to measure detailed changes in the US labor market during the first few months of the Pandemic Recession.[1] In the current pandemic, data from ADP have many advantages over other data sources. First, ADP processes payroll for about 26 million US workers each month (about 20 percent of total US private employment). As discussed in Cajner and others (2018, 2020) and Grigsby, Hurst, and Yildirmaz (forthcoming), the ADP data are representative of the US workforce along many labor market dimensions. First, the sample sizes are orders of magnitudes larger than most household surveys, which measure individual labor market outcomes at monthly frequencies. Second, the ADP data are available at weekly frequencies. As a result, statistics on the labor market can be observed in almost real time. This facilitates high-frequency analysis such as examining employment responses when states lift closure restrictions on certain industries. Third, the ADP data link to both workers and firms, which permits study of worker recall. The data also include worker and firm characteristics that allow for the estimation of the distributional effects of the recession across demographic group, industry, firm size, and location. Finally, the data include administrative measures of wages that are free from measurement error, facilitating the study of nominal wage adjustments. Collectively, the ADP data allow for a detailed analysis of high-frequency changes in labor market conditions in the first months of the current Pandemic Recession, complementing the data produced by US statistical agencies.

We find that paid US private sector employment declined by 21 percent between mid-February and late April 2020 and then rebounded partially thereafter. As of late June, US employment was still 13 percent below February levels. About 30 percent of the employment decline through mid-April was driven by business shutdowns. However, some of these businesses started coming back during May and June, albeit at a smaller size. About one-third of the increase in US paid employment since the late April trough can be attributed to the reopening of businesses that

---

1. Importantly, our series are constructed from the ADP micro data and are distinct from the National Employment Report (NER), the monthly employment series published jointly by ADP and Moody's which has the goal of predicting Bureau of Labor Statistics (BLS) employment numbers. The ADP micro data tracked the last recession remarkably well; online appendix figure A1 shows that monthly employment changes using ADP micro data closely match the monthly employment changes reported in the BLS's Current Employment Statistics (CES) survey during the fifteen years prior to the Pandemic Recession.

temporarily closed. Employment declines through April were largest for businesses with fewer than fifty employees, with closures and reopenings playing an even larger role for this size group. We also document that reentering businesses are primarily bringing back their original employees. Finally, we find that despite a staggering 50 percent of all continuing businesses substantively shrinking between February and June, over 10 percent of businesses actually grew during this time period.

Importantly, we also show employment declines were disproportionately concentrated among lower wage workers. Segmenting workers into wage quintiles, we show that more than 35 percent of all workers in the bottom quintile of the wage distribution lost their job—at least temporarily—through mid-April. The comparable number for workers in the top quintile was only 9 percent. Through late June, bottom quintile workers still had employment declines of 20 percent relative to February levels, but many previously nonemployed workers had been recalled to their prior employer. We also find that employment declines were about 4 percentage points larger for women than for men. Very little of the differences across wage groups or gender can be explained by business characteristics such as firm size or industry. Finally, we show that states that reopened earlier had larger employment gains in the reopening sectors.

The massive decline in employment at the lower end of the wage distribution implies meaningful selection effects when interpreting aggregate data. For example, we document that average wages of employed workers rose sharply—by over 6 percent—between February and April, consistent with official data. However, all of this increase is due to the changing composition of the workforce. After controlling for worker fixed effects, worker base wages during the beginning of the recession have been flat. Moreover, we find evidence that businesses were much less likely to increase the wages of their workers and slightly much more likely to cut the wages of their workers during the first four months of the Pandemic Recession. We find that nearly 7 million continuously employed workers received a nominal wage cut between March and June 2020.[2]

---

2. Our paper complements many recent papers that use a variety of different data sources to track labor market outcomes during the recent recession. A sampling of those papers includes Bartik, Bertrand, Cullen and others (2020), Bartik, Bertrand, Lin and others (2020), Barrero, Bloom, and Davis (2020), Bick and Blandin (2020), Brynjolfsson and others (2020), Chetty and others (2020), Dingel and Neiman (2020), Coibion, Gorodnichenko, and Weber (2020), Kahn, Lange, and Wiczer (2020), and Kurmann, Lalé, and Ta (2020). As discussed above, our ADP data have advantages over the data used in many of these other papers in that they are nationally representative, have large sample sizes, track both employment and

I. Data and Methodology

We use anonymized administrative data provided by ADP. ADP is a large international provider of human resources services including payroll processing, benefits management, tax services, and compliance. ADP has more than 810,000 clients worldwide and now processes payroll for more than 26 million individual workers in the United States per month. The data allow us to produce a variety of metrics to measure high-frequency labor market changes for a large segment of the US workforce. A detailed discussion of the data and all variable definitions can be found in the paper's online appendix.

We use two separate anonymized data sets—one measuring business-level outcomes and another measuring employee-level outcomes—to compute high-frequency labor market changes. The business-level data set reports payroll information during each pay period. Each business's record is updated at the end of every pay period for each ADP client.[3] The record consists of the date payroll was processed, employment information for the pay period, and many time-invariant business characteristics such as North American Industry Classification System (NAICS) industry code. Business records include both the number of paychecks issued in a given pay period ("paid" employees) and the total number of individuals employed ("active" employees). Paid employees include any workers issued regular paychecks during the pay period as well as those issued bonus checks or any other payments. Active employees include paid employees as well as workers with no earnings in the pay period (such as workers on unpaid leave or workers who are temporarily laid off).

The data begin in July 1999 but are available at a weekly frequency only since July 2009. As shown in Cajner and others (2018), ADP payroll data appear to be quite representative of the US economy; the data modestly overrepresent the manufacturing sector and large businesses, but we emphasize that coverage is substantial across the entire industry and size distribution. While some forms of selection into ADP cannot be

---

wages, and allow for the joint matching of individual workers to individual businesses. For overlapping questions, our findings are mostly similar to the results in these other papers. When results differ, we discuss further in the text.

3. Note that we use the terms *business* and *firm* throughout the paper to denote ADP clients. Often, entire firms contract with ADP. However, sometimes establishments or units within a firm contract separately. The notion of business in our data is therefore a mix of US Census Bureau notions of an establishment (i.e., a single operating business location) and a firm (i.e., a collection of establishments under unified operational control or ownership).

observed (i.e., certain types of firms choose to contract with ADP), we ensure representativeness in terms of observables by reweighting the data to match Statistics of U.S. Businesses (SUSB) employment shares by firm size and two-digit NAICS industry; a further discussion can be found in the online appendix. For businesses that do not process payroll every week (for example, businesses whose workers are paid biweekly), we create weekly data by assuming the payroll in the missing intermediate period is what is observed in the next period for which the business processes payroll. We then build a weekly time series of employment for each business.[4]

The business-level data report payroll aggregates for each business. For a very large subset of businesses, we also have access to their anonymized de-identified individual-level employee data.[5] That is, we can see detailed anonymized payroll data for individual workers. As with the business data, all identifying characteristics (names, addresses, etc.) are omitted from our research files. Workers are provided an anonymized unique identifier by ADP so that they may be followed over time. We observe various additional demographic characteristics such as the worker's age, gender, tenure at the business, and residential state location. We also can match the workers to their employer. As with the business-level data described above, we can observe the industry and business size of their employer.

The benefits of the employee data relative to the business data described above are threefold. First, we can explore employment trends by worker characteristics such as age, gender, initial wage levels, and worker residence state. This allows us to discuss the distributional effects of the current recession across different types of workers. Second, the individual-level data allow us to measure additional labor market outcomes such as worker wages as well as recall rates of a given worker as businesses start to reopen. Finally, the panel structure of the data permits analysis of individual wage dynamics. In all the work that follows, we will indicate whether we are

---

4. The methodology we adopt for this paper differs slightly from that used in our previous work with the ADP business-level data (see, for example, Cajner and others 2018, 2020). In particular, in light of the extreme employment changes during the beginning of the Pandemic Recession, in the present work we do not seasonally adjust the data, and we measure employment changes of surviving businesses, closing businesses, and reopening businesses relative to mid-February levels rather than constructing longer-term time series.

5. Unlike the business-level data, the data for our employee sample skew toward employees working in businesses with at least fifty employees. These are the same data used in Grigsby, Hurst, and Yildirmaz (forthcoming). While the data come from employees mostly in businesses with more than fifty employees, there is representation in these data for employees throughout the business size distribution. Again, we weight these data so that they match aggregate employment patterns by industry and firm size from the SUSB.

Figure 1. Aggregate Paid and Active Employment

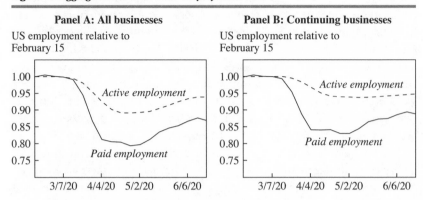

Panel A: All businesses   Panel B: Continuing businesses

US employment relative to February 15

US employment relative to February 15

Source: ADP anonymized payroll records and authors' calculations.

Notes: The solid black line in panel A shows the trend in paid payroll employment for all businesses. The dashed black line in panel A shows the trend in active employment for all businesses. Panel B shows the same patterns for businesses that continually make scheduled payroll payments throughout the entire sample period starting on February 15.

using the business-level data or the employee-level data for our analysis. Unless indicated otherwise, we report weighted results.[6]

II. Employment Changes in the Pandemic Recession

This section presents weekly labor market indexes in the United States compiled from the ADP business-level micro data. Panel A of figure 1 shows our estimated aggregate employment changes spanning the payroll week covering February 15 through late June.[7] Importantly, this panel shows employment changes at both continuing businesses and businesses that have shut down (i.e., those not issuing any paychecks during regularly scheduled pay periods), where shutdowns could reflect either permanent or temporary inactivity. The indexes plot employment levels relative to

6. For all aggregate results, the weighted employment changes found in both data sets are nearly identical during the beginning of the Pandemic Recession.

7. For all figures based on the business-level data, we report two-week trailing moving averages to smooth through volatility that results from offsetting pay frequencies across ADP businesses, the majority of which are biweekly but not all occurring on the same weeks. Also, these results—like all results in the paper—are weighted to match SUSB employment (treating the ADP businesses as firms). In the online appendix, we show results weighting to match Quarterly Census of Employment and Wages employment (treating the ADP businesses as establishments).

February 15 levels without seasonal adjustment. The figure shows the evolution for paid employees (solid line) and active employees (dashed line). Between mid-February and the labor market trough in late April, paid employment in the United States fell by 20.6 percent, and active employment fell by about 11 percent. The sharper drop in paid employment is to be expected if many businesses initially placed their workers on temporary layoff. Since mid-April, paid employment has increased by 7.4 percentage points through June 20. However, as of late June, paid employment in the United States was still about 13 percent below its level at the start of the recession. Importantly, the bulk of the rebound occurred in May, and the pace of job gains slowed measurably toward the end of June. As we highlight below, the employment increases from mid-April until the end of June are associated with many states starting to reopen their businesses.

The job loss numbers in the ADP data are broadly consistent with employment data published in the BLS's Current Employment Statistics (CES) survey for overlapping weeks. The CES, which measures employment during the week containing the twelfth of the month, estimated private employment declines of 1 million in March and 18.9 million in April, followed by rebounds of 3.7 million in May and 5.4 million in June (not seasonally adjusted). In our measure of total paid employment, focusing on the pay periods corresponding with CES reference weeks, we observe employment declines of about 1.2 million in March and 23.9 million in April followed by rebounds of 3.8 million in May and 5.3 million in June.[8]

Panel B of figure 1 shows employment losses for continuing businesses. We define continuing businesses in a given week as those businesses who have continually made scheduled payroll payments between February 15 and that week. Notice that paid employment for continuing businesses declined by 16.9 percent through late April before rebounding through late June, leaving paid employment 11.2 percent below mid-February levels. The differences between panels A and B highlight the importance of firm closures (which may be temporary) in driving employment declines through late April and the importance of those firms reopening in driving the increase in employment during May and June. Continuing firms accounted for about three-quarters of the employment losses through late

---

8. These numbers were computed using our estimated employment declines multiplied by total US private sector employment in February 2020. The corresponding numbers for active employment were −0.7 million, −13.1 million, +1.6 million, and +4.4 million for March, April, May, and June, respectively.

Figure 2. Employment Change by Business Size

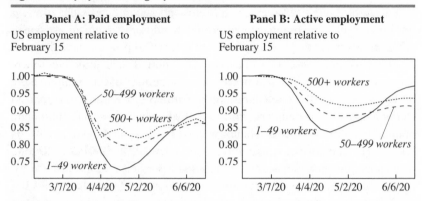

Source: ADP anonymized payroll records and authors' calculations.

Notes: Panel A shows the trend in payroll employment for each size grouping. Panel B shows the same patterns for active employment.

April. We further explore the importance of business shutdown and reentry to aggregate employment trends in section V.

It is worth mentioning the active employment series shown in figure 1. Recall that active employment measures the number of workers in payroll databases, including those not receiving pay in a given pay period.[9] Active employment among *continuing* businesses actually declined by about 0.5 million jobs between the April and May CES reference periods while other measures showed gains; in other words, businesses in continuous operation trimmed their active employees in the payroll databases, on net, even while aggregate paid employees increased. This pattern hints at important gross employment flows underlying the net numbers we highlight: even while employment has resumed net growth (driven largely by the return of temporarily inactive workers), many businesses were shedding jobs.

Much attention has been given to the preservation of small businesses in the current recession. The roughly $2 trillion stimulus package signed into law on March 27 made special provisions to support small businesses through a large expansion in federal small business loans, and a second tranche of small business loan appropriations was signed on April 24. Figure 2 plots the change in employment by initial business size relative to February 15. The figure shows that businesses with fewer than fifty

---

9. Importantly, we do not observe active employment of firms not issuing paychecks; that is, active employment is necessarily zero among firms that have shut down.

employees reduced both paid employment (panel A) and active employment (panel B) at a faster rate than their larger counterparts throughout March and April. However, businesses of all sizes saw massive employment declines during the first few months of the current recession. Businesses with fewer than fifty employees saw paid employment declines of more than 25 percent through April 18, while those with between fifty and 500 employees and those with more than 500 employees, respectively, saw declines of 15–20 percent during that same time period and reached troughs a week or two later than the smallest businesses.[10] Notably, the growth in paid employment since late April has been much larger for smaller businesses. Between late April and late June, smaller businesses increased employment by 17 percent (of February 15 levels). Businesses with more than fifty employees increased employment by between 4 percent and 7 percent during the same time period. As employment is rebounding, it is the smaller firms that are primarily increasing employment. Again, as we highlight below, much of this differential growth for smaller firms is due to the reopening of smaller firms that temporarily shuttered during the state-imposed shutdowns.

Figure 2 hides interesting heterogeneity across businesses even within size classes. In figure 3, we report the entire distribution of employment changes within and across business size classes, limiting our focus to businesses that survive through this time period (continuers) so we can study a meaningful growth distribution. For each initial employment size class, we report percentiles of employment change between February 15 and June 20, where percentiles are constructed from the employment-weighted business distribution.

Starting on the left-hand side of figure 3, the tenth percentile business within every size class saw declines of at least 50 percent, with the largest class (at least 500 employees) seeing a decline of about 98 percent. These are large firms that essentially shut down, keeping only a handful of original employees on payroll. Even the smallest business size class (1–49) saw substantial declines. The facts that small businesses saw even more overall employment declines (as highlighted in figure 2) and employment changes in the bottom decile of continuing firms were smaller for small businesses suggest that most of the total decline in employment for

10. The somewhat jagged variation in employment changes for the larger businesses is an artifact of the heterogeneity of varying payroll frequencies. In our employee-level data, we can control for the pay frequency of a given worker exactly and such small week-to-week variations are smoothed out.

Figure 3. The Distribution of Employment Change by Business Size among Survivors

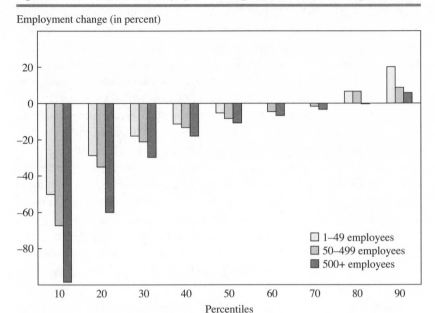

Employment change (in percent)

Percentiles

- ☐ 1–49 employees
- ◻ 50–499 employees
- ■ 500+ employees

Source: ADP anonymized payroll records and authors' calculations.
Notes: Shutdown businesses are excluded. Change in employment is measured between February 15 and June 20.

businesses with fewer than fifty employees is due to business closures. Conversely, all business size groups experienced positive growth at the ninetieth percentile. Even during the Pandemic Recession, some firms added net employment.

Between the extremes, we also observe a wide range of businesses whose employment is close to unchanged. Among the smallest size group at least 10 percent of businesses had little employment change (those spanning the sixtieth through the seventieth percentiles). Similarly a large swath of midsize and larger businesses experienced only modest changes (those spanning the sixtieth through the eightieth percentiles saw changes of less than 7 percent). Taken together, figure 3 reveals striking heterogeneity in the experiences of businesses, even within size classes.[11] The

11. We observe qualitatively similar results when focusing on active employment instead of paid employment, though the distribution of changes in all directions is notably narrower.

Table 1. Paid Employment Changes by Industry (in percent)

Industry	Feb 15–April 25	Feb 15–June 20
Arts, Entertainment and Recreation	−50.7	−31.7
Accommodation and Food Services	−45.4	−26.8
Retail Trade	−28.9	−17.5
Other Services	−25.1	−14.6
Transportation and Warehousing	−21.8	−20.5
Real Estate, Rental and Leasing	−21.0	−16.9
Information Services	−17.7	−11.3
Wholesale Trade	−17.5	−12.8
Administrative and Support	−16.8	−15.5
Health Care and Social Assistance	−16.5	−10.3
Educational Services	−16.2	−18.9
Construction	−13.8	−4.0
Manufacturing	−12.6	−10.4
Professional, Scientific, and Tech Services	−12.1	−8.3
Finance and Insurance	−1.2	−4.9

Source: ADP anonymized payroll records and authors' calculations.

Notes: Total decline (inclusive of shutdowns) in paid employment for all firms in each two-digit NAICS industry. All changes are relative to February 15, 2020. Data from the business-level sample. Weekly data (without two-week moving average).

median surviving small businesses (less than fifty employees) declined 5 percent, while the medium and large business median declines were 8 and 11 percent, respectively.

The results by firm size are not overly surprising in light of the industry results documented next. The industries that were hit hardest in the beginning of the Pandemic Recession also tend to be the industries with the smallest businesses as documented by Hurst and Pugsley (2011). Table 1 shows employment changes by two-digit NAICS industries during two time periods: February 15 to April 25 (the aggregate employment trough, prior to states starting to reopen) and February 15 to June 20 (i.e., the entire period). These results are shown in columns 1 and 2 of the table, respectively. The largest declines in employment were in sectors that require substantive interpersonal interactions. Through late April, paid employment in both the arts, entertainment and recreation and accommodation and food services sectors (i.e., leisure and hospitality) fell by more than 45 percent while employment in retail trade fell by almost 30 percent. The other services industry, which includes many local or neighborhood businesses like laundromats and hair stylists, also experienced declines in employment of 25.1 percent through late April. Despite a boom in emergency care treatment within hospitals, the health care and social assistance industry experienced a 16.5 percent decline in employment through late April. Industries that employ higher-educated workers—like finance and insurance—saw smaller initial employment declines.

Since bottoming out in late April, most sectors have seen some recovery in employment. Much of the relatively larger increases are in sectors where reopenings have occurred. For example, most states started reopening manufacturing and construction sectors in early May. These sectors saw employment gains of about 20 percent and 70 percent, respectively, of their initial employment losses. Large recoveries are also seen in some of the sectors that experienced the largest initial declines, such as accommodation and food services, retail trade, and other services. Businesses in these three sectors started opening up during May as many states started to lift restrictions on restaurants, retail outlets, and personal service businesses such as barbershops, beauty parlors, and nail salons. Despite states reopening and employment rebounding slightly, employment in these sectors still remains significantly depressed relative to mid-February levels. Notice that, as travel remained depressed and schools remained closed, employment in the transportation and education sectors had not seen the rebound found in retail trade or food services through June 20. Another sector which saw a large rebound is health care and social assistance, which recovered nearly 40 percent of lost employment by the end of June as hospitals and other health providers have attempted to start returning to normal activities.[12]

III. Distributional Effects across Workers

In this section, we document the heterogeneity in job loss across different types of workers using our employee sample. We begin by exploring the labor market outcomes for workers at different points of the base wage distribution at the beginning of the current downturn. We first segment workers by their initial place in the wage distribution. Specifically, we use early February data to define wage quintiles for our analysis based on a worker's administrative base hourly wage. We pool together hourly and salaried workers when making our quintiles. For hourly workers, we use their exact hourly wage. For salaried workers, we assume they work forty hours per week when computing their hourly wage. For weekly (biweekly) salaried individuals, this is just their weekly (biweekly) base administrative

---

12. In the online appendix, we provide a table of the weekly employment and wage changes by two-digit sector from February through June to facilitate the calibration of various models of the Pandemic Recession.

Figure 4. Employment Changes by Initial Wage Quintile and Gender

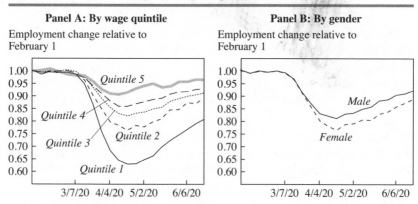

Source: ADP anonymized payroll records and authors' calculations.
Notes: Employment declines measured relative to early February. Data for this figure use the employee-level sample.

contracted earnings divided by 40 (80). We hold these thresholds fixed throughout all other weeks of our analysis. The nominal thresholds for the quintiles are $13.50, $16.41, $24.53, and $32.45 per hour.[13]

Panel A of figure 4 shows the employment changes for workers in different wage quintiles relative to early February. As seen from the figure, employment declines in the initial stages of this recession are disproportionately concentrated among lower wage workers. Workers in the bottom quintile of the wage distribution experienced a staggering 37 percent decline in employment between early March and late April. Employment for this group had partially rebounded through late June, but their employment remained depressed by roughly 20 percent relative to mid-February levels. Conversely, employment of workers in the top quintile of the wage distribution declined nearly 10 percent through the end of April. Only about 4 percent of these top earning workers remained out of work through late June. The employment losses during the Pandemic Recession have been disproportionately concentrated among lower wage workers.

13. These cutoffs match well the distribution of wages in the 2019 March Supplement of the Current Population Survey (CPS). Computing hourly wages as annual earnings last year divided by annual hours worked last year, the twentieth, fortieth, sixtieth, and eightieth percentile of hourly wages (measured in nominal dollars per hour) in the 2019 CPS were $12.00, $17.10, $24.00, and $36.10 (authors' calculation).

How much of the larger decline in employment among low-wage workers can be attributed to the industrial composition of the COVID-19 shock? Low-wage workers are more likely to work in restaurants, retail, and leisure services and are also more likely to work in smaller businesses. To assess whether differential exposure to the recession by business characteristics (industry and business size) or worker characteristics (age and location) can explain the differential pattern across either gender or the wage distribution, we further exploit the panel nature of our data and estimate a linear probability model of monthly employment for a given worker at a given firm on wage quintile dummies and detailed controls for industry and business size.[14] Specifically, we measure whether the employee is paid at that firm at the beginning of each given month.

The baseline separation probability between February and March is 6.1 percentage points higher for bottom quintile earners than for top quintile earners. After controlling for only wage quintile fixed effects, bottom quintile earners were 21.5 percentage points less likely to be employed by their February employer in the first two weeks of April relative to top quintile earners, reflecting the patterns in panel A of figure 4. Including industry and firm size fixed effects reduces the gap in excess separation rates between bottom quintile earners and top quintile earners only slightly to 19.1 percentage points. Therefore, a differential firm size and industry mix can explain 12.2 percent (1 − 19.1/21.5) of the gap in job loss between low-wage and high-wage workers during the beginning of this recession, but a substantial gap remains even after accounting for firm size and industrial composition. However, including controls for worker age further reduces the gap in excess separation probabilities between low-wage and high-wage workers to 16.5 percentage points. As highlighted in the online appendix, younger workers were more likely to be displaced during the early part of the recession, and younger workers systematically have lower wages. Overall, we conclude that there is a substantial difference in the behavior of low- and high-wage workers during the early stages of the Pandemic Recession. Only a small part of these differences can be accounted for by differences in industry, business size, and age.

Panel B of figure 4 plots employment changes by gender. Through late April, women experienced a decline in employment that was 4 percentage points larger than men (about 22 percent versus 18 percent). The gap

---

14. The online appendix discusses the details of this specification as well as plotting the coefficients and standard errors from the regression output.

remained roughly constant through late June. These patterns stand in sharp contrast to prior recessions where men experienced larger job declines. Historically, male-dominated industries such as construction and manufacturing contract the most during recessions. However, as noted above, this recession is hitting a different set of industries, including retail, leisure, and hospitality industries. Can the differential industry declines explain the gender differences in employment losses? In the online appendix, we again exploit the panel nature of our data to assess this question. Less than half a percentage point of the 4–5 percentage point difference can be explained by industry. In other words, even within detailed industries, women are experiencing larger job declines relative to men. The fact that industry or other firm characteristics do not explain the gender difference in employment declines is interesting in its own right. Future research using household level surveys with additional demographic variables can explore whether other facets of the pandemic—such as the increased need for child care—explains some portion of the gender gap in employment losses during this recession.

IV. Wage Changes during the Pandemic Recession

Figure 5 shows the trends in wages in the economy during the pandemic recession. The solid line creates a wage index by measuring the mean contract per period wage rate of all working individuals in the economy.[15] Since the start of the recession, observed average wages in the ADP sample grew by nearly 6 percent through mid-May. As highlighted in Solon, Barsky, and Parker (1994), the changing composition of workers over the business cycle can distort measures of wage cyclicality.[16] As seen from panel A of figure 4, workers at the bottom of the wage distribution were much more likely to have employment reductions than those at the top of the wage distribution. From March through the end of April, the sample became more selected toward higher-earning individuals, while the reverse happened thereafter.

---

15. Contract per period wages are the contracted per hour wage rate for workers paid hourly and the contracted per period weekly or biweekly earnings for salaried workers (depending on pay frequency). The online appendix outlines the wage concept in greater detail.

16. Grigsby (2019) documents that measured growth in average wages has become countercyclical during the last few recessions. He documents that the changing selection of workers during the recent recessions has been responsible for the observed countercyclicality of wages.

Figure 5. Trend in Base Wages, Controlling for Selection

Average US wage relative to February 15

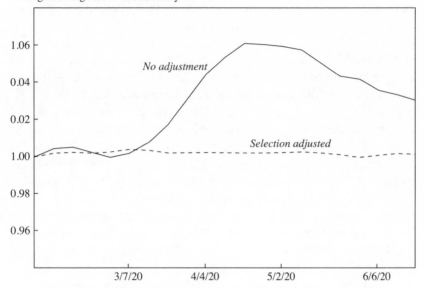

Source: ADP anonymized payroll records and authors' calculations.
Notes: The solid line averages base wages across all employed workers in each period. The dashed line controls for selection by measuring the base wage of a given worker over time.

To assess the importance of this selection, we again exploit the panel nature of the ADP data. In particular, we compute individual wage growth for a sample of continuing workers between pay periods t and $t + 1$. By considering individual wage *growth* rather than *levels*, we restrict attention to workers who are in the sample in consecutive periods, thereby purging the wage series of the principal form of selection. We then produce a selection-adjusted wage index by chain-weighting this average wage growth from the reference week ending February 15. The result of adjusting for selection in this way is shown in the dashed line in figure 5. Two things are of note. First, despite the rapid nominal wage growth for the average employed worker (solid line), there is essentially no nominal wage growth for continuing workers during this period (dashed line). In other words, all of the observed aggregate wage growth is due to selection. Second, the selection effects are largest through late April when employment declines were largest. Since late April there has been a decline in aggregate average unadjusted wages as employment has disproportionately increased for lower wage workers. These patterns also reveal themselves within industries. In the online appendix, we present employment, mean base wage, and selection-adjusted wage indexes by two-digit NAICS industry. In every industry, selection-adjusted base wages are much flatter than average wages, with the selection-adjusted wage falling in many industries. The flat composition-adjusted wages in figure 5 suggest that nominal wage growth has actually slowed. Normally, over a period of a few months, nominal wages increase as some workers receive their regularly scheduled wage adjustments, while wage cuts are exceedingly rare.

This was not the case at the beginning of the Pandemic Recession. Figure 6 provides a summary comparison of the employee wage adjustment patterns in 2019 (darker bars) and 2020 (lighter bars). Panel A plots the share of continuously employed workers who receive a base wage cut in our sample. Specifically, it plots the share of workers who were employed with a given firm in both March and June who saw declines in their base per period pay rate between March and June. The first column shows that 6.2 percent of these workers saw wage declines between March and June of 2020. This stands in stark contrast to the patterns for 2019, when just 1.6 percent of workers saw wage cuts between these same months. Base wage cuts are a remarkable feature of the labor market in the Pandemic Recession.

Of course, many workers separated from their job over this time period. Overall, we find that 5.3 percent of all workers in our sample who were employed in March (regardless if they remained employed through June) saw a base wage cut between March and June. Given that total US employment at the beginning of March was 128 million workers, this amounts to approximately 6.8 million workers receiving base wage cuts in addition to the tens of millions more who lost their job.

Of course, firms may choose to forgo scheduled wage increases without actually cutting workers' wages. Studying such wage freezes is made more complicated by the fact that most continuously employed workers only receive one base wage change per year (Grigsby, Hurst, and Yildirmaz forthcoming). However, as highlighted in Grigsby, Hurst, and Yildirmaz (forthcoming), most firms adjust their base wages annually in a given month. For example, some firms always provide annual base wage adjustments in April while others do their adjustments in July. To study wage freezes during the beginning of the Pandemic Recession, we create a sample of firms who made at least 75 percent of their 2019 base wage changes in March, April, May, or June. These are firms for which March through June are their normal base wage adjustment months.

Figure 6. Probability of Base Wage Cuts and Freezes in 2019 and 2020
by Base Wage Quintile

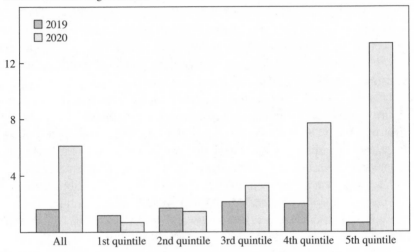

Panel A: Probability of wage cut

Percent with base wage decrease

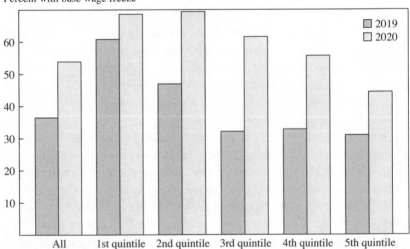

Panel B: Probability of wage freeze

Percent with base wage freeze

Source: ADP anonymized payroll records and authors' calculations.
Notes: Panel A includes all workers employed with the same firm in both March and June. The sample for panel B consists of workers at firms that usually adjust wages in March–June and restricts the sample to firms that made 75 percent of their annual wage changes for their employees in 2019 during March, April, May, or June.

We plot the probability that workers receive a wage freeze (i.e., zero base wage change) in these firms in panel B of figure 6. Column 1 shows that these firms adjusted the base wages of roughly 64 percent of their continuously employed workers from March through June of 2019 (i.e., kept the wages fixed for 36 percent of their employees). This number is similar to the decadelong average of base wage changes within the firms in the ADP employee sample found in Grigsby, Hurst, and Yildirmaz (forthcoming). Moreover, essentially all base wage changes in 2019 were increases; these firms only decreased the nominal wages of 0.7 percent of their workers during these months of 2019. However, during the same four months in 2020, these same firms froze the wages of 58 percent of their workers. In addition to the millions of base wage cuts observed in March to June, millions of workers have seen zero base wage changes at firms due to make their annual wage adjustment.[17]

The 6.3 percent of workers receiving nominal base wage cuts during the Pandemic Recession is of similar magnitude to the 6 percent found by Grigsby, Hurst, and Yildirmaz (forthcoming) during the Great Recession. However, many firms have yet to make their scheduled wage adjustments in 2020, and it remains to be seen whether such base wage cuts will continue. Similarly, during the Great Recession, over half of workers still received nominal wage increases. So far during the Pandemic Recession, base wages are increasing much less and decreasing slightly more than they did during the Great Recession.

The remaining columns of figure 6 show the probability of a wage cut (panel A) and the probability of a wage freeze (panel B) for workers in different initial wage quintiles. Wage freezes were more common throughout the wage distribution in 2020 relative to 2019. However, while employment losses were concentrated among low-wage workers (figure 4), nominal wage cuts were disproportionately concentrated among higher wage workers. More than three-quarters of all nominal wage cuts were concentrated in workers in the top two deciles of the wage distribution. For this sample, 13.4 percent of all workers in the top wage quintile received a nominal wage reduction between March and June 2020.

17. Nine percent of workers at these firms saw wage cuts between March and June of 2020. The full histogram of base wage changes for these firms in 2019 and 2020 is shown in the online appendix.

Table 2. Decomposition of Employment Growth in Shutdown and Reentering Businesses

Week	Continuers	New entry	Ever shut down	Shut down and reentered	Total
2/15/2020	0.0	0.0	0.0	0.0	0.0
2/22/2020	0.5	0.1	−0.1	0.0	0.5
2/29/2020	0.1	0.3	−0.3	0.0	0.1
3/07/2020	−0.1	0.5	−0.6	0.0	−0.1
3/14/2020	−0.6	0.6	−1.0	0.1	−0.9
3/21/2020	−4.4	0.7	−1.9	0.1	−5.4
3/28/2020	−10.7	0.8	−3.4	0.1	−13.2
4/04/2020	−15.0	1.0	−4.8	0.1	−18.8
4/11/2020	−15.0	1.1	−5.7	0.2	−19.4
4/18/2020	−14.8	1.2	−6.1	0.2	−19.6
4/25/2020	−15.8	1.2	−6.4	0.5	−20.6
5/02/2020	−15.8	1.3	−6.6	0.8	−20.3
5/09/2020	−14.4	1.5	−6.8	0.9	−18.8
5/16/2020	−12.5	1.6	−6.9	1.2	−16.6
5/23/2020	−11.7	1.8	−7.0	1.6	−15.4
5/30/2020	−11.6	2.0	−7.2	2.1	−14.7
6/06/2020	−10.5	2.2	−7.4	2.4	−13.3
6/13/2020	−9.7	2.3	−7.5	2.6	−12.4
6/20/2020	−10.3	2.3	−7.9	2.7	−13.1

Source: ADP anonymized payroll records and authors' calculations.

Notes: Decomposition of total employment growth into employment contributions from continuously operating firms, newly entering firms, firms that were shut down at some point since February 15, and firms that were shut down but subsequently reentered. Data from the business-level sample. Percentages expressed in terms of February 15 employment.

V. Business Shutdown, Reentry, and Worker Recall

So far, most of our results combine employment changes for businesses that suspend operations (whether temporarily or permanently) and businesses that continue operating. Separating these groups is useful: a primary determinant of the speed of recovery from this crisis may be the extent to which irreversible disinvestments occur. This question has come to the forefront recently as employment has increased. Are business closures permanent? How much of the employment increase has occurred as the result of businesses reopening or firms recalling workers that were temporarily laid off?

Table 2 shows the decomposition of aggregate employment growth into the contributions from continuers (employment at firms that operated continuously since February 15), entry (employment at firms that did not exist in our sample on February 15), shutdown (initial employment at firms that shut down at any point since February 15), and reentry (employment at firms that shut down at some point since February 15 but subsequently reopened). The sum of these four contributions equals total aggregate paid employment growth. To create this table we use our business-level sample and report all contributions as percent of total employment as of February 15. We define a firm as "shutting down" if they issued no paychecks during a week in which we would expect them to have done so (given past pay frequency patterns). We define a firm as "reentering" if it had shut down and started paying its workers again.

On June 20, job losses at firms that operated continuously contributed 10.3 percentage points out of 13.1 percent total employment decline since mid-February (as highlighted in figure 1).[18] As of June 20, 7.9 percent of mid-February employment was shut down at some point and 2.7 percent of (mid-February) employment that was previously shut down had returned by June 20. In other words, one-third of employment in firms that had shut down at some point during the first few months of the pandemic had returned by late June. The difference between shutdown and reentry columns in table 2 measures the employment in firms that have remain closed and the change in employment at reentering firms (the former component accounts for most of the difference). Newly entering firms added 2.3 percent (of February levels) to employment through late June, though we caution against interpreting these figures in terms of genuine new business formation.[19]

Between April 25 and June 20, aggregate employment increased by 7.5 percentage points (relative to February 15 levels). About three-quarters of that growth (5.5 out of 7.4 percentage points) was due to employment gains in continuing firms, and about one-third (2.2 out of 7.4 percentage points) was due to employment contributions of firms that reopened.[20] The findings suggest that the reopening of temporarily shuttered businesses contributed meaningfully to aggregate employment gains during May and June.

---

18. The numbers under "Continuers" in table 2 differ slightly from those in panel B of figure 1 due to different normalizations. In figure 1 we normalize the series by employment in *continuing firms* in February 2020 while in this table we normalize the series by total employment across *all* firms in February 2020.

19. Note that entry does not necessarily correspond to new firm formation; it could simply capture existing firms newly contracting with ADP or firms that existed at some point in the past, were closed during February, and later reopened again, for example, seasonal businesses. We do note, however, that Census Bureau data on new business applications with planned wages described by Haltiwanger (2020) indicate that application rates had returned to their 2019 pace by early June.

20. The employment gains from newly entering businesses during May and early June and the employment losses from businesses that newly shuttered in May and early June roughly offset each other.

Figure 7. Employment in Shutdown and Reentered Firms

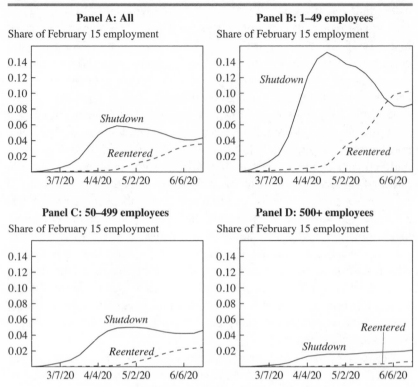

Source: ADP anonymized payroll records and authors' calculations.

Notes: Solid line indicates the share of February 15 employment at firms that were shut down as of each date; dashed line indicates the share of February 15 employment at firms that had shut down and then reentered. The sample of firms is defined as of mid-February and is followed over time. Shutdown firms are defined as those where no payroll was processed.

Panel A of figure 7 shows the dynamics of employment at currently shutdown (solid line) and reentered (dashed line) businesses for all businesses during the recession. Specifically, the solid lines in each panel measure the employment lost in currently shutdown firms during each pay period. The dashed line shows the employment gains coming from reentering firms. Panel A shows the employment losses associated with business shutdown for the US economy peaked in late April. Since then, as highlighted in table 2, some of these shuttered firms have reopened, contributing to aggregate employment growth. As of late June, there is still 4 percent of February employment in firms that are still shut down. Notably, however, the decline in shutdown employment from its April peak is smaller in magnitude than the employment generated by reentry (about 2 percentage points versus nearly 4 percentage points), reflecting the fact that shutdowns continued to occur even after mid-April.

In the online appendix, we additionally show that firm shutdown disproportionately affected low wage workers. By the end of April, approximately three times as many bottom quintile workers were in firms that have shut down than were top quintile workers. This partly reflects differences in firm closure by industry: firms in the entertainment and accomodation and food service industries were most likely to shut down in our sample.

The remaining panels in figure 7 show firm shutdown and reentering patterns by business size. Business shutdown was much more prominent among smaller firms, with shutdown firms contributing about 15 percent of the initial employment decline by late April among those businesses with fewer than fifty employees. However, many of these small businesses had reopened through late June. As seen in figure 2, total paid employment in small businesses increased by nearly 17 percentage points (relative to February levels) between mid-April and late June. Employment growth in firms that temporarily shuttered—that is, shuttered and then reopened—contributed about half of the employment gains among businesses with less than fifty employees from mid-April through the end of June. Businesses with 50–499 employees saw lower, but still notable, levels of shutdown, peaking around 5 percent of initial employment. Shutdown has been subdued among the largest firms, though it is noteworthy that the series had not peaked and had continued to gradually increase through late June.

When businesses reenter, they may not hire back all of their preexisting workforce. Figure 8 explores this possibility. Panel A plots the distribution of firm employment at reentry relative to the firm's employment during early February, weighting each firm by its initial size. The figure shows that about 60 percent of returning firms are smaller than they were in the beginning of February. The median reentering firm reopened with 86 percent of its initial employment, while the mean firm only has 78 percent of its initial employment. We present versions of this figure weighting firms by their February employment in the online appendix. That employment-weighted figure shows that returning large firms disproportionately return smaller: the employee-weighted median reentering firm has 65 percent of its February employment. Although firm reentry is contributing to a recovery in overall employment, these reentering firms are operating below their initial capacity. In part, this may be due to firms allowing individuals to return to work in stages in order to minimize social contact in the office.

Figure 8. Employee Recall in Reentering Firms

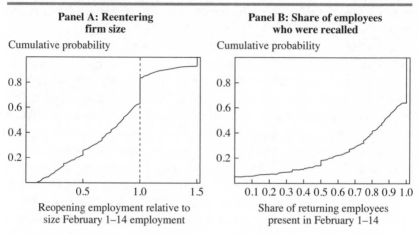

Panel A: Reentering firm size

Cumulative probability

0.8
0.6
0.4
0.2

0.5   1.0   1.5

Reopening employment relative to
size February 1–14 employment

Panel B: Share of employees who were recalled

Cumulative probability

0.8
0.6
0.4
0.2

0.1 0.2 0.3 0.4 0.5 0.6 0.7 0.8 0.9 1.0

Share of returning employees
present in February 1–14

Source: ADP anonymized payroll records and authors' calculations.

Notes: The sample consists of those firms that existed in early February 2020, temporarily shut down, and then subsequently reopened (i.e., resumed paycheck issuance). Employment measurements are through late June.

Monitoring this subcapacity operation will be important to the overall recovery dynamics.

When businesses return, they can choose to either rehire their prior workforce or seek new employees. Panel B of figure 8 shows the share of returning businesses' workforce that was previously employed with that same business in the first two weeks of February. Such workers represent "recalls." Again, the distribution is weighted by initial business size. In almost half of reentering firms the new workforce comprises at least 90 percent of employees who worked in the firm in early February. Hardly any firms reenter without having their workforce comprising at least half of the workers who were with the firm in early February. The results in this figure suggest that the overwhelming majority of reentering businesses are seeking to avoid costly searching by simply rehiring from their initial workforce. Again, most of these businesses are still well below their initial size, so as the recovery continues they may be able to bring back more of their initial workers.

As we highlight throughout, firm shutdown has not been the only source of employment declines at the beginning of this recession. Continuing employees have also seen enormous employment declines followed by small employment increases over the last few months. As these continuing firms recover, they too face a choice of whether to rehire existing employees

Figure 9. Growth of Continuing Businesses

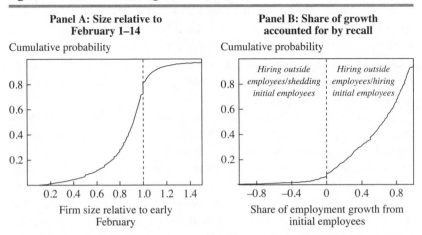

Panel A: Size relative to
February 1–14

Cumulative probability

Panel B: Share of growth
accounted for by recall

Cumulative probability

Firm size relative to early
February

Share of employment growth from
initial employees

Source: ADP anonymized payroll records and authors' calculations.
Notes: Panel A plots the distribution of business employment in late June relative to the first two weeks of February. Panel B plots firm-level distribution of the share of firm growth of continuing businesses accounted for by recall of previously employed workers. Firm growth measured between the firm's trough employment after March 11 and late June. *Recall* defined as hiring workers who were employed by the firm in the first two weeks of February. Throughout attention is limited to firms whose trough employment occurred after March 11. In panel B, attention is limited to firms that add at least ten employees.

or seek outside employment. Panel A of figure 9 plots the distribution of the current firm size for firms that contracted during the beginning of the recession but then subsequently started growing again. Specifically, we consider the growth in employment between the week in which a continuing firm has its lowest observed employment (after some contraction) and the final week of our sample (the end of June). We then calculate the firm's current size relative to its size in mid-February. The figure shows that the median growing continuing firm is currently at a size that is 10 percent lower than its mid-February level. Consistent with the patterns in figure 3, roughly 15 percent of these growing firms are now larger than they were in mid-February.

Panel B shows the share of trough-to-peak employment growth for continuing businesses accounted for by recalling previously employed workers. For each growing continuing firm, we calculate the share of this employment growth accounted for by growth in workers who were employed by the firm in the first two weeks of February. Note that this share can be negative if the business continues to shed existing workers while simultaneously hiring new outside workers. Finally, to remove noise from small-growth firms, we consider only continuing firms that grow by at least ten workers from their trough to peak.[21] The figure shows that roughly 90 percent of firms grow at least in part by recalling existing workers. Almost 10 percent of continuing firms hired exclusively from recall.[22] However, the complement of these findings is also interesting. Almost 10 percent of continuing firms are growing from external hires, even as they shed their initial workforce. Even in these uncertain times, there remains some worker churn. The fact that workers are being reallocated among existing business during the Pandemic Recession is consistent with the findings in Barrero, Bloom, and Davis (2020).

Overall, firm shutdown was an important driver of employment losses at the beginning of the Pandemic Recession, and firm reopening is likewise contributing to the labor market recovery. However, reentering firms operate at far below capacity, only hiring back a fraction of their prior workforce. Although both continuing and shutdown firms principally recall their prior employees to spur growth at this stage of the recovery, many continuing firms are also looking toward external labor markets for their hiring.

VI. Employment Gains and State Reopening

Figure 10 explores the effects of states reopening certain sectors on employment. To facilitate exposition, we create two groups of states—a set of large states that broadly opened in late April or early May and a set of large states that broadly opened in late May and early June.[23] For the set of states opening early we pool data from Florida, Georgia, and Texas. These states opened restaurants and lifted stay-at-home orders between April 24 and May 4. For the set of states opening later we pool data from Illinois, Pennsylvania, Virginia, and Washington. The late-opening states opened restaurants and lifted stay-at-home orders after May 31. Our results focus on one sector where reopening had the most direct effect: the food and accommodation sector (NAICS 72).

21. We present the distribution of these recall shares for firms that grow by at least one or five employees in the online appendix.
22. These findings are broadly consistent with the results in Fujita and Moscarini (2017) showing the importance of employee recall in prior recessions.
23. We focus on large states because there is less noise in employment fluctuations at the state-by-industry level within the ADP data. We use our employee sample for this analysis so that we can measure state of residence. There are small differences in aggregate employment declines by sector between our business sample and our employee sample given the slightly different sampling frames.

Figure 10. State Reopening and Employment: Accommodation and Restaurant Sector

Employment change relative to February 1

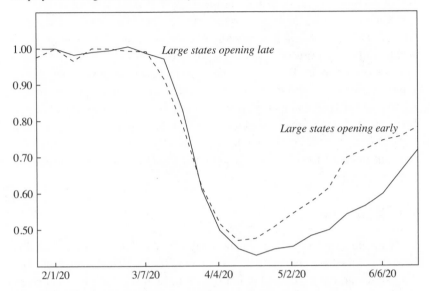

Source: ADP anonymized payroll records and authors' calculations.
Notes: Employment in NAICS Industry 72 (Accommodation and Food Service). Dashed line indicates
a set of large states that opened in late April or early May (Florida, Georgia, Texas); solid line indicates
a set of large states that opened in late May or early June (Illinois, Pennsylvania, Virginia, Washington).
Data come from the ADP employee sample.

The figure shows that employment in restaurants and accommodations fell similarly through mid-April in both state groupings. Starting in late April, employment in this sector within the states opening early increased faster than employment in the states opening later. The state groups start to diverge during the week of April 18, which was a week prior to the Georgia reopening of in-person dining. Given that the state openings were announced in advance, firms started ramping up some employment prior to the actual date of opening. This qualitative pattern is not overly surprising.

The quantitative patterns are, however, noteworthy. First, even in the states that opened early, employment in this sector is still more than 20 percent below February levels as of late June. Opening, per se, does not guarantee employment will fully rebound in this sector. If individuals are concerned about contracting the virus in public places, the demand for these types of services may remain depressed even as these sectors start to reopen. Second, employment in these sectors within states that opened late started to increase even prior to those states reopening. The increase was modest but suggests that demand was increasing (perhaps for take-out meals) even prior to official reopenings. These demand effects could interact with disease trends within the state that could also prompt states to lift stay-at-home orders. Additionally, the expectation of reopening likely resulted in some firms bringing back workers early to prepare for serving customers in person. Researchers seeking to attach a causal quantitative interpretation of employment gains associated with state reopening should do so cautiously. Finally, employment in this sector had almost converged between the two groups of states as of late June. Again, this suggests that once states reopen, employment in previously constrained sectors will rise but demand forces will still prevent employment from returning to prerecession levels.

VII. Conclusion

In this paper, we use high-frequency payroll data from ADP to track the behavior of the labor market in the early part of the Pandemic Recession. The data show an unprecedented collapse in employment from mid-February through late April with employment falling by 21 percent relative to early February levels. As states started to reopen, employment rebounded partially. As of late June, employment was still 13 percent below February levels. The employment declines as of late June were massive relative to past recessions; during the Great Recession employment troughed at 7 percent of prerecessionary levels.

Our results highlight that the employment losses were disproportionately concentrated among smaller firms and lower wage workers. Much of the fiscal stimulus implemented during the early part of the recession was targeted toward these groups. Job losses, in percentage terms, had converged between smaller and larger businesses as of late June (relative to prerecession levels). Many previously shuttered businesses—particularly smaller businesses—reopened during May and June, bringing back laid-off workers. This could be consistent with government stimulus provided through programs like the Paycheck Protection Program (PPP) allowing some smaller businesses to survive the beginning of the recession during the mandated shutdowns. However, further research will be needed to try to causally isolate the effects of PPP on small business employment.

One finding of ours that needs to be monitored going forward is how the Pandemic Recession is affecting wages of workers who did not get displaced. During the first few months of the recession, we have shown that many workers are receiving nominal cuts to their contracted wage while many others are receiving pay freezes. The extent of nominal wage cuts and wage freezes are large relative to nonrecessionary years and are even larger than what was observed in the Great Recession. How broader measures of compensation adjust—including components such as bonuses, performance pay, and fringe benefits—is worth monitoring as the recession continues. Our initial findings suggest that both the employment adjustments and the wage adjustments are large relative to prior recessions.

ACKNOWLEDGMENTS We thank Sinem Buber, Mita Goldar, and Matthew Levin from ADP for their support on the project. We also thank Steve Davis, Jan Eberly, and Jonathan Parker for comments on prior drafts. As part of the University of Chicago data use contract, ADP reviewed the paper prior to distribution with the sole focus of making sure that the paper did not release information that would compromise the privacy of their clients or reveal proprietary information about the ADP business model. The views expressed in the paper are the authors' and do not necessarily reflect the views of ADP. Additionally, the analysis and conclusions set forth here are those of the authors and do not indicate concurrence by other members of the research staff or the Federal Reserve Board of Governors.

References

Barrero, Jose Maria, Nicholas Bloom, and Steven J. Davis. 2020. "COVID-19 Is Also a Reallocation Shock." In the present volume of *Brookings Papers on Economic Activity*.

Bartik, Alexander W., Marianne Bertrand, Zoë B. Cullen, Edward L. Glaeser, Michael Luca, and Christopher T. Stanton. 2020. "How Are Small Businesses Adjusting to COVID-19? Early Evidence from a Survey." Working Paper 26989. Cambridge, Mass.: National Bureau of Economic Research.

Bartik, Alexander W., Marianne Bertrand, Feng Lin, Jesse Rothstein, and Matt Unrath. 2020. "Measuring the Labor Market at the Onset of the COVID-19 Crisis." In the present volume of *Brookings Papers on Economic Activity*.

Bick, Alexander, and Adam Blandin. 2020. "Real-Time Labor Market Estimates during the 2020 Coronavirus Outbreak." Working Paper.

Brynjolfsson, Erik, John J. Horton, Adam Ozimek, Daniel Rock, Garima Sharma, and Hong-Yi TuYe. 2020. "COVID-19 and Remote Work: An Early Look at US Data." Working Paper 27344. Cambridge, Mass.: National Bureau of Economic Research.

Cajner, Tomaz, Leland D. Crane, Ryan A. Decker, Adrian Hamins-Puertolas, and Christopher Kurz. 2020. "Improving the Accuracy of Economic Measurement with Multiple Data Sources: The Case of Payroll Employment Data." In *Big Data for 21st Century Economic Statistics*, edited by Katharine G. Abraham, Ron S. Jarmin, Brian Moyer, and Matthew D. Shapiro. Chicago: University of Chicago Press.

Cajner, Tomaz, Leland D. Crane, Ryan A. Decker, Adrian Hamins-Puertolas, Christopher Kurz, and Tyler Radler. 2018. "Using Payroll Processor Microdata to Measure Aggregate Labor Market Activity." Finance and Economics Discussion Series 2018–005. Washington: Board of Governors of the Federal Reserve System. https://doi.org/10.17016/FEDS.2018.005.

Chetty, Raj, John N. Friedman, Nathaniel Hendren, Michael Stepner, and the Opportunity Insights Team. 2020. "How Did COVID-19 and Stabilization Policies Affect Spending and Employment? A New Real-Time Economic Tracker Based on Private Sector Data." Working Paper 27431. Cambridge, Mass.: National Bureau of Economic Research.

Coibion, Olivier, Yuriy Gorodnichenko, and Michael Weber. 2020. "Labor Markets during the COVID-19 Crisis: A Preliminary View." Working Paper 27017. Cambridge, Mass.: National Bureau of Economic Research.

Dingel, Jonathan I., and Brent Neiman. 2020. "How Many Jobs Can Be Done at Home?" Working Paper 26948. Cambridge, Mass.: National Bureau of Economic Research.

Fujita, Shigeru, and Giuseppe Moscarini. 2017. "Recall and Unemployment." *American Economic Review* 107, no. 12: 3875–916.

Grigsby, John. 2019. "Skill Heterogeneity and Aggregate Labor Market Dynamics." Working Paper. Chicago: University of Chicago.

Grigsby, John, Erik Hurst, and Ahu Yildirmaz. Forthcoming. "Aggregate Nominal Wage Adjustments: New Evidence from Administrative Payroll Data." *American Economic Review*.

Haltiwanger, John. 2020. "Applications for New Businesses Contract Sharply in Recent Weeks: A First Look at the Weekly Business Formation Statistics." Working Paper. College Park: University of Maryland. http://econweb.umd.edu/~haltiwan/first_look.pdf.

Hurst, Erik, and Benjamin Wild Pugsley. 2011. "What Do Small Businesses Do?" *Brookings Papers on Economic Activity*, Fall, 73–118.

Kahn, Lisa B., Fabian Lange, and David G. Wiczer. 2020. "Labor Demand in the Time of COVID-19: Evidence from Vacancy Postings and UI Claims." Working Paper 27061. Cambridge, Mass.: National Bureau of Economic Research.

Kurmann, André, Etienne Lalé, and Lien Ta. 2020. "The Impact of COVID-19 on U.S. Employment and Hours: Real-Time Estimates with Homebase Data." Working Paper. https://www.lebow.drexel.edu/sites/default/files/1588687497-hbdraft0504.pdf.

Solon, Gary, Robert Barsky, and Jonathan Parker. 1994. "Measuring the Cyclicality of Real Wages: How Important Is Composition Bias?" *Quarterly Journal of Economics* 109, no. 1: 1–25.

NATALIE COX
Princeton University

ARLENE WONG
Princeton University

PETER GANONG
University of Chicago

DIANA FARRELL
JPMorgan Chase Institute

PASCAL NOEL
University of Chicago

FIONA GREIG
JPMorgan Chase Institute

JOSEPH VAVRA
University of Chicago

ERICA DEADMAN
JPMorgan Chase Institute

Initial Impacts of the Pandemic on Consumer Behavior: Evidence from Linked Income, Spending, and Savings Data

ABSTRACT   We use US household-level bank account data to investigate the heterogeneous effects of the pandemic on spending and savings. Households across the income distribution all cut spending from March to early April. Since mid-April, spending has rebounded most rapidly for low-income households. We find large increases in liquid asset balances for households throughout the income distribution. However, lower-income households contribute disproportionately to the aggregate increase in balances, relative to their prepandemic shares. Taken together, our results suggest that spending declines

Conflict of Interest Disclosure: The authors did not receive financial support from any firm or person for this paper or from any firm or person with a financial or political interest in this paper. They are currently not officers, directors, or board members of any organization with an interest in this paper. While working on this paper, coauthors Pascal Noel and Peter Ganong were academic fellows with the JPMorgan Chase Institute (JPMCI) and received financial compensation for providing research advice on public reports produced by the JPMCI. Coauthors Fiona Greig, Diana Farrell, and Erica Deadman are currently employees of JPMCI. JPMCI provided the data for this report and reviewed these data to avoid disclosure of personal identifying information, as well as the disclosure of firm intellectual property, and that the research output is consistent with the scope of the initial proposal. Discussant Jonathan Parker is an unpaid consultant at JPMCI where he does work for the Institute and has access to the data for research purposes utilized by the authors. The views expressed in this paper are those of the authors, and do not necessarily reflect those of the JPMorgan Chase Institute, Princeton University, or the University of Chicago.

Figure 1. Aggregate Consumption and Savings

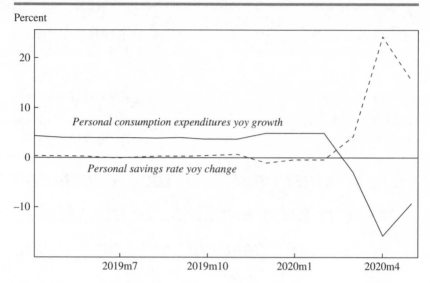

Percent

Source: BEA.
Note: Year-over-year growth calculated from monthly Bureau of Economic Analysis data.

in the initial months of the recession were primarily caused by direct effects of the pandemic, rather than resulting from labor market disruptions. The sizable growth in liquid assets we observe for low-income households suggests that stimulus and insurance programs during this period likely played an important role in limiting the effects of labor market disruptions on spending.

The COVID-19 pandemic led to a large and immediate decline in US aggregate spending and an increase in aggregate private savings (see figure 1). In this paper, we use anonymized bank account information of millions of Chase customers to measure the microeconomic dynamics underlying these aggregate patterns. Specifically, we use our household-level account data to explore how spending and savings over the initial months of the pandemic vary with household-specific demographic characteristics, such as prepandemic income and industry of employment.

Measuring and understanding the link between income, spending, and savings is useful for understanding the causes and dynamics of this recession. For instance, the relationship between individual income, spending, and savings can shed light on the role of supply factors (such as shutdowns and reducing activities with high infection risk) versus demand factors (such as Keynesian spillovers across sectors as unemployed workers reduce spending). Understanding these factors can be informative about the effectiveness of different stimulus policies for targeting different households and businesses. Many data sets have already been used to study the dynamics of geographic level spending during the pandemic, but aggregated relationships may or may not be identical to those at the individual household level at which economic behavior is ultimately determined.[1] Our paper provides an initial step in analyzing these household-level dynamics.[2]

Focusing first on aggregate results, we find that overall spending fell over 35 percent in the second half of March. In April, spending began to increase from its nadir, but it remained substantially depressed through the end of our sample on May 30. Declines in nonessential spending accounted for most of the declines in spending.[3] Amongst nonessential categories, declines were particularly large for restaurants, hotel accommodations, and clothing and department stores. Amongst essential categories, declines were most dramatic for health care, ground transportation, and fuel. Reassuringly, these patterns are similar to those found using other aggregate sources of spending data.[4] However, this also implies that these results do not rely on the unique features of our micro data, so they are not the main contribution of our paper.

We next turn to results which *do* rely on our micro data linking household-level observables on income, spending, and savings. First, we find that during the initial stages of the pandemic in March, there are extremely large declines in spending for all quartiles of the prepandemic income distribution.[5] Spending by the top quartile of the income distribution falls

---

1. See, for example, Chetty and others (2020).

2. To be clear, our current analysis does not run regressions at the household level, but it does crucially rely on individual household data to define groups and outcomes of interest. We also focus for now on sorting households by prepandemic characteristics like income level, rather than by changes during the pandemic.

3. We define these categories precisely later, but loosely speaking nonessential stores are those which are subject to government restrictions as a result of the pandemic.

4. See, for example, EarnestResearch, Where States Stand: Measuring the Reopenings One Step at a Time, https://www.earnestresearch.com/where-states-stand-measuring-the-reopening-one-step-at-a-time/; Baker and others (2020); Opportunity Insights Economic Tracker, https://tracktherecovery.org/, accessed June 15, 2020; Facteus, Insights on Changing Consumer Behavior FIRST Report, https://www.facteus.com/reports/first-report, accessed June 15, 2020; and Karger and Rajan (2020).

by modestly more than any other quartile (in percentage terms). However, this difference is small relative to the broad decline in spending by all income groups. Beginning in mid-April when aggregate spending begins to recover, substantial differences by income emerge: spending recovers much more rapidly for low-income households than for high-income households so that large differences arise by the end of May. We show that these relationships between income and spending over the pandemic hold both in general, as well as within narrow geographic areas like zip codes.[6]

Second, we explore differences in spending by individuals' industry of employment. This variation is interesting because industries vary substantially in both their exposure to labor market disruptions and in average income levels. Exploiting joint variation in industry of employment and household income is thus helpful for better understanding the source of heterogeneity in spending patterns. We find that spending cuts are pervasive, with declines for workers in all industries of employment. Consistent with the patterns we find by income, workers in industries with low average pay initially cut spending slightly less and then have spending which recovers more rapidly. For example, grocery store workers have the smallest declines in spending and the most rapid rebound, while white-collar professional workers' spending is recovering more slowly. We then further split workers within given industries of employment by their individual prepandemic income levels. We find that income levels appear to matter more for spending than industry of employment. For example, low-income workers in all industries have rapid increases in spending in mid-April, while these increases are muted for high-income workers.

Finally, we turn to evidence on the distribution of household savings over the pandemic to provide further insight into the effects of changing income and spending on household liquidity. To the best of our knowledge, we are the first paper to explore these distributional effects. Aggregate savings have increased substantially over the last two months. Information on the underlying distribution of increases is useful for understanding the sources and consequences of this increase. There are several forces during the pandemic that likely affected aggregate savings rates: (1) as discussed above, spending has fallen. This decline is most dramatic at the top of the

---

5. As we discuss more in section II, since our data arise from bank account information, we undersample the very lowest income households, but the sample is otherwise broadly representative.

6. High- and low-income people live in different locations, which might have different exposure to the pandemic. Using within zip code variation shows that income-spend relationships are not driven by confounding effects of physical location.

income distribution, which will tend to boost savings for these households; (2) massive increases in unemployment have reduced labor income, and these effects are especially concentrated on low-income workers. This will tend to reduce savings for low-income households; (3) stimulus and social insurance programs like Economic Impact Payments (EIPs) and expanded unemployment insurance (UI) provide transfers which represent a larger share of income for low- than high-income households. This will tend to increase liquidity and savings by low-income households; (4) delayed tax filing dates may increase short-term savings if those who owe money delay filing more often than those who are owed refunds.

Consistent with aggregate savings data, we find a large initial increase in savings during the pandemic. By the end of May 2020, average liquid balances are 36 percent higher than at the same point in 2019. While increases in liquid balances are pervasive throughout the income distribution, we find that lower-income households contribute disproportionately to the aggregate increase in balances, relative to their initial prepandemic shares. That is, liquid balances at the end of May are slightly more equally distributed over the income distribution than liquid balances in February. However, in dollar terms, high-income households contribute most to the aggregate increase in savings.

Taken together, our results suggest several conclusions. First, labor market disruptions were unlikely to be a primary factor driving initial spending declines during the recession. Overall declines in spending were much larger than what could be explained by the rise in unemployment in this recession, given historical relationships. Furthermore, spending actually declines by less for households with greater exposure to labor market disruptions. This does not mean that labor market disruptions have no effects on spending or that demand spillovers are unimportant, but it does suggest that at least in these initial months of the recession, the direct effects of the pandemic are the primary factor driving spending.

Second, the composition of typical spending is important for understanding spending declines. Aggregate spending declines by more in nonessential sectors which are more exposed to shutdowns and health risk. Furthermore, spending declines more for high-income households, who tend to consume more of these nonessential goods in normal times.

Third, various stimulus and social insurance programs like EIPs and expanded UI likely played a sizable role in helping to stabilize spending and liquid balances, especially for low-income households. Since fiscal stimulus was ramped up at the same time that many states began to reopen, it is difficult to disentangle general reopening effects from effects of this fiscal stimulus by looking just at aggregate spending. However, stimulus checks and expanded UI benefits represent a larger share of monthly income for low-income workers than for high-income workers, and would thus naturally explain the more rapid recovery in spending we observe for low-income workers. Finally, expanded transfers could also explain the disproportionate increase in savings that we observe for lower-income households. It is important to note that many of these transfer programs are likely temporary; the EIPs are a one-off stimulus, while the expanded component of UI benefits is slated to end in late July 2020. Households may be less likely to immediately consume, and more likely to save, these payments because they are nonpermanent.

It is important to emphasize that our evidence for now focuses on time-series patterns for relatively aggregated household groups, and so we do not provide any causal evidence on the strength of any particular channels driving spending decisions. Thus, our evidence is suggestive rather than conclusive on this front. The early patterns we find in this paper may also change as the pandemic progresses and new policy decisions are made. Future work exploring even more detailed household-level results as this recession progresses will hopefully shed further light on the economic consequences of this pandemic and associated policy responses.

I. Data Description

Our analysis of spending and checking account balances is based on the universe of transactions from Chase checking accounts, debit cards, and credit cards through May 30, 2020. Our main measure of total spending includes all debit and credit card purchases as well as cash withdrawals. In robustness checks in the online appendix we show that our conclusions are similar if we add paper checks to our measure of total spending.[7] While we observe credit, debit, cash, and check transactions, we are still working to process electronic checking account transactions such as ACH payments, and so this type of spending is not included in our analysis. For all checking accounts, we also observe checking account balances.

---

7. We do not include paper checks in our main analysis for two reasons. First, we do not know whether the checks reflect spending, debt payments, or transfers. Second, due to delays in depositing and processing checks, there is a lag between when the check was used and when it appears as a withdrawal in the bank account. Hence, it is hard to interpret the patterns of paper check outflows at the high frequency we use in this analysis.

Table 1. Income Distribution and Credit Card Spending

	Income quartiles			
	Quartile cutoffs ($)	*Mean income ($)*	*Sample with Chase credit card (%)*	*Avg. weekly credit card spend ($)*
Quartile 1	12,000–27,707	20,948	30	205
Quartile 2	27,707–41,255	34,185	36	228
Quartile 3	41,255–63,462	50,927	46	329
Quartile 4	63,462 +	108,914	57	639
N	5,014,672			

Source: JPMorgan Chase Institute.

We impose income and activity screens in order to focus on a sample of individuals who primarily use their Chase account to manage their finances. Specifically, we filter on those who have a nonbusiness account, had at least five checking account transactions and at least three card transactions in every month between January 2018 and March 2020, and had at least $12,000 in labor income in both 2018 and 2019.[8] This leaves us with a sample of just over five million individuals.

We measure labor income using information on payroll direct deposits. We further measure industry of employment based on the payer associated with direct deposits in February 2020. However, there is an important caveat that we can match the payer associated with payroll income to an identified payer for only 24 percent of households, and most of these payers tend to be large employers. Finally, it is important to note that while we observe labor income through February 2020, we are still working to process and interpret data on labor income and government transfers during the pandemic. As a result, data on income change during the pandemic are not available for our current analysis. For this reason, we report various results based on prepandemic income, but do not yet have results on how spending has responded to individual income changes.

Given that our sample is drawn from account holders at a single financial institution, we use income data from the Current Population Survey (CPS) to measure how representative they are of the US population. Table 1 reports quartiles of the labor income distribution for our sample. Figure A.12 in the online appendix plots the average labor income by quartile for the Chase sample compared to average labor income for the CPS population (adjusted

---

8. We have explored different thresholds on transactions, and results are similar.

for income and payroll taxes since the Chase measure is posttax). This figure suggests that our sample is broadly representative, although it somewhat overstates income at the lowest end of the distribution and slightly under-states income at the highest end of the distribution. The overstatement at the lowest end of the distribution is due to two factors. First, reliable measure-ment requires us to impose a minimum threshold of $12,000 in labor income.[9] In the CPS, 7.7 percent of households have labor income below this cutoff. They would be excluded from our analysis.[10] Second, every household in our data set has a bank account. Therefore, we do not include unbanked households, who are disproportionately low-income. The FDIC reports that 6.5 percent of US households did not have a bank account in 2017.[11] A final caveat for our analysis is that we report *average* outcomes in terms of spending and liquid balances by income quartile. However, there may be heterogeneity *within* quartiles. For example, not all households were eligible for EIPs and some unemployed households faced long delays in receiving UI payments. For all these reasons, our findings that average spending and average balances are relatively higher for low-income households should not be interpreted to mean that *all* low-income house-holds are doing relatively well during the pandemic. There is compelling evidence that this is not the case (Bitler, Hoynes, and Schanzenbach 2020).

Our data are unique in their size, sample coverage, and in their individual-level view of income, spending, and balances. Other data sources used to research the consumer response to COVID-19 tend to be aggregated over region, store, or time (Earnest, Womply, or Affinity), which limits the analysis of household balance sheet dynamics. By observing covariates at the individual level, like geography and industry of employment, we can also directly control for confounding factors that might be correlated with income and changes in spending. For example, our data can be used to look at how spending varies with income within narrow geographic areas like zip codes, and thus help control for the fact that high-income locations differ from low-income locations along a number of dimensions. Our data

---

9. We require at least $12,000 in labor income since it is difficult to distinguish truly low-income households from mismeasured higher income households without reliably captured direct deposits.

10. After conditioning on households with labor income above $12,000 in the CPS, mean and median income in the bottom quartile of our sample is very similar to mean and median income in the bottom quartile of the CPS.

11. See 2017 FDIC National Survey of Unbanked and Underbanked Households, Executive Summary.

also allow us to look at how spending changes by income groups within industry of employment.

Our sample, which captures households across the income distribution, complements the work done using Facteus data (Karger and Rajan 2020; Alexander and Karger 2020) and proprietary Fintech data (Baker and others 2020) which are primarily focused on low-income households. Finally, the size of the Chase customer base allows for additional precision when calculating statistics of interest as well as for substantially more disaggregated data cuts, relative to data sets with smaller sample sizes. Our data are closest in structure to that in Andersen and others (2020), which uses similar bank account data from a Scandinavian bank. The most important distinction is that our data cover US households, and thus a dramatically different institutional environment with different social safety nets and government responses to the pandemic.

II. Household Spending

II.A. Overall Change in Spending

We begin by measuring the change in total spending. Online appendix A.1 provides changes in spending for each of the components of total spending (credit card, debit card, and cash), as well as paper checks. The top panel of figure 2 plots the 2020 to 2019 year-over-year percentage change in weekly spending. The bottom panel shows the average dollar amount of spending in 2020 and 2019. Changes in spending follow a distinctive pattern: spending is stable through the beginning of March, then declines precipitously by over 35 percent relative to 2019 from the second through fourth week of March. The size of the spending drop is largely consistent with other estimates from similar data sources during the same time frame.[12] These declines are somewhat larger than the aggregate spending declines in figure 1, but this is not particularly surprising. Personal consumption expenditures include substantial spending on components like housing services, which likely had little to no decline. Spending showed signs of recovery in May, but remains roughly 15 percent below pre-pandemic levels as at the end of May.

---

12. See for example, Baker and others (2020); Opportunity Insights Economic Tracker, https://tracktherecovery.org/, accessed June 15, 2020; and Facteus, Insights on Changing Consumer Behavior FIRST Report, https://www.facteus.com/reports/first-report, accessed June 15, 2020.

Figure 2. Average Spending Changes

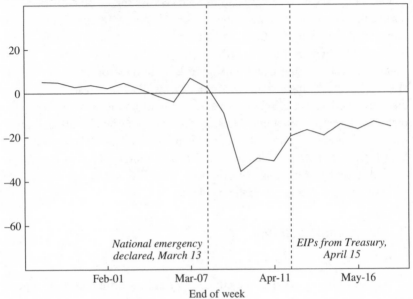

Year-over-year percent change in total spending per household

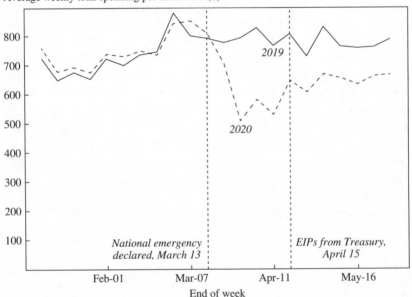

Average weekly total spending per household ($)

Source: JPMorgan Chase Institute.

The timing of the initial spending drop mirrors the spread of the virus and staggered national implementation of government social distancing orders. A national emergency was declared on March 13, 2020. Over the following three weeks, the number of states with stay-at-home orders increased from zero to forty-five. The prevalence of COVID-19 also increased dramatically over the course of March.

At the same time, the drop in spending also closely tracks the pattern of initial job losses. Unemployment insurance (UI) claims began spiking in the third week of March, with more than 20 million UI claims filed by April 11. Conversely, spending begins to recover in the weeks after April 15 when a majority of EIPs arrive and as many of the unemployed workers who file claims in March and early April begin to receive benefits (Chetty and others 2020). This raises a question of how much of the drop in spending is due to the pandemic itself, the social distancing policies, or income losses.

It is useful to calibrate the size of the spending drop relative to what we have observed among those who lose a job involuntarily during normal times. Ganong and Noel (2019) measure the spending drop around job loss among UI recipients, and observe an initial spending drop of roughly 6 percent. In other words, the spending drop in March 2020 is roughly six times larger than the average household spending drop in the first month of unemployment for UI recipients in normal times. This puts into perspective how dramatic the spending drop is and suggests that the pandemic and policies aimed at preventing its spread are contributing substantially to the drop in spending.

II.B. Change in Household Spending by Categories

While figure 2 shows a sharp drop in aggregate spending over March and April, there is reason to think that specific spending categories would be differentially impacted. Many nonessential businesses, like bars and salons, were closed by state and local governments. Similarly, stay-at-home orders limited the ability of individuals to travel. Beyond the mechanical effect of social distancing regulations, individuals may also have independently curtailed spending in certain categories to avoid risk of infection or as a response to income loss.

While we do not have information on debit card or cash spending by categories, we do have detailed category splits for credit card spending. We begin by disaggregating total credit card spending into essential and nonessential categories, as commonly defined in state stay-at-home orders. Figure 3 shows a dramatic difference in the path of essential and

Figure 3. Credit Card Spending on Essential and Nonessential Categories

Year-over-year percent change in credit card spending per household

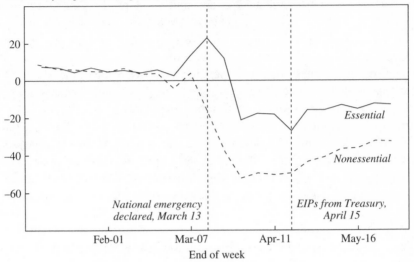

Average credit card spending per household ($)

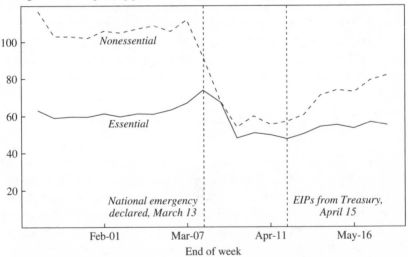

Source: JPMorgan Chase Institute.

Note: State social distancing orders that restricted nonessential goods and services used to categorize spending. Essential category includes fuel, transit, cash, drug stores, discount stores, auto repair, groceries, telecom, utilities, insurance, and health care. Nonessential category includes department stores, other retail, restaurants, entertainment, retail durables, home improvement, professional and personal services, and miscellaneous. Although flights, hotels, and rental cars are sometimes categorized as essential and not technically closed, they are included in the nonessential category because they are affected by stay-at-home restrictions on nonessential travel.

Table 2. Credit Card Spending Changes for Essential and Nonessential Categories

	Essential		Nonessential	
	Share of spending (%)	*Year-over-year change (%)*	*Share of spending (%)*	*Year-over-year change (%)*
April 2019	35		65	
April 2020	46	−18	54	−49
Contribution to aggregate drop in spending	16		84	

Source: JPMorgan Chase Institute.

Note: Percent contribution to aggregate drop in spending is calculated as (% drop in category A) × (baseline share of category A) / (% drop in aggregate).

nonessential spending. Essential spending spiked in early March as households stockpiled goods like groceries. It then fell substantially before eventually stabilizing at a year-over-year decline of around 15 percent.[13] In contrast, spending on nonessential categories fell sharply throughout March, bottoming at a decline of just over 50 percent, and then began to slowly recover through late April and May.

Given the fact that households were ordered to stay at home except to make essential trips in most states, one might ask why households were still spending roughly $50 a week on nonessential categories in April. First, there was variation in both the degree of closures and in what was deemed nonessential across locations. Second, our spending categories do not map perfectly to each specific nonessential category. Third, households may be able to switch some nonessential services from in-person to remote, for example, from movie theater entertainment to online streaming or from in-restaurant dining to take-out.

We also quantify how much each category contributed to the aggregate drop in credit card spending. Table 2 shows what share of aggregate spending went toward essential and nonessential categories before and during the pandemic. Multiplying the prepandemic shares by their relative percentage drops, we find that nonessential spending accounted for 84 percent of the aggregate decline, and essential spending accounted for 16 percent.

13. The downward spike in year-over-year essential spending in the week ending April 18, 2020 likely arises because of the timing of Easter, which occurred during this week in 2020 but during the previous week in 2019. Many grocery stores are closed on Easter, which may explain a dip during this week in 2020 relative to the same week in 2019, which did not include the Easter closures.

To further illustrate the divergence in spending patterns across categories, we split essential and nonessential spending into more disaggregated categories in figure 4. Total essential spending spiked by roughly 20 percent in early March before dropping by 20 percent by the end of March. However, there is a wide range of spending responses among goods and services deemed essential. In the first few weeks of March there was a temporary surge in spending on groceries, discount stores, and pharmacies. Spending at grocery stores, which contributes the largest share of total essential spending, remained elevated through the end of our sample, aside from a brief decline in the week including Easter, when many grocery stores are closed. In contrast, spending fell in several other essential categories like hospital, other health care, transit and ground transportation, and fuel. Total dollar declines in these categories exceed the dollar increases in grocery spending, so that overall essential spending declines. Focusing on nonessential spending, declines are strongest in restaurants, hotel accommodations, and clothing and department stores. Overall, these results largely mirror those computed in other aggregate data sets and provide reassurance that our data are consistent with external evidence.

II.C. Heterogeneity in Spending Changes by Income

SPENDING CHANGES OVER THE INCOME DISTRIBUTION   We next explore whether spending reductions (both in aggregate and by category) vary with prepandemic income. We stratify our sample into income quartiles based on total labor inflows in 2019.[14] For context, those in the bottom quartile make less than $28,000 in take-home labor income per year, while those in the top quartile earn more than $63,000. As discussed in section I, our bottom quartile misses unbanked households and the 8 percent of US households with labor income below $12,000, since we cannot reliably measure their income.

Figure 5 plots the year-over-year change in spending for each quartile, both in percentage and dollar terms. The top income quartile reduces spending by about 39 percent, or $400, by the fourth week of March, while the bottom quartile reduces spending by 32 percent, or $100. The difference in the spending drop between income quartiles is starker in dollar terms than percentages, since high-income households have a higher baseline level of spending. However, divergence in spending over the income distribution starting in the second half of April is more striking. By the end

---

14. In future work, we plan to explore also the relationship to income changes during the pandemic.

Figure 4. Credit Card Spending Growth across Spending Categories

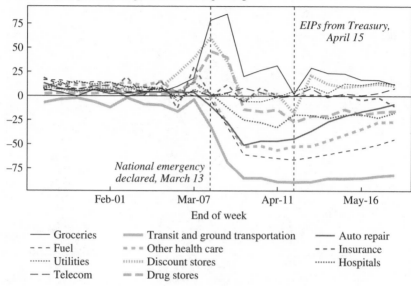

Essential spending

Year-over-year percent change in credit card spending

EIPs from Treasury, April 15

National emergency declared, March 13

End of week

—— Groceries	▬▬ Transit and ground transportation	—— Auto repair
- - - Fuel	▪ ▪ ▪ Other health care	- - - Insurance
·········· Utilities	···· Discount stores	········· Hospitals
— — Telecom	▬ ▬ Drug stores	

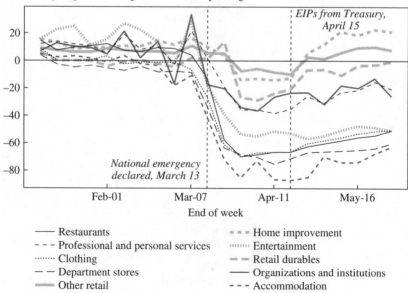

Nonessential spending

Year-over-year percent change in credit card spending

EIPs from Treasury, April 15

National emergency declared, March 13

End of week

—— Restaurants	▪ ▪ ▪ Home improvement
- - - Professional and personal services	········ Entertainment
········ Clothing	▬ ▬ Retail durables
— — Department stores	—— Organizations and institutions
▬▬ Other retail	- - - Accommodation

Source: JPMorgan Chase Institute.

Figure 5. Spending by Income Quartiles

Year-over-year percent change in total spending per household

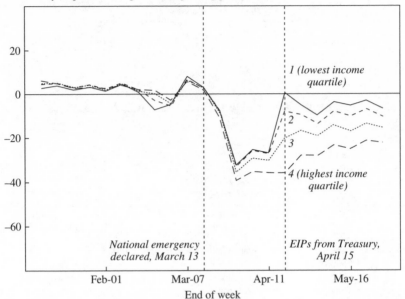

Average weekly total spending per household ($)

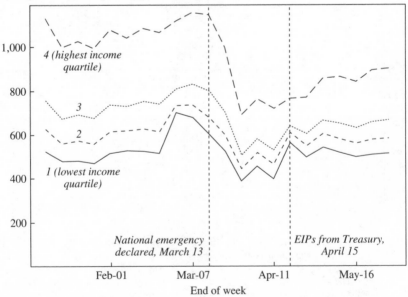

Source: JPMorgan Chase Institute.

of April, the decline in spending partially recovers, with the recovery most pronounced for the lowest income quartiles. The recovery in spending for the lowest income quartiles occurs in the same week when many stimulus payments are made in mid-April. The timing of the divergence in spending by income suggests that stimulus payments may have played an important role in restoring the ability of low-income households to maintain spending during the pandemic.

Online appendix A.2 provides the spending changes over the income distribution by form of payment (debit, credit, cash, and check). We observe similar patterns of spending changes across all forms of payments.

Table A.1 in the online appendix reports the cumulative change in spending by income quartile in 2020 relative to 2019 for the eleven pandemic weeks in our data set between March 15 and May 30. The highest income quartile contributes disproportionately to the change in spending, accounting for 37 percent of initial spending and 50 percent of the spending decline. As a result, the share of spending for the highest income quartile declined.

While the results so far show that households with higher income cut spending by more and have slower recoveries in spending than low-income households, it is important to note that income is correlated with many other factors which might also affect spending responses, so these are not necessarily causal relationships. One particular concern in the context of the pandemic is that income is correlated with physical location, and locations vary in the strength of the pandemic. In particular, high-income individuals tend to live in cities, which have greater disease burden and more restrictive shutdowns. This means that the relationship between income and spending dynamics could reflect features of where high-income households live, rather than effects of income itself.[15]

To differentiate the role of income from the role of physical location, we look at the relationship between income and spending over the pandemic within narrow geographic areas. In particular, we compute the following regression:

$$\frac{C_{2020,z,q} - C_{2019,z,q}}{\overline{C}_{2019,q}} = Quartile_q + ZIP_z + \varepsilon_{z,q},$$

15. Note that measuring spending at the geography level rather than household level introduces additional concerns on this front: high-income households are more likely to leave cities than low-income households in response to the pandemic, which might induce spurious declines in spending in locations with many high-income households prior to the pandemic.

where $c_{t,z,q}$ is average spending per customer with t as the year (for the time period April 15–May 28), z is zip code, and q is the income quartile. We take two steps to minimize the influence of outliers. First, note that the denominator is $\bar{c}_{2019,q}$ which uses everyone in the income quartile. This prevents having one very large or very small ratio from skewing our results. Second, $c_{t,z,q}$ is Winsorized at the 1st and 99th percentile. We focus primarily on specifications with geography z equal to five-digit zip codes but also explore more aggregated three-digit zip codes to again limit the influence of measurement error.

Comparing odd columns in table 3 without geographic fixed effects to even columns with fixed effects shows that relationships between income and spending over the pandemic within zip codes are very similar to unconditional relationships. That is, high-income households cut spending more during the pandemic relative to low-income households living in the same zip code.[16] The similarity of results with and without fixed effects shows that these relationships are not driven by any observed or unobserved differences across locations where high- and low-income households live.

Finally, we further decompose the decline in credit card spending by income quartiles into essential and nonessential categories.[17] Figures 6 and 7 show that the spending declines for essential categories are indistinguishable across income groups, while nonessential credit card spending diverges more across income groups.

Although all households cut spending dramatically, the fact that high-income households cut spending by somewhat more may be surprising. Recent research suggests that lower-income households work in jobs that are harder to perform at home, require higher physical proximity, and therefore may be more impacted by distancing restrictions (Mongey, Pilossoph, and Weinberg 2020). Perhaps as a result, recent evidence from administrative ADP data shows that job losses were four times larger for workers in the bottom income quintile than those in the top income quintile, with a staggering 35 percent employment decline for the lowest-income workers (Cajner and others 2020). In response to greater income losses, we might have expected lower-income workers to have cut their spending by more. In fact, we find the reverse: higher-income households cut their spending by slightly more and their spending recovers more slowly.

---

16. Note that our information on address is as of early 2020.

17. Unfortunately, as mentioned above, we do not have the spending split by categories for the other forms of payment (debit, cash, and check).

Table 3. Income-Spend Relationships within Geography

	Dependent variable: spending growth							
	(1)	(2)	(3)	(4)	(5)	(6)	(7)	(8)
Income Q2	-0.032*	-0.028*	-0.048*	-0.039*	-0.035*	-0.034*	-0.032*	-0.033*
	(0.004)	(0.004)	(0.002)	(0.001)	(0.003)	(0.002)	(0.009)	(0.008)
Income Q3	-0.080*	-0.079*	-0.118*	-0.092*	-0.094*	0.085*	-0.082*	-0.081*
	(0.004)	(0.004)	(0.002)	(0.001)	(0.003)	(0.002)	(0.009)	(0.008)
Income Q4	-0.154*	-0.142*	-0.217*	-0.161*	-0.179*	-0.159*	-0.149*	-0.147*
	(0.004)	(0.004)	(0.002)	(0.001)	(0.003)	(0.002)	(0.009)	(0.008)
Constant	-0.043*		-0.047*		-0.049*		-0.061*	
	(0.003)		(0.001)		(0.002)		(0.006)	
Inclusion of geography fixed effects	NO	YES	NO	YES	NO	YES	NO	YES
Number of observations	70,189	70,189	70,189	70,189	25,432	25,432	3,608	3,608
Adjusted R^2	0.024	0.235	0.238	0.557	0.137	0.506	0.082	0.272

Source: JPMorgan Chase Institute.

Note: Year-over-year spending growth regression for the period April 15–May 28, 2020, for individual geography times income quartiles on income quartile dummies with and without geography fixed effects. Columns 1 and 2 define geography as five-digit zip codes and equal weight. Columns 3 and 4 use five-digit zip codes and are weighted by number of customers in each zip code times income quartile. Columns 5 and 6 use equal weights and five-digit zip codes but are restricted to zip code times income quartiles with at least twenty customers. Columns 7 and 8 use equal weights and define geographies as three-digit zip codes.

Significance: * $p < 0.01$.

Figure 6. Share of Credit Card Spending Decline Accounted for by Essential and Nonessential Credit Card Spending by Income Quartiles

Year-over-year percent change in essential spending

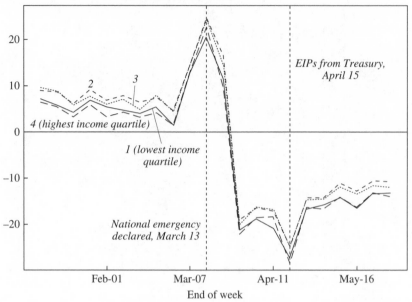

Year-over-year percent change in nonessential spending

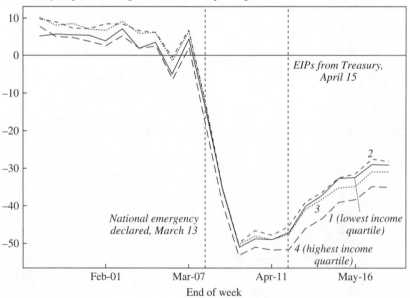

Source: JPMorgan Chase Institute.

Figure 7. Reduction in Essential versus Nonessential Spending by Income Quartiles

Income quartile

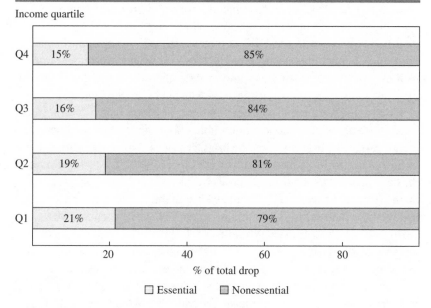

% of total drop

☐ Essential   ▨ Nonessential

Source: JPMorgan Chase Institute.

Differences between high- and low-income households in the composition of spending may be one reason why spending falls by more for high-income households. Nonessential categories represent a larger share of spending for high-income households—67 percent of spending in April 2019 for households in the top income quartile—compared to 59 percent for those in the bottom income quartile. In addition, higher-income households have slightly larger drops in their essential spending. Together, these facts imply that reductions in nonessential spending account for a somewhat larger share of total spending declines for high- versus low-income households (85 percent compared to 79 percent, figure 7). Since these nonessential categories are most affected by the pandemic shutdowns, overall spending of higher-income households may be more affected by supply-side restrictions. In other words, the effective price of consumption rises more for higher-income households relative to lower-income households. Thus, the composition of spending of higher-income households likely contributed to the larger decline in their spending. As discussed above, the widening of these initial spending declines during the recovery phase may reflect an important role for economic stimulus and transfer programs. The stimulus checks that began to arrive in April amount to a larger share of total income for a low-income household than for a high-income household. Ganong, Noel, and Vavra (2020) also show that the $600 expansion in UI benefits enacted through Federal Pandemic Unemployment Compensation (FPUC) boosted wage replacement rates to well over 100 percent for many low-income unemployed workers, providing a substantial income boost once they began receiving benefits.

Finally, higher-income households may be more exposed to negative wealth effects. Higher-income households hold more financial assets, and therefore are exposed to declines in asset prices during the initial stages of the pandemic. However, wealth effects are unlikely to be a key driver of the heterogeneous spending responses by income, given previous estimates on the strength of wealth effects together with the fact that the stock market had recovered most of its pandemic-related losses by the end of May.

CHANGE IN SPENDING BY INDUSTRY OF EMPLOYMENT We next examine whether workers in sectors most affected by employment disruptions adjust spending in ways that differ from workers in less affected sectors.

Figure 8 plots spending changes by industry of employment, for each industry where we have significant sample size. We aggregate to industries at the two-digit NAICS code. The one exception is retail, which we break out into grocery stores, drug stores, and discount stores—generally considered essential businesses and kept open under social distancing policies—and clothing and department stores, which were generally deemed nonessential businesses and where layoffs have been greater (Cajner and others 2020).

Overall, it is hard to discern systemic patterns between spending declines and the distribution of employment losses by industries. It is true that essential workers like those in grocery stores exhibit smaller spending declines. At the same time, professionals exhibit the largest spending declines, even though many jobs in this category can more easily be performed remotely.

While industry of employment is closely related to job losses, it is important to note that it is also highly correlated with income levels and that this may be explaining some of these differences.[18] For example, grocery store workers are typically low-income, while professional workers are typically high-income. In this sense, patterns when splitting by industry of employment in many ways mirror those when splitting by income: the

---

18. See online appendix table A.6.

Figure 8. Spending Changes Split by Industry of Employment

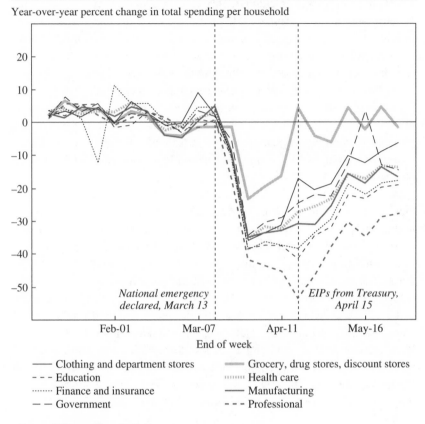

Year-over-year percent change in total spending per household

National emergency
declared, March 13

EIPs from Treasury,
April 15

End of week

—— Clothing and department stores   ▬▬ Grocery, drug stores, discount stores
- - - Education   ·········· Health care
········ Finance and insurance   —— Manufacturing
— — Government   - - - Professional

Source: JPMorgan Chase Institute.

largest drops in spending and slowest recoveries occur in higher-income industries of employment.

To provide a further sense of the separate role of income and industry, in figure A.11 in the online appendix, we compute spending by industry of employment separately for workers in the highest and lowest quartile of prepandemic income. Comparing variation across industries within income quartile in figure A.11 to variation across industries without conditioning on income in figure 8 shows that controlling for income substantially reduces the role of industry of employment. Similarly, comparing the same colored line between panels (a) and (b) in figure A.11 versus comparing different lines in figure 8 also shows that income generally has a greater correlation with spending dynamics than does industry of employment.

One potential interpretation is that the income channel accounts for only a small share of spending changes through the end of May. This may not be surprising given the magnitude of the spending decline. As mentioned previously, we document that average household spending fell over 35 percent, while the typical unemployed worker receiving UI only cuts spending around 6 percent in normal times (Ganong and Noel 2019).

However, there are several reasons for caution in concluding that income losses play a small role in spending effects. First, industry of employment may not fully proxy for job loss in our sample. To the extent that we can ascertain industry of employment primarily for employees of large firms, we may not be capturing the income losses for employees of small businesses.

Second, current conditions of the pandemic make comparing the magnitude of the spending response in April 2020 to that of UI recipients during normal times highly uncertain. On the one hand, the economic situation is highly uncertain, and labor markets weakened at an unprecedented pace. This might cause the unemployed to cut spending by more than during normal unemployment spells. On the other hand, as a result of the CARES Act, UI benefits are much more generous in level and duration, and available to many more workers. Furthermore, sizable stimulus checks were also sent out in April. These income supports might buffer against labor-income-related spending declines if this stimulus continues. The more rapid recovery of spending for low-income households suggests this channel is at work. The rest of the paper looks at the behavior of household savings to provide additional evidence on these channels.

III. Household Liquid Balances

Given the unprecedented reduction in spending across income and industries documented above, we next explore whether there were changes in the distribution of household liquid balances. Figure 1 shows that aggregate private savings increased substantially over the pandemic, reflecting the combination of large declines in spending and large increases in government transfers from stimulus programs. However, there are reasons to think that the pandemic could have heterogeneous impacts on household savings and substantial resulting effects on the distribution of wealth: households experiencing job loss may draw down on savings (or further draw on sources of borrowing), while those with job security may be essentially forced to save more, as consumption of many nonessential goods and services is more restricted. In addition, stimulus payments and other income support programs represent a larger share of prepandemic income for low-income households than for high-income households.

To explore these effects, we calculate how the distribution of end-of-week balances in household checking accounts evolved during the pandemic. Specifically, we explore how various unconditional moments of checking account balances evolved as well as how balances changed across the income distribution and by industry of employment. While checking account balances are only a subset of total savings and wealth, they represent some of the most liquid and easily accessible cash on hand available for households to smooth consumption and self-insure. A large literature has shown that liquid assets of this form play a crucial role in consumption. Furthermore, checking account balances have the practical advantage of being precisely and easily measured since checking accounts are one of our primary data sources.

We begin by plotting the average level of liquid balances, and the percentage year-over-year change from January through the end of May 2020. Figure 9 shows that by the last week of May, average balances increased by 33 percent year-over-year, or about $1,500 relative to earlier in the year. This increase is consistent with the large increase in the personal savings rate shown in figure 1 and with the growth in the stock of commercial bank deposits shown in online appendix figure A.13.[19] Much of the year-over-year growth in checking balances occurred during and after the week when most EIP stimulus checks were deposited, which suggests that the increase was driven by these income inflows, in addition to the reduced spending we documented in the previous section.[20]

Figure 10 plots additional moments of the distribution of liquid balances over time. The top panel shows that increases in liquid balances are pervasive, with increases observed at various percentiles of the distribution. The dollar increase in balances is greater for households with larger initial prepandemic balances. However, it is important to note that scale effects would be expected to drive that type of pattern: for example, if all balances double, the accounts with the largest initial balances will have the largest absolute increases. The bottom panel shows that the lower end of the distribution is growing more than the top end of the distribution. Interestingly,

19. Note that figure 9 should not be compared directly to the personal savings rate in figure 1, since aggregate personal savings is a flow variable while checking account balances are a stock variable.

20. We further decompose this trend into checking account inflows and outflows in the online appendix.

Figure 9. Level and Year-on-Year Change in Average Checking Account Balances

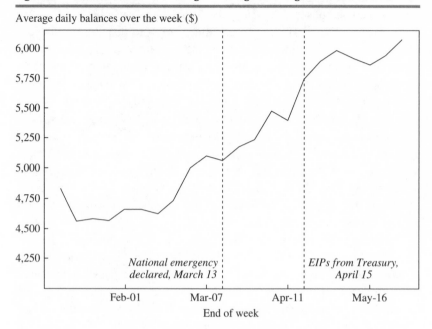

Average daily balances over the week ($)

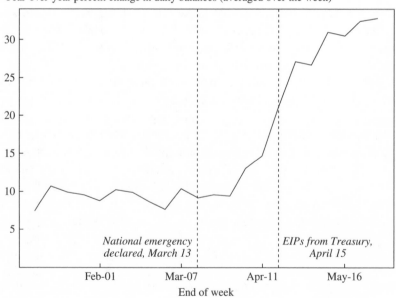

Year-over-year percent change in daily balances (averaged over the week)

Source: JPMorgan Chase Institute.

Figure 10. Change in Distribution of Checking Account Balances

Average daily balances over the week ($)

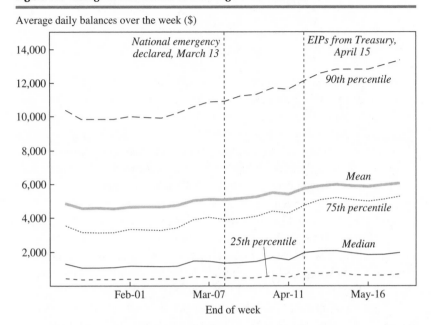

Year-over-year percent change in daily balances (averaged over the week)

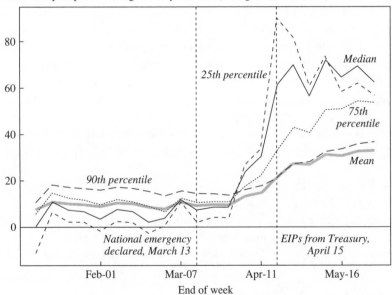

Source: JPMorgan Chase Institute.

the year-over-year growth for lower percentiles shoots up around the time of stimulus payments and then trends down. This suggests that households with low initial liquidity received a large increase in liquidity from stimulus payments, but they may be fairly rapidly using up this additional cash.

While the results in Figure 10 show that increases in liquid balances are pervasive, it is interesting to explore the relationship with pre-pandemic income. In particular, it is useful to know whether the increase in aggregate liquid balances was primarily driven by gains at the top of the income distribution (e.g., by individuals who cut spending most dramatically while generally maintaining labor income), or by gains at the bottom of the income distribution (e.g., individuals who cut spending somewhat less and faced larger declines in labor market income, but also had larger government transfers). Figure 11 plots checking account balances (in levels and growth rates) by income quartiles. Similar to the unconditional distribution of balances, we see pervasive increases in balances with increases observed for all groups. Also similar to the unconditional distribution, there are clear scale effects: the highest income quartile posted the largest dollar gains of around $2,000. The lowest income quartile increased balances by more than $1,000, which was the largest increase in year-on-year percentage terms.

Given these scale effects, what should we conclude about the relative role of high- versus low-income households in driving the increase in liquid wealth? One way to answer this question is to compare each group's contribution to the aggregate increase, relative to that group's initial share of savings. If all groups' savings grow by the same amount, then each group's contribution to the aggregate increase is equal to its initial share and the wealth distribution is unchanged. If low-income households have higher savings growth, then they will contribute more to the aggregate increase than their initial share and wealth inequality will decline.

To explore this more formally, table 4 reports the initial balances in February 2020, the increase in balances from February to May, and the final balances in May for each income quartile. Unsurprisingly, higher income quartiles contribute more to the level and change in total liquid balances, since these households have much more liquid wealth. For example, 51.5 percent (12.02/23.35) of total liquid balances come from the top income quartile.

It is also true that the top income quartiles drive the majority of the increase in liquid balances over the pandemic (36 percent), but

Figure 11. Change in Average Checking Account Balances by Income Quartile

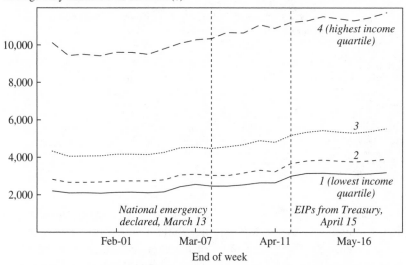

Average daily balances over the week ($)

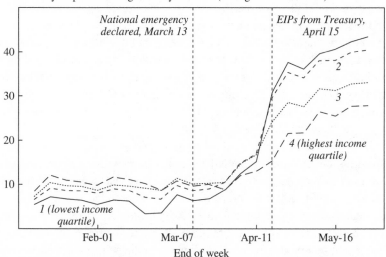

Year-over-year percent change in daily balances (averaged over the week)

Source: JPMorgan Chase Institute.

Note: This figure plots both average dollar balances and year-on-year percentage change in checking account balances by income quartile. Balance increases are larger in dollar terms for high-income households (who have higher prepandemic balances), and in percent terms for low-income households (who have lower prepandemic balances).

Table 4. Decomposition of Total Liquid Balances Changes by Income Quartile

	Initial balances ($ billion)	*Share of initial balances (%)*	*Increase in balances ($ billion)*	*Share of increase in balances (%)*	*Final balances ($ billion)*	*Share of final balances (%)*
Quartile 1	2.67	11.4	1.28	19.0	3.95	13.1
Quartile 2	3.44	14.7	1.39	20.7	4.83	16.1
Quartile 3	5.22	22.3	1.60	23.8	6.82	22.7
Quartile 4	12.02	51.5	2.45	36.4	14.47	48.1
Total	23.35	100.0	6.72	100.0	30.07	100.0
Top decile	7.19	30.8	1.305	19.4	8.49	28.2
Top 1 percent	1.84	7.9	0.294	4.4	2.13	7.1

Source: JPMorgan Chase Institute.
Note: Initial balances are computed in February 2020 and final balances are calculated in May 2020.

importantly, this increase is less than proportional to the initial share of liquid wealth held by the top quartile. Table 4 shows that lower-income quartiles are actually driving more of the aggregate increase in balances than would be expected from their initial balance shares, so liquid wealth inequality decreases between February and May. This provides a concrete sense in which the poor are disproportionately increasing savings relative to the rich during this pandemic. While this shift in the wealth distribution toward low-income households may not seem huge, it implies a more than three percentage point decline in the share of liquid wealth held by the richest quartile occurring over a matter of weeks. One important caveat is that we only measure checking account balances. If higher-income households transferred more assets out of the checking account, it is possible that we understate the increase in their total assets.[21]

This increase in savings for the poor very likely reflects the fact that stimulus checks and expanded UI benefits provide a disproportionate increase in income for these households. This also means that this shift may reverse in the near future if stimulus is reduced. For example, the expanded federal supplement to UI which has led to replacement rates above 100 percent for many families, is set to expire at the end of July 2020. The magnitude of the additional spending drop induced by initial disease avoidance and social distancing restrictions may also dominate the consumption response caused solely by income loss. This could lead to an

21. On the other hand, if delayed tax payments contributed to the growth in cash balances among high-income families, liquid asset growth could be short-lived.

Figure 12. Growth of Balances by Industry of Employment

Year-over-year percent change in daily balances (averaged over the week)

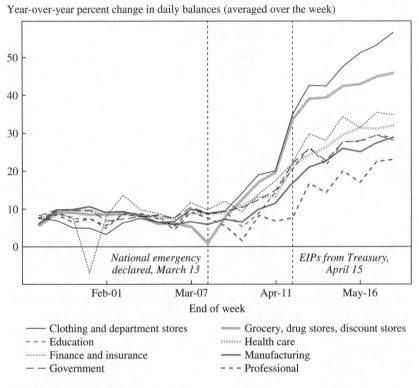

National emergency declared, March 13

EIPs from Treasury, April 15

End of week

—— Clothing and department stores
- - - Education
········ Finance and insurance
— — Government

▒▒▒ Grocery, drug stores, discount stores
▒▒▒▒ Health care
—— Manufacturing
- - - Professional

Source: JPMorgan Chase Institute.

increase in savings, even for those experiencing job loss, but it might not continue as social distancing is relaxed.

Finally, figure 12 shows liquid balance growth by industry of employment. While increases are again pervasive, we find that grocery store and department store workers have the largest growth in checking account balances. This is directly in line with checking account growth by income, since these are also the lowest income industries in our split.

IV. Conclusion

We find that all individuals across the income distribution cut spending at the start of the pandemic. These declines are massive relative to typical spending responses to unemployment. While high-income households cut spending more than low-income households, these differences are small relative to the huge common declines in spending. However, beginning in mid-April, substantial differences by income emerge: while spending begins to recover for all groups, it does so much more rapidly for the lowest income quartile. Similar patterns emerge when cutting by industry of employment, with workers in all industries initially cutting spending dramatically and then workers in low-wage industries seeing spending recover more quickly.

One limitation of this paper is that Chase micro data on income during the pandemic period are still being processed at the time of writing and are not yet available for analysis. We therefore turn to public-use data to explore how the income distribution has changed in recent months. Specifically, we simulate how income has likely changed in the first few months of the pandemic using statutory provisions of the CARES Act, information from the CPS, and the unemployment insurance calculator in Ganong, Noel, and Vavra (2020). Although *labor income* fell the most for lower-income households, we estimate that *total income,* including transfers, actually increased the most for those at the bottom of the income distribution for two reasons. First, the EIPs were a flat payment and therefore constituted a larger share of income for low-income households. Second, because the temporary $600 supplement to UI benefits under the CARES Act is the same for all unemployed workers, it drives up the replacement rate and resulting income disproportionately for low-income workers. In fact, UI benefits now replace more than 100 percent of lost earnings for low-income households (Ganong, Noel, and Vavra 2020). The details of this simulation are described in the online appendix.

Figure 13 juxtaposes simulation-based estimates of the change in income alongside the change in spending from figure 2. There is a suggestive correlation between the pattern of income changes and the relative pattern of spending changes. Spending falls the least for the group receiving the most income support, and decreases the most for the group with the least income support. In future work, when Chase micro data on income during the pandemic become available, we plan to explore the joint dynamics of income and spending at the household level to better understand these patterns.

Two other pieces of evidence in our paper suggest that government income support could be driving spending during this period. First, the timing of the more rapid rebound in spending for low-income households coincides closely with the timing of EIP stimulus and expanded UI benefits, suggesting an important role for government support in stabilizing spending during the pandemic, especially for low-income workers.

Figure 13. Estimated Changes in Income and Spending by Income Quartiles

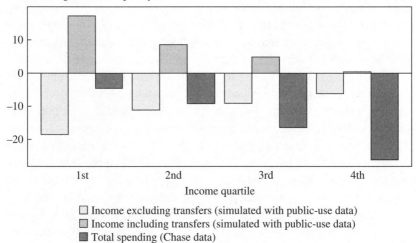

Percent change relative to prior year

☐ Income excluding transfers (simulated with public-use data)
▨ Income including transfers (simulated with public-use data)
■ Total spending (Chase data)

Source: JPMorgan Chase Institute.
Note: The change in income compares March, April, and May 2020 to average quarterly income in the prior year. The change in income reflects the decline in labor income, the EIPs, and unemployment benefits. The change in spending compares April 15–May 30 to spending in the same period in the prior year. Our estimate focuses on this narrower time horizon after the most immediate impacts of the lockdown—which depressed spending across the income distribution—had subsided.

Second, while increases in liquid balances are widespread during the pandemic and driven in large part by general declines in spending, we see that households at the bottom end of the income distribution—who see the largest stimulus relative to prepandemic income—have the largest growth in liquid savings during this period. As a result, liquid wealth inequality falls between February and May.

Taken together, our results suggest that labor market disruptions were unlikely to be a primary factor driving spending declines in these initial months of the recession. Many of the effects of labor market disruptions on spending were likely offset by sizable fiscal stimulus and insurance programs. Instead, direct effects of the pandemic were likely the primary factor driving overall declines in spending. Our analysis does not claim to disentangle the effect of pandemic-related channels—that is, regulatory shutdowns versus disease prevalence and fear of infection—on the spending decline. It instead focuses on the impact of income changes brought about by job loss and government transfers.

There are some important cautionary implications for future policy. First, it is important to note that even though aggregate spending has recovered substantially from its nadir, it remains well below normal. Spending on May 31st, when our sample currently ends, remains very low in absolute terms, even when compared to spending declines in other severe episodes like the Great Recession. Spending has partially recovered, but still remains severely depressed relative to prepandemic levels. Policy makers should thus not be too quick to conclude that the economy has rapidly recovered to normal. Even more importantly, our results suggest that an important share of this spending recovery has in fact been driven by aggressive fiscal stimulus and insurance payments. While we see a large spike in savings for low-income households immediately after the EIP, these increases may erode as the EIP gets used and if UI benefits get scaled back. This suggests that new support may be needed to maintain spending for low-income, vulnerable households in the near future. Phasing out broad stimulus too quickly could potentially transform a supply-side recession driven by direct effects of the pandemic into a broader and more persistent recession caused by declines in income and aggregate demand.

ACKNOWLEDGMENTS   We thank Therese Bonomo, Peter Robertson, and Tanya Sonthalia for their outstanding analytical contributions to the report. We thank Jonathan Parker, Jan Eberly, and Erik Hurst for helpful discussions. We are additionally grateful to Samantha Anderson, Maxwell Liebeskind, Robert McDowall, Shantanu Banerjee, Melissa Obrien, Erica Deadman, Sruthi Rao, Anna Garnitz, Jesse Edgerton, Michael Feroli, Daniel Silver, Joseph Lupton, Chris Knouss, Preeti Vaidya, and other members of the JPMorgan Chase Institute for their support, contributions, and insights.

References

Alexander, Diane, and Ezra Karger. 2020. "Do Stay-at-Home Orders Cause People to Stay at Home? Effects of Stay-at-Home Orders on Consumer Behavior." Working Paper 2020-12. Chicago: Federal Reserve Bank of Chicago.

Andersen, Asger, Emil Hansen, Niels Johannesen, and Adam Sheridan. 2020. "Pandemic, Shutdown and Consumer Spending: Lessons from Scandinavian Policy Responses to COVID-19." ArXiv:2005.04630. Ithaca, N.Y.: Cornell University.

Baker, Scott R., R. A. Farrokhnia, Steffen Meyer, Michaela Pagel, and Constantine Yannelis. 2020. "How Does Household Spending Respond to an Epidemic? Consumption during the 2020 COVID-19 Pandemic." Working Paper 26949. Cambridge, Mass.: National Bureau of Economic Research. http://www.nber.org/papers/w26949.

Bitler, Marianne, Hilary Hoynes, and Diane Schanzenbach. 2020. "The Social Safety Net in the Wake of COVID-19." In the present volume of *Brookings Papers on Economic Activity*.

Cajner, Tomaz, Leland D. Crane, Ryan A. Decker, John Grigsby, Adrian Hamins-Puertolas, Erik Hurst, Christopher Kurz, and Ahu Yildirmaz. 2020. "The U.S. Labor Market during the Beginning of the Pandemic Recession." Working Paper 27159. Cambridge, Mass.: National Bureau of Economic Research. https://www.nber.org/papers/w27159.

Chetty, Raj, John N. Friedman, Nathaniel Hendren, Michael Stepner, and the Opportunity Insights Team. 2020. "How Did COVID-19 and Stabilization Policies Affect Spending and Employment? A New Real-Time Economic Tracker Based on Private Sector Data." Working Paper 27431. Cambridge, Mass.: National Bureau of Economic Research. https://www.nber.org/papers/w27431.

Ganong, Peter, and Pascal Noel. 2019. "Consumer Spending during Unemployment: Positive and Normative Implications." *American Economic Review* 109, no. 7: 2383–424. https://www. aeaweb.org/articles?id=10.1257/aer.20170537.

Ganong, Peter, Pascal Noel, and Joseph Vavra. 2020. "US Unemployment Insurance Replacement Rates during the Pandemic." Working Paper 2020-62. Chicago: Becker Friedman Institute for Economics. https://bfi.uchicago.edu/wp-content/uploads/BFI_WP_202062-1.pdf.

Karger, Ezra, and Aastha Rajan. 2020. "Heterogeneity in the Marginal Propensity to Consume: Evidence from Covid-19 Stimulus Payments." Working Paper 2020-15. Chicago: Federal Reserve Bank of Chicago. https://www. chicagofed.org/publications/working-papers/2020/2020-15.

Mongey, Simon, Laura Pilossoph, and Alex Weinberg. 2020. "Which Workers Bear the Burden of Social Distancing Policies?" Working Paper 2020-51. Cambridge, Mass.: National Bureau of Economic Research. https://www.nber.org/papers/w27085.

Comments and Discussion

COMMENT BY
JONATHAN A. PARKER Following the identification of a novel form
of coronavirus in China at the end of 2019, COVID-19 has spread rapidly
around the world causing death and economic destruction. On March 13,
2020, with hundreds of new cases identified each day (soon to be thousands), the United States declared a national emergency. In response both
to the spreading virus and to government-ordered partial shutdowns, significant swaths of the US economy simply stopped during much of April.
As the spread of the virus was slowed in the late spring and early summer,
the reductions in economic activity have been partially reversing. These
two excellent papers present some of the first broad-based, quantitative
measurement of the massive disruption and partial rebound of employment and consumer spending during the first few months of this pandemic
recession. They should be a good guide for what is happening now at the
end of July, as new cases currently number in the tens of thousands.

In this discussion, I will first briefly describe how aggregate consumption and income have reacted during these first few months that followed
COVID-19 reaching the United States, and then compare these measures to
the average consumption and income responses documented in each of the
two papers. But the main contributions of these papers lie in the careful
analysis of the heterogeneous impact of the pandemic using high-quality,
large microeconomic data sets.[1] So, second, I will emphasize what I take as
the two main lessons from the combination of the papers. During this initial
period of the pandemic, the economic collapse is almost entirely due to the

---

1. Both papers treat the related literature well, and I choose not to use my space
comparing these papers to other rapid-response analyses of the economic effects of COVID-19
using micro data.

Figure 1. Real Personal Disposable Income and Personal Consumption Expenditures

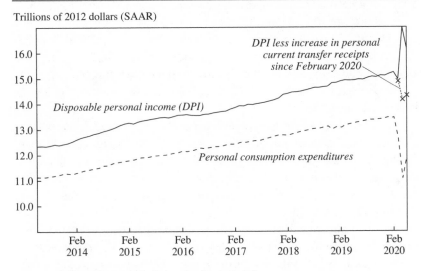

Trillions of 2012 dollars (SAAR)

DPI less increase in personal current transfer receipts since February 2020

Disposable personal income (DPI)

Personal consumption expenditures

Feb 2014   Feb 2015   Feb 2016   Feb 2017   Feb 2018   Feb 2019   Feb 2020

Sources: Bureau of Economic Analysis and authors' calculations.

pandemic directly. That is, whether one defines the shutdown of some sectors of the economy "demand" (e.g., people do not want to consume certain goods) or "supply" (e.g., certain firms cannot produce), the key point is that the papers show that the collapse in consumption is not due to, or amplified by, current income losses, and that the declines in employment are not due to, or amplified by, current low income or liquidity. The other lesson is that this lack of observable propagation through incomes and reduced demand is significantly due to the large policy response. These lessons apply only to these first few months. The pandemic is continuing, and I expect that this recession will slowly turn from a pandemic shutdown into a more typical recession and exhibit the usual economic propagation of recessions through demand channels.

Since these lessons lean more heavily on the consumption results, in the last part of my discussion, I will highlight a few other interesting findings about the decline in employment, and conclude with a few thoughts about real-time analysis by academic economists and economic policy going forward.

Figure 1 shows the disruption that this caused the economy as documented in aggregated statistics. Aggregate personal consumption expenditures (the dashed line) fall by about 6 percent from February to March and then decline precipitously from March to April by 12.2 percent, reaching a level not seen since about seven years earlier. Both to emphasize how rapid and large this decline is, and because I hope never to have the opportunity to write a sentence like this again, let me note that this implies that real personal consumption expenditures declined by 79.1 percent at an annual rate between March and April 2020. Consumption subsequently rebounded in June, rising by 8.1 percent to roughly 11 percent below its February level.

These numbers are broadly consistent with the patterns shown in Cox and colleagues mapped into monthly averages, with two exceptions. First, the high-frequency nature of the paper's data—a significant contribution of the paper—shows some evidence for a spike in spending that occurs before the shutdown, possibly as people stock up ahead of expected increases in infection rates, store closures, and shelter-in-place orders.[2] Second, the paper documents a larger decline in consumption from February to March and a smaller decline from March to April than in the Bureau of Economic Analysis (BEA) data. In favor of the results in Cox and colleagues is that the month-to-month timing of consumption expenditures in official statistics is not particularly reliable. A major source of the data, for example, is a survey of retail establishments about sales volumes in which establishments can choose different time horizons over which to report sales amounts, over-lapping horizons that must then be unpacked by the BEA to create monthly data. On the other hand, the Chase data capture only Chase customers and omit certain types of consumer spending. Using account-level data requires that one infer whether an outflow is consumption, saving, or debt payment from the observed counterparty. Paper checks do not have readily observable counterparties, nor do electronic funds transfers (EFTs) in this paper. One might also be concerned that the pandemic changed the means of payment for different types of consumption.[3]

Figure 1 further shows that disposable personal income (solid line) falls slightly in March and then *rises* by 13.6 percent in April before falling back down slightly in June. The personal savings rate—the difference between the two series as a percent of disposable income—rose to more than 30 percent in April, a number consistent with the unprecedented use of the word *unprecedented* during this pandemic.

---

2. See also Baker and others (2020).

3. That said, cash withdrawals are measured in consumption both before and after the pandemic, so that switches in the composition of spending between cash and cards should only affect the allocation of spending to categories (Cox and colleagues, figure 4).

Figure 2. Consumption and Income by Ex Ante Income Level

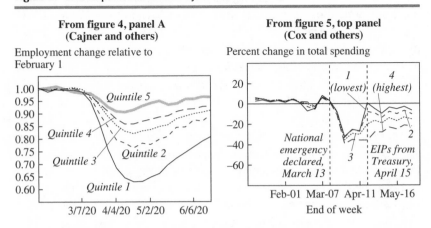

From figure 4, panel A
(Cajner and others)

Employment change relative to
February 1

From figure 5, top panel
(Cox and others)

Percent change in total spending

Sources: ADP anonymized payroll records and authors' calculations (left); JPMorgan Chase Institute (right).

However, the increase in disposable personal income looks like good news, and nothing like the labor market disruptions documented by Cajner and colleagues. The reason for this discrepancy is that government transfers increased by $231 billion from March to April ($2.8 trillion at an annual rate!) mostly due to the disbursement of economic relief payments. The final line (solid with x's) on figure 1 removes the increase in current transfer receipts since February from the disposable personal income series and shows that income less these transfers declined by 2.3 percent in March and then 4.9 percent in April before slightly rebounding by 1 percent in May.

These declines in income are large for one-month movements, but are still slightly lower than one might infer from Cajner and colleagues. The most likely cause of this discrepancy is the difference in populations. The BEA data include government workers and retirees for example, whose regular incomes, as best we know, experienced less of an impact early in the pandemic. This highlights a difference not just between the aggregate data and the population studied by Cajner and colleagues, but also between the populations studied by the two papers. That said, I will now pretend the papers cover the same people and measure what we want them to measure, two assumptions that appear reasonable given the size of the pandemic shock and the point I want to emphasize.

Figure 2 simply reproduces the two figures in the two papers that show changes over time by quintiles or quartiles of the ex ante income distribution. The figure on the left, from Cajner and colleagues, shows that there are dramatically larger declines in employment for ex ante lower income workers. The figure on the right, from Cox and colleagues, shows that there are not larger declines in spending for ex ante lower income workers. The implication: *the initial aggregate collapse of consumption during these months was driven by the unwillingness or inability of people to consume rather than by declines in income.*

The second main point: the most important reason that low-income (harder hit) households have not on average had to cut consumption on average by more than high-income households appears to be the increase in government transfers (economic relief payments, automatic stabilizers, and extended UI benefits). While this point is suggested by figure 1, Cox and colleagues show two important pieces of evidence in favor of this conclusion. First, consumer spending jumps up significantly at exactly the same time that most of the Economic Relief Payments—a major part of the policy response—were disbursed. Second, the paper shows that low-income households maintained substantial liquidity during these first few months despite significant income losses.

Let me note one caveat about the evidence for these conclusions. As shown in the left panel of figure 2, Cajner and colleagues show that employment has rebounded more strongly for ex ante low-income workers (although it remains below its prepandemic level). Further, the paper also shows that wage cuts are more common among high-income workers. Thus, my reading may be exaggerating somewhat the differences in income losses by ex ante income level. If there were only small differences in income, then we would expect little difference in spending responses across income levels and be less confident in the conclusion that income losses in general were not substantially holding back the economy.

My juxtaposition of the results of the two papers in figure 2 can be complemented by a similar comparison of the set of results in the two papers by industry. The pandemic shut down certain industries, and both papers nicely document how this has caused quite different income losses across workers. Yet again, we see little differences in consumption of households who work in different industries.

This conclusion implies that for the first few months of the pandemic in the United States, the goal of policy should have been insurance rather than stimulus. And policy largely met this insurance need. Policy surely also contributed to the lack of economic damage from a collapse in spending, but it did not stimulate the economy beyond this point, which I think is appropriate. When from a public health perspective (and so a welfare perspective), it is optimal to shut down some sectors of the economy, then there is a reduced multiplier from government transfers and income support. In the typical recession, stimulus tends to raise purchases the most for the goods for which demand fell the most. So stimulus tends to generate spending that leads to hiring or maintaining employment for the workers most affected by the recession, who then tend to turn around and maintain consumption instead of cutting it. This is the Keynesian multiplier. However, when some employers are shuttered for health reasons, no stimulus is spent there, so any increase in demand and in resultant incomes go to those workers and industries who are already the least affected.

Further, unlike in a typical recession, when a sector of the economy is temporarily shut down, everyone in that sector with the same skills is out of work at the same time. While some workers can gain employment by moving across industries, if the shutdown is temporary, there is little benefit to having people searching for work which requires employers to on-board and train people whose skills are a poor match for the job at hand. Instead, as emphasized by Guerrieri and others (2020), fiscal targeted transfers are an important part of optimal policy as pandemic insurance. Only once the pandemic is past and as the economy reopens, to the extent that we are in a recession or a slow recovery, then more traditional demand stimulus may be beneficial.

There are also many more fascinating details in each paper, but I only have space to discuss two and will focus on Cajner and colleagues, which I have focused slightly less on up to now.

First, data on average wages show that they have risen substantially in the crisis so far, a point that has received a fair bit of attention. One can only measure wages for employed workers. Cajner and colleagues show that the average wage rises precisely because, as I focused on above, low-wage workers disproportionately lost their jobs. The paper shows that in fact, wages for continuing workers are on average unchanged through these first few months of the recession. The paper also shows that this constant average wage masks lots of different wage changes, and indeed a substantial share of workers have experienced wage reductions.[4] This finding sheds light on the theoretical factors that may constrain wage reductions in typical recessions. In particular, menu costs models predict that wages are more flexible in response to large shocks. Further, in such models, aggregate wage adjustment is slowed by strategic complementarities

---

4. For example, most senior faculty at MIT experienced a (temporary, we hope) wage cut for 2020, a first as far as I know.

and non-simultaneous adjustments. Both modelling ingredients thus predict that wages are more flexible in response to large and simultaneous economic shocks to firms, which is what this early evidence appears to show.

Second, the pandemic has had significantly different impacts on workers by gender. Cajner and colleagues show a much larger decline in the employment of women than men. Further, this difference is largely unrelated to the fact that women and men tend to work in different industries and at different sized firms. As such, in addition to the unequal burden of childcare and housework as the pandemic has shuttered schools, women may experience longer-lasting and more serious consequences from the labor market shutdown (Alon and others 2020).

Before concluding, I wanted to both praise and make a few suggestions for the conduct of research in this new world in which academic economists work with private-sector companies and conduct nearly real-time analysis, sometimes now directly for high-quality journals like the BPEA. Real-time analysis used to be purely the purview of newspapers, Gallup-type survey firms, and economists in bank research departments that had access to data and produced analyses for clients. And these organizations do still tend to produce analyses of important economic events first.[5] These early analyses partly lay out key questions and partly set narratives that persist in our understanding of events. The involvement of academics in this process is a boon. We can expand the resources available for these analyses, and also add a set of skills and knowledge—about theory, causation, and economic behavior—that can improve these analyses.

But these benefits should also involve some changes in how we operate. First, our usual strengths—the added value of academics—is about getting things right, at the cost of being slow. We are often trusted because we are correct, which involves being diligent, careful, and taking our time. We have to protect that trust, which means being clear that rapid analysis of firm data is not the same product as established research based on painstaking analysis. To be clear, I praise both papers in this regard. Each is extremely careful to delineate its strengths and to clearly state caveats.

Second, we have to be careful ourselves not to take early narratives (like my main conclusions in this discussion) as final truths. As an example, the latest Commerce Department estimate is that the homeownership rate

5. Bank of America, for example, produced an analysis of the spending caused by the economic relief payments on April 22, within days of the first payments being distributed; Michelle Meyer and Anna Zhou, "COVID-19 and the Consumer: Data through April 16," Bank of America Data Analytics.

rose by more than 3 percent between the first and second quarters of 2020. The pandemic has played havoc with the collection of lots of economic data, and I will go out on a limb and say that this large an increase in home-ownership is very, very unlikely. Another example is that it has taken academics many years and many papers to overturn the early media consensus that the subprime crisis caused the financial crisis. And we are still—more than a decade later—parsing the relative roles of lending standards, low interest rates, and optimistic beliefs in the housing bubble, which is great. We, and many of the first contributors, have a dogged persistence to refine early findings and get to the truth. But early findings are more persistent the farther one looks from the core researchers. So, to again try to be clear, I have no reason to doubt the results in these papers, but we as a field need to avoid first-impressions bias, and I look forward to updating and refining my understanding from future analyses of the data from more companies and from traditional representative surveys.

To conclude let me return to interpreting the main lessons of these papers. The dramatic aggregate declines in employment and consumption appear to be due to choices rather than responses to low incomes or liquidity. The income declines represent a combination of responses to the pandemic: government policies, motivated by a desire to stop or at least slow the spread of the disease, and human behaviors that incorporate the additional motivation of self-preservation.[6] The effects of the income declines on consumption appear, in the data so far, to have been largely mitigated by fiscal insurance policies.

REFERENCES FOR THE PARKER COMMENT

Alon, Titan, Matthias Doepke, Jane Olmstead-Rumsey, and Michèle Tertilt. 2020. "This Time It's Different: The Role of Women's Employment in a Pandemic Recession." Working Paper 13562. Bonn: Institute of Labor Economics. http://ftp.iza.org/dp13562.pdf.

Andersen, Asger Lau, Emil Toft Hansen, Niels Johannesen, and Adam Sheridan. 2020. "Pandemic, Shutdown and Consumer Spending: Lessons from Scandinavian Policy Responses to COVID-19." ArXiv:2005.04630v1. https://arxiv.org/pdf/2005.04630.pdf.

6. My reading of the literature so far is that, given the individual responses that already occur in response to the disease, there are few medium-term economic costs of government policies that shut down economic activity, at least on average outcomes, and there are substantial benefits in terms of health and lives saved from the disease (Andersen and others 2020; Correia, Luck, and Verner 2020).

Baker, Scott R., Robert A. Farrokhnia, Steffen Meyer, Michaela Pagel, and
    Constantine Yannelis. 2020. "How Does Household Spending Respond to an
    Epidemic? Consumption during the 2020 COVID-19 Pandemic." *Review of
    Asset Pricing Studies* 10, no. 4: 834–62.
Correia, Sergio, Stephan Luck, and Emil Verner. 2020. "Pandemics Depress the
    Economy, Public Health Interventions Do Not: Evidence from the 1918 Flu."
    Working Paper. https://papers.ssrn.com/sol3/papers.cfm?abstract_id=3561560.
Guerrieri, Veronica, Guido Lorenzoni, Ludwig Straub, and Iván Werning. 2020.
    "Macroeconomic Implications of COVID-19: Can Negative Supply Shocks
    Cause Demand Shortages?" Working Paper 26918. Cambridge, Mass.: National
    Bureau of Economic Research. https://www.nber.org/papers/w26918.

GENERAL DISCUSSION   Adriana Kugler appreciated Cox and coauthors' simulation to estimate changes in income from stimulus policy, and she considered the possibility that Cajner and coauthors could employ a similar simulation to estimate the effects of Paycheck Protection Program (PPP) payments for firms. She postulated that PPP payments could help explain the trajectory of firm size and the nature of employment rebounds being primarily recall-driven (as opposed to being driven by new hires). She proposed that researchers explore the timing differentials that occurred in the implementation of the stimulus to verify this idea.

Kugler also commented on the breakdown of employment changes by gender in Cajner and coauthors' presentation, wondering if perhaps the idiosyncratic effects of the pandemic within individual sectors have been responsible for job losses being concentrated against women. She raised the possibility that using three-digit industry codes, as opposed to two-digit or one-digit codes, could be useful in answering this question.

Lastly, Kugler turned back to Cox and coauthors' paper, suggesting the potential for this study to focus more strongly on differences in pandemic unemployment assistance and relief transfers by state. Kugler proposed a more in-depth exploration of how individual states differed in their program implementation timing, worker composition, welfare infrastructure, and welfare qualification criteria and how those differences drove the results of the paper. Kugler concluded by urging both groups of authors to detail more explicitly the effects of the Coronavirus Aid, Relief, and Economic Security (CARES) Act and general government policy on their respective analyses.

Olivier Blanchard reiterated the finding from Cox and coauthors that saving has increased at the top of the income distribution during the pandemic, noting that he found it particularly striking. He asked the authors and discussant if they had any general predictions for the consumption behavior of the rich in the future.

Hilary Hoynes commended the authors of both papers for examining how their respective analyses found different results for different groups and for articulating important levels of heterogeneity in the trends they observed. She raised the possibility that certain individuals were left out of the samples in each study, a problem she believed was particularly concerning for Cox and coauthors. She questioned if economically disadvantaged Americans, who are disproportionately likely to lack the bank accounts necessary to be included in the JPMorgan Chase data, were properly represented in the study. Similarly, Hoynes pointed out that the lowest income quartile in the study was limited to those with $12,000 or more, again raising the possibility that the sample did not accurately represent the most vulnerable Americans. She echoed discussant Jonathan Parker's comment that cautioned against drawing strong conclusions based on this issue and promoted the papers to be presented later in another conference session (Han and coauthors and Bitler and coauthors) for their results that focused on the poorest Americans.

David Wilcox continued along a similar line of thought. He asked if Cox and coauthors had any information regarding indicators of financial distress for the households in their sample, such as potential delinquencies on rent or a mortgage. He cautioned against concluding that relief measures had succeeded in staving off financial distress in the absence of measures of these indicators to confirm such a conclusion. Wilcox also noted that communities of color have been disproportionately harmed by COVID-19 and asked if it would be possible to examine the data along racial and ethnic lines to draw out additional insights.

Daron Acemoglu suggested to Cox and coauthors that they could use a shift-share composition analysis to explain the differences in their results across income groups. He noted that certain types of consumption would decline more than others because of social distancing (among other pandemic-related factors) and that those types of consumption are not homogeneously distributed across income brackets. Acemoglu proposed that understanding how the composition of different income groups' consumption was affected by the pandemic will be important for understanding changes in savings and consumption as the economy turns toward recovery.

Claudia Sahm was unable to comment directly due to technical difficulties, but moderator James Stock summarized from a comment she posted via the teleconference platform. According to Stock, Sahm said she strongly disagreed with a sentiment expressed by Jonathan Parker urging moderation in the responses of economists, and she exhorted the conference to take action with respect to solving the pressing crises of the pandemic.

Wendy Edelberg said she agreed with Sahm that economists had an imperative to act and also agreed with Parker in cautioning against drawing conclusions too quickly. Turning to her central point, she argued that if one looked at how much consumption by low-income workers changed relative to high-income worker consumption, one might be led to believe that consumption in low-income households was not particularly affected by changes in income. She noted that such a conclusion would upend standard conceptions of marginal propensities to consume and how they differ among the rich and the poor. However, she pointed out that such an understanding would largely require ignoring the actual levels to which low-income consumption fell. Edelberg asked whether, by looking at how much consumption fell for low-income individuals, economists could gain new understandings of marginal propensities to consume among the poor. She concluded by noting that such lessons could have implications for the design of future stimulus policies and for determining whether or not stimulus payments to low-income individuals would largely be spent or saved.

Alessandro Rebucci asked if it was possible to determine the extent to which the pandemic differently affected the markets for goods and for services. He noted that services have been affected more than goods. He continued by commenting on the importance of understanding what has driven saving behavior in the pandemic, and he asked if increases in saving have been more due to precautionary saving in response to increased uncertainty or to declines in nonessential and conspicuous consumption, like vacation spending, due to the lockdowns and travel restrictions. He argued that understanding these drivers is important to form expectations about the recovery and also for policy design.

Ryan Decker, a coauthor on the Cajner paper, represented his colleagues in answering questions. He first noted, in relation to Sahm's comment and the related discussion, that while there has been pressure to release results quickly, he felt confident in his team's ability to work with ADP data. To illustrate this point, he noted that they have released papers using those data going back to 2018 and have other forthcoming papers that have been subject to rigorous academic scrutiny. He credited Wilcox for helping guide the research team to using the ADP data set.

In response to questions about the PPP, Decker said that his team's paper did not specifically examine that initiative. He pointed toward work that David Autor, Crane, and colleagues were presenting the same day at an

Automatic Data Processing, Inc., conference, examining PPP and analyzing how small and large businesses had different experiences with the program.

Lastly, Decker responded to an earlier comment about industry coverage, affirming that his data set was comprehensive across industries, and said that his team's findings about employment differences by gender held true even within detailed industries.

Peter Ganong, a coauthor on the Cox paper, fielded questions for his research team. He directed attention to a figure from his presentation, a bar plot showing changes in debit card spending, income without transfers, and income with transfers ("Estimated changes in income and spending," on figure 13 of his team's presentation).

First, Ganong answered questions regarding the representativeness of the sample in his study, noting that it was comprised of bank account data, and that roughly 95 percent of Americans have bank accounts.[1] He commented that this obviously left out some Americans, particularly low-income ones. Additionally, he affirmed the point raised by Hilary Hoynes, that individuals had to have at least $12,000 in labor income to be included in the sample. As a result, if, prior to the COVID-19 pandemic, an individual earned less than $1,000 per month, they would not be represented in the study sample. Ganong elaborated, stating that the lowest quartile of individuals in the study had annual post-tax labor incomes between $12,000 and $24,000, so while many low-income individuals were represented in the study, those with the lowest incomes were not.

Second, Ganong turned to questions regarding how his study calculated income changes, and what assumptions he and his team made regarding the receipt of unemployment insurance and stimulus. Briefly, he noted that while not all stimulus checks had gone out at that time (referring to economic impact payments), enough had for that fact not to be a large source of uncertainty. What was more important, Ganong said, was the fact that some states have been slower than others in processing unemployment insurance claims and in issuing unemployment insurance payments. He noted that their study does not assume that everyone left unemployed in the pandemic has received unemployment insurance but instead uses information from the Department of Labor to infer the fraction of unemployed Americans receiving unemployment insurance. He stated this was roughly 50 percent in April and 75 percent in May.

---

1. Economic Inclusion, "FDIC Survey of Household Use of Banking and Financial Services," 2019, https://economicinclusion.gov/surveys/.

Finally, Ganong turned to questions regarding heterogeneity in the team's sample. Noting that the average consumption in the lowest quartile of the sample remained *approximately* constant, this did not mean that every individual in this quartile had constant consumption but rather that some people increased their consumption and some people decreased their consumption. He then concluded briefly in response to Wilcox's earlier point, saying that the JPMorgan Chase Institute is engaged in studies regarding mortgage delinquency and that while those considerations were not in his team's line of research, they would be addressed by others soon.

SESSION TWO
Safety Net Programs and Poverty

JEEHOON HAN
Zhejiang University

BRUCE D. MEYER
University of Chicago

JAMES X. SULLIVAN
University of Notre Dame

Income and Poverty in the COVID-19 Pandemic

ABSTRACT   This paper addresses the economic impact of the COVID-19 pandemic by providing timely and accurate information on the impact of the current pandemic on income and poverty to inform the targeting of resources to those most affected and assess the success of current efforts. We construct new measures of the income distribution and poverty with a lag of only a few weeks using high-frequency data from the Basic Monthly Current Population Survey (CPS), which collects income information for a large, representative sample of US families. Because the family income data for this project are rarely used, we validate this timely measure of income by comparing historical estimates that rely on these data to estimates from data on income and consumption that have been used much more broadly. Our results indicate that at the start of the pandemic, government policy effectively countered its effects on incomes, leading poverty to fall and low percentiles of income to rise across a range of demographic groups and geographies. Simulations that rely on the detailed CPS data and that closely match total government payments made show that the entire decline in poverty that we find can be accounted for by the rise in government assistance, including unemployment insurance benefits and the Economic Impact Payments. Our simulations further indicate that of those losing employment the vast majority received unemployment insurance,

Conflict of Interest Disclosure: The authors did not receive financial support from any firm or person for this paper or from any firm or person with a financial or political interest in this paper. They are currently not officers, directors, or board members of any organization with an interest in this paper. No outside party had the right to review this paper before circulation. The views expressed in this paper are those of the authors, and do not necessarily reflect those of Zhejiang University, the University of Chicago, or the University of Notre Dame.

though this was less true early on in the pandemic, and receipt was uneven across the states, with some states not reaching a large share of their out of work residents. Updated results during the pandemic for a subset of the tables in this article can be found at povertymeasurement.org.

The start of the COVID-19 pandemic in the United States quickly resulted in an unprecedented decline in economic activity with employment and earnings plummeting. At the same time, the federal government responded with tax rebates in the form of Economic Impact Payments (EIPs), small business loans, and an unprecedented expansion of unemployment insurance as part of the Coronavirus Aid, Relief, and Economic Security (CARES) Act and related stimulus legislation that, all told, committed more than $3 trillion to countering the effects of the COVID-19 pandemic. Whether this response has been adequate to offset the losses and what net effect it may have on income and poverty remain unclear. To ensure that the government can track the income changes of the American population overall and by demographic group to target and calibrate its fiscal response most effectively requires timely information on income and poverty. Unfortunately, official estimates of income and poverty for 2020 will not be available until September 2021. These official statistics will be of little use to federal, state, and local policymakers who need to decide quickly how to allocate scarce resources to minimize COVID-19's impact on vulnerable populations. Thus, this crisis calls for timely and accurate information on the impact of the current pandemic (as well as future shocks) on the economic well-being of individuals and families.

To address the gap in critical, real-time information we construct new measures of the income distribution and income-based poverty with a lag of only a few weeks using high-frequency data for a large, representative sample of US families and individuals. We rely upon the Basic Monthly Current Population Survey (Monthly CPS), which includes a greatly underused global question about annual family income. A clear advantage of using the Monthly CPS to estimate changes in income and poverty is that the quick release of these data allows us to understand the immediate impact of macroeconomic conditions and government policies. For example, given data release dates, analyses of income from the Monthly CPS would have revealed the negative impact of the Great Recession a full fourteen months before official estimates indicated an increase in poverty. Our approach generates immediately useful income and poverty estimates for the overall population, as well as how these rates vary by demographic groups and geography. We also validate this new and timely measure of family income by comparing estimates that rely on these data to estimates from data on income that have been used much more broadly and that have a long historical track record. Our validations will help other researchers understand the advantages and limitations of using more timely income data to understand changes in economic well-being.

Our initial evidence indicates that at the start of the pandemic, government policy effectively countered its effects on incomes, leading poverty to fall and low percentiles of income to rise across a range of demographic groups and geographies. Our evidence suggests that income poverty fell shortly after the start of the COVID-19 pandemic in the United States. In particular, the poverty rate, calculated each month by comparing family incomes for the past twelve months to the official poverty thresholds, fell by 1.5 percentage points from 10.9 percent in the months leading up to the pandemic (January and February) to 9.4 percent in the three most recent months (April, May, and June). This decline in poverty occurred despite that fact that employment rates fell by 14 percent in April (online appendix figure 1)—the largest one-month decline on record. The declines in poverty are evident for most demographic groups, although we find some evidence that poverty declines most noticeably for those who report their race as neither white nor Black and those who have a high school education or less.

Our simulations using the detailed and nationally representative CPS data indicate that government programs, including the regular unemployment insurance (UI) program, the expanded UI programs, and the EIPs, can account for more than the entire decline in poverty, which would have risen by over 2.5 percentage points in the absence of these programs. These programs also helped boost incomes for those further up the income distribution, but to a lesser extent. Evidence based on actual dollars spent on these programs indicates that most eligible families received the EIP, and that the expanded coverage of unemployment insurance reached the vast majority of those desiring to work who were unable to do so. However, the states were slow to reach many without work and some states were still unable to reach a large share of their population even three months after the initial employment decline.

This study generates some of the first evidence on how the COVID-19 pandemic is affecting the economic well-being of individuals and families in the United States, and which groups are affected most. Economists have long examined the impact of large macroeconomic shocks, such as recessions (Grusky, Western, and Wimer 2011) or pandemics (Almond 2006; Almond and Mazumder 2005). However, due to the limited availability of data making it difficult to study major shocks as they evolve, past research has necessarily mostly happened long after the events occurred. Our study provides a template for the future understanding of large economic shocks as they happen. This paper also addresses important survey methodology questions, such as whether the patterns of annual income from a monthly survey align with the patterns for income from annual surveys that are the source for official statistics, and how responses to a single, global question about income compare to estimates of total income from questions about many income sources. Understanding the validity of survey-measured income is critically important given the prominent role it plays in economic research.

I. Discerning the Impact of COVID-19

The impact of the pandemic on the labor market was swift and severe. Employment rates (online appendix figure 1) dropped sharply, by more than 8 percentage points (14 percent), in April, the largest one-month decline on record. At the same time earnings fell by more than 10 percent (online appendix figure 2). Although both earnings and employment bounced back somewhat in May and June, they remain well below the levels at the start of 2020.

The two most direct ways that federal policies worked to offset this sudden decline in earnings were through EIP and the expansion of UI benefits. The EIP provided $1,200 to individuals with income less than $75,000 and to single parents (heads of household) with income below $112,500, and they provided $2,400 to married couples with income less than $150,000. Recipients were also eligible to receive an additional $500 for each qualifying child. For those with income above these thresholds, the payments were reduced by 5 percent of the income that exceeded the threshold.

EIPs started the second week of April, with the early checks going to those with the lowest adjusted gross income. As shown in online appendix figure 3, the Internal Revenue Service had sent EIPs to nearly 90 million individuals by April 17, and to an additional 63 million individuals over the next five weeks. As of June 3, 159 million payments had been processed.[1]

---

1. IRS, "159 Million Economic Impact Payments Processed" (press release), www.irs. gov/newsroom/159-million-economic-impact-payments-processed-low-income-people-and-others-who-arent-required-to-file-tax-returns-can-quickly-register-for-payment-with-irs-non-filers-tool.

Additional relief was made available to those who lost their job through expanded UI benefits. The CARES Act, which was passed in late March, created the Pandemic Unemployment Compensation (PUC) program, which provided an additional $600 per week to claimants on top of the usual benefit. These PUC payments expired at the end of July 2020. The CARES Act also extended eligibility for benefits to groups not covered by the traditional UI program, such as the self-employed, part-time workers, and those who did not have a long enough work history to qualify for the traditional program (Pandemic Unemployment Assistance, PUA), and it extended by thirteen weeks the duration of UI benefits for a regular claim (Pandemic Emergency Unemployment Compensation, PEUC).

An unprecedented number of individuals have filed for these benefits during the pandemic. As shown in online appendix figure 4, initial claims shot up starting in mid-March. For the week ending April 4, 6.2 million initial claims were filed. Between the weeks ending March 21 and June 20, more than 50 million initial claims were filed. According to the Bureau of the Fiscal Service of the US Treasury, UI payments never exceeded $3 billion in a single month from February 2019 through February 2020.[2] In March 2020, these payments jumped to $4.2 billion, and then to $48.4 billion in April, $93.7 billion in May, and $115.7 billion in June.

Together these policies have the potential to significantly boost family incomes and lift many families, at least temporarily, out of poverty. Consider a family of four with two adults and two children whose family income comes entirely from the earnings of the head of the household. If the head's earnings do not change after the start of the pandemic and the family receives the maximum EIP in April, then this family would be lifted out of poverty (i.e., their income for the past twelve months would exceed the poverty threshold for a family of this size and composition) in April as long as their income exclusive of EIP was within 90 percent of the poverty line. Moreover, the onetime EIP would be sufficient to keep such a family's income over the past twelve months above the poverty line for an entire year, through March 2021. Alternatively, if, in addition to the EIP, the head of such a family lost his or her job in April 2020 and collected UI benefits as well as the additional $600 per week through July 2020, then such a family would have income above the poverty line in

2. US Treasury, Daily Treasury Statement, https://datalab.usaspending.gov/dts/?start=20050609&end=20200617&frequency=mtd&category=Unemployment%20Insurance%20Benefits. accessed July 23, 2020.

April and for the following nine months as long as their pre-COVID-19 earnings (and therefore income) were within 80 percent of the poverty line.[3]

II. Earlier Work on Timely Measures of Income and Poverty

While there is an extensive literature that examines income and poverty measurement and trends, summarized in Ruggles (1990), Citro and Michael (1995), Meyer and Sullivan (2012), and Burkhauser and others (2019), none of these studies have addressed the long delay in the availability of nationally representative income data, and very few have used the data from the Monthly Current Population Survey (Monthly CPS). Bergmann and Coder (2010) use the Monthly CPS to construct a poverty measure based on earnings and imputed UI benefits for the period from 2005 to 2009. A few researchers have used the Monthly CPS to generate timely estimates of income and compare these estimates to the CPS Annual Social and Economic Supplement (ASEC). However, this work has focused on median income (Green and Coder 2020) and provided only very limited validation of its measures. Thus, there is surprisingly little precedent for our timely, validated measure of income and poverty.

III. Data and Methods

We rely on income to measure poverty in this situation, despite two of us having argued for more than fifteen years that, for historical (as opposed to timely) research, consumption should be preferred. However, we have never argued that consumption should be exclusively used. Income and consumption data are complements and there are situations where each is likely to be more informative than the other. Given that detailed, comprehensive and representative consumption data are not available in a timely fashion, the income data are an important source.[4] Furthermore, the short-run aspects of this pandemic, in which consumption is likely to move independently of short-run changes in income, make income of interest in its own right. Examining short-term changes in income during the pandemic allows us to examine whether the concomitant decline in consumption is due to a shortfall in current income or another explanation, such as a

---

3. This calculation assumes that the head collects UI benefits equal to half of pre-separation earnings.

4. If the Bureau of Labor Statistics follows the same schedule as in recent years, nationally representative data on consumption for 2020 from the Consumer Expenditure Survey would not be released until September 2021.

limited opportunity to consume certain goods and services or uncertainty over future income streams.

Our new measures of the income distribution and income-based poverty rely on data from the Monthly CPS, which collects information on labor market outcomes and demographic characteristics from a representative sample of about 40,000 to 50,000 households.[5] Interviews are conducted during the calendar week containing the nineteenth of the month. The survey provides the timeliest nationally representative data available for family income. The Monthly CPS has been collecting information about income for nearly forty years. Thus, we can observe the cyclical patterns of income and its association with other variables long before the onset of the COVID-19 pandemic, which is helpful for understanding the validity of the income data, as it allows us to compare income and other observable characteristics from these data to those from many other historical data series. To capture changes in income before and after the start of the pandemic, we will focus on data from the January 2020 survey through the June 2020 survey, although for some analyses we also report more historical estimates.

III.A. Analysis Sample

Our analyses focus on a subset of individuals from the Monthly CPS because we do not observe family income for all individuals for several reasons. In online appendix table 1, we report the number of households and individuals that are in the survey for each month of 2020 and how these numbers change as we restrict the sample. First, housing units selected to be in the CPS are typically only asked this question in the first and fifth interview months that they are in the survey (housing units are in the CPS sample for eight months over a sixteen-month period—four months on, eight months off, and four months on).[6] Second, the total income question is asked only in reference to the family income of the householder's family, so we do not observe this income information for individuals in the household who are outside the householder's family (i.e., unrelated individuals and unrelated subfamilies), which accounts for about 5 percent of individuals in the first or fifth interview month. Finally, during our sample

---

5. We obtained the Monthly CPS data through IPUMS-CPS (Flood and others 2020).

6. CPS households that do not provide an answer to this income question in their first or fifth month are asked this question in subsequent months. Thus, about 3 percent of households in these other months are asked and respond to the family income question. Otherwise, in the public use files, the value of family income in these other months is just carried over from the response in either the first or fifth month.

period, between 23 and 28 percent of individuals in the first or fifth months of the survey do not have a response to the family income question. Although the Census Bureau provides imputed values of income for those who do not respond, we do not include these observations in our analysis. As a result of these restrictions, we observe family income from respondents in their first or fifth month in the survey for a monthly sample ranging from 8,999 households and 20,822 individuals in February 2020 to 6,149 households and 14,383 individuals in April 2020.

An important issue to consider for analyses of income before and after the start of the pandemic is that concerns about COVID-19 may have affected survey responses. Due to health concerns, the Census Bureau shifted the survey collection method for the Monthly CPS from in-person to phone interview for some households in March 2020 and for nearly all households in April 2020. Households in their first and fifth interview month are most affected by this change because interviews in these two months are usually conducted in-person, whereas interviews in other months are normally conducted via phone. For example, in January 2020, 66 percent of the households in their first or fifth month were interviewed in person.

In online appendix table 2, we examine how the change in the survey method affects the survey nonresponse rate as well as the composition of the sample across interview months between February and June 2020. The first row shows that the nonresponse rates in the April, May, and June 2020 surveys were substantially higher than that in February 2020 for all interview months. However, this rise was most noticeable for households in their first month, and to some extent for those in their fifth month. That the rise in survey nonresponse rates is more noticeable for those in their first or fifth month than for those in other months suggests that the shift from in-person to telephone interviews may have had an impact on response rates. We also see a rise in item nonresponse for the family income question, although this rise is much less pronounced than the rise in survey nonresponse.

These patterns might be problematic if survey or item nonresponse is not random. To consider whether there might be selection into non-response, we examine the observable characteristics of the sample across interview months before and after the onset of the pandemic, restricting the sample to individuals who are included in the householders' families with non-imputed family income. Most of the characteristics that we report in online appendix table 2 are similar pre- and post-onset of COVID-19 regardless of interview month. However, there is some evidence that individuals in the first interview month in April, May, and June 2020 are slightly more educated and less likely to be in a single parent family than those in the first interview month pre-COVID-19. These small differences suggest that changes in survey response rates may have resulted in a slightly more advantaged sample of first month responders in the most recent survey months though further analysis suggests the differences are not substantive.[7]

To be cautious, we address concerns about possible changes in sample representativeness in two ways. First, for our main analyses we re-weight the samples from March through June so that observable characteristics—family type, age of head, and education of head—for these months match those in January and February, as explained in online appendix I. As an additional robustness check, we also report results for a sample that includes only individuals in their fifth month interview, as the change in nonresponse rates and demographic characteristics across recent months is smaller for this group.

III.B. Family Income in the Monthly CPS

Our primary analyses rely on a global question in the Monthly CPS about total cash income for the householder's family for the previous twelve months. Specifically, the question asks the respondent to report:

> total combined income during the past 12 months . . . of all members [of the family]. This includes money from jobs, net income from business, farm or rent, pensions, dividends, interest, social security payments and any other money income received . . . by members of [the family] who are 15 years of age or older.[8]

This global family income question from the Monthly CPS aligns closely with the definition of total cash income from the CPS ASEC, which is used for official poverty and income statistics, although family income from the

---

7. For our main sample (first and fifth month respondents), we reject the joint hypothesis that the demographic characteristics in online appendix table 2 (not including income and employment) are the same for those in April, May, and June as compared to those in January and February (p-value $< .01$). However, when we regress unemployment on these characteristics for a sample of those in the other interview months, and use the estimates from this model to predict unemployment for our main sample across survey months, the mean predicted values are virtually the same throughout our sample period, differing by less than 0.024 percentage points (0.96 percent). They are also virtually the same as the mean predicted values for the other interview months that did not move from in-person to telephone interviews, suggesting that the change in interview mode did not affect sample composition substantively.

8. "Basic CPS Items Booklet: Labor Force Items," https://www2.census.gov/programs-surveys/cps/techdocs/questionnaires/Labor%20Force.pdf.

CPS ASEC is calculated as the sum of responses to questions about many different components of income. Because interviews take place in the third week of the month, we assume that the respondent includes income from the interview month in their response to the question. Making this distinction is important for determining when we should expect to see this measure of family income reflect the effects of the pandemic. For example, respondents to the April CPS arguably included negative income shocks that occurred or government payments that were received during the first few weeks of April. During these weeks, UI claims grew sharply and the first wave of EIPs were distributed.

It is also unclear whether the responses to this question give equal weight to each of the previous twelve months, or whether greater weight is given to income in more recent months. If there is telescoping, that is, more accurate recall of more recent income, then the most recent responses to the income question in the Monthly CPS are more likely to capture the effects of the pandemic. Investigating whether there is evidence of telescoping in the Monthly CPS family income data is an important area for future research.

Rather than reporting a specific amount for total income, respondents in the Monthly CPS choose among sixteen categorical income ranges. For the bottom part of the income distribution, the income ranges are fairly small. Below $15,000 there are five categories, and from $15,000 to $40,000 the intervals are $5,000 wide. To calculate our estimates of poverty and various percentiles of the income distribution, we convert this categorical response into a continuous measure by randomly selecting values of family income from families in the CPS ASEC from the same survey year who have incomes that fall in that same income range and who have some similar demographic characteristics. In online appendix I we provide the details for this imputation procedure, as well as comparisons of family income in the Monthly CPS to family income in the CPS ASEC (see section V for additional analyses of the validity of the income measure from the Monthly CPS).

III.C. Measures of Income Poverty and the Income Distribution

Our estimates of poverty compare our measure of family income for the twelve months immediately preceding the interview from the Monthly CPS to the official poverty threshold for each family, which varies by family size and composition. We use the official poverty thresholds for the year that aligns with the most recent month of the reference period in the Monthly CPS. For example, since the most recent month of the reference period for respondents to the April 2020 CPS falls in 2020, we use the "official" 2020 poverty thresholds to calculate poverty for these respondents.[9]

There are many limitations of the official measure that numerous studies have noted, such as its adjusting thresholds over time using a price index that overstates inflation; its omission of taxes, tax credits, and in-kind benefits such as food stamps and housing subsidies; and its peculiar equivalence scale (Citro and Michael 1995; Meyer and Sullivan 2012; Burkhauser and others 2019). These limitations are less relevant for the short-term changes in poverty that are the focus of this study as long as the errors do not change quickly over time. For example, although price index bias significantly affects estimates of changes in poverty over several decades (Meyer and Sullivan 2012), such bias is negligible for changes in poverty within a year. While we do not incorporate noncash programs into our analyses because the Monthly CPS does not include data on receipt of such benefits, these programs may play an important role in replacing lost earnings during the pandemic. See Bitler, Hoynes, and Schanzenbach (2020) for more discussion of the importance of these programs.

Because the sudden disruption in economic activity affected families at all income levels, and many families were eligible to receive government relief benefits, we also investigate how other points in the distribution of income, beyond those near the poverty line, change during the pandemic. In particular, we look at changes in family income for the 10th, 25th, 50th, and 75th percentiles. For these analyses, we adjust the income measures for family size and composition using the Citro and Michael (1995) recommended equivalence scale and account for inflation using the personal consumption expenditures chain-type price index (PCEPI).

IV. Changes in Poverty and the Income Distribution during the COVID-19 Pandemic

In figure 1 we report the poverty rate as well as a three-month moving average of this rate, for the period from January 2019 to June 2020. Then, in table 1, we focus in on the estimates for each month between January and June of 2020, as well as the change in poverty between the pre- and post-onset of COVID-19 periods defined as January–February 2020 and April–June 2020, respectively.

9. To obtain "official" thresholds for 2020, we adjust the 2019 thresholds for inflation using the CPI-U, which is the price index the Census Bureau uses to adjust the official thresholds for inflation on an annual basis.

Figure 1. Poverty Rates from the Monthly CPS, 2019–2020

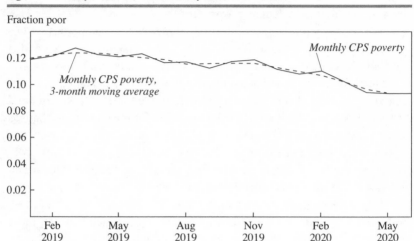

Source: Monthly CPS.

Note: The sample includes individuals who are included in the householders' families and those in their first or fifth month in the survey. Individuals who have imputed income in the Monthly CPS are excluded. The three-month moving average is calculated as the unweighted average of poverty rates in month $t - 1$, t, and $t + 1$. The statistics are weighted using fixed demographic weights since March 2020.

The results in figure 1 indicate that poverty was falling fairly steadily in the period leading up to the pandemic. Between November 2019 and February 2020, poverty fell by 0.9 percentage points. This decline then accelerates once the pandemic hits. Between the pre and post periods poverty fell by 1.5 percentage points (or about 14 percent), and this difference is statistically significant.[10] The estimates for each month in table 1 suggest that poverty fell in March, which could be interpreted as surprising given that the CARES Act was passed after the CPS interviews for this month. However, this decline was a continuation of a pronounced downward trend, and unemployment had barely started to rise by that point. Furthermore, we caution against making too much of one-month changes given the imprecision of these estimates.

To determine whether the labor market shock and the government response affected certain demographic groups differently, we explore the heterogeneity of poverty rates across groups defined by age (0–17, 18–64,

10. We find similar results to those discussed in this section when we restrict the sample to only responders in their fifth interview month, but do not re-weight recent months to hold demographic characteristics fixed (online appendix tables 5 and 7).

Table 1. Poverty Rates, Monthly CPS, 2020

Month	January	February	March	April	May	June	Change since start of pandemic
Full sample	10.8%	11.0%	10.2%	9.4%	9.3%	9.3%	−1.5%
	(0.5)	(0.5)	(0.5)	(0.6)	(0.6)	(0.6)	(0.5)
Number of individuals	20,020	20,822	16,733	14,383	14,236	14,391	
Age							
Age 0–17	15.3%	15.3%	16.3%	14.4%	13.2%	13.1%	−1.7%
	(1.0)	(1.0)	(1.2)	(1.4)	(1.4)	(1.3)	(1.0)
Age 18–64	9.8%	9.9%	8.5%	8.0%	8.4%	8.4%	−1.6%
	(0.4)	(0.4)	(0.5)	(0.6)	(0.6)	(0.5)	(0.4)
Age 65+	7.7%	8.7%	7.6%	7.1%	6.6%	7.1%	−1.3%
	(0.6)	(0.6)	(0.6)	(0.6)	(0.6)	(0.7)	(0.6)
Race							
White	9.4%	9.2%	8.7%	7.8%	8.3%	7.9%	−1.3%
	(0.5)	(0.5)	(0.6)	(0.6)	(0.6)	(0.6)	(0.5)
Black	18.2%	20.8%	21.3%	18.7%	16.1%	18.2%	−1.9%
	(1.6)	(1.7)	(2.1)	(2.5)	(2.2)	(2.2)	(1.8)
Other	12.4%	12.1%	9.0%	9.5%	9.1%	8.6%	−3.2%
	(1.5)	(1.6)	(1.4)	(1.9)	(2.2)	(1.7)	(1.6)
Gender							
Male	10.3%	10.1%	8.7%	8.7%	8.5%	8.8%	−1.5%
	(0.5)	(0.5)	(0.5)	(0.7)	(0.6)	(0.7)	(0.5)
Female	11.3%	11.9%	11.7%	10.1%	10.1%	9.9%	−1.6%
	(0.5)	(0.5)	(0.6)	(0.7)	(0.7)	(0.7)	(0.6)
Head Education							
H.S. degree or below	20.9%	20.3%	20.5%	19.5%	18.1%	17.0%	−2.4%
	(1.1)	(1.1)	(1.3)	(1.6)	(1.4)	(1.3)	(1.1)
Some college or above	6.0%	6.4%	5.3%	4.7%	5.3%	5.9%	−0.9%
	(0.4)	(0.4)	(0.4)	(0.5)	(0.6)	(0.6)	(0.4)

Source: Monthly CPS.

Note: The sample includes individuals who are included in the householders' families and who are in their first or fifth month in the survey. Individuals with imputed income are excluded from the sample. Change since the start of the pandemic is calculated as the difference between the poverty estimate from the pooled sample for the April, May, and June CPS surveys and the poverty estimate from the pooled sample for the January and February CPS surveys: (Apr + May + Jun) − (Jan + Feb). The statistics are weighted using fixed demographic weights since March 2020. Standard errors are clustered at the household level.

and 65+), race (white, Black, and other), gender, and the educational attainment of the head of the household (high school degree or below and some college or above). Poverty fell for all three groups, with declines of 1.7 percentage points (11.1 percent) for individuals age 0–17, 1.6 percentage points (16.1 percent) for individuals age 18–64, and 1.3 percentage points (17.1 percent) for individuals age 65 and older. The declines in poverty are statistically significant for the two older groups, but they are not significantly different from each other. We also see declines in poverty for all racial and gender groups and all groups defined by the educational attainment of the head. Those in the other race group (neither white nor Black) experienced the largest drop in poverty—a decline of 3.2 percentage points or 25.6 percent—followed by those with low-educated heads who experienced a decline of 2.4 percentage points or 11.3 percent.[11] Both of these changes are statistically significant. However, we cannot reject the hypothesis that the declines in poverty are the same for all race or all education groups.

We also considered how changes in poverty differed depending on how hard states were hit early on from the pandemic or by differences in states' policy responses. For example, we looked at the patterns separately for states with high and low COVID-19 death rates, states that implemented stay-at-home orders early versus late, states that announced a state of emergency early versus late, and states with high versus low recipiency rates for unemployment insurance. The recipiency rate, the percentage of unemployed workers who receive UI benefits, is a standard measure of the generosity of state UI programs (Wandner 2018). The details for how we split these samples are in online appendix I. The results for these subgroups are reported in online appendix table 6. We find evidence that poverty rates declined for all these groups. The decline is most noticeable for the states that issued initial stay-at-home orders later. Poverty rates for those in this group declined by 2.3 percentage points. And although this decline is statistically significant, we cannot reject the hypothesis that this decline is the same as that for those in states that issued these orders earlier. In fact, none of the differences across these groups are statistically significant.

Looking beyond poverty estimates, we also consider how the COVID-19 pandemic affected different points in the distribution of income. In figure 2

---

11. The other race group includes American Indian, Alaska Native, Native Hawaiian or other Pacific Islander (16 percent based on the May 2020 survey), Asian (58 percent), and two or more races reported (26 percent).

Figure 2. Percentiles of Family Income from the Monthly CPS, 2019–2020

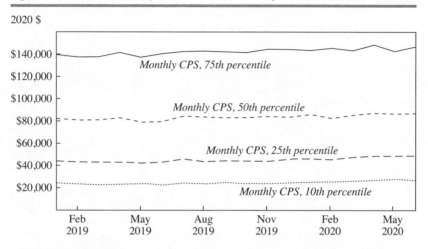

Source: Monthly CPS.
Note: The sample includes individuals who are included in the householders' families and those in their first or fifth month in the survey. Individuals who have imputed income in the Monthly CPS are excluded. The family income is equivalence-scale adjusted and equivalized to a family with two adults and two children. The income is adjusted over time using the personal consumption expenditures chain-type price index and is expressed in May 2020 dollars. The statistics are weighted using fixed demographic weights since March 2020.

we report estimates of the 10th, 25th, 50th, and 75th percentiles of family income (equivalized to a family with two adults and two children) for the period from January 2019 to June 2020. Then, in table 2, we report estimates of the 25th percentile for each month between January and June of 2020, as well as changes in the 25th percentile between the pre- and post-onset of COVID-19 periods. Results analogous to those in table 2, but for the 50th and 75th percentiles, are reported in online appendix tables 8 and 9.

The results in figure 2 show that income for each of the percentiles we report remains flat for the period from January 2019 through February 2020. Then, incomes start to rise after that. The 25th percentile of family income increased from about $46,000 in January and February to about $49,000 in April, May, and June, a statistically significant increase of about $3,000, or 6.4 percent (table 2).[12] This increase seems reasonable given the government benefits low income families were potentially eligible for,

12. The January number is about 1.75 times the federal poverty line for a family of four.

Table 2. Twenty-Fifth Percentile, Monthly CPS, 2020

Month	January	February	March	April	May	June	Change since start of pandemic
Full sample	$46,246	$45,546	$47,763	$48,796	$48,821	$48,977	$2,965
	(820)	(814)	(885)	(1,054)	(1,281)	(1,311)	(906)
Number of individuals	20,020	20,822	16,733	14,383	14,236	14,391	
Age							
Age 0–17	$38,577	$37,417	$35,598	$39,311	$40,996	$41,163	$2,669
	(1,319)	(1,146)	(1,741)	(2,100)	(1,319)	(2,317)	(1,302)
Age 18–64	$49,928	$49,691	$53,605	$54,844	$54,274	$54,165	$4,689
	(1,249)	(905)	(1,262)	(1,264)	(1,359)	(1,557)	(1,072)
Age 65+	$47,398	$46,477	$49,074	$48,437	$50,499	$48,391	$2,045
	(988)	(956)	(1,070)	(1,436)	(1,564)	(1,220)	(1,101)
Race							
White	$50,216	$49,050	$51,934	$52,927	$52,754	$53,162	$3,184
	(1,118)	(934)	(1,220)	(1,289)	(1,200)	(1,606)	(1,161)
Black	$31,051	$30,280	$29,289	$35,359	$34,836	$32,864	$3,460
	(1,560)	(1,432)	(1,815)	(3,471)	(2,059)	(1,976)	(1,751)
Other	$44,044	$43,970	$48,199	$52,727	$45,574	$49,314	$5,344
	(3,150)	(2,294)	(1,812)	(4,231)	(4,107)	(4,584)	(3,305)
Gender							
Male	$47,469	$47,976	$50,707	$51,886	$50,969	$50,451	$3,258
	(867)	(874)	(1,173)	(1,370)	(1,272)	(1,527)	(1,028)
Female	$45,378	$43,588	$45,391	$47,221	$46,705	$47,367	$2,600
	(783)	(796)	(1,082)	(909)	(1,145)	(1,299)	(785)
Head Education							
H.S. degree or below	$29,323	$30,082	$29,713	$30,186	$33,144	$31,896	$2,160
	(799)	(920)	(895)	(1,469)	(1,359)	(1,365)	(1,093)
Some college or above	$62,750	$61,390	$64,412	$66,108	$64,360	$64,033	$2,850
	(1,628)	(1,309)	(1,713)	(1,660)	(1,877)	(1,425)	(1,320)

Source: Monthly CPS.

Note: The sample includes individuals who are included in the householders' families and who are in their first or fifth month in the survey. Individuals with imputed income are excluded from the sample. The family income is equivalence-scale adjusted and equivalized to a family with two adults and two children. The income is adjusted over time using the personal consumption expenditures chain-type price index and is expressed in May 2020 dollars. Change since the start of the pandemic is calculated as the difference between the poverty estimate from the pooled sample for the April, May, and June CPS surveys and the poverty estimate from the pooled sample for the January and February CPS surveys: (Apr + May + Jun) − (Jan + Feb). The statistics are weighted using fixed demographic weights since March 2020. The standard errors are bootstrapped and clustered at the household level.

including a $3,400 EIP (for a married couple with two children) and UI benefits that included a $600 per week top off.

We also see a rise in income at higher percentiles, although the extent of the rise is smaller as we move up the distribution. Median income (online appendix table 8) rose by about $2,500 (2.8 percent) during this period and this rise is statistically significant. At the 75th percentile (figure 2 and online appendix table 9), incomes rose more modestly, by about $1,300 (0.9 percent), and this rise is not statistically significant. A rise in income at the 75th percentile would not be too surprising given that those with incomes at this level would potentially still be eligible for the expanded government benefits. The equivalized income values for the 75th percentile are about $145,000 for a married couple with two children and about $65,000 for an individual. These values are below the income thresholds for receiving the full amount of the EIP.

As with our results for poverty, we find consistent evidence that income rose between the pre- and post-onset of COVID-19 periods for all of the subgroups that we consider (table 2 and online appendix table 10), and in nearly all cases the rise is statistically significant, although the estimates of these changes across groups are not significantly different from each other.

IV.A. The Effect of Government Policy Changes in Income

That we find poverty declined and income rose in the first few months after the start of the pandemic, despite the fact that earnings fell sharply, suggests that the government policy response to the pandemic had a substantial effect on income. We can estimate the direct impact of payments to individuals by calculating the differences in poverty and other income statistics relying on measures of family income that alternatively include and exclude the government benefits. Since we directly observed income including the benefits, we only need to calculate a second, counterfactual income measure that subtracts those benefits. Although we do not directly observe receipt of the EIP and the expanded UI benefits, we have sufficient information in the Monthly CPS to calculate the potential benefits that each family could receive—annual income, family size and structure, and unemployment status and duration.

In particular, for our sample from the April, May, and June CPS we impute benefits for the three main government programs that directly transferred cash income to individuals and families—the EIP, the Pandemic Unemployment Compensation (PUC) program, and the Pandemic Unemployment Assistance (PUA) program—as well as for regular UI, as these payments also expanded significantly after the start of the pandemic.

Our approach will also account for benefits from the Pandemic Emergency Unemployment Compensation (PEUC) program that extended by thirteen weeks the duration of UI benefits, although this program affected a small number of claimants during our sample period.

Imputing EIP is straightforward as nearly all income eligible individuals and families received such payments. We calculate the appropriate benefit amount based on family income, size, and composition. On aggregate our imputation method accurately captures total EIP paid out, but we cap our imputed benefits to match these aggregates. See online appendix II for a detailed description of our procedure.

Because the expanded UI programs reach well beyond the traditional unemployed, we need to allocate UI benefits to a broad set of individuals who are not currently working. In fact, if we only allocated benefits to those who were unemployed, total benefits would fall far short of the total dollars paid out. Thus, we impute regular UI benefits for a subset of individuals who report being unemployed (not working and looking for work) except those who were previously self-employed. For PUA, we impute benefits for a subset of individuals who were unemployed but were previously self-employed, as well as those who report being absent from work due to health reasons, family responsibilities, child care problems, and other reasons, and those who want a job but did not look for work over the past four weeks because: (1) they believed no work was available in their area of expertise, (2) they could not find a job, (3) of family responsibilities, (4) they could not arrange child care, or (5) of other reasons. While a large fraction of these groups is likely to be eligible for some form of unemployment insurance, there are some individuals who are eligible for UI whom we will miss. For example, we do not observe complete employment histories, so we will miss those who received UI benefits in the twelve months prior to the interview but had already become reemployed by the time of the interview. To ensure that we allocate the appropriate amount of UI benefits paid, we cap the number of individuals (selected at random) to which we impute benefits so that the total dollars of benefits we impute matches administrative totals.[13] Because the likelihood that individuals receive UI conditional on being monetarily eligible differs considerably across states, we allow the cap to vary across states based on state UI

---

13. US Treasury, Daily Treasury Statement, https://datalab.usaspending.gov/dts/?start=20050609&end=20200617&frequency=mtd&category=Unemployment%20Insurance%20Benefits. accessed July 23, 2020.

recipiency rates as explained in online appendix II. See online appendix II for more details on our procedure.

Using these imputed benefits, we calculate changes in the share of individuals with family incomes below the poverty line and multiples of the poverty line using income with and without these benefits. In the first row of table 3 we report our main poverty estimates from table 1. These estimates are based on reported total annual family income, and therefore, in theory, include EIP and both the expanded and regular UI benefits. We then calculate poverty, subtracting from income these government benefits for our April, May, and June CPS samples. In the last column we report the change in poverty between January 2020 and June 2020 for each measure of poverty. When all of these government policies are excluded, we find that poverty rises by 2.7 percentage points between January and June, and this rise is statistically significant. In other words, not only do the government programs account for the entire decline in poverty that we observe, but in their absence, poverty would have risen sharply.

To determine the relative contribution of these programs in reducing poverty we exclude each of them separately. These calculations indicate that while both UI and the EIP played an important role in staving off a rise in poverty, the EIP played a somewhat larger role. When we exclude these payments, the poverty rate for June is 1.1 percentage points higher than January. If, instead, we exclude all UI programs but keep the EIP, then the rise in poverty is 0.8 percentage points. If we exclude only the expanded UI benefits (PUC and PUA), then poverty between January and June increases slightly by 0.1 percentage points, but the poverty rate in June in this counterfactual scenario is still much higher (1.6 percentage points) than the actual estimate for June.

In the remaining panels of table 3 we consider the effects of these policies on higher points in the income distribution: 200 percent, 300 percent, and 500 percent of the poverty line. As we move up the income distribution, the effect of the policies decreases in percentage terms, which is expected given the targeted nature of these programs and that the fixed value of these payments is a smaller fraction of family income. The estimates in the top panel suggest that the effect of all programs was to reduce poverty by 30.6 percent (from 13.5 percent to 9.3 percent). These combined programs reduced the fraction of families with income below 200 percent of the poverty line by 13.6 percent. Both the EIP and UI contributed to reducing the fraction below 200 percent of the poverty line. Further up the income distribution, government programs increased income, but the effects were smaller. The effect of all programs was to reduce the fraction

Table 3. Poverty Rates with and without COVID-19-Related Government Payments, Monthly CPS, 2020

Month	January	February	March	April	May	June	June–January
Panel A. Income less than 100% FPL							
Actual poverty	10.8%	11.0%	10.2%	9.4%	9.3%	9.3%	−1.5%
	(0.5)	(0.5)	(0.5)	(0.6)	(0.6)	(0.6)	(0.8)
w/o EIP and all				11.1%	11.6%	13.5%	2.7%
UI programs				(0.7)	(0.7)	(0.7)	(0.8)
w/o EIP and				11.0%	11.4%	13.3%	2.5%
PUC/PUA				(0.7)	(0.7)	(0.7)	(0.8)
w/o EIP				10.8%	10.7%	11.9%	1.1%
				(0.7)	(0.7)	(0.7)	(0.8)
w/o all UI				9.6%	9.9%	11.6%	0.8%
programs				(0.6)	(0.6)	(0.7)	(0.8)
w/o PUC/PUA				9.6%	9.8%	10.9%	0.1%
				(0.6)	(0.6)	(0.6)	(0.8)
Panel B. Income less than 200% FPL							
Actual poverty	29.1%	29.3%	27.8%	27.4%	27.4%	26.9%	−2.1%
	(0.7)	(0.7)	(0.8)	(0.9)	(0.9)	(0.9)	(1.1)
w/o EIP and all				29.0%	30.4%	31.2%	2.1%
UI programs				(0.9)	(0.9)	(0.9)	(1.1)
w/o EIP and				28.9%	30.2%	30.6%	1.5%
PUC/PUA				(0.9)	(0.9)	(0.9)	(1.1)
w/o EIP				28.9%	29.3%	29.4%	0.3%
				(0.9)	(0.9)	(0.9)	(1.1)
w/o all UI				27.6%	28.4%	28.5%	−0.6%
programs				(0.9)	(0.9)	(0.9)	(1.1)
w/o PUC/PUA				27.5%	28.1%	28.3%	−0.8%
				(0.9)	(0.9)	(0.9)	(1.1)
Panel C. Income less than 300% FPL							
Actual poverty	45.0%	46.7%	45.0%	43.8%	44.5%	45.1%	0.1%
	(0.7)	(0.7)	(0.8)	(0.9)	(0.9)	(0.9)	(1.2)
w/o EIP and all				45.0%	47.6%	48.0%	3.0%
UI programs				(0.9)	(0.9)	(0.9)	(1.2)
w/o EIP and				45.0%	47.3%	47.7%	2.7%
PUC/PUA				(0.9)	(0.9)	(0.9)	(1.2)
w/o EIP				44.9%	46.6%	46.6%	1.6%
				(0.9)	(0.9)	(0.9)	(1.2)
w/o all UI				44.0%	45.4%	46.4%	1.4%
programs				(0.9)	(0.9)	(0.9)	(1.2)
w/o PUC/PUA				44.0%	45.1%	46.1%	1.1%
				(0.9)	(0.9)	(0.9)	(1.2)

Table 3. Poverty Rates with and without COVID-19-Related Government Payments, Monthly CPS, 2020 (*Continued*)

Month	January	February	March	April	May	June	June–January
Panel D. Income less than 500% FPL							
Actual poverty	69.9%	69.5%	69.3%	68.3%	69.6%	69.7%	−0.2%
	(0.6)	(0.6)	(0.7)	(0.8)	(0.8)	(0.8)	(1.0)
w/o EIP and all				69.1%	71.5%	71.0%	1.1%
UI programs				(0.8)	(0.8)	(0.8)	(1.0)
w/o EIP and				69.1%	71.5%	70.9%	1.0%
PUC/PUA				(0.8)	(0.8)	(0.8)	(1.0)
w/o EIP				69.0%	71.0%	70.6%	0.7%
				(0.8)	(0.8)	(0.8)	(1.0)
w/o all UI				68.4%	70.1%	70.2%	0.3%
programs				(0.8)	(0.8)	(0.8)	(1.0)
w/o PUC/PUA				68.4%	70.0%	70.1%	0.2%
				(0.8)	(0.8)	(0.8)	(1.0)

Source: Monthly CPS.

Notes: The sample includes individuals who are included in the householders' families and who are in their first or fifth month in the survey. Individuals with imputed income are excluded from the sample. The statistics are weighted using fixed demographic weights since March 2020. FPL = federal poverty line. Standard errors are clustered at the household level. See online appendix II for the details on the imputation of EIPs and UI payments.

below 300 percent of the poverty line by 6.2 percent, and the fraction below 500 percent of the poverty line by 1.8 percent.

Our simulations also allow us to provide evidence on other important questions related to how the government response to the pandemic affected individuals and families. In particular, we can examine the extent to which eligible families received benefits and explore which demographic groups were more or less likely to actually receive benefits. Although we do not observe actual receipt of these benefits in our data, we have good information on the total amount of benefits that were given out each month, and we have reasonably good information on who is likely to be eligible from the CPS.

Given the broad eligibility for EIP that was based mainly on income, imputing such benefits is straightforward. Although there was some concern about barriers for certain groups of individuals in receiving these benefits, our simulations suggest that by the third week of June, most eligible individuals and families received such payments. If we allocate payments to all eligible families in the June CPS, the weighted sum of these benefits is $276 billion, which is only about 3 percent more than

Table 4. Imputed Cumulative Stimulus and UI Payments (Billion $) and Receipt Rates

Month	Program	Simulated eligible amount ($)	Payments from administrative data ($)	Simulated receipt amount ($)	Dollar receipt rate (%)	Person receipt rate (%)
April	EIP	274	160	162	59	59
	PUA	47		2	5	5
	Regular UI	26		10	37	37
	PUC	90		20	22	23
	Total UI	164	32.4	31.7	19	23
May	EIP	279	259	260	93	93
	PUA	54		21	39	38
	Regular UI	41		27	68	65
	PUC	142		74	52	52
	Total UI	237	122	122	52	52
June	EIP	278	267[a]	278	100	100
	PUA	48		40	82	81
	Regular UI	49		43	87	86
	PUC	164		138	84	84
	Total UI	261	224	220	84	84

Sources: Monthly CPS; IRS; and US Treasury.

Notes: The simulated eligible amount is the weighted total cumulative dollars of benefits that we would impute if all eligible persons received benefits. Payments from administrative data reflect the total cumulative dollars paid out based on data from the IRS or US Treasury (2020). Simulated receipt amount reflects the total imputed benefits capped to match the administrative data totals (except for the EIP in June). The person receipt rate is calculated as the fraction of those designated as eligible that were allocated imputed benefits for that program.

a. This amount is through June 3, 2020.

the actual amount of payments through June 3, 2020 ($267 billion) as reported by the IRS.[14]

For UI, our caps on total benefits imputed are binding in each month, indicating that we have more individuals who are designated as eligible for regular UI or PUA than we impute to receive these benefits, with the gap much more pronounced in the early months. For example, in May, 38 percent of those eligible for PUA were allocated an imputed benefit, while 65 percent of those eligible for regular UI received benefits (table 4). By June, these receipt rates were much higher—81 percent for PUA and 86 percent for regular UI—indicating that the majority of those who lost employment received benefits by this point. We should emphasize that

14. US Department of the Treasury, "Treasury, IRS Announce Delivery of 159 Million Economic Impact Payments" (press release), https://home.treasury.gov/news/press-releases/sm1025.

Table 5. Imputed UI Receipt Rates by Recipiency Rate Tercile and Month

Month	UI Type	Recipiency rate tercile	Receipt rate (%)
April	PUA	1	6
		2	4
		3	5
	Regular UI	1	29
		2	38
		3	43
May	PUA	1	23
		2	40
		3	50
	Regular UI	1	46
		2	65
		3	81
June	PUA	1	54
		2	91
		3	95
	Regular UI	1	62
		2	95
		3	99

Sources: Monthly CPS; US Department of Labor.

Note: Terciles of state recipiency rate are determined using regular UI recipiency rates by state for the first quarter of 2020.

many of those that we consider eligible likely are not truly eligible due to having quit, being new entrants, or not satisfying the PUA requirements. Thus, the true receipt rate may be higher than these allocation percentages. To double check our assessment of the reach of UI in the pandemic, we compared published counts of UI claims to estimates of those out of work. This analysis corroborates the main takeaways from our simulations (see online appendix II and online appendix table 15). There was a slow initial response of state UI programs in the pandemic, but by June the vast majority of those out of work were reached by the expanded UI system.

We further break down these receipt rates, separating states into groups defined by terciles of the state-level recipiency rate from the first quarter of 2020 (table 5). The recipiency rate is commonly taken as an indicator of how welcoming the state is to UI claims—those with low rates are thought of as discouraging claims and being more aggressive in disqualifying applicants. These results show that receipt rates differed considerably across these groups. For example, in May, for those in the bottom tercile of recipiency rates, 23 percent of those eligible for PUA were allocated imputed benefits, while 50 percent of those in the top tercile were allocated benefits. For regular UI, these rates were 46 percent for the bottom tercile and 81 percent for the top tercile. In June, the receipt rates rose for PUA to 54 percent for the bottom tercile and 95 percent for the top tercile, while the corresponding receipt rates for regular UI were 62 percent and 99 percent.

Clearly there are large differences in receipt rates between states that are traditionally unwelcoming to UI claims with a low recipiency rate and those with a high recipiency rate. These differences in state recipiency rates have implications for how well the UI system reaches certain demographic groups. For example, because the low recipiency rate states have a higher share of the population that is Black (17 percent in the lowest tercile compared to 12 percent in the highest tercile), Black Americans have been treated less well by the UI system than white Americans.

V. Comparisons of Family Income Data from the Monthly CPS to Other Sources

Because the Monthly CPS family income data have been rarely used to measure income or poverty, we benchmark them and examine their accuracy by comparing them to alternative sources of data on income. We consider how these different sources of income align both in levels and in trends. We are also interested in assessing whether monthly updates to an annual measure of income or poverty, which we can do with the Monthly CPS data, anticipate changes that are later revealed by survey data that are only available annually, such as the CPS ASEC. We are further interested in whether within-year variation in family income from the Monthly CPS aligns with data from other sources. These comparisons will provide information that will allow researchers to identify the strengths and weaknesses of these vital, but rarely used, public-use data and aid their use and interpretation.

The most direct comparison for the Monthly CPS is the Annual Social and Economic Supplement (ASEC) to the CPS, as this survey is administered as a supplement to a subset of the Monthly CPS samples from February, March, and April. The CPS ASEC is the source of official income statistics in the United States. The questions in both surveys are designed to capture a similar concept of income: pretax money income. One important distinction between these measures is that the Monthly CPS measure relies on a single, global question about income over the past twelve months from all sources and all individuals in the householder's family, while CPS ASEC income is derived from information on more than twenty-five different income sources in the household for the previous calendar year

Figure 3. Poverty Rates from the Monthly CPS and the Annual Social and Economic Supplement of the CPS, 2005–2020

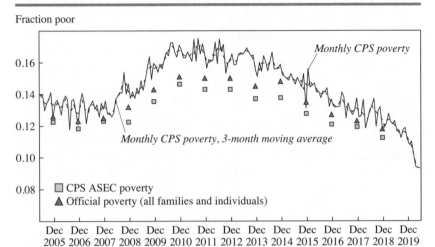

Sources: Monthly CPS; Annual Social and Economic Supplement of the CPS.

Notes: The Monthly CPS and CPS ASEC samples include individuals who are included in the householders' families. The Monthly CPS sample is restricted to individuals with non-imputed income who are in their first or fifth month in the survey. The three-month moving average is calculated as the unweighted average of poverty rates in month $t - 1$, t, and $t + 1$. The statistics are weighted using fixed demographic weights since March 2020.

for all individuals age fifteen and above. Thus, comparisons of income in the Monthly CPS to income in the CPS ASEC can shed light on the extent to which global questions about income can capture income from many different sources.

To assess the comparability of patterns across these different sources, in figure 3 we report income poverty using both the Monthly CPS and the CPS ASEC for the period from 2005 through 2020. For the CPS ASEC estimates, we restrict the sample to individuals in householder families only, because this is the sample for which we observe income in the Monthly CPS. For comparison, we also report the official US poverty rate, which is derived from the CPS ASEC data. The only difference between these two measures from the CPS ASEC is that the official measure also includes individuals who are outside the householder's family. Because our sample from the Monthly CPS is much smaller than that from the CPS ASEC, and is therefore noisier, we also report a three-month moving average of the Monthly CPS poverty rate. For all measures, the x-axis indicates the most recent month of the income reference period. Thus, we plot the estimates from the CPS ASEC in December of each year because the reference period is the calendar year, but for the Monthly CPS we plot the estimates in the interview month.

The results in figure 3 indicate that individuals in householder families have lower poverty than other individuals—the official poverty rate is about 1 percentage point higher than the measure from the CPS ASEC that excludes individuals outside the householder's family. The poverty estimates from the Monthly CPS are higher than the comparable measures from the CPS ASEC, typically by 1 to 2 percentage points. This difference in levels suggests that the more detailed income questions that are asked in the CPS ASEC capture more income than the single, global questions about family income. For changes over time, however, the patterns are quite similar across these two series. For example, between December 2007 and December 2010, annual CPS ASEC poverty rose by 19 percent, while annual Monthly CPS poverty (three-month moving average) rose by 25 percent. Between December 2014 and December 2018, CPS ASEC poverty fell by 18 percent while Monthly CPS poverty fell by 21 percent. In fact, the annual poverty rates estimated from these two sources— comparing CPS ASEC estimates of poverty to those from the December CPS—are highly correlated. Between 2005 and 2018, the correlation between these two measures of poverty is 0.91.

Figure 3 also shows the advantage of using the Monthly CPS to provide timely estimates. The first evidence of the negative impact of the Great Recession on official poverty did not come until September of 2009, when official poverty estimates (and the CPS ASEC data) were released for calendar year 2008. With the Monthly CPS, however, we see annual poverty rising as soon as June of 2008—an estimate that could have been calculated in July of 2008, a full fourteen months before the official estimates became available. The timely Monthly CPS data mean that we can already see how poverty was changing in the months leading up to and shortly after the start of the COVID-19 pandemic, and we will continue to get an early look at how economic well-being changes as macroeconomic circumstances evolve over the coming months.

In figure 4, we report the trends for various percentiles of real family income for both the Monthly CPS and the CPS ASEC for the period from 2005 through 2020. Again, we see that CPS ASEC income exceeds Monthly CPS income, but for each of the percentiles we report, the changes over time are quite similar for the two data sources.

Another way to consider the accuracy of the Monthly CPS income measure compared to the CPS ASEC income measure is to examine the

Figure 4. Percentiles of Family Income from the Monthly CPS and the Annual Social and Economic Supplement of the CPS, 2005–2020

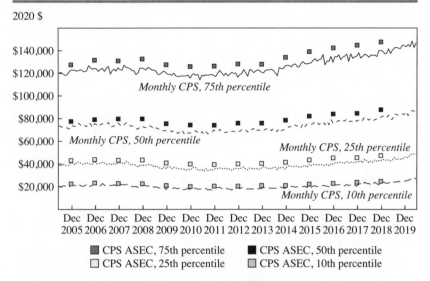

2020 $

Dec Dec Dec Dec Dec Dec Dec Dec Dec Dec Dec Dec Dec Dec Dec
2005 2006 2007 2008 2009 2010 2011 2012 2013 2014 2015 2016 2017 2018 2019

■ CPS ASEC, 75th percentile   ■ CPS ASEC, 50th percentile
□ CPS ASEC, 25th percentile   □ CPS ASEC, 10th percentile

Sources: Monthly CPS; Annual Social and Economic Supplement of the CPS.
Notes: The Monthly CPS and CPS ASEC samples include individuals who are included in the householders' families. The Monthly CPS sample is restricted to individuals with non-imputed income who are in their first or fifth month in the survey. The family income is equivalence-scale adjusted and equivalized to a family with two adults and two children. The income is adjusted over time using the personal consumption expenditures chain-type price index and is expressed in May 2020 dollars. The statistics are weighted using fixed demographic weights since March 2020.

dispersion of each measure. It is common to model a variable that is measured with error as the sum of a true component plus an error component that is uncorrelated with the true component. In such a case, greater dispersion means more error. The standard deviation, variance, and coefficient of variation of the income measures from the two sources can be found in the online appendix table 12. This table indicates that the standard deviation of the Monthly CPS measure is about 9 percent lower than the ASEC measure, while the coefficient of variation is about 2 percent higher, suggesting that there is little difference in the amount of measurement error in the two income sources.

We also compare income in the Monthly CPS to income in the Consumer Expenditure Survey (CE). The CE is a nationally representative survey that is the most comprehensive survey of consumption data in the United States. It is a rotating panel survey that interviews about 7,000 families each quarter. While the focus of the survey is spending data, it also collects

Figure 5. Poverty Rates from the Monthly CPS and the Consumer Expenditure Surveys, 2014–2018

Fraction poor

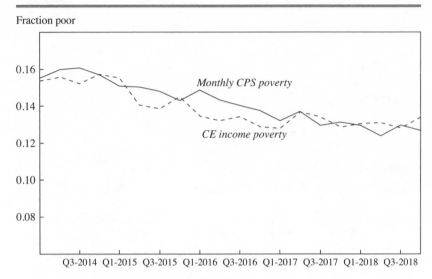

Q3-2014 Q1-2015 Q3-2015 Q1-2016 Q3-2016 Q1-2017 Q3-2017 Q1-2018 Q3-2018

Sources: Monthly CPS; Consumer Expenditure Survey.
Note: Poverty rates are calculated for each survey quarter. The Monthly CPS sample includes individuals who are included in the householders' families and those in their first or fifth month in the survey. Individuals who have imputed income in the Monthly CPS are excluded. The CE income is calculated as the before-tax income less food stamps.

information on family income. The nice feature of this comparison is that the CE interviews families throughout the year with the reference period for the income questions being the previous twelve months, which aligns with the reference period for the Monthly CPS income question. For the period from the first quarter of 2014 through the end of 2018, we report in figure 5 estimates of annual income poverty on a quarterly basis using the CE data alongside the estimates from the Monthly CPS, aggregated up to the quarter. As shown in figure 5, the long-term trends in poverty from the Monthly CPS line up very closely with those from the CE. Between the first quarter of 2014 and the last quarter of 2018, poverty fell by 18 percent using data from the Monthly CPS and by 13 percent using data from the CE. The annual poverty rates estimated from these two sources are highly correlated. During this period, the correlation between these two measures of poverty is 0.84. These patterns suggest that changes in family income that are captured in the Monthly CPS are consistent with other, commonly used, nationally representative data sources.

VI. Relation to Other Information on Income and Well-Being during the Pandemic

In recent months, a flood of near real-time data has shed light on aspects of the changes in economic well-being of the population during the very early stages of the pandemic. At least two patterns are notable about this research. First, the other sources of evidence, from surveys as well as administrative sources, are largely consistent with, or can be reconciled with, the evidence in this paper. Second, while these other sources provide important information about how the economic circumstances of individuals and families have changed during the pandemic, the evidence we present from the Monthly CPS has important advantages.

Consistent with our results, the Bureau of Economic Analysis (BEA) Personal Income and Outlays data (currently available through June 2020 and shown in online appendix figure 5) indicate that real disposable personal income fell by 2 percent in March but rebounded to rise by 13 percent in April, calculated as the change from the previous month in both cases. Although it fell in May, personal income remains well above its level in March. The BEA also reported that real personal consumption expenditures fell by 13 percent in April, followed by modest increases in May and June. Cox and others (2020) and Chetty and others (2020) also find a decline in April in spending as recorded in bank accounts or aggregated credit records, respectively, though they both find an uptick in May. Cox and others (2020) also find that savings increased early in the pandemic especially for those with low previous income. They conclude that the initial decline in consumption they observe is not due to a decline in income from labor market shocks. Other evidence suggests credit card debt, personal loans, and even borrowing from pawn shops declined (Dalton and Andriotis 2020). The rise in income and savings can be reconciled with the initial decline in consumption because the opportunities for spending were limited by stay-at-home orders and travel bans, as well as personal choices to avoid contracting or spreading the virus, and uncertainty about future income streams and other factors. Thus, the income rise that we find is consistent with other evidence.

While aggregated national accounts or financial records yield useful information on aggregate changes in consumption, they do not provide disaggregated estimates of economic well-being by demographic group, which is important for understanding which groups are hurt the most by the pandemic. Distributional statistics such as income percentiles or poverty rates that are needed to assess who is affected by the pandemic also cannot be obtained from these data. Household financial records have the potential to provide disaggregated and distributional detail, but are not representative of the entire population, importantly missing a substantial segment of the population without bank accounts.

There are important and timely new survey sources that provide invaluable information on other domains, but they have little or no information on income. These surveys include the Census Bureau's Household Pulse Survey, the Federal Reserve Bank's SHED, and the Data Foundation's COVID Impact survey (see online appendix table 13 for details on these surveys). These surveys do not collect data on current income. The most recent wave of the SHED does ask about changes in income from the previous month. However, the interviews from this wave occurred in early April, prior to the distribution of most of the government benefits that we consider. The COVID Impact survey (Bauer 2020) finds an increase in food insecurity when compared to a different earlier survey while the Census Bureau's Household Pulse Survey (US Census Bureau 2020) finds high rates of inability to pay rent, for example. These sources, as well as evidence on food bank usage, suggest increased hardship after the pandemic. We should emphasize that the profound disruptions from the pandemic such as the closures of schools, stores, churches, and other facilities, the uncertainty about future income streams, concerns about the health of family and friends, and other disruptions could lead to increases in hardship. An uptick in deprivation could be real, though there are reasons to be less certain of the magnitude of any change over time given the different source of the pre- and post-pandemic information. In terms of policy, the important fact gained from this paper is that the increase in deprivation is not due to the overall income loss, but rather due to other disruptions of the pandemic, including possibly the unevenness of the income flows. Furthermore, given the evidence that small changes in wording or question order can have large impacts on survey results, having data from a survey that has been fielded in the same form for decades allows us to be more certain about any implications from our evidence than we could when using a new survey without historical benchmarks.

VII. Discussion and Conclusions

Despite a dramatic slowdown in the labor market, our results indicate that poverty fell, and percentiles of income rose in the early months of the pandemic, using the only available source of representative and timely income data for the US population. We further show that in the absence of the stimulus payments and expanded unemployment insurance, poverty would have risen sharply. Although expanded government programs helped stave off a rise in poverty, many of these benefits were onetime or are temporary, so future estimates of income will depend on how the availability of these benefits changes going forward.

While we show that reported annual income increased at all percentiles, this improvement in the overall distribution of income is still consistent with a share of families experiencing substantial income drops. Given the observed data, a substantial short-run fall for a small number of families would have to be combined with small increases for a much larger number.

These changes are based on an annual measure of income. The annual reference period will average out potentially large swings in income from month-to-month because much of the government relief was onetime or temporary. Ideally, we would also examine high-quality nationally representative income data for shorter time periods, but these data do not exist. Short-run decreases in income for those without savings or another buffer can lead to substantial increases in hardship.

Our simulations also provide evidence on the extent to which eligible families received government benefits. Comparisons to aggregate payments indicate that most eligible families received EIPs by June. For UI, many of those who were eligible did not receive benefits in the early months of the pandemic. By June, however, a large majority of those eligible had received benefits. These receipt rates, however, differed noticeably across states, which has important implications for which demographic groups were more or less likely to actually receive benefits. For example, because the low recipiency rate states have a higher share of the population that is Black, Black Americans that were eligible for UI were less likely to receive. Examining further the differences in the coverage of UI across demographic groups is an interesting topic for future research.

A number of potential biases in our results are worth noting. We suspect there is some tendency, it is unclear how strong, to emphasize recent income patterns in reporting on the past year. Such a bias would mean that our estimates more closely approximate changes in income over a shorter horizon than the nominal one-year reference period. We also suspect that the shift in income from earnings, a well-reported source of income, to unemployment insurance, a poorly reported source, means that we may have understated any improvements or overstated any declines in income. In recent years, about 90 percent of earnings has been reported in the CPS, as opposed to only about 60 percent of unemployment insurance

(Meyer, Mok, and Sullivan 2015). We should also note that our timely estimates of poverty are less precise that the official poverty estimates because they are only available for a subset of respondents and are based on a single, global income question.

This study has important implications for both policy and future research. A better, more timely understanding of income and poverty will help federal, state, and local policymakers allocate scarce resources to minimize the impact of COVID-19 (and future pandemics or other economic shocks) on vulnerable populations. In addition, by assessing the validity of these new measures using several sources of income, this study lays the foundation for future work on timely poverty measurement and allows others to understand the strengths and weaknesses of these vital, but rarely used, public-use data.

ACKNOWLEDGMENTS   We would like to thank our discussant, Abigail Wozniak, and the editors for helpful feedback; Chris Kelly and Josie Donlon for excellent research assistance; Anna Brailovsky for helpful comments; the NSF for financial support for this project; and the Russell Sage Foundation, Alfred P. Sloan Foundation, Charles Koch Foundation, and the Menard Family Foundation for their support of the Comprehensive Income Dataset Project. We would also like to thank Bill Evans for sharing data on state-level COVID-19-related mortality rates and state policies.

References

Almond, Douglas. 2006. "Is the 1918 Influenza Pandemic Over? Long-term Effects of In Utero Influenza Exposure in the Post-1940 US Population." *Journal of Political Economy* 114, no. 4: 672–712.

Almond, Douglas, and Bhashkar Mazumder. 2005. "The 1918 Influenza Pandemic and Subsequent Health Outcomes: An Analysis of SIPP Data." *American Economic Review* 95, no. 2: 258–62.

Bauer, Lauren. 2020. "The COVID-19 Crisis Has Already Left Too Many Children Hungry in America." Blog post, May 6, The Hamilton Project. https://www.hamiltonproject.org/blog/the_covid_19_crisis_has_already_left_too_many_children_hungry_in_america.

Bergmann, Barbara, and John Coder. 2010. "Developing Monthly Poverty Estimates Based on the Monthly Current Population Survey Labor Force Public Use Files: A Report on Methods and Results." Working Paper. Stanford, Calif.: Stanford Center on Poverty and Inequality. https://inequality.stanford.edu/sites/default/files/coder_poverty.pdf.

Bitler, Marianne P., Hilary W. Hoynes, and Diane Whitmore Schanzenbach. 2020. "The Social Safety Net in the Wake of COVID-19." In the present volume of *Brookings Papers on Economic Activity*.

Burkhauser, Richard V., Kevin Corinth, James Elwell, and Jeff Larrimore. 2019. "Evaluating the Success of President Johnson's War on Poverty: Revisiting the Historical Record Using a Full-Income Poverty Measure." Working Paper 26532. Cambridge, Mass.: National Bureau of Economic Research. https://www.aei.org/wp-content/uploads/2019/12/Burkhauser-Corinth-Elwell-Larrimore-President-Johnson-War-on-Poverty-WP-1.pdf.

Chetty, Raj, John N. Friedman, Nathaniel Hendren, Michael Stepner, and the Opportunity Insights Team. 2020. "Real-Time Economics: A New Platform to Track the Impacts of COVID-19 on People, Businesses, and Communities Using Private Sector Data." Working Paper. Cambridge, Mass.: Mossavar-Rahmani Center for Business and Government. https://www.hks.harvard.edu/centers/mrcbg/programs/growthpolicy/real-time-economics-new-platform-track-impacts-covid-19-people.

Citro, Constance F., and Robert T. Michael, eds. 1995. *Measuring Poverty: A New Approach*. Washington: National Academy Press.

Cox, Natalie, Peter Ganong, Pascal Noel, Joseph Vavra, Arlene Wong, Diana Farrell, and Fiona Greig. 2020. "Initial Impacts of the Pandemic on Consumer Behavior: Evidence from Linked Income, Spending, and Savings Data." Working Paper. Chicago: Becker Friedman Institute for Economics. https://bfi.uchicago.edu/wp-content/uploads/BFI_WP_202082.pdf.

Dalton, Matthew, and AnnaMaria Andriotis. 2020. "Consumers, Flush with Stimulus Money, Shun Credit-Card Debt." *Wall Street Journal*, August 2. https://www.wsj.com/articles/consumers-flush-with-stimulus-money-shun-credit-card-debt-11596373201.

Flood, Sarah, Miriam King, Renae Rodgers, Steven Ruggles, and J. Robert Warren. 2020. *Integrated Public Use Microdata Series, Current Population Survey: Version 7.0* [data set]. Minneapolis: IPUMS. https://doi.org/10.18128/D030. V7.0.

Green, Gordon, and John Coder. 2020. "Household Income Trends December 2019." Sentier Research, LLC. http://econintersect.com/pages/releases/release. php?post=202002061323.

Grusky, David B., Bruce Western, and Christopher Wimer, eds. 2011. *The Great Recession.* New York: Russell Sage Foundation.

Meyer, Bruce D., Wallace K. C. Mok, and James X. Sullivan. 2015. "Household Surveys in Crisis." *Journal of Economic Perspectives* 29, no. 4: 199–226. https:// www.aeaweb.org/articles?id=10.1257/jep.29.4.199.

Meyer, Bruce D., and James X. Sullivan. 2012. "Winning the War: Poverty from the Great Society to the Great Recession." *Brookings Papers on Economic Activity,* Fall, 133–83.

Ruggles, Patricia. 1990. *Drawing the Line: Alternative Poverty Measures and Their Implications for Public Policy.* Washington: Urban Institute Press. http:// webarchive.urban.org/publications/203516.html.

US Census Bureau. 2020. "Household Pulse Survey Interagency Federal Statistical Rapid Response Survey to Measure Effects of the Coronavirus (COVID-19) Pandemic on the United States Household Population." https://www2.census. gov/programs-surveys/demo/technical-documentation/hhp/2020_HPS_Background.pdf.

Wandner, Stephen A., ed. 2018. *Unemployment Insurance Reform: Fixing a Broken System.* Kalamazoo, Mich.: W. E. Upjohn Institute for Employment Research. https://research.upjohn.org/up_press/249/.

MARIANNE P. BITLER
University of California, Davis

HILARY W. HOYNES
University of California, Berkeley

DIANE WHITMORE SCHANZENBACH
Northwestern University

The Social Safety Net in the Wake of COVID-19

ABSTRACT   The COVID-19 crisis has led to spiking unemployment rates with disproportionate impacts on low-income families. School and child-care center closures have also meant lost free and reduced-price school meals. Food prices have increased sharply, leading to reduced purchasing power for families with limited income. The Families First Coronavirus Response Act and the Coronavirus Aid, Relief, and Economic Security Act constituted a robust response, including expansions to unemployment insurance (expansions in eligibility and a $600 per week supplement), a onetime payment of $1,200 per adult and $500 per dependent, an increase in SNAP payments, and the launch of the Pandemic EBT program to replace lost school meals. Despite these efforts, real-time data show significant distress—notably, food insecurity rates have increased almost three times over the pre-COVID-19 rates and food pantry use has also spiked. In this paper, we explore why there is so much unmet need despite a robust policy response. We provide evidence

Conflict of Interest Disclosure: The authors did not receive financial support from any firm or person for this paper or from any firm or person with a financial or political interest in this paper. Marianne P. Bitler was paid by the California Department of Public Health for research and analysis of the WIC Program as it relates to vendors; however the analysis did not focus on WIC participation and food spending behavior because of economic shocks, but rather on how changes among vendors impact participant shopping behavior. Hilary W. Hoynes is a member of the board of directors for MDRC and the California Budget and Policy Center. They are currently not officers, directors, or board members of any organization with an interest in this paper. No outside party had the right to review this paper before circulation. The views expressed in this paper are those of the authors, and do not necessarily reflect those of Northwestern University, the University of California, Berkeley, or the University of California, Davis.

for three explanations: (1) timing—relief came with a substantial delay, due to overwhelmed unemployment insurance (UI) systems and the need to implement new programs; (2) magnitude—payments outside UI are modest; and (3) coverage gaps—access is lower for some groups, and other groups are statutorily excluded.

The COVID-19 crisis has hit low-income families especially hard. As unemployment rates have spiked overall, they have risen even higher for those with lower levels of education, and for Black and Hispanic individuals. Other aspects of the crisis have a disproportionate impact on low-income families as well; for example, low-income families are more likely to be headed by a single mother, and a higher share of women have lost jobs than during prior recessions. Closures of schools and child-care centers have meant that large numbers of low-income children have lost access to free or reduced-price meals. Food prices have increased sharply leading to a reduction in the purchasing power of families' limited income.

Two pieces of legislation, the Families First Coronavirus Response Act and the Coronavirus Aid, Relief, and Economic Security (CARES) Act, include important provisions to respond to these historic job losses. Four elements are particularly relevant in our context. First, there were substantial expansions to unemployment insurance (UI): a $600 per week universal supplement, a thirteen-week extension of eligibility, and expanded eligibility for self-employed and gig economy workers and those without sufficient earnings for normal UI. Second, a onetime payment of $1,200 per adult ($2,400 for a married couple) plus $500 per dependent child under seventeen was implemented (with phaseouts for high-income families). Third, all Supplemental Nutrition Assistance Program (SNAP) payments were raised to the maximum benefit level, averaging a $165 increase in monthly benefits for households receiving increases. Fourth, a new program, Pandemic EBT (P-EBT), was launched to provide direct payments to the millions of families whose children lost access to free and reduced-price meals while their schools were closed.

Despite these efforts, many individuals and families are suffering. Food insecurity rates have increased sharply over the pre-COVID-19 rates with almost a quarter of families reporting their food "just didn't last" and they did not have money to buy more. Seven percent of adults reported receiving help from a food pantry in the prior week, with Feeding America (the national organization of food pantries) reporting a 60 percent increase in need and many news outlets documenting long lines of individuals waiting to obtain food assistance.[1] Adverse mental health conditions have worsened, with rates of depression and anxiety much higher than pre-COVID-19 levels. While it will be many months before we have a clear picture of how family incomes are changing, it is evident from the available real-time data that there currently remains tremendous unmet need.

Why do we see so much need and distress despite a policy response of unprecedented magnitude? In this paper, we examine this question and provide evidence for three explanations. First, there is the timing of the response; many relief payments, especially to low-income families, came with a substantial delay, and the income shock could not be weathered without hardship (or emergency charity aid) for those who lacked savings or access to credit. Payment delays have been driven by overwhelmed UI systems, the need to engineer new programs, and application requirements for the most disadvantaged families built into the delivery system. To the extent that these are factors, we should see improvements as administrative capacity and payments increase across time, though of course hardship may increase once again when emergency payments are rolled back. Second, outside of the UI system, the magnitude of payments made to low-income families was relatively modest—averaging $30 to $40 per week—and may not have been sufficient to offset increased need. Third, there are coverage gaps in the response, and some who were hit by the economic shock had no recourse from existing safety net programs. Importantly, despite expansions intended to make UI coverage more universal than it has traditionally been, the limited real-time data suggest that there are still many unemployed workers who are not receiving UI.

Furthermore, and more structurally, over the past several decades the United States has steered its social safety net, which has always been less far-reaching and less funded compared to other rich countries, to focus on work. Through the shift from cash assistance to earnings supplements, and through adding work requirements to programs designed to meet basic food and healthcare needs, the United States has built a social safety net that delivers less insurance and has placed more emphasis on incentivizing work and topping up low earnings. The current system may meet need

---

1. Feeding America, https://www.feedingamerica.org/take-action/coronavirus; "Feeding America Network Stays Resilient during COVID-19 Crisis," press release, May 12, 2020, https://www.feedingamerica.org/about-us/press-room/feeding-america-network-stays-resilient-during-covid-19-crisis.

during times of low unemployment, but it is ill-suited to protect against job loss and high unemployment. Cash welfare payments for the nondisabled are extremely limited and are either not countercyclical or only very slightly so (Bitler and Hoynes 2016; Bitler, Hoynes, and Iselin 2020). While SNAP payments typically can quickly increase in response to rising need, the benefits are modest, and recent policy changes—tying SNAP receipt to work for some groups and making it more difficult for immigrants to participate—will dampen SNAP's countercyclical impact if not waived. As a result, there are many who are likely falling through holes in the safety net.

This analysis leads us to two sets of recommendations. In terms of policies that need to be addressed now, the emergency policies expanding UI and SNAP and replacing missed school meals should be extended and adapted to the ongoing crisis. In addition, following the successful policies of the 2009 stimulus, it would be advisable to increase maximum SNAP benefits by 15 percent. Because UI and SNAP only serve a limited subset of those in need, another round of stimulus payments may also be in order, potentially targeted more narrowly to low-income families.

Second, there must be more structural policy changes to our work-based social safety net that enable it to function more effectively in economic downturns. The UI system should be updated to reach a larger share of unemployed workers, including the self-employed and those with inconsistent work histories. Because the level and coverage of programs should be expanded during recessions, we recommend building more effective countercyclicality into these key safety net programs, with policy changes automatically triggered by increases in the unemployment rate and shutting off when economic recovery takes place. Federal and state data systems should be harmonized to facilitate automation of relief payments to all eligible recipients.

I. The COVID-19 Shock to Economic Well-Being

To begin, we deploy the available data to monitor the current, real-time measures of household well-being, with particular attention to the disadvantaged population.[2]

To understand who is at risk under COVID-19 for needing new or increased access to the social safety net, we start by describing the extent

---

2. Han, Meyer, and Sullivan (2020) and Parolin, Curran, and Wimer (2020) use available data to estimate real-time measures of poverty.

of job loss. We use the monthly Current Population Survey (CPS) to document increases in unemployment across education groups (Blau, Koebe, and Meyerhofer 2020; Montenovo and others 2020) pooling the data for twenty-four months ending in June 2020, limiting the sample to age 18–64, and estimating a model with calendar month dummies (to control for seasonality) and month dummies for the four months beginning in March 2020. In online appendix table 1 panels B-E, we present the estimated coefficients on the COVID-19 month dummies (March, partially treated; April; May and June); each provides estimates for the effect of the crisis on labor market outcomes, and net of typical seasonal patterns.[3] As has been widely discussed, the current crisis has made it difficult to measure unemployment, and the Bureau of Labor Statistics has documented a spike in the share recorded as having jobs but not being at work and also in those not in the labor force but wanting work, many of whom should likely be classified as unemployed instead.[4] In light of this, in online appendix table 1 we present five outcome measures for the estimated COVID-19 shock, each showing changes relative to February 2020 (netting out the previous year): unemployed (column 1); unemployed or having a job and not at work (column 2); unemployed, having a job and not at work, or not in the labor force (column 3); has a job and not at work (column 4); and not in the labor force (column 5).[5] Our preferred measure is the most expansive and is shown in column 3. Overall, by April 2020 there was a 14.1 percentage point increase in the share unemployed or with a job but not at work or not in the labor force (or an 8 percentage point increase in unemployed) and an 11.2 percentage point increase for those unemployed or with a job but not at work. The labor market shock has been significantly greater for those with lower levels of education. The increase in April unemployment (for our preferred measure) was 17.8 percentage points for those with high school or less compared to 8.8 percentage points for those with a college degree or more. Because children's exposure to

---

3. The baseline comparison we suggest is to February 2020, but of course, the regression results would be the same as long as the omitted month is not during March–June.

4. https://www.bls.gov/cps/employment-situation-covid19-faq-may-2020.pdf. The BLS has documented that some share of those reporting they have a job but are not at work likely are unemployed given ideal definitions of these measures and also notes similar concerns for those not in the labor force due to COVID-19. Some who would like to have work but are not measured as in the labor force reached record levels during the crisis, likely due to closures, stay at home orders, and concerns about engaging in the labor market (also noted in the BLS FAQ).

5. For completeness the table also shows estimates for has a job and not at work (column 4), and not in the labor force (column 5).

economic shocks has been shown to have long-lasting health and economic consequences (Hoynes and Schanzenbach 2018), we also analyze
changes in children's exposure to the crisis as measured by changes in labor
market status for adults age 18–64 in their household.[6] As shown in
online appendix table 2, children in households with a household head with
high school degree or less experienced a 10.1 percentage point increase in
the likelihood they lived with an adult who was unemployed, with a job but
not at work, or not in the labor force in April; compared to 6.9 percentage
points for children with a household head with a college degree. These
striking inequalities in the extent of the economic shock across education
groups continue through May and June 2020 and are evident for all of the
labor market measures. This result—that recessions increase unemployment more for lower education groups than higher education groups—
is a recurring feature of US business cycles (Hoynes, Miller, and Schaller
2012; Aaronson and others 2019).

Also important to the underlying context is that these economic indicators increased more and did so more quickly during the COVID-19
crisis, compared to the Great Recession (see online appendix figures 1a
and 1b).[7] The (official) unemployment rate spiked to 14.7 percent in April
2020 and has remained above 10 percent through July during COVID-19,
while it reached 10 percent for only a single month in the Great Recession. Prices for food at home have increased quickly during COVID-19
driven in large part by the largest single-month increase in nearly forty-five
years in April.[8]

Next, we move beyond labor market outcomes to examine real-time
measures of family economic well-being. We start by analyzing food
insecurity, a summary measure indicating that a household does not have
reliable access to the food they need due to lack of resources. Usually,
a household's food insecurity status is categorized based on their answers
to an eighteen-item questionnaire, ranging from how often the household
worried that their food would run out before there was money to buy more,
to whether a child in the household has gone for a day without eating

---

6. Note that unlike measures about own labor force participation and employment status,
these measures are not mutually exclusive, as a child living with more than one adult can live
with adults with various employment outcomes.

7. The online appendix figures differ in when the series documenting unemployment
rates and price changes in the Great Recession begins, with 1a starting at the beginning of the
Great Recession and 1b showing the run-up to the unemployment peak.

8. These price increases do not include increased time and hassle costs of obtaining food
for many families during COVID-19.

due to lack of money for food. Food insecurity rates can be thought of as a measure of economic (lack of) well-being, and the time series pattern is highly correlated with unemployment rates (Schanzenbach and Pitts 2020).

During the COVID-19 pandemic, surveys collecting real-time data have not asked the entire battery of food security questions, but instead have asked only a few questions drawn from the survey. We show estimates from three waves of the COVID Impact Survey, which asked respondents whether the following statement was often true, sometimes true, or never true for their household over the past 30 days: "The food that we bought just didn't last, and we didn't have money to get more." We code a respondent as being food insecure if they report that the statement was often or some-times true. To compare food insecurity rates during COVID-19 to the past, we calculate the share answering yes to the same question in the National Health Interview Survey (NHIS). The NHIS asks the full food security questionnaire, but we limit the analysis to responses to the single item asking whether the respondent agrees that their food "just didn't last."[9]

Figure 1 displays trends in food insecurity rates for households over-all and for those with children.[10] For respondents overall, rates of food insecurity increased sharply from 11 percent in 2018 (the latest available NHIS estimate) to 23 percent in April 2020. Low-income families with children have been hit particularly hard during this period, between the loss of free and subsidized school meals due to school closures and particu-larly elevated unemployment rates among women. This is reflected in even greater elevation in food insecurity among respondents with children, from 13 percent in 2018 to 34 percent in April 2020.[11] The large increase in (seasonally adjusted official) unemployment, from 3.5 percent in February to 14.7 percent in April—an out of sample prediction with strong linearity

9. Like the COVID Impact Survey, the NHIS also asks about experiences in the past 30 days. To make the data series comparable, we weight the NHIS at the respondent level; the COVID Impact Survey only provides respondent-level weights. In general, in the NHIS the share answering that their food "just didn't last" is consistently 1.24 (overall) to 1.27 (with children) times the food insecurity rate based on the full questionnaire; see online appendix table 3.

10. Online appendix figure 2 shows increases in food hardship measures using the Census Bureau's Household Pulse Survey compared with the Current Population Survey's Food Security Supplement. The Household Pulse Survey asks a different question from the food security questionnaire and inquires about the past seven days. Results are qualitatively similar.

11. Karpman, Zuckerman, and Gonzalez (2018) find that food insecurity rates are higher in self-administered online surveys than they are in telephone or in-person interviews, which they theorize is in part due to reduced social desirability bias, suggesting that the self-administered versions might be more accurate descriptions of respondents' well-being.

Figure 1. Food Insecurity Rates, 2011–2018 and during COVID-19

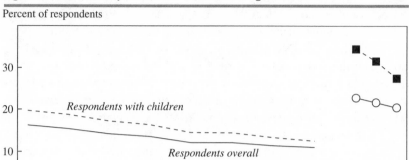

Percent of respondents

Source: Authors' tabulations from the National Health Interview Survey (NHIS) and the COVID Impact Survey.

Note: The solid (dashed) line is the annual average share of respondents (respondents with children) reporting that over a thirty-day period it was sometimes or often the case that their "food just didn't last" and that they didn't have money to get more, calculated from the NHIS 2011–2018. The three connected round (square) dots are share of respondents (respondents with children) reporting monthly, calculated from the COVID Impact Survey collected April 20–26, May 4–10, and May 30–June 8. Statistics are respondent-weighted.

assumptions to be sure—explains more than half of the increase in food insecurity. Some of the remaining unexplained increase in food insecurity may be due to the sharp increase in food prices (online appendix figure 1) or loss of free or reduced-price school meals due to school closures.[12] Food insecurity rates remain elevated but have come down somewhat from their April peak, with overall rates of 22 percent in May and 20 percent in June (32 percent and 27 percent for respondents with children, respectively).

Other measures of real-time hardship are also elevated. Figure 2 displays the share of households reporting receipt of emergency food from a food bank, food pantry, or church, based on an annual time series 2002–2018 drawn from the CPS-Food Security Supplement collected each December that asks about receipt of emergency food over the past month. The solid

---

12. While many schools continued to offer grab-and-go meals, according to our calculations from the Census Household Pulse Survey fewer than 10 percent of households with children report receiving "free meals through the school or other programs aimed at children." Ananat and Gassman-Pines (2020) find that 11 percent of low-income families reported picking up a grab-and-go meal at their child's school in the first weeks of school closures. Usually 58 percent of students are eligible for free or reduced-price meals at school.

Figure 2. Households Receiving Food from a Food Bank/Pantry or Church

Percent

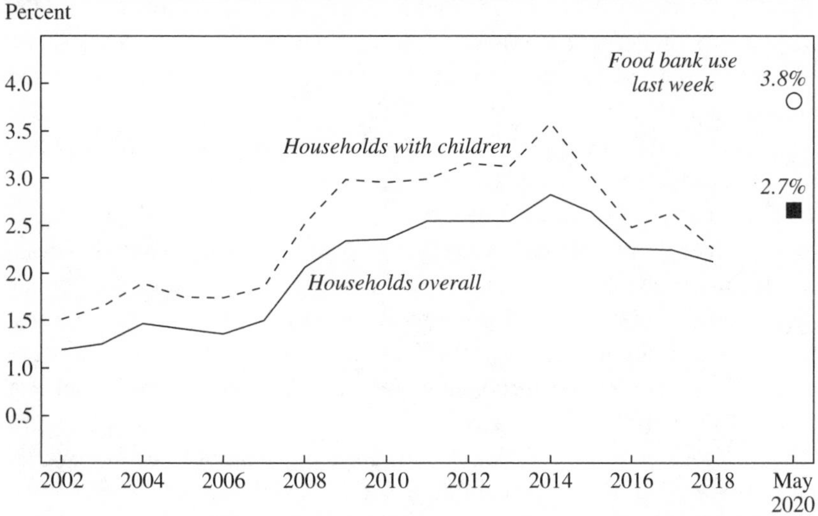

Source: Authors' tabulations of CPS Food Security Supplement (CPS-FSS) and Census Pulse Survey.
Notes: The share of households (solid) or households with children (dashed) who reported using a food bank, pantry, or church sometime in the last month from the CPS-FSS for December 2002–2018. The square (circle) plots the share of households (households with children) who received a meal from a food pantry, food bank, or church in the past week, based on the Census Pulse Survey pooled across April 23–May 26. Statistics are weighted to be representative of all US households, using household weights in the CPS-FSS and calculating pseudo-household weights in the Census Pulse Survey by dividing the respondent weight by the number of adults in the household.

and dashed lines present trends for households overall and for those with children. The previous peak, in 2014, showed 2.8 percent of households receiving emergency food (3.6 percent for households with children) per month. The point estimates for the COVID-19 period represent responses from the Census Household Pulse Survey (averaged across months May through July 2020), which asked respondents to report on emergency food from these sources over the past week. Comparing across data sources, *weekly* receipt of free food is at or above its previous peak *monthly* rate reaching 4.3 percent of households (6.3 percent of those with children).[13]

In addition, measures of mental health are also being tracked in real time during COVID-19 and show elevated rates of distress across three

13. The COVID Impact Survey also asks about receipt of food over the past seven days from a food pantry and finds even higher estimates—6.8 percent for respondents overall and 8.3 percent among those with children, averaged across their three waves of data collected from April to June.

categories: whether the respondent had little interest in doing things; whether the respondent felt down, depressed, or hopeless; or whether the respondent felt nervous, anxious, or worried. During COVID-19, the share of adults reporting mental health problems in the past week has increased compared with rates from 2017–2018, suggesting serious distress.[14] Rates are generally higher among those with lower levels of education, and this gradient persists during COVID-19 (see online appendix table 4).

The Census Household Pulse Survey also asks respondents to rate their confidence in their ability to pay for basic needs in the coming weeks. In May, more than half of respondents indicated they are not "very confident" in their ability to pay for the food they need in the next four weeks, with 9 percent indicating they are "not at all confident." These rates are uniformly higher among respondents with children and are higher among respondents with lower levels of education (see online appendix table 5). Among those who have a rent or mortgage payment, 43 percent overall and 51 percent of those with children did not have "high confidence" that they could make their next payment. Together, the evidence suggests that households and individuals are struggling across a variety of dimensions during COVID-19.

II. The Policy Response: How Much Money Is Going to Whom and When?

Between the Families First Coronavirus Response Act (passed March 18) and the CARES Act (passed March 27), more than $1 trillion have been allocated in relief and assistance nationally. Four elements are particularly important for lower-income families: expansions to SNAP, the new P-EBT program that provides payments to compensate for missed school meals, expansions to UI, and the onetime economic impact payments (EIP). As we will show, these four policies account for about $600 billion and are the main response of direct payments to households. Here we track what we know about the magnitude of these benefits, who they went to, and the timing of their activation.

By design, and even without congressional action, SNAP is structured to respond quickly to increased need. Households that newly become eligible due to unemployment or other loss of income can apply for SNAP and generally receive benefits within thirty days. Indeed, across states, SNAP

---

14. The 2017–2018 data measures are for the past two weeks.

participation increased more between February and April in states with larger increases in unemployment rates (see online appendix figure 3) following the pattern found in prior downturns (Bitler and Hoynes 2016).[15] Additionally, during COVID-19 Congress made temporary changes that increased both participation and (for many participants) benefit levels. Usually, SNAP benefits are reduced as a household's income increases, with a maximum monthly benefit in fiscal year 2021 of about $170 per person reduced by 30 cents for each additional dollar in income (after allowable deductions).[16] While state and federal health emergencies are in progress, states can award all SNAP participants the maximum benefit (a provision known as the Emergency Allotment). This increases SNAP spending (holding participation constant) and provides an average increase in benefits of 40 percent to those on SNAP with higher incomes, such as the working poor (for whom SNAP tops up earnings) who have been at particular risk for job loss. To date there has been no benefit increase for the most disadvantaged SNAP recipients who were already receiving the maximum benefit. Additionally, states are temporarily allowed to extend eligibility periods for currently participating households for six months—under normal circumstances recipients are required to reapply for benefits every 6 to 12 months—so offices already stretched by health-related office closures and the need to socially distance could concentrate on screening new applicants. This temporary policy change increased SNAP participation by reducing the flows *out* of the program during the pandemic.

As a result, SNAP spending and participation are increasing with unprecedented speed, as shown in figure 3, but as we show below, the magnitude is small relative to UI and the economic impact payment. Although national data on SNAP participation only come with some lag, the figure presents the percentage increase in SNAP participation (dark solid line) across forty-three states that have released their data for April or May (these states account for 97 percent of SNAP participation). Relative to February, SNAP participation increased by 12 percent in April, and by 17 percent by May. For comparison, SNAP participation increases during the Great Recession are shown as the dark dotted line. It took 9 months to see the same SNAP participation increase during the Great Recession,

15. Worth noting, Florida experienced the largest increase in SNAP participation, likely due in part to their strong administrative system for SNAP developed to quickly deploy Disaster-SNAP after hurricanes. Rosenbaum (2020) provided SNAP data.

16. The maximum benefit for a family of four in fiscal year 2021 is $680 or $170 per person (USDA 2020).

Figure 3. Percentage Increase in SNAP Participation and Spending Since Business Cycle Peak: COVID-19 versus Great Recession

Percent increase in SNAP participants, spending since business cycle peak

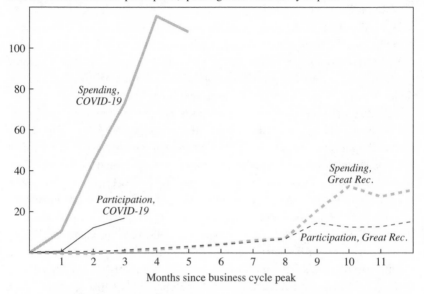

Months since business cycle peak

Source: Authors' calculations of Great Recession spending and caseload data, and February 2020 caseload data, from USDA, Food and Nutrition Service, SNAP Data National Level Annual Summary.

Notes: Growth in caseloads in March–May 2020 calculated from states that have reported caseload data as of July 31, 2020. Forty-three states released April SNAP participation (42 states in May), and these states made up 97 percent of all SNAP participation in February. Growth in SNAP spending in 2020 is reported in Daily Treasury Statements through July 31, 2020. All series are plotted as growth by month since the business cycle peak, which was December 2007 for the Great Recession and February 2020 for the COVID-19 recession.

but of course unemployment also grew more slowly during that recession.[17] SNAP spending (light solid line) is calculated using daily Treasury statements and compares spending on SNAP by month through July relative to spending in February. Some of the spending increase is due to the new P-EBT program, which provides benefits patterned after SNAP to families who lost access to free or reduced-price meals due to school closures. By the end of July, SNAP spending has more than doubled. Our calculations suggest about 20 percent of the increase is explained by increases in participation, 40 percent is due to paying all participants the maximum

17. Online appendix figure 4 shows the growth of SNAP spending and participation for the twelve months leading up to the unemployment rate peak during the Great Recession. The patterns are qualitatively similar.

benefit, and 40 percent is from P-EBT payments. Some of this increase will end once state and federal health emergencies end. Spending grew much more slowly during the Great Recession (light dotted line) and increased substantially when the 15 percent increase in maximum SNAP benefits authorized by Congress as part of the American Recovery and Reinvestment Act stimulus package was implemented.

The congressional policy response also included large expansions to UI, including a $600 per week supplement, a 13-week extension of fully federally funded benefits, and an expansion of eligibility for self-employed and gig-economy workers and other patches to reach workers who were previously excluded from eligibility (under the new Pandemic Unemployment Assistance or PUA program).[18] The number of UI participants has increased to record levels, with 34.5 million total continuing claims through the week ending July 4, as shown in online appendix figure 5. After their early May peak, regular continuing claims have started to decrease while PUA claims, after considerable delay in initiation, started to increase.

The onetime economic impact payments included in the CARES Act provide $1,200 per adult ($2,400 for a married couple) and $500 per dependent under 17. This was structured as a fully refundable tax credit, phased out beginning at annual incomes of $150,000 for married couples, $112,000 for head of household filers, and $75,000 for single filers. The Treasury provided automatic payments for all who filed federal taxes in tax years 2018 or 2019 as well as many elderly or disabled individuals receiving payments through Social Security or Veteran's Affairs programs.[19] However, entire families that included any immigrant adult without a Social Security number were ineligible, thus excluding many citizen children and spouses (if not in the military). The initial payments were made to those with direct deposit information during the week of April 17 and paper checks followed more slowly after that.

Putting this all together, figure 4 shows weekly spending on economic impact payments, UI, and SNAP (including P-EBT) calculated from daily Treasury statements.[20] The increase in UI payments has averaged

18. The federal government also is funding the "waiting" week for UI, so benefits get out more quickly, and most states suspended search requirements for obtaining UI during the health crisis through May at least.

19. Some of the Social Security Administration groups had to submit forms to receive dependent payments.

20. Here we follow Tedeschi (2020), who estimates economic impact payments and UI payments by calculating year-over-year changes by week. We also use this approach for SNAP spending.

Figure 4. Weekly Spending on Unemployment Insurance, Economic Impact Payments, and SNAP

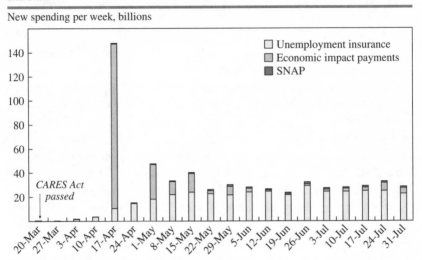

New spending per week, billions

Source: Authors' tabulations of Daily Treasury Statements through July 31 for SNAP, unemployment insurance benefits, and IRS tax refunds to individuals.

Notes: We difference expenditures from the inflation-adjusted same-week payments in 2019 to net out the seasonality in payments and to separate economic impact payments from usual tax refunds. We censor economic impact payments at zero prior to the week of April 17.

$23.5 billion per week from May through July. We estimate $131 billion in economic impact payments were made in mid-April when the direct deposit payments were made, with smaller amounts paid in subsequent weeks as the paper checks rolled out. Increases in SNAP, the only program with payments narrowly targeted to low-income families, hover around $1 billion per week, with some weekly fluctuation due to variation across states in the timing of monthly SNAP benefit payments and disbursal of P-EBT benefits. Between these three categories of spending, nearly $600 billion in new expenditures occurred between April and July—almost $360 billion through UI, $220 billion through economic impact payments, and just over $16 billion in new spending came through SNAP.[21]

There is some emerging evidence that these payments are helping alleviate hardship. For example, unemployed workers who report receiving UI have lower levels of food insecurity than do those who unsuccessfully attempted to receive UI. Food insecurity rates reported in the COVID

21. Online appendix figure 6 shows cumulative weekly spending using the same data.

Impact Survey dropped from 23 percent in April to 20 percent in June for respondents overall, and from 34 percent to 27 percent among respondents with children (figure 1). Furthermore, new evidence finds that receipt of P-EBT payments decreases measures of food hardship (Bauer and others 2020). Despite noteworthy improvements, these measures are still extremely elevated, and are generally worse for families with children, and for Black and Hispanic respondents.

III. With This Policy Response, Why Is There Need?

Given the policy response to date, why do we see such large unmet economic need? There are three driving factors: delays in the receipt of payments that were authorized, modest benefit levels (for programs other than UI), and holes in coverage. In this section, we describe elements of the policy implementation, including slow rollout, cumbersome administrative processes, as well as more structural deficiencies.

The available real-time evidence shows that despite high levels of aggregate claims, many workers, especially those with low levels of education, are not receiving UI. We establish this finding from survey and administrative data sources, and it is consistent with experiences during previous recessions. Panel A of table 1 presents data from week 3 of COVID Impact Survey data collected May 30–June 6.[22] We tabulate data on receipt of UI and SNAP among workers reporting being on furlough. The survey asks "In the past 7 days, have you either received, applied for, or tried to apply for any of the following forms of income assistance, or not?" and the interviewer asks about UI and SNAP. The table presents the responses separately for those with a high school education or less, some college, or a college degree or more. The results show striking disparities in access to UI payments; among furloughed persons with a high school degree or less, 42 percent were receiving UI compared to 52 percent for those with a college degree or more. And this disparity in access to UI is consistent with prior recessions. Panel B of table 1 presents a similar gradient for the Great Recession using the 2008 Panel of the Survey of Income and Program Participation (SIPP). Using the sample of individuals in short-term unemployment near the trough of the Great Recession, 29 percent of those with a high school degree or less were receiving UI compared to 47 percent of college

22. COVID Impact Survey: Version 1, National Opinion Research Center, University of Chicago, https://www.norc.org/Research/Projects/Pages/covid-impact-survey.aspx.

Table 1. Program Receipt among the Unemployed

	Any UI (%) (1)	Any SNAP (%) (2)	Both UI and SNAP (%) (3)	Neither (%) (4)
Panel A: Furloughed individuals, June 2020				
≤ High school	42	11	6	52
Some college	55	24	18	38
Bachelor degree or higher	52	9	6	46
Panel B: Short-term unemployed individuals, 2008				
≤ High school	29	29	6	48
Some college	37	21	5	47
Bachelor degree or higher	47	6	3	50

Source: Authors' tabulations of the COVID Impact Survey (panel A) and the 2008 SIPP Panel (panel B).
Note: We tabulate data on receipt of UI and SNAP, where the survey asks "In the past 7 days, have you either received, applied for, or tried to apply for any of the following forms of income assistance, or not?" The sample consists of those reporting they are unemployed due to furlough at the time of the survey. Panel B includes individuals age 20–59 who were unemployed and looking for work for at least a week in the first month of wave 6 of the 2008 SIPP (January–April 2010) and had been unemployed for fewer than four months. Receipt of UI and SNAP is measured for the first month of wave 6. UI refers to own receipt and SNAP refers to receipt within the household. All statistics are weighted to be representative of the adult population.

graduates. It is also important to note that this table suggests that there is only partial overlap between UI and SNAP receipt among the unemployed/ furloughed, and a substantial share obtain SNAP but not UI. Around half of furloughed (during COVID-19) or short-term unemployed (during the Great Recession) report receiving neither UI nor SNAP.

To explore why UI does not reach all unemployed workers, now and in previous recessions, we use the 2019 CPS Annual Social and Economic Supplement (which covers the 2018 calendar year) and the 2020 UI calculator in Ganong, Noel, and Vavra (2020) to simulate the share of individuals age 20–59 with positive earnings who would be eligible for UI (under normal UI rules, i.e., without federal expansions) if they became unemployed.[23] There are sharp disparities in eligibility, with much lower

23. The code for the Ganong, Noel, and Vavra (2020) calculator is available at https:// github.com/ganong-noel/ui_calculator. Ganong, Noel, and Vavra (2020) also present eligibility estimates using their calculator; their approach differs slightly from ours. They focus on all workers who are US citizens, have hourly wage and salary earnings above the federal minimum wage, and who are eligible for UI based on their earnings history. Our sample differs in that we restrict the sample to workers age 20–59 and expand it to include all workers regardless of immigration status and with any positive earnings, not just those with wage and salary earnings above the federal minimum wage. When estimating potential eligibility should they be laid off and average weekly benefits, we treat workers who are likely unauthorized immigrants as ineligible for UI benefits. We also ignore self-employment income in determining UI eligibility and benefits.

eligibility rates for those in lower-income families (see online appendix figure 7). For workers in families with income below 100 percent of poverty, only 63 percent are eligible for UI compared to 87 percent among all workers. Among those with income below poverty, 14 percent of the ineligible are unauthorized (not eligible to work legally), another 7 percent are ineligible due to being self-employed, and 17 percent are authorized and have wage and salary earnings, but do not meet the work history requirements.[24] Importantly, the new PUA provisions in the CARES Act have attempted to fill the gap in eligibility for the self-employed and those with insufficient work history so it is possible that more of these 7 + 17 percent now have UI eligibility; changes have not altered ineligibility rates for unauthorized workers. Thus, as many as 14 percent of those under the poverty level may still be ineligible under the best-case scenario. In addition, there is widespread variation in the share of those unemployed who obtain UI conditional on being eligible. O'Leary and Wandner (2020) report that in 2018, the share of the eligible unemployed receiving UI ranged from 10.5 percent in North Carolina to 95 percent in Rhode Island. Murray and Olivares (2020) report that states with higher rates of pre-COVID-19 UI utilization among those eligible are paying out more claims in the COVID-19 era, suggesting a role for administrative burdens.

Next, we turn to real-time administrative data to assess how the UI system responded to this unprecedented increase in unemployment. Ideally we would present, weekly and by state, the number of persons receiving regular UI, PUA, and the $600 supplement, along with the dates of initiation for the new programs. While we (and others) have made valiant attempts to assemble this, as of this writing there is no systematic data source available to identify this information. One approach is to use Department of Labor reports of weekly continuing claims. However, many concerns have been raised about the use of continuing claims to capture the number of recipients, particularly for PUA. First, the count of continuing claims is the number of weeks times people, not the number of people; this is particularly problematic when there are delays in processing and back payments are issued with first payments.[25] Second, continuing claims can include claimants who are still pending a determination and denials can occur after this stage (Hedin, Schnorr, and von Wachter 2020). Additionally, PUA continuing claims appear to be inconsistently reported during the

---

24. We follow Passel (2007) to identify survey respondents as unauthorized immigrants.
25. For example, if it takes four weeks to process the claim when the first payment is made, it will count "4" in continuing claims that week due to the back pay.

COVID-19 crisis.[26] Another approach is to use Department of Labor reports of weekly initial claims, yet these also have weaknesses, including subsequent denials, double counting due to returning to UI after brief return to work, and, particularly for PUA, capturing possible fraud.[27]

Despite these data challenges, the available evidence clearly points to significant delays, especially in the rollout of PUA across states. This is not surprising, as states had to design entirely new methods to ensure eligibility for PUA, and states varied widely in their administrative capacity and the need for social distancing in the early months of the pandemic. Additionally, for a state to receive federal reimbursements for PUA, its recipients must be ineligible for state UI. In practice, in some states PUA applicants must apply to and be rejected from the regular UI program before they could separately apply for PUA, leading to further delays. Using information from state press releases, we can document significant delays and wide differences in when PUA was first paid out, ranging from as early as March in New Hampshire (which had passed a program expanding UI to the self-employed even before the CARES Act), to April 30 in California, to May 11 in West Virginia, and May 26 in Kansas.[28] States also varied in the timing of their payment of the federal supplemental $600 weekly payment (FPUC) which was meant to go to all UI recipients.

Using less granular monthly data, we can also calculate for the United States a more reliable measure of the UI *utilization rate* by taking the ratio of "first UI payments" available monthly for regular and PUA UI from the Department of Labor (currently through May 2020 for all states

26. Take Florida for example: the first initial claim reported to Department of Labor for PUA was for the week ending June 27 despite an April 25 press release announcing people could start applying for PUA. Additionally, there have been no continuing claims reported as data were downloaded August 9, yet the state data dashboard reports they have paid out $453 million of PUA as of August 9. Using data shared by Murray and Olivares (2020) and Cajner and others (2020), we document similar discrepancies between the timing of when the first week first claims were reported to the Department of Labor and when states reported that they started accepting PUA claims, with at least twenty-three states accepting PUA applications at least seven days before the first week of initial claims was reported to Department of Labor, and with the average difference being twenty-nine days. We thank them for generously sharing their data.

27. For example, the state of Ohio froze 270,000 claims as of August 7 in order to investigate fraud at a time when about 500,000 PUA claims had been paid, and the US Labor Department inspector general raised concerns about fraud in a May 26 Alert Memorandum.

28. Many states also started by sending PUA applicants the minimum payment (plus, where relevant the additional $600 federal payment), and then later determined actual payment eligibility amounts and sent back payments where appropriate.

reporting PUA first payments) to the total number of unemployed.[29] First payments get around the problem of subsequent denials as well as being an unduplicated count of recipients. Combining regular state UI and PUA first payments, we find that 6.4 percent of the unemployed had received a first payment in March, rising to 53.9 percent in April and 84.9 percent in May (see online appendix table 6). If we limit to payments for PUA, we find 1.6 percent of the unemployed received a first payment by April 2020 rising to 11 percent in May.

In summary, the combination of real-time survey and administrative data, the historical patterns, and policy changes during COVID-19 suggest that while UI is serving the majority of the unemployed, it is far from universal. During COVID-19, UI has been slow to reach the unemployed and there is a sizeable share—disproportionately those with low levels of education—who are not receiving benefits. This is consistent with available pre-COVID-19 evidence.

Coverage was incomplete for the economic impact payments as well. According to the daily Treasury statements (shown in online appendix figure 6), cumulative payments for the onetime economic impact payments ($1,200 per adult and $500 per child under 17) through the end of July 2020 are around $215 billion. However, despite the apparent universality of the payment for those with income below the high-income phase-out level, the design of the payment scheme has left out the most disadvantaged Americans. First, the law excludes immigrant families who are deemed ineligible if any adult or spouse lacks a Social Security number (unless the family included a member of the military).[30] Second, the payments were sent automatically, with no additional action, for tax filers (in 2018 or 2019) and those receiving benefits from the Social Security Administration or Veterans Affairs. Marr and others (2020) estimate that 12 million nonfilers are eligible for the relief payment but did not automatically receive it. Instead, to receive these payments individuals are required to apply for the payment through a new IRS nonfiler tool. This nonfiler population is a disadvantaged group with low incomes, and an

29. Regular and PUA UI first payments come from the 902P and 5159 forms from the Department of Labor, respectively. Pandemic Emergency Unemployment Compensation first payments are very small, so we exclude them from the graphs. For the denominator we use CPS monthly estimates of those unemployed (adjusted for changes in those with a job but not at work and not in the labor force over the previous year).

30. Also ineligible are adult dependents, 17-year-olds, and college students whom their parents can claim as dependents.

Figure 5. Timing of Pandemic Assistance Payments for P-EBT

Share of children participating in National School Lunch Program
living in states disbursing P-EBT (percent)

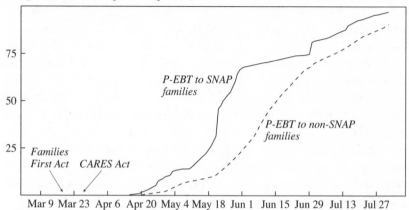

Source: Bauer and others (2020), and authors' calculations from state departments of health services.
Note: The solid (dashed) line displays the share of children who participate in the National School
Lunch Program who live in states that have disbursed P-EBT payments to families receiving free or
reduced-price meals who also participate in SNAP (do not participate in SNAP).

estimated three-quarters of them are eligible for SNAP or Medicaid. Based
on the Urban Institute Coronavirus Tracking Survey, wave 1—fielded
between May 14 and May 27—41 percent of adults with income below
poverty reported that they had not received their economic impact payment
compared with 27 percent among those with income between 100 and
250 percent of poverty and 14 percent among those with income between
250 and 400 percent of poverty (Holtzblatt and Karpman 2020).

Another source of delay in benefits reaching needy families came
from having to create a new program in the midst of the pandemic. When
schools across the United States closed in mid-March, 30 million students
lost daily access to free or reduced-price school meals. To offset this loss,
Congress authorized the new P-EBT program to provide food benefits
to families who lost subsidized school meals. In order to participate,
though, states had to set up and receive approval from the USDA for this
completely new program. Payments came out slowly, as shown in figure 5. Two months after the Families First Act authorized the program,
very few states had made payments; about 15 percent of eligible families
lived in states where P-EBT benefits began being dispersed to those on

SNAP (where preexisting debit cards could be used), and fewer than 10 percent lived in states where non-SNAP recipients eligible for school meals programs were dispersing P-EBT benefits. Many states did not make retroactive payments until June or July.

In sum, this discussion illustrates the delays and incomplete coverage in the policy response. Also, among those eligible we have incomplete take-up of these programs. Why? This is a direct result of the "application-based" policy environment. Across the different relief provisions, some payments were made automatically (recovery rebate for previous tax filers, increase in SNAP benefit for existing participants) while others required application (UI, recovery rebate for some nonfilers, P-EBT for those not on SNAP in some states). Decades of research show that take-up rates are incomplete when an application is required. Individuals need to know about the programs to access them (Currie 2006). Administrative hassles are built into many programs and contribute to the less-than-complete take-up (Herd and Moynihan 2019). In addition, as the COVID-19 crisis has highlighted, states have made policy choices that result in differential capacity to quickly enroll newly unemployed individuals.

IV. Putting the Policy Response in the Context of the Broader Social Safety Net

The COVID-19 crisis has been met with an extraordinary economic policy response. It is important to understand, though, that the US social safety net—the foundation beneath this policy response—has been redesigned in recent decades in ways that have made it less responsive to economic downturns. In the years following the Great Recession, many states have reduced the generosity of their UI programs. Median replacement rates to low-income workers are below 50 percent in many states (online appendix figure 8), providing very limited earnings replacement. More generally, our social safety net has shifted toward a work-conditioned social safety net, using earnings subsidies to increase incomes among workers but offering relatively little out-of-work assistance (to those not elderly or disabled). These changes have been ushered in through the 1996 welfare reform law, expansions to the earned income tax credit (EITC), and, for some populations, work requirements for SNAP. More recently, work requirements have been adopted in some states for Medicaid and regulations implemented to expand SNAP work requirements. The result is a social safety net with an emphasis on promoting and rewarding work, a system that may be adequate during times of low unemployment but provides too little insurance against job loss and economic shocks.[31]

Recent work by Bitler, Hoynes, and Iselin (2020) and Bitler and Hoynes (2016) summarizes how participation in SNAP, UI, the EITC, and cash welfare varies with the unemployment rate at the state level, and how that has changed over time. In the period since 2007, only UI shows a robust countercyclical response, with a 1 percentage point increase in unemployment leading to an 18 percent increase in UI spending (Bitler, Hoynes, and Iselin 2020). SNAP has a weaker response, with a 1 percentage point increase in the unemployment rate leading to a 7 percent increase in SNAP spending. Neither the work-conditioned EITC nor cash welfare systematically change in response to the economy. In other words, despite its important role in reducing poverty, the EITC is poorly suited to insure consumption against job loss.[32]

Overall, the literature shows that on the eve of the COVID-19 crisis, the safety net was providing uneven and incomplete protection. While UI is strongly countercyclical overall, not all unemployed workers receive benefits, including undocumented immigrants and those with inconsistent work histories. Cash welfare does not respond to aggregate economic need, and the EITC is not designed to provide insurance against job loss. SNAP does have the capacity to expand during economic downturns, but benefits are modest, and since its benefits are food vouchers they are only partially fungible. In addition, recent policy changes risk further dampening the protective effects of SNAP by imposing stricter work requirements among nondisabled adults without dependents and reducing participation among immigrants and families with mixed immigration status.[33]

---

31. For reference, antipoverty effects of existing programs in 2018 for children, adults with and without children, and the elderly are presented in online appendix figure 9. The EITC has the largest antipoverty impact for children and adults who live with them, followed by SNAP, housing assistance, and school meals. Among the elderly and childless adults, Social Security overwhelmingly has the largest antipoverty effect.

32. Bitler, Hoynes, and Kuka (2017) show that lack of cyclicality of the EITC masks two opposing responses: a procyclical effect for single filer EITC recipients (whose EITC payment falls or is lost altogether with economic shocks) and a countercyclical effect for married filers (or more generally those with higher predicted earnings) for whom a labor market shock can bring them down into EITC eligibility.

33. When labor market conditions are poor, states can waive SNAP time limits when particular economic conditions (based on employment statistics in the state or local area) are met, so that food assistance is not conditional on employment during bad economic times. The Trump Administration issued a new rule effective April 1, 2020, making it more difficult to obtain time-limit waivers. Importantly, the new rule requires that states have elevated unemployment rates for at least the previous twelve months, slowing the ability of the program to respond to immediate need at the onset of an economic downturn.

V. Needed Policies Moving Forward

Our analysis leads us to two sets of recommendations. The first set of recommendations relates to changes that need to occur in the short-term to address the current recession. The increased payments authorized by Congress for UI, SNAP, and for missed school meals have been crucial if incomplete responses, but all are in danger of not being continued as cases continue to surge at the time of this writing. For example, the $600/week UI supplement was allowed to expire at the end of July, and PUA (covering the self-employed) is scheduled to expire at the end of December. The temporary increase in SNAP payments is not tied to the state of the economy, but instead is only authorized through the duration of national and state health emergencies. P-EBT has not yet been extended into the 2020 school year for students who are engaged in remote learning. This potential rollback in support is occurring despite an unemployment rate that still exceeds the maximum rates experienced in the Great Recession. It is too soon to phase down increased payments that provide crucial relief to families experiencing hardships. The current policy response, in particular those applying to UI and SNAP, should remain in place and be phased out only as the economic emergency recedes.

As a general matter, we have designed a safety net that needs an additional boost during recessions. Usual state UI systems generally provide low payments (as a share of wages) for a short duration. SNAP benefits are modest and are intended to supplement other food resources. The EITC tops up low earnings but is not countercyclical. Because these limitations are known, and since there is a high cost both to policy uncertainty and to delays in relief payments, we think it is wise to build automatic expansions into key safety net programs during recessions, as proposed in Boushey, Nunn, and Shambaugh (2019). For example, following the successful policies of the 2009 stimulus, maximum SNAP benefits should be increased by 15 percent (thereby reaching those most disadvantaged recipients who did not gain from the current SNAP expansions). In order to support a work-based safety net, the UI system should be redesigned to provide more insurance and to reach a larger share of disadvantaged unemployed workers during recessions, for example by making permanent the pandemic expansions to UI that extended coverage to self-employed and gig workers and to those with limited work histories, although this may require rethinking the UI tax system for these groups. We need to build a harmonized federal and state data system to facilitate automated relief payments to all eligible Americans. For example, information from state-administered SNAP and Medicaid data systems should have been available to the Treasury to facilitate EIPs for this group. Finally, this crisis has made clear the need for states to increase their administrative capacity for their programs, particularly UI.

VI. Conclusions

The COVID-19 recession is unlike previous recessions due to its depth and speed of onset. In response to this shock, Congress enacted a number of smart short-term fixes to the safety net that have improved its ability to insure low-income families during this recession, including increasing UI payments and extending eligibility, increasing SNAP payments to some participants, sending cash relief payments (EIP), and introducing a new program to replace missed school meals (P-EBT). Without question, these policies have improved the responsiveness of the safety net to this crisis and have reduced suffering that would have occurred without these actions.

Even with these valuable policy responses, there is still tremendous unmet need. Food insecurity has sharply increased, as has the share of families relying on emergency food pantries. Some excess suffering occurred because much of the policy response was slow to roll out and reach needy families. The available yet incomplete data suggest a sizeable subset who experienced shocks and have not received safety net payments; for example, some workers who lost their jobs are not receiving benefits from UI or SNAP. In addition, there remain great economic risks if additional policy responses are removed too quickly, because the underlying US safety net does not provide adequate protection during recessions.

ACKNOWLEDGMENTS   We thank Seth Murray and Edward Olivares for sharing data on the timing of PUA claims, and Tomaz Cajner, Andrew Figura, Brendan Price, David Ratner, and Alison Weingarden for sharing their code and data on this. Raheem Chaudhry, Danea Horn, Abigail Pitts, and Natalie Tomeh provided excellent research assistance. We thank Lisa Barrow, Stacy Dean, Robert Moffitt, Zach Parolin, Brendan Price, Dottie Rosenbaum, Jesse Rothstein, Geoff Schnorr, Jay Shambaugh, Louise Sheiner, Tim Smeeding, Ernie Tedeschi, Till von Wachter, Justin Wolfers, and Abigail Wozniak for helpful comments.

References

Aaronson, Stephanie R., Mary C. Daly, William L. Wascher, and David W. Wilcox. 2019. "Okun Revisited: Who Benefits Most from a Strong Economy?" *Brookings Papers on Economic Activity*, Spring, 333–404.

Ananat, Elizabeth O., and Anna Gassman-Pines. 2020. "Snapshot of the COVID Crisis Impact on Working Families." *Econofact*, March 30. https://econofact.org/snapshot-of-the-covid-crisis-impact-on-working-families.

Bauer, Lauren, Abigail Pitts, Krista Ruffini, and Diane Whitmore Schanzenbach. 2020. *The Effect of Pandemic EBT on Measures of Food Hardship*. Washington: The Hamilton Project, Brookings Institution. https://www.hamiltonproject.org/assets/files/P-EBT_LO_7.30.pdf.

Bitler, Marianne, and Hilary Hoynes. 2016. "The More Things Change, the More They Stay the Same? The Safety Net and Poverty in the Great Recession." *Journal of Labor Economics* 34, no. S1: 403–4. https://www.journals.uchicago.edu/doi/abs/10.1086/683096.

Bitler, Marianne, Hilary Hoynes, and John Iselin. 2020. "The Cyclicality of Cash and Near Cash Transfer Programs." *National Tax Journal* 73, no. 3: 759–80.

Bitler, Marianne, Hilary Hoynes, and Elira Kuka. 2017. "Do In-Work Tax Credits Serve as a Safety Net?" *Journal of Human Resources* 36, no. 2: 358–89.

Blau, Francine, Josefine Koebe, and Pamela Meyerhofer. 2020. "Essential and Frontline Workers in the COVID-19 Crisis." *Econofact*, April 30. https://econofact.org/essential-and-frontline-workers-in-the-covid-19-crisis.

Boushey, Heather Ryan Nunn, and Jay Shambaugh. 2019. *Recession Ready: Fiscal Policies to Stabilize the American Economy*. Washington: The Hamilton Project, Brookings Institution. https://www.hamiltonproject.org/papers/recession_ready_fiscal_policies_to_stabilize_the_american_economy.

Cajner, Tomaz, Andrew Figura, Brendan Price, David Ratner, and Alison Weingarden. 2020. "Reconciling Unemployment Claims with Job Losses in the First Months of the COVID-19 Crisis." Finance and Economics Discussion Series 2020–55. Washington: Board of Governors of the Federal Reserve. https://www.federalreserve.gov/econres/feds/reconciling-unemployment-claims-with-job-losses-in-the-first-months-of-the-covid-19-crisis.htm.

Currie, Janet. 2006. "The Take Up of Social Benefits." In *Poverty, the Distribution of Income, and Public Policy*, edited by Alan Auerbach, David Card, and John Quigley. New York: Russell Sage Foundation.

Ganong, Peter, Pascal Noel, and Joseph Vavra. 2020. "US Unemployment Insurance Replacement Rates during the Pandemic." Working Paper 27216. Cambridge, Mass.: National Bureau of Economic Research. https://www.nber.org/papers/w27216.

Han, Jeehoon, Bruce D. Meyer, and James X. Sullivan. 2020. "Income and Poverty in the COVID-19 Pandemic." In the present volume of *Brookings Papers on Economic Activity*.

Hedin, Thomas J., Geoffrey Schnorr, and Till von Wachter. 2020. "An Analysis of Unemployment Insurance Claims in California during the COVID-19 Pandemic." Policy Brief. Los Angeles: California Policy Lab. https://www. capolicylab.org/publications/june-11th-analysis-of-unemployment-insurance-claims-in-california-during-the-covid-19-pandemic/.

Herd, Pamela, and Donald Moynihan. 2019. *Administrative Burden: Policymaking by Other Means.* New York: Russell Sage Foundation.

Holtzblatt, Janet, and Michael Karpman. 2020. "Who Did Not Get the Economic Impact Payments by Mid-to-Late May, and Why?" Washington: Urban Institute. https://www.urban.org/research/publication/who-did-not-get-economic-impact-payments-mid-late-may-and-why.

Hoynes, Hilary, Doug Miller, and Jessamyn Schaller. 2012. "Who Suffers During Recessions?" *Journal of Economic Perspectives* 26, no. 3: 27–48. https://www. aeaweb.org/articles?id=10.1257/jep.26.3.27.

Hoynes, Hilary, and Diane Whitmore Schanzenbach. 2018. "Safety Net Investments in Children." *Brookings Papers on Economic Activity*, Spring, 89–132.

Karpman, Michael, Stephen Zuckerman, and Dulce Gonzalez. 2018. *The Well-Being and Basic Needs Survey: A New Data Source for Monitoring the Health and Well-Being of Individuals and Families.* Washington: Urban Institute. https:// www.urban.org/sites/default/files/publication/98919/the_well-being_and_basic_ needs_survey_1.pdf.

Marr, Chuck, Kris Cox, Kathleen Bryant, Stacy Dean, Roxy Caines, and Arloc Sherman. 2020. *Aggressive State Outreach Can Help Reach the 12 Million Non-Filers Eligible for Stimulus Payments.* Washington: Center on Budget and Policy Priorities.

Montenovo, Laura, Xuan Jiang, Felipe Lozano Rojas, Ian Schmutte, Kosali Simon, Bruce Weinberg, and Cody Wing. 2020. "Unequal Employment Impacts of COVID-19." *Econofact,* June 1. https://econofact.org/unequal-employment-impacts-of-covid-19.

Murray, Seth, and Edward Olivares. 2020. "Job Losses during the Onset of the COVID-19 Pandemic: Stay-at-Home Orders, Industry Composition, and Administrative Capacity." Working Paper. Social Science Research Network, June 18. http://dx.doi.org/10.2139/ssrn.3633502.

O'Leary, Christopher J., and Stephen A. Wandner. 2020. "An Illustrated Case for Unemployment Insurance Reform." Working Paper 19-317. Kalamazoo, Mich.: Upjohn Institute. https://research.upjohn.org/up_workingpapers/317/.

Parolin, Zachary, Megan Curran, and Christopher Wimer. 2020. "Forecasting Estimates of Poverty during the COVID-19 Crisis." Poverty and Social Policy Brief 4, no. 6. New York: Center on Poverty and Social Policy, Columbia University. https://www.povertycenter.columbia.edu/s/Forecasting-Poverty-Estimates-COVID19-CPSP-2020.pdf.

Passel, Jeffrey. 2007. "Unauthorized Migrants in the United States: Estimates, Methods, and Characteristics." Working Paper 57. Paris: OECD Working Party on Migration. https://www.oecd-ilibrary.org/social-issues-migration-health/ unauthorized-migrants-in-the-united-states_110780068151.

Rosenbaum, Dottie. 2020. "Boost SNAP to Capitalize on Program's Effectiveness and Ability to Respond to Need." Washington: Center on Budget and Policy Priorities.

Schanzenbach, Diane Whitmore, and Abigail Pitts. 2020. *Estimates of Food Insecurity during the COVID-19 Crisis: Results from the COVID Impact Survey, Week 1 (April 20–26, 2020).* Evanston, Ill.: Institute for Policy Research, Northwestern University. https://www.ipr.northwestern.edu/documents/reports/food-insecurity-covid_week1_report-13-may-2020.pdf.

Tedeschi, Ernie. 2020. "U.S. Fiscal Tracker: Major Disbursements Fall to $31 Billion." Evercore ISI Macro Note, June 12.

US Department of Agriculture (USDA). 2020. "Supplemental Nutrition Assistance Program (SNAP) Fiscal Year (FY) 2021 Maximum Allotments and Deductions." https://fns-prod.azureedge.net/sites/default/files/media/file/FY21-Maximum-Allotments-Deductions.pdf.

Comments and Discussion

COMMENT BY
ABIGAIL WOZNIAK I will briefly summarize these two papers before turning to consider how to interpret the two papers together.

Han, Meyer, and Sullivan seek to provide closer-to-real-time estimates of income for the full range of US households in order to track poverty in a more timely manner over the course of the pandemic. Normally, US poverty is assessed annually using official statistics collected in the March Annual Social and Economic Supplement of the Current Population Survey (CPS ASEC). Han and colleagues point out that this measurement process means that official estimates of 2020 poverty will not be available until September 2021.

The innovation in Han and colleagues is to use data already available from major US household surveys to generate household-level estimates of monthly income for a large, representative sample. These data are responses to the monthly CPS question on total household income from all sources. The official poverty statistics rely on a detailed breakdown of income by source available only in the ASEC, but Han and colleagues demonstrate in their figures 3 and 4 that various moments of the income distribution track closely with one another whether constructed using the ASEC or the monthly income measures. The idea that these data can be used to provide more timely readings on the evolution of the income distribution is a great insight, and Han and colleagues do a thorough job demonstrating that these data deserve our attention.

After establishing this approach, Han and colleagues use the monthly income reports to analyze changes in the US income distribution in the first months of the COVID-19 pandemic. Their findings are striking. Fundamentally, they find that poverty rates in the COVID-19 contraction have departed from the pattern set in previous downturns: instead of rising

146

in the contraction, as has been the case in past recessions, poverty rates at the onset of the COVID-19 contraction actually fell. They document that, by their new measure, poverty rates fell by 0.9 percentage points from November 2019 to February 2020, then by another 0.8 percentage points from February to March, and by a similar amount from March to April 2020, before stabilizing at about 9.3 percent for April, May, and June. In total, Han and colleagues report a 1.5 percentage point decline in poverty, concentrated in March and April, as shown in their table 1.

Han and colleagues credit this pattern to a federal aid response that was unprecedented in its speed and scale. To assess the role of these programs, Han and colleagues create estimates of aid received by households under the main pandemic assistance programs: Economic Impact Payments (EIPs), Pandemic Unemployment Compensation (PUC), and Pandemic Unemployment Assistance (PUA). To generate these estimates, they assume that households received EIPs and UI benefits as allowed by statute, but they cap the total amount allocated to match administrative total disbursements by randomly excluding eligible recipients. Their estimates suggest that this suite of support payments can fully account for the income changes they document. Hence, their paper implies that the federal response was large enough to more than fully reverse what would likely have been an increase in poverty rates and a decline in incomes at many lower deciles. They conclude that "the increase in deprivation [as reported in the media and other studies] is not due to the overall income loss, but rather due to other disruptions of the pandemic."

Bitler and colleagues use several data sources to examine this increase in deprivation more closely. They focus on three measures of well-being and economic security, deriving from different sources. These are unemployment (from recent monthly CPS), food insecurity, and mental health (both from the weekly US Census Household Pulse and the COVID Impact Surveys). They find large declines in these measures of well-being. Consistent with other research, they document a substantial rise in unemployment between March and April 2020 in the CPS, with the sharpest increases among already lower earning groups. They also document large increases in self-reported food insecurity and worsening mental health.

Bitler and colleagues then explore connections between these changes in well-being and benefits disbursement. This is challenging, since little individual- or household-level data are available on who has received state or federal support and at what levels. Bitler and colleagues therefore rely on past cyclical patterns to gauge the extent to which benefits may have reached eligible recipients. From there, they can assess remaining unmet need. Little evidence on mental health is available for nationally representative populations over past business cycles, but much is known about the cyclicality of benefits receipt through unemployment insurance (UI) and SNAP, due in part to earlier research from the authors. Using past estimates on the sensitivity of food insecurity to changes in unemployment over the cycle, Bitler and colleagues estimate that the rise in reported food insecurity in the first months of the pandemic is in line with earlier cycles. Consistent with this relationship, they show that SNAP disbursements have risen more in states with larger increases in unemployment.

Evidence on where UI payments have gone is still somewhat difficult to come by. Bitler and colleagues rely on eligibility rules to show that large shares of workers are not eligible for UI payments, even under the expanded provisions of the CARES Act. These include particularly large shares of the lowest earning workers as well as many immigrants. They also point to a range of barriers preventing households from receiving the Economic Impact Payments; these include known delays in distribution, complexity in delivery, and statutorily ineligible groups. Bitler and colleagues argue that ultimately a range of barriers to access, specific provisions to exclude certain groups, and administrative challenges mean that benefits distribution is likely to have so far missed large portions of the US population. This lack of support, they argue, is a likely contributor to declining economic security and mental health.

I describe these as two great papers that lead to one big puzzle. How can the economic condition and overall well-being of so many families have declined so sharply (as identified in Bitler and colleagues) if incomes have risen appreciably for a large portion of the lower earners in the distribution (as identified in Han and colleagues)? One way to try to interpret this tension is to step back and consider the papers as providing evidence on different signals of a general underlying household well-being concept. This concept could be defined narrowly as the ability to cover current essential expenses, or more broadly, as the ability to continue with prior consumption levels with little disruption. In my view, both teams are focused on a concept most like the former, but it is important to acknowledge that the latter concept may be relevant for answers given by survey respondents.

If we accept that the teams are trying to identify measures of financial security that allow Americans to cover essential expenses, then the different assessments they offer could be driven by three factors: (1) one of the signals may be wrong, in that it is biased to the extent that it provides the wrong sign; (2) both signals could be correct, but they could be representative of different US households that are experiencing COVID-19-era changes and support differently (i.e., a composition difference); or (3) they could represent different facets of financial security, and these could be changing in different ways. I will address each of these possibilities in the remainder of this comment before concluding with a discussion of their likelihood as well as lessons for policymakers to take from this uncertain data environment.

ON THE POSSIBILITY OF BIAS IN THE DATA SIGNALS Of course, all data come with error, but what I am concerned with in the case of these two papers is the possibility that one of the sources is biased, to a degree that it is giving us the wrong sign in the pandemic environment. Both teams take great care to demonstrate the validity of their measures. Han and colleagues show that the CPS basic monthly measure of annual income they use produces poverty rates and income quantiles that are strongly consistent—particularly in changes—with the more detailed annual income measure from the March ASEC and other sources. Bitler and colleagues use a suite of data sources and show that these all provide measures broadly consistent with one another. In this case their signal does not derive from just one source, so this can increase confidence in the direction it indicates.

However, data from both teams contain features that raise questions. Bitler and colleagues' data sources, while broadly consistent with one another, sometimes differ in the levels of deprivation they indicate, and sometimes by a large amount.[1] The evidence on deprivation also comes from pandemic-era sources, which may less than perfectly compare to prepandemic sources, as Han and colleagues note. Han and colleagues' data show that half the decline in poverty rates in the first half of 2020 comes in March, prior to the distribution of most administrative benefits but after sharp declines in employment had begun. Table 1 shows the timing of the CPS survey from which Han and colleagues take their monthly measures of total income. The table shows that the March survey week occurred while the CARES Act was still being debated. In the same week, almost 3 million unemployment insurance claims were filed. Since the income measure is based on a twelve-month lookback period, a decline in poverty rates and rise in annual income for lower percentiles between February and March 2020 would have had to be driven by substantial increases in labor income in the first few weeks of March.

Han and colleagues note that poverty was on a downward trend prior to March 2020, and the March decline may reflect this, as well as normal month-to-month measurement error. However, in light of this pattern it is

---

1. See also Winship and Rachidi (2020).

Table 1. Policy and Data Timeline

	Week	Events	Initial UI claims (NSA, millions)
March	1		0.20
	2		0.25
	3	CPS survey week, CARES debated	2.9
	4	CARES passed	6
April	1		6.2
	2	PUC disbursements begin	5.0
	3	EIPs begin, over half disbursed; PUA begins	4.3
	4	CPS survey week, Census Pulse survey begins	3.5
May	1	Fewer than 15 states have begun PUA	2.9
	2		2.4
	3		2.2
	4	CPS survey week	1.9
	5		1.6

Source: Nunn, Parsons, and Shambaugh (2020); FRED.

Notes: CPS = Current Population Survey; PUC (Pandemic Unemployment Compensation) are additional payments through traditional unemployment insurance (UI); PUA (Pandemic Unemployment Assistance) are payments to workers who would not qualify for traditional UI under current statutes; EIPs = Economic Impact Payments. Week 1 is the full week containing the first of the month. Subsequent weeks are those fully included in the month. UI claims are from the end of the designated week.

worth considering whether the CPS monthly income data might contain additional error, perhaps unique to the pandemic. One source of error might be re-timing. Respondents may have anticipated the benefits payments they later received under the CARES Act. This source of error is likely not a concern for overall policy conclusions, at least if respondents correctly anticipate their payments. Other sources of error would pose more significant problems for interpreting the rise in incomes in spring 2020 as fully due to real increases from support payments. One example of this would be a change in recall bias, perhaps due to the pandemic. If the pandemic heightens awareness of one's full stream of income—perhaps because respondents have recently reviewed their income to gauge their financial cushion—then some of the rise in incomes may be spurious. The pandemic itself may change how respondents answer survey questions, even those that have been fielded consistently prior to the pandemic. The same caveat applies to Bitler and colleagues. In their case, survey changes in food insecurity and mental health from prepandemic levels may be driven by the pandemic's effects on perceptions of security (economic and otherwise), rather than its actual effects on household income. This issue is clearly illustrated by substantial misclassification of workers based on their responses to the question of "employed, not at work" versus "on layoff" outlined by the US Bureau of Labor Statistics (2020).

Some of this discrepancy could be alleviated with information from administrative sources. Detailed administrative data on which individuals received CARES Act payments would allow the teams to assess whether their estimates of the contribution of these payments to financial security were correct.

ON THE POSSIBILITY OF RELEVANT COMPOSITION AND CONCEPT DIFFERENCES Differences in the composition of respondents across surveys are another possible source of differing conclusions. In this case, it is possible that the surveys capture respondents who are experiencing the implications of the pandemic differently, leading them to provide conflicting indicators of the overall change in financial security. While this is possible, it seems unlikely. Both teams use data sources that are likely to provide representative estimates for the US population as a whole. Moreover, Han and colleagues show that the poverty declines they identify are, for the most part, very broad based. Notably, they write, "we cannot reject the hypothesis that the declines in poverty are the same for all race or all education groups." If particular subpopulations were driving the difference between their aggregate results and those in BHS, it should be the case that some significant populations did not experience poverty declines. But this is not the case.

The different picture of COVID-19 impacts on financial security across the two papers could also be the result of surveying on different concepts. The concept of food security, for example, is different from the concept of total annual income over the past twelve months. Changes in the two concepts could be diverging in the pandemic environment. While this is possible in principle, if true, this would mean the COVID-19 recession has deviated from a long-standing pattern. In a typical recession, poverty rates, unemployment, and food insecurity all rise, as shown in Bitler and colleagues. Bitler and colleagues also show that reported food insecurity has in fact risen in line with its patterns in earlier recessions when calibrated against the rise in unemployment. So, although it is possible that income has risen for many lower earning households while at the same time their food security and ability to make timely housing payments has fallen, the historic (and practical) connections between these measures mean the current measurement situation would be very unusual.

CONCLUDING ASSESSMENT AND LESSONS FOR POLICYMAKERS Both sets of authors have a preferred explanation from the three I have outlined.

The discussion by Han and colleagues in section VI allows for two explanations—different concepts and wrong-signed signal provided by one of the series—to be true.[2] Bitler and colleagues seem to favor the different composition explanation. In their section III, they assess the ways in which the payments that Han and colleagues estimate in their earnings simulations may not have been paid out as assumed, for a range of reasons, and find evidence that in spite of significant federal aid, many individuals and households received little. This is broadly similar to arguing that the income series and the deprivation series are picking up changes for different groups of Americans. We are in an environment that—if not entirely unprecedented—is unmatched in the modern data-gathering era. It is therefore probably still too soon to say definitively why these sources are providing different pictures of US household financial security.

However, in addition to the many good points both teams have made, it is also worth considering an explanation from economic theory. Normally, a rise in income for low earners would reduce financial insecurity for those households, leading to declines in food insecurity and improved housing stability. However, this is not a normal time. Instead of using added income on recurring expenses, households may be trying to preserve at least some of their additional income for anticipated coming hardships. With the expiration of federal CARES Act benefits at the end of July, and the ongoing historically elevated unemployment insurance claims, it looks like households who anticipated limited additional federal support and ongoing hardship would have been correct.

Economic theory would have predicted these households would try to smooth the temporary added income they received in the spring. This is not a definitive test, but patterns in food insecurity (figure 1) and delayed housing payments (figure 2) over the course of late April through July suggest this may be the case. These series show little variation in the shares of households facing these situations, despite the phase in and out of substantial portions of the CARES Act benefits payments over this period. This would be the case if households attempted to smooth the additional income they received starting in April. Looking specifically at food insecurity due

---

2. More precisely, Han and colleagues argue that the survey data showing elevated levels of hardship based on food insecurity and deferred or missed rent and mortgage payments are unreliable as indicators of true hardship for a variety of reasons related to comparability challenges. They suggest instead that "the profound disruptions from the pandemic . . . could lead to increases in hardship" through other channels. However, I find that two major pandemic-era surveys provide evidence highly consistent with one another and with a major pre-COVID-19 source (Swaziek and Wozniak 2020).

Figure 1. Food Insecurity in the United States during COVID-19

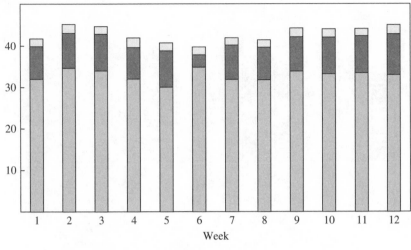

Food insecurity by type

Percent

Week

☐ Often not enough to eat
■ Sometimes not enough to eat
▨ Enough, but not always the kinds of food wanted to eat

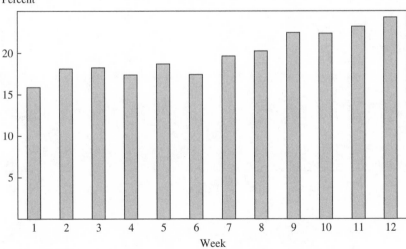

Couldn't afford to buy more food

Percent

Week

Source: US Census Household Pulse Survey.
Notes: Survey week 1 (April 23–May 5) through week 12 (July 16–21). Top panel: share of all respondents reporting food insecurity, by severity. Bottom panel: share of all respondents listing financial constraints as the reason for their food insecurity.

Figure 2. Housing Expense Insecurity in the United States during COVID-19

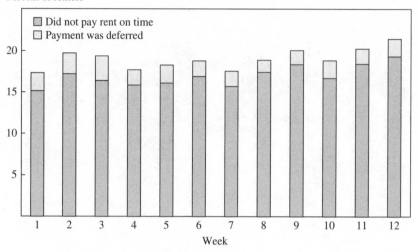

Rent payment last month

Percent of renters

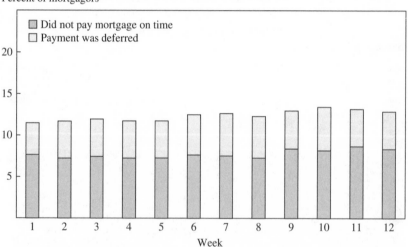

Mortgage payment last month

Percent of mortgagors

Source: US Census Household Pulse Survey.
Notes: Survey week 1 (April 23–May 5) through week 12 (July 16–21).

to financial constraints, the figure shows that, if anything, this begins rising six to eight weeks after the initiation of EIPs and while expanded UI payments were still in place. Also, the share of respondents reporting food insecurity due to supply disruptions (not shown) declines over the same period. These patterns seem at odds with Han and colleagues' suggestion that ongoing pandemic disruptions are more responsible for high levels of food insecurity than is direct financial need. Further evidence suggesting smoothing behavior by households is documented in Cox and others (2020). They find that liquid balances grew for most US households starting in March, and the increase was disproportionately driven by lower-wage earners.

At this point, neither team has a source that can, with great confidence, summarize the financial security position of US households. We must carefully analyze the imperfect signals these data give us and assess whether historic direct financial supports to US households are doing what they are intended to do in real time. The fact that the United States does not have a more robust data infrastructure at this critical time is beyond unfortunate. It means we will get some important questions wrong, with lasting consequences. One lesson from these two papers is that policymakers should consider statistical reform along the lines presented in Heggeness (2020).

Fortunately, in spite of differences, the two projects align on a number of other implications for policymakers. Policymakers should design supports to address known dimensions of distress in an auto-stabilized way, so that support declines only as the economy recovers, rather than leaving households to guess the likely path of future benefits. The data suggest that large shares of Americans are facing food and housing insecurity in spite of massive income infusions. Policies to address this distress should potentially target these basic needs specifically. Bitler and colleagues have many suggestions, particularly for ways to strengthen food supports. Policymakers should also carefully monitor changes in prices that might differentially affect housing and food expenditures, potentially making households less secure on these dimensions even as incomes rise. Finally, efforts to monitor income and other measures of financial security should continue in a robust way through the pandemic, in order to guide ongoing policy decisions.

REFERENCES FOR THE WOZNIAK COMMENT

Cox, Natalie, Peter Ganong, Pascal Noel, Joseph Vavra, Arlene Wong, Diana Farrell, and Fiona Greig. 2020. "Initial Impacts of the Pandemic on Consumer Behavior: Evidence from Linked Income, Spending, and Savings Data." In the present volume of *Brookings Papers on Economic Activity*.

Heggeness, Misty. 2020. "The Need for Data Innovation in the Time of COVID-19."
    Policy brief. Opportunity and Inclusive Growth Institute, Federal Reserve Bank
    of Minneapolis. https://www.minneapolisfed.org/article/2020/the-need-for-data-
    innovation-in-the-time-of-covid-19.

Nunn, Ryan, Jana Parsons, and Jay Shambaugh. 2020. "Incomes Have Crashed.
    How Much Has Unemployment Insurance Helped?" Blog post, May 14,
    Brookings. https://www.brookings.edu/blog/up-front/2020/05/13/incomes-have-
    crashed-how-much-has-unemployment-insurance-helped/.

Swaziek, Zachary, and Abigail Wozniak. 2020. "Disparities Old and New in US
    Mental Health during the Covid-19 Pandemic." *Fiscal Studies* 43, no. 3: 709–
    32.

US Bureau of Labor Statistics. 2020. "Frequently Asked Questions: The Impact
    of the Coronavirus (COVID-19) Pandemic on the Employment Situation for
    May 2020." June 5. https://www.bls.gov/cps/employment-situation-covid19-
    faq-may-2020.pdf.

Winship, Scott, and Angela Rachidi. 2020. *Has Hunger Swelled?* Washington:
    American Enterprise Institute.

GENERAL DISCUSSION   Steven Davis commented on the concerning increase in food insecurity during the COVID-19 pandemic, especially considering the recent and substantial expansion of government income support programs. If the data on food insecurity prove correct, Davis noted that the increase is an indictment of unemployment insurance and SNAP policy implementation. He stated that, in his view, the economics profession in general has devoted too little attention to policy execution. The evidence presented here suggests that recent income support policies have failed to meet their goals despite huge expenditures.

Jason Furman questioned to what extent are people not receiving benefits they are eligible for as a result of problems with execution versus to what extent people are not eligible for benefits because of policy design. Furman then furthered his question by remarking that the policy priority could be to continue to operate under the same eligibility criteria and just expand benefits rather than change eligibility.

He also noted that he has heard that lines at food banks may be as long as they are because people are seeking precautionary savings—that people who could afford food are receiving food donations in order to save money in case they can't save later. People are more able to wait in long food bank lines because of the lower opportunity cost of time during the pandemic. Furman asked the authors if these interpretations have any merit in the discussion of increased food insecurity.

Janice Eberly directed the authors to questions in the teleconferencing platform's chat function regarding the large number of unemployed workers who have not received unemployment benefits, according to the survey.

Jay Shambaugh noted, for the paper by Han, Meyer, and Sullivan, that the stimulus checks as authorized by the CARES Act could not go to immigrants or tax households with an immigrant member. He asked the authors how they dealt with this exclusion. He also noted that undocumented immigrants were ineligible for the stimulus checks and unemployment insurance. Shambaugh then mentioned a comment in the paper regarding offsetting biases and wondered if these biases of income support ineligibility were biased toward people living near or far below the poverty line. He remarked that the paper by Bitler, Hoynes, and Schanzenbach presented disproportionate UI nonreceipt at the very low end of the income range and questioned if the authors had imputed benefit income to people who did not receive any benefits.

Shambaugh then asked Diane Schanzenbach how and to what extent food availability and pricing at the beginning of the quarantine, when there were shortages in staples and SNAP-eligible foods at grocery stores, had an impact on food insecurity.

In response to questions regarding the increase in food insecurity, Bruce Meyer argued that there may be many reasons for this trend besides a decline in income. He noted the decline in overall spending and the increase in uncertainty about the future. Meyer acknowledged evidence that the food insecurity measure has problems, including its peculiar time series patterns and inconsistency with other measures of well-being.[1] He argued that researchers should stop measuring unemployment insurance receipt using self-reports because of evidence indicating that people underreport receipt of benefits. Meyer referenced the Current Population Survey's weighted report of receipt and the demonstrated and growing share of recipients that do not report their unemployment insurance income. He noted that this paper's calculations only assume that a fraction of the unemployed received unemployment insurance to match the total dollars paid out according to Treasury totals.

Meyer also responded to concerns about program ineligibility for undocumented immigrants by mentioning that they are less than 3 percent of the American population, according to the latest Pew estimates. He said it is unlikely that in the near future there will be policies directed toward

---

1. Bruce D. Meyer and James X. Sullivan, "Levels and Changes in Income Poverty, Consumption Poverty and Material Well-Being: A Response to Shaefer and Rivera (2017)," working paper, 2018, https://www3.nd.edu/~jsulliv4/Meyer_Sullivan_response.pdf.

undocumented immigrants and that the group is not large enough to explain overall income patterns. Meyer remarked that there is sensible concern about states being unable to get increased benefits out to people. He also argued that more-targeted policies can address concerns over whom current programs exclude.

Hilary Hoynes responded to the questions about the paper she coauthored. She first addressed the conversation on to what extent people do not receive benefits because they are ineligible. Hoynes referenced Shambaugh's remark on the exclusion of households with an ITIN filer from receiving the relief payments. She also referenced Schanzenbach's comment on UI eligibility rules and noted that lots of people are excluded from income support programs.

Hoynes then addressed questions about the nonreceipt of benefits as a result of implementation problems. She noted that the relief payment went to households that had filed taxes in 2018 and 2019 and to those receiving Social Security or veterans' payments. Hoynes referenced a Center on Budget and Policy Priorities estimate that 12 million individuals were eligible for relief payments but did not receive them.[2] This group is disproportionately composed of those on SNAP or Medicaid and low earners. She added that implementation with automation can be more effective in providing more people with their benefits by removing administrative hurdles.

Hoynes responded to a question from Peter Ganong in the chat function about how much of the UI slowdown is truly a slowdown versus cases of ineligibility. Hoynes pointed to administrative records and survey data Schanzenbach shared that show the increase in UI receipt, demonstrating the timing delay in implementation. She stated that this timing issue is very important for people facing unemployment. Hoynes mentioned that the best administrative data looking at heterogeneity are from the California Policy Lab, and the data on initial applications and their conversions to payments show the same gradients across disadvantaged groups as they did in previous recessions.[3] These gradients are persistent across all US economic cycles, though it is unclear how the challenges of getting online and completing reporting in this instance have affected recent data.

2. Chuck Marr, Kris Cox, Kathleen Bryant, Stacy Dean, Roxy Caines, and Arloc Sherman, *Aggressive State Outreach Can Help Reach the 12 Million Non-Filers Eligible for Stimulus Payments* (Washington: Center on Budget and Policy Priorities, 2020).

3. Thomas J. Hedin, Geoffrey Schnorr, and Till von Wachter, "An Analysis of Unemployment Insurance Claims in California during the COVID-19 Pandemic," policy brief (Los Angeles: California Policy Lab, 2020), https://www.capolicylab.org/wp-content/uploads/2020/06/June-11th-Analysis-of-CA-UI-Claims-During-the-COVID-19-Pandemic.pdf.

PINELOPI KOUJIANOU GOLDBERG
Yale University

TRISTAN REED
World Bank

The Effects of the Coronavirus Pandemic in Emerging Market and Developing Economies: An Optimistic Preliminary Account

ABSTRACT   Early in 2020, the general expectation was that the coronavirus pandemic's effects would be more severe in developing countries than in advanced economies, on both the public health and economic fronts. Preliminary evidence as of July 2020 supports a more optimistic assessment. To date, most low- and middle-income countries have a significantly lower death toll per capita than richer countries, a pattern that can be partially explained by younger populations and limited obesity. On the economic front, emerging market and developing economies (EMDEs) have seen massive capital outflows and large price declines for certain commodities, especially oil and nonprecious metals, but net capital outflows are in line with earlier commodity price shocks. While there is considerable heterogeneity in how specific countries will be affected in the short and medium run, we are cautiously optimistic that financial markets in the largest EMDEs, especially those not reliant on energy and metal exports, could recover quickly—assuming the disease burden is ultimately not as dire in these countries. In the long run, the highest costs may be due to the indirect effects of virus containment

Conflict of Interest Disclosure: The authors did not receive financial support from any firm or person for this paper or from any firm or person with a financial or political interest in this paper. Pinelopi Goldberg was chief economist of the World Bank Group until March 2020, received compensation from the World Bank in that capacity, and is currently a nonresident senior fellow at the Peterson Institute for International Economics. Tristan Reed is an economist for the World Bank. They are currently not officers, directors, or board members of any organization with an interest in this paper. No outside party had the right to review this paper before circulation. The views expressed in this paper are those of the authors and do not necessarily reflect those of the World Bank or Yale University.

policies on poverty, health, and education as well as the effects of accelerating deglobalization on EMDEs. An important caveat is that there is still considerable uncertainty about the future course of the pandemic and the consequences of new waves of infections.

A s the COVID-19 health crisis spread throughout the world to reach low- and middle-income countries in South Asia, sub-Saharan Africa, and Latin America, the international community became increasingly anxious about potentially catastrophic effects of the crisis there. In the early months of 2020, the consensus was that such countries would be hit much harder than advanced economies on both the public health and economic fronts. The managing director of the International Monetary Fund (IMF), Kristalina Georgieva, noted in an IMF podcast on April 9: "Just as the health crisis hits vulnerable people hardest, the economic crisis is expected to hit vulnerable countries hardest" (Georgieva 2020). The president of the World Bank Group, David Malpass, estimated that the COVID-19 crisis would push 60 million people in developing countries into extreme poverty (World Bank 2020a). And in a recent poll of Chicago Booth IGM's Economic Experts Panel, the majority of polled economists (including one of the coauthors of this study) agreed that the "economic damage from the virus and lockdowns will ultimately fall disproportionately hard on low- and middle-income countries."[1] Against this backdrop, the message of this paper is cautiously optimistic: we find that, to date, developing countries have fared relatively well in terms of public health outcomes. And even on the economic front, while it is premature to make any predictions regarding the medium- and long-term economic effects of the crisis, there are encouraging signs. As a caveat to our optimism, we acknowledge that the health crisis has not yet played out and there is still considerable uncertainty about the future course of the pandemic and the likelihood of future infection waves. Our optimism regarding the short run is counterbalanced by our concern regarding the long-run impact of the crisis arising from the indirect effects of containment policies, especially the disruption of health and education services and increase in extreme poverty, as well as from the acceleration of the deglobalization trend with its trade and immigration policy implications.

The paper provides preliminary evidence on the public health and short-run economic effects of the COVID-19 crisis in developing countries

---

1. Chicago Booth Initiative on Global Markets, "COVID-19 and the World Economy," May 5. www.igmchicago.org/surveys/covid-19-and-the-world-economy-2/.

along with some speculation about the long run. The term *developing countries* will be used throughout the paper to include all emerging market and developing economies (EMDEs). We start with an important qualifier: EMDEs include an enormously diverse set of societies and economies. In the context of the COVID-19 crisis in particular, it is useful to keep in mind that the set contains countries such as Vietnam, which as of July 15, 2020, reports zero deaths due to COVID-19 and has generally been minimally affected by the crisis; Brazil, which as of July 15 reports 75,523 deaths; and Zimbabwe, which has just five intensive care unit (ICU) beds (Murthy, Leligdowicz, and Adhikari 2015), yet as of July 15, reports only twenty deaths due to COVID-19.[2] Nevertheless, what these countries have in common, both from a public health and an economic standpoint, seems in the context of the current crisis more important than how they differ. On the public health front, a distinct characteristic of many EMDEs is the low capacity of the health care sector as proxied by number of hospital beds, amount of medical equipment, and number of medical personnel. On the economic front, the very term *developing* countries signifies vulnerabilities that make these countries potentially more susceptible to economic contraction following a health crisis. Further, while adverse economic effects in advanced economies are due to these countries' (justified) efforts to contain the virus, adverse economic effects in EMDEs are to be expected due to spillovers from advanced economies' policies, independent of EMDEs' own policies. EMDEs' own health and economic policies can amplify or reduce these spillover effects, but they cannot avoid them.

Our analysis is structured in two parts corresponding to the public health and economic effects respectively. We start by examining how well countries have fared in the current crisis from a public health perspective. Our measure of COVID-19 outcomes is deaths per million. We chose this measure both because it is widely available and because—measurement challenges notwithstanding—it is less susceptible to concerns regarding biases that plague statistics on positive case counts or hospitalizations. We document a robust positive association between per capita income and deaths per million: the higher the per capita income, the higher the number of deaths per million.

An immediate concern is that this pattern could reflect measurement error, specifically the capacity to correctly identify cause of death, or data manipulation that is correlated with income. However, the

---

2. "Coronavirus Pandemic (COVID-19)," Our World in Data, https://ourworldindata.org/coronavirus.

differences between advanced and developing countries are too large to be driven by (mis)measurement alone. Some specific examples illustrate the contrast: as of July 15, 2020, the United States had 423 deaths per 1 million people; the United Kingdom had 664; France, 461; Brazil, 355; Mexico, 282; South Africa, 75; Nigeria, 4; India, 18; Indonesia, 14; Philippines, 15; and Vietnam, zero.[3] Such big differences across countries make it unlikely that the positive relationship between per capita deaths and per capita income reflects mismeasurement alone or data manipulation. While there is strongly suggestive evidence, based on anecdotes and periodic adjustments to official death statistics, that deaths are undercounted, there is no evidence that this undercounting is systematically correlated with per capita income or the stage of development more generally. Arguments could go either way. On one hand, developing countries tend to have lower statistical capacity (though the death statistics are generally considered reliable), and some of them have limited resources for testing (a precondition for correctly identifying the cause of death), although—as we show in the next section—on average, low-income countries have more comprehensive testing programs than the rest of the world. On the other hand, a consistent source of mismeasurement in the case of COVID-19 has been the omission of deaths in nursing homes and long-term care facilities for the elderly. Such facilities tend to be less prevalent in developing countries, making this source of mismeasurement less relevant to them. Therefore, on net, it is not clear that mismeasurement is systematically correlated with development. Similarly, while deliberate data manipulation, especially in countries with no free press, is a concern, it is less clear that it is correlated with stage of development.[4]

The global cross-country comparison exhibits the exact opposite pattern from what has been widely documented within countries at specific locations: at the global level, the COVID-19 burden seems to fall disproportionately on richer countries; within municipalities, however, it is the socioeconomically disadvantaged groups who suffer the most.[5] The spatial pattern of coronavirus mortality is interesting as it may provide insight

3. "Coronavirus Pandemic (COVID-19)," Our World in Data, https://ourworldindata.org/coronavirus.

4. A potential approach for dealing with death undercounting would be to look at excess deaths. We discuss the problems with this approach in the next section (I.A).

5. The spatial pattern of COVID-19 mortality within countries exhibits the same pattern. For example, in Italy, it was Lombardy, one of the wealthiest regions of the country, that had the highest death toll. Similarly, in the United States, New York State, New York City in particular, had one of the highest deaths per capita rates in the country; but within New York City, it was the socioeconomically disadvantaged who were affected the most.

both into the political economy of policy responses (and resistance to them) and into appropriate policies going forward. Our analysis demonstrates that a large part (but not all) of this positive correlation between countries' per capita income and deaths per million can be explained through demographics (age) and obesity. Whatever the source of this pattern, it gives a ray of hope to governments with fewer resources: it suggests that tragic as the loss of life may have been, it was not as large as anticipated. This is positive, both because lives were spared and because it means that—to the extent that this pattern does not change in the future—countries may be able to ease containment measures and focus on the economic fallout that has been significant.

Next, we examine the short-run economic effects. We focus on financial data, since financial markets reacted immediately to the COVID-19 news and available data reflect this reaction; in contrast, data on macroeconomic variables become available with a delay and currently exist for only a handful of countries. Early March saw unprecedented portfolio outflows from EMDEs accompanied by sharp depreciations of several currencies, an increase in bond spreads, and a collapse of commodity prices and, with them, of revenues from commodity exports. These developments raised serious concerns about the solvency and general economic prospects of several EMDEs. However, data from subsequent months present a more optimistic picture. Based on estimates of broader measures of capital we show that while capital outflows have been severe, net flows are within the range observed during earlier commodity price crises, for instance, the collapse in the oil price beginning in 2014. Solvency issues have been temporarily addressed through a debt service standstill, spreads have come down, commodity prices have increased, and financial markets seem calmer and more confident than in March. Aggressive central bank operations in the United States and Europe have reassured markets and may keep EMDE borrowing costs at bay in the future. Overall, the picture that emerges from available financial data is that while the current situation facing developing countries is grim, it may not be fundamentally different from past crises. To date, the most adverse economic impacts have been due to the collapse of oil prices, and it is the countries most exposed to oil price exports that have been most affected. The oil price collapse was itself the result of two shocks, the demand collapse due to the health crisis and the price war between Russia and Saudi Arabia (which may in turn have been triggered by anticipation of the demand collapse, although tensions with Russia predate the COVID-19 crisis). At any rate, the insight that reliance on commodity exports makes certain resource-rich developing countries particularly vulnerable to external crises is neither novel nor specific to the current public health crisis.

There is substantial uncertainty regarding the medium- and long-run effects of COVID-19 on developing countries, but we offer some thoughts in the last part of the paper. Particularly for small economies, these effects will depend on how soon advanced economies recover. In addition, they will depend on EMDEs' own policies, which will be disproportionately important in larger economies. Most EMDEs have adopted lockdowns and mobility restrictions similar to those in advanced economies in order to contain the spread of the virus. While such policies have adverse economic effects in all countries, their long-term impacts in developing countries may prove substantially more severe if they lead to lower school attendance among some groups of their populations, especially girls, fewer vaccinations (e.g., for measles) among children, and higher child and maternal mortality due to the disruption of health care services. The severity of these effects will depend on the extent and duration of current lockdown measures. Preliminary evidence based on phone surveys suggests substantial loss in employment and income and cutbacks in food consumption in countries with few cases and deaths relative to other parts of the world. Hence, in the poorest countries, the indirect impact of the coronavirus pandemic may prove substantially more severe than its direct death toll. Finally, the economic future of developing countries will depend also on how trade and immigration policies evolve in advanced economies in the coming years. If developed countries turn inward and borders remain closed, EMDEs will have to rely on themselves more than ever. Overall, it seems that, to date, EMDEs have weathered the COVID-19 crisis better than expected. But the biggest challenges may await them post-crisis, necessitating a process of structural adjustment and the rethinking of their development strategies in a world with less international integration.

We caution that the results presented in the paper are as of July 15. The health crisis started later in South Asia, Africa, and Latin America than in Europe and North America. Accordingly, it has not yet played out in the EMDEs in these parts of the world, and it is possible, indeed likely, that our estimates could change in the coming months as several countries in Latin America, especially Brazil and Mexico, have seen an acceleration in new infections and deaths during May and June. Furthermore, several developing countries—for example, India and South Africa—have experienced a spike in infections in the first two weeks of July. Nevertheless, the death rates in India and South Africa, as well as in the overwhelming majority of countries in Asia and Africa, remain substantially lower than those in the average advanced economy, by orders of magnitude. Therefore, and for reasons we explain in the next section, we are cautiously optimistic that our main conclusions may not be reversed; for this to happen, infections and deaths in EMDEs would have to accelerate at an extremely fast pace in the next months or continue for a very long time. Such rapid acceleration has not been observed so far, but the coronavirus has repeatedly surprised us, and there is no guarantee that it will not happen in the future. Were this to happen, the message of this paper would not only be reversed, it would be devastating. For it would mean that the costly containment strategies developing countries followed so far would have failed to contain the virus. Developing countries would have paid the cost of mobility restrictions, school closures, and so on, only to find themselves in the same place as advanced economies with a delay of a few months. The human and economic cost of such a scenario is unfathomable.

I. The Public Health Crisis and Response

The first part of our analysis describes how the public health crisis and response so far has played out differently across countries. We first review the hypotheses proposed at the onset of the crisis before turning to an econometric analysis of the data.

I.A. Initial Hypotheses

Initially, there was uncertainty about how the health crisis would play out in EMDEs. The prevailing view was that the disease burden would be much higher in countries with fewer resources to fight the virus. However, there were also reasons for optimism that the effects could be milder than in advanced economies.

First, low connectivity of some countries might allow for earlier containment. International air travel seeded national outbreaks, with some of the first cases in Europe imported in January by a tour group from Wuhan, China (Olsen and others 2020), and a resident of France who had traveled to the city for business (Stoecklin and others 2020); the majority of cases in New York City in early March are thought to have originated in Europe (Gonzalez-Reiche and others 2020). Early modeling of importation risk to sub-Saharan Africa from certain Chinese provinces suggested risk would be less in low-income and lower-middle-income economies compared to upper-middle-income economies, given fewer flights (Gilbert and others 2020).[6]

Second, the observation that the outbreak was initially concentrated in the cooler regions of Europe, the United States, and China has led some to argue that the SARS-CoV-2 virus may be transmitted more slowly in warmer climates (Araujo and Naimi 2020; Sajadi and others 2020). During the 2003 outbreak of the preceding coronavirus SARS-CoV-1 only three cases were ever detected in India and only one case was ever detected in sub-Saharan Africa, in South Africa.[7] The conclusion that climate may protect tropical and subtropical countries is highly speculative however; even if warmer climate does slow transmission, there is no evidence it will do so enough to suppress the outbreak in the absence of other measures such as social distancing (Kissler and others 2020).

Third, developing countries have substantially younger populations. According to the United Nations Population Division (2019), while 17.5 percent of the Italian population is over age 70, that number is 5.6 percent for Peru and 2.2 percent for Ethiopia. Advanced age has been documented extensively as a leading risk factor for severe COVID-19 illness and mortality (Zhou and others 2020; Jordan, Adab, and Cheng 2020; Zheng and others 2020), suggesting that lower-income countries may ultimately face a lower disease burden. Modeling by epidemiologists also appears to reflect this hypothesis. Barnett-Howell and Mobarak (2020) analyze the disease burden predicted by Walker and others (2020), who account for differences in the age distribution, and show that predicted rates of mortality are substantially higher among Organization for Economic Cooperation and Development (OECD) countries compared to EMDEs.

Fourth, obesity, the prevalence of which increases with income, is another risk factor for severe illness (Simonnet and others 2020; Lighter and others 2020; Sattar, McInnes, and McMurray 2020). According to the most recent age-standardized estimates from the World Health Organization (WHO), in the United States 36.2 percent of adults are obese (i.e., have a body mass index ≥ 30). In Mexico, this number is 28.9 percent;

---

6. Despite China being the focus of this initial work, Skrip and others (2020) find that the majority of imported cases across forty countries in sub-Saharan Africa were individuals who had recently traveled from Europe (66.1 percent of imported cases) rather than Asia (19.7 percent) or the Americas (7.2 percent).

7. "Summary of Probable SARS Cases," World Health Organization, https://www.who.int/csr/sars/country/table2004_04_21/en/.

Figure 1. Risk Factors for Severe COVID-19 Illness and the Public Health Response

**Risk factors for severe COVID-19 illness
average by income group**

Population over age 70 (%)

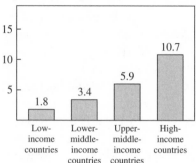

Obesity prevalence (% of adults)

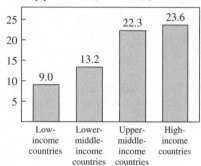

**Public health response
average by income group**

Days before first death that action is taken

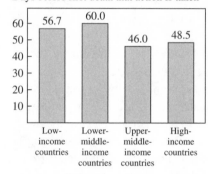

Positive test ratio (%)

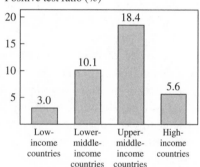

Sources: UN Population Prospects; World Health Organization; Blavatnik School of Government, University of Oxford, https://www.bsg.ox.ac.uk/research/research-projects/coronavirus-government-response-tracker; Our World in Data, https://ourworldindata.org/coronavirus.

in Ghana, it is 10.9 percent; and in Vietnam, it is 2.1 percent.[8] Figure 1 shows the average values of the share of the population over age 70 and obesity prevalence across countries within each of the World Bank's four groupings of countries by national income: low income, lower-middle income, upper-middle income, and high income. For both factors there is a clear positive relationship with income. For obesity, though average prevalence

8. "Global Health Observatory Data Repository," World Health Organization, https://apps.who.int/gho/data/node.main.A900A?lang=en.

increases monotonically with income group, upper-middle-income countries have similar prevalence to high-income countries (i.e., 22.3 percent versus 23.6 percent, respectively).

Fifth, the virus arrived in many EMDEs with a delay of one to two months, allowing the authorities to draw on lessons from other countries, and in some cases take earlier action. A key insight from epidemiology is that more lives are saved if suppression measures (those that force the effective reproduction number (R_t) below one, so that the virus will die out) are taken earlier, when there have been fewer deaths (Walker and others 2020). Using the Oxford COVID-19 Government Response Tracker and deaths reported on the website Our World in Data, it is possible to calculate how early in each national epidemic first action was taken.[9] For instance, Kenya began screening international air passengers for temperature and symptoms on January 20, sixty-seven days before the first death on March 27, and well in advance of its first confirmed case on March 14. France, on the other hand, took its first action on January 23, also by screening international air passengers, but this was only twenty-three days before its first death on February 15, and only two days before its first confirmed case on January 25.

The lower left-hand panel of figure 1 shows the average days before first death that action is taken across the four national income groups, where action is defined as the "containment and health response" index rising above zero for the first time, typically due to information campaigns or screening of international passengers. To avoid dropping countries with zero confirmed deaths from the sample, which would bias these averages downward, for such countries we set the date of first death equal to the most recent date deaths are observed (July 15). Uganda, for example, has no deaths as of this writing and took its first action on January 20, so we record the days before first death action is taken as 152, the number of days between their first action and July 15.

The delay in arrival of the virus may have given countries more time to prepare infrastructure for COVID-19 testing. The challenge is daunting. Test, trace, and isolate (TTI) programs, which the WHO recommends as part of a comprehensive response to the virus, are estimated to require one

---

9. Blavatnik School of Government, University of Oxford, COVID-19 Government Response Tracker, https://www.bsg.ox.ac.uk/research/research-projects/coronavirus-government-response-tracker; "Coronavirus Pandemic (COVID-19)," Our World in Data, https://ourworld indata.org/coronavirus. All values of infections and deaths reported in this paper are from Our World in Data.

contact tracer for every 1,000 people (Association of State and Territorial Health Officials 2020). In Nigeria, this implies that about 200,000 tracers would be needed to implement TTI nationally, as well as technological systems for recording and sharing information and a budget for their salaries, personal protective equipment, transportation, and tests. While many countries, including Nigeria, do have experience with large-scale public health initiatives such as immunization campaigns—for example, Burkina Faso was able to inoculate 11 million people or 96 percent of the population age 1–29 against meningitis in only ten days (Djingarey and others 2015)—such initiatives require substantial resources and planning.

A useful proxy for testing capacity is the positive test rate, that is, the share of tests which come back positive. Jha, Tsai, and Jacobson (2020) suggest authorities should seek to achieve a positive test rate of less than 10 percent. If too many tests come back positive, it is likely that many cases are being missed. If only a small share of tests are returned positive, it seems reasonable to conclude that testing is sufficient for the case load (unless one has been testing people who are less likely to be infected, for example, if only people with means could afford to be tested). For context, using again the data from Our World in Data as of July 15, 2020, the ratio of confirmed cases to total tests in Sweden is 13.3 percent and 8.5 percent in the United States. In South Korea and New Zealand, two advanced economies noted for highly effective test and trace programs, the ratio is 1.06 percent and 0.35 percent respectively. The lower right-hand panel of figure 1 shows that the average value of the ratio is actually lowest in low-income countries, at 3.0 percent, compared to 5.6 percent in high-income countries. While far fewer tests have been completed in low-income countries, by this measure, which corrects for the number of cases, low-income countries have the most comprehensive testing programs in the world. Zimbabwe, for instance, has a test positive rate of 1.5 percent. Vietnam, a lower-middle-income country, has the lowest test positive rate at 0.10 percent and, as of July 15, zero confirmed deaths. Nigeria, also a lower-middle-income country, raises the average for its group with a much higher test positive rate of 17.0 percent. Upper-middle-income countries have the highest average positive test rate, at 18.4 percent, driven specifically by certain Latin American countries such as Brazil, which has a 90.4 percent test positive rate, and Ecuador, which has a 50.7 percent rate. Testing in these countries is clearly insufficient for the case load.

Ironically, though low connectivity and a younger population have often been described as challenges for developing countries, here they may turn out to be a blessing. Unfortunately, there are also compelling reasons for pessimism: the effects of the pandemic could be more severe than in advanced economies.

First and foremost is the lower to nonexistent capacity of the health care system. Available data suggest Zambia and Zimbabwe each have just five ICU beds available to treat severely ill patients (Murthy, Leligdowicz, and Adhikari 2015). Looking at the most recent values of the broader measure of all hospital beds, most of which will not be equipped for intensive care, the Philippines has one bed per thousand people while Japan has 13.4, according to the World Bank World Development Indicators (WDI). Assuming for the moment equal prevalence of illness across populations, this implies if Japan were able to "flatten the curve" and avoid overwhelming the health care system, the Philippines would need to reduce the rate of new infections by a further 92.5 percent to avoid overwhelming its own system.[10]

Second, many of the policies that have been tried with relative success in advanced countries may be harder to implement in developing countries. Lockdowns and social distancing may be less effective in settings with high population density and high poverty (e.g., urban slums) or in multigenerational or polygamous households. Further, as noted by Ravallion (2020), the world's poor are highly dependent on casual day labor for survival and have little in the form of savings or food stocks, implying they will have stronger incentives to leave their homes, even when governments ask them not to.

Taken as a whole, this discussion suggests there was substantial uncertainty initially as to whether the direct health impacts of COVID-19 would be worse in developing countries. In the rest of this section, we investigate the various hypotheses described above more rigorously using a linear regression. Specifically, we estimate the following equation:

$$(1) \qquad \ln(\text{deaths per million})_i = \beta_0 + \rho \ln(\text{GDP per capita})_i \\ + f(\text{time since 1st death})_i + X_i'\beta + \varepsilon_i,$$

where i indexes countries, X_i' is a vector of explanatory variables, and ε_i is an error term.

Given that the pandemic is ongoing, one concern is whether the effects we document are due to countries being earlier or later on the curve. Mechanically, countries accumulate deaths as times passes, so countries

---

10. The calculation is $92.5 = (1 - 1/13.4) \times 100$.

Figure 2. Reported COVID-19 Deaths per Capita

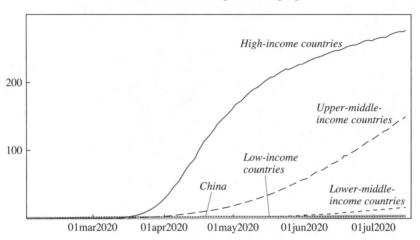

Total COVID-19 deaths per million people

Source: Our World in Data, https://ourworldindata.org/coronavirus.

that started having cases and deaths earlier in the year will have a larger death toll. To account for this mechanical effect, we control for the time since the first death was observed in each country through a square root function. This functional form is motivated by the pattern observed in several countries that seem to be toward the end of their infection and death curves (e.g., European countries).[11] This approach seems adequate at present but would have to be revisited if countries faced a second wave of infections. One day, when the pandemic is over, the above regression should be run without controlling for this mechanical effect.

Before reviewing the data and regression estimates, we graph the COVID-19 deaths per million people in figure 2 by World Bank income group classification. To date, the picture in EMDEs seems to vindicate the optimists. Middle- and low-income countries seem to be on a very different curve than high-income countries. The graph clearly shows the earlier outbreak of the health crisis in high-income countries. But even accounting for this difference in timing, deaths in EMDEs are growing much more slowly over time. This is especially true for low-income and lower-middle-income countries. The curve for upper-middle-income countries rises more steeply starting in May, reflecting the rising deaths in Latin America,

11. We also experimented with a linear function with no significant impact on the results.

Figure 3. National Income and COVID-19 Deaths per Million

COVID-19 deaths per million people (USA = 1)

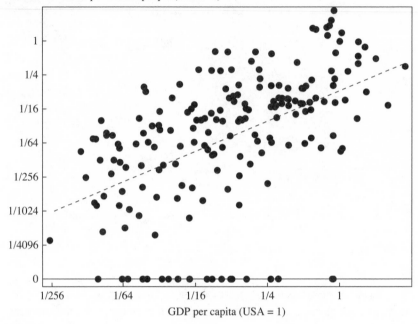

GDP per capita (USA = 1)

Sources: Our World in Data, https://ourworldindata.org/coronavirus; World Bank World Development Indicators.
Note: Ordinary least squares fit shown as dashed line.

especially in Brazil. That curve excludes China, which is shown separately, as the very low death rate in China would dominate the graph, obfuscating the recent deaths in Latin America. Even taking this rise into account, it seems unlikely that middle- and low-income countries will catch up to high-income countries.

A different way to assess the raw differences between advanced and developing economies is shown in figure 3, which displays the raw correlation between deaths per million and national income as of July 15. Deaths per million is strongly and positively correlated with per capita income. At present, the numbers across advanced and developing economies differ by orders of magnitude. Almost every country with per capita income one-sixteenth of the United States has one-sixteenth the deaths per million of the United States *or fewer.* While infections and deaths in Brazil and Mexico are rising fast, so that the death rates in these countries may catch up to the United States eventually, for the rest of the countries, it would take a fast acceleration of deaths over a prolonged period of time for the pattern we document to be reversed. India and South Africa, for example, have experienced a spike in infections in the first two weeks of July. However, the death rates in these countries remain orders of magnitude smaller than in advanced countries, at about 18 deaths per million and 75 deaths per million respectively (as of July 15). Of course, there is always the possibility of new waves, especially as countries are gradually opening up.

As we discussed above, the large differences between high- and low-income countries make it unlikely that these patterns are driven by death undercounting in low-income countries. Figure 2 reinforces this message as it shows that advanced and developing countries differ not only in terms of death rate levels; their respective curves also look very different, with developing countries, especially lower-middle-income and lower-income countries, exhibiting much flatter curves. This pattern is intriguing from an epidemiological perspective as it may indicate different transmission patterns—heterogeneous basic reproduction numbers, R_0—across countries. At any rate, it is hard to reconcile with the hypothesis that the differences we document are due to data manipulation or systematic undercounting in lower-income countries.

A potential approach for dealing with death undercounting would be to look at excess deaths over a certain period of time, as was done, for example, in the *Economist* (2020) or by Wu and others (2020) in the *New York Times* for selected cities and countries. Excess death data provide support for the view that COVID-19 deaths are undercounted in both advanced and developing countries. However, due to the lack of mortality times series, excess deaths cannot be computed for most developing countries. In addition, the interpretation of excess deaths is not clear: such deaths capture both the direct mortality effects of COVID-19 and the indirect effects due, for example, to the disruption of non-COVID-19 health care services, the pandemic's effects on mental disease and suicides, the increase (or decrease) of violence, the increase (or decrease) of car accidents, and so on. This may explain why South Africa, for instance, exhibits zero excess deaths as of July 9, 2020, while official statistics report 3,720 cumulative deaths attributed to COVID-19 as of that date (Wu and others 2020).

A final note is that our regression makes no statement about indirect human costs of the pandemic because of lockdowns. Ray and Subramanian (2020) write eloquently on this topic in the context of India, stating: "Lives lost through violence, starvation, indebtedness and extreme stress, are invisible, in the sense that they will diffuse through category and time" (13). These deaths are not accounted for in our measure of COVID-19 deaths per million. One attempt to capture them would be to look at the aforementioned excess deaths relative to previous monthly averages and to ask how many of them can be explained by confirmed cases and how many reflect the indirect death toll of the pandemic. Unfortunately, as noted earlier, the mortality time series required for this analysis are not available systematically for EMDEs. Moreover, given existing concerns regarding mismeasurement, it is not clear whether excess deaths that go beyond confirmed cases capture undercounting of COVID-19 deaths or the indirect death toll of the pandemic.

I.B. Data

Here we briefly review the data used, summary statistics of which are presented in table 1. COVID-19 deaths per million are from the COVID-19 data set on Our World in Data and are compiled based on statistics released by the European Centre for Disease Prevention and Control (ECDC). As noted earlier, our regressions include a function of days since first death to account for the mechanical fact that countries accumulate more deaths with time. This variable is set to zero for countries with no deaths to date. These data are also taken from Our World in Data.

The days since first death function is meant to capture the mechanical effect of time on deaths, but it may also be a proxy for a different channel. Late exposure to the virus may have been the result of developing countries' lower connectivity to the rest of the world. The late arrival of the virus resulting from lower connectivity may have given developing countries extra time to prepare and to take measures to contain the spread of the disease. To separate this channel from the mechanical effect of time, we use three variables. First, we use two proxies for connectivity: the international flight arrivals per 1,000 people in December 2019 and January 2020 (also broken down by origin, i.e., flights from China and flights from Schengen Area) and the imports per capita in 2019. These measures are taken from Flightradar24 (a commercial flight tracking service) and from the United Nations Comtrade Database, respectively. We experimented with alternative measures (e.g., exports or the sum of imports and exports) with no difference in the results. Further, we use information on the timing of the first response based on the Oxford COVID-19 Government Response Tracker. Specifically, we use the time between the first time the government in a certain country acted related to COVID-19 and the first death in that country to measure the speediness of response. Note that for several countries, this variable takes negative values as these countries acted before experiencing even a single death.

In addition to the timing of the first public health response, we also investigate the strength of the response, measured alternatively by the government response for containment and health response index reported in the Oxford COVID-19 Government Response Tracker, and reductions in time spent in the workplace and public transit, relative to the median value for the corresponding day of the week during the five-week period from January 3 to February 6, 2020, as reported by Google.[12] Further, we use a contract tracing comprehensiveness index, which is reported by Oxford University as part of their government health and containment response index; a value of zero indicates no contact tracing, a value of 2 indicates contacts of all cases are traced, and a value of 1 indicates limited tracing.

GDP per capita is measured in constant 2010 US dollars and taken from the World Bank WDI. The health variables—population over age 70, obesity, and smoking and diabetes prevalence—are from the WHO. PM2.5 air pollution and hospital beds per thousand people are from the World Bank WDI. Population density of largest urban center is as reported by the Global Human Settlement Layer Urban Centre Database.

We include various measures of institutional capacity. Data on testing come from Our World in Data. Finally, we also examine measures of the extent to which either autocracy or democracy is institutionalized in the country from the Polity IV Project database. According to these data, monarchies such as Saudi Arabia and Eswatini (previously Swaziland) have autocracy scores of 9 and 10, while China has a score of 7. Countries scoring 10 for democracy include Mongolia and Germany, while South Africa is 9 and the United States has a score of 8. All these countries are rated zero for the extent of institutionalized autocracy. The relationship between COVID-19 deaths and political and social features of the state is studied by Bosancianu and others (2020), though they do not include these indicators. We also include an index of statistical capacity developed by the World Bank, ranging from zero to 100, in order to test whether measurement specifically can account for deaths per million. For this index, which is not available for high-income countries, we set the value for all high-income countries equal to the maximum, 97, so that the index has the greatest possible potential to explain the association between income and deaths per million.

12. "COVID-19 Community Mobility Reports," accessed July 15, 2020; https://www.google.com/covid19/mobility/2020.

Table 1. Summary Statistics

	N	Mean	SD	Min.	Max.
Confirmed COVID-19 deaths per million people	197	59	147	0	1,238
Days since first death (= 0 if no deaths)	197	76	32	0	161
Real GDP per capita (2010 USD)	189	17,699	26,542	211	195,880
Population over age 70 (%)	182	6.1	4.8	0.7	22
Obesity prevalence (% of adults)	177	18	8.9	2.1	38
Smoking prevalence (% of adults)	139	21	9.5	2	46
Diabetes prevalence (% of adults)	193	8.0	4.2	1	22
PM2.5 air pollution ($\mu g/cm^3$)	183	28	19	5.9	100
Hospital beds per thousand people	185	3.1	2.8	0.1	19
December and January international flight arrivals per 1,000 people	197	1.3	2.8	0.0002	18
December and January flight arrivals from China per 1,000 people	197	0.02	0.05	0.000005	0.3
December and January flight arrivals from Schengen Area per 1,000 people	197	0.3	1.0	0.00001	6.7
Imports per capita (USD)	162	5,983	8,775	71	65,708
Imports from China per capita (USD)	161	561	936	6.0	8,802
Imports from Schengen Area per capita (USD)	162	8,367	12,815	81	74,585
Days before first death that action is taken	169	53	34	−79	171
Containment and health response four weeks after first death (0–100)	151	75	14	17	100
Workplace mobility decline four weeks after first death (%)	121	−45	20	−90	5
Public transit mobility decline four weeks after first death (%)	121	−57	19	−93	−5
General cancellation of public events four weeks after first death (= 1)	152	0.9	0.3	0	1
Containment and health response ninety days after first death (0–100)	37	70	13	46	94

Population per km² in largest urban center	173	6,511	3,397	1,172	19,843
Persons per household	144	3.9	1.4	2.1	8.7
COVID-19 tests per 1,000 people	83	42	50	0.5	267
Positive test ratio (%)	83	9.3	17	0.1	117
Contact tracing comprehensiveness index (0–2)	151	1.3	0.7	0	2
Statistical capacity (0–100)	195	75	19	27	97
Institutionalized democracy (0–10)	148	6.0	3.7	0	10
Institutionalized autocracy (0–10)	148	1.6	2.7	0	10
February precipitation (mm/day)	197	2.8	2.4	0.03	13
March precipitation (mm/day)	197	2.4	2.1	0.02	12
April precipitation (mm/day)	197	2.6	2.2	0.03	13
May precipitation (mm/day)	197	3.0	2.7	0.06	19
Nonimported cases of SARS-CoV-1 (= 1)	197	0.03	0.2	0	1
Nonimported cases of MERS-CoV (= 1)	197	0.05	0.2	0	1

Actual rainfall for February to May 2020 is measured using data from the National Oceanic and Atmospheric Administration. Precipitation for each country is measured in average millimeters per day using the Climate Prediction Center Merged Analysis of Precipitation data set, which reports values on a 2.5 by 2.5 degree grid obtained by combining satellite estimates and gauge data (Xie and Arkin 1997). Values on the grid are averaged within administrative boundaries.[13] As an alternative to using data on temperature, we use distance to equator as a proxy for weather and climate; this variable is measured in degrees latitude from the centroid of the national administrative boundaries reported by Natural Earth.

Finally, it has been hypothesized that exposure to prior epidemics may have conferred to some developing countries "trained immunity."[14] To investigate this hypothesis, we use information on prior SARS-CoV-1 and MERS-CoV infections. Locations of nonimported SARS-CoV-1 are Canada, China, Mongolia, the Philippines, Singapore, and Vietnam, as reported by the WHO. Locations of nonimported MERS are Bahrain, Iran, Jordan, Kuwait, Lebanon, Oman, Saudi Arabia, United Arab Emirates, and Yemen, as reported by the Centers for Disease Control and Prevention.

I.C. Regression Results

Table 2 reports the results of estimating several specifications of equation (1) using ordinary least squares. Additional specifications are reported in the online appendix. Before taking logs of deaths per million we have added 0.0219 to the value for twenty countries with zero confirmed deaths, so that they are not dropped from estimation, treating them as if they experienced 2.9 deaths per 100 million people. This number was selected so that these countries have exactly $1/(4 \times 4096)$ deaths per million of the United States, implying that the Y-axis tick on which they sit in figure 3 is evenly spaced from the others above it. The full sample includes 189 observations of deaths per million and GDP per capita.

13. Country values are calculated in two steps. First, inverse distance weighted interpolation is used to generate a 1 by 1 degree grid of monthly rainfall values; a power coefficient equal to 5 is applied to the distance measure, so that interpolated points reflect mainly the nearest values. This step is necessary because the boundaries of several small countries do not contain any point on the original 2.5 by 2.5 degree grid. Second, rainfall on all points within the 1 by 1 degree grid are averaged within the administrative boundaries of each country.

14. Netea and others (2020) define "trained immunity" as a biological process by which activation of the innate immune system can result in enhanced responsiveness to subsequent triggers—a de facto innate immune memory.

We present this regression with the important qualifier that the dependent variable (deaths per million) continually changes, and hence the results may change in the future. Column 1 reports the coefficient on the log of per capita income in the absence of any additional explanatory variables X_i. Here the coefficient $\rho = 0.891$ (SE = 0.102), suggests that for a 1 percent increase in income there is approximately a 0.9 percent increase in deaths per million, corresponding to the linear fit displayed graphically in figure 3. Further, the R^2 (which has been adjusted for the number of explanatory terms in the model) is 0.24, indicating that roughly one-fourth of the variation in deaths per million is explained by income.

We now add additional variables sequentially to unpack this relationship. In column 2 we add the square root of days since first death (which is set to zero for those twenty-one countries with zero confirmed deaths) to account for the mechanical effect that countries later in the pandemic will have accumulated more deaths. The adjusted R^2 rises to 0.628, suggesting timing of arrival explains a substantial part of the overall variation in deaths. The coefficient $\rho = 0.617$ (SE = 0.078) has fallen, consistent with the fact that EMDEs experienced their first death later but remains statistically significant below 1 percent and is sizable in magnitude.

In column 3 we add two risk factors for severe COVID-19 illness: the share of the population over age 70 and obesity prevalence. Notably, since accurate body mass index data are difficult to come by for representative samples of the confirmed cases within countries (Lighter and others 2020), our cross-country regression presents a novel opportunity to investigate the contribution of obesity to COVID-19 mortality. The element of β corresponding to the coefficient on the age variable is positive and significant, equal to 0.089 (SE = 0.029), suggesting that for a 1 percentage point increase in the population over 70, deaths per million increase by about 0.9 percent. The element of β corresponding to the coefficient on obesity is also positive and significant, equal to 0.052 (SE = 0.022), suggesting that for a 1 percentage point increase in obesity prevalence, deaths per million increase by about 0.5 percent. The coefficient $\rho = 0.216$ (SE = 0.126) falls substantially relative to the previous specifications, suggesting that the high initial correlation between income and deaths can be explained by just the two risk factors for severe illness (age and obesity) and the time of virus's arrival.

In table A2 of the online appendix, we explore specifications that include additional health covariates (smoking prevalence, diabetes prevalence, as well as a measure of particulate matter pollution since pollution may increase asthma prevalence). We consistently find no statistically

Table 2. Regression of (Log) COVID-19 Deaths per Million People on Country Covariates

	(1)	(2)	(3)	(4)	(5)	(6)	(7)	(8)	(9)	(10)
Ln(real GDP per capita)	0.891*** (0.102)	0.617*** (0.078)	0.216* (0.126)	0.706*** (0.090)	0.759*** (0.121)	0.221* (0.124)	0.422*** (0.158)	0.499* (0.280)	0.451*** (0.152)	0.246 (0.226)
Square root of since first death (= 0 if no deaths)		0.611*** (0.035)	0.538*** (0.039)	0.473*** (0.074)	0.139 (0.186)	0.417*** (0.067)	0.364*** (0.073)	0.204 (0.211)	0.362*** (0.078)	0.439*** (0.127)
Population over age 70 (%)			0.089*** (0.029)			0.109*** (0.029)	0.125*** (0.032)	0.091** (0.041)	0.072 (0.048)	0.154** (0.076)
Obesity prevalence (% of adults)			0.052** (0.022)			0.063*** (0.022)	0.068*** (0.022)	0.060* (0.031)	0.062*** (0.022)	0.146*** (0.023)
Days before first death that action is taken				−0.009* (0.005)	−0.012* (0.006)	−0.007 (0.005)	−0.005 (0.004)	−0.001 (0.005)	−0.007* (0.004)	0.022** (0.009)
Containment and health response four weeks after first death (0–100)					−0.012 (0.013)					
Workplace mobility decline four weeks after first death (%)					−0.040*** (0.013)					
Public transit mobility decline four weeks after first death (%)					0.016 (0.016)					
Ln(Population density in largest urban center)							1.124*** (0.354)	1.847*** (0.541)	1.224*** (0.359)	2.007*** (0.540)

	(1)	(2)	(3)	(4)	(5)	(6)	(7)	(8)	(9)	(10)
Ln(COVID-19 tests per 1,000 people)								0.583**		
								(0.234)		
Contact tracing comprehensiveness index (0–2)								-0.557**		
								(0.264)		
February precipitation (mm/day)									-0.080	-0.006
									(0.104)	(0.140)
March precipitation (mm/day)									0.269**	0.248
									(0.108)	(0.184)
April precipitation (mm/day)									-0.079	-0.516***
									(0.110)	(0.177)
May precipitation (mm/day)									0.068	0.241**
									(0.067)	(0.101)
Distance to equator (degrees latitude)									0.026*	-0.003
									(0.014)	(0.020)
Constant	-5.887***	-8.560***	-5.962***	-7.720***	-4.947***	-4.972***	-16.264***	-22.625***	-17.974***	-25.827***
	(0.910)	(0.675)	(0.846)	(0.916)	(1.865)	(0.906)	(3.647)	(5.106)	(3.709)	(5.674)
Adjusted R^2	0.243	0.628	0.610	0.606	0.443	0.617	0.618	0.563	0.637	0.636
Observations	191	189	171	165	119	156	154	82	154	154
Population weighted	No	No	No	No	No	No	No	No	No	Yes

Note: Standard errors are robust to heteroskedasticity.

***$p < 0.01$; **$p < 0.05$; *$p < 0.1$

significant effect of these variables on deaths per million, once age and obesity are controlled for. Moreover, they often have counterintuitive signs (column 1 in table A2). Health care capacity (as measured by hospital beds per 1,000 people) is also insignificant (column 2 in table A2), but with a negative sign, as expected. We also consider a specification that controls for the hypothesized "trained immunity" effect through dummies indicating countries had nonimported cases of SARS-CoV-1 and MERS-CoV (column 4 in table A2). We find a large, negative, and statistically significant effect of SARS-CoV-1 on deaths per million. The coefficient on MERS-CoV is negative, but not significant. Importantly, the inclusion of these covariates has no effect on the remaining coefficients, and on the income coefficient—hence, it does not help explain the positive correlation between deaths and income. The SARS-CoV-1 dummy acts as a proxy for countries in East Asia, which have much lower death rates, and may therefore also capture factors other than trained immunity. For this reason, we do not include it in other specifications. In general, we avoid using country dummies (or variables that effectively act as country dummies), since we estimate a cross-country regression, and country dummies wipe out relevant variation in our covariates.

In columns 4 and 5 of table 2, we omit the two risk factors (age and obesity) and control instead for the public health policy response. In column 4, we add just one variable that measures the days before first death that action is taken by the government on the public health response. Whereas before we had been controlling for when the virus arrived in the country (through days since first death), we are now also controlling for the time at which the government responded. As expected, the coefficient on this variable is negative, and it is statistically significant at the 10 percent level. The coefficient $\rho = 0.706$ (SE = 0.090) has risen and is again statistically significant. Conditional on the timing of first death and government action, there is still a strong positive correlation between income and deaths per million, meaning that while early action may help reduce deaths, it does not explain why developing countries have had lower death rates to date. In column 5, we examine whether the strength of lockdown measures mattered in addition to the timing of first action by adding both the value of the containment and health response index and observed changes in mobility from workplaces and on public transit. Note that because the mobility reports are not available for all countries in our sample, we lose some observations, and hence columns 4 and 5 are not directly comparable.

Nevertheless, the results in column 5 provide some useful insights. Both our proxy for early action and the decline in workplace mobility are found to have a negative and significant impact on deaths per capita. However, the inclusion of mobility controls further increases the correlation between deaths per capita and income. A recent piece by Maire (2020) may explain why. Maire (2020) finds that low-income and lower-middle-income countries had lower compliance (i.e., decline in mobility) conditional on the policy stringency index than the rest of the countries. Hence, it does not appear that developing countries have contained the death toll because of lower mobility—in contrast, it seems that they have a lower death rate *despite* not reducing mobility.

In columns 6–10, we reintroduce the two risk factors, age and obesity, that were shown to have a significant impact on cross-country differences. Given that mobility reports are not available for all countries in our sample (and that they do not appear to explain why developing countries have lower death rates anyway), we omit mobility from these specifications but always include the early action control (timing of first policy response). The latter always has the expected negative sign but is significant only in column 9. Columns 7–10 introduce one additional variable, the population density in a country's largest urban center. This variable has a large positive and significant effect in all specifications as expected. Further, average household size does not significantly predict death rates conditional on the density of the largest urban center (column 3 in online appendix table A2). Interestingly, however, once population density is introduced, the correlation between deaths and income (which had become small once age and obesity were controlled for) reappears, though it is substantially lower than in the initial specifications that do not control for risk factors. This suggests that, once again, developing countries do not have fewer deaths because they have fewer dense cities; they have fewer deaths *despite* having some of the densest cities in the world.[15]

In column 8, we add the (log) number of tests per 1,000 and the contact tracing comprehensiveness index. Unfortunately, the number of observations drops to 82, so we cannot draw any definitive conclusions based on this specification. The coefficient on the contact tracing index is negative and significant, suggesting that this approach is effective in reducing the death rate. The coefficient on the testing measure is positive and significant. Given that testing is not random, the interpretation of this coefficient is not straightforward. On one hand, one could interpret the positive sign as

15. The top twenty urban centers by population density are in the Democratic Republic of the Congo, Ethiopia, India, Indonesia, Nigeria, Niger, and Pakistan (https://ghsl.jrc.ec.europa.eu/ghs_stat_ucdb2015mt_r2019a.php).

suggesting that when more tests are conducted, more COVID-19 deaths are detected. On the other hand, given that most countries faced testing capacity constraints, many of them rationed testing and made tests available only to those who were likely to be infected. In this case, higher infection and death rates would be the reason for more testing—a classic case of reverse causality. Despite this ambiguity in the interpretation of the testing coefficient, we note that the coefficients on the other covariates (age, obesity, and population density of the largest city) remain unaffected. The correlation with income persists ($\rho = 0.499$; SE = 0.280). For the reasons we mentioned above, we do not view the results in column 8 as conclusive. But if one were to take them at face value, they would suggest that the lower death rates in developing countries are attributable to several factors: younger populations, lower obesity, more contact tracing, possible mismeasurement. However, the puzzle of developing countries' lower death rates, as reflected in the positive correlation of the death rate with income, remains. Column 5 of table A2 in the online appendix reports an additional specification, in which one more covariate is added to those of column 8 in table 2: the positive test ratio. Interestingly, once the positive test rate is included, the coefficient on income drops and is no longer significantly different from zero. The coefficients on both testing measures are positive and significant. In both cases, a causal interpretation of these effects is not possible. But if one interpreted the test positive rate as a measure of the capacity of the testing system (rather than a measure of the infections rate), then the positive coefficient would support the view that higher testing capacity (reflected in a lower testing ratio) is associated with fewer deaths. As noted earlier, many low-income countries have some of the most comprehensive testing programs in the world, given their disease burden.

In columns 9 and 10, we add controls for weather and climate. The specifications in these two columns are identical, but column 10 reports population-weighted regressions. In column 9, precipitation in March enters with a positive sign and it is significant. This is likely because several South American countries with high death rates—namely, Brazil, Ecuador, and Peru—also experienced substantial precipitation in March. Distance to equator, which is a proxy for cooler temperature and lower humidity (among many other things), also has a positive and statistically significant effect on the death rate, providing some support for the hypothesis that warm climate might slow the virus or even suppress it. The population-weighted results are similar with two differences: the signs and statistical significance of the weather variables change; and, more interestingly, the correlation with income is much smaller and statistically insignificant ($\rho = 0.246$; SE = 0.226). The coefficients on age and obesity, while qualitatively similar to those in previous specifications, now double in magnitude. These results are robust to excluding the two most populous countries in our sample, India and China.

The online appendix tables report additional robustness checks. The effects of age, obesity, and population density of the largest urban center remain robust. In table A1, we include various controls for connectivity. The controls are mostly insignificant, except for flight arrivals from China, which is a proxy for China (as this measure includes domestic flights in China). Not surprisingly, the associated coefficient is negative and significant as China has had a lower death rate. Similarly, in one specification in column 4, flight arrivals from the Schengen Area have a large (positive) impact on death, but this variable is a likely proxy for European countries, which have had a particularly high death toll. For the reasons given earlier, we avoid variables that act as country dummies. Notably, the inclusion of the connectivity measures does not significantly affect either the income or the time since first death variables. In table A2 we consider further covariates and specifications. Column 6 includes a control for statistical capacity. Although statistical capacity is not statistically significant, its inclusion reduces the coefficient on income to 0.323, providing some support for the hypothesis that some part of the positive correlation between income and death rate may be due to measurement (countries with higher statistical capacity report more deaths). Column 9 in table A2 includes controls for the regime type. Though the coefficient on democracy is positive, and the coefficient on autocracy is negative, suggesting democracy may have made controlling the disease harder, as some have speculated for instance in the context of the United States, these effects are not statistically significant.

In table A3, we explore additional specifications, several of which leave out the time since first death variable since this variable may be absorbing the effect of policy actions. It is interesting to note that if we include only the two risk factors (age and obesity) that have turned out to be most important in the majority of our specifications, we can explain approximately one-third of the variation in death rates (column 1). Controlling for these two factors alone reduces the correlation of death rates with GDP from 0.891 in the very first specification of table 2 to 0.335 in column 2 of table A3—hence almost two-thirds of the correlation between income and death rate we initially reported can be attributed to these two factors alone. But this correlation rises again once we control for population density in the largest urban center (column 3). The finding that population density, while important, reinforces rather than solves the puzzle of lower death rates in developing countries, is one of the most robust findings of our analysis.

I.D. Tentative Conclusions

Between table 2 and the tables in the online appendix, we have explored thirty different specifications for regressions explaining cross-country variation in death rates. The three covariates that are consistently found to have a large and statistically significant impact on deaths per million are age, obesity, and population density in the largest urban center. The first two can explain a large part (almost two-thirds) of the positive correlation between income and deaths per million. In contrast, population density in the largest urban center tends to increase the correlation between income and death rate, deepening the puzzle of why developing countries have lower death rates; developing countries have a lower death toll despite having some of the world's densest cities.

Some of the specifications support the view that policy, especially early action and contact tracing, can explain cross-country differences, but the associated results are either based on few observations or not robust. Along the same lines, we find some support for the claim that death undercounting could partially explain lower death rates, but controlling for such undercounting through a measure of statistical capacity (or the more controversial tests per million measure) still does not significantly reduce the correlation between income and death rates.

We highlight two more robust findings. First, no matter what covariates one includes, the correlation between per capita income and deaths per million proves extremely robust; it always has a positive sign and is statistically significant in all but one specification. Hence, part of the lower death toll in developing countries to date remains a puzzle. Second, the other variable that has consistently had a large, statistically significant impact on the death rate is (the square root of) time since first death. As explained earlier, we feel compelled to include this variable in the regressions to control for the mechanical effect of time on the accumulation of deaths. But this variable also serves as a proxy for other relevant factors, for example, the transmission process. Figure 2 shows clearly that compared to high-income countries, the path of COVID-19 has been very different in middle- and low-income countries; not only do the latter have lower deaths per capita at any point in time, the entire curve of COVID-19 progression looks different (much flatter). This pattern is consistent with the hypothesis of heterogeneous R_0's (see Ellison 2020)—in this case across country income groups. In column 4 of table A3, we explore this hypothesis by allowing for different coefficients on the time since first death variable across different country income groups. The results support the premise of heterogeneous—across country groups—transmission processes, with low-income countries exhibiting the slowest and advanced economies exhibiting the fastest COVID-19 progression. However, it is not clear what accounts for these different patterns. It is possible that the demographic factors we identified as having high explanatory power for death rates affect death rates not only through case fatalities but also through transmission (this would be, for example, the case if younger people are not only less likely to die from COVID-19, but also less likely to transmit it because they don't exhibit severe symptoms). Alternatively, it is possible that different R_0's across income groups reflect different policies, though given the heterogeneity of policy responses across the world, the exact mechanism behind this hypothesis is itself a puzzle. At any rate, we believe that the differences across country income groups we document are intriguing and may prove useful to epidemiologists in the future. For example, it would be interesting to calibrate a model with heterogeneous R_0's to specifically investigate the question of what type of heterogeneity would lead to the patterns we document in this paper. We leave this undertaking to future research.

We conclude, tentatively, that to date, the public health care crisis in EMDEs has not been as severe as initially feared. No matter what the reason for this is, it is good news. It means that fewer lives were lost. It also means that—to the extent this pattern is not reversed in the future—developing countries may be able to focus on the economic situation, to which we turn in the next section.

II. The Economic Crisis

In the second part of this article, we turn to the economic crisis, drawing on the financial data available at this early moment.

II.A. Short and Medium Run

EMDEs could face years of economic hardship due both to suppression measures, the continued duration of which is uncertain, and to spillover effects from a global recession. In advanced economies, the hope was that once countries brought the public health crisis under control, they would manage the economic crisis. For smaller economies especially, the decline in commodity export revenues and remittances from migrants to advanced

Figure 4. Nonresident Purchases (Sales) of EM Stocks and Bonds

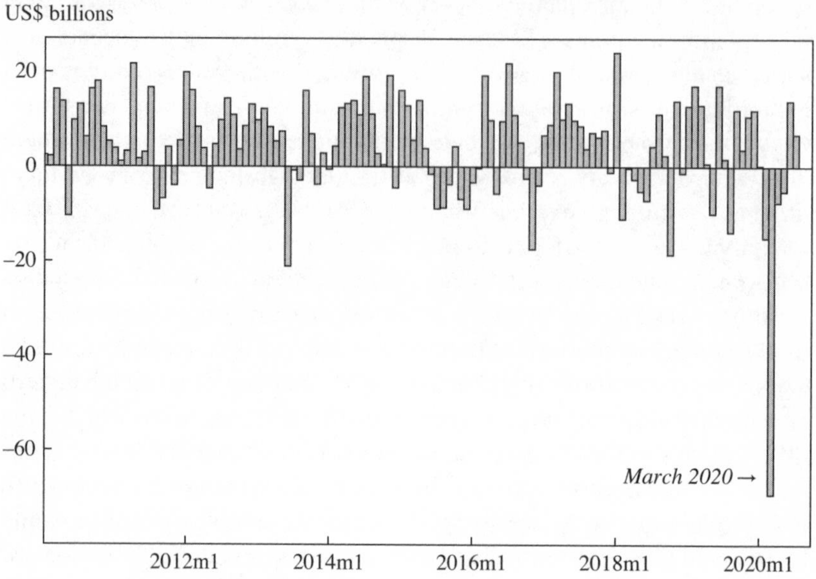

US$ billions

March 2020 →

Source: Institute of International Finance.

economies implies that the economic effects could be grave, even if they manage to control the virus.

We structure the discussion of the short- and medium-run economic effects in three parts. We first discuss external vulnerabilities focusing on financial markets. Next, we discuss preliminary evidence on the effects of countries' own containment policies. Finally, we offer some thoughts on policy implications.

EXTERNAL VULNERABILITIES Given limited availability of data on macroeconomic variables at this early moment, we start by discussing financial data, which highlight how the external environment facing EMDEs has changed. We consider first international capital flows. Some sales of EMDEs' assets were expected, as is typical during periods of increased global risk aversion (Kalemli-Özcan 2019). The initial reaction of capital markets to COVID-19 news in March however was unprecedented. Figure 4 shows that in the month of March $69.4 billion of emerging market stocks and bonds were sold by nonresidents, the largest monthly outflow of portfolio investment that has ever been recorded by the Institute of International Finance (IIF). Outflows of this so-called hot money can cause instability in the financial system, as they cause devaluations that increase the risk that governments and corporations will not be able to honor liabilities denominated in foreign currency (Das and others 2020).

As shown in figure 5, these March outflows coincided with a substantial increase in hard currency bond spreads. Though the increase was shared across corporate and sovereign bonds, sovereigns were hit particularly hard. At a time precisely when governments faced large emergency spending needs, access to international capital markets almost disappeared. In several cases (e.g., Nigeria, Mexico) sovereigns had been trading at a spread over corporates, suggesting the market already viewed these governments as a greater risk than private firms in these countries.

Examining the movement of bond spreads highlights the limitations facing international institutions attempting to support EMDEs during this crisis. On March 23, Group of Twenty (G-20) finance ministers and central bank governors held a conference call and stated their willingness to support developing economies through the IMF and World Bank Group. This is exactly the moment when spreads peaked in most countries, suggesting these statements perhaps eased some anxieties about the increased risk of sovereign and corporate default. However, on April 15, when the G-20 announced its detailed action plan, the main initiative of which was to offer less-developed countries the option of forbearance—delayed payment—on bilateral loans, sovereign spreads again increased, for instance, in Nigeria and Ethiopia. Spreads also increased in Brazil and Mexico, even though these countries were ineligible for forbearance under the G-20 proposal, which focused on the poorest countries. Under the terms proposed, countries could request to suspend loan payments from May 1, 2020, until the end of the year. Private creditors were encouraged to offer similar terms, if countries requested them. Though interest would continue to accrue, leaving the net present value of the loans unchanged, forbearance still effectively increases maturities, introducing greater risk. It seems that the market evaluated this additional risk relative to the counterfactual of on-time payment rather than default; the spreads in Ethiopia, Nigeria, and Pakistan (and to a lesser degree in Brazil and Mexico) increased immediately after the G-20 forbearance announcement. Though these spreads have come down in the meantime, for now, apart from subsidized direct finance through multilateral development banks, the international community has not been able to reduce substantially the higher borrowing costs EMDEs now face in private markets.

The greatest concern is that higher borrowing costs will make each country's emergency response more difficult to finance. Beyond short-run risks to financial stability, concerns about a massive capital flight may be

Figure 5. Hard Currency Bond Spreads in Emerging Markets

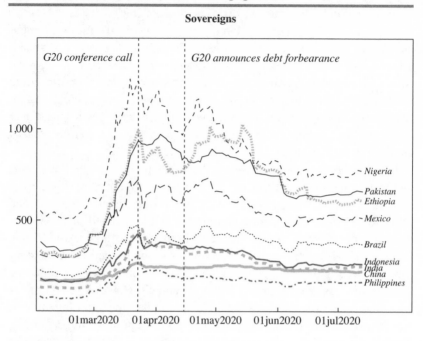

Sovereigns

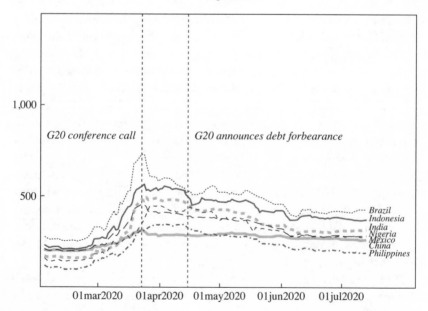

Corporates

Source: J. P. Morgan Markets.

exaggerated. The top panel of figure 6 shows estimates of overall net capital flows from fifteen major EMDEs over the same time period as portfolio investment flows that were shown in figure 4.[16] By this broader measure, which includes also direct investment and banking flows, total net capital outflows in March 2020, though more than $100 billion, were for these fifteen countries of comparable magnitude as in late 2015, during that year's trough in the oil price, which is included in the panel for reference. Flows therefore were large but not unprecedented. The bottom panel of figure 6 reports accumulated net capital flows for select countries over the most recent year, as a multiple of GDP. Even accounting for recent outflows, India and Indonesia, for instance, have still accumulated 2 percent and 4.5 percent of GDP respectively in new capital since last year. Country-level trends in net capital accumulation do not appear to have changed.

An interesting feature of figure 6 is the strong correlation between overall net capital flows to EMDEs and the oil price over the last decade. While we do not claim there is a simple causal relationship between the two, this observation raises the possibility that some of the capital outflows in March—and the financial distress of EMDEs more broadly—may be linked to the decline in commodity prices rather than the pandemic per se. The collapse in the oil price, also in early March, was the result of a supply shock related to a price war between Saudi Arabia and Russia—the full extent of the collapse in oil demand emerged only shortly thereafter. In support of the hypothesis that oil prices specifically were a contributor to the EMDE sell-off, Saudi Arabia experienced by far the largest year-on-year decline in overall net capital flows as a share of GDP, by −8.1 percent, among all EMDEs tracked by the Institute of International Finance. Outflows from that country alone accounted for 22 percent of the value of net capital flows in the month of March.

16. We focus on net flows in the tradition of Calvo (1998). Some authors (for example, Forbes and Warnock 2012; Brunnermeier and others 2012; Broner and others 2013) have made the case for also keeping track of gross cross-border capital flows, as gross flows provide a more appropriate measure of risk sharing across countries and global financial integration. We return to this issue at the end when we discuss the long-run risks associated with deglobalization. These estimates are produced by the IIF. The advantage of the IIF data is that they are available at high frequency, while balance of payments data are available only on a quarterly basis. We emphasize that figure 6 is based on estimates rather than actual data. However, the IIF estimates have tracked balance of payment data closely in the past, as shown in the supplementary figures for selected countries in the online appendix.

Figure 6. Overall Net Capital Flow to Emerging Markets

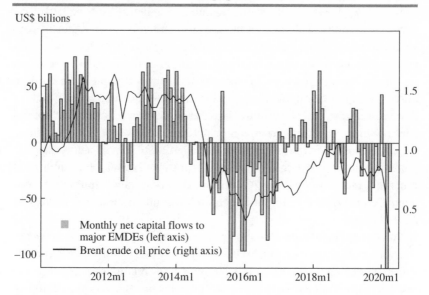

US$ billions

Accumulated net flows over most recent year

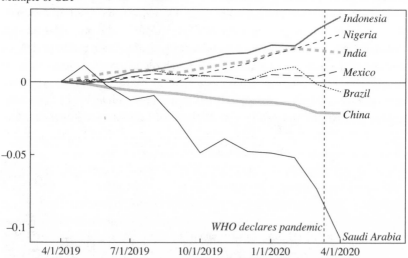

Sources: Institute of International Finance; World Bank Commodity Markets Outlook.

Notes: Overall net capital flows include all types of flows from both residents and nonresidents covering portfolio flows (i.e., purchases or sales of stocks and bonds), banking flows, direct investment, and other components of the financial account in a nation's balance of payments and are equal to the change in the current account, excluding central bank reserve operations. Monthly net capital flows in the top panel are the sum of net flows to Argentina, Brazil, Chile, China, Egypt, India, Indonesia, Malaysia, Mexico, Nigeria, Poland, Saudi Arabia, South Africa, Turkey, and Ukraine.

Some of the economic effects of the crisis in EMDEs may not be dissimilar from a standard commodity price shock. Figure 7 shows how prices of energy, metals, and various agricultural commodities have changed from the start of the pandemic until July 15. Crude oil has been the biggest loser. In May, it was down more than 50 percent since the last year, but then recovered, to be approximately 40 percent lower than last year. Though gold prices have risen—unsurprising at a time of global risk aversion—prices of the base metals copper, aluminum, and tin as a group declined by approximately 20 percent between January and May 2020. Natural gas also experienced a drop in price, but rapidly recovered this loss during the month of April. By July 15, all of these commodity prices had recovered, with the price of copper even higher than a year before. Effects on agricultural products have been more varied, with sharp declines in the prices of cocoa, cotton, and sugar during March, but sharp spikes in the prices of coffee and rice. All these prices as of July 15 had returned to roughly where they were in the previous year.

Figure 8 summarizes the exposure of countries, by income group, to four risk factors for an external recession, including a collapse in commodity prices. These four factors are agricultural raw materials exports, natural resource rents, international tourism receipts, and remittances, all measured as a share of GDP. The United Nations predicts a global decline in international tourism arrivals by 60–80 percent in 2020 (United Nations World Tourism Organization 2020), and the World Bank predicts a 20 percent decline in remittances (Ratha and others 2020) to low- and middle-income countries specifically. Among these risk factors, low-income countries are most exposed to the decline in commodity prices, with natural resource rents accounting for 12.4 percent of GDP, compared to just 2.6 percent in high-income countries. Though low-income countries export more agricultural raw materials as a share of GDP relative to other income groups, the value of these exports, just 1.6 percent, pales in comparison to their revenues from natural resources. Though international tourism receipts are worth more to low-income countries than agricultural raw materials, at 2.8 percent of GDP, tourism is still predominantly an export of high-income countries, where receipts account for 11.8 percent of GDP. Remittances are most important in low- and lower-middle-income countries, though in both income groups the value of natural resource rents is greater.

These observations, which are not new, suggest the downside for EMDEs due to external factors is likely to play out through familiar channels. Smaller economies highly dependent on commodity prices and remittances will suffer the most. In larger economies, where growth is determined to

Figure 7. Commodity Prices

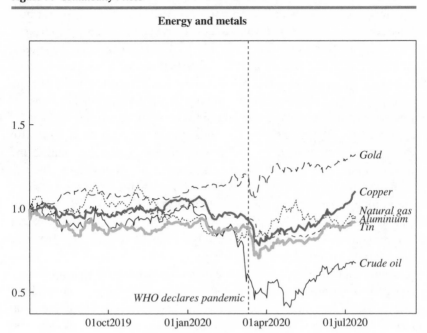

Energy and metals

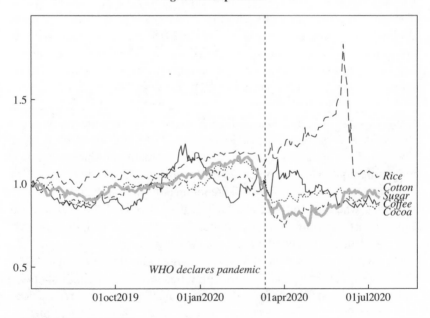

Agricultural products

Figure 8. Risk Factors for Exposure to External Recession

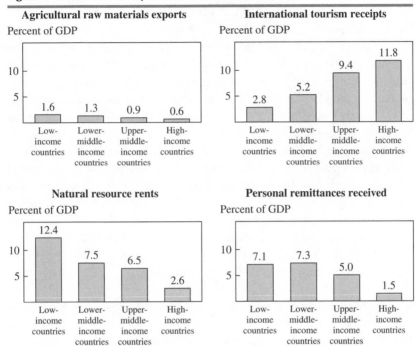

Source: World Bank World Development Indicators.

a greater extent by local demand, the speed of economic recovery will depend on how quickly the public health crisis passes. If the COVID-19 disease burden is ultimately not as dire in these countries—as we have suggested in the previous section it may not be—this observation leaves us cautiously optimistic that the largest EMDEs, especially those not reliant on energy and metal exports, could recover quickly.

This view is reflected to a certain extent in growth forecasts. For example, in the *World Economic Outlook Update, June 2020*, the IMF predicts −3 percent real GDP growth for 2020 in EMDEs, relative to −8 percent growth in advanced economies. The IMF also expects what could be called a *V*-shaped recovery, with 5.4 percent global growth in 2021 (IMF 2020). The World Bank estimates in *Global Economic Prospects* (2020b) are overall more pessimistic, but they too predict a less severe output contraction in EMDEs relative to advanced economies: in 2020, EMDEs are predicted to see growth of −2.5 percent while advanced economies are predicted to see growth of −7 percent. Commodity exporters face growth of −4.5 percent compared to the rest of EMDEs, who are predicted to see growth of −1 percent (World Bank 2020b). Of course, we do not mean to be overly sanguine. Declines in growth, even when they do not turn negative for individual countries, have a tremendous cost in lower-income countries. Mahler and others (2020) expect that the pandemic will push 49 million people into extreme poverty in 2020, causing the first increase in the global poverty rate since the Asian financial crisis in 1998.

EFFECTS OF COUNTRIES' OWN CONTAINMENT POLICIES Just as in advanced economies, some of the most severe economic effects of the pandemic will be due to containment measures, especially general and prolonged lockdowns. As a first look at the effects so far, figure 9 shows year-on-year changes in real GDP for EMDEs that have already reported actual values for the first quarter of 2020. The figure allows one to judge the losses so far relative to the gains of the previous three quarters. Given the economic effects are likely not to have appeared until after the first COVID-19 cases and subsequent lockdowns, countries are separated into two panels: on the top are those with their first case before February 15, and on the bottom are those with their first case after February 15. China, which had its first confirmed case in the fourth quarter of 2019, appears to have fared the worst, as expected, with a −6.8 year-on-year decline in income. In the Philippines, the pandemic erased three-quarters of GDP growth that had been even faster than that of China, so that it experienced essentially 0 percent year-on-year growth. Vietnam, Indonesia, and Morocco, where the virus arrived in the second half of the quarter, all experienced declines in income, but not enough to erase gains from 2019.

Losses in the second quarter of the year of course are expected to be much worse, as stay-at-home orders have now spanned much of the quarter, though as of May many countries are tentatively reopening. The experience of China, which first issued stay-at-home recommendations early in the quarter on January 23, provides guidance for how large these second quarter losses might be. China experienced −36.5 percent annualized real GDP growth in the first quarter of 2020 according to the National Bureau of Statistics. This corresponds to a $((1 - 0.365)^{1/52} - 1) \times 100 = -0.86$ percent loss of income per week. Rounding up slightly to account for the fact that stay-at-home orders did not span the whole quarter, 1 percent of GDP is a very rough estimate of the potential income lost per week of lockdown.

While we are awaiting official data, several phone surveys provide an early picture of economic losses. Relative to official statistics, these surveys have the advantage of capturing (at least part of) the informal sector

Figure 9. Real Gross Domestic Product

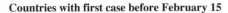

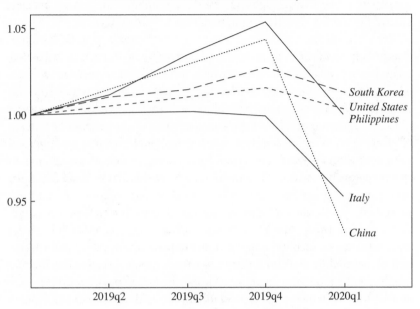

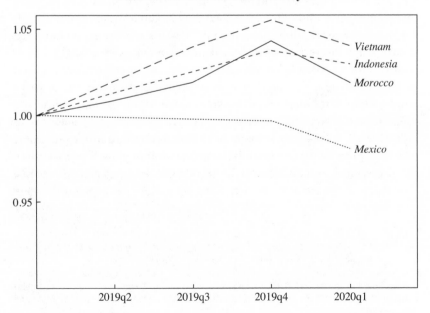

Source: Haver Analytics.

which is prevalent in developing countries. On the other hand, one may worry about potential selection as owning a smartphone is a prerequisite for survey participation. Such selection may imply that the poorest segments of countries' populations may not be represented.

Even with this caveat in mind, the reported losses appear devastating. Indicatively, according to the World Bank's Living Standards Measurement Study (LSMS) for Nigeria, which was released in early June 2020, 42 percent of respondents reported that they were not currently working due to COVID-19, mostly in the commerce, service, and agriculture sectors (though they were employed prior to the onset of the crisis); 79 percent of respondents reported that their households' total income had decreased since mid-March; and 51 percent of households reported reducing food consumption because of falling income.[17] Results from the LSMS for Ethiopia paint a similar picture (Wieser and others 2020). Surveys from several other sub-Saharan countries (Kenya, Uganda, Sierra Leone, Senegal, etc.) as well as from South Asia (India, Pakistan, Nepal) consistently report loss of work and income along with disruptions to education and routine health care and difficulties meeting basic nutritional needs.[18] The income loss in conjunction with rising food prices in some countries and the risk of desert locust damage to crops in others (East Africa in particular) have led to heightened food insecurity. According to the Famine Early Warning Systems Network (2020), forty-six countries are on food security alert and four countries are on famine alert, including Nigeria, which, in addition to the income losses resulting from mobility restrictions, saw rising imported staple food prices resulting from the depreciation of its currency.

POLICY IMPLICATIONS What can be done? As noted by Loayza and Pennings (2020), it is impossible to stimulate an economy under lockdown. In the short run, the focus must be on the public health response and support for the poor and vulnerable. Happily, countries are rising to the task. Up to 124 countries globally have launched cash transfer programs, which are planned for an average duration of three months. These transfers are also sizable in value, especially in low-income countries where they provide on average for 47 percent of monthly GDP per capita; this value

---

17. COVID-19 National Longitudinal Phone Survey 2020: Nigeria 2020, World Bank, https://microdata.worldbank.org/index.php/catalog/3712/related-materials.

18. See, for example, a survey in Senegal by the Center for Global Development (Le Nestour and Moscoviz 2020); various reports on India's Centre for Monitoring Indian Economy website: https://economicoutlook.cmie.com/; and a *Quartz Africa* report on Nigeria (Kazeem 2020).

is 27 percent in lower-middle-income countries and 22 percent in upper-middle-income countries (Gentilini and others 2020). Many countries have also introduced support for small and medium-sized enterprises to stem the collapse of employment relationships, in the form of concessional lending, approvals of debt payment deferral, and direct wage subsidies (Freund and Garcia Mora 2020).

In the medium term, macroeconomic stimulus will be required. Unfortunately, fiscal multipliers in developing countries are very small (Kraay 2020). Monetary policy could in principle be employed, but monetary transmission is weak. One question is whether unconventional monetary policy, through quantitative easing, may be useful. Monetary authorities in several countries have indeed begun purchasing bonds in the open market. Such actions, however, appear more motivated by a desire to stabilize bond markets rather than lower interest rates per se. In Indonesia and South Africa, for instance, two countries with ongoing operations, the policy rate is still above 3 percent. These monetary authorities still have room to reduce rates through conventional means.

Overall, the greatest challenge facing EMDEs is limited fiscal space. If the pandemic is not contained and the next months are spent cycling in and out of lockdown, direct transfers to the poor and support to small and mid-sized enterprises will need to be funded. Without recovery in global demand, small states dependent on commodity exports and remittances will be those least able to fund these transfers. With declining tax revenues, for all countries alike the only option will be to borrow at exorbitant rates. Lower rates induced by emergency central bank operations in advanced economies could induce a hunt for yield that eventually drives rates lower in EMDEs. Indeed, historical evidence shows that monetary policy and low interest rates in advanced economies are an important driver of positive spillovers and capital inflows to EMDEs (Kalemli-Özcan 2019). Consistent with this view, the smaller sales of portfolio securities by nonresidents in April compared to March could be due in part to the United States lowering the policy rate from 0.65 percent to 0.05 percent in April, which, all else being equal, should increase demand for higher-yield EMDE bonds. This hunt for yield cannot tell the whole story, however. Positive purchases of portfolio securities by nonresidents returned only in June, at which point the effective federal funds rate had increased very slightly to 0.08 percent. This suggests the role of an additional factor, most likely a reduction in global risk aversion, in bringing capital back to EMDEs. Whether it is the hunt for yield or the reduction in global risk aversion that brings capital back to the EMDEs, this is good news for these countries if it persists in the future. On the other hand, slow growth in advanced economies is typically associated with less capital flow to EMDEs (Calvo, Leiderman, and Reinhart 1996; Koepke 2019), suggesting further news about a protracted health crisis in advanced economies could lead to persistence in high borrowing costs for EMDEs. In the next year, the fate of EMDEs will depend on whether and how quickly the virus is controlled at home and abroad.

Finally, EMDEs and the international community at large will have to deal with the unfolding debt crisis. The current consensus is that the debt service standstill agreed to in April is a step in the right direction but not enough for addressing the solvency issues of heavily indebted countries—indeed the plan does not forgive debt, it merely postpones service. Further, the scope of the agreement is limited as it does not apply to many middle-income countries that may face debt sustainability issues in the coming months. Even within the set covered by the debt standstill, according to the IMF, of seventy-seven countries that are eligible for debt relief under the agreement, only twenty-two have requested forbearance so far, out of fear that debt relief would affect their credit ratings. During May, Moody's had placed two participating countries (Ethiopia and Pakistan) on a negative watch, citing specifically the G-20's call for private sector creditors to participate in the debt standstill on comparable terms to official creditors. Moreover, there are concerns that without mandatory private creditor participation, funds made available by debt relief will be used to service private creditor debt rather than expenses related to the COVID-19 crisis.

While there is wide agreement that private creditor participation is a prerequisite for progress, it is less clear how to achieve such participation. Several supplementary or alternative approaches have been proposed, ranging from debt jubilee to major restructuring of current obligations, which will need to be evaluated over the coming months on a case-by-case basis. Any proposed solution has to trade off substantive debt relief against concerns about moral hazard and the prospect of raising borrowing costs even further. Notably, many countries that today face a high risk of external debt distress are the same countries whose debt was forgiven under the Heavily Indebted Poor Countries Initiative, which commenced in 1996. At this point, there is still uncertainty as to which countries will face insolvency and to what extent solvency problems are due to the COVID-19 pandemic as opposed to longer-term structural problems. Against this background, one of the main advantages of the debt standstill is that it gives relevant stakeholders time to evaluate the situation.

II.B. Long Run

The evidence we have presented so far suggests that EMDEs have weathered the COVID-19 crisis better than originally expected. However, considerable uncertainty remains regarding the long run.

The main source of uncertainty is, of course, on the public health side. A second wave of pandemic in the fall would plunge the world economy into an even deeper crisis. But even in the absence of a second wave, the gradual reopening of countries worldwide as infections subside poses challenges for developing countries. Many (but not all) of them adopted strict containment policies proactively. As they start reopening their economies and borders, there is considerable risk of importing infections from abroad, setting in motion the contagion process many had feared. Vigilant quarantines for those entering from abroad combined with testing and tracing may help mitigate this concern.

On the economic side, the long-run prospects of EMDEs will depend to a large extent on how quickly capital returns and how fast advanced economies recover. Both are highly uncertain in the face of the challenges that advanced economies themselves face. But independent of how recovery plays out in advanced countries, the developing countries' own domestic policies will shape their future. Here the big unknown is how large and persistent the indirect effects of their virus containment policies will turn out to be.

In their effort to prevent or contain the virus spread most developing countries adopted policies similar to those in advanced economies, including nationwide lockdowns. While these policies have a big economic cost everywhere, their effects are particularly severe in developing countries, in part because most of these countries do not have the fiscal or monetary space to compensate those most adversely affected.[19] As noted earlier, several preliminary accounts from low-income settings report substantial loss of income, unemployment, and difficulties in meeting nutritional needs. Whether these effects are only temporary or will persist in the future will be hard to assess in a systematic way given that the majority of people in developing countries are employed in the informal sector.[20] This means not

19. See Ray and Subramanian (2020) for a preliminary report of the effects of the lockdown in India on the country's economy, and Barnett-Howell and Mobarak (2020), who argue lockdowns may not be an optimal policy in lower income settings.

20. The International Labor Office estimates that about 60 percent of the workforce in EMDEs is employed in the informal sector; in Africa, this figure is estimated to be between 80 and 90 percent (International Labor Office 2018).

only that the formal, employer-based safety network cannot reach most of the population in developing countries but also that their experience will not be accurately reflected in future official employment statistics and GDP measures. Tracing the long-term effects of the crisis on people's livelihoods in developing countries will therefore require longer-term, academic-style research involving household surveys that contain information on informal employment and earnings.

Perhaps the most worrisome long-term impacts of the coronavirus pandemic will be in the areas of education and health care. School closures are particularly problematic in settings where students do not have access to computers or the internet, so that online learning is not an option. Current estimates suggest that only 29 percent of low-income countries provide distant learning for their students; in contrast, 90 percent of high-income countries provide some type of program (Carvalho and Hares 2020). Worse, there are reasons to fear that this halting of education may not be temporary. Experience from the Ebola crisis taught us that when schools reopened, not all students returned: many younger girls dropped out permanently.[21] If this experience repeats itself in the current crisis, the long-run effects of temporary school closings on women's education could be detrimental with potentially important implications for fertility. Furthermore, there are serious concerns about the indirect effects of the health crisis on child and maternal mortality. An early analysis of the pandemic's indirect effects by Roberton and others (2020) predicts substantial increases in maternal and child deaths due to reductions in coverage of labor and delivery and sick child care.[22] A retroactive analysis of the Ebola crisis by Elston and others (2017) finds that such indirect effects were more severe than the direct impact of the Ebola crisis itself. Along the same lines, health care disruptions may have long-run effects if they lead to persistent discontinuations of malaria treatments or basic immunizations, especially among children. In many developing countries, extended campaigns have been necessary to persuade people to embrace vaccinations and put their children on an immunization schedule. Disrupting this schedule, even if only temporarily, may cause them not to return to clinics, halting if not

21. Bandiera and others (2019) find that in Sierra Leone, young girls in highly disrupted villages experienced a persistent 16 percentage point drop in school enrollment post-crisis, while out-of-wedlock pregnancies increased.

22. The study predicts that reductions in health coverage of around 15 percent for six months would result in 253,500 additional child deaths and 12,190 additional maternal deaths, while reductions of around 45 percent for six months would result in 1,157,000 additional child deaths and 56,700 additional maternal deaths.

reversing progress in this area. In general, many effects that in high-income settings would be reasonably viewed as temporary may have long-lasting or permanent consequences in low-income settings.

Finally, the future of EMDEs will depend on the changing attitudes toward globalization in advanced economies. Experience, especially from East Asia, suggests that trade played an important role in the growth and development of low- and middle-income countries. In a recent paper (Goldberg and Reed 2020), we find that trade, especially with high-income countries, has been an important contributor to poverty reduction. However, the growth of trade has slowed down considerably since the global financial crisis, and the last five years have seen a strong political backlash against multilateralism and globalization in many advanced countries, culminating in the US-China trade war. At the same time, automation has led to concerns that the traditional comparative advantage of low-skill, low-wage developing countries in the production of basic manufacturing may become less relevant in the future and that the days of offshoring are over. This is the backdrop against which the COVID-19 crisis unfolded. The pandemic has intensified preexisting deglobalization trends and has led to new calls for protectionism based on novel arguments involving independence and resilience of global value chains. Similarly, restrictions on the movement of people (i.e., immigration) are now being justified on public health grounds, which could harm remittance flows. On the financial side, there is a risk that the crisis will lead to large reductions in gross capital flows, that is, smaller capital inflows by foreigners and smaller capital outflows by domestic residents in EMDEs. Existing research (Broner and others 2013) suggests that during crises, reductions in gross flows are often substantially larger than reductions in net flows. This implies a reduction in countries' ability to finance domestic investments with foreign funds as well as to share idiosyncratic domestic risk with foreigners. As advanced countries are increasingly turning inward, closing their borders to goods, people, and capital from lower-income countries, EMDEs may have to rely on themselves more than ever. Domestic reforms promoting structural adjustment in response to the new realities may be the only path toward long-term recovery.

III. Concluding Remarks

Our preliminary assessment of the COVID-19 crisis as it is unfolding in developing countries may seem too optimistic. We do not argue that the situation in EMDEs is rosy; rather, our claim is that it is not as dire as initially feared. This has important policy implications. On the public health side, while there is still considerable uncertainty about the future, the better than expected record of many developing countries to date suggests that, to the extent that these countries do not face new waves of infections and their health systems do not get overburdened, they may be able to devote more resources to addressing the economic fallout of the crisis. Furthermore, it suggests that many countries may be able to lift strict containment policies, such as nationwide, prolonged lockdowns or school closings that have particularly high costs in low-income settings. Of course, the situation will need to be monitored closely for outbreaks of infections, and containment measures may have to be reintroduced periodically. On the economic side, there are encouraging signs as financial markets have stabilized and commodity prices are trending upward. We are more concerned about long-run effects arising from the shutting down of economies: the loss of education among girls, the suspension of vaccinations among children, the falling back into poverty of those living close to subsistence. Above all, we are concerned about the implications that advanced economies turning inward will have for the growth and development of poorer countries. These effects are hard to quantify in the short run but may prove the most tragic legacy of the COVID-19 crisis in developing countries in the long run.

ACKNOWLEDGMENTS   We thank our discussants, Şebnem Kalemli-Özcan and Michael Kremer, as well as the editor, Janice Eberly, for many useful comments on an earlier draft. We are also grateful to the United Kingdom Department for International Development for sharing with us their weekly "C19 Economic Evidence Roundups" with up-to-date information on the impact of the crisis in several developing countries.

References

Araujo, Miguel B., and Babak Naimi. 2020. "Spread of SARS-CoV-2 Coronavirus Likely to Be Constrained by Climate." MedRxiv. https://doi.org/10.1101/2020. 03.12.20034728.

Association of State and Territorial Health Officials. 2020. "A Coordinated, National Approach to Scaling Public Health Capacity for Contact Tracing and Disease Investigation," https://www.astho.org/COVID-19/A-National-Approach-for-Contact-Tracing/.

Bandiera, Oriana, Niklas Buehren, Markus Goldstein, Imran Rasul, and Andrea Smurra. 2019. "The Economic Lives of Young Women in the Time of Ebola: Lessons from an Empowerment Program." Working Paper 8760. Washington: World Bank. https://papers.ssrn.com/sol3/papers.cfm?abstract_id=3344844.

Barnett-Howell, Zachary, and Ahmed Mushfiq Mobarak. 2020. "The Benefits and Costs of Social Distancing in Rich and Poor Countries." ArXiv:2004.04867. Ithaca, N.Y.: Cornell University.

Bosancianu, Constantin Manuel, Kim Yi Dionne, Hanno Hilbig, Macartan Humphreys, Sampada Kc, Nils Lieber, and Alexandra Scacco. 2020. "Political and Social Correlates of Covid-19 Mortality." Berlin Social Science Center.

Broner, Fernando, Tatiana Didier, Aitor Erce, and Sergio Schmukler. 2013. "International Capital Flows during Crises: Gross Matters." VoxEU/CEPR, March 28. https://voxeu.org/article/international-capital-flows-during-crises-gross-matters.

Brunnermeier, Markus K., José De Gregorio, Philip Lane, Hélène Rey, and Hyun Song Shin. 2012. "Banks and Cross-Border Capital Flows: Policy Challenges and Regulatory Responses." VoxEU/CEPR, October 7. https://voxeu.org/article/banks-and-cross-border-capital-flows-policy-challenges-and-regulatory-responses.

Calvo, Guillermo A. 1998. "Capital Flows and Capital-Market Crises: The Simple Economics of Sudden Stops." *Journal of Applied Economics* 1, no. 1: 35–54.

Calvo, Guillermo A., Leonardo Leiderman, and Carmen M. Reinhart. 1996. "Inflows of Capital to Developing Countries in the 1990s." *Journal of Economic Perspectives* 10, no. 2: 123–39.

Carvalho, Shelby, and Susannah Hares. 2020. "More from Our Database on School Closures: New Education Policies May Be Increasing Educational Inequality." Center for Global Development. https://www.cgdev.org/blog/more-our-database-school-closures-new-education-policies-may-be-increasing-educational.

Das, Mitali, Şebnem Kalemi-Özcan, Damien Puy, and Liliana Varela. 2020. "Emerging Markets' Hidden Debt Risk." *Project Syndicate*, May 20. https://www.project-syndicate.org/commentary/covid19-emerging-market-firms-foreign-currency-debt-risk-by-mitali-das-et-al-2020-05?barrier=accesspaylog.

Djingarey, Mamoudou H., Fabien V. K. Diomandé, Rodrigue Barry, Denis Kandolo, Florence Shirehwa, Clement Lingani and others. 2015. "Introduction and Roll-out of a New Group A Meningococcal Conjugate Vaccine (PsA-TT) in African Meningitis Belt Countries, 2010–2014." *Clinical Infectious Diseases* 61, suppl. 5: S434–41.

Economist. 2020. "Tracking COVID-19 Excess Deaths across Countries." July 15. https://www.economist.com/graphic-detail/2020/04/16/tracking-covid-19-excess-deaths-across-countries.

Ellison, Glenn. 2020. "Implications of Heterogeneous SIR Models for Analyses of COVID-19." Working Paper 27373. Cambridge, Mass.: National Bureau of Economic Research.

Elston, James W. T., Christopher Cartwright, Patricia Ndumbi, and John Wright. 2017. "The Health Impact of the 2014–15 Ebola Outbreak." *Public Health* 143:60–70.

Famine Early Warning Systems Network. 2020. "Food Assistance Outlook Brief." https://fews.net/sites/default/files/documents/reports/May%202020_FAOB_Public.pdf.

Forbes, Kristin J., and Francis E. Warnock. 2012. "Capital Flow Waves: Surges, Stops, Flight, and Retrenchment." *Journal of International Economics* 88, no. 2: 235–51.

Freund, Caroline, and Alfonso Garcia Mora. 2020. "Keeping the Lights On: Supporting Firms and Preserving Jobs from Crisis through Recovery." Blog post, April 30, World Bank. https://blogs.worldbank.org/psd/keeping-lights-supporting-firms-and-preserving-jobs-crisis-through-recovery.

Gentilini, Ugo, Mohamed Almenfi, Ian Orton, and Pamela Dale. 2020. "Social Protection and Jobs Responses to COVID-19: A Real-Time Review of Country Measures." Washington: World Bank. April 17. https://openknowledge.worldbank.org/handle/10986/33635.

Georgieva, Kristalina. 2020. "Confronting the Covid-19 Crisis." IMF Podcasts, April 9. https://www.imf.org/en/News/Podcasts/All-Podcasts/2020/04/09/md-curtain-raiser-2020-sms.

Gilbert, Marius, Giulia Pullano, Francesco Pinotti, Eugenio Valdano, Chiara Poletto, Pierre-Yves Boëlle and others. 2020. "Preparedness and Vulnerability of African Countries against Importations of COVID-19: A Modelling Study." *The Lancet* 395, no. 10227: 871–77.

Goldberg, Pinelopi K., and Tristan Reed. 2020. "Income Distribution, International Integration and Sustained Poverty Reduction." Working Paper 9324. Washington: World Bank.

Gonzalez-Reiche, Ana S., Matthew M. Hernandez, Mitchell J. Sullivan, Brianne Ciferri, Hala Alshammary, Ajay Obla and others. 2020. "Introductions and Early Spread of SARS-CoV-2 in the New York City Area." *Science* 369, no. 6501: 297–301.

International Labor Office. 2018. *Women and Men in the Informal Economy: A Statistical Picture.* Geneva: International Labor Organization. https://www.ilo.org/global/publications/books/WCMS_626831/lang—en/index.htm.

International Monetary Fund. 2020. *World Economic Outlook Update, June 2020: A Crisis Like No Other, an Uncertain Recovery.* Washington: International Monetary Fund.

Jha, Ashish K., Thomas Tsai, and Benjamin Jacobson. 2020. "Why We Need at Least 500,000 Tests per Day to Open the Economy—and Stay Open." Pandemics Explained. Providence, R.I.: Brown School of Public Health. https://globalepidemics.org/2020/04/18/why-we-need-500000-tests-per-day-to-open-the-economy-and-stay-open/2020.

Jordan, Rachel E., Peymane Adab, and K. K. Cheng. 2020. "Covid-19: Risk Factors for Severe Disease and Death." *The BMJ* 368. https://doi.org/10.1136/bmj.m1198.

Kalemli-Özcan, Şebnem. 2019. "U.S. Monetary Policy and International Risk Spillovers." Working Paper 26297. Cambridge, Mass.: National Bureau of Economic Research.

Kazeem, Yomi. 2020. "Ordinary Nigerians Are Filling the Country's Major Social Welfare Gaps amid Coronavirus." *Quartz Africa*, April 24. https://qz.com/africa/1843839/nigerias-coronavirus-lockdown-is-hitting-poor-families-hard/.

Kissler, Stephen M., Christine Tedijanto, Edward Goldstein, Yonatan H. Grad, and Marc Lipsitch. 2020. "Projecting the Transmission Dynamics of SARS-CoV-2 through the Postpandemic Period." *Science* 368, no. 6493: 860–68.

Koepke, Robin. 2019. "What Drives Capital Flows to Emerging Markets? A Survey of the Empirical Literature." *Journal of Economic Surveys* 33, no. 2: 516–40.

Kraay, Aart. 2020. "How Large Is the Government Spending Multiplier? Evidence from World Bank Lending." *Quarterly Journal of Economics* 127, no. 2: 829–87.

Le Nestour, Alexis, and Laura Moscoviz. 2020. "Five Findings from a New Phone Survey in Senegal." Blog post, April 24, Center for Global Development. https://www.cgdev.org/blog/five-findings-new-phone-survey-senegal.

Lighter, Jennifer, Michael Phillips, Sarah Hochman, Stephanie Sterling, Diane Johnson, Fritz Francois, and Anna Stachel. 2020. "Obesity in Patients Younger than 60 Years Is a Risk Factor for Covid-19 Hospital Admission." *Clinical Infectious Diseases* 71, no. 15: 896–97. https://doi.org/10.1093/cid/ciaa415.

Loayza, Norman V., and Steven Pennings. 2020. "Macroeconomic Policy in the Time of COVID-19: A Primer for Developing Countries." Research and Policy Briefs 28. Washington: World Bank. https://openknowledge.worldbank.org/handle/10986/33540.

Mahler, Daniel Gerszon, Christoph Lakner, R. Andres Castaneda Aguilar, and Haoyu Wu. 2020. "The Impact of COVID-19 (Coronavirus) on Global Poverty: Why Sub-Saharan Africa Might Be the Region Hardest Hit." Blog post, April 20, World Bank Data Blog. https://blogs.worldbank.org/opendata/impact-covid-19-coronavirus-global-poverty-why-sub-saharan-africa-might-be-region-hardest.

Maire, Julien. 2020. "Factors That Explain Mobility across Countries during COVID-19 Crisis." Manuscript.

Murthy, Srinivas, Aleksandra Leligdowicz, and Neill K. J. Adhikari. 2015. "Intensive Care Unit Capacity in Low-Income Countries: A Systematic Review." *PloS One* 10, no. 1: e0116949. https://doi.org/10.1371/journal.pone.0116949.

Netea, Mihai G., Jorge Domínguez-Andrés, Luis B. Barreiro, Triantafyllos Chavakis, Maziar Divangahi, Elaine Fuchs and others. 2020. "Defining Trained Immunity and Its Role in Health and Disease." *Nature Reviews Immunology* 20:375–388. https://doi.org/10.1038/s41577-020-0285-6.

Olsen, Sonja J., Meng-Yu Chen, Yu-Lun Liu, Mark Witschi, Alexis Ardoin, Clémentine Calba and others. 2020. "Early Introduction of Severe Acute Respiratory Syndrome Coronavirus 2 into Europe." *Emerging Infectious Diseases* 26, no. 7: 1567–70.

Ratha, Dilip K., Supriyo De, Eung Ju Kim, Sonia Plaza, Ganesh Kumar Seshan, and Nadege Desiree Yameogo. 2020. "COVID-19 Crisis through a Migration Lens." Migration and Development Brief 32. Washington: World Bank. http://documents.worldbank.org/curated/en/989721587512418006/COVID-19-Crisis-Through-a-Migration-Lens.

Ravallion, Martin. 2020. "On the Virus and Poor People in the World." Blog post, April 2, Economics and Poverty. https://economicsandpoverty.com/2020/04/02/on-the-virus-and-poor-people-in-the-world/2020.

Ray, Debraj, and S. Subramanian. 2020. "India's Lockdown: An Interim Report." Working Paper 27282. Cambridge, Mass.: National Bureau of Economic Research.

Roberton, Timothy, Emily D. Carter, Victoria B. Chou, Angela R. Stegmuller, Bianca D. Jackson, Yvonne Tam, Talata Sawadogo-Lewis, and Neff Walker. 2020. "Early Estimates of the Indirect Effects of the COVID-19 Pandemic on Maternal and Child Mortality in Low-Income and Middle-Income Countries: A Modelling Study." *The Lancet* 8, no. 7: E901–8.

Sajadi, Mohammad M., Parham Habibzadeh, Augustin Vintzileos, Shervin Shokouhi, Fernando Miralles-Wilhelm, and Anthony Amoroso. 2020. "Temperature, Humidity, and Latitude Analysis to Estimate Potential Spread and Seasonality of Coronavirus Disease 2019 (COVID-19)." *JAMA Network Open* 3, no. 6: e2011834. https://doi.org/10.1001/jamanetworkopen.2020.11834.

Sattar, Naveed, Iain B. McInnes, and John J. V. McMurray. 2020. "Obesity a Risk Factor for Severe COVID-19 Infection: Multiple Potential Mechanisms." *Circulation* 142, no. 1: 4–6.

Simonnet, Arthur, Mikael Chetboun, Julien Poissy, Violeta Raverdy, Jerome Noulette, Alain Duhamel and others. 2020. "High Prevalence of Obesity in Severe Acute Respiratory Syndrome Coronavirus-2 (SARS-CoV-2) Requiring Invasive Mechanical Ventilation." *Obesity* 28, no. 7: 1195–99.

Skrip, Laura A., Prashanth Selvaraj, Brittany Hagedorn, Andre Lin Ouédraogo, Navideh Noori, Dina Mistry, Jamie Bedson, Laurent Hébert-Dufresne, Samuel V. Scarpino, and Benjamin Muir Althouse. 2020. "Seeding COVID-19 across Sub-Saharan Africa: An Analysis of Reported Importation Events across 40 Countries." MedRxiv. https://doi.org/10.1101/2020.04.01.20050203.

Stoecklin, Sibylle Bernard, Patrick Rolland, Yassoungo Silue, Alexandra Mailles, Christine Campese, Anne Simondon and others. 2020. "First Cases of Coronavirus Disease 2019 (COVID-19) in France: Surveillance, Investigations and Control Measures, January 2020." *Eurosurveillance* 25, no. 6.

United Nations Population Division. 2019. "World Population Prospects 2019." https://population.un.org/wpp/Download/Files/1_Indicators%20(Standard)/ EXCEL_FILES/1_Population/WPP2019_POP_F07_1_POPULATION_BY_ AGE_BOTH_SEXES.xlsx.

United Nations World Tourism Organization. 2020. "International Tourist Numbers Could Fall 60–80% in 2020." https://www.unwto.org/news/covid-19-international-tourist-numbers-could-fall-60-80-in-2020.

Walker, Patrick G. T., Charles Whittaker, Oliver J. Watson, Marc Baguelin, Kylie E. C. Ainslie, Sangeeta Bhatia and others. 2020. "Report 12: The Global Impact of COVID-19 and Strategies for Mitigation and Suppression." London: Imperial College London MCR Center for Global Infectious Disease Analysis.

Wieser, Christina, Alemayehu A. Ambel, Tom Bundervoet, and Asmelash Haile. 2020. *Monitoring COVID-19 Impacts on Households in Ethiopia: Results from a High-Frequency Phone Survey of Households*. Washington: World Bank. https://openknowledge.worldbank.org/handle/10986/33824.

World Bank. 2020a. "100 Countries Get Support in Response to COVID-19 (Coronavirus)." Press release, May 19. https://www.worldbank.org/en/news/ press-release/2020/05/19/world-bank-group-100-countries-get-support-in-response-to-covid-19-coronavirus.

World Bank. 2020b. *Global Economic Prospects*. Washington: World Bank. https://www.worldbank.org/en/publication/global-economic-prospects.

Wu, Jin, Allison McCann, Josh Katz, and Elian Peltier. 2020. "109,000 Missing Deaths: Tracking the True Toll of the Coronavirus Outbreak." *New York Times*, June 10. https://www.nytimes.com/interactive/2020/04/21/world/coronavirus-missing-deaths.html.

Xie, Pingping, and Phillip A. Arkin. 1997. "Global Precipitation: A 17-year Monthly Analysis Based on Gauge Observations, Satellite Estimates, and Numerical Model Outputs." *Bulletin of the American Meteorological Society* 78, no. 11: 2539–2558.

Zheng, Zhaohai, Fang Peng, Buyun Xu, Jingjing Zhao, Huahua Liu, Jiahao Peng and others. 2020. "Risk Factors of Critical and Mortal COVID-19 Cases: A Systematic Literature Review and Meta-analysis." *Journal of Infection* 81, no. 2: e16–e25.

Zhou, Fei, Ting Yu, Ronghui Du, Guohui Fan, Ying Liu, Zhibo Liu and others. 2020. "Clinical Course and Risk Factors for Mortality of Adult Inpatients with COVID-19 in Wuhan, China: A Retrospective Cohort Study." *The Lancet* 395, no. 10229:1054–62. https://doi.org/10.1016/S0140-6736(20)30566-3.

Comments and Discussion

COMMENT BY
ŞEBNEM KALEMLI-ÖZCAN The paper by Goldberg and Reed is an early account of the experience of emerging market and developing economies (EMDEs) with the COVID-19 crisis. The paper focuses both on health and economic fronts. The key message of the paper is that, as of July 15, 2020, EMDEs have fared relatively well. The authors argue that on the health front, the low number of deaths in EMDEs can be explained by the fact that EMDEs have younger populations and lower obesity rates. On the economic front, Goldberg and Reed draw upon the experience of EMDEs with world prices during the previous crises and compare this experience with the current prices given the lack of real-time data on economic quantities. They argue that COVID-19 is playing out as a typical commodity bust for the EMDEs and conclude that the short-run economic effects will be limited. They further argue that the medium- and long-run effects can be devastating due to the indirect effects of the containment and lockdown policies on education and health. The authors caution that their conclusions can be reversed if infections and deaths accelerate in EMDEs.

I am an optimist and hope to see the effects of this pandemic on EMDEs to be limited. However, I would be more cautious than the authors and argue that it is too early to decide on the health and economic costs of the pandemic in EMDEs based on what we know so far. My main argument rests on two premises. First, treating EMDEs as a group to decide on short-run health and economic costs might be misleading. This grouping would mean that we rely on cross-country variation that mixes developing economies (DEs), such as Ghana and Ethiopia—which are among the world's poorest countries—with emerging markets (EMs), such as Brazil, Mexico, and Turkey. Large emerging markets such as Turkey and Mexico are Organization for Economic Cooperation and Development (OECD) countries and part of the Group of Twenty (G-20). If we treat them as a group, we will be underestimating the external dimension of this crisis on these countries from three angles: (1) COVID-19 is not only a commodity price shock for EMs, where most EMs are commodity importers and not exporters. These EMs suffer from capital outflows and depreciating currencies with a detrimental effect on their large foreign currency debts (Cakmakli and others 2020). Since COVID-19 involves a large risk-off shock in financial markets, it is not surprising that the immediate effect on EMs will be capital outflows and depreciations. With the low external demand from advanced countries and disruptions in the global supply chains, the impact of the pandemic on such EMs' economies will not mainly come from the bust in the commodity prices. (2) Many DEs in Africa are far less traveled to than large EMs such as Brazil and Mexico, which experienced many cases and an increasing number of deaths since June 2020. (3) In terms of external debt patterns, EMs and DEs differ drastically, where DEs' debt is owed to official creditors and hence has a better chance to be reduced via schemes like organized debt moratoriums, whereas a large part of the EMs' debt is owed to private creditors. In addition, the main borrowing sector in EMs is not the sovereign, as in DEs, but the private sector (Avdjiev and others 2017). Policies aimed at reducing the burden of sovereign-to-sovereign debt versus private-to-private debt have to be different.

Second, cross-country regressions compare countries' average outcomes. To understand the health and economic effects of a fast moving and highly uncertain crisis such as COVID-19, we need to use time-variation from within these countries. As these data will be limited, we need to combine such inference with estimates from economic-epidemiological models for EMDEs and also draw upon historical experiences as much as we can.

The policy implications will differ given the different narratives about the effects of the pandemic in EMDEs. If the external dimension of the crisis were to be misread, and consequently the health and economic impact were thought to be limited in the short run, then the policy recommendation will be to argue against containment and lockdown policies, since those policies will have adverse effects on education and health in the long run as argued by the authors. However, if the short-run health and economic impact were to be larger, then strict lockdown policies early in the pandemic might be the only way to avoid such large losses, by taking the disease under control quickly, at the same time giving policymakers time to invest in testing and tracing strategies to be used effectively once the economies reopen.

To detail my arguments, I am going to start with figure 1, which shows the number of new daily cases for EMDEs and advanced economies (AEs) based on data from Johns Hopkins University. The figure separates China out of the EMDEs as the disease is under control there. The figure clearly shows the fast increase in infections in EMDEs relative to AEs, with a late start. This means that if we only focus on a number of deaths metric as done in the paper, we will miss the evolution of the epidemic. It might be that the populations of EMDEs are healthier than AEs' populations, and so deaths may increase at a slower rate going forward. We do not know. However, the speed of the increase in new cases is noteworthy, suggesting it might be only a matter of time before we see more deaths in EMDEs. We can see the speed by comparing top and bottom panels that both plot the same data from different dates; the top panel plots the cases as of June 22, and the bottom panel plots the same data as appeared in the column by Martin Wolf in the *Financial Times* on June 9, 2020.

In order to understand the mechanics of the key finding in the paper, namely, that rich countries have more deaths, I have performed a few additional analyses using Goldberg and Reed's data. I plot below in figure 2 results from the same regression that the authors run using their data from countries on the top panel and using micro data from US counties on the bottom panel. It is clear that while rich countries have more deaths as shown in the paper and here in the top panel, rich counties have fewer deaths as shown with the positive relation between the poverty rate and the number of COVID-19 deaths at the county level in the bottom panel.

This shows that GDP variables in the cross-country regressions capture something else, not income, and that something else is positively correlated with income. Goldberg and Reed argue that the missing variables that are positively correlated with GDP are demographics and health. They show that upon controlling for fractions of the older population and obesity rate in a country, the GDP variable becomes insignificant and cannot explain the COVID-19 deaths anymore. Instead, now countries with older populations and countries with higher obesity rates are the ones with higher COVID-19 deaths. Since EMDEs have lower obesity rates and younger populations, their death rates are low according to these results.

Of course, there are other potential suspects that are positively correlated with GDP and can explain the lower deaths in EMDEs. For example, the late arrival of the pandemic to EMDEs should be able to explain the lower

Figure 1. COVID-19 New Daily Cases from EMDEs and AEs

New COVID-19 cases
(daily average over previous 7 days; updated June 22)

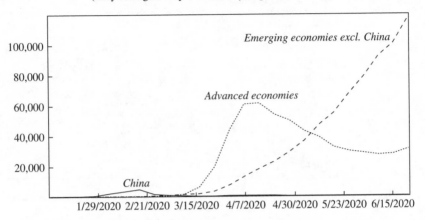

COVID-19 is now taking off in emerging and developing countries
Daily new COVID-19 cases (thousands)

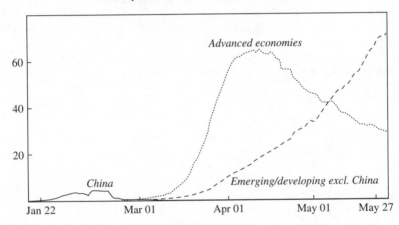

Source: Johns Hopkins University (top); Wolf (2020) (bottom).

Figure 2. COVID-19 Deaths and Income

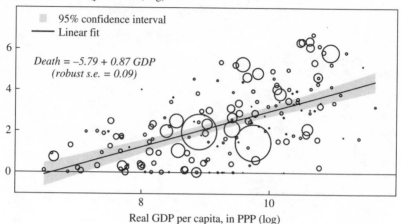

COVID-19 and income across countries

COVID-19 deaths (per million, log)

Real GDP per capita, in PPP (log)

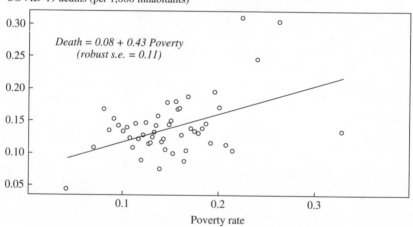

COVID-19 and poverty across US counties

COVID-19 deaths (per 1,000 inhabitants)

Poverty rate

Source: Chen and others (2020).
Notes: Top panel shows unweighted regression. Bottom panel shows binned plot with state fixed effects.

Table 1. Additional Dependent Variables Affecting COVID-19 Deaths per Million

	(1)	(2)	(3)
Ln (GDP per capita)	0.56**	0.35**	0.29
	(0.23)	(0.17)	(0.19)
Days since first death	0.46***	0.45***	0.38*
	(0.10)	(0.08)	(0.23)
Ln (COVID-19 tests/1,000)	0.35*	0.67***	0.73***
	(0.20)	(0.14)	(0.15)
Test ratio		0.05***	0.05***
		(0.01)	(0.01)
Contact Tracing Index			−0.48**
			(0.20)
R^2	0.50	0.62	0.67

Source: Author's calculations.
*$p < .10$; **$p < .05$; ***$p < .01$.

deaths. Or, it could be that there is widespread misreporting in EMDEs relative to AEs in terms of deaths. The authors control for these and still find a strong effect of demographics and health. It can also be the case that in EMDEs there is better contact tracing as individual liberties might be more limited in those countries. In fact, in my analysis that uses the authors' data, I found out that testing and contact tracing can explain the GDP effect on COVID-19 deaths in EMDEs. This result is striking as these variables have a strong negative effect on COVID-19 deaths, independent of the effects of demographics and health. As shown in table 1, conditional on testing and the late arrival of the pandemic, contact tracing is negatively correlated with GDP, as EMDEs did a better job than AEs in this regard. This can explain lower deaths in EMDEs, and it renders the positive effect of GDP insignificant. These results are reassuring in terms of the positive effects of the right public health policies; since the pandemic arrived later to EMDEs, they had more time to prepare, obtained more knowledge, and observed the policy mistakes in other countries. By introducing the right public health policies early on, they might have reduced the number of deaths.

The lower number of deaths in EMDEs so far does not mean that the short-run economic impact is limited. In fact, I would argue that in spite of the limited number of deaths, the short-run economic impact has been devastating for EMDEs as far as we can observe. The lack of real-time data on GDP and capital flows makes the exact measurement of the short-run economic impact hard, but we can put together bits and pieces of information for a coherent picture that shows large economic costs in EMDEs so far.[1]

The first step to understand the economic costs for EMDEs is to realize that this shock is a multitude of shocks for these countries and not only a commodity price bust, as argued by Goldberg and Reed. It is a health shock, external supply shock, external demand shock, and capital flow shock. All these shocks combined will lead to depreciating exchange rates and output losses. In the absence of real-time data on GDP and capital flows, I will use data from surveys that track industrial production to proxy for GDP and rely on historical dynamics of capital flows during EMDEs' crises combined with models to estimate the short-run economic impact.

Figure 3 plots data from a Purchasing Managers' Index (PMI) survey that tracks production both in manufacturing and services sectors and almost in real time (released with a one-to-two-month delay). Both panels show that there is very little difference between EMDEs and AEs in terms of short-run economic output losses in these sectors. Using similar data and making projections, the International Monetary Fund (IMF) has a similar argument in the World Economic Outlook (WEO) for June. Compared to the WEO for April, the IMF (2020) is projecting a deeper recession in 2020 and slower recovery in 2021 in the June WEO. They argue that no country will be spared where global growth will decline −4.9 percent in 2020. In fact, growth in EMDEs will decline −5 percent (excluding China) and a cumulative hit to GDP growth over 2020–2021 in EMDEs is expected to exceed that in AEs given the limited policy space of EMDEs (IMF 2020). For the few countries for which we know the second quarter GDP, the numbers confirm the devastating short-run economic impact. Mexico's economy contracted 17.3 percent in the second quarter compared with the previous three months (Webber 2020).

What about capital flows? Given the absence of balance of payments data we cannot know what is going on with total capital flows until later in the year. Many, including Goldberg and Reed, use alternative high frequency real-time data on portfolio flows from the Institute of International Finance (IIF) that show record portfolio equity outflows since February 2020 (around $100 billion). Although unprecedented, portfolio equity is not an important asset class for EMDEs, constituting less than

---

1. Second quarter GDP and balance of payments data for capital flows will only be available later in the year. Since the pandemic started at the end of first quarter in EMDEs, the first quarter GDP will not be informative.

Figure 3. Production in Manufacturing and Services: EMDEs and AEs

PMI: Manufacturing – output

Index; >50 = expansion; sa

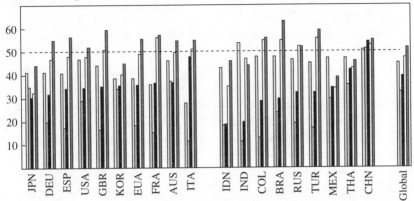

PMI: Services – business activity

Index; >50 = expansion; sa

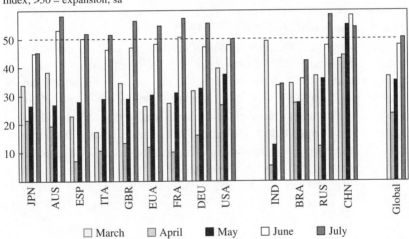

Source: PMI data from IHS Markit.

20 percent of total capital flows (Avdjiev and others 2017). IIF data also show that there are portfolio debt outflows of around $30 billion from EMDEs since February 2020. This amount is not unprecedented as it is much less than what came out of EMDEs during the global financial crises of 2008.[2]

Both of these types of portfolio flows are now stabilized, and it seems like there are not large outflows from other asset classes. In EM (DE) countries more than 60 percent (70 percent) of capital flows are in debt, and the rest is in equity, mostly in foreign direct investment (FDI) (Avdjiev and others 2017). The share of loans in this debt is more than 60 percent for EMs and more than 80 percent for DEs. These figures suggest that cross-border bank loans and corporate loans play an overwhelming role in total capital flows to EMDEs. We know from previous EMDEs crises which were much smaller risk-off shocks than COVID-19 that these asset classes are sensitive to risk-off shocks, and real troubles start when banks and corporates start losing the foreign capital in large amounts.

To make this case, figure 4 plots capital flows by nonresidents to corporate, bank, and sovereign sectors during the global financial crisis and taper tantrum on the top and middle panels, and during COVID-19 on the bottom panel, using thirty-four EMDEs.[3] During the global financial crisis and taper tantrum events, foreign investors in EMDEs pulled out of domestic banking sectors the most, as well as the corporate sectors to a certain extent. However, adjustments to debt flows were limited during the COVID-19 shock. If anything, they were mostly out of the sovereign sector, as flows to the banking sector held stable. Since these data are mainly for the first quarter of 2020, it also includes large inflows into EMDEs (especially to corporates) in January and February before the crisis fully took hold. Updated data for the second quarter of 2020 may reveal larger declines in inflows, including to banks, as experienced during previous crises. The reason why foreign investors left sovereign

---

2. IIF data only cover portfolio equity and portfolio debt flows. IIF data are also available only for a limited set of countries. IIF collects real-time data either through central banks who report real-time portfolio flows or use fund-level data from Bloomberg. For example, for bond flows, IIF only includes India, Indonesia, Thailand, South Africa, Hungary, Turkey, Mexico, Poland, and Ukraine. For countries whose data are not available, IIF does a valuation adjustment to stocks to nowcast the portfolio flows. The larger set of countries in which they track NET capital flows does not provide real data but an estimate based on the current account and reserves. As we know from previous EM crises, what matters is gross flows and not the current account, especially gross banking flows and corporate flows, both of which IIF data will not cover.

3. The figure is adapted from Avdjiev and others (2017).

Figure 4. Gross Capital Flows during EMDE Crises

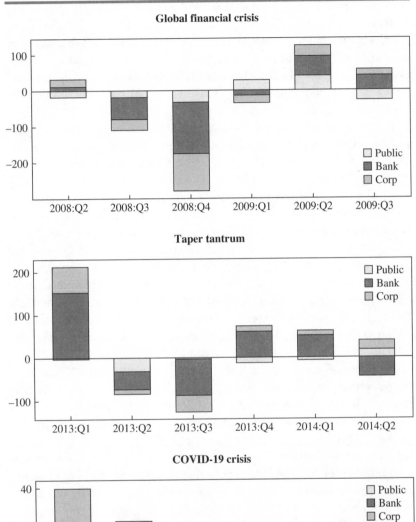

Source: Avdjiev and others (2017).

bond markets first might be because they expect higher sovereign defaults given the limited fiscal space of many EMs' governments. The reason why banking and corporate flows held stable during the COVID-19 crisis so far is probably the immense stimulus by the US Federal Reserve that increased the global US dollar liquidity, which in turn reduces the funding costs of domestic and global banks. Historical evidence shows that US monetary policy is an important driver of positive spillovers and capital inflows to EMDEs (e.g., Kalemli-Özcan 2019).

If the economic costs are larger in the short run than assumed by the authors, then the policy advice on the lockdown and containment measures may need to be revisited. The literature so far emphasizes the optimality of full lockdown policies in terms of controlling the disease as soon as possible so that infection rates go down and supply and demand normalizes (Acemoglu and others 2020; Alvarez, Argente, and Lippi 2020; Farboodi, Jarosch, and Shimer 2020; Eichenbaum, Rebelo, and Trabandt 2020). Most of the literature focuses on closed economy models and may not be appropriate for EMDEs, where full lockdowns may not be practical as argued by Goldberg and Reed. However, open economy versions of these closed economy epidemiological models show that the importance of full lockdown is even bigger as external demand is very important for EMDEs. The economic losses under partial lockdowns are higher for EMDEs (11 percent of GDP) relative to full lockdown (5.8 percent of GDP) (Cakmakli and others 2020). This is because the full lockdown recovers both domestic and external demand faster as the fear factor goes down with lower infection rates. A full lockdown controls the disease in thirty-nine days and lowers the number of deaths tremendously as shown in figure 5. This figure is adopted from Cakmakli and others (2020). The top panel shows deaths under no lockdown and each partial lockdown based on stringency or leakage. The bottom panel shows the number of deaths under full lockdown, where the version with leakage is shown with a dotted line. As shown with gray shaded areas, it takes much longer to control the disease with partial lockdowns leading to a higher number of deaths. Economic costs are larger under partial lockdowns as demand never gets normalized. These results hold even if lockdowns leak and cannot be enforced fully as typical in EMDEs. In real-time data, Goolsbee and Syverson (2020) show that no lockdowns or ending lockdowns early are not powerful tools for restarting growth so long as individuals continue to fear infection and keep demand low. Figure 5 shows the same result based on estimates from an epidemiological-economic model and shows that full lockdowns are most effective in reducing infections and so reducing

Figure 5. Number of Deaths under Full and Partial Lockdowns

1,000 persons

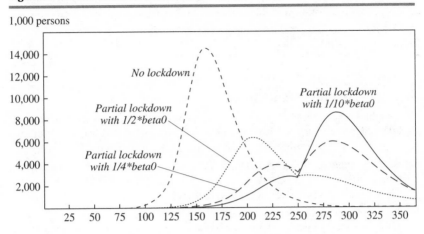

1,000 persons

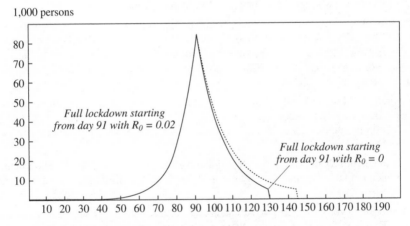

Source: Cakmakli and others (2020).

the fear factor. As these full lockdowns can normalize the demand sooner, their economic costs are lower than partial or no lockdowns.

Of course, as argued by Goldberg and Reed, lockdowns are blunt policy instruments that cause social and economic damage and may not even be fully implemented in an EMDE setting with informal firms and small living spaces. Still, if lockdowns are done early enough, they can help to save lives, as shown most notably by African countries (*Financial Times* 2020). All countries need a set of policies to keep infections low after the early lockdowns as no country can keep full lockdowns forever. The only countries who have done this so far are the East Asian countries with mandated masks, strict social distancing, obsessive hygiene, testing, contact tracing, and isolating once they reopen. Most of these East Asian countries are EMDEs and are good examples of success, though for different reasons than the authors emphasize.

REFERENCES FOR THE KALEMLI-ÖZCAN COMMENT

Acemoglu, Daron, Victor Chernozhukov, Iván Werning, and Michael D. Whinston. 2020. "Optimal Targeted Lockdowns in a Multi-Group SIR Model." Working Paper 27102. Cambridge, Mass.: National Bureau of Economic Research.

Alvarez, Fernando E., David Argente, and Francesco Lippi. 2020. "A Simple Planning Problem for COVID-19 Lockdown." Working Paper 26981. Cambridge, Mass.: National Bureau of Economic Research.

Avdjiev, Stefan, Bryan Hardy, Şebnem Kalemli-Özcan, and Luis Servén. 2017. "Gross Capital Flows to Banks, Corporates, and Sovereigns." Working Paper 23116. Cambridge, Mass.: National Bureau of Economic Research.

Cakmakli, Cem, Selva Demiralp, Şebnem Kalemli-Özcan, Sevcan Yesiltas, and Muhammed A. Yildirim. 2020. "COVID-19 and Emerging Markets: An Epidemiological Model with International Production Networks and Capital Flows." Working Paper 27191. Cambridge, Mass.: National Bureau of Economic Research.

Chen, Sophia, Deniz O. Igan, Nicola Pierri, and Andrea F. Prebitero. 2020. "Tracking the Economic Impact of COVID-19 and Mitigation Policies in Europe and the United States." Working Paper 20/125. Washington: International Monetary Fund.

Eichenbaum, Martin S., Sergio Rebelo, and Mathias Trabandt. 2020. "The Macroeconomics of Epidemics." Working Paper 26882. Cambridge, Mass.: National Bureau of Economic Research.

Farboodi, Maryam, Gregor Jarosch, and Robert Shimer. 2020. "Internal and External Effects of Social Distancing in a Pandemic." Working Paper 27059. Cambridge, Mass.: National Bureau of Economic Research.

Financial Times. 2020. "Africa Needs More Help with Its Pandemic Response." July 27. https://www.ft.com/content/1af2ff7c-d9c4-47fd-972c-6a6cb2fda8dd.

Goolsbee, Austan, and Chad Syverson. 2020. "Fear, Lockdown, and Diversion: Comparing Drivers of Pandemic Economic Decline 2020." Working Paper 27432. Cambridge, Mass.: National Bureau of Economic Research.

International Monetary Fund (IMF). 2020. *"World Economic Outlook Update, June 2020: A Crisis Like No Other, An Uncertain Recovery."* Washington: International Monetary Fund. https://www.imf.org/en/Publications/WEO/Issues/2020/06/24/WEOUpdateJune2020.

Kalemli-Özcan, Şebnem. 2019. "US Monetary Policy and International Risk Spillovers." In *Economic Policy Symposium Proceedings: Challenges for Monetary Policy*. Jackson Hole, Wyo.: Federal Reserve Bank of Kansas City.

Webber, Jude. 2020. "Mexico's Economy Records Fifth Straight Quarterly Contraction." *Financial Times,* July 30. https://www.ft.com/content/1e25c567-66c3-44e0-86ed-54805a5d6503.

Wolf, Martin. 2020. "COVID-19 Will Hit Developing Countries Hard." *Financial Times,* June 9. https://www.ft.com/content/31eb2686-a982-11ea-a766-7c300513fe47.

COMMENT BY

MICHAEL KREMER   Goldberg and Reed's paper makes two key claims. First, it shows that there have been fewer documented COVID-19 deaths in low- and lower-middle-income countries than in the rest of the world. Second, it argues that many of the economic costs of the epidemic are less severe than anticipated but that lockdown policies have generated large economic costs. This suggests that low-income countries may want to consider moving from blanket lockdown policies to smart containment strategies.

Understanding why there have been fewer confirmed COVID-19 deaths in low-income countries is critical for policymaking. Goldberg and Reed focus on demographics and obesity. This comment tries to draw attention to some other possible explanations with a focus on the paper's discussion of epidemiology.

Much like macroeconomists, epidemiologists typically use models and calibrate them using micro data. This paper employs a complementary approach of using cross-country data. There are advantages to combining these approaches. The findings in this paper indicate some limitations of the most basic epidemiological models. Instead, they suggest that it might be better to consider more complex models that could generate the observed data, while leading to very different policy implications.

It is useful to begin by considering the canonical epidemiological model for diseases like COVID-19, known as SIR, or the susceptible-infected-recovered model:

$$dS = -\beta IS/N$$

$$dI = \beta IS/N - \gamma I$$

$$dR = \gamma I$$

where S denotes the number of susceptible people, I denotes the number of infected people, R denotes the number of recovered people, and the total population (N) is normalized to one.

When a susceptible person meets an infected person, transmission occurs with probability β. The number of infected people grows when there is an infection event and decreases when an infected person recovers, which occurs with a rate γ (we will ignore deaths here). The change in the number of recovered people is therefore γ multiplied by the number of infected people.

In this standard model, R_0—the number of new infections caused by an infected individual in a native population—is β/γ. If this is greater than one, the disease will spread, otherwise, the disease will not take off. We can estimate R_0 by looking at the initial doubling time (accounting for length of time between infections). For COVID-19, many studies take the data from the Wuhan province in China and the Lombardy region in Italy and estimate a relatively high rate of R_0, such as 2.5 or 3.0 (Riou and Althaus 2020; Vollmer and others 2020).

In these models, the initial growth is close to exponential, but later there are fewer susceptible people, and therefore infected individuals are less likely to meet and infect the susceptible ones. The epidemic slows down and eventually reaches the stage of herd immunity, when $1/R_0$ people are susceptible. Still some transmission still happens beyond this point, but the disease starts to die off. An R_0 of 2.5 suggests that 60 percent of the people will need to be infected before the disease slows down. This indicates a fairly pessimistic picture for the pandemic.

The next question is how to include mortality in the model. One possibility is to allow the total deaths to be equal to the number of people who are ever infected multiplied by the infection-fatality rate. We know from micro data that elderly people and obese people are more likely to succumb to COVID-19. Looking at the difference in death rates by demographics using Chinese data (Verity and others 2020), we would expect a fivefold difference between developed countries and low-income countries in mortality solely based on the fact that there are less elderly people in very poor countries.[1] While differences in obesity prevalence might strengthen this effect, there could be factors increasing the mortality in poorer countries, such as weaker health systems or higher air pollution. So, it is reasonable to expect roughly a fivefold difference. However, the actual

---

1. We reweighted the Chinese estimates of age-specific mortality (Verity and others 2020) by age distribution in other countries based on the 2019 UN World Population Prospects, assuming all age groups have the same infection rate. The infection-fatality rate then ranges from an average of 0.25 percent in low-income countries to 1.24 percent in high-income countries.

Figure 1. Daily COVID-19 Deaths per Million Inhabitants

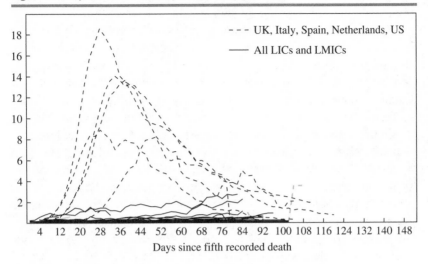

Days since fifth recorded death

Source: Lea (2020).
Note: LICs are low-income countries; LMICs are lower-middle-income countries.

differences are much larger (see figure 1). The death rate in the United Kingdom is almost fifty times greater than the death rate in low- and middle-income countries.

The main regressions in the paper focus on cumulative deaths. However, it is possible to extract more information by taking advantage of the time path in mortality. One can observe much flatter curves for low- and lower-middle-income countries compared to OECD countries. The rapid exponential growth seen in high-income countries has not been replicated in low- and middle-income countries. If this was driven solely by a lower fatality rate, we would have the same shape of the curve, but it would be one-fifth as large at any point. However, the curve appears to have a different shape and a different trajectory, which cannot be explained by differences in the death rate alone. One could argue that demographics affect the infection rate, but this would probably go the opposite way; older people probably go out less and hence are less likely to contract the virus.

One reason for a lower curve could be that the demographics and mortality rate may be working differently in different countries. In India, Mexico, and South Africa the share of deaths among the elderly is lower than in high-income countries, even after adjusting for demographics. The difference is quite stark with 90 percent of deaths in the United Kingdom among the elderly to just over 50 percent (ranging from 51 percent to 65 percent after reweighting by demographic structure) in India, Mexico, and South Africa.[2] It would be interesting to further explore the hypothesis that in low- and middle-income countries other risk factors not found in the high-income countries may be driving mortality. A competing explanation is that deaths are underreported in the older population in low- and middle-income countries relative to high-income countries. However, this would make the curve lower but would not explain it being flatter.

Another possible reason for the curve being lower in low- and middle-income countries is measurement error. However, as Goldberg and Reed argue, the effect seems too large to be explained solely by this. In addition, for measurement error to explain the flatness as well as the height of the curve, there would need to be an implausible downward trend in the fraction of reported COVID-19 deaths. While it is plausible that in low-income countries many COVID-19 deaths are not attributed to the virus, it is harder to explain why the fraction of reported COVID-19 deaths would decline over time.

Another explanation could be a shorter gap between the epidemic arriving and lockdown measures. Under a standard epidemiological model, assuming the contact rates return to normal after a lockdown, countries will move toward herd immunity just as they would in the absence of a lockdown. That does not seem to be happening in low- and middle-income countries. There is considerable uncertainty in the data so we should be cautious, and there are more complex stories one could tell. However, if we take the data in this paper, the policy variables do not seem sufficient to explain the results.

I suggest an alternative, speculative hypothesis. There are many reasons to think that epidemiological parameters might be heterogeneous across communities. There are high-risk places such as meatpacking plants. People who are regularly present in those places are therefore at higher risk. We also know that there are factors affecting transmission that are

2. See United Nations Department of Economics and Social Affairs, "2019 Revision of World Population Prospects," https://population.un.org/wpp/; United Kingdom Office for National Statistics, "Deaths Registered Weekly in England and Wales, Provisional," up to week ending August 28, https://www.ons.gov.uk/peoplepopulationandcommunity/birthsdeath sandmarriages/deaths/datasets/weeklyprovisionalfiguresondeathsregisteredinenglandandwales, accessed September 4, 2020; Indian Ministry of Health and Family Welfare, "Updates on COVID-19," press release, May 21, https://pib.gov.in/PressReleseDetail.aspx?PRID=1625744; and Secretaría de Salud de México, "Información Referente a Casos COVID-19 en México" [database], https://datos.gob.mx/busca/dataset/informacion-referente-a-casos-covid-19-en-mexico, accessed September 4, 2020.

Figure 2. Heterogeneous versus Homogeneous Models: An Example

Infected

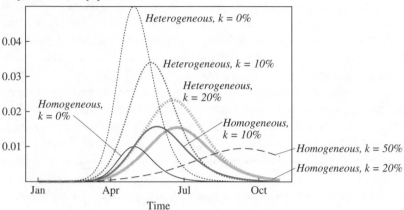

Proportion of total population

Heterogeneous, k = 0%

0.04

Heterogeneous, k = 10%

0.03

*Heterogeneous,
k = 20%*

*Homogeneous,
k = 0%*

0.02

*Homogeneous,
k = 10%*

0.01

Homogeneous, k = 50%

Homogeneous, k = 20%

Jan   Apr   Jul   Oct

Time

Recovered

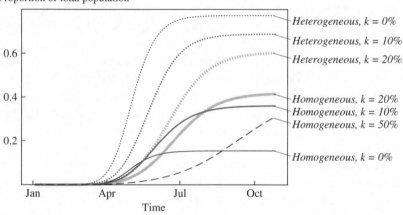

Proportion of total population

Heterogeneous, k = 0%

Heterogeneous, k = 10%

0.6

Heterogeneous, k = 20%

Homogeneous, k = 20%

0.4

Homogeneous, k = 10%

Homogeneous, k = 50%

0.2

Homogeneous, k = 0%

Jan   Apr   Jul   Oct

Time

Source: Author's calculations.

correlated with income, such as temperature, home ventilation, time spent outdoors, and the patterns of social interaction. So, let us consider a model with different types of subcommunities and limited interaction across these groups. Imagine, for example, there is a high transmission subcommunity that is 20 percent of the population with an R_0 of 2.6 and a low transmission subcommunity with an R_0 of 0.8.

Under the canonical SIR models, the epidemic will take off in the region where R_0 is 2.6 but not in the subcommunity where R_0 is 0.8. The overall R_0 for the country would be close to 2.6, leading to the conclusion that between 60 and 70 percent of the population will need to be infected before herd immunity can be reached. In fact, only 60 percent to 70 percent of the high R_0 communities would be infected before herd immunity is reached. This is consistent with some of the data we see, without necessarily implying that policy played a key role.

In a world with heterogeneity, the optimal policy is very sensitive to parameters. For example, let us assume that governments can put in place containment measures that generate economic costs but cut the rate of spread by 25 percent. If the high R_0 groups have already reached herd immunity and R_0 in the low spreader group is less than one, containment measures are unnecessary. On the other hand, if the low transmission group has an R_0 of 1.2 without containment policies, relaxing the containment measures would enable further spread.

It is important to add that the high heterogeneity in R_0 and behavior change are not the only two hypotheses that can account for a lower herd immunity threshold. There is some evidence of susceptibility to the disease being much lower in children than in adults and the elderly. One recent estimate of the susceptibility of children (Davies and others 2020) is that it is half of that in adults. It could be that children do get sick just as easily as the adults but experience a very different course of the disease. There is even a possibility that many of them are immune. The hypothesis of preexisting immunity has been raised by other recent papers (Le Bert and others 2020). If it is true, it would also lead to a lower herd immunity threshold.

The competing hypotheses mentioned are not easy to distinguish from each other using macro, summary-level data of the type we are discussing here, especially given the inherent biases and various forms of under-reporting. All these hypotheses indicate that the growth rate of the epidemic will decrease over time, earlier than what a simple epidemiological model would predict. But at a minimum, we can still use these data to quantify the extent of departure from "simple" epidemiological models (in which we account for demographics, obesity, government policy, etc.) and if such a discrepancy occurs, evaluate whether it varies from country to country.

One cause for possible optimism is that we often talk about lockdown measures as a binary variable, when there are in fact many different poli-cies that vary in their likely impacts on the spread of the disease, as well as in their economic, social, and overall health impacts. There are some fairly low-cost measures, like wearing masks or restrictions on nightclubs where the virus spreads easily. On the other hand, there are measures like shutting down trade or childhood immunization, both of which have very high economic or social costs while not doing much to prevent the spread of the epidemic.

If there is a lot of uncertainty about the model and about the parameters, repeated prevalence surveys could be used to track the epidemic over time. With these, one could progressively relax the restrictions with the lowest epidemiological risks and the highest economic benefits. It would require monitoring the growth rate of infections throughout this process and applying stricter restrictions if it approaches one.

This approach makes sense for an individual country trying to control the epidemic, and allows us to learn during the process. The hypothesis that heterogeneity in epidemiological parameters could explain the lower prevalence in low- and middle-income countries is one of many, and there is not yet strong evidence to support it. However, prevalence surveys could reveal patterns suggesting that, for example, rural areas of low-income countries have an R_0 below one even without containment. In that case, a policymaker could adopt fairly relaxed policies in those areas. On the other hand, for dense or low-income urban populations, it could be the case that R_0 is greater than one unless there are containment policies in place, in which case we do need those restrictions.

It is important to mention that while COVID-19 has brought devastating consequences on its own, containment policies can also cause a huge burden to the population. It is essential to understand where and in which situations the containment policies are necessary, as well as which policies are the most effective. By using real-time data from representative prevalence surveys to inform our decisions, we can choose policies that are capable of bolstering the recovering economies while avoiding the economic and social consequences of blanket lockdowns. At the same time, we also need to ensure that these policies are effective in preventing an unacceptable spread of the disease.

REFERENCES FOR THE KREMER COMMENT

Davies, Nicholas G., Petra Klepac, Yang Liu, Kiesha Prem, Mark Jit, CMMID COVID-19 Working Group, and Rosalind M. Eggo. 2020. "Age-Dependent Effects in the Transmission and Control of COVID-19 Epidemics." *Nature Medicine* 26:1205–11. https://doi.org/10.1038/s41591-020-0962-9.

Le Bert, Nina, Anthony T. Tan, Kamini Kunasegaran, Christine Y. L. Tham, Morteza Hafezi, Adeline Chia, and others. 2020. "SARS-CoV-2-Specific

T Cell Immunity in Cases of COVID-19 and SARS, and Uninfected Controls." *Nature* 584:457–62. https://doi.org/10.1038/s41586-020-2550-z.

Lea, Nick. 2020. "State of the COVID-19 pandemic, 24th June 2020." Unpublished presentation. London: Foreign, Commonwealth and Development Office.

Riou, Julien, and Christian L. Althaus. 2020. "Pattern of Early Human-to-Human Transmission of Wuhan 2019 Novel Coronavirus (2019-NCoV), December 2019 to January 2020." *Eurosurveillance* 25, no. 4. https://doi.org/10.2807/1560-7917.ES.2020.25.4.2000058.

Verity, Robert, Lucy C. Okell, Ilaria Dorigatti, Peter Winskill, Charles Whittaker, Natsuko Imai, and others. 2020. "Estimates of the Severity of Coronavirus Disease 2019: A Model-Based Analysis." *Lancet Infectious Diseases* 20, no. 6: 669–77. https://doi.org/10.1016/S1473-3099(20)30243-7.

Vollmer, Michaela, Swapnil Mishra, H. Juliette T. Unwin, Axel Gandy, Thomas A. Melan, Valerie Bradley, and others. 2020. *Report 20: A Sub-National Analysis of the Rate of Transmission of COVID-19 in Italy.* London: Imperial College COVID-19 Response Team. https://doi.org/10.25561/78677.

GENERAL DISCUSSION   Daron Acemoglu followed up on Michael Kremer's comments, noting that heterogeneous infection rates across groups have major implications for the spread of diseases and that these implications can be difficult to untangle. He stated that the R_0 values estimated at the beginning of an infection event tend to be inaccurate because high-R_0 groups generally get infected first and then recover, resulting in different infection patterns during subsequent periods. Acemoglu continued by stating that density is a huge determinant of R_0 values, noting the cases of severe COVID-19 spread in New York City and London. In contrast to these cases, he pointed out that in many EMDEs, much of the population lives in lower-density areas, which will be a major determinant of how the COVID-19 pandemic unfolds in these countries.

Pinelopi Goldberg responded by addressing some of the issues with data brought up during Şebnem Kalemli-Özcan's and Kremer's comments and alluded to by Acemoglu. She stated that while it is likely that the number of deaths in EMDEs is undercounted, comparing the COVID-19 death curves in EMDEs to those in advanced economies in figure 2 reveals that the curves are entirely different shapes, not just at different levels. As undercounting would lead to similarly shaped but lower curves, this difference in curve shapes suggests that the low number of reported deaths in EMDEs is not solely due to data issues. Goldberg went on to emphasize that there still needs to be more testing. She stated that there are currently major issues with the data on number of cases by country, as these data are driven mostly by the number of tests done in a country, not by actual patterns of COVID-19 cases.

In response to Acemoglu's initial comments, Goldberg then pointed out that the paper controls for the population density of the largest urban center in each country and that this variable was included in the preferred specification along with age, obesity, and time since first death. She noted that it could be fruitful to explore a specification including variables for both the density of the largest urban center in a country and the density of the entire country. Goldberg also stated that it would be of interest to further examine the impact of the time since first death variable and that, overall, more granular data would be useful. In response to Kremer's comments regarding epidemiological modeling, Goldberg stated that there has been substantial pushback against modeling during this pandemic because many models have had significant shortcomings and have needed to be revised.

Regarding Acemoglu's comments on density, Tristan Reed remarked that his and Goldberg's analysis explored both the density of the largest urban city in a country and the density of the entire country in different specifications, and the density of the largest urban city had greater predictive power. He then explained that in the specification that included GDP per capita, time since first death, age, obesity prevalence, and urban density, the coefficient on GDP per capita became significant and rose in comparison to the specification including only GDP per capita, time since first death, age, and obesity prevalence. This means that EMDEs have fewer cases despite having high urban density, rather than *because of* low density.

Goldberg then speculated on the effects of various government policies meant to counteract the spread and severity of the pandemic. Despite the analysis finding no significant effect of early policy response on deaths from COVID-19, she stressed that her takeaway was not that policy is unimportant but that the nuanced effects of policies were not captured in current data. She described as examples the cases of Vietnam and Peru. At the time of discussion, June 25, Vietnam had zero deaths from COVID-19 despite sharing a border with China, due in part to effective policies that imposed checks on travelers early in the pandemic and managed to prevent the spread of the virus. In contrast, Peru also adopted policies to address the pandemic relatively quickly, but the virus spread widely regardless, perhaps due to slums and a large informal sector that made policies ineffective. Goldberg argued that these two cases show that policy implementation, rather than just policy adoption, had the most impact on reducing the spread and severity of COVID-19 within countries. Implementation, however, is not captured in their quantitative data.

Kalemli-Özcan pointed out that, in regards to government policies, partial lockdowns have potentially higher annual costs than full lockdowns because partial lockdowns tend to last longer since infection rates remain higher than in a full lockdown. She continued by saying that changes to demand will have a large impact on costs of the pandemic and that external demand in particular will be extremely important for some EMDEs. Furthermore, Kalemli-Özcan argued that current debt relief policies will be ineffective at alleviating economic hardships in many EMDEs because many of these countries have substantial debt owed to private creditors, who are not included in relief policies. Instead, she posited that capital outflows will be more important for EMDEs than their debt stock, as it will be harder to roll over the debt with private creditors during increased capital outflows, an argument she also expanded on in her earlier comment.

Marianne Bertrand then shared her thoughts on large urban centers in EMDEs, stating that her intuition was that these areas should have the largest numbers of deaths due to COVID-19. She asked why the results found in the paper seemed to go against this intuition, with EMDEs experiencing fewer deaths from COVID-19 despite having large, dense urban centers. Goldberg agreed that the results went puzzlingly against intuition and responded by stating that she and Reed had no definitive answer for this trend. Kremer suggested that, because being outdoors seems to substantially reduce transmission of the virus, deaths may be lower in EMDEs despite the density of urban areas because buildings, especially in warm-climate areas, may be highly ventilated. People in these countries may also spend more time outdoors, again due to temperature. He also stated that temperature itself may have some impact on the transmissibility of the virus, but findings in this area of research are mixed.

Raquel Fernández suggested that the extent and use of public transportation might be an important explanatory factor for this urban density trend and asked whether the authors had explored this as a variable. Goldberg responded that she and Reed had not included a public transportation variable, as no global data exist for public transportation. Instead, they explored a variable for change in mobility and found an effect on deaths with the inclusion of this variable. Reed specified that the mobility data come from Google. Kalemli-Özcan stated that it was important to note that the Google mobility data only cover people with phones connected to Google and that there is therefore less data coverage in EMDEs, where many people may not have smartphones or use Google.

Kalemli-Özcan continued by emphasizing the importance of looking at gross capital flows to understand the economic impact of crises, as she stated in her earlier comments. Goldberg responded that while the focus on gross capital flows provides some interesting opportunities for analysis, she and Reed also focused on other measures of economic impact, including net capital flows and commodity prices. Her takeaway from their analysis of these measures is that the COVID-19 economic shock is comparable to previous crises and that the economic shock to EMDEs is likely to play out through familiar channels.

Kalemli-Özcan then spoke on the importance of global policy coordination to ensure that the economic impact of COVID-19 will not be catastrophic. Goldberg agreed with this but pointed out that there is little global willingness to help EMDEs. Instead, the global economic shock of COVID-19 has provided countries with an excuse to focus on domestic economies. Because of this current lack of external help and global coordination, in the long term, she and Reed are pessimistic about economic recovery in EMDEs.

Reed continued by arguing that at the start of the pandemic, a major concern was that EMDEs would need to spend massively to respond to the virus and support locked down populations and that few countries had the fiscal space to do so. However, if the infection rate is lower in EMDEs, as his and Goldberg's paper suggests, this massive amount of expenditure may not be necessary. Reed emphasized that fiscal space remains a concern. Recent debt standstills will help some in this regard, and he argued that there is still time for bond markets to return to normal and expand the borrowing capacity of EMDEs.

SESSION FOUR
Labor Markets and the Economics
of Non-pharmaceutical Interventions

ALEXANDER W. BARTIK
University of Illinois at Urbana-Champaign

MARIANNE BERTRAND
University of Chicago

FENG LIN
University of Chicago

JESSE ROTHSTEIN
University of California, Berkeley

MATTHEW UNRATH
University of California, Berkeley

Measuring the Labor Market at the Onset of the COVID-19 Crisis

ABSTRACT   We use traditional and nontraditional data to measure the collapse and partial recovery of the US labor market from March to early July, contrast this downturn to previous recessions, and provide preliminary evidence on the effects of the policy response. For hourly workers at both small and large businesses, nearly all of the decline in employment occurred between March 14 and 28. It was driven by low-wage services, particularly the retail and leisure and hospitality sectors. A large share of the job losses in small businesses reflected firms that closed entirely, though many subsequently reopened. Firms that were already unhealthy were more likely to close and less likely to reopen, and disadvantaged workers were more likely to be laid off and less likely to return. Most laid-off workers expected to be recalled, and this was predictive of rehiring. Shelter-in-place orders drove only a small share of job losses. Last, states that received more small business loans from the Paycheck Protection Program and states with more generous unemployment insurance benefits had milder declines and faster recoveries. We find no evidence that high unemployment insurance replacement rates drove job losses or slowed rehiring.

Conflict of Interest Disclosure: The authors did not receive financial support from any firm or person for this paper or from any firm or person with a financial or political interest in this paper. The authors utilized data provided by Homebase, which were made available to a large number of academics and have not been restricted in their use in any way. They are currently not officers, directors, or board members of any organization with an interest in this paper. No outside party had the right to review this paper before circulation. The views expressed in this paper are those of the authors, and do not necessarily reflect those of the University of California, Berkeley, the University of Chicago, or the University of Illinois, Urbana-Champaign.

239

he COVID-19 pandemic hit the US labor market with astonishing speed. The week ending March 14, 2020, there were over 250,000 initial unemployment insurance claims—about 25 percent more than the prior week, but still below January levels. Two weeks later, there were over 6 million claims. This shattered the pre-2020 record of 1.07 million, set in January 1982. Claims remained above 1 million for nineteen consecutive weeks, and over 60 million claims were filed by the end of October. The unemployment rate shot up from 3.5 percent in February to 14.7 percent in April, and the number of people at work fell by about 25 million.

The United States' labor market information systems are not set up to track changes this rapid. The primary official measures of the state of the labor market are two monthly surveys, the Current Population Survey (CPS) of households and the Current Employment Statistics (CES) survey of employers. Each collects data about the second week of the month. In 2020, an enormous amount changed between the second week of March and the second week of April.

In this paper, we attempt to describe the labor market in what may turn out to be the early part of the COVID-19 recession, compare the labor market downturn to previous recessions, and provide some evidence on the policies enacted in response to the downturn. We combine data from the traditional government surveys with nontraditional data sources, particularly daily work records compiled by Homebase, a private sector firm that provides time clocks and scheduling software to mostly small businesses. We link the Homebase work records to a survey answered by a subsample of Homebase employees. We supplement the Homebase data with data on firms with more than 100 employees from Kronos, another private sector firm providing time clock, scheduling, and other services. We use the Homebase and Kronos data to measure the high-frequency timing of the March-April contraction and the gradual April-early July recovery. We use CPS and Homebase data to characterize the workers and businesses most affected by the crisis. And we use Homebase data as well as data on physical mobility from SafeGraph, based on electronic tracking of mobile phones, to measure the effects of state shelter-in-place orders and other policies (in particular, the Paycheck Protection Program and unemployment insurance generosity) on employment patterns from March to early July.

We are not the only ones studying the labor market at this time. Allcott and others (2020), Alon and others (2020), Cajner, Crane, and others (2020),

Cajner, Figura, and others (2020), Chetty and others (2020), Cortes and Forsythe (2020), Dey and others (2020), Forsythe and others (2020), Goolsbee and Syverson (2020), Gupta and others (2020), Kurmann, Lalé, and Ta (2020), Lin and Meissner (2020), and Mongey, Pilossoph, and Weinberg (2020) all conduct exercises that are related to ours. There are surely many others that we do not cite here. Our goal is neither to be definitive nor unique, but merely to establish basic stylized facts that can inform the policy response to, and future research on, the crisis.

The paper proceeds as follows. Section I describes our data sources. Section II provides an overview of the labor market collapse and subsequent partial recovery. In section III, we explore who was affected by the collapse, investigating characteristics of workers that predict being laid off in March and April, then being reemployed thereafter. Section IV uses event study models to examine the effects of non-pharmaceutical interventions (i.e., shelter-in-place and stay-at-home orders) on hours worked in the Homebase data and on physical mobility. Section V examines the impacts of the roll-out of unemployment insurance expansions at the state level and of the Paycheck Protection Program on Homebase hours. We conclude in section VI.

I. Data

We rely on three primary sources to measure the evolution of the labor market during the first half of 2020, supplementing with additional measures that provide context.

First, we use the CES survey of employers, the source of official employment counts, to track industry-level employment changes at a monthly frequency. Second, we use the CPS, a monthly survey of about 60,000 households that is the source of the official unemployment rate. Respondents are asked each month about their activities during the week containing the twelfth of the month. The most recent available data are from the June survey. By matching interviews with the same households in consecutive months, we identify workers who were employed in March but not in April, or who were out of work in April or May but reemployed in May or June.

We combine these official data sources with daily data from a private firm, Homebase, which provides scheduling and time clock software to tens of thousands of small businesses that employ hundreds of thousands of workers across the United States and Canada. The time clock component of the Homebase software measures the exact hours worked each day for each hourly employee at the client firms. Employers are identified by their industry and location.

Homebase's customers are primarily small firms in food and drink, retail, and other sectors that employ hourly workers (see online appendix A). The time clock data largely cover hourly workers within those firms. The Homebase subpopulation is highly relevant to the current moment, as the pandemic seems to have most affected the industries and small businesses that form the Homebase clientele. Indeed, we show that the employment collapse was much more dramatic in the Homebase sample than in the labor market as a whole.

When analyzing the Homebase data, we focus on US-based firms that were already Homebase clients before the onset of the pandemic. We define a base period as the two weeks from January 19 to February 1, and scale hours in subsequent weeks as a fraction of hours worked during this period.[1] We consider a firm to have shut down if in any week (Sunday to Saturday) it had zero hours reported by all of its hourly workers, and to have reopened if, following a shutdown, it again appears with positive hours.

We supplement the Homebase data with information from a survey of workers. Survey invitations were sent starting May 1 to everyone who had signed into the Homebase software as a user since February 2020. We use survey responses received by July 7, matched to the administrative records for the same workers, and we limit this group to workers with positive hours in the base period and only one Homebase client employer since January 19, 2020. Among the roughly 426,000 workers meeting this description, approximately 1,700 (0.4 percent) responded to our survey. Despite the low response rate, online appendix table B1 shows that the survey respondents are roughly representative of all Homebase workers on the (limited set of) dimensions on which we can compare them. However, survey respondents are somewhat positively selected on hours worked at the Homebase employer (online appendix figure B1) and hence may be more representative of the "regular" workforce at these employers. Online appendix table B2 summarizes demographic characteristics for survey respondents.

---

1. We exclude from all analyses any individual daily observations with more than twenty reported hours.

II. Overview of the Labor Market Collapse

Between February and April 2020, the unemployment rate (not seasonally adjusted) spiked by 10.6 percentage points, reaching 14.4 percent, while the employment rate fell by over 9 percentage points. These two-month changes were roughly 50 percent larger than the cumulative changes over more than two years in the respective series in the Great Recession. In sharp contrast to past recessions, the February–April unemployment increase was entirely driven by increases in the share of workers who expected to be recalled to their former positions; the share who were looking for new jobs shrunk slightly. The temporary layoff share of the unemployed has never previously exceeded 30 percent, but rose to nearly 80 percent in April.[2] Employment and unemployment recovered a small amount in May, but remained in unprecedented territory.

The usual labor market categories are not well suited to pandemic conditions, and the official unemployment rate understated the amount of joblessness. The share who were employed but not at work grew by 3.3 percentage points from March to April.[3] The Bureau of Labor Statistics (BLS) believes much or all of this increase derives from misclassification of people who should have been counted as on temporary layoff; if they had been classified that way, the unemployment rate in April would have been 19.2 percent instead of 14.4 percent (BLS 2020, item 14). Similarly, labor force nonparticipation rose, with many of the new nonparticipants saying that they wanted jobs but were not actively looking for work or were not available to take jobs (BLS 2020, item 18). It seems likely that many of these were kept out of work by the pandemic and would otherwise have been counted as unemployed. If they had been included as well, the adjusted unemployment rate in April would have been well above 20 percent.

2. See https://fred.stlouisfed.org/graph/?g=x5O2 for a long time series using CPS data. Hedin, Schnorr, and von Wachter (2020) use administrative records from the California unemployment insurance system to explore the characteristics of unemployment insurance applicants. They find that over 90 percent of new claimants in late March reported that they expected to be recalled to their prior jobs, up from around 40 percent in February. The share expecting recalls gradually declined after late March, to around 70 percent at the end of May, but this nevertheless indicates that many of the job losses may not be permanent, and is consistent with the increase in temporary layoffs measured by the CPS.

3. See https://www.hamiltonproject.org/blog/who_are_the_potentially_misclassified_in_ the_employment_report.

Figure 1. The Labor Market Collapse

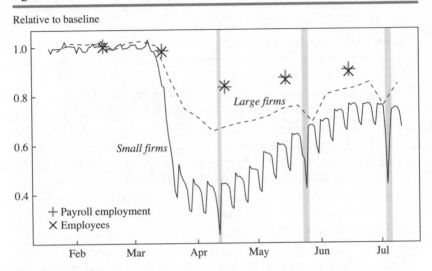

Source: Homebase; Kronos; CES; CPS.

Notes: The small firms series shows daily total hours worked across all firms in Homebase data, as a fraction of average hours worked on the same day of the week in the January 19–February 1 base period. The sample includes firms (defined at the firm-industry-state-MSA level) that recorded at least eighty hours in the base period. The large firms series shows weekly punches (shifts) among hourly workers at firms with more than 100 employees, from Kronos data, as a share of the average during the January 20–February 2 base period. Payroll employment and employees series show monthly estimates from the official CES and CPS surveys, respectively, scaled as a share of their January levels. Vertical bars mark the weekends containing Easter, Memorial Day, and the Fourth of July.

Monthly statistics are inadequate to understanding the rapidity of the labor market collapse. Figure 1 plots daily total hours worked at Homebase's client firms. We also plot three lower-frequency comparisons: (1) weekly counts of shifts worked by hourly workers at larger firms (>100 employees) as measured in data collected by Kronos, another similar firm that serves larger employers; (2) payroll employment from the CES; and (3) monthly household employment from the CPS. In all four series, we report employment measures relative to a base period in late January.[4] Total hours worked at Homebase firms fell by approximately 60 percent between the beginning and end of March, with the bulk of this decline between March 13 and March 24. The nadir seems to have been around the second week of April. Hours then grew slowly and steadily through

---

4. The base period is January 19–February 1 in the Homebase data, January 20–February 2 in the Kronos data, and January in the CES and CPS data.

mid-June. They made up about half of the lost ground by the third week of June, but then fell back again slightly in late June and early July.[5]

The time pattern for larger firms in the Kronos data is more muted but quite similar in shape. The most rapid decline in employment occurred in the last two weeks of March, the nadir of employment occurred in the second week of April, and firms recovered about 50 percent of their employment losses by the third week of June. The lower-frequency CES and CPS data are also consistent with these patterns, with the employment trough in April in both series and a roughly 50 percent recovery by June. The most notable difference between the series is the magnitude of the overall employment decline, around 16 percent in the CES and CPS, 34 percent in the Kronos sample, and 60 percent in the Homebase data. As we discuss below, this likely reflects a combination of differences in industry coverage and firm size, with the smaller firms in food, drink, and retail that are the bulk of Homebase clients experiencing the most severe employment declines during this downturn.

III. Who Are the Unemployed? Who Are the Rehired?

In this section we explore the distribution of the job losses across industries, firms, and workers.

III.A. Industry

Figure 2 uses CES data to show the two-month decline in employment from February to April, by major industry. The service sector, and particularly its low-wage segment, experienced by far the largest drop in employment. In leisure and hospitality, which includes restaurants and hotels, employment fell by nearly half between February and April. Other services, which include repair and maintenance services, personal and laundry services, and services to private households, were the second most impacted, with more than 20 percent of employment lost by April. Workers employed in retail trade were also disproportionately exposed.[6]

---

5. There are clear day-of-week effects in the Homebase data as well: Homebase employment is lower on weekends than on weekdays since the onset of the crisis, relative to the day-of-week pattern in the base period. These reductions are largest in the holiday weeks of Easter, Memorial Day, and the Fourth of July.

6. Online appendix figure C1 shows monthly changes in 2020. Consistent with figure 1, employment recovered somewhat in May and June, with the recovery concentrated in the same sectors that saw the largest declines.

Figure 2. Employment Change in Great Recession and 2020, by Sector

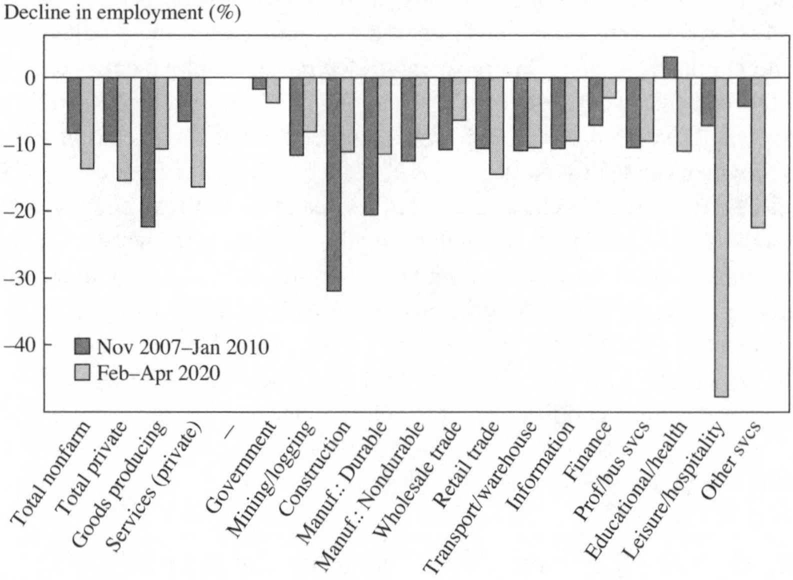

Decline in employment (%)

Nov 2007–Jan 2010
Feb–Apr 2020

Total nonfarm / Total private / Goods producing / Services (private) / Government / Mining/logging / Construction / Manuf.: Durable / Manuf.: Nondurable / Wholesale trade / Retail trade / Transport/warehouse / Information / Finance / Prof/bus svcs / Educational/health / Leisure/hospitality / Other svcs

Source: CES.
Notes: Payroll employment by industry or aggregate; the first four categories are aggregates that include many of the remaining series. Not seasonally adjusted.

Figure 2 also shows the cumulative decline in employment between November 2007 and January 2010. Job loss in 2020 was about 60 percent larger than in the whole of the Great Recession, and the sectoral composition was quite different. Construction and durable goods manufacturing declined the most in the Great Recession, while low-wage services were relatively insulated.

III.B. Firm Closings and Reopenings

An advantage of Homebase data over the CPS, beyond their high frequency, is that they enable us to link workers to their employers. We use this link to separate the observed change in total hours into three channels: firm shutdowns, layoffs, and cuts in hours. We define a firm as having fully shut down in a given week if the Homebase data record zero employees clocking in at that firm during that week. Among firms that have not shut down, we count layoffs as the proportional change in the number of workers with positive hours in a week, relative to the

Figure 3. Hours Changes at Homebase Firms by Week

Percent change in hours attributable to each form of contraction

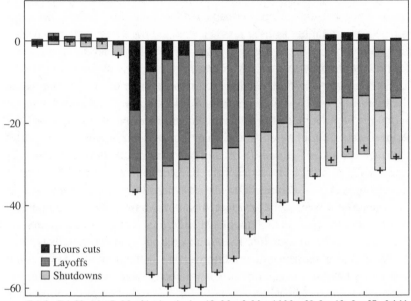

Source: Authors' analysis of Homebase data.

Notes: Changes in total hours worked at Homebase firms that were active between January 19 and February 1, relative to weekly hours during that period, decomposed into three sources: those due to firm closures, changes in the number of workers at continuing firms, and changes in average hours among remaining workers. The contribution of firm closure is measured by summing up baseline hours of firms that are shut down (with zero recorded hours) each week. The contribution of headcount changes (layoffs) is the proportionate change in the number of workers at continuing firms, multiplied by those firms' hours during the baseline period. The contribution of changes in average hours is the proportionate change in hours per worker at continuing firms, multiplied by baseline firm hours. Markers indicate the cumulative net effect, combining all three. Lightly shaded bars mark the weeks containing Easter, Memorial Day, and the Fourth of July.

baseline. Last, we define hours cuts as the reduction in average hours, relative to the baseline period, among workers remaining employed at still operating firms.[7]

Figure 3 reports the percent change in hours each week since early February attributable to these three channels. Except for the first week

---

7. Some firms that appear to us to have shut down may have retained some non-hourly workers who do not use the Homebase software to track their time, so should properly be classified as layoffs at continuing firms.

of the labor market collapse, reductions in hours per worker as defined above have accounted for a very minor part of the change in total hours at Homebase businesses.[8] Instead, the decline in total hours came primarily from firms that closed entirely and from reductions in the number of workers at continuing firms. Layoffs accounted for a larger share in March and shutdowns in April, but thereafter the two have had about the same quantitative impact on "missing hours."[9]

We next use the Homebase data to assess the role of firm reopenings in the (partial) recovery. Of the roughly 42,000 unique firms in our baseline sample, about 40 percent shut down for at least one week by April 4.[10] About 70 percent of these firms have reopened for at least a week after that date (though 10 percent have since closed again). In online appendix figure C2, we report the distribution of hours at ever-closed businesses through July 11, as a share of total baseline hours at these businesses. In the most recent week, total hours at these firms remain close to 55 percent below their baseline level. About two-thirds of these missing hours are attributable to businesses that remain closed; the remainder reflects businesses that have reopened at a reduced scale. Of the roughly 45 percent of hours that have been regained, a vast majority have come from rehiring of workers that had been employed by the business before the shutdown. However, the share attributable to new hires has been slowly trending up over time, reaching almost a quarter by the week of July 5–11. It is worth noting that Homebase firms have high turnover rates even in good times; in fact, the share of hours being worked by new hires is lower in 2020 than over similar periods in 2018 and 2019 (see online appendix figure C3).

The Homebase data also allow us to investigate which businesses were more likely to shut down as well as take an early look into which firms are most likely to make it through the crisis. We consider two employer characteristics: size, defined as the employer's total number of unique employees

---

8. We conjecture that the large role for hours reductions in mid-March is an artifact created by mid-week layoffs or firm closings. When workers stop working in the middle of a week, our method counts that as a reduction in weekly hours that week and as a layoff or firm closing the following week. Consistent with this, online appendix figure C4 shows that the distribution of workers' hours fell the first week of the collapse but returned to normal the following week and has been quite stable through the year to date.

9. Online appendix figure C5 shows firm exits using a stricter definition that counts firms as exiting only if they do not return by mid-July. In 2018 and 2019, about 2 percent of firms exited Homebase each month. In March 2020, about 15 percent exited. After early April, the exit rate was similar to prior years.

10. Another 10 percent shut down for at least one week between April 5 and mid-July, mostly in mid-April.

Figure 4. Likelihood of Firm Closure and Reopening by Firm Size and Precrisis Growth Rate

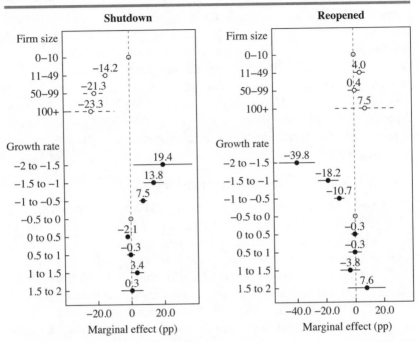

Source: Authors' analysis of Homebase data.
Notes: Marginal effects and confidence intervals from two logit models, with state and industry fixed effects. Left panel: all firms in the Homebase data; the outcome is an indicator for the firm shutting down (recording zero hours) for at least one week between March 8 and April 4. Right panel: firms that shut down by April 4; the outcome is an indicator for subsequently reporting positive hours before July 11. Firm size is the number of unique employees in the base period (January 19–February 1). The growth rate is the change in the number of employees between January 2019 and January 2020, divided by the average of these two periods. Marginal effects are evaluated for a professional services firm in California with up to ten employees in the base period and a growth rate of −.5 to 0. Left panel: $N = 24,872$; right panel: $N = 9,594$.

in the January 19–February 1 base period, and growth rate, which we define as the change in the number of employees between January 2019 and January 2020 divided by the average of the beginning and end-point levels, a ratio that is bounded between −2 and 2.

Figure 4 reports marginal effects from logit models for the likelihood of the firm shutting down by April 4, and, for firms that did, for the likelihood of reopening by July 11, controlling for state and industry fixed effects. Larger firms were much less likely to shut down than smaller firms. Conditional on having shut down, larger firms are also somewhat more likely to have reopened by mid-July, though this is not statistically significant. Most interesting is how the likelihood of shutting down and reopening is predicted by employer growth between January 2019 and January 2020. Businesses that were struggling before COVID-19 have much increased odds of shutting down during the COVID-19 crisis and of remaining closed. Three non-mutually exclusive explanations are that these businesses might have been particularly low on cash and unable to withstand the shock (Bartik and others 2020); that they may have been de-prioritized by banks when they applied for Paycheck Protection Program (PPP) funding; or that the COVID-19 crisis sped up the pruning of some of the less productive businesses in the economy (Barrero, Bloom, and Davis 2020).

III.C. Worker-Level Job Loss and Rehiring

We next explore which workers are most likely to lose their jobs and subsequently be rehired, using both CPS and Homebase data. We estimate multivariate logit models that include a range of worker characteristics as predictors, along with fixed effects for states and major industry groupings. Our first model, in columns 1–2 of table 1, includes all CPS respondents who worked in March and takes as the outcome the absence of work in April, while the second, in columns 3–4, is estimated on those not working in April and May and takes work in the following month as the outcome of interest.

The analysis reveals systematic differences across socio-demographic groups in the likelihood of having stopped work in April. We see a strong U-shaped pattern in age for job loss. Workers who are over 65 years old (or 16 to 25, respectively) were 14.2 (7.8) percentage points more likely to exit work in April than otherwise similar workers aged 26–37. There is also a strong education gradient: Workers without high school degrees were 10.9 percentage points more likely to have stopped working in April than otherwise similar college graduates. Black, Asian, and Hispanic workers were, respectively, 4.8, 5.4, and 1.7 percentage points more likely to exit work in April than otherwise similar white workers. Finally, married individuals were less likely to lose jobs and women were more likely to do so. We do not observe systematic differences based on parental status, for either men or women.

These inequities in the distribution of job loss were for the most part not offset by rehiring in May or June. In particular, older workers, Black and Asian workers, single workers, and women, each more likely to lose their jobs in April, were also less likely to start work again in May or June. On the other hand, there is no clear education gradient in rehiring.

The remaining columns of table 1 repeat the analyses of job loss and rehiring, now using the Homebase data. We link the administrative records on hours worked to the worker survey, which provides demographic information. We define layoff and rehiring somewhat differently, thanks to the higher frequency data: a worker is counted as leaving work if he or she worked in the base period in January but had at least one week with zero hours between March 8 and April 25; then, for these workers, we classify as rehired those who returned to work and recorded positive hours at some point after April 18. Note that we do not distinguish in these definitions between firms that closed entirely and workers who were laid off from continuing firms, nor similarly between rehires at reopening versus continuing firms.

Perhaps unsurprisingly, given the small sample size, few of the estimated effects are statistically significant. However, a few patterns emerge. We see a much higher likelihood of layoff among those without a high school degree and much lower likelihood among those in managerial positions. We also see that workers with children were relatively spared from layoffs. In addition, while Hispanic workers are less likely to be laid off, we also see that, as in the CPS data, Black workers are notably less likely to be rehired.

The survey data we collected also allow us to understand more fully the experiences and expectations of the Homebase workers. Twenty-one percent of the sample reported having experienced a layoff because of COVID-19, while 31 percent report having been furloughed, and 21 percent report hours reductions. Less than 10 percent report having made a decision to not work or work less, with most of those saying it was to protect themselves or their family members from exposure to the virus. Less than 10 percent of the workers whose hours and employment status were negatively impacted by COVID-19 report being paid for any of the hours that they are not working. Among these negatively impacted workers, nearly 60 percent report that their employers encouraged them to file for unemployment insurance. This was notably higher (77 percent) among laid-off workers than among furloughed workers (66 percent) or workers who experienced reduced hours (35 percent). Fifty-two percent of workers that have been laid off report that their employer has expressed a desire to hire them back. Among workers that have been negatively impacted by COVID-19, only about a quarter report looking for work. The modal reason for not searching is an expectation of being rehired; only 7 percent attribute their lack of job search to financial disincentives to work. Among the people that expected to be rehired (when the surveys were conducted, largely in early May), the modal expected rehire date was June 1 (33 percent), followed by July 1 (26 percent).

Table 1. Worker Characteristics and Job Loss and Rehiring in Current Population Survey and Homebase Samples

	CPS				Homebase					
	Stopped work in April		Started work in May or June		Stopped work mid-March to late April		Started work after stopping			
	Marg. effect	SE	Marg. effect	SE	Marg. effect	SE	Marg. effect	SE	Marg. effect	SE
Age										
16–25	**0.078**	(0.011)	−0.002	(0.016)	−0.008	(0.043)	0.060	(0.042)	0.010	(0.029)
26–37	—		—		—		—		—	
38–49	−0.010	(0.007)	−0.009	(0.015)	−0.027	(0.047)	0.034	(0.051)	0.061	(0.054)
50–64	**0.019**	(0.008)	−0.026	(0.014)	−0.011	(0.049)	−0.045	(0.049)	−0.010	(0.034)
65 and over	**0.142**	(0.015)	**−0.066**	(0.018)	0.096	(0.078)	−0.041	(0.074)	0.000	(0.049)
Education Level										
Less than high school	**0.029**	(0.011)	−0.016	(0.017)	**0.178**	(0.064)	−0.007	(0.057)	−0.034	(0.038)
High school	—		—		—		—		—	
Some college	**−0.016**	(0.006)	−0.014	(0.012)	0.013	(0.037)	−0.001	(0.037)	−0.019	(0.026)
Bachelor degree or higher	**−0.080**	(0.009)	−0.025	(0.013)	−0.015	(0.041)	−0.070	(0.042)	−0.054	(0.042)
Race										
Black	**0.048**	(0.010)	**−0.074**	(0.015)	−0.024	(0.054)	**−0.196**	(0.059)	−0.054	(0.044)
Asian	**0.054**	(0.012)	**−0.053**	(0.018)	−0.059	(0.072)	0.081	(0.066)	0.038	(0.060)
Native American	0.029	(0.022)	−0.019	(0.038)	0.111	(0.145)	−0.043	(0.118)	−0.012	(0.081)
Hispanic	**0.017**	(0.008)	−0.015	(0.013)	**−0.096**	(0.045)	−0.021	(0.044)	0.006	(0.031)

Married	**-0.022**	(0.005)	**0.041**	(0.012)	0.033	(0.036)	0.050	(0.041)	0.034	(0.037)
Female	**0.034**	(0.007)	**-0.028**	(0.012)	-0.013	(0.042)	0.025	(0.039)	-0.024	(0.027)
Child	male	-0.005	(0.011)	0.019	(0.022)	**-0.158**	(0.066)	-0.002	(0.064)	-0.048	(0.042)
Child under 10	male	0.002	(0.012)	0.002	(0.023)						
Child	female	0.008	(0.010)	-0.009	(0.019)	**-0.098**	(0.046)	0.040	(0.049)	0.010	(0.034)
Child under 10	female	0.019	(0.012)	0.010	(0.022)						
Occupation										
Manager	**-0.072**	(0.008)	0.031	(0.020)	**-0.244**	(0.056)	0.071	(0.082)	0.037	(0.076)
Expected to be rehired										
Likely									**0.400**	(0.123)
N	31,692		11,387		1,620		1,217		650	

Source: CPS; Homebase.

Notes: Each pair of columns reports marginal effects and standard errors from a separate logit regression, controlling for two-digit industry and state effects (not reported here). In the CPS sample, the model for leaving work in April is limited to those who were at work in March; the model for starting work in May or June is limited to those who were not working the prior month. The models include gender by presence-of-children interactions; we report the marginal effects of children separately for males and females. In the Homebase sample, the model for stopping work is for an indicator for at least one week with zero hours between mid-March and late April, among those in our sample with positive hours in late January who responded to the worker survey. The models for starting work after stopping are for having positive hours in a subsequent week, among those with zero hours in a week; the final model limits to those who were not working at the time of the survey. Marginal effects are evaluated for an unmarried, childless, male, white, non-Hispanic individual age 26–37 with a high school diploma in a nonmanagerial occupation in the professional and technical services industry in California. Bold effects are significant at the 5 percent level.

Respondents were also asked if they would return to their employer if offered the opportunity. Three-quarters of respondents said they would go back. Job satisfaction is an important correlate of this response. For example, 80 percent of workers who strongly agreed with the statement "I liked my manager" would plan to go back if asked, compared with 67 percent who only somewhat agreed with this statement. Also, 89 percent of workers who strongly agreed with "I was satisfied with my wages" would plan to go back to their prior employer if asked, compared to 67 percent who only somewhat agreed with this statement.

In the final columns of table 1, we assess how expectations about rehiring relate to the likelihood of being rehired (defined as above). We reestimate the logit for rehiring, limiting the sample to those who were out of work at the time of the survey and adding an indicator for expecting to be rehired. Workers who believed it was likely they would be rehired were 40 percentage points more likely to be rehired subsequently than were otherwise similar workers in the same industry and state who believed a rehiring was unlikely. These results indicate that workers had access to predictive information about the odds of a maintained firm-worker match that may have helped at least some of them better manage through what was otherwise a period of massive disruption and uncertainty. The converse of this, though, is that the workers who have not yet been rehired disproportionately consist of those who never expected to be, making it less likely that further recovery will lead to additional rehiring.

IV. Evaluating Non-pharmaceutical Interventions

Many firm closures were closely coincident with state closure orders and other non-pharmaceutical interventions, and policy has generally proceeded on the assumption that many firms will reopen when these orders are lifted. It is not evident, however, that firms closed or remain closed only because of government policy. Closures reflected increased awareness about the threat posed by COVID-19, and consumers, workers, and firms might have responded to this information with or without government orders. Following closings, many businesses may have been permanently damaged and may not reopen even when conditions improve. Moreover, insofar as consumer behavior rather than state orders is the binding constraint on demand for firm services, the mere lifting of an order may not be enough to restore adequate demand.

In this section, we study the relationship between state labor market outcomes and so-called shelter-in-place and stay-at-home orders (which we refer to collectively as "shutdown orders") that restrict the public and private facilities that people can visit to essential businesses and public services. This type of intervention is both the most prominent of the non-pharmaceutical interventions and the one that may have the largest direct effects on economic activity. We test the importance of these directives on firms' hours choices, as captured by the Homebase data. We use event study models, using both contrasts between states that did and did not implement shutdown orders and variation in the timing of these orders to identify the effect of orders on hours worked. We also estimate event studies of the effect of the *lifting* of public health orders, which need not be symmetric to the effect of imposing them.

Stay-at-home and reopen orders are sourced directly from government websites.[11] We define a stay-at-home order as any order that requires residents to stay at home or shelter in place. Orders that conveyed COVID-19-related guidelines but did not require residents to shelter in place are excluded.[12] In states that had stay-at-home orders, we define reopen orders as the first lifting of any of the shutdown-related restrictions on business activities, and time them to the effective date.[13] Online appendix figure C6 shows the number of states with active shutdown orders between the start of March and the present. California was the first state to impose a shutdown order, on March 19. The number of active orders then rose quickly, reaching 44 in early April. It was stable for about three weeks, then began to decline as some states started to reopen in late April and early May. By June 1, all states had reopened.

Stay-at-home orders can reduce employment simply by prohibiting nonessential workers from going to work. They can also have indirect effects operating through consumer demand, which may relate to public awareness of COVID-19, willingness of consumers to visit businesses, and COVID-19 caseloads. Consequently, we supplement our event study analysis of hours data from Homebase with data on mobility, which

---

11. They most commonly come from centralized lists of executive orders; see, for example, "Executive and Administrative Orders," Illinois.gov, https://www2.illinois.gov/government/executive-orders. In some cases they come from centralized lists of public health and COVID-19-related orders; see, for example, "Public Health Orders and Executive Orders," New Mexico Department of Health, https://cv.nmhealth.org/public-health-orders-and-executive-orders/.

12. See, for example, "Stay Safe, Stay Home Directive," Coronavirus Utah.gov, https://coronavirus.utah.gov/stay-at-home/.

13. Results are similar when we define reopening as the lifting of the original shelter-in-place order.

captures in part the willingness of customers to visit businesses in person. We measure overall mobility using SafeGraph data on visits to public and private locations between January 19 and July 11, 2020, including only locations that recorded positive visits during our base period, January 19–February 1. We normalize the raw count of visits by the number of devices that SafeGraph sees on each day to control for the differences in the count of visits related to SafeGraph's ability to track devices, then rescale relative to the base period.

We estimate event-study models of the effect of shutdown and reopen orders (considered separately) on log hours worked from Homebase and log SafeGraph visits.[14] Each outcome is measured at the state-by-day level. The shutdown model is estimated on data from February 16 to April 19, while the reopen order model is estimated on data from April 6 through July 11. We regress each outcome on full sets of state and date fixed effects, state-specific trends, and a series of "event time" indicators for days relative to the date of the order ranging from −7 (corresponding to 7 days before the event) to the maximum observed in the data, either +31 (corresponding to 31 days after the event) for shutdown orders or +82 (for 82 days after the event) for reopening events.

We report these results in figure 5.[15] The top panel reports the event study estimates for the shutdown (solid line) and reopen (dotted line) models, while the bottom panel reports the time effects from these specifications to aid interpretation of the magnitude of the event-study estimates in the top panel. Each panel includes two sub-panels, one for each of our outcomes.

Starting with the estimates for the relationship between shutdown orders and hours in the left side of the top panel of figure 5, we see that hours worked fell immediately following the orders, stabilizing at a decline of roughly 12 log points by the third day after the shutdown order.

---

14. We do not formally estimate the interaction of the different outcomes, but simply estimate reduced-form effects of orders on each. For examples of studies that do examine interactions among outcomes, see Chernozhukov, Kasahara, and Schrimpf (forthcoming) and Allcott and others (2020).

15. We have also reestimated the event study models without state-specific trends; see online appendix figure C7. An implicit assumption of event study models is that in the absence of orders any differences among states would have grown linearly with calendar time. We have also estimated weighted event studies (Ben-Michael, Feller, and Rothstein 2019) that rely on matching to identify control states with similar counterfactual trends. While traditional event study models can be poorly behaved in the presence of heterogeneous treatment effects (Goodman-Bacon and Marcus 2020; Callaway and Sant'Anna 2019), weighted event studies are not subject to this problem.

Figure 5. Event Study Estimates of the Effect of Imposition and Lifting of Shelter-in-Place Orders

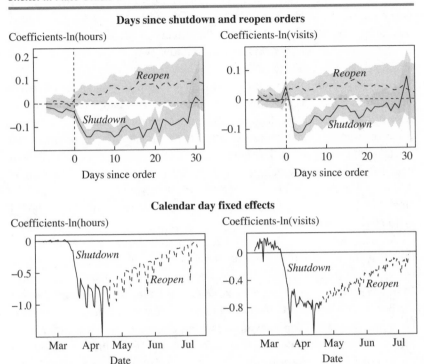

Source: Authors' analysis of Homebase and SafeGraph data.

Notes: Samples for the shutdown event studies consist of state-by-day observations from February 16 to April 19. Samples for the reopening event studies consist of state-by-day observations from April 6 to July 11; states that never had shelter-in-place orders are excluded. Specifications include full sets of state and calendar date effects as well as state-specific trends. We exclude (normalize to zero) the effects for event times less than −7. The shutdown calendar time effects are normalized to zero on February 16. The reopening effects are normalized to align with the shutdown estimates on April 13. Shaded areas show 95 percent confidence intervals for the event time effects.

In our model for physical visits, we see an uptick in visits on the date of the shutdown announcement, possibly reflecting trips to buy groceries or other supplies, followed by a sharp, roughly 15 log-point decline after the shutdown orders are implemented.

Both hours and visits slowly recover after the shutdown order, returning to the level of non-shut-down states by about a month after the initial order. This may reflect adjustment of firms or workers to the restrictions, reduced compliance, or reduced enforcement of restrictions after they were put into place. The solid lines in the top panel of figure 5 report results from the corresponding specifications for reopen orders. We see that reopen orders have the opposite effect of shutdown orders, with hours and visits rising 6 to 8 log points in the first ten days after the orders and growing steadily thereafter. The estimates imply that the effects of shutdown orders, about 12 log points, are largely erased within about two weeks after the orders are lifted.

How should we interpret the magnitudes of the estimates in the top panel of figure 5? One way to think about them is to compare the estimates of the effects of shelter-in-place orders to the calendar date effects from the same specifications, which reflect other determinants of the outcomes that are common to all states. The bottom panel of figure 5 reports the calendar date effects from the specifications reported in the top panel. The sample windows for the two models overlap for the period April 6–19, and we show both, normalizing the reopen order estimates to align with the layoff estimates on April 13.

As expected, given the results in section I above, the calendar date effects show extremely large reductions in hours (about 100 log points at the weekend trough and 60–75 log points on weekdays) and visits in late March. These are much larger than the effects of the orders reported in the top panel. The estimated effect of shutdown orders on log hours (log visits) is about one-sixth (one-seventh) as large as the pure calendar time effects.[16] These results imply that, at least in the short run, shutdown and reopen orders account for only a modest portion of the changes in labor markets and economic activity during the crisis; the overall patterns have more to do with broader health and economic concerns affecting product demand and labor supply rather than with shutdown or reopen orders themselves.[17]

Two caveats are important to keep in mind when interpreting our finding that shutdown and reopen orders play only a modest role in the labor market effects of COVID-19. First, shutdown orders may have

16. For example, for hours, the event time effect of shutdown orders is about −12 log points, as discussed above. By contrast, the calendar time effects for late March and early April are around −75 log points on weekdays, and even larger on weekends.

17. Consistent with this interpretation, when we estimate event studies models that also include effects of school closing events, which should not have had direct effects on small businesses but may have had a larger signaling value about the importance of reducing contact, we find larger effects of these events (online appendix figure C8). Nevertheless, even the combined effect of shelter-in-place and school closing orders is no more than half as large as the pure calendar time effects, and only about a third as large during the labor market trough in the second week of April.

spillover effects on other states not captured in our model. In particular, the first shutdown orders may have played a role in signaling the seriousness and potential risk associated with COVID-19, even if subsequent shutdown orders had more muted effects. Second, over longer time horizons, if shutdown orders reduce caseloads, this may result in labor market improvements that counteract to some extent the negative effects that we estimate here. Explorations of these more complicated medium- and long-run interactions of shutdown orders, labor market activity, social distancing, and caseloads are beyond the scope of our analysis here. Several papers, including Chernozhukov, Kasahara, and Schrimpf (forthcoming) and Allcott and others (2020), have investigated these interactions by combining treatment effect estimates like those here with epidemiological and economic models that specify the relationships among our outcomes to estimate how the full system responds over time to shutdown orders.

V. Evaluating Economic Policy Responses

The Coronavirus Aid, Relief, and Economic Security (CARES) Act was signed on March 27, with over $2 trillion allocated to a range of provisions aimed at supporting the labor market and economy through the early stages of the crisis. In this section, we present descriptive evidence regarding the relationship between two components of CARES—its enhancement of unemployment benefits and the Paycheck Protection Program (PPP) loans to small businesses—and labor market outcomes. While our analyses do not have strong causal designs, they are suggestive about the likely short-run impacts.

The CARES Act included many provisions aimed at expanding and enhancing unemployment insurance benefits. Pandemic Unemployment Assistance (PUA) extended unemployment benefits to independent contractors and others who did not have enough earnings history to qualify for regular unemployment insurance, and Pandemic Emergency Unemployment Compensation (PEUC) provided additional weeks of benefits for those whose regular benefits have run out. A third major component is Federal Pandemic Unemployment Compensation (FPUC), which added $600 to every weekly unemployment benefit payment.

The primary goal of these expansions was to aid workers who had been thrown out of their jobs by the pandemic and the associated public health measures. By all accounts, they were successful: average personal income rose by an unprecedented amount in April, though this likely masks important heterogeneity. But they also affect the labor market in two offsetting ways. First, unemployment insurance plays a broadly stimulative effect, supporting consumption of displaced workers (Ganong and Noel 2019; Rothstein and Valletta 2017) and thus demand for goods and services. Second, enhancements and extensions of unemployment benefits may reduce the incentive for displaced workers to search for work. This may slow rehiring, and could even lead to more job loss; although workers who quit their jobs are not eligible for unemployment insurance (UI), workers who would prefer to receive unemployment benefits instead of remaining on the job might persuade their employers to implement layoffs rather than going into debt to keep the business open.

These moral hazard concerns have focused on FPUC, which was controversial from the start. The $600 amount was chosen to raise the UI replacement rate to around 100 percent for the average US worker. Because many workers, particularly those displaced in March and April, earn less than the average, and because the FPUC payment did not vary with prior earnings, many workers faced replacement rates well in excess of 100 percent. Ganong, Noel, and Vavra (2020) find that the median replacement rate was 145 percent and that 76 percent of workers unemployed in the past would have qualified for replacement rates greater than 100 percent under FPUC. Anecdotally, some employers reported that laid-off workers were unwilling to return to work, even when businesses reopened, because this would mean a loss in income (Morath 2020).

We take two strategies for evaluating the effects of the expansions of UI under the CARES Act. One uses across-state variation, and the other uses variation in the timing of the rollout of two components of the CARES unemployment insurance expansions.

We begin with the across-state comparison. Ganong, Noel, and Vavra (2020) document wide variation across states in unemployment insurance replacement rates under CARES, with a low median replacement rate of 119 percent in Arizona and a high of 165 percent in Oklahoma. We divide states into four groups by the median replacement rate, following Ganong, Noel, and Vavra (2020, appendix table 1), and investigate whether either the employment collapse or rehires vary across these groups. Variation in the replacement rate comes from two sources: differences in state wage distributions, and differences in the generosity of states' preexisting unemployment insurance benefit formulas. Neither is random, so differences across states may capture other state characteristics that correlate with these factors. We also explore estimates that control for census division fixed effects, which may capture some of the most important differences among states.

Figure 6. Hours Trends by State Median Unemployment Insurance Benefit Replacement Rate and Round 1 PPP Amount

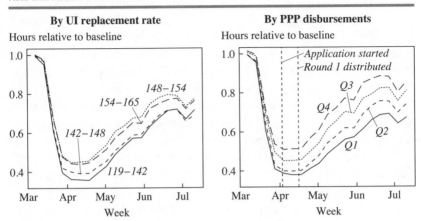

Source: Authors' analysis of Homebase data.
Notes: Unemployment Insurance replacement rates, expressed as percentages of weekly earnings, are from Ganong, Noel, and Vavra (2020, table A-1) and include CARES Act supplements to benefits. Washington, DC, is excluded, as Ganong, Noel, and Vavra (2020) do not report UI data for it. For PPP graph, states are ranked by the amount of PPP loans under $150,000 to firms in NAICS industries 44 and 72 (food and drink and retail) approved on or before April 16, divided by the total payroll (in dollars) of establishments under size fifty in these industries in 2018:Q1, from the County Business Patterns data. The first quartile has the smallest amount.

The left panel of figure 6 shows the time series of Homebase hours, relative to the late January base period, for each of the four groups. The states with the lowest replacement rates saw the steepest collapse of hours in March, and recovered no more quickly thereafter. This is not the pattern one would expect if either were driven by labor supply responses to UI generosity, although as noted, other differences across states may confound this estimate.

We can use a similar strategy to develop descriptive evidence about the forgivable small business loans provided under the PPP. Like the UI programs, PPP was rolled out very quickly and somewhat haphazardly. It relied on banks to disburse loans to their existing customers, and banks varied in their preparedness to process applications quickly. Moreover, the program was initially under-funded: loan applications opened on April 3, and the initial appropriation was exhausted by April 16. (Additional loans from a second round of PPP funding started being provided on April 27.) There was substantial variability across areas in the amount of loans processed during the short initial application window. We classify states into four quartiles by the amount of PPP loans by April 16 for small firms (loans under $150,000) in the retail and food and drink industries, divided by total payroll in small businesses in these industries in March 2018. This ratio is over 160 percent larger in the top quartile of states than in the bottom. Again, this variation is not random, as greater small business distress may have led to higher take-up of PPP loans. But the very short, chaotic period between the opening of applications and the exhaustion of funds suggests that some of the variation likely reflects idiosyncratic factors related to existing banking relationships and bank preparation (and willingness) to handle the loans rather than any response to pandemic conditions.

The right panel of figure 6 shows hours worked by the four PPP quartiles. The trough in hours is lower in the states that received the least PPP money (as a share of potentially covered payroll), and these states also saw slower recoveries than states that received more funds. This is consistent with a protective effect of PPP loans. However, a substantial gap is already apparent at the beginning of April, before the PPP loan window opened, suggesting that other factors may confound this comparison.

One factor that could confound the comparison is differences in the industry or worker mix across states. To explore this, we turn again to logit models for job loss and rehiring, akin to those reported earlier. Online appendix table C1 reports several estimates in both the CPS and the Homebase data. Each model includes the controls listed in table 1 as well as industry fixed effects, but we replace the state fixed effects from those specifications with indicators for three of the four quartiles of states by PPP volumes and by UI replacement rates. In even-numbered columns, we also add fixed effects for the nine census divisions, so that comparisons are only among nearby states. Patterns are generally similar to what was seen in figure 6. Higher PPP volumes and higher UI replacement rates are associated with fewer layoffs; higher PPP volumes are also associated with faster rehiring. The states with the lowest UI replacement rates did have somewhat faster rehiring in the CPS data, but this merely matches their greater layoffs, and in any case is not replicated in the Homebase data.

A second strategy for assessing the impact of UI benefits, though not PPP, is to exploit differences in the rollout of benefit enhancements across states. While most of the current benefit enhancements were authorized as part of the CARES Act and workers across the country became eligible for them at the same time, the actual rollout of FPUC and PUA was staggered: states took several weeks to reprogram computer systems to make the additional FPUC payments, and longer to set up whole new application and eligibility determination processes for PUA. Claimants should have received benefits that were retroactive to the beginning of the programs, but the liquidity benefits would not arrive until the payments were actually made, and it is plausible that any labor supply response, which would have depended on knowledge of the program, did not fully manifest until the payments actually appeared.

Online appendix figure C11 shows event study plots for the two treatments' effects on hours worked. Both are estimated using a balanced sample of states and calendar dates, running from February 16 to July 11, and include full sets of state, calendar time, and event time indicators. We also control for the presence of an active stay-at-home order. We see little sign that hours changed following the initiation of payments under either program. If anything, PUA might have had a very small positive effect, the opposite of the decline in labor supply that concerned critics.

VI. Conclusion

We are only in the very early stages of the economic recession induced by the COVID-19 pandemic, and much of its story remains to be written. Yet, data accumulated over the last four months already illustrate some important facts and lay out important questions for future research and suggest directions for policy responses.

The labor market collapse triggered by the COVID-19 pandemic was unprecedented in its speed, with the bulk of the job losses happening in a matter of just two weeks. As we show above, there is little evidence that shutdown orders or school closures promulgated by states by themselves played a major role in this collapse. Instead, crescendoing public health concerns in the middle of March, and their subsequent implications for product demand in the "in-person" sectors, appear to be the principal drivers.

The labor market recovered quickly from mid-April through mid-June before plateauing as the virus surged. The recovery, though very partial and interrupted, allowed many workers to return to their prior places of employment within a few months' time. Nevertheless, many firms remain closed and many workers have not returned. It is likely, and the data we report already suggest, that the displaced workers that were left out from this very early stage of the recovery will face a steeper challenge reentering the labor market. Firm-worker matches are going stale, and many of the former employers appear unlikely to reopen. A potential second wave of closings only elevates these concerns.

The speed of the recession underscores the limitations of ad hoc policy responses, and the importance of automatic programs. By the time the

CARES Act passed on March 27, millions of workers had already been displaced, and tens of thousands of firms had already shuttered. It then took several more weeks to implement the various CARES support provisions. Moreover, when CARES was passed, many anticipated that the economic crisis would be short. The FPUC program (the $600 supplement to UI benefits) was set to expire at the end of July, while PPP loans were meant to support firms for only eight weeks. As of this writing, it appears that the period of economic weakness will last much longer, particularly as the COVID-19 public health crisis proved not to be as short-lived as initially anticipated. Policy responses with built-in triggers tied to economic conditions could adjust flexibly and automatically to the evolving situation.

The COVID-19-induced labor market collapse has also been unique in its sectoral composition, hitting mainly (at least in this early stage) the low-wage services and retail sectors of the economy. This is a sharp contrast with the recessions of the recent past, which have hit the higher-paid construction and manufacturing sectors hardest. Furthermore, our data show that within these already low-wage sectors the least advantaged workers have been most negatively affected. Both access to formal credit and the informal safety net (assets and savings, borrowing from family and friends) are likely to be particularly weak for the young, less educated, disproportionally nonwhite workers that have lost work since the pandemic hit. There is a high risk that many in this group will experience deep distress, absent additional policy responses to strengthen the formal safety net before labor demand recovers. In this regard, our evidence above does not suggest any adverse effects of higher unemployment insurance replacement rates on employment in early summer. This suggests that (as in the Great Recession; see Rothstein 2011) concerns about moral hazard effects may be overstated, and that labor demand is the more important determinant of employment outcomes thus far. Whether or not this pattern will hold when the public-health risks of COVID-19 recede is also an important topic for future work.

A central policy concern and question for future research is whether the long-term economic losses associated with mass layoffs in the service and retail sectors, where turnover is generally higher and workers may have less firm-specific human capital, will be as large as those caused by mass layoffs in sectors such as manufacturing, where turnover is generally lower and workers may have more firm-specific human capital.

Another topic for future study concerns the concentration of job losses in businesses that shut down entirely. An important fact that emerges from our early analysis is that firms that were struggling before COVID-19 were much more likely to shut down at the peak of the (first wave) of the pandemic and also much less likely to reopen during the recovery. This suggests a cleansing effect of the recession, but the causes and consequences of this pattern remain to be determined. It is possible that the delayed government response to expand support to small businesses played a role, making it impossible for businesses that were already low on cash before COVID-19 to build a financial bridge until the PPP money became available. It is also possible that banks prioritized healthier firms in their decision to extend PPP loans. The loan-level data that were recently released mask the identity of small borrowers, but future research with identified data about loans to small businesses may help in sorting out these hypotheses.

Altogether, our findings show that this recession has differed sharply from other recent downturns in its speed, the types of firms and workers it affected, workers' beliefs about its longevity and their likelihood of recall, as well as in the nature and size of the policy response. Combining nontraditional sources with traditional labor market data has been key in understanding and responding to the downturn so far, and will remain so as circumstances continue to change rapidly going forward.

ACKNOWLEDGMENTS We thank Justin Germain, Nicolas Ghio, Maggie Li, Salma Nassar, Greg Saldutte, and Manal Saleh for excellent research assistance. We are grateful to Homebase (joinhomebase.com), and particularly Ray Sandza and Andrew Vogeley, for generously providing data. We also thank David Gilbertson for tabulations of Kronos data. Caroline Buckee and Victor Chernozhukov provided extremely valuable comments as discussants. We thank Lucas Finamor for pointing out a coding error in an early version of these analyses.

References

Allcott, Hunt, Levi Boxell, Jacob Conway, Billy Ferguson, Matthew Gentzkow, and Benjamin Goldman. 2020. "Economic and Health Impacts of Social Distancing Policies during the Coronavirus Pandemic." *Social Science Research Network.* https://dx.doi.org/10.2139/ssrn.3610422.

Alon, Titan, Matthias Doepke, Jane Olmstead-Rumsey, and Michele Tertilt. 2020. "This Time It's Different: The Role of Women's Employment in a Pandemic Recession." Working Paper. IZA Institute for Labor Economics. https://www.iza.org/publications/dp/13562/this-time-its-different-the-role-of-womens-employment-in-a-pandemic-recession.

Barrero, Jose Maria, Nicholas Bloom, and Steven J. Davis. 2020. "COVID-19 Is Also a Reallocation Shock." In the present volume of *Brookings Papers on Economic Activity.*

Bartik, Alexander W., Marianne Bertrand, Zoë B. Cullen, Edward L. Glaeser, Michael Luca, and Christopher T. Stanton. 2020. "How Are Small Businesses Adjusting to COVID-19? Early Evidence from a Survey." *Proceedings of the Natural Academy of Sciences* 117, no. 30: 17656–66.

Ben-Michael, Eli, Avi Feller, and Jesse Rothstein. 2019. "Synthetic Controls and Weighted Event Studies with Staggered Adoption." ArXiv:1912.03290. Ithaca, N.Y.: Cornell University.

Bureau of Labor Statistics. 2020. "Frequently Asked Questions: The Impact of the Coronavirus (COVID-19) Pandemic on the Employment Situation for April 2020." https://www.bls.gov/cps/employment-situation-covid19-faq-april-2020.pdf.

Cajner, Tomaz, Leland D. Crane, Ryan A. Decker, John Grigsby, Adrian Hamins-Puertolas, Erik Hurst, Christopher Kurz, and Ahu Yildirmaz. 2020. "The US Labor Market during the Beginning of the Pandemic Recession." In the present volume of *Brookings Papers on Economic Activity.*

Cajner, Tomaz, Andrew Figura, Brendan M. Price, David Ratner, and Alison Weingarden 2020. "Reconciling Unemployment Claims with Job Losses in the First Months of the COVID-19 Crisis." Washington: Board of Governors of the Federal Reserve System. https://www.federalreserve.gov/econres/feds/reconciling-unemployment-claims-with-job-losses-in-the-first-months-of-the-covid-19-crisis.htm.

Callaway, Brantly, and Pedro H. C. Sant'Anna. 2019. "Difference-in-Differences with Multiple Time Periods." Working Paper. http://conference.iza.org/conference_files/EVAL_2019/28549.pdf.

Chernozhukov, Victor, Hiroyuki Kasahara, and Paul Schrimpf. Forthcoming. "Causal Impact of Masks, Policies, Behavior on Early Covid-19 Pandemic in the U.S." *Journal of Econometrics.*

Chetty, Raj, John N. Friedman, Nathaniel Hendren, Michael Stepner, and the Opportunity Insights Team. 2020. "How Did COVID-19 and Stabilization Policies Affect Spending and Employment? A New Real-time Economic Tracker Based on Private Sector Data." Working Paper 27431. Cambridge,

Mass.: National Bureau of Economic Research. https://www.nber.org/papers/w27431.

Cortes, Guido Matias, and Eliza C. Forsythe. 2020. "The Heterogeneous Labor Market Impacts of the Covid-19 Pandemic." Working Paper 20-327. Kalamazoo, Mich.: Upjohn Institute for Employment Research. https://research.upjohn.org/up_workingpapers/327/.

Dey, Matthew, Mark A. Loewenstein, David S. Piccone Jr., and Anne E. Polivka. 2020. "Demographics, Earnings, and Family Characteristics of Workers in Sectors Initially Affected by COVID-19 Shutdowns." *Monthly Labor Review*, US Bureau of Labor Statistics, June. https://doi.org/10.21916/mlr.2020.11.

Forsythe, Eliza, Lisa Kahn, Fabian Lange, and David G. Wiczer. 2020. "Labor Demand in the Time of COVID-19: Evidence from Vacancy Postings and UI Claims." Working Paper 27016. Cambridge, Mass.: National Bureau of Economic Research. https://www.nber.org/papers/w27061.

Ganong, Peter, and Pascal Noel. 2019. "Consumer Spending during Unemployment: Positive and Normative Implications." *American Economic Review* 109, no. 7: 2383–424.

Ganong, Peter, Pascal Noel, and Joseph Vavra. 2020. "US Unemployment Insurance Replacement Rates During the Pandemic." Working Paper 2020-62, August. Chicago: Becker-Friedman Institute, University of Chicago.

Goodman-Bacon, Andrew, and Jan Marcus. 2020. "Using Difference-in-Differences to Identify Causal Effects of COVID-19 Policies." *Survey Research Methods* 14, no. 2. 153–58.

Goolsbee, Austin, and Chad Syverson. 2020. "Fear, Lockdown, and Diversion: Comparing Drivers of Pandemic Economic Decline 2020." Working Paper 27432. Cambridge, Mass.: National Bureau of Economics Research. https://www.nber.org/papers/w27432.

Gupta, Sumeha, Laura Montenovo, Thuy D. Nguyen, Felipe Lozano Rojas, Ian M. Schmutte, Kosali I. Simon, Bruce A. Weinberg, and Coady Wing. 2020. "Effects of Social Distancing Policy on Labor Market Outcomes." Working Paper 27280. Cambridge, Mass.: National Bureau of Economic Research.

Hedin, Thomas J., Geoffrey Schnorr, and Till von Wachter. 2020. "An Analysis of Unemployment Insurance Claims in California during the COVID-19 Pandemic." Policy Brief. Los Angeles: California Policy Lab. https://www.capolicylab.org/publications/june-11th-analysis-of-unemployment-insurance-claims-in-california-during-the-covid-19-pandemic/.

Kurmann, André, Etienne Lalé, and Lien Ta. 2020. "The Impact of COVID-19 on U.S. Employment and Hours: Real-Time Estimates with Homebase Data." Working Paper. http://www.andrekurmann.com/hb_covid.

Lin, Zhixian, and Christopher M. Meissner. 2020. "Health vs. Wealth? Public Health Policies and the Economy During COVID-19." Working Paper 27099. Cambridge, Mass.: National Bureau of Economic Research. https://www.nber.org/papers/w27099.

Mongey, Simon, Laura Pilossoph, and Alex Weinberg. 2020. "Which Workers Bear the Burden of Social Distancing Policies? Working Paper 27085. Cambridge,

Mass.: National Bureau of Economic Research. https://www.nber.org/papers/w27085.

Morath, Eric. 2020. "Coronavirus Relief Often Pays Workers More Than Work." *Wall Street Journal*, April 28. https://www.wsj.com/articles/coronavirus-relief-often-pays-workers-more-than-work-11588066200.

Rothstein, Jesse. 2011. "Unemployment Insurance and Job Search in the Great Recession." *Brookings Papers on Economic Activity*, Fall, 143–210.

Rothstein, Jesse, and Robert G. Valletta. 2017. "Scraping By: Income and Program Participation after the Loss of Extended Unemployment Benefits." *Journal of Policy Analysis and Management* 36, no. 4: 880–908.

SUMEDHA GUPTA
Indiana University–Purdue University Indianapolis

KOSALI SIMON
Indiana University

COADY WING
Indiana University

Mandated and Voluntary Social Distancing during the COVID-19 Epidemic

ABSTRACT The COVID-19 epidemic upended social and economic life in the United States. To reduce transmission, people altered their mobility and interpersonal contact, and state and local governments acted to induce social distancing through across-the-board policies. The epidemic and the subsequent social distancing response led to high unemployment and to efforts to reopen the economy using more-targeted virus mitigation policies.

This paper makes five contributions to studying epidemic policy and mobility. First, we review COVID-19 research on mobility, labor markets, consumer behavior, and health. Second, we sketch a simple model of incentives and constraints facing individuals. Third, we propose a typology of government social distancing policies. Fourth, we review new databases measuring cellular mobility and contact. Fifth, we present regression evidence to help disentangle private versus policy-induced changes in mobility.

During the shutdown phase, large declines in mobility occurred before states adopted stay-at-home (SAH) mandates and in states that never adopted them, suggesting that much of the decline was a private response to the risk of infection. Similarly, in the reopening phase mobility increased rapidly, mostly preceding official state reopenings, with policies explaining almost none of the increase.

Conflict of Interest Disclosure: The authors did not receive financial support from any firm or person for this paper or from any firm or person with a financial or political interest in this paper. They are currently not officers, directors, or board members of any organization with an interest in this paper. No outside party had the right to review this paper before circulation. The views expressed in this paper are those of the authors and do not necessarily reflect those of Indiana University.

D uring the first half of 2020, social distancing became the primary strategy in the United States for reducing the spread of SARS-CoV-2, which is the virus that causes COVID-19. Basic information about the threat posed by the epidemic started to become clear when early cases and deaths occurred in January and February. In March, the level of human physical mobility fell substantially across the country (Gupta, Nguyen, and others 2020). Mobility started to recover somewhat in May and June as initial fears regarding hospital capacity surges diminished (Kowalczyk 2020) and scientific knowledge regarding lower-risk ways of interacting emerged.[1] People started to resume some aspects of regular life, but at the time this article was prepared, mobility still remained far below its pre-epidemic levels.

The prevailing level of mobility is generated in part by the private decisions people make in response to the health threat posed by the epidemic. But state and local governments have also adopted a variety of mandates and regulations to reduce mobility even further. The production of higher levels of social distance and lower levels of physical mobility is not a typical goal for democratic governments. Normally, governments act to encourage and protect freedom of mobility and assembly. During the epidemic, social distancing is valuable because it helps control the epidemic. Unfortunately, the pre-COVID-19 academic literature provides little guidance on which policy levers governments can use to produce the most social distance at the lowest economic cost. And existing economic and public health data systems do not provide much information on patterns of physical mobility and contact, which makes it hard to optimize social distancing policies in an iterative fashion. There may be substantial value in research that identifies principles that can guide policy and perhaps support the development of better-targeted social distancing strategies.

In a series of research papers, we have measured levels of physical mobility using high-frequency data, and we have used the data to assess the role of state and local public policies in shaping levels of social distancing. Our overarching goal is to develop knowledge on the underlying factors that make some distancing policies more effective than others (Gupta, Montenovo, and others 2020; Nguyen and others 2020; Montenovo and others 2020; Lozano Rojas and others 2020; Bento and others 2020; Gupta, Nguyen, and others 2020). In this paper, we provide an overview of social distancing policies, review the literature on what is known to

---

1. Centers for Disease Control and Prevention, "Coronavirus (COVID-19)," https://www.cdc.gov/coronavirus/2019-ncov/index.html.

date of the effects of social distancing key outcomes, explain a collection of new data sources that can be used to track levels of mobility, and present a core set of empirical results from the shutdown and reopening phases of the epidemic.

The paper is in seven parts. Section I discusses the literature on social distancing and physical mobility in the context of the COVID-19 epidemic. Most of the literature is very recent, and we attempt to summarize the key questions, empirical strategies, and conclusions that have emerged so far. In section II, we sketch a microeconomic model of household production and choice that incorporates physical contact and infection risk into the agent's decision process. The model is very simple and abstracts from many features of the real world. However, it helps clarify the incentives and constraints that affect decisions to engage in physical contact with others, and it suggests broad principles that might be used to guide the design of social distancing policies. Section III reviews the long list of public policies that state and local governments have actually adopted during the epidemic and explains how we organized and grouped these policies to facilitate empirical analysis. Section IV provides an overview of the cell signal–based data sources that we are using to measure mobility patterns across states and over time.

These mobility data are not perfect measures of the underlying behavior of interest. We look at different measures from several sources. But at their core, all of the measures are constructed by tracking (anonymously) the physical location of smart devices. They proxy human mobility under the assumption that smart devices change locations because people carry them from one place to the next. But mobility measures generally do not reveal whether a person who changes locations remains six feet away from other people during the trip. Mobility measures also don't indicate whether the person wore a mask or how often they washed their hands. Despite their limitations, cell phone–based mobility data are probably the best proxy measure of social distancing currently available. One of the main advantages of our line of research is the use of multiple measures from multiple data systems. This provides some ability to assess the robustness of our results.[2] Section V lays out the event study framework we use in much of

2. It is possible that future researchers will have access to richer data on how person-to-person contact is changing. For example, it is conceivable that data harvested from video recordings might provide information on how often people touch each other to shake hands, hug, exchange objects, and so on. Data like these could provide important insight into behavior during the epidemic.

our empirical work. We present results in section VI and offer conclusions in section VII.

I. Related Research

In the four months since the start of the epidemic in the United States, the social science literature on the epidemic and the policy response has grown very rapidly. The papers in the emerging literature are organized around a collection of broad research questions: (1) How has the epidemic affected the way people interact with each other and with physical spaces? (2) How has the response to the epidemic affected the level of economic activity? (3) How much of the change in mobility and economic activity is generated by private responses to the health and safety threat from the virus, and how much of this change has been induced by public policies themselves? (4) How have various public policies and private responses affected the downstream severity of the epidemic?

The first two questions are essentially descriptive. They have been answered using a combination of existing and new data sources. Research on questions about physical mobility and person-to-person contact has a long history in the literature on infectious disease epidemiology. But the conventional methods used in that literature are not well suited to monitoring population behaviors in real time. The COVID-19 epidemic has led to heavier reliance on data harvested from smart devices, mapping applications, and financial transactions. These data sources have expanded the set of concepts that can be brought into the surveillance system, but it is still not clear how different types of information are useful for public health decision making. Understanding the strengths and weaknesses of new data sources is one of the key challenges in the literature. Balancing the value of high-frequency and low-frequency measures for monitoring the state of the epidemic is another overarching concern.

The third and fourth questions are concerned with the causal effects of public policies adopted during the epidemic, and to some extent with the causal effect of changes in knowledge about the state of the epidemic. One line of work, the mobility literature, is concerned with the first-stage effects of policy on transmission-related behaviors. Another line of work is essentially about the possible unintended consequences of the same policies. Research on the effects of distancing policies on labor market outcomes and consumer behavior falls into this category. A third line of work is concerned with the way that different policy responses have shaped the course of the epidemic as measured by COVID-19 caseloads and deaths. In all three streams of work, event studies and generalized difference-in-differences designs have emerged as the main strategy for trying to isolate the causal effects of policy changes. These designs are natural given the setting and available data. However, they rely on strong assumptions that may fail in some circumstances and not others.

In the online appendix, we include two tables that summarize key pieces of information from a large set of working papers and recently published articles. Online appendix table A1 lists papers that provide estimates of the effects of one or more COVID-19 shutdown policies. To the extent possible, we report the main quantitative effect estimate provided in each paper. But we caution the reader that these "treatment effect" estimates do not correspond to a common structural parameter. We should not expect the magnitude of the policy effects to be the same across studies based on different outcome measures, different policy definitions, and different time horizons. Not all of the studies we examined offer estimates of the effects of COVID-19 policies. Online appendix table A2 gives a summary of these papers; there is no column for a specific quantitative effect size, but these papers provide useful context and are organized by the same subtopics as the first table.

I.A. Pre-COVID-19 Epidemiological Research on Mobility

Prior to the COVID-19 epidemic, the economic and public health data systems in the United States were not set up to measure close physical interactions at a level of frequency and detail necessary to provide nearly real-time information about human movement and mixing during an epidemic (Buckee and others 2020). However, infectious disease researchers have made heavy use of information from social contact surveys. These are point-in-time (cross-sectional) household or individual surveys that collect detailed information on each respondent's daily contacts with other people who have specific age and gender attributes (Mossong and others 2008; Bento and Rohani 2016; Prem, Cook, and Jit 2017). Static social contact surveys have proven to be useful for studying endemic diseases and seasonal diseases that occur fairly reliably in a population because sudden disruptions of behavior are not expected.

Contact surveys are most often used to estimate age-specific contact matrices, which are a way to describe the frequency of contact between people from different age strata in a given population (Mossong and others 2008; Prem, Cook, and Jit 2017). Survey-based estimates of contact matrices are used to build more sophisticated models of the spread of infectious diseases within and between populations with different demographic and geographic structures (Mossong and others 2008; Rohani, Zhong, and King 2010; Bento and Rohani 2016; Prem, Cook, and Jit 2017). Incorporating information on the contact structure of a population produces structural models that more successfully explain shifts in disease prevalence over time and across age groups. Models that ignore the contact structure in a population may misinterpret the epidemiological processes that determine the spread of the disease. Although contact surveys provide useful information about the average contact patterns in a population, they are costly, slow, and may suffer from recall bias and coverage gaps (Mossong and others 2008; Prem, Cook, and Jit 2017). Thus, researchers generally do not use contact surveys to empirically track behavioral changes during an epidemic. Likewise, we are not aware of any studies that use repeated waves of a contact survey to estimate the effects of social distancing policies on contact patterns. That said, things may be different during the COVID-19 epidemic. For example, in recent work on COVID-19, Jarvis and others (2020) fielded a longitudinal contact survey that collected data on the same people each week for sixteen weeks. They compare their COVID-19-era contact data with data from an earlier cross-sectional contact survey collected in 2006 and find substantial changes in the contact patterns since 2006.

Although contact surveys may still play an important role, they are a cumbersome way to monitor the population in real time during an epidemic. In a major outbreak, it is critical to assess the effects of public policies and informational events on the individual behaviors that shape contact patterns. One alternative to surveys that has proven valuable are aggregate mobility data, such as the smart device data we use in this paper. Wesolowski and others (2012) pioneered the use of cell phone records to understand the role of human travel patterns on the spread of malaria in Kenya. They found that human travel facilitates the spread of malaria parasites much farther than possible through mosquito dispersal alone. Information about the importance of specific travel routes in spreading the epidemic provides a guide for policy efforts to reduce transmission. More recently, Wesolowski and others (2015) used cell phone data to study the role of travel patterns on the spread of *Dengue virus* during an epidemic in Pakistan in 2013. They found that previous model-based descriptions of human mobility did not perform well in describing the travel patterns captured by the cell phone data and that incorporating the cell phone travel data led to epidemiological models that were more accurate in explaining the spread of the epidemic over time and across locations. Wesolowski and others (2016) offer a review of the emerging role of cell phone data in the study of infectious diseases and epidemics.

Aggregate mobility data provide a way to measure the intensity of movement within and between specific geographic locations. However, the underlying data are harvested from convenient sources, like cell phone records, which may not be representative of the population in the way that a formal survey sample might be. The mobility measures that can be constructed from aggregate data also lack the careful attention to construct validity that is a feature of the measures available in well-designed contact surveys. Despite these limitations, the aggregate data allow researchers to measure mobility using a daily time series available at various geographic levels of detail. These time series data can be compared with pre-epidemic baselines and can be used as a foundation for policy analysis based on interrupted time series and difference-in-differences research designs. They offer nearly real-time insight into the extent to which people are complying with various kinds of social distancing initiatives (Wesolowski and others 2015). Although aggregate data are still relatively new, previous work shows that they can be integrated with other epidemiological data and has explored methods that account for spatial and temporal dependence to support accurate inferences regarding dynamics on scales appropriate to pathogens and their human hosts (Keeling and Rohani 2008).

The pre-COVID-19 literature provides clear empirical evidence that human movement shapes transmission dynamics (Bharti and others 2015). The details depend on the pathogen, of course. But research suggests that travel and mobility-related behaviors are important in both introducing novel pathogens into susceptible populations and in determining how easily the pathogen spreads by altering the frequency of contact between infected and susceptible individuals (Wesolowski and others 2016). For example, Mari and others (2012) examine the role of travel patterns and waterways on spread of cholera. And Gog and others (2014) study the spread of the 2009 influenza epidemic in the United States. They find that models that account for both spatial diffusion and local school opening dates fit the data the best. There is also evidence from the pre-COVID-19 data-driven studies that social distancing policies can reduce the magnitude of an epidemic (Bootsma and Ferguson 2007; Hatchett, Mecher, and Lipsitch 2007). In addition, Ferguson and others (2005) use a simulation model to assess alternative strategies for containing an influenza epidemic in Asia. They find—for specific disease parameters—that strategies that combine antiviral medication with social distancing interventions are most successful.

I.B. Mobility Patterns and Social Distancing–Related Behaviors

One of the most active strands of social science research on the COVID-19 epidemic is concerned with how mobility patterns have changed in response to the risk of infection and in response to state and local social distancing policies. The literature has come to a consensus that human mobility dropped precipitously in mid-March, very early in the shutdown sequence and around the time of the March 13 national emergency proclamation (Gupta, Nguyen, and others 2020; Cronin and Evans 2020). The mid-March decline is large and quite sudden. Most studies have used high-frequency data sources derived from smart device apps. These data sources do not have a long history of use in economics. As we mentioned in the discussion of pre-COVID-19 research, epidemiologists have been using similar data to study epidemics since at least Wesolowski and others (2012). So far, the emerging economics literature on mobility and social distancing has focused on simple descriptive time series work and on quasi-experimental estimates of the effects of state and local policies on mobility patterns. Although there is overlap between the methods used in the economics and epidemiology literature, it is probably fair to say that the epidemiology literature focuses less on the determinants of mobility and more on the role of prevailing mobility patterns in the dynamics of a given epidemic. They use cell phone data to build better structural models of the epidemic across time and space. Economists have focused somewhat more on the idea that mobility patterns are an outcome that public policies are trying to change in the population.

One concern in the literature on mobility is that the smart device users underlying the mobility measures are unlikely to be a representative sample from the population. However, the sample size underlying the data is at least 10 percent of the US population, and the timing and size of the fall in mobility seem to be similar regardless of the mobility data and concept used in individual studies. That is, the basic time series is similar for measures of staying at home, going in to work, average distance traveled, percent of individuals who travel out of state or out of county, indexes of how much foot traffic occurs in certain types of establishments, and so on.

Some studies—such as our own—estimate how much of the change is attributable to various state and local social distancing policies. The literature has devoted the most attention to the effects of stay-at-home (SAH) mandates, which occurred later in the shutdown sequence implemented in most states. Although there are a few outlier results, most studies find that SAH policies reduced measured mobility by about 5–10 percent within the first week after the policy was implemented (Abouk and Heydari 2020; Alexander and Karger 2020; Andersen 2020; Chen and others 2020; Cicala and others 2020; Cronin and Evans 2020; Dave and others 2020; Elenev and others 2020; Engle, Stromme, and Zhou 2020; Goolsbee and Syverson 2020; Lin and Meissner 2020; Painter and Qiu 2020; Gupta, Nguyen, and others 2020).

The outsize attention to SAH mandates makes sense since they have proven to be the most controversial laws and they seem to be nominally the most restrictive. However, some studies have also examined the effects of other policies, like school closures, which often happened sooner. But it may be hard to reliably separate the effects as multiple policies were implemented sequentially (but in close proximity in time) and sometimes even simultaneously.

I.C. Labor Market Outcomes

The losses of employment since the start of the COVID-19 epidemic are massive. There were 20.5 million job losses in April alone and rapid increases in unemployment insurance (UI) applications (Lozano Rojas and others 2020; Montenovo and others 2020). The unemployment rate rose from 4.4 percent in March to 14.7 percent in April. Also, many people may have dropped out of the labor market (Coibion, Gorodnichenko, and Weber 2020b) and would not be captured in unemployment statistics. The unprecedented increase in initial UI claims in the early part of the pandemic was largely across the board and occurred in all states, suggesting that the economic disruption was driven by both the health shock itself and the state policies to induce social distancing (Lozano Rojas and others 2020; Gupta, Montenovo, and others 2020). On average, the literature notes a modest 2–8 percent increase in UI claims due to state policies, with business closures having a larger effect than stay-at-home orders (Forsythe and others 2020; Kong and Prinz 2020; Lozano Rojas and others 2020).

The timeline and nature of job losses is noteworthy. Relative to the timing of the human mobility reduction, job market losses occurred later (Gupta, Montenovo, and others 2020). It is possible that labor market responses were delayed partly because of increases in the number of workers who reported that they were "employed but absent from work" in the monthly Current Population Surveys (CPS). That is, people may have been temporarily unemployed but expecting to be recalled to the same jobs. This could have led to an undercount of point-in-time unemployment levels.

Surprisingly, research suggests that workers who remained employed during the early epidemic did not experience much change in hours worked or earnings (Cheng and others 2020; Gupta, Montenovo, and others 2020). During the shutdown period employment declines were steeper for Hispanics, workers age 20 to 24, and those with high school degrees and some college. Pre-epidemic sorting into occupations with more potential for remote work and industries that were deemed essential explain a large share of gaps in recent unemployment for key racial, ethnic, age, and education subpopulations (Montenovo and others 2020).

As of this writing, since April, there have been reductions in the number of new unemployment claims and signs of improved labor market performance. Studies note that the official state reopenings have contributed a modest 0–4 percent increase in employment; decreases in job loss among those employed were smaller (Cheng and others 2020; Chetty and others 2020). Moreover, the majority of those who were reemployed appear to have returned to their previous employment, with the rate of reemployment decreasing with time since job loss. Lastly, the groups that had the highest unemployment rates in April—Hispanic and Black workers, youngest and oldest workers, and women—have had the lowest reemployment rates (Cheng and others 2020). These racial and ethnic labor market disparities are important because they add to already existing disparities in the extent of the health tolls of COVID-19 (Benitez, Courtemanche, and Yelowitz 2020; McLaren 2020; Hooper, Nápoles, and Pérez-Stable 2020).

I.D. Consumer Spending

Research to date consistently finds that consumer spending also fell by approximately 35 percent in mid-March (Chetty and others 2020; Alexander and Karger 2020). The decline in spending occurred despite close to $2 trillion in additional federal spending as of July for COVID-19 economic support. Rates of food insecurity have also climbed substantially (Bitler, Hoynes, and Schanzenbach 2020). Consumer spending may have fallen in part because people reduced their demand for consumption goods that require high levels of social interaction. That is, efforts to avoid transmitting and contracting the virus is probably part of the story. However, spending may also have been affected by the timing of federal stimulus payments, enhanced unemployment benefits, and the consequences of state shutdown and reopening policies.

Research documents that in addition to spending having declined immediately and dramatically, there are important shifts in the composition of people's consumption bundles. Consumer spending at small businesses and large retail outlets has fallen. But spending on orders of food has been rising (Alexander and Karger 2020). The decline in consumer spending happened across the country (Alexander and Karger 2020; Baker and others 2020; Chetty and others 2020) and is highly correlated with a self-reported measure of whether a person was under a lockdown (Coibion, Gorodnichenko, and Weber 2020a).

Despite declines in spending and high rates of food insecurity, federal stimulus spending appears to have ensured an actual fall in the poverty rate after the start of the pandemic, relative to pre-pandemic levels (Han, Meyer, and Sullivan 2020). This is noteworthy, as the start of the pandemic occurred in a strong growing economy, thus it will be important to monitor consumer spending rebounds and implications for financial health.

I.E. Health Outcomes

The foremost objective of state social distancing policies on the whole has been to mitigate the spread of SARS-CoV-2. A major concern is that if the virus is allowed to spread too quickly, local health care systems could be overwhelmed. Even a slower spread of the virus could lead to tremendous loss of life.

Overall, the emerging literature seems to agree that the intense social distancing that occurred between mid-March and mid-April did indeed "flatten the curve" during the early months of the epidemic. The estimated effect of state policies on case and death rates vary somewhat depending on the specific policy measure examined in the study and also on the time frame of the study. However, most studies estimate a 20–60 percent reduction in cases and deaths (Chernozhukov, Kasaha, and Schrimpf 2020; Dave and others 2020; Friedson and others 2020; Jinjarak and others 2020) and a 2–9 percent reduction in daily growth rates of cases and deaths (Courtemanche and others 2020; Lyu and Wehby 2020; Wang and others 2020; Yehya, Venkataramani, and Harhay 2020) as a result of mandatory policies and informational events.

I.F. Research Related to Reopening

Declining case and death rates have been critical to determine when states can safely reopen—the CDC recommended two weeks of steady decline in cases and deaths prior to lifting any social distancing mandates. Our work finds that human mobility, although still below the pre-COVID-19 level, started to recover somewhat prior to official state reopenings and then increased by a further 1–8 percent in response to official state reopenings (Nguyen and others 2020). Again, both voluntary behavior and mandates appear to guide behavior. The relatively modest increase in mobility following reopenings is not surprising since the risk of infection has not changed. Moreover, state reopenings cannot be viewed as the reversal of state closures.[3] Although states varied in the exact timing of their closure mandates, once implemented, school closures or stay-at-home orders were relatively homogeneous across the states. In contrast, state reopenings have varied a great deal in nature—immediate versus phased reopenings, sectors or industries that initially reopened, and capacity limits on businesses. Despite a slow and partial return to economic activity, reports from the summer note a surge in cases and deaths following reopenings (Vervosh and Healy 2020; Witte and Guarino 2020).

If rates of cases and deaths continue to grow, states will be faced with the difficult decision to implement second rounds of shutdowns, which research finds can be effective in curbing the spread but are also economically very costly. During the fall of 2020, states appeared to be pursuing a more nuanced policy stance based on adaptive behaviors like mask wearing, maintaining six feet of distance from others, capacity limits, and implementing designated business hours for the at-risk subpopulations, such as the elderly, to minimize interaction with others. Since significant voluntary social distancing occurred in response to information about COVID-19 in mid-March, we would expect that individuals would voluntarily adopt these practices as well to lower their risk of infection. However, the large voluntary increases in social distancing in the early days of the epidemic hide considerable heterogeneity in behavioral response to the threat of infection along lines of political affiliation, race, and other socioeconomic and demographic characteristics (Aksoy, Ganslmeier, and Poutvaara 2020; Allcott and others 2020; Huang and others 2020; Mongey and Weinberg 2020).

II. Theoretical Framework

In epidemiology, the dominant paradigm for analyzing an infectious disease outbreak is the susceptible-infected-recovered (SIR) model (Kermack and McKendrick 1927), which examines dynamics of an epidemic that arise as a population moves through disease-relevant states. This model does

3. Based on authors' collection of dates of implementation and expiry of state stay-at-home orders and official reopening timelines we note that in only three states—Florida, Idaho, and Missouri—did official state reopenings coincide with the lifting of stay-at-home orders. In most cases stay-at-home orders and school closures expired after the date of initial reopenings (Nguyen and others 2020; COVID-19 US State Policy Database, www.tinyurl.com/statepolicies).

not provide much insight into the way that an epidemic might alter the behavior of people in a population. The economic epidemiology literature nests a micro-level model of individual behavior inside the SIR framework to try to model how the role of endogenous self-protection behaviors might alter the dynamics of an epidemic (Philipson 1996; Kremer 1996; Geoffard and Philipson 1996; Philipson 2000). A much larger literature in economics explores individual choices and investments that affect health (Grossman 1972, 2000). This literature allows health to affect the utility function directly and also indirectly as an input into many other activities that people value. A key point is that health is not the only thing that people value, and it is common for people to make trade-offs between health and other objectives. Indeed, a major subfield examines the economics of risky health behaviors such as smoking, drug use, risky sex, poor diet, and dangerous driving (Cawley and Ruhm 2011; Viscusi 1993).

In this section, we sketch a simple microeconomic model in which a utility-maximizing agent allocates time and resources between activities with different risks of infection with SARS-CoV-2. The basic model is built on the household production model introduced by Becker (1965). The starting point is a utility function defined over a set of commodities or experiences; inputs to the production of these commodities may require physical interaction with others, which may diminish the production of health. We focus on a utility function defined over three commodities:

$$u = u(z, o, h)$$

In the model, z is a vector of regular commodities, such as housing, home-cooked meals, or in-restaurant dining with friends; o represents market work (occupation), which pays a wage that determines the value of a person's time and shapes the person's budget constraint, but also enters the utility function directly; h represent a person's health status.

Each of the commodities in the utility function must be produced with market goods, time, and physical interaction with others. To make these relationships concrete, use $j \in (z, o, h)$ to index the three commodities. Let x_j be an input vector of market goods that may be used in the production of commodity j. Let p_x be the vector of market prices associated with the market inputs. The variable e_j represents the quantity of a person's time (effort) that is devoted to the production of commodity j. Finally, d_j measures physical interaction (distance) with nonhousehold members involved in the production of commodity j. The person produces the regular commodities z using the production function $z = z(x_z, e_z, d_z)$. Similarly, the person produces the market work (occupation) commodity by combining market goods (e.g., a computer, suitable clothing, a car), time, and physical interaction with nonhousehold members using a production function $o = o(x_o, e_o, d_o)$.

The health production function is somewhat different because it may depend on the infection risk associated with the physical interactions a person makes in the production of the other commodities. For simplicity, we assume that all physical interactions generate the same risk, and we ignore spillovers from behaviors of others in the community. Let $D = \sum_j d_j$ represent the total amount of physical interaction with nonhousehold members that the person experiences across all of their home production activities. The health production function is $h = h(x_h, e_h, \rho D)$. In the model, ρ is an infectious disease risk parameter normalized so that $\rho = 1$ for the health risk associated with physical interaction with other people during "normal" times. We assume that $\dfrac{\partial h}{\partial \rho D} < 0$, which means that health is declining with physical interaction with other people and with the level of infectious disease risk at that time and local area.[4]

The model sets up a trade-off between health and the production and consumption of other commodities that raise utility but also require potentially health-damaging exposure to the virus. The COVID-19 epidemic can be viewed as an exogenous change in the prevailing level of the infectious disease parameter ρ. The epidemic does not alter anyone's utility function or production technology. But people faced with higher values of ρ may nevertheless choose a new mix of commodities to produce and consume.

To pay for market goods, at prices p_x, the person relies on earned and unearned income. Suppose that M is the person's nonlabor income, w is his or her wage rate, and e_o is hours devoted to occupational work. As above, x_j represents the vector of inputs used in the production of commodity j. The person's budget constraint is $x_z' p_x + x_o' p_x + x_h' p_x = M + w e_o$, where e_o is the amount of time the person devotes to market work. In addition to the

---

4. In our main analysis, we focus on a utility function with a single health commodity. But it is also logical to view h as a vector of health commodities, each element of which may have a production function that depends on physical interaction in a different way. For example, we might say that $h = (m, r)$ is a vector consisting of mental health (m) and respiratory health (r). Then $m = m(x_m, e_m, \rho_m D)$ and $r = r(x_r, e_r, \rho_r D)$ would represent mental health and respiratory health production functions, respectively. In this case, it might be reasonable to expect that $\dfrac{\partial m}{\partial \rho_m D} > 0$ even though $\dfrac{\partial r}{\partial \rho_r D} < 0$ so that physical interaction improves mental health and worsens respiratory health.

financial budget constraint, the person has a fixed time endowment so that the sum of time spent in market work and across the production of various commodities must satisfy $T = e_z + e_o + e_h$. The person's problem is to max $u(z, o, h)$, subject to (1) $x_z' p_x + x_o' p_x + x_h' p_x = M + we_o$, (2) $T = e_z + e_o + e_h$, (3) $z = z(x_z, e_z, d_z)$, (4) $o = o(x_o, e_o, d_o)$, and (5) $h = h(x_h, e_h, \rho D)$.

Writing out first-order conditions and solving the system of equations would lead to a collection of demand functions for each market input, time use, and level of physical interaction with other people. These demand curves are derived from the person's demand for commodities (z), occupational work (o), and health (h). Let $x_z = x_z (p, w, F, \rho)$ be the person's derived demand for market good inputs into the production of z. Likewise, let $e_z = e_z(p, w, F, \rho)$ represent demand for time devoted to the production of z. And let $d_z = d_z(p, w, F, \rho)$ be the person's demand for physical interaction in order to produce z. Similar input demand functions are defined for inputs required to produce the occupational work commodity (o) and to produce health (h).

In this framework, the COVID-19 epidemic amounts to an external increase in ρ, which is the infection risk generated by physical interaction with other people. Marginal increases in ρ affect utility through the effect of infection risk on health production. However, larger changes in ρ may also generate indirect effects on utility through behavioral changes in the demand for other commodities, market goods, and time uses.

The private responses to the epidemic are captured by partial derivatives of the various demand functions. For example, $\dfrac{\partial d_j}{\partial \rho}$ is the effect of an increase in infection risk on the person's demand for physical interaction involved in producing commodity j. Typically, we expect $\dfrac{\partial d_j}{\partial \rho} < 0$ so that infection risk will reduce the demand for physical interaction as an input to other commodities.

The model suggests that an increase in infection risk leads to fewer physical interactions even in the absence of any government policies. Further, the fall in demand for physical interaction is likely to alter the demand for market goods and services that people tend to consume in conjunction with physical interaction. The nature of these changes depends on the commodity production functions. Physical interaction may be a close substitute for market goods in the production of some commodities. In these cases, an increase in infection risk (ρ) will increase the demand for substitute market inputs. In other cases, physical interaction and market goods may be complements in the production function. Then rising infection risk will tend to reduce demand for the market goods that are complements to physical interaction. Similar patterns hold for time use. The change in demand for market goods, time use, and interaction do not flow from a change in preferences. The issue is that people cannot produce certain commodities as safely as they did in the past. In this sense, the disruption from the epidemic flows from a negative supply shock.

Individual reductions in physical interaction may confer benefits on other people. The positive externalities may justify government policies to promote social distancing. One class of social distancing policies would target physical interactions directly. For example, the government might levy a tax on physical interaction, issue advice and mandates that attach stigma to interactions, or regulate the group size of interactions. These policies will tend to reduce the demand for physical interaction, but they will also affect the demand for various input goods and services.

A different class of policies might focus on market goods that are viewed as strong complements to physical distancing. For example, the government might levy higher taxes on various kinds of public transit, admission to parks and beaches, or restaurant meals. Tax instruments like this have not been widely used during the epidemic. Instead, governments have tended to mandate that certain types of goods and services may not be sold during the epidemic. Closing restaurants and bars reduces demand for the input goods directly but also could reduce demand for physical distancing, which is a complement to visits to these establishments.

A third class of policies might target the infection risk parameter. For example, governments might require people to wear masks during physical interactions. A successful mask policy could be represented as a factor that diminishes the realized effect of the infection risk parameter. For instance, people wearing masks might produce health $h = h(x_h, e_h, \alpha \rho D)$, where $0 < \alpha < 1$ is the effect of the mask and the "effective" infection risk is now $\alpha \rho < \rho$. At current margins, infection risk mitigation policies might increase the demand for physical interaction and for the goods and services that go along with it. These kinds of policies may have important economic benefits because they would help resolve the supply shock in the economy.

The model we examine here treats infection risk as an aggregate parameter and focuses on the way that changes in infection risk might affect demand for physical interaction, market goods, and time use. A richer model would specify a health production function that varied with characteristics of the person, perhaps including factors like age and preexisting health conditions that make a person particularly sensitive to COVID-19. In that setting, the magnitude of private responses to changes in infection risk would vary across people, and there would be a case for more-targeted government interventions that focused not only on goods and interactions but also on people with higher health costs of infection.

III. Government Policies during the Epidemic

In this section, we provide an overview and rough typology of the strategies that state and local governments have used during the shutdown and reopening phase of the epidemic.

III.A. Typology of Policies during Shutdown

We assembled data on state- and county-level events and social distancing policies using information from several policy tracking projects, including the National Governors Association, Kaiser Family Foundation, national media outlets, the data file by Fullman and colleagues, and Raifman and Raifman (2020).[5] We began with a large collection of fifteen to twenty separate policies that are tracked by one or more outlets. However, many policies, such as state laws banning utility cancellations for nonpayment of bills, are unlikely to directly affect mobility in a major way. In addition, most tracking services record different degrees of the same type of policy, such as gathering restrictions by the size of the group affected or closures of different types of economic activity. Policy trackers also differ occasionally in whether they follow only mandates or also reported government recommendations.

Given the difficulty of estimating effects of a large number of policies at once, one of our first tasks was to organize and structure data on the core public policy instruments that state governments have been using during the epidemic.[6] We reduced the raw number of policies under consideration by assessing which mandates and information events were logically connected with individual behaviors related to mobility and social distancing. We were also guided by the joint timing of policy changes, whether a policy was adopted by a large number of states, and whether there was concordance about the timing and nature of the policy across multiple sources.

---

5. "State COVID-19 Data and Policy Actions," Kaiser Family Foundation, https://www.kff.org/coronavirus-covid-19/issue-brief/state-covid-19-data-and-policy-actions/, accessed July 2020; Fullman and others, "State-Level Social Distancing Policies in Response to COVID-19 in the US," version 1.04 [data set], http://www.covid19statepolicy.org.

6. In Gupta, Nguyen, and others (2020) we follow county policymaking as well, although there was much less activity on that front; we focus only on state policies here.

Most of our empirical work distinguishes two broad types of state informational events and government mandates. The informational events we consider are the announcement of the state's first COVID-19 case and death; we collect these dates through the CDC website, other repositories, and by searching news outlets. Public information events may induce people to voluntarily engage in individual behaviors that mitigate transmission, including social distancing, frequent hand washing, and mask wearing. Government mandates consist of a considerable set of state-level policies related to emergency declarations, school and business closures, and stay-at-home orders. Most of our work revolves around the date at which these mandates became active. However, we often also consider the date of announcement as a sensitivity check and to assess the possibility of anticipatory responses. On average, the announcement and implementation dates were usually about two days apart.[7]

The six state mandates we tracked, listed here, are roughly in the order in which they rolled out across states.

Emergency declarations: these include state of emergency, public health emergency, and public health disaster declarations. All states issued these policies by March 16, 2020. The federal government issued an emergency declaration on March 13, 2020. States may use these declarations in order to pursue other policies, such as school closure, to access federal disaster relief funds, or to allow the executive branch to make decisions for which they would usually need legislative approval. By statute, states are able to exercise additional powers when they issue emergency declarations. In a typical state, governors are able to declare an emergency, and usually do so for weather-related cases, although some states, such as Massachusetts in 2014, have invoked public health emergencies in order to address addiction-related issues (Haffajee, Parmet, and Mello 2014). In some states, city mayors also may issue emergency declarations. In our conceptual framework, emergency declarations are typically the earliest form of state policy that might induce a mobility response; however, we think that emergency declarations are best viewed as an information instrument that signals to the population that the public health situation is serious and that they should act accordingly.

School closures: some school districts closed prior to state-level actions; however, by April 7, 2020, all fifty states had issued statewide school closure

---

7. COVID-19 US State Policy Database, www.tinyurl.com/statepolicies.

rulings.[8] While school closure policies would reduce some travel (of children and staff), they could reduce adult mobility as well if parents changed work travel immediately as a result. School closures may also contribute to a sense of precaution in the community. Although many spring break plans were canceled, it is possible we might also capture increased travel due to school closures.

Restaurant restrictions and partial nonessential business (NEB) restrictions: these policies were also fairly widespread, with forty-nine states having such restrictions by April 7.[9] This law would directly restrict movement due to the inability to dine at locations other than one's home.

Gathering recommendations or restrictions: these policies range from advising against gatherings, to allowing gatherings as long as they are not very large, to cancellation of all gatherings of more than a few individuals. There was a lot of action on this front: forty-eight states enacted gatherings policies. In principle, these laws would reduce mobility in a manner similar to restaurant closings. However, gathering restrictions are hard to enforce, and they rely on cooperation from residents. Their effects on mobility patterns are apt to be negligible, and we generally do not focus on these policies in our empirical work.

Nonessential business (NEB) closures: NEB closures typically occurred when states had already conducted partial closings and then opted to close all nonessential businesses. Thirty-one states acted in this area during our study period. NEB closures could have fairly large effects, as they reduce where purchases happen and also reduce work travel. Moreover, they provide a binding constraint on individual behavior; even those not voluntarily complying with social distancing recommendations had fewer locations to visit.

Stay-at-home (SAH): these policies (also known as shelter-in-place laws) are the strongest and were the last of the closure policies to be implemented. SAH mandates may reduce mobility in very direct and obvious ways. A few states also enacted curfews specifying the hours when individuals can

---

8. Verified through Fullman and others, "State-Level Social Distancing Policies in Response to COVID-19 in the US," version 1.04 [data set], http://www.covid19state policy.org; "Map: Coronavirus and School Closures in 2019–2020," *Education Week*, https://www.edweek.org/ew/section/multimedia/map-coronavirus-and-school-closures.html, accessed April 10, 2020.

9. Fullman and others, "State-Level Social Distancing Policies in Response to COVID-19 in the US," version 1.04 [data set], http://www.covid19statepolicy.org.

leave their homes. However, we do not classify curfew policies as equivalent to SAH mandates. Several states have not issued an SAH mandate in any part of the state (Vervosh and Healy 2020); as of April 3, these included Arkansas, Iowa, Nebraska, North Dakota, Oklahoma, South Dakota, and Wyoming.

The state policies adopted during the shutdown phase occurred very rapidly. With an eye toward econometric models, we worked to understand the order and timing of the sequence of policies and to assess the extent to which it is feasible to meaningfully separate the effects of different policies. Figure 1 shows how the share of the US population that was subject to each social distancing policy evolved over time.[10]

Emergency declarations appear early and separate from the other policies. However, school closures, gathering restrictions, and restaurant and nonessential business closings often coincide so closely in time that it seems infeasible to identify their effects separately in a regression analysis. Given the information on the sequence and timing of state policies, we condensed the six major policy events to a set of four major events during the shutdown phase: state first cases and deaths, emergency declarations, school closures, and stay-at-home mandates.

As this section demonstrates, there are some principles we use for selecting which of the large number of different state policies currently discussed in the COVID-19 policy literature we should track in our research on mobility. The key decision factor was ensuring close connections to our theoretic framework while considering (informally) whether we could plausibly separate the effects of these policies.

III.B. Typology of Reopening Policies

We collected and coded data on state reopening policies, starting with descriptions of reopening plans in the *New York Times*. We gathered additional information on the reopening schedules for each state through internet searches.[11] We consider two primary reopening dates: date of announcement of upcoming reopenings and date of actual reopening. We define the state's reopening date as the earliest date at which that state issued a reopening policy of any type. The dates we determined as the first reopening event for

---

10. Figure 2.2 in Gupta, Nguyen, and others (2020) shows the timeline of the policy changes that occurred in each state, and figure 3.2 shows the timing of the first cases and deaths by state. There we show that the first COVID-19 case in a state is easily set apart in timing from the other policies, as is the first COVID-19 death.

11. We provide the reopening policies information we have compiled from various sources at https://github.com/nguyendieuthuy/ReOpeningPlans.

Figure 1. US Population Covered by State Closure and Reopening Policies

US population (percent)

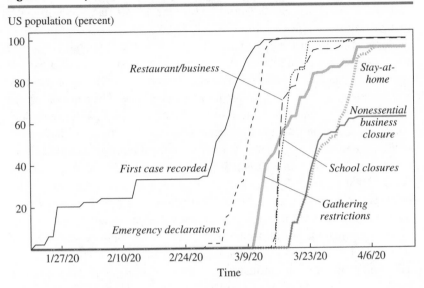

US population (percent)

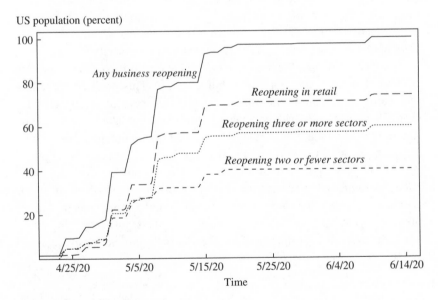

Source: Authors' compilations.
Note: Data cover January 20 to June 15, 2020.

each state are identical to the ones depicted in figures used by the *New York Times*.[12] Starting with South Carolina, by June 15, all states had officially reopened in some phased form.

Some states never formally adopted a stay-at-home order, but even these states implemented partial business closures (e.g., restaurant closures) and some nonessential business restrictions. Of course, measures of mobility and economic activity have fallen in these states as well because of private social distancing choices. In addition, the lack of an official closure does not mean that state governments cannot take actions to try to hasten the return to regular levels of activity. For example, South Dakota did not have a statewide stay-at-home order, but the governor announced a "back to normal" plan that set May 1 as the reopening date for many businesses. Our study period to examine the effect of reopenings on mobility commences on April 15 to ensure that we capture reopenings across all states.

Most reopening policies have been centered around seven areas of economic activity: outdoor recreation, retail, restaurant, worship, personal care, entertainment, and industry activities. However, the pace at which states have reopened each of these sectors has varied a lot. Some states reopened most businesses and industries immediately, while others have adopted a much more phased approach.[13] Retail, recreation, and restaurants have often reopened first, frequently only at limited capacity (see figure 1).

South Carolina was the first state to reopen, on April 20. It was also one of the last states to adopt a stay-at-home order.[14] This April 20 reopening was partial, allowing retail stores to open at 20 percent of capacity. By April 30, twelve states had reopened to some degree (Alabama, Mississippi, Tennessee, Montana, Oklahoma, Alaska, Georgia, Michigan, Minnesota, Vermont, Wisconsin, and South Carolina). Eleven more states reopened on May 1; by May 13, a total of forty states had reopened. By June 30 all states had undergone at least the first stage of reopening. In most of our reopening analyses the study period ends on June 15, which means that we are able to estimate impacts for at least thirty days post-reopening using variation from all fifty states and the District of Columbia for phase 1 and phase 2 reopening policies.

---

12. "See Coronavirus Restrictions and Mask Mandates for All 50 States," *New York Times*, https://www.nytimes.com/interactive/2020/us/states-reopen-map-coronavirus.html, accessed June 23, 2020.

13. Alaska, Connecticut, Washington, D.C., Iowa, Indiana, Louisiana, Maryland, Missouri, New Hampshire, Nevada, South Dakota, and Wyoming reopened initially by opening five or more of the seven sectors.

14. Although it issued an emergency declaration fairly early (March 13), South Carolina did not issue a stay-at-home order until April 7 (see Gupta, Nguyen, and others 2020).

Stay-at-home orders and nonessential business closures are related but distinct. Several states issued stay-at-home mandates after they issued orders closing all nonessential businesses or after closing some nonessential businesses (such as gyms) and closing restaurants for on-site dining. Although for the most part, stay-at-home orders coincided with orders to close all nonessential businesses, restaurants and other select categories of business closures started well before stay-at-home orders. Many business closures started in mid-March, along with school closures (see figure 2). Timing of reopenings has been within 24 hours of lifting stay-at-home orders in only seven states (Connecticut, Florida, Idaho, Kansas, Montana, Pennsylvania, and Utah; see table 1 for details).[15] In the remaining states, reopening frequently preceded official expiry of stay-at-home orders on average by a month (thirty-two days).

The top panel of figure 1 shows that by June 15 all US states had adopted some form of reopening policy. However, the pace of reopening has been gradual and varied. The bottom panel of figure 1 shows that by June 15, nearly 74 percent of the population lives in states that opened the retail sector, but only 60 percent is in states that opened three or more sectors that we track.[16] However, seventeen states pursued a more limited strategy by opening only one or two sectors.[17]

States that either implemented fewer social distancing measures or implemented those measures later also tended to reopen earlier, based on time since the first of four major social distancing measures—nonessential business closures, restaurant closures, social gathering restrictions, and stay-at-home orders or advisories. These results may reflect either a lack of political desire to engage in distancing or a more limited outbreak (Andersen 2020; Adolph and others 2020; Allcott and others 2020).

IV. Mobility Data

The data sets typically used in public health research do not provide high-frequency measures of social interaction. To make progress, our research program has made heavy use of data from at least four commercial cell signal aggregators who have provided their data for free to support COVID-19

15. COVID-19 US State Policy Database, www.tinyurl.com/statepolicies.
16. Following the *New York Times*, we track outdoor recreation, retail, food and drink establishments, personal care establishments, houses of worship, entertainment venues, and industrial areas.
17. There were seven states where we could not clearly identify the sectors that would be affected by the reopening decision.

Figure 2. State Policy and Information Timelines (January 15 to June 15, 2020)

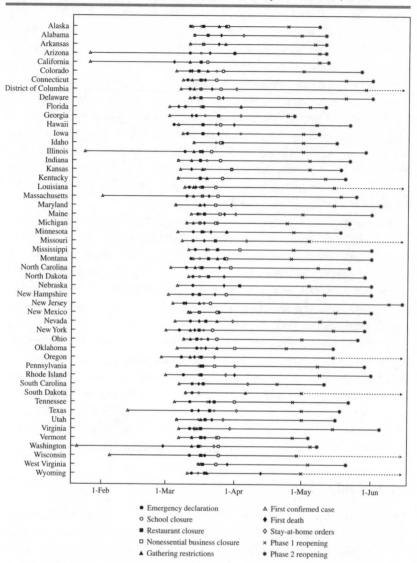

Source: Authors' compilations.
Note: Continuing arrows denote states yet to enter phase 2 of reopening.

research. Each company has several different measures of mobility, which may capture a different form of underlying behavior, with different implications for the transmission of the virus and economic activity. In addition, each company collects data from potentially different sets of app users, and it is possible that some of the cell signal panels are more mobile than others. Given these complexities, it is important to examine several measures of mobility both to assess the robustness and generality of a result and to provide opportunities to learn from differences in results across measures. In this paper, we discuss results based on data from Apple's Mobility Trends Reports, Google's Community Mobility Reports, PlaceIQ, and SafeGraph.

Apple's Mobility Trends Reports are published daily and reflect requests for driving directions in Apple Maps.[18] The measure we use tracks the volume of driving directions requests per US state compared to a baseline volume on January 13, 2020; no county-level equivalent is available.

We extract state-level measures of mobility from Google's Community Mobility Reports, which contain county-level data as well.[19] We use the data that reflect the percent change in visits to places within a geographic area, including grocery and pharmacy, transit stations (public transport hubs such as subway, bus, and train stations), retail and recreation (e.g., restaurants, shopping centers, and theme parks), places of work, and residential (places of residence). The baseline for computing these changes is the median level of activity on the corresponding day of the week from January 3 to February 6, 2020.

We use two anonymized, aggregated location exposure indexes from PlaceIQ data: (1) a mixing index that, for a given day, detects the likely exposure of a smart device to other devices in a county or state on a given day, and (2) out-of-state and out-of-county travel indexes that measure, among smart devices that pinged in a given geographic location, the percent of these devices that pinged in another geographic location at least once during the previous fourteen days.[20]

18. Apple Mobility Trends Reports, https://www.apple.com/covid19/mobility, accessed June 22, 2020.

19. Google, COVID-19 Community Mobility Reports, 2020, https://www.google.com/covid19/ mobility, accessed June 22, 2020.

20. Victor Couture, Jonathan I. Dingel, Allison E. Green, Jessie Handbury, and Kevin R. Williams, Exposure Indices Derived from PlaceIQ Movement Data [data set], 2020, https://github.com/COVIDExposureIndices/COVIDExposureIndices.

Table 1. State Social Distancing–Related Policy Enactment and Information Event Dates

	Emergency declarations	School closures	Restaurant/ other restrictions	Gathering restrictions (any)	Nonessential business closures	First confirmed case	First death	Stay-at-home orders	Initial reopenings	Phase 2 reopenings
Alabama	11-Mar-20	16-Mar-20	17-Mar-20	28-Mar-20	24-Mar-20	13-Mar-20	27-Mar-20	4-Apr-20	30-Apr-20	11-May-20
Alaska	13-Mar-20	19-Mar-20	20-Mar-20		20-Mar-20	12-Mar-20	25-Mar-20	28-Mar-20	24-Apr-20	8-May-20
Arizona	11-Mar-20	17-Mar-20	19-Mar-20			26-Jan-20	24-Mar-20	31-Mar-20	8-May-20	11-May-20
Arkansas	11-Mar-20	16-Mar-20	20-Mar-20			11-Mar-20	20-Mar-20		6-May-20	11-May-20
California	4-Mar-20	19-Mar-20	15-Mar-20	19-Mar-20	11-Mar-20	26-Jan-20	4-Mar-20	19-Mar-20	8-May-20	12-May-20
Colorado	10-Mar-20	23-Mar-20	17-Mar-20	26-Mar-20	19-Mar-20	5-Mar-20	12-Mar-20	26-Mar-20	1-May-20	27-May-20
Connecticut	10-Mar-20	17-Mar-20	16-Mar-20	23-Mar-20	12-Mar-20	8-Mar-20	18-Mar-20	23-Mar-20	20-May-20	17-Jun-20
Delaware	11-Mar-20	16-Mar-20	16-Mar-20	25-Mar-20	13-Mar-20	11-Mar-20	21-Mar-20	24-Mar-20	20-May-20	15-Jun-20
DC	13-Mar-20	16-Mar-20	16-Mar-20	24-Mar-20	16-Mar-20	7-Mar-20	26-Mar-20	1-Apr-20	29-May-20	
Florida	9-Mar-20	16-Mar-20	17-Mar-20	30-Mar-20	3-Apr-20	1-Mar-20	6-Mar-20	3-Apr-20	4-May-20	5-Jun-20
Georgia	14-Mar-20	18-Mar-20	24-Mar-20		24-Mar-20	2-Mar-20	12-Mar-20	3-Apr-20	24-Apr-20	27-Apr-20
Hawaii	4-Mar-20	23-Mar-20	17-Mar-20	25-Mar-20	16-Mar-20	6-Mar-20	31-Mar-20	25-Mar-20	7-May-20	22-May-20
Idaho	13-Mar-20	3-Apr-20	17-Mar-20		17-Mar-20	13-Mar-20	24-Mar-20	25-Mar-20	1-May-20	16-May-20
Illinois	9-Mar-20	23-Mar-20	16-Mar-20	25-Mar-20	25-Mar-20	24-Jan-20	26-Mar-20	21-Mar-20	1-May-20	29-May-20
Indiana	6-Mar-20	17-Mar-20	16-Mar-20	21-Mar-20	13-Mar-20	6-Mar-20	17-Mar-20	25-Mar-20	4-May-20	22-May-20
Iowa	9-Mar-20	19-Mar-20	16-Mar-20	24-Mar-20	12-Mar-20	8-Mar-20	16-Mar-20		1-May-20	8-May-20
Kansas	12-Mar-20	18-Mar-20	18-Mar-20		17-Mar-20	7-Mar-20	12-Mar-20	30-Mar-20	4-May-20	18-May-20
Kentucky	6-Mar-20	16-Mar-20	16-Mar-20	26-Mar-20	19-Mar-20	6-Mar-20	16-Mar-20	26-Mar-20	11-May-20	20-May-20
Louisiana	11-Mar-20	16-Mar-20	17-Mar-20	23-Mar-20	13-Mar-20	9-Mar-20	14-Mar-20	23-Mar-20	15-May-20	5-Jun-20
Maine	10-Mar-20	17-Mar-20	17-Mar-20	24-Mar-20	13-Mar-20	12-Mar-20	20-Mar-20	1-Apr-20	1-May-20	1-Jun-20
Maryland	5-Mar-20	16-Mar-20	16-Mar-20	23-Mar-20	16-Mar-20	5-Mar-20	18-Mar-20	30-Mar-20	15-May-20	5-Jun-20
Massachusetts	15-Mar-20	16-Mar-20	18-Mar-20	25-Mar-20	18-Mar-20	1-Feb-20	27-Mar-20	24-Mar-20	18-May-20	8-Jun-20
Michigan	10-Mar-20	16-Mar-20	16-Mar-20	23-Mar-20	13-Mar-20	10-Mar-20	18-Mar-20	24-Mar-20	24-Apr-20	22-May-20
Minnesota	13-Mar-20	18-Mar-20	17-Mar-20			6-Mar-20	21-Mar-20	28-Mar-20	27-Apr-20	18-May-20
Mississippi	13-Mar-20	23-Mar-20	17-Mar-20		23-Mar-20	11-Mar-20	18-Mar-20	3-Apr-20	27-Apr-20	1-Jun-20

State									
Missouri	14-Mar-20	20-Mar-20	24-Mar-20	31-Mar-20	11-Mar-20	19-Mar-20	6-Apr-20	4-May-20	16-Jun-20
Montana	12-Mar-20	16-Mar-20	20-Mar-20	28-Mar-20	13-Mar-20	27-Mar-20	28-Mar-20	26-Apr-20	1-Jun-20
Nebraska	10-Mar-20	16-Mar-20	17-Mar-20	30-Mar-20	3-Mar-20	25-Mar-20		4-May-20	1-Jun-20
Nevada	13-Mar-20	16-Mar-20	20-Mar-20		11-Mar-20	27-Mar-20	31-Mar-20	9-May-20	29-May-20
New Hampshire	13-Mar-20	3-Apr-20	19-Mar-20		6-Mar-20	27-Mar-20	28-Mar-20	11-May-20	1-Jun-20
New Jersey	13-Mar-20	16-Mar-20	16-Mar-20	28-Mar-20	2-Mar-20	23-Mar-20	21-Mar-20	9-Jun-20	15-Jun-20
New Mexico	9-Mar-20	18-Mar-20	16-Mar-20	21-Mar-20	4-Mar-20	10-Mar-20	24-Mar-20	16-May-20	1-Jun-20
New York	11-Mar-20	16-Mar-20	16-Mar-20	24-Mar-20	11-Mar-20	25-Mar-20	22-Mar-20	15-May-20	29-May-20
North Carolina	12-Mar-20	16-Mar-20	17-Mar-20	21-Mar-20	5-Mar-20	16-Mar-20	30-Mar-20	8-May-20	22-May-20
North Dakota	7-Mar-20	18-Mar-20	16-Mar-20	20-Mar-20	1-Mar-20	14-Mar-20		1-May-20	29-May-20
Ohio	9-Mar-20	17-Mar-20	15-Mar-20	24-Mar-20	9-Mar-20	20-Mar-20	24-Mar-20	1-May-20	26-May-20
Oklahoma	15-Mar-20	17-Mar-20	25-Mar-20	26-Mar-20	6-Mar-20	19-Mar-20		24-Apr-20	15-May-20
Oregon	8-Mar-20	16-Mar-20	17-Mar-20		28-Feb-20	14-Mar-20	23-Mar-20	15-May-20	4-Jun-20
Pennsylvania	6-Mar-20	16-Mar-20	17-Mar-20	23-Mar-20	6-Mar-20	18-Mar-20	1-Apr-20	8-May-20	29-May-20
Rhode Island	9-Mar-20	16-Mar-20	16-Mar-20		1-Mar-20	1-Apr-20	28-Mar-20	9-May-20	1-Jun-20
South Carolina	13-Mar-20	16-Mar-20	18-Mar-20		7-Mar-20	16-Mar-20	7-Apr-20	20-Apr-20	4-May-20
South Dakota	13-Mar-20	16-Mar-20		6-Apr-20	10-Mar-20	10-Mar-20		1-May-20	
Tennessee	12-Mar-20	20-Mar-20	23-Mar-20	1-Apr-20	5-Mar-20	21-Mar-20	1-Apr-20	27-Apr-20	22-May-20
Texas	13-Mar-20	23-Mar-20	21-Mar-20	21-Mar-20	13-Feb-20	16-Mar-20		1-May-20	18-May-20
Utah	6-Mar-20	16-Mar-20	18-Mar-20	16-Mar-20	6-Mar-20	22-Mar-20	27-Mar-20	1-May-20	16-May-20
Vermont	12-Mar-20	16-Mar-20	17-Mar-20	17-Mar-20	7-Mar-20	14-Mar-20	24-Mar-20	27-Apr-20	4-May-20
Virginia	13-Mar-20	18-Mar-20	17-Mar-20	25-Mar-20	7-Mar-20	19-Mar-20	30-Mar-20	15-May-20	5-Jun-20
Washington	29-Feb-20	17-Mar-20	16-Mar-20	25-Mar-20	21-Jan-20	29-Feb-20	23-Mar-20	5-May-20	8-May-20
West Virginia	12-Mar-20	18-Mar-20	17-Mar-20	25-Mar-20	5-Feb-20	19-Mar-20	24-Mar-20	4-May-20	21-May-20
Wisconsin	16-Mar-20	16-Mar-20	17-Mar-20	24-Mar-20	17-Mar-20	29-Mar-20	25-Mar-20	29-Apr-20	11-May-20
Wyoming	13-Mar-20	16-Mar-20	19-Mar-20		11-Mar-20	13-Apr-20	20-Mar-20	1-May-20	11-May-20

Source: Authors' compilations based on Fullman and others, "State-Level Social Distancing Policies in Response to COVID-19 in the US," version 1.04 [data set], http://www.covid19statepolicy.org; the public use map and tracker of K-12 school closures (*Education Week*), *New York Times*, and data we collected on the timing of the first COVID-19 case announcements from media reports in each state.

Notes: Data are current as of June 15, 2020.

We use SafeGraph data to measure the median hours spent at home by devices as well as the number of devices at the census block group level that are detected at a typical work location during the day or to have left the house. We aggregate these to state by-day levels.

V. Econometric Framework

Let Y_{st} be a measure of mobility in state s on date t. E_s is the start date of a closure/reopening policy in state s. $TSE_{st} = t - E_s$ is the number of days between t and the adoption date. We fit the following event study regression model:

$$Y_{st} = \sum_{a=-30}^{-2} \alpha_a 1(TSE_{st} = -a) + \sum_{b=0}^{30} \beta_b 1(TSE_{st} = b) + W_{st}\sigma + \theta_s + \gamma_t + \epsilon_{st}.$$

In the model, θ_s is a state fixed effect, which captures time-invariant differences in outcomes across states. γ_t is a date fixed effect, which represents a common trend. W_{st} is a vector of state times day measures of temperature and precipitation, which helps adjust for seasonality. ϵ_{st} is a residual error term, and α_a and β_b trace out deviations from the common trends that states experience in the days leading up to and following a given policy event. Standard errors allow for clustering at the state level.

Our main specifications are based on a balanced panel of states. The models are not weighted, and our estimates reflect the average state rather than the average person. The composition of states contributing to event study coefficients is quite stable for a range of thirty days before and after the event. The calendar time covered by the event studies varies somewhat across outcomes and is described along with each set of results. To help summarize results, we assess the presence of a pre-trend based on the statistical significance of the pre-policy event study coefficients. In our summary results, we say that a measure exhibits a pre-trend if at least 30 percent of the coefficients in the pre-period were statistically significant.

We also use the event study models to decompose the overall change in mobility over time into a share explained by state-level policy changes and a share explained by secular trends that are not associated with state policies. To understand the counterfactual exercise, let $\hat{y}_{st}$ be the fitted value for state s on date t from the estimated event study regression. These fitted values are a model-based estimate of what actually happened in the state. Let $y_{st}^* = \widehat{y}_{st} - \sum_{b=0}^{30} \hat{\beta}_b 1(TSE_{st} = b)$ be an estimate of the counterfactual mobility outcome that would have prevailed in the absence of the state policy. We compute the daily cross-state average of the fitted values and counterfactual estimates to form two national time series of mobility outcomes. A close correspondence between the realized time series and the counterfactual time series would indicate that changes in mobility are mainly from secular trends rather than policy.

VI. Results

VI.A. Trends in Mobility

The collection of graphs in figure 3 shows the national and state-level time series for a subset of the mobility measures we follow in Gupta, Nguyen, and others (2020) and Nguyen and others (2020). The dashed black line indicates the "smoothed" (seven-day moving average) national average (not weighted by state population). Each of the lines on a graph represents a state. The state lines darken in the middle for the time period when the state implemented a stay-at-home (SAH) order, and then they change again when the state implements its first reopening stage. This provides a convenient way to observe when the changes in mobility occurred relative to the policy dates.

The overall pattern of results is very consistent across the different measures of mobility. The top left panel of figure 3 shows the mixing index. Weekend patterns and other seasonal effects are visible, when all lines move together. There is a substantial drop in mixing around mid-March, when the index falls more than 73.4 percent between March 1 and April 14. The top right panel of figure 3 shows the average out-of-county travel measure, which fell by 33.4 percent between March 1 and April 14. The bottom left panel of figure 3 shows trends for hours spent at home, which is a state-level average of census block group medians. Time at home increased 60.6 percent between March 1 and April 14. The springtime is typically associated with more mobility and interaction, so any decline during this period is abnormal.[21]

The graphs in figure 3 show that states with no SAH mandates also experienced large declines in mobility as well as subsequent increases after

21. Data for recent years (2018–2019) from the US Department of Transportation for (seasonally unadjusted) vehicle miles traveled show that the March value is typically 20 percent higher than February's value (US Department of Transportation 2020).

Figure 3. Trend in Mobility Changes

(a) Mixing index

Mixing index

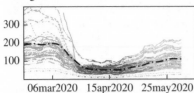

Source: PlaceIQ　　　Y-axis is truncated at 400

(b) Average out-of-county movement

Total out-of-county movement

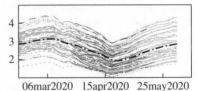

Source: PlaceIQ

(c) Requests for driving directions

Request for driving direction

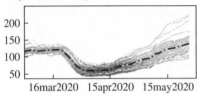

Source: Apple Mobility

(d) Fraction at work

Fraction at work

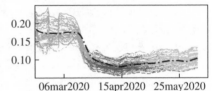

Source: SafeGraph Aggregated Mobility Metrics

(e) Retail and recreation

Mobility to retail/recreation

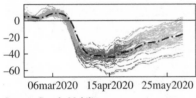

Source: Google Mobility

(f) Grocery and pharmacy

Mobility to grocery/pharmacy

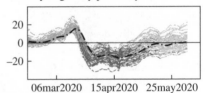

Source: Google Mobility

(g) Median hours at home

Median hours at home

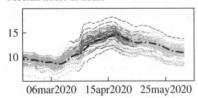

Source: SafeGraph Aggregated Mobility Metrics

(h) Fraction leaving home

Fraction left the house

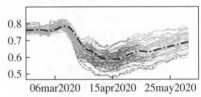

Source: SafeGraph Aggregated Mobility Metrics

Source: Authors' calculations based on data from Apple Mobility, Google Mobility, SafeGraph Aggregated Mobility Metrics, and PlaceIQ smart device.

Notes: Each line represents a state, indicating when the state implemented stay-at-home orders (middle) and change after phase 1 of reopening (right). The thick black line represents a smoothed seven-day moving average of the states.

mid-April. Indeed, states with no SAH policies at all had declines in movement almost as dramatic as in other states. Furthermore, most states with SAH mandates experienced major declines in mobility even before the SAH mandates went into effect.

VI.B. Mandate Effects

Estimates of the event studies evaluating the effect of closure policies and informational events on each of the mobility measures are presented in Gupta, Nguyen, and others (2020). In figure 4 we graphically present the event study coefficients of the effect of state policies and informational events on the mixing index available from PlaceIQ. As noted in section IV the mixing index captures the concentration of devices in particular locations and provides the closest proxy for social distancing and thus transmission. The results suggest that the concentration of devices in particular locations does not trend differentially in the period leading up to any policy or information event. However, we do not find statistically significant evidence that the policy or information events have induced substantial changes in mixing at the state level except for a large effect of emergency declarations. The event study coefficients imply that emergency declarations reduced the state-level mixing index by about 52 percent after twenty days, relative to the value of the index on March 1, which is the baseline reference period for all percent effects reported for closure events. The coefficients show a similar pattern for first deaths, but it is not statistically significant.

Table 2 provides a summary of the results of the event study regressions for each outcome and policy or information event, including additional ones for which figures and tables of coefficients are reported in Gupta, Nguyen, and others (2020). Table 2 has a row for each state outcome variable and a column for each policy or information event. The top panel shows the effect size five days after the event, expressed as a percentage of the average value of the outcome variable on March 1, 2020. The bottom panel shows the effect size after twenty days, also expressed as a percentage of the average outcome on March 1. We indicate the effects that are statistically significant at the 5 percent level or better and where parallel trends hold. The cells that are shaded in grey have possible violations of the differential pre-trends assumption and should be largely overlooked; we do not indicate statistical significance for them. First death announcements also carry a large coefficient but it is statistically not significant; school closures and stay-at-home laws have statistically insignificant and wrong-signed coefficients.

Figure 4. Effects of Mitigation Policies and Information Events on Mixing Index

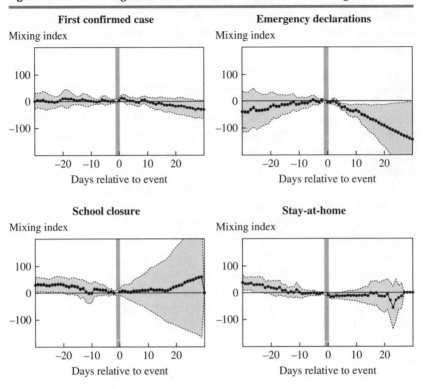

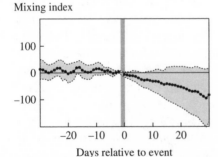

Baseline dependent variable mean = 178.64, std. dev. = 97.59

Source: PlaceIQ Geolocation Data.

Notes: The plots present event study regression coefficients with 95 percent confidence intervals. The dependent variable shows the state's index for mixing (average amount of mixing within its census block groups). Standard errors are clustered at the state level. Full event study estimates available in Gupta, Nguyen, and others (2020).

Table 2. Effect Sizes: Percentage Magnitude Effects of the Policy and Informational Events on Social Distancing Measures

	1. Effects of mitigation policies and informational events				
	First confirmed case	*Emergency declarations*	*School closures*	*Stay-at-home*	*First death*
	Effects after 5 days				
Mixing index	1	−14***	4	−7	−11
Median hours at home	−1*	6***	1	5	3*
Fraction leaving home	1**	−1*	−1	−5	−2***
Total out-of-state movement	−2	−1	−4**	−1	0
Total out-of-county movement	−1	−2**	−4***	−3	−2
	Effects after 20 days				
Mixing index	−10	−52***	13	−8	−31
Median hours at home	−2	27***	3	11	9**
Fraction leaving home	2	−13***	−3	−9	−7***
Total out-of-state movement	−9	−3	−13	1	5
Total out-of-county movement	−2	−8***	−9***	−2	−6*

	2. Effects of state initial reopenings	
	Announcement of initial reopening	*Initial reopening*
	Effects after 5 days	
Mobility measures	(%)	(%)
Request for driving directions	−6	−3
Mobility to retail/recreation	3	3
Mobility to grocery/pharmacy	8	9
Mobility to transit stations	0	9
Mobility to workplace	2	3**
Fraction at work	−3*	2
Fraction left home	1**	1**
Mixing index	−2	5
Out-of-state movement	−2	0
Out-of-county movement	−1	0
Absence of mobility measures		
Stay in residential areas	−1	−4**
Median hours at home	−1*	−1***

(*continued on next page*)

Table 2. Effect Sizes: Percentage Magnitude Effects of the Policy and Informational Events on Social Distancing Measures (*Continued*)

	Announcement of initial reopening	Initial reopening
	Effects after 20 days	
Mobility measures	(%)	(%)
Request for driving directions	−15	−15
Mobility to retail/recreation	8	4
Mobility to grocery/pharmacy	8	4
Mobility to transit stations	0	−6
Mobility to workplace	4	1
Fraction at work	2	1
Fraction left home	4***	1
Mixing index	20	−4
Out-of-state movement	−1	−8
Out-of-county movement	2	0
Absence of mobility measures	(%)	(%)
Stay in residential areas	−5	−4
Median hours at home	−3***	−3***

Source: Authors' calculations.

Notes: Each cell is from a separate regression. Grey-shaded cells denote violation of pretreatment parallel trends—we do not denote statistical significance for these cells. Effect sizes for closures are estimated using coefficients in the event study tables presented in Gupta, Nguyen, and others (2020), divided by the dependent variable value as of March 1, 2020. Effect sizes for reopenings are estimated using coefficients in the event study tables presented in Nguyen and others (2020), divided by the dependent variable value as of April 15, 2020.

*** $p < .01$; ** $p < .05$; * $p < .10$.

VI.C. Reopening Effects

In a manner similar to the event studies for the closure policies, we present results for the initial reopening dates, starting in figure 5. The two panels display effects first where the policy date is the announcement of the reopening and second for the actual reopening date. There is a pattern (although not statistically significant) of what appears to be a nonparallel trend prior to the actual reopening date, but it is fairly flat prior to the announcement date. None of the estimates are statistically significant, even after the policy is effective, although nonsignificant coefficients are consistent with an increase in movement after the announcement date. This helps illustrate our finding that it is important to consider a variety of mobility measures to assess the impact of the policies. Table 2 shows that although the mixing index is not statistically precise, there are several other outcomes that are and that do not violate pre-trends concerns. The effect sizes here are, however, considerably smaller than in the closure period. One reason for that may be that in the reopening phase we do not have informational

Figure 5. Effects of Announcement and Effective Date of Initial Reopening
on Mixing Index

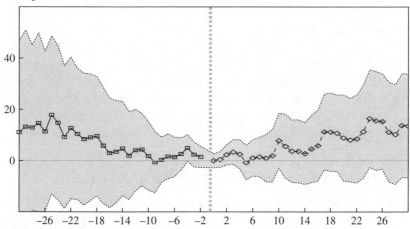

Announcement of initial reopening

Mixing index

Baseline DV mean = 44.02, std. dev. = 19.31

Days relative to reopening

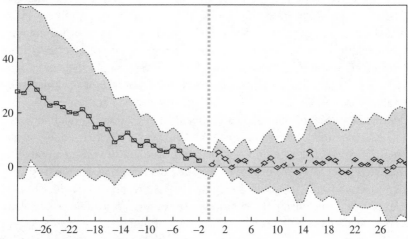

Initial reopening

Mixing index

Baseline DV mean = 44.02, std. dev. = 19.31

Days relative to reopening

Source: PlaceIQ (April 9 to June 11, 2020).

Notes: The plots present event study regression coefficients with 95 percent confidence intervals. The dependent variable shows the state's index for mixing (average amount of mixing within its census block groups). Standard errors are clustered at the state level. Full event study estimates available in Nguyen and others (2020).

events occurring in the same way they did during the closure period. We do not study the impact of changing rates of COVID-19 cases or deaths, as those were often directly referred to as conditions for reopening.

The overall message from table 2 for the reopening dates is that estimates are fairly similar whether we use the announcement date or the actual reopening date and that effect sizes are fairly small at both five days and twenty days, on the order of 1–4 percent. These are not surprising results, given the very limited nature of initial reopening phases. The small effects overall also could mask larger effects in certain situations; event study estimates are summaries of each state's experience (Wing, Simon, and Bello-Gomez 2018), and Nguyen and others (2020) show that effects are larger in states that were the last to close businesses and also differ along a number of other dimensions.

VI.D. The Role of Secular Trends (National Sentiment)

One way to interpret our results is to use the event study coefficients to tease apart the amount of the actual change in mobility that occurred during the closure or reopening time periods into shares explained by state actions, relative to secular changes in sentiment due to other factors. Figure 6 and table 3 show estimates of this decomposition for the mixing index during the shutdown phase. We used event study regressions to estimate the effects of emergency declarations on the mixing index outcome. The solid line in figure 6 shows how the national average mixing index actually changed over time. The dashed line is an estimate of the counterfactual path of the mixing index, which removes the policy effects from the model. The time trends captured by the model imply that the mixing index would have increased substantially in the absence of the emergency declarations. Table 3 shows that the emergency declaration event study coefficients account for about 65 percent of the observed decline in the mixing index that occurred between the first week of March and the second week of April. The remaining 35 percent was due to secular trends that occurred separately from state emergency declarations. Decompositions like this one imply that both policy and private responses (secular trends) played a key role during the shutdown. However, the specific policy share versus secular share varies across measures of mobility.

We used this same strategy to examine the state reopening policies. Figure 7 and table 4 show decomposition results for the mixing index and the fraction of people who leave home during the day. The solid lines in figure 7 show how the mixing index (top panel) and the fraction leaving home (bottom panel) evolved between mid-April and mid-June. Both

Figure 6. Change in Social Distancing (Mixing Index) Attributed to
Emergency Declarations

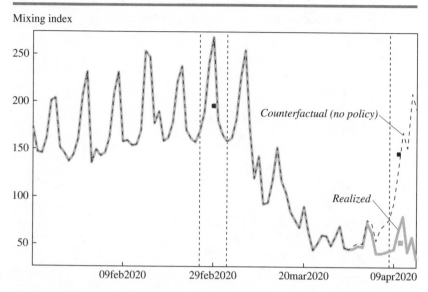

Source: PlaceIQ Geolocation Data.

Notes: Corresponding to figure 5, calendar time trends of the predicted lines, with and without the policy event time terms set to zero, are shown for the mixing index measure of mobility and the emergency declarations policy measure.

Table 3. Estimated Effects of Emergency Declarations on Mixing Index

	February 26–March 3	April 8–April 14	Change
Actual mixing index	194.3	51.9	−142.4
Counterfactual mixing index (no policy)	194.3	144.9	−49.4
Secular share of change			0.35
Policy share of change			0.65

Source: Authors' calculations based on decomposition of changes in mobility to share attributable to state emergency declarations and those resulting from secular trends.

Notes: Related estimates plotted in figure 6.

measures rose substantially during the reopening phase. The dashed lines show counterfactual estimates of the path of each index in the absence of the event study state reopening effects. The results suggest that the reopening policies had almost no influence on the rise of the mixing index. The growth in that variable is almost completely attributable to a nationwide secular trend that occurred separately from reopening events. In contrast, the model suggests that state reopening events did alter the evolution of

Figure 7. Change in Social Distancing (Mixing Index and Fraction Leaving Home) Attributed to Initial Reopening

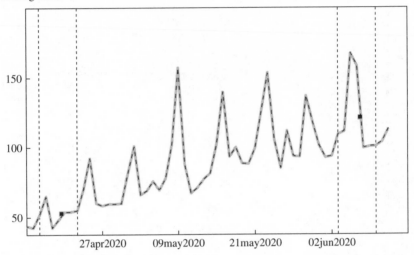

Estimated effects of initial reopening on mixing index

Mixing index

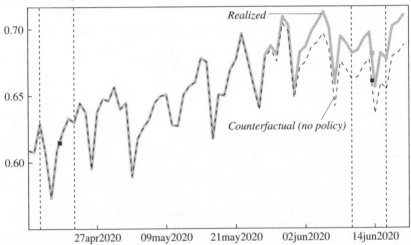

Estimated effects of initial reopenings on fraction leaving home

Fraction leaving home

Sources: PlaceIQ Geolocation Data; SafeGraph Aggregated Mobility Metrics.

Notes: Corresponding to figure 5, top panel shows calendar time trends of the predicted lines, with and without the policy event time terms set to zero, for the mixing index measure of mobility and the emergency declarations policy measure. Bottom panel provides specific values discussed in the text.

Table 4. Estimated Effects of Reopening on Social Distancing

	April 17–April 23	June 10–June 16	Change
Actual Mixing Index	53.2	121.2	68.0
Counterfactual Mixing Index (No policy)	53.2	121.5	68.3
Secular share of change			1.0
Policy share of change			0.0
Actual Fraction Leaving Home	0.6	0.7	0.1
Counterfactual Fraction Leaving Home (No policy)	0.6	0.7	0.0
Secular share of change			0.69
Policy share of change			0.31

Source: Authors' calculation based on decomposition of changes in mobility to share attributable to state initial reopening policy and those resulting from secular trends.

Notes: Related estimates plotted in Figure 7.

the fraction leaving home measure of mobility. Table 4 shows that the fraction leaving home grew from about 60 percent to 70 percent between late April and mid-June. About 31 percent of that increase is attributable to the reopening policies because of how much time had passed before policies were adopted. The remaining 69 percent of the change might have happened even in the absence of state policies, given the common trends implied by the model. These results again suggest that both private responses (secular trends) and state-level policies have played a role in generating recent increases in mobility; however, the magnitude or share of policy effects varies across measures of mobility, and the policy share is perhaps somewhat smaller during the reopening phase than during the shutdown phase.

VII. Conclusion

We examine human mobility responses to the COVID-19 epidemic and to the policies that arose to encourage social distancing. A simple theoretical framework suggests that people will increase social distance in reaction to information and apprehension regarding the virus, not just in response to state closure or reopening mandates.

We examine closures first, finding that information-based policies and events such as first cases had the largest effects. This does not imply that these laws and events would always have such impacts, as it is possible people simply react to the earliest of the policies, and more restrictive policies like stay-at-home orders happened fairly late. Early state policies appeared to convey information about the epidemic, suggesting that even the policy response operates partly through a voluntary channel.

Given that most states have now undertaken some steps to reduce the lockdown, we are able to compare mobility during the closure to mobility during the reopenings. Even though the reopenings are gradual, often with capacity limits for each sector, we find that mobility increases a few days after the policy change. There is some evidence that reopenings lead people to increase the number of different locations they visit, rather than increase the total time they are outside their home. Finally, we observe that the largest increases in mobility occur in states that were late adopters of closure measures and thus had these mandates in place for the shortest amount of time. This suggests that closure policies may have represented more of a binding constraint in the late-adopting states. Together, these four observations provide an assessment of the extent to which people in the United States are resuming movement and physical proximity as the COVID-19 pandemic continues. Given the high costs of broad closures, it behooves researchers to examine possible targeted approaches.

Our own empirical work and our review of the emerging literature support several broad conclusions. First, the epidemic has led to a massive change in human mobility and contact patterns. This change happened quite early and suddenly and largely across the board. Although much of the decline in mobility appears to be a private response to changing health conditions, research also suggests that state and local social distancing policies have helped further depress mobility. Second, measures of economic activity related to both labor market outcomes and consumer spending have changed dramatically in response to the epidemic. The fall in consumer spending occurred despite a large increase in federal spending. The fall in spending occurred throughout the country and does not seem to have been moderated by state and local policies. The decline in employment happened a bit later than the immediate mobility and spending effects, but here as well the evidence suggests that social distancing policies are not associated with large differences in labor market outcomes across localities. Third, there is fairly consistent evidence that the state social distancing policies have helped improve health outcomes as measured by cases and deaths.

The literature on the COVID-19 epidemic has developed at a very rapid pace. The crisis is still only a few months old, but an active research community and new availability of data have contributed to our understanding of the way people are responding to both public health conditions and public policy constraints. But there is still much work to be done. States started reopening their economies by mid-April. School reopenings were a pressing decision. As of July, there was evidence that caseloads and deaths were beginning to rise again. Congress also debated another round of economic aid to protect society financially against the damage caused by the epidemic. It is not clear how long the country can maintain such low levels of physical mobility and such high levels of unemployment. The next phase of the epidemic may call for more targeted policies that mitigate the spread of the virus with less disruption.

ACKNOWLEDGMENTS The authors thank the BPEA for financial support. The paper has benefited from guidance from Caroline Buckee, Victor Chernozhukov, James Stock, and other conference participants. We also thank colleagues Ana Bento, Thuy Nguyen, Shyam Raman, Byungkyu Lee, and Felipe Lozano Rojas, our coauthors of the study "Tracking Public and Private Responses to the COVID-19 Epidemic: Evidence from State and Local Government Actions," NBER Working Paper 27027, which served as a foundation for the current paper. We also thank our coauthors of related research papers examining the labor market effects of the COVID-19 pandemic which have informed the current study: Wei Cheng, Xuan Jiang, Laura Montenovo, Ian Schmutte, and Bruce Weinberg.

References

Abouk, Rahi, and Babak Heydari. 2020. "The Immediate Effect of COVID-19 Policies on Social Distancing Behavior in the United States." Working Paper. https://papers.ssrn.com/sol3/papers.cfm?abstract_id=3571421.

Adolph, Christopher, Kenya Amano, Bree Bang-Jensen, Nancy Fullman, and John Wilkerson. 2020. "Pandemic Politics: Timing State-Level Social Distancing Responses to COVID-19." MedRxiv. https://www.medrxiv.org/content/10.1101/2020.03.30.20046326v1.

Aksoy, Cevat Giray, Michael Ganslmeier, and Panu Poutvaara. 2020. "Public Attention and Policy Responses to COVID-19 Pandemic." Working Paper 13427. Bonn, Germany: Institute of Labor Economics. http://ftp.iza.org/dp13427.pdf.

Alexander, Diane, and Ezra Karger. 2020. "Do Stay-at-Home Orders Cause People to Stay at Home? Effects of Stay-at-Home Orders on Consumer Behavior." Working Paper 2020-12. Federal Reserve Bank of Chicago. https://www.chicagofed.org/publications/working-papers/2020/2020-12.

Allcott, Hunt, Levi Boxell, Jacob C. Conway, Matthew Gentzkow, Michael Thaler, and David Y. Yang. 2020. "Polarization and Public Health: Partisan Differences in Social Distancing during the Coronavirus Pandemic." *Journal of Public Economics* 191.

Andersen, Martin S. 2020. "Early Evidence on Social Distancing in Response to COVID-19 in the United States." Working Paper. https://papers.ssrn.com/sol3/papers.cfm?abstract_id=3569368.

Baker, Scott R., Robert A. Farrokhnia, Steffen Meyer, Michaela Pagel, and Constantine Yannelis. 2020. "How Does Household Spending Respond to an Epidemic? Consumption during the 2020 COVID-19 Pandemic." *Review of Asset Pricing Studies.*

Becker, Gary S. 1965. "A Theory of the Allocation of Time." *Economic Journal* 75, no. 299: 493–517.

Benitez, Joseph A., Charles J. Courtemanche, and Aaron Yelowitz. 2020. "Racial and Ethnic Disparities in COVID-19: Evidence from Six Large Cities." Working Paper 27592. Cambridge, Mass.: National Bureau of Economic Research. https://www.nber.org/papers/w27592.

Bento, Ana I., Thuy Nguyen, Coady Wing, Felipe Lozano-Rojas, Yong-Yeol Ahn, and Kosali Simon. 2020. "Evidence from Internet Search Data Shows Information-Seeking Responses to News of Local COVID-19 Cases." *Proceedings of the National Academy of Sciences* 117, no. 21: 11220–22.

Bento, Ana I., and Pejman Rohani. 2016. "Forecasting Epidemiological Consequences of Maternal Immunization." *Clinical Infectious Diseases* 63, suppl. 4: S205–12.

Bharti, Nita, Xin Lu, Linus Bengtsson, Erik Wetter, and Andrew J. Tatem. 2015. "Remotely Measuring Populations during a Crisis by Overlaying Two Data Sources." *International Health* 7, no. 2: 90–98.

Bitler, Marianne P., Hilary W. Hoynes, and Diane Whitmore Schanzenbach. 2020. "The Social Safety Net in the Wake of COVID-19." In the present volume of *Brookings Papers on Economic Activity.*

Bootsma, Martin C. J., and Neil M. Ferguson. 2007. "The Effect of Public Health Measures on the 1918 Influenza Pandemic in U.S. Cities." *Proceedings of the National Academy of Sciences* 104, no. 18: 7588–93.

Buckee, Caroline O., Satchit Balsari, Jennifer Chan, Mercé Crosas, Francesca Dominici, Urs Gasser, and others. 2020. "Aggregated Mobility Data Could Help Fight COVID-19." *Science* 368, no. 6487: 145–46.

Cawley, John, and Christopher J. Ruhm. 2011. "The Economics of Risky Health Behaviors." In *Handbook of Health Economics, Volume 2*, edited by Mark V. Pauly, Thomas G. Mcguire, and Pedro P. Barros. Amsterdam: North-Holland.

Chen, M. Keith, Yilin Zhuo, Malena de la Fuente, Ryne Rohla, and Elisa F. Long. 2020. "Causal Estimation of Stay-at-Home Orders on SARS-CoV-2 Transmission." Working Paper. Los Angeles: UCLA Anderson School. https://www.anderson.ucla.edu/faculty_pages/keith.chen/papers/WP_StayAtHomeOrders_and_COVID19.pdf.

Cheng, Wei, Patrick Carlin, Joanna Carroll, Sumedha Gupta, Felipe Lozano Rojas, Laura Montenovo, and others. 2020. "Back to Business and (Re)Employing Workers? Labor Market Activity during State COVID-19 Reopenings." Working Paper 27419. Cambridge, Mass.: National Bureau of Economic Research. https://www.nber.org/papers/w27419.

Chernozhukov, Victor, Hiroyuki Kasaha, and Paul Schrimpf. 2020. "Causal Impact of Masks, Policies, Behavior on Early COVID-19 Pandemic in the U.S." Working Paper. https://www.medrxiv.org/content/10.1101/2020.05.27.20115139v5.

Chetty, Raj, John N. Friedman, Nathan Hendren, Michael Stepner, and the Opportunity Insights Team. 2020. "How Did COVID-19 and Stabilization Policies Affect Spending and Employment? A New Real-Time Economic Tracker Based on Private Sector Data." Working Paper 27431. Cambridge, Mass.: National Bureau of Economic Research. https://www.nber.org/papers/w27431.

Cicala, Steve, Stephen P. Holland, Erin T. Mansur, Nicholas Z. Muller, and Andrew J. Yates. 2020. "Expected Health Effects of Reduced Air Pollution from COVID-19 Social Distancing." Working Paper 27135. Cambridge, Mass.: National Bureau of Economic Research. https://www.nber.org/papers/w27135.

Coibion, Olivier, Yuriy Gorodnichenko, and Michael Weber. 2020a. "Labor Markets during the COVID-19 Crisis: A Preliminary View." Working Paper 27017. Cambridge, Mass.: National Bureau of Economic Research. https://www.nber.org/papers/w27017.

Coibion, Olivier, Yuriy Gorodnichenko, and Michael Weber. 2020b. "The Cost of the COVID-19 Crisis: Lockdowns, Macroeconomic Expectations, and Consumer Spending." Working Paper 27141. Cambridge, Mass.: National Bureau of Economic Research.

Courtemanche, Charles, Joseph Garuccio, Anh Le, Joshua Pinkston, and Aaron Yelowitz. 2020. "Strong Social Distancing Measures in the United States Reduced the COVID-19 Growth Rate." *Health Affairs* 39, no.7: 1237–46.

Cronin, Christopher J., and William N. Evans. 2020. "Private Precaution and Public Restrictions: What Drives Social Distancing and Industry Foot Traffic in the

COVID-19 Era?" Working Paper 27531. Cambridge, Mass.: National Bureau of Economic Research. https://www.nber.org/papers/w27531.

Dave, Dhaval M., Andrew I. Friedson, Kyutaro Matsuzawa, and Joseph J. Sabia. 2020. "When Do Shelter-in- Place Orders Fight COVID-19 Best? Policy Heterogeneity Across States and Adoption Time." Working Paper 27091. Cambridge, Mass.: National Bureau of Economic Research. https://www.nber.org/papers/w27091.

Elenev, Vadim, Luis Quintero, Alessandro Rebucci, and Emilia Simeonova. 2020. "Staggered Adoption of Nonpharmaceutical Interventions to Contain COVID-19 across U.S. Counties: Direct and Spillover Effects." Working Paper 20-06. Baltimore: Johns Hopkins University, Carey Business School. https://papers.ssrn.com/sol3/papers.cfm?abstract_id=3657594.

Engle, Sam, John Stromme, and Anson Zhou. 2020. "Staying at Home: Mobility Effects of COVID-19." Working Paper. https://papers.ssrn.com/sol3/papers.cfm?abstract_id=3565703.

Ferguson, Neil M., Derek A. T. Cummings, Simon Cauchemez, Christophe Fraser, Steven Riley, Aronrag Meeyai, Sopon Iamsirithaworn, and Donald S. Burke. 2005. "Strategies for Containing an Emerging Influenza Pandemic in Southeast Asia." *Nature* 437:209–14.

Forsythe, Eliza, Lisa B. Kahn, Fabian Lange, and David Wiczer. 2020. "Labor Demand in the Time of COVID-19: Evidence from Vacancy Postings and UI Claims." *Journal of Public Economics* 189.

Friedson, Andrew I., Drew McNichols, Joseph J. Sabia, and Dhaval M. Dave. 2020. "Did California's Shelter in Place Order Work? Early Evidence on Coronavirus-Related Health Benefits." Discussion Paper 13160. Bonn: Institute of Labor Economics. http://ftp.iza.org/dp13160.pdf.

Geoffard, Pierre-Yves, and Tomas Philipson. 1996. "Rational Epidemics and Their Public Control." *International Economic Review* 37, no. 3: 603–24.

Gog, Julia R., Sébastien Ballesteros, Cécile Viboud, Lone Simonsen, Ottar N. Bjornstad, Jeffrey Shaman, Dennis L. Chao, Farid Khan, and Bryan T. Grenfell. 2014. "Spatial Transmission of 2009 Pandemic Influenza in the US." *PLoS Computational Biology* 10, no. 6: 1–11.

Goolsbee, Austan, and Chad Syverson. 2020. "Fear, Lockdown, and Diversion: Comparing Drivers of Pandemic Economic Decline 2020." Working Paper 27432. Cambridge, Mass.: National Bureau of Economic Research. https://www.nber.org/papers/w27432.

Grossman, Michael. 1972. "On the Concept of Health Capital and the Demand for Health." *Journal of Political Economy* 80, no. 2: 223–55.

Grossman, Michael. 2000. "The Human Capital Model." In *Handbook of Health Economics 1A*, edited by Anthony J. Culyer and Joseph P. Newhouse. Amsterdam: North-Holland.

Gupta, Sumedha, Laura Montenovo, Thuy D. Nguyen, Felipe L. Rojas, Ian M. Schmutte, Kosali I. Simon, Bruce A. Weinberg, and Coady Wing. 2020. "Effects of Social Distancing Policy on Labor Market Outcomes." Working Paper 27280.

Cambridge, Mass.: National Bureau of Economic Research. https://www.nber. org/papers/w27280.

Gupta, Sumedha, Thuy D. Nguyen, Felipe L. Rojas, Shyam Raman, Byungkyu Lee, Ana Bento, Kosali I. Simon, and Coady Wing. 2020. "Tracking Public and Private Response to the COVID-19 Epidemic: Evidence from State and Local Government Actions." Working Paper 27027. Cambridge, Mass.: National Bureau of Economic Research. https://www.nber.org/papers/w27027.

Haffajee, Rebecca, Wendy E. Parmet, and Michelle M. Mello. 2014. "What Is a Public Health 'Emergency'?" *New England Journal of Medicine* 371, no. 11: 986–88.

Han, Jeehoon, Bruce D. Meyer, and James X. Sullivan. 2020. "Income and Poverty in the COVID-19 Pandemic." In the current volume of *Brookings Papers on Economic Activity.*

Hatchett, Richard J., Carter E. Mecher, and Marc Lipsitch. 2007. "Public Health Interventions and Epidemic Intensity during the 1918 Influenza Pandemic." *Proceedings of the National Academy of Sciences* 104, no. 18: 7582–87.

Hooper, Monica Webb, Anna María Nápoles, and Eliseo J. Pérez-Stable. 2020. "COVID-19 and Racial/Ethnic Disparities." *JAMA* 323, no. 24: 2466–67.

Huang, Vincent S., Staci Sutermaster, Yael Caplan, Hannah Kemp, Danielle Schmutz, and Sema K. Sgaier. 2020. "Social Distancing Across Vulnerability, Race, Politics, and Employment: How Different Americans Changed Behaviors before and after Major COVID-19 Policy Announcements." Working Paper. https://www.medrxiv.org/content/10.1101/2020.06.04.20119131v1.

Jarvis, Christopher I., Kevin Van Zandvoort, Amy Gimma, Kiesha Prem, Petra Klepac, G. James Rubin, and W. John Edmunds. 2020. "Quantifying the Impact of Physical Distance Measures on the Transmission of COVID-19 in the UK." *BMC Medicine* 18:1–10, article no. 124.

Jinjarak, Yothin, Rashad Ahmed, Sameer Nair-Desai, Weining Xin, and Joshua Aizenman. 2020. "Accounting for Global COVID-19 Diffusion Patterns, January-April 2020." Working Paper 27185. Cambridge, Mass.: National Bureau of Economic Research. https://www.nber.org/papers/w27185.

Keeling, Matt J., and Pejman Rohani. 2008. *Modeling Infectious Diseases in Humans and Animals.* Princeton, NJ: Princeton University Press.

Kermack, William O., and A. G. McKendrick. 1927. "A Contribution to the Mathematical Theory of Epidemics." *Proceedings of the Royal Society of London. Series A, Containing Papers of a Mathematical and Physical Character* 115, no. 772: 700–21.

Kong, Edward, and Daniel Prinz. 2020. "Disentangling Policy Effects Using Proxy Data: Which Shutdown Policies Affected Unemployment during the COVID-19 Pandemic." *Journal of Public Economics* 189.

Kowalczyk, Liz. 2020. "After the Surge: Hospitals Prep to Bring Back Regular Patients While Virus Cases Linger." *Boston Globe*, May 2. https://www.bostonglobe.com/2020/05/02/nation/hospitals-next-phase-recruiting-back-regular-patients-while-allaying-fears-about-mingling-with-coronavirus/.

Kremer, Michael. 1996. "Integrating Behavioral Choice into Epidemiological Models of AIDS." *Quarterly Journal of Economics* 111, no. 2: 549–73.

Lin, Zhixian, and Christopher M. Meissner. 2020. "Health vs. Wealth? Public Health Policies and the Economy during COVID-19." Working Paper 27099. Cambridge, Mass.: National Bureau of Economic Research. https://www.nber.org/papers/w27099.

Lozano Rojas, Felipe, Xuan Jiang, Laura Montenovo, Kosali I. Simon, Bruce A. Weinberg, and Coady Wing. 2020. "Is the Cure Worse than the Problem Itself? Immediate Labor Market Effects of COVID-19 Case Rates and School Closures in the US." Working Paper 27127. Cambridge, Mass.: National Bureau of Economic Research. https://www.nber.org/papers/w27127.

Lyu, Wei, and George L. Wehby. 2020. "Shelter-in-Place Orders Reduced COVID-19 Mortality and Reduced the Rate of Growth in Hospitalizations." *Health Affairs* 39, no. 9: 1–7.

Mari, L., E. Bertuzzo, L. Righetto, R. Casagrandi, M. Gatto, I. Rodriguez-Iturbe, and A. Rinaldo. 2012. "Modelling Cholera Epidemics: The Role of Waterways, Human Mobility and Sanitation." *Journal of the Royal Society Interface* 9, no. 67: 376–88.

McLaren, John. 2020. "Racial Disparity in COVID-19 Deaths: Seeking Economic Roots with Census Data." Working Paper 27407. Cambridge, Mass.: National Bureau of Economic Research. https://www.nber.org/papers/w27407.

Mongey, Simon, and Alex Weinberg. 2020. "Characteristics of Workers in Low Work-from-Home and High Personal-Proximity Occupations." White Paper. Chicago: University of Chicago, Becker Friedman Institute for Economics. https://bfi.uchicago.edu/wp-content/uploads/BFI_White-Paper_Mongey_3.2020.pdf.

Montenovo, Laura, Xuan Jiang, Felipe Lozano Rojas, Ian M. Schmutte, Kosali I. Simon, Bruce A. Weinberg, and Coady Wing. 2020. "Determinants of Disparities in COVID-19 Job Losses." Working Paper 27132. Cambridge, Mass.: National Bureau of Economic Research.

Mossong, Joël, Niel Hens, Mark Jit, Phillippe Beutels, Kari Auranen, Rafael Mikolajczyk, and others. 2008. "Social Contacts and Mixing Patterns Relevant to the Spread of Infectious Diseases." *PLoS Medicine* 5, no. 3: 381–91.

Nguyen, Thuy D., Sumedha Gupta, Martin Andersen, Ana Bento, Kosali I. Simon, and Coady Wing. 2020. "Impacts of State Reopening Policy on Human Mobility." Working Paper 27235. Cambridge, Mass.: National Bureau of Economic Research. https://www.nber.org/papers/w27235.

Painter, Marcus O., and Tian Qiu. 2020. "Political Beliefs Affect Compliance with COVID-19 Social Distancing Orders." Working Paper. https://papers.ssrn.com/sol3/papers.cfm?abstract_id=3569098.

Philipson, Tomas. 1996. "Private Vaccination and Public Health: An Empirical Examination for US Measles." *Journal of Human Resources* 31, no. 3: 611–30.

Philipson, Tomas. 2000. "Economic Epidemiology and Infectious Diseases." In *Handbook of Health Economics 1B*, edited by Anthony J. Culyer and Joseph P. Newhouse. Amsterdam: North-Holland.

Prem, Kiesha, Alex R. Cook, and Mark Jit. 2017. "Projecting Social Contact Matrices in 152 Countries Using Contact Surveys and Demographic Data." *PLoS Computational Biology* 13, no. 9: 1–21.

Raifman, Matthew A., and Julia R. Raifman. 2020. "Disparities in the Population at Risk of Severe Illness from COVID-19 by Race/Ethnicity and Income." *American Journal of Preventive Medicine* 59, no. 1: 137–39.

Rohani, Pejman, Xue Zhong, and Aaron A. King. 2010. "Contact Network Structure Explains the Changing Epidemiology of Pertussis." *Science* 330, no. 6006: 982–85.

US Department of Transportation. 2020. *July 2020 Traffic Volume Trends.* Washington: Federal Highway Administration, Office of Highway Policy Information. https://www.fhwa.dot.gov/policyinformation/travel_monitoring/20jultvt/.

Vervosh, Sarah, and Jack Healy. 2020. "Holdout States Resist Calls for Stay-at-Home Orders: 'What Are You Waiting For?'" *New York Times,* April 3. https://www.nytimes.com/2020/04/03/us/coronavirus-states-without-stay-home.html.

Viscusi, W. Kip. 1993. "The Value of Risks to Life and Health." *Journal of Economic Literature* 31, no. 4: 1912–46.

Wang, Yang, Han Chen, Van Ngo, and Xueming Luo. 2020. "Causal Chain: Shelter-in-Place, Social Distancing, and Spread of COVID-19." Working Paper. https://papers.ssrn.com/sol3/papers.cfm?abstract_id=3634613.

Wesolowski, Amy, Caroline O. Buckee, Kenth Engø-Monsen, and C. J. E. Metcalf. 2016. "Connecting Mobility to Infectious Diseases: The Promise and Limits of Mobile Phone Data." *Journal of Infectious Diseases* 214, suppl. 4: S414–20.

Wesolowski, Amy, Nathan Eagle, Andrew J. Tatem, David L. Smith, Abdisalan M. Noor, Robert W. Snow, and Caroline O. Buckee. 2012. "Quantifying the Impact of Human Mobility on Malaria." *Science* 338, no. 6104: 267–70.

Wesolowski, Amy, Taimur Qureshi, Maciej F. Boni, Pål Roe Sundsøy, Michael A. Johansson, Syed Basit Rasheed, Kenth Engø-Monsen, and Caroline O. Buckee. 2015. "Impact of Human Mobility on the Emergence of Dengue Epidemics in Pakistan." *Proceedings of the National Academy of Sciences* 112, no. 38: 11887–92.

Wing, Coady, Kosali Simon, and Ricardo A. Bello-Gomez. 2018. "Designing Difference in Difference Studies: Best Practices for Public Health Policy Research." *Annual Review of Public Health* 39:453–69.

Witte, Griff, and Ben Guarino. 2020. "It's Not Only Coronavirus Cases That Are Rising. Now COVID Deaths Are, Too." *Washington Post*, July 17. https://www.washingtonpost.com/national/its-not-only-coronavirus-cases-that-are-rising-now-covid-deaths-are-too/2020/07/17/193006e8-c868-11ea-8ffe-372be8d82298_story.html.

Yehya, Nadir, Atheendar Venkataramani, and Michael O. Harhay. 2020. "Statewide Interventions and COVID-19 Mortality in the United States: An Observational Study." *Clinical Infectious Diseases.*

Comments and Discussion

SUMMARY OF COMMENT

VICTOR CHERNOZHUKOV provided oral comments. He congratulated the authors on providing such rapid and innovative data on economic activity early in the pandemic.

His comments focused on some of the challenges of estimating the effect of non-pharmaceutical interventions (NPIs) on economic activity. He presented weekly correlations between seven distinct NPIs (state-level data, March through May 2020). Nearly all the correlations exceeded 0.8, and several exceeded 0.9, indicating scope for omitted variable bias in regressions by Gupta, Simon, and Wing and by Bartik and colleagues, which considered only a subset of NPIs. Another econometric challenge is that the policies considered in these data were "hard" policies that took effect at a specific known date, while policies that changed behavior more gradually were excluded. Policies that induce gradual behavioral change, if not measured and included, would induce patterns that these regressions could misattribute as endogenous self-protection. As an example, Chernozhukov turned to some of his own research with Hiro Kasahara and Paul Schrimpf on use of masks.[1] They found a large effect of masking orders on cases, deaths, and mobility, both through a direct channel and through a behavioral channel. These and other econometric considerations led him to speculate that both papers—by Gupta, Simon, and Wing and Bartik and colleagues—could underestimate the effect of policies on economic activity.

1. Victor Chernozhukov, Hiroyuki Kasahara, and Paul Schrimpf, "Causal Impact of Masks, Policies, Behavior on Early COVID-19 Pandemic in the U.S.," *Journal of Econometrics* 220, no. 1 (2021): 23–62.

COMMENT BY

CAROLINE BUCKEE The deadly COVID-19 pandemic emerged in early 2020 and, in the absence of effective treatments or a vaccine, led to the unprecedented implementation of socially and economically disruptive non-pharmaceutical interventions around the world. In the two papers by Bartik and colleagues and by Gupta, Simon, and Wing the impact of these interventions on employment and human behavior, respectively, are examined, and in both papers, the authors use data streams from mobile phones to measure social and economic activity in relation to the dynamics of the labor force and public health policies around the United States. The comments below reflect my background as an infectious disease epidemiologist and as a researcher who has been using mobile phone data to monitor movement patterns in the context of disease modeling for nearly a decade. I have focused on two aspects that are relevant to both studies: the importance of spatially heterogeneous disease burden and the use of mobile phone data as a proxy for human behavior.

THE IMPORTANCE OF SPATIAL HETEROGENEITIES IN THE BURDEN OF COVID-19 Both studies examine economic and behavioral time series data in relation to policies that were implemented to slow the transmission of SARS-CoV-2. As they find, and as others have observed (Badr and others 2020), people across the country reacted strongly to the declaration of a national emergency on March 13 regardless of local policies. Almost any measure of mobility or other behavior is likely to show this rapid countrywide decline in activity in response to the threat of the pandemic. Most analyses, including these two, have concluded that the synchronization of behavior may have resulted from individuals acting based on national and global information about the pandemic rather than local policies. Indeed, Bartik and colleagues note that their results with respect to labor markets and economic activity "have more to do with broader health and economic concerns affecting product demand and labor supply" than with the timing of specific policies.

However, the trajectory of the epidemic in the United States has been characterized by distinct geographic heterogeneities within and between individual states, among different demographics, and even within cities (Kissler and others 2020). These heterogeneities reflect the spatial progression of the epidemic across the country, starting in Seattle and New York before moving into the south and middle of the country over the summer, as well as remarkable local heterogeneities resulting from income and racial inequalities. Both of these types of heterogeneity have implications for the interpretation of economic and mobility data because decision making by individuals generating the data reflect very different experiences of the disease itself.

Although people's behaviors in response to the national lockdowns were relatively synchronized across the country, their perceptions of the risks posed from COVID-19 are likely to have been strongly dependent on their personal, local experiences. People in New York may have experienced illness or death among friends and loved ones or witnessed the fatigue and desperation of health workers in their communities. In contrast, recent seroprevalence estimates suggest that even by June, much of the Midwest had not yet experienced any significant SARS-CoV-2 transmission (Anand and others 2020). Not only would this have an impact on individuals' real and perceived risks from COVID-19 but also on their sense that the economic and social hardships experienced as a result of interventions were justified. To the extent that compliance and reaction to non-pharmaceutical interventions will depend on perceived risks, as we have seen in the context of Ebola in West Africa (Peak and others 2018), many of the nationwide metrics analyzed in these studies may mask significant regional heterogeneity. In particular, the speed and behavioral response to reopening, including consumer behavior, people leaving home and mixing socially, and the likelihood that individuals look for work and re-open their businesses, may have shown significant regional variation.

The second important spatial heterogeneity in disease incidence and burden is highly local and reflects structural disparities between neighborhoods that fall along socioeconomic and racial lines. Indeed, Bartik and colleagues find significant differences in employment and rehiring between different racial groups and income levels. Just as regional differences in disease burden may have had an impact on state-level economic and behavioral metrics, local differences in the experience of disease and death from COVID-19 are likely to have been pronounced among these economic categories. Consistent with nationwide racial disparities in mortality due to COVID-19 (Bassett, Chen, and Krieger 2020), analyses of COVID-19 deaths in Cook County, Illinois, found startling mortality rate differences due to COVID-19 between neighborhoods depending on poverty and race, varying from 14.1 per 100,000 in wealthy neighborhoods among white people, to 135.1 per 100,000 in poor neighborhoods among Hispanic and Latinx people (Feldman and Bassett 2020; Acosta and Irizarry 2020). A seroprevalence study among pregnant women in New York City in April showed a cumulative incidence of 11 percent in Manhattan versus 26 percent in South Queens, for example (Kissler and others 2020). In that study we showed that local differences in commuting behavior, measured using mobility data from Facebook users, was strongly correlated with seroprevalence. Thus, both mobility behavior related to employment and COVID-19-related illness and death have had an impact even on people living in the same city differently.

Studies aiming to understand social and economic decisions made by individuals in relation to public health and other policies—as both studies presented here seek to do in different ways—may therefore gain important insights if they account for the dramatic differences between individuals in their local experience of the epidemic when interventions were imposed or lifted.

THE USE OF MOBILITY DATA FROM PRIVATE COMPANIES AS A PROXY FOR HUMAN ACTIVITY Both Bartik and colleagues and Gupta, Simon, and Wing derive quantitative behavioral estimates from SafeGraph data, and Gupta, Simon, and Wing go further and use multiple different sources of activity data (for example, from Google and Apple) from mobile phones. Gupta, Simon, and Wing note that while mobility data from mobile phones have become relatively routine among infectious disease epidemiologists, they are still quite rare in other fields. While mobile phone data are a useful nearly real-time proxy for human behaviors, including for monitoring human behavior during this pandemic, there are a number of important issues that—in my opinion—make it challenging to directly use derived metrics in a quantitative, statistical analysis.

Gupta, Simon, and Wing discuss some of these caveats, including the representativeness of the data with respect to demographic structure, but it is important to outline some of the other systematic biases that may have an impact on analyses. These have been reviewed in the context of COVID-19 in Grantz and others (2020) and Oliver and others (2020), and a standardization of mobility metrics of this kind has been called for (Kishore and others 2020).

So-called ad tech data, such as the data from SafeGraph, can be distinguished from other data sources, including Google, Apple, Facebook, or data from mobile operators. Ad tech data derive from advertisements associated with the use of particular apps on smart phones, and the data from individuals are processed and packaged by multiple companies before they are analyzed. This creates opacity around the biases and details of individual data sets, including missingness, and data imputation or inference is often performed prior to release of the data. Therefore, even an investigation of the biases in the data becomes impossible for research groups using the data. Indeed, unlike data from Facebook, for example, where data quality or missingness is sometimes reported, this imputation step means that uncertainty in the SafeGraph estimates is impossible to ascertain.

Demographic biases are clearly an issue, because most mobility data from mobile phones reflect smart phone users only, who skew young and wealthy (mobile operator data are an exception because they include "dumb phone" subscribers, which is why operator data are often more appropriate in low-income settings). With respect to representativeness, unlike Google or Facebook, ad tech data providers often report their "monthly active users" (MAU), but this can be misleading. For example, 1 million monthly active users is not the same as a longitudinal sample of 1 million individuals because a user may appear infrequently or only once in the data set, and the number of users can vary dramatically from day to day. This high turnover is rarely reported, making it difficult to quantify uncertainty associated with any particular day and location. There are, in addition, geographic variations in representativeness that cannot be accounted for. For example, by comparing Facebook data to SafeGraph data across the United States, we find that while Facebook reports missingness in rural counties, SafeGraph imputes data and reports no missingness (personal communication).

Demographic and geographic representativeness aside, mobility metrics derived from these data sets—such as the mixing index used by Gupta, Simon, and Wing—are difficult to interpret. Standardized analytical frameworks, particularly validated ones, are still absent for this kind of data (Kishore and others 2020). Interpreting mixing indexes and other metrics of mobility is also complicated by the fact that in a large, geographically diverse country, the same movement patterns may represent very different behaviors in urban versus rural locations. Out-of-county travel, for example, is hard to interpret in the absence of spatial context, even when compared to a baseline, because it may depend on the spatial layout of grocery stores and so on. Gupta, Simon, and Wing include multiple metrics and data sources as a way to confirm their findings, which makes sense, but since all the metrics are likely to be biased in the same ways (reflecting smart phone users) there may still be bias unaccounted for. Taken together, although the qualitative findings are important and useful, these issues with uncertainty about data quality and representativeness and the rigor of particular derived metrics mean that making sense of effect sizes from time series and statistical analyses is challenging.

CONCLUSIONS Both studies track the behavioral and economic impacts of the unprecedented public health interventions that were put in place due to COVID-19 earlier this year. As we move into autumn and face a long winter with possible renewal of various behavioral interventions, understanding how people and the economy will respond is critical. Mobile phone data are a valuable source of information about human activity, although they are a loose proxy for the contacts that spread the virus and likely to be increasingly difficult to interpret epidemiologically against the backdrop of layered interventions such as masking. I don't necessarily expect the reaction to future lockdowns to recapitulate the behavioral dynamics we saw in the spring, not only because the economic and political situation is different now, but also, crucially, because now there are hardly any US communities that have not suffered significant illness and death due to COVID-19, and this will change the social and political acceptability of interventions.

REFERENCES FOR THE BUCKEE COMMENT

Acosta, Rolando J., and Rafael A. Irizarry. 2020. "Monitoring Health Systems by Estimating Excess Mortality." MedRxiv. https://www.medrxiv.org/content/10.1101/2020.06.06.20120857v2.

Anand Shuchi, Maria Montez-Rath, Jialin Han, Julie Bozeman, Russell Kerschmann, Paul Beyer, Julie Parsonnet, and Glenn M. Chertow. 2020. "Prevalence of SARS-CoV-2 Antibodies in a Large Nationwide Sample of Patients on Dialysis in the USA: A Cross-Sectional Study." *The Lancet* 396, no. 10259: 1335–44. https://doi.org/10.1016/S0140-6736(20)32009-2.

Badr, Hamada S., Hongru Du, Maximilian Marshall, Ensheng Dong, Marietta M. Squire, and Lauren M. Gardner. 2020. "Association between Mobility Patterns and COVID-19 Transmission in the USA: A Mathematical Modelling Study." *The Lancet Infectious Diseases* 20, no. 11: 1247–54. https://doi.org/10.1016/S1473-3099(20)30553-3.

Bassett, Mary T., Jarvis T. Chen, and Nancy Krieger. 2020. "Variation in Racial/Ethnic Disparities in COVID-19 Mortality by Age in the United States: A Cross-Sectional Study." *PLoS Medicine* 17, no. 10: e1003402. https://doi.org/10.1371/journal.pmed.1003402.

Feldman, Justin M., and Mary T. Bassett. 2020. "The Relationship between Neighborhood Poverty and COVID-19 Mortality within Racial/Ethnic Groups (Cook County, Illinois)." MedRxiv. https://www.medrxiv.org/content/10.1101/2020.10.04.20206318v1.

Grantz, Kyra H., Hannah R. Meredith, Derek A. Cummings, C. Jessica E. Metcalf, Bryan T. Grenfell, John R. Giles, and others. 2020. "The Use of Mobile Phone Data to Inform Analysis of COVID-19 Pandemic Epidemiology." *Nature Communications* 11, article no. 4961. https://doi.org/10.1038/s41467-020-18190-5.

Kishore, Nishant, Mathew V. Kiang, Kenth Engø-Monsen, Navin Vembar, Andrew Schroeder, Satchit Balsari, and Caroline Buckee. 2020. "Measuring Mobility to Monitor Travel and Physical Distancing Interventions: A Common Frame-work for Mobile Phone Data Analysis." *The Lancet Digital Health* 2, no. 11: e622-e628. https://doi.org/10.1016/S2589-7500(20)30193-X.

Kissler, Stephen M., Nishant Kishore, Malavika Prabhu, Dena Goffman, Yaakov Beilin, Ruth Landau, and others. 2020. "Reductions in Commuting Mobility Correlate with Geographic Differences in SARS-CoV-2 Prevalence in New York City." *Nature Communications* 11, article no. 4674. https://doi.org/10.1038/s41467-020-18271-5.

Oliver, Nuria, Bruno Lepri, Harald Sterly, Renaud Lambiotte, Sébastien Deletaille, Marco De Nadai, and others. 2020. "Mobile Phone Data for Informing Public Health Actions across the COVID-19 Pandemic Life Cycle." *Science Advances* 6, no. 23: eabc0764. https://doi.org/10.1126/sciadv.abc0764.

Peak, Corey M., Amy Wesolowski, Elisabeth zu Erbach-Schoenberg, Andrew J. Tatem, Erik Wetter, Xin Lu, and others. 2018. "Population Mobility Reductions Associated with Travel Restrictions during the Ebola Epidemic in Sierra Leone: Use of Mobile Phone Data." *International Journal of Epidemiology* 47, no. 5: 1562–70. https://doi.org/10.1093/ije/dyy095.

GENERAL DISCUSSION   Jason Furman inquired about the nature of job loss over time. Furman remarked that it is possible that if weekly unemployment insurance (UI) claims remain high throughout the summer, then those unemployment spells may be different in nature. For example, he posited that some initial job losses could be primary, direct effects of the COVID-19 pandemic but that it is possible subsequent job losses could be the result of more traditional recession forces. Furman speculated that by determining this distinction between types of job loss, policy-makers may be able to gain insights into how and when those jobs might be recovered.

Hilary Hoynes speculated whether it would be possible to link the private sector Homebase data used in the paper with recently published data from the Treasury Department on the Paycheck Protection Program (PPP). Hoynes suggested it would be interesting to see if there could be a way to see to what extent the PPP affected labor market outcomes for workers in the Homebase data. More specifically, she wondered whether such a linking could shed light on whether PPP loans accomplished certain goals policymakers had for it (e.g., keeping workers connected to their employers).

Adding to this conversation, Marianne Bertrand pointed out that the Treasury Department plans to release detailed data on the name of firms, location, firm size, and so on, for the larger loans (above $150,000). She pointed out that when these data become available, it could be possible to link the firms in the Treasury Department's PPP loan data with the firms in the Homebase data set.

Simon Mongey shared a resource from the Philadelphia Federal Reserve Bank on the PPP loans.[1]

Stephen Goss asked the discussant Caroline Buckee about the effects of seasonality and weather on the spread of the coronavirus. He mentioned that some observers have pointed to Brazil, which, being in the Southern Hemisphere and currently in the midst of winter, has still seen a surge in cases. Goss inquired whether Brazil's experience might provide insights into what sort of experience the United States and the European Union (EU) may have with the virus as our seasons begin to change. He speculated whether the EU's current relative success in controlling the virus may be short-lived as the weather begins to change.

Henry Aaron asked whether improved treatment methods are being incorporated into models. He remarked that it seems much of the conversation has surrounded spread and deaths but not much on changes in treatment.

In response to Goss's comments, Buckee says that because other coronaviruses do exhibit seasonal effects, it is likely that this strand may be affected by seasonality, but to a limited degree. The much more relevant way that seasonality will play a role is in the gathering of people indoors as a result of the colder weather in the fall and winter months. Buckee worried about the potential surge in cases that may result if many of the social interactions that have occurred outdoors during the summer continue indoors in the fall. In particular, she was concerned about schools reopening in the fall without the proper precautions being taken. As for the comparison between the United States and the EU, Buckee argued that the difference in success with dealing with the virus has largely been an effect of policy choices: lack of increased testing capacity, issues surrounding social response and messaging, and so on.

Addressing Aaron's question, Buckee replied that changes in treatment methods have not shown through in the data, largely because there have not been many significant breakthroughs in treatments. In addition to the many ongoing trials, Buckee referred specifically to a recent trial of dexamethasone that showed a 30 percent reduction in deaths among people on ventilators. However, she pointed out that many of those trial results haven't been

1. "SBA_PPP," public data tables on the Payroll Protection Program by the US Small Business Administration, GitHub, https://github.com/RocArm/SBA_PPP?fbclid=IwAR0hHw_lJObIzRoroYWLhWU7RcpiXDszdIkdsMCRz3VLKNMQ4GSsngUwBw.

rolled out widely yet, which is why she didn't think that these trials were having a major impact on treatment and the death rate. A related point that Buckee made in this conversation was that a large share of deaths early on in the pandemic occurred in nursing homes and assisted care facilities. More recently, as states have begun reopening, the largest surge in cases has been among young people, who have a lower mortality rate anyway.[2] In light of these two trends, Buckee commented that it's difficult to disentangle whether that change reflects a demographic shift, differences in social distancing behavior, or household structure differences in different geographic areas as the epidemic spreads across the country. Buckee concluded that while it can be hard to discern exactly what's happening, these trends will be important moving forward.

Austan Goolsbee highlighted a recent paper that he and Chad Syverson have put out that uses county-level lockdown policies (rather than state-level policies).[3] Goolsbee claimed that their paper finds that looking at county-level policies as opposed to state-level ones seems to matter a fair amount: many of the hardest-hit counties implemented policies well before their states did. Goolsbee mentioned that by doing a horse race on the two levels of policy, they find that the local level appears to be far more influential. He concluded by saying that he and his coauthor have posted the data publicly for anyone to use.

Alessandro Rebucci pointed out he has a paper where he and his coauthors analyze the relationship between partisanship and state-level heterogeneity in compliance with non-pharmaceutical interventions (NPIs).[4] Their empirical evidence shows that preferences and attitudes toward "free" interactions are an additional factor in the decision problem. Responding to this point, Bertrand commented that it would be interesting to think about heterogeneity of order effects between Democratic versus Republican states. She speculated that one can imagine that a truly enforced order in a Republican state may matter more than in a Democratic state if people in

---

2. Julie Bosman and Sarah Mervosh, "As Virus Surges, Younger People Account for 'Disturbing' Number of Cases," *New York Times*, June 25, 2020, https://www.nytimes.com/2020/06/25/us/coronavirus-cases-young-people.html.

3. Austan Goolsbee and Chad Syverson, "Fear, Lockdown, and Diversion: Comparing Drivers of Pandemic Economic Decline 2020," working paper 27432 (Cambridge, Mass.: National Bureau of Economic Research, 2020).

4. Alexander Chudik, M. Hashem Pesaran, and Alessandro Rebucci, "Voluntary and Mandatory Social Distancing: Evidence on COVID-19 Exposure Rates from Chinese Provinces and Selected Countries," research paper 20-03 (Baltimore: Johns Hopkins Carey Business School, 2020), https://papers.ssrn.com/sol3/papers.cfm?abstract_id=3576703.

Democratic states take the disease more seriously and are adjusting their behavior even absent an order to do so.

Jesse Rothstein thanked both of the discussants and the participants for their helpful comments. Responding to Furman's comment, Rothstein mentioned that the data used in the paper did not allow for that distinction to be drawn, but he pointed to Till von Watcher's recent paper analyzing California UI claims data.[5] Rothstein mentioned that Hedin, Schnorr, and von Wachter find that the first waves of UI claims were concentrated among workers with less educational attainment and workers in specific industries and that subsequent waves of UI claims tended to be more representative of the broader labor force, potentially supporting Furman's hypothesis.

Alexander Bartik echoed Rothstein's thanks and responded to a few participants' points in particular. Building on Rothstein's response to Furman, Bartik highlighted the figure in their paper that shows payroll employment by month and industry. He emphasized that this figure showed that in the early weeks of the pandemic, the leisure and hospitality industry in particular was hard hit; the data at that time had not shown a spread to certain industries (e.g., durable goods, manufacturing, construction, etc.). However, Bartik acknowledged that the data may change in the coming months.

Bartik responded to Hoynes by stating that currently that sort of linking is not yet possible, but that he and his coauthors are working with scholars at Harvard to conduct a survey of the firms in the Homebase data to see if they can use quasi-experimental methods to accomplish a similar goal with regards the PPP loan data. He also pointed to work being done by Granja and others, who have looked into PPP disbursement and employment effects.[6]

Bartik acknowledged that several participants raised the issue of the paper's focus being only on the shutdown orders. He said that they did this for a variety of reasons but that they plan to incorporate the fuller set of policies into future analysis. Given the nature of Homebase data, he pointed out that they should be able to analyze relatively fine measures of timing. He wanted to clarify that they are not taking a strong stance on

5. Thomas J. Hedin, Geoffrey Schnorr, and Till von Wachter, "California Unemployment Insurance Claims during the COVID-19 Pandemic," policy brief (Los Angeles: California Policy Lab, 2020).

6. Joao Granja, Christos Makridis, Constantine Yannelis, and Eric Zwick, "Did the Paycheck Protection Program Hit the Target?," working paper, April 26, 2020, https://papers.ssrn.com/sol3/papers.cfm?abstract_id=3585258.

the time effects of information per se, but that their interpretation of those effects was that they reflected reduced consumer demands for in-person services. Bartik pointed out that this reduced consumer demand could, in part, be a function of schools being closed, since school closings change how parents consume in-person services.

Lastly, Bartik commented that although they had not done it yet, it is possible for them to look at their Homebase sample for 2018 and 2019, which could bolster their analysis.

Sumedha Gupta also thanked all of the participants and said that she greatly appreciated their feedback. Responding to Buckee's comments, Gupta acknowledged that she agreed with many of her points, especially regarding the heterogeneity of the data sources. She pointed out that their paper addresses many of these differences in the data sets, which is why they chose to look at all of them in an effort to capture the whole story and to see if that story is consistent. Since, thus far, much of the data they have looked at have been consistent, Gupta felt confident in claiming the direction (even if not the magnitude) of the effect. Gupta also pointed out that some of their analysis did look at some local (rural versus urban) differences. She also highlighted that their analysis found interesting differences when looking at indoor versus outdoor activity.

Responding to Victor Chernozhukov's comments, Gupta expressed interest in learning more about his bias correction approach and stated that she intended to look into some of the papers he recommended to see if they can implement it.

Gupta also acknowledged that there is difficulty in parsing out the timing differences between the state of emergency declarations versus stay-at-home orders, especially since it all happened in about a three-week period. Furthermore, Gupta posited that although it can be quite difficult to disentangle the effects of each of the public policies, she and her coauthors think of the emergency declaration as a sort of "reduced form" effect for several of the other policies; in other words, it is almost as if the emergency declarations triggered the start of many of the other policies. However, Gupta still recognized the importance of doing estimations by including controls for the different policies as well as the need to have linearized, event time studies to see the effects for all of the policies simultaneously.

Gupta concluded by stating that their main takeaway is that while there has clearly been a policy response (regardless of how wide-ranging the policies one chooses to include), their data seem to suggest the larger effect has been a private response to this pandemic.

SESSION FIVE
Macroeconomics and Epidemiology

JOSE MARIA BARRERO
Instituto Tecnológico Autónomo de México

NICHOLAS BLOOM
Stanford University

STEVEN J. DAVIS
University of Chicago

COVID-19 Is Also a Reallocation Shock

ABSTRACT   We develop several pieces of evidence about the reallocative effects of the COVID-19 shock on impact and over time. First, the shock caused three to four new hires for every ten layoffs from March 1 to mid-May 2020. Second, we project that one-third or more of the layoffs during this period are permanent in the sense that job losers won't return to their old jobs at their previous employers. Third, firm-level forecasts at a one-year horizon imply rates of expected job and sales reallocation that are two to five times larger from April to June 2020 than before the pandemic. Fourth, full days working from home will triple from 5 percent of all workdays in 2019 to more than 15 percent after the pandemic ends. We also document pandemic-induced job gains at many firms and a sharp rise in cross-firm equity return dispersion in reaction to the pandemic. After developing the evidence, we consider implications for the economic outlook and for policy. Unemployment benefit levels that exceed worker earnings, policies that subsidize employee retention irrespective of the employer's commercial outlook, and barriers to worker mobility and business formation impede reallocation responses to the COVID-19 shock.

The COVID-19 pandemic and efforts to contain the virus have exacted a staggering economic toll in countries around the world. China's economy shrank 6.8 percent in the first quarter of 2020 on a year-on-year

Conflict of Interest Disclosure: The authors did not receive financial support from any firm or person for this paper or from any firm or person with a financial or political interest in this paper. They are currently not officers, directors, or board members of any organization with an interest in this paper. No outside party had the right to review this paper before circulation. The views expressed in this paper are those of the authors, and do not necessarily reflect those of the Instituto Tecnológico Autónomo de México, Stanford University, or the University of Chicago.

basis, and eurozone economies shrank at a 14.8 percent annualized rate. In the United States, nearly 28 million persons filed new claims for unemployment benefits over the six-week period ending April 25. The US economy shrank an annualized rate of 5.0 percent in the first quarter of 2020 and 32.9 percent in the second quarter (BEA 2020). Yet, even as much of the economy shut down, many firms expanded in response to pandemic-induced demand shifts. As Bender and Dalton (2020) put it in the *Wall Street Journal*, "the coronavirus pandemic is forcing the fastest reallocation of labor since World War II, with companies and governments mobilizing an army of idled workers into new activities that are urgently needed." That is, COVID-19 is a major reallocation shock.

We develop evidence on the extent, character, and timing of the reallocative aspects of the COVID-19 shock for the US economy. We start by quantifying the near-term reallocative impact on business staffing outcomes, drawing on two special questions fielded in the April 2020 Survey of Business Uncertainty (SBU). One question asks (as of mid-April) about the coronavirus impact on own-company staffing since March 1, and another asks about the anticipated impact over the ensuing four weeks. Cumulating responses over firms and across these two questions, the data say that pandemic-related developments caused near-term layoffs equal to 12.9 percent of March 1 employment and new hires equal to 3.9 percent. In other words, the COVID-19 shock caused three new hires in the near term for every ten layoffs. Similarly, the Job Openings and Labor Turnover Survey (JOLTS) reports more than four hires for every ten layoffs in March and April. This large volume of new hires amid a tremendous employment contraction aligns well with payroll statistics reported by Cajner and others (2020), with Census Bureau statistics on gross business formation, and with anecdotal evidence of large pandemic-induced increases in labor demand at some firms.

Next, we construct projections for the permanent layoff share of recent job losses. As a first step, we draw on questions about layoff status put to employers in the SBU, to unemployment benefit claimants in California, and to households in a *Washington Post*–Ipsos survey. The first two sources indicate that about 23 percent of layoffs from March to May 2020 were seen as permanent at the time, and the rest were seen as temporary. (The *Washington Post*–Ipsos survey yields a figure of 20 percent.) Historically, many layoffs perceived as temporary when they happen do not result in recalls. Adjusting for this pattern, we project that roughly one-third or more of COVID-19-induced layoffs will be permanent in the sense that job losers don't return to their old jobs at their former employers. Because we use historic evidence on how temporary layoffs convert to actual recalls, our adjustment could be too small or too large for the current episode. In addition, the conversion rate will surely depend on how long it takes to resolve the COVID-19 health crisis and for the economy to recover. Still, our key message in this regard is clear: many jobs lost in the wake of the COVID-19 pandemic are gone for good.

We also use SBU data to develop novel measures of expected reallocation activity. Specifically, we aggregate over firm-level employment forecasts to calculate the following quantity: gross expected job gains at firms that anticipate growing over the next year plus gross expected job losses at firms that anticipate shrinking over the next year minus the absolute value of the expected aggregate employment change. Dividing this quantity by aggregate employment yields our measure of the expected excess job reallocation rate at a one-year look-ahead horizon. It rises from 1.5 percent of employment in January 2020 to 5.4 percent in April. This April value is 2.4 times the pre-COVID average and is the highest value in the short history of the series. Using firm-level sales forecasts at a one-year horizon, we find a similar pattern: the expected excess reallocation rate rises from an average of just under 1 percent of sales before the pandemic to more than 5 percent from April to June 2020. These forward-looking measures reinforce the view that COVID-19 is a major reallocation shock.

Next, we draw on special questions in the May 2020 SBU to quantify the anticipated shift to working from home after the coronavirus pandemic ends, relative to the situation that prevailed before it struck. To do so, we first asked firms about the share of full workdays performed at home by their full-time employees in 2019. (Responses to this question for the prepandemic situation align well with worker responses to similar questions about working from home in the 2017–2018 American Time Use Survey.) We then asked firms what they anticipate about the share of full workdays performed at home after the pandemic ends. Comparing responses to the before and after questions, firms expect that full workdays performed at home will triple. This expected tripling will involve shifting one-tenth of all full workdays from business premises to residences— one-fifth for office workers. Since the scope for working from home rises with wages, the shift in worker spending power from business districts to locations near residences is even greater.

Finally, we consider time series evidence on the dispersion in monthly equity returns across US-listed firms. Return dispersion relates less directly to future reallocation activity, but its availability over several decades helps us put the COVID-19 episode in perspective. Whether measured by the interquartile range or the standard deviation of returns in the value-weighted distribution, the dispersion in equity returns jumps sharply in March 2020, reaching levels last seen during the financial crisis of 2008–2009 and the dot.com bust of the early 2000s. These three episodes exhibit the highest return dispersion in our sample period, which starts in 1984.

After presenting the evidence, we consider implications for the economic outlook and for policy responses to the pandemic. As of late July 2020, it is nearly five months since the COVID-19 recession began in earnest. Even if medical advances or natural forces bring an end to the health crisis in the near future, there are sound economic reasons to think that pandemic-induced shifts in consumer spending patterns, working arrangements, and business practices will partly stick. First, millions of households have tried online shopping and delivery services in recent months. Some find they like it and will continue to value the convenience and (perceived) safety after the pandemic ends. Second, according to our survey evidence, more than half of all employees worked from home as of May 2020. This mass experiment has pushed workers and organizations to invest in becoming more effective at working from home, which is a source of persistence in the new working arrangements. Barrero, Bloom, and Davis (2020) also find that most workers have been positively surprised by their productivity at home and want to continue working from home one or more days per week after the pandemic. Third, after turning to virtual meetings out of necessity, many businesses are likely to see them as an easier, cheaper option to travel and in-person meetings in some circumstances. A persistent drop in business travel has profound implications for travel and hospitality industries. Fourth, the pandemic knocked down regulations that had stymied a shift from in-person to virtual interactions, especially in health care services. These economic forces and mechanisms suggest that much of the near-term reallocative impact of the pandemic will persist. If the COVID-19 pandemic lingers for many more months, or if new pandemic threats emerge, it will further drive and entrench recent shifts in consumer spending patterns, working arrangements, and business practices.

Historically, creation responses to major reallocation shocks lag the destruction responses by a year or more. Partly for this reason, we anticipate a drawn-out economic recovery from the COVID-19 shock, even if the pandemic is largely controlled in the next few months. Multiple forces contribute to delayed creation, as we discuss. Policy responses to major shocks and inherited features of the policy landscape can further stretch out the creation response, slowing the recovery. In this regard, we discuss five aspects of US policy that retard creation responses to the pandemic-induced reallocation shock: unemployment benefit levels that exceed earnings for many American workers, policies that subsidize employee retention irrespective of employers' longer-term outlook, land-use restrictions that inhibit the reallocation of jobs and workers, occupational licensing restrictions the impede mobility across occupations and states, and regulations that inhibit business formation and expansion.

I. Evidence

I.A. Gross Hiring and Business Formation in the Pandemic's Immediate Wake

The top part of table 1 presents two questions about the impact of COVID-19 on staffing levels in the April 2020 SBU, fielded April 13–24. One question asks about impact on own-company staffing levels since March 1, 2020, and the other asks about the anticipated impact over the next four weeks. For each question, the survey instrument allows responses in five categories: number of permanent layoffs, with no expectation of recall; number of temporary layoffs and furloughs; hires of new employees; cuts to the number of contractors and leased workers; and additions to the number of contractors and leased workers. Cumulating the responses to these two questions and aggregating over firms yields a near-term net contraction (exclusive of quits) equal to 10.8 percent of March 1 employment. Ninety-two percent of this net contraction happened between March 1 and the mid-April survey response period, and the rest is anticipated to happen over the ensuing four weeks. Using JOLTS statistics to impute quits, we obtain a net staffing reduction equal to 14.2 percent of March 1 employment, which is similar to the fall in active employment among continuing firms that Cajner and others (2020, fig. 2, panel B) find over the same time period in tabulations of ADP payroll records.

Despite the huge negative employment impact of the pandemic and lockdown, the coronavirus shock caused sizable gross staffing gains over the span of two and a half months: new hires equal to 3.9 percent of March 1 employment and new contractors and leased workers equal to 0.2 percent. SBU data also say the COVID-19 shock caused gross staffing reductions equal to 14.9 percent of March 1 employment (18.3 percent inclusive of quits), mostly due to temporary layoffs and furloughs. The undersampling of young firms in the SBU, the omission of new firms from the sample frame, and lower survey response rates of highly stressed firms are reasons to think our estimates of gross staffing changes are downwardly biased.

Table 1. Gross Staffing Changes in Reaction to the COVID-19 Pandemic

Survey questions: We would also like to ask how developments related to the coronavirus are affecting staffing levels at your firm:

—Since March 1, we made the following staffing changes in response to developments related to the coronavirus (response options as indicated below).

—Over the next four weeks, we expect to make the following staffing changes in response to developments related to the coronavirus (response options as indicated below).

Survey response period: April 13–24, 2020.

	From March 1 to mid-April	Over next four weeks	Cumulative
Net staffing change, exclusive of quits	−10.0	−0.9	−10.8
	(1.18)	(2.02)	(2.63)
Net staffing change, with imputed quits	−12.5	−1.9	−14.2
Gross staffing reductions, exclusive of quits	10.9	4.0	14.9
	(1.16)	(0.69)	(1.62)
Gross staffing reductions, with imputed quits	13.4	5.0	18.3
Permanent layoffs	0.9	0.7	1.5
	(0.18)	(0.23)	(0.34)
Temporary layoffs and furloughs	8.5	2.9	11.4
	(0.95)	(0.49)	(1.28)
Cuts in contractors and leased workers	1.6	0.5	2.0
	(0.63)	(0.36)	(0.85)
Imputed quits	2.5	0.9	3.4
Gross staffing increases	0.9	3.1	4.1
	(0.16)	(1.88)	(2.05)
Hires of new employees	0.8	3.0	3.9
	(0.16)	(1.88)	(2.04)
Additions to contractors and leased workers	0.1	0.1	0.2
	(0.03)	(0.05)	(0.06)
Number of survey responses	368	341	335

Source: Authors' calculations using data from the April 2020 Survey of Business Uncertainty.

Notes: Entries are activity-weighted means, expressed as a percent of employment on March 1. Standard errors in parentheses. According to data from the Job Opening and Labor Turnover Survey, there were 0.2314 quits per layoff in March 2020 and 0.2191 in April. We multiply these fractions by the SBU layoff rates in the table to obtain imputed quits.

We can restate our results about gross staffing gains and losses in terms that are less sensitive to these sources of bias. In particular, table 1 implies that coronavirus-related developments caused about three new hires for every ten layoffs. If we include contractors and leased workers, the ratio is about 2.7 gross staffing gains for every ten gross staffing reductions. JOLTS data for March and April show 4.6 hires for every ten layoffs. Similarly, Cajner and others (2020) find a high incidence of new hires in ADP data for April and May 2020. While it might seem surprising to find so many hires amid the sharpest employment contraction since records began, simultaneous large-scale hiring and separations are a ubiquitous feature of US labor markets.[1]

JOLTS data on job openings also point to large-scale hiring plans in the immediate wake of the COVID-19 pandemic. There were about 6.2 million job openings in the US private sector on the last (business) days of January and February 2020, 5.3 million on the last day of March, and 4.3 million on the last day of April. In other words, job openings after the pandemic struck were about 69 to 85 percent as large as before it struck. In this regard, it's important to note that the JOLTS concept of job openings excludes positions open only to internal transfers, positions to be filled by recalls from temporary layoffs, and positions that are not available to start within thirty days. According to JOLTS data, actual hires in April 2020 were 70 percent of actual hires in February. Thus, JOLTS statistics confirm that large-scale hiring activity, actual and planned, continued during the pandemic recession, though at a much-reduced pace. This statistical evidence aligns well with anecdotal evidence of large pandemic-induced labor demand increases at some firms, detailed in online appendix C.

Census Bureau statistics on gross business formation also point to gross hiring activity in the near-term wake of the pandemic. These statistics derive from administrative data on applications for a new employer identification number (EIN) on IRS Form SS-4. Figure 1 reports statistics for "high-propensity" applications, which are the subset of applications for a new EIN that the Census Bureau regards as having a high propensity to hire paid employees. The figure makes three points. First, gross business formation in the second half of March and in April was down 20 to 38 percent relative to the same week in 2019. While depressed, business formation did not dry up in the immediate wake of the COVID-19 shock. Second, new business applications began to recover in May, and by late May were down less than 5 percent from a year earlier. Third, business formation continued to rise in June, surpassing both year-earlier values and the pace of business formation in early 2020. In sum, new business formation was greatly depressed, but not moribund, in the wake of the COVID-19 shock. It recovered in May and surpassed prepandemic levels in June.

I.B. Projecting the Permanent Layoff Share of COVID-19 Job Losses

According to table 1, employers perceived 23.5 percent of their layoffs from March 1 to mid-May as permanent at the time of job loss.

---

1. See, for example, Davis, Faberman, and Haltiwanger (2006) and Lazear and Spletzer (2012).

Figure 1. High-Propensity Business Applications in 2020 and Percent Change Relative to 2019

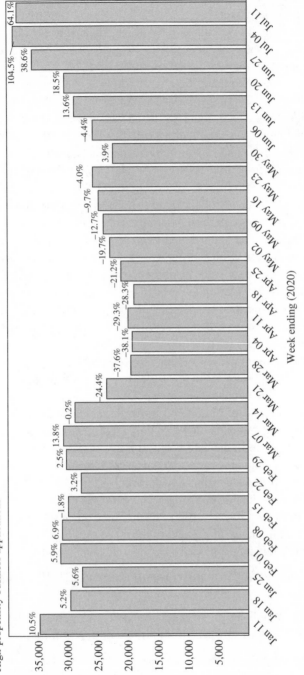

High-propensity business applications

Week ending (2020)

Source: Weekly Business Formation Statistics, https://www.census.gov/data/experimental-data-products/weekly-business-formation-statistics.html; US Census Bureau.
Notes: These statistics derive from administrative data on applications for a new employer identification number (EIN) on IRS Form SS-4. Characteristics of applicants indicating high-propensity include (a) being from a corporate entity; (b) hiring employees, purchasing a business, or changing organizational type; (c) providing a first wages paid date (planned wages); or (d) having a NAICS industry code in manufacturing (31–33), retail stores (44), health care (62), or restaurants/food service (72). Year-on-year percent changes in the number of high-propensity business applications relative to the same week in 2019 given as percentages above each bar.

A *Washington Post*–Ipsos survey of 8,086 American adults fielded from April 27 to May 4, 2020, finds that 20 percent of layoffs were seen as permanent.[2] Claimants for unemployment benefits in California from March to May 2020 perceived 23.2 percent of their job losses as permanent as of the filing date.[3] In online appendix A, we develop two estimates for the permanent layoff share of job losses between March and April 2020 using the Current Population Survey (CPS). Our lower CPS-based estimate of 26 percent arises by treating persons absent from work with pay for "other reasons" as on temporary layoff. Our higher estimate of 34 percent treats these persons as employed. A survey of 500 hiring decisionmakers commissioned by Upwork and fielded April 22–28 finds that 47 percent of recent layoffs were perceived as permanent.[4]

As we discuss in online appendix A, it is challenging to estimate the permanent layoff share of job losses using CPS data.[5] The 47 percent figure from the Upwork survey is an outlier, and we are inclined to discount it. We prefer the permanent layoff figures derived from the SBU, *Washington Post*–Ipsos poll, and California unemployment claimants, which are quite similar. Thus, we use SBU figures in our base case projections for the fraction of pandemic-induced job losses that ultimately turn out to be permanent in the sense that the job loser does not return to a job at his or her previous employer. Recall that 27.9 million Americans filed new claims for unemployment benefits in the six weeks ending April 25. Multiplying 27.9 million by the 23.5 percent permanent layoff share in the SBU yields over 6.5 million permanent layoffs.

Of course, there remains tremendous uncertainty about the economic outlook. For many firms, today's cash-flow problems will become tomorrow's insolvencies, and temporary layoffs will become permanent.[6] The longer the pandemic persists, the longer it will take for the economy to

---

2. See the *Washington Post*–Ipsos poll, conducted online April 27–May 4, 2020, https://context-cdn.washingtonpost.com/notes/prod/default/documents/7a39185f-8222-4e28-9528-5741ebb137ad/note/2e5183d3-9f6f-45a1-84ab-7f2532c8c5fb.#page=1, question 26. Another 3 percent of respondents express no opinion as to whether they will be re-hired by their more recent employer.

3. Muhammad Akhtar and Till von Wachter kindly supplied the California data. See online appendix B.

4. See the Upwork 2020 Future Workforce Report (slides), www.slideshare.net/upwork/2020-future-workforce-report/1.

5. Online appendix A also explains why the headline CPS statistic for the share of unemployed persons on temporary layoffs is not a sound estimate for the permanent layoff share of job losses.

6. For anecdotal evidence of how temporary layoffs are becoming permanent in the wake of COVID-19, see Morath (2020).

recover and the larger the share of recent layoffs that will turn out to be permanent. To get a sense of the fraction of layoffs that will lead to actual recalls, we turn to historical evidence from two sources. Using a sample of unemployment insurance (UI) recipients in Missouri and Pennsylvania from 1979 to 1981, Katz and Meyer (1990) find that 72 percent of UI recipients who initially anticipated recall were actually recalled. In addition, 13 percent of ex ante permanent layoffs were, in fact, recalled. Giuseppe Moscarini kindly provided us with alternative estimates based on Survey of Income and Program Participation data from 1990 to 2013 and the analysis in Fujita and Moscarini (2017). He estimates that 87.5 (6.6) percent of layoffs perceived as temporary (permanent) at the time of job loss led to actual recalls.

Applying the Katz and Meyer (1990) figures to statistics in the "Cumulative" column in table 1 implies actual recalls equal to $(0.72)[11.4/14.9] + 0.13[(1.5 + 2.0)/14.9] = 58$ percent of gross staffing reductions. This calculation adjusts for permanent layoffs that result in recalls and treats cuts in contractors and leased workers like permanent layoffs. According to this calculation, 42 percent of gross staffing reductions in table 1 will result in permanent layoffs. Applying the 42 percent figure to the 27.9 million new claims for unemployment benefits in the six weeks ending on April 25 yields 11.7 million permanently lost jobs. This number does not include later job losses caused by the COVID-19 shock. Applying instead the recall rates from Moscarini yields 32 percent as the realized permanent layoff share of COVID-19-induced job losses. While there is uncertainty about the share of pandemic-induced job losses that will ultimately result in permanent layoffs, that should not distract from the key point: many millions of jobs lost during the pandemic recession will result in permanent layoffs.

I.C. Constructing Forward-Looking Reallocation Measures

We now use SBU data to construct forward-looking reallocation measures. For this purpose, we rely on monthly SBU questions that elicit subjective forecast distributions over own-firm future outcomes at a one-year look-ahead horizon. (More precisely, the forecast horizon is twelve months for employment and four quarters for sales.) The survey instrument also gathers data for current and past outcomes. See Altig, Barrero and others (2020) for more information.

Let $E_t L_{i,t+12}$ denote the expected level of employment in month $t + 12$ at firm i implied by its subjective forecast distribution at t. Define the corresponding month t expected employment growth rate at a twelve-month look-ahead horizon as the arc change rate,

$$E_t g_{i,t+12} = \frac{E_t L_{i,t+12} - L_{it}}{0.5\left(L_{it} + E_t L_{i,t+12}\right)},$$

where all quantities on the right side derive from survey responses in month t.[7] Denote the firm's activity weight as $z_{it} \equiv 0.5(L_{it} + E_t L_{i,t+12})$ and aggregate activity as $Z_t = \sum_i z_{it}$. Let S_t^+ and S_t^- denote the sets of firms at t with positive and negative values, respectively, for $E_t g_{i,t+12}$.

We compute the expected excess job reallocation rate in month t as

$$E_t X_{t+12}^{jobs} = \sum_{i \in S_t^-}\left(\frac{z_{it}}{Z_t}\right)\left|E_t g_{i,t+12}\right| + \sum_{i \in S_t^+}\left(\frac{z_{it}}{Z_t}\right)\left|E_t g_{i,t+12}\right| - \left|\sum_i \left(\frac{z_{it}}{Z_t}\right)E_t g_{i,t+12}\right|,$$

where the first term on the right side is the expected gross job destruction rate over the twelve-month forecast horizon, the second term is the expected gross job creation rate, and the third term is the absolute value of the expected net aggregate growth rate.[8] This statistic quantifies the volume of cross-firm job reallocation in excess of what's required by the aggregate change. Equivalently, we can calculate twice the minimum of expected gross job gains and losses and divide by the simple average of current and expected employment to obtain a rate. This equivalent calculation makes clear that our measure quantifies *simultaneous* creation and destruction.[9] We compute the expected excess sales reallocation rate in an analogous manner.[10]

7. This growth rate measure is symmetric about zero, bounded between -2 and 2, and equal to log changes up to a second-order Taylor series approximation. Growth rates computed this way aggregate exactly when combined with suitable weights, given by the simple mean of initial and (expected) terminal levels. They also accommodate births, deaths, and continuers in an integrated manner. This approach to growth rate measurement and aggregation has become standard in the literature on business-level dynamics. See Davis and Haltiwanger (1999).

8. In practice, we Winsorize the z_{it} values at 500 and the $E_t g_{i,t+12}$ values at the 1st and 99th percentiles of the distribution of expected employment growth rates in data pooled over the period from October 2014 to December 2018. These thresholds follow Altig, Barrero, and others (2020).

9. For example, if three firms forecast employment changes of -3, -1, and zero, excess reallocation is zero. Alternatively, if three firms forecast employment changes of -3, -1, and 2, then excess reallocation is 4. If current employment is 4 for each firm, the expected excess reallocation rate is 36.4 percent in this example. See Davis and Haltiwanger (1999) for additional discussion.

10. For sales, we Winsorize z_{it} at the 90th percentile of its distribution in the pooled sample from September 2016 to April 2020. We Winsorize $E_t g_{i,t+12}$ at the 1st and 99th percentiles of the distribution of expected sales growth rates in the pooled sample for the period from October 2014 to December 2018. See Altig, Barrero, and others (2020) for an explanation of how we obtain arc percentage changes and implied levels of expected future sales from SBU data on the forecast distribution over future sales growth rates.

Since we use SBU data to construct our forward-looking reallocation measures, we would like some assurance that the underlying firm-level data contain meaningful forecasts. In this regard, Altig, Barrero, and others (2020) and Barrero (2020) show that firm-level growth rate expectations in the SBU data are highly predictive of realized growth rates. Moreover, firm-level subjective uncertainty measures in the SBU response are highly predictive of the magnitudes of their forecast errors and future forecast revisions. Using survey questions with the same design as the SBU questions, a revision under way of Bloom and others (2017) finds that plant-level growth rate expectations in the Census Bureau's Manufacturing and Organizational Practices Survey are also highly predictive of realized outcomes. These studies give us confidence that our forward-looking reallocation measures reflect meaningful forecasts of firm-level growth rates.

That said, there are good reasons to think that our SBU-derived measures understate the expected reallocation rate on average and that they also understate the rise in expected reallocation activity in the wake of the pandemic. First, the SBU undersamples younger firms, which have much higher reallocation rates than mature firms. Second, highly stressed firms are less likely to respond to surveys, which leads to an understatement of expected destruction activity.[11] Third, we cannot sample firms that enter in the future, which causes an understatement of expected creation activity. Thus, we regard our estimates of forward-looking reallocation rates as conservative in terms of both average levels and the pandemic-induced response.

I.D. Expected Excess Reallocation Rates

Table 2 summarizes expected reallocation rates before and after the COVID-19 pandemic hit the US economy, and figure 2 displays monthly rates from September 2016 onward.[12] The pre-COVID expected excess job reallocation rate averages 0.97 percent for sales and 2.23 percent for jobs. It rises from 1.54 percent in January 2020 to 5.37 percent in April, which is 2.4 times the pre-COVID-19 mean. The upward jump from March to April is the largest move in the short history of the series. The expected sales reallocation rate jumps from 0.24 percent in January 2020

---

11. In line with this remark, the survey response rates among active SBU panelists are 57 percent in January 2020, 60 percent in February, 57 percent in March, and 52 percent in April, where active panelists are those who responded to the survey at least once in the previous six months.

12. The SBU first went to field in October 2014, but the early monthly samples were small and our formulation of the look-ahead questions did not stabilize until September 2016.

Table 2. Expected Growth and Excess Reallocation Rates at One-Year Forecast Horizons, Average Values of Monthly Statistics for the Indicated Time Periods

	Expected growth rates		Expected excess reallocation rates	
	Sales	*Jobs*	*Sales*	*Jobs*
September 2016 to January 2020	4.37	1.59	0.97	2.23
April to June 2020	−0.57	1.04	5.62	4.52

Source: Authors' calculations using data on firm-level forecasts in the Survey of Business Uncertainty.
Notes: We first use the firm-level forecasts to compute activity-weighted statistics for each month. We then compute the simple mean over months of each statistic for the indicated time period to obtain the table entries. Figures 2 and C.1 (in the online appendix) plot the monthly values. For the period from April to June 2020, we have 386 firm-level observations for jobs and 361 for sales.

Figure 2. Expected Excess Reallocation Rates at One-Year Forecast Horizons, Monthly

Percent

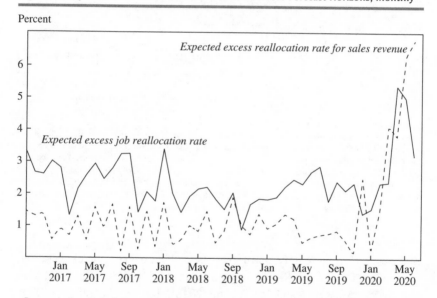

Source: Authors' calculations using data from the Survey of Business Uncertainty.

to 4.11 percent in March and above 6 percent in May and June. The March through June values are also the highest in the history of the series, and several times the pre-COVID mean. In sum, our forward-looking measures confirm that COVID-19 is a large reallocation shock.

Several other countries conduct surveys that could be used to construct forward-looking reallocation measures like the ones in figure 2. The UK Decision Maker Panel, a monthly survey that began in August 2016, includes questions patterned after the ones in the SBU (Bloom and others 2018).

Figure 3. Working from Home

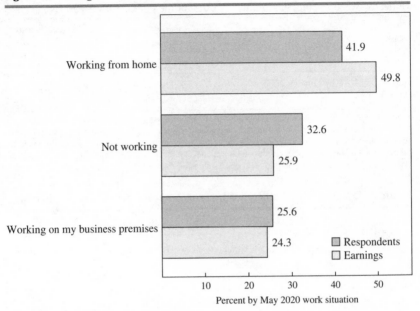

Percent by May 2020 work situation

Source: Survey by QuestionPro on behalf of Stanford University.
Notes: Survey fielded May 21–29, of 2,500 US residents age 20–64, earning more than $20,000 per year in 2019. Survey question read: "Currently (this week) what is your work status?" Response options: "Working on my business premises," "Working from home," "Still employed and paid, but not working," "Unemployed, but expect to be recalled to my previous job," "Unemployed, and do not expect to be recalled to my previous job," and "Not working, and not looking for work." We reweight the sample to match the share of individuals at the level of cells defined by the cross-product of earnings interval, state, and industry (using the current or most recent job) in CPS data from 2010 to 2019.

Surveys in Germany, Italy, and Japan also collect data on the expectations of firm-level variables. See Guiso and Parigi (1999), Bachmann and Elstner (2015), Massenot and Pettinicchi (2018), Tanaka and others (2020), and Chen and others (2019). Thus, it is feasible to construct forward-looking excess reallocation time series for several countries, which would be quite helpful in evaluating their predictive content and usefulness for policymakers.

I.E. The Shift to Working from Home

COVID-19 precipitated a mass social experiment in working from home. To quantify this phenomenon, we surveyed 2,500 US residents age 20–64 who earned more than $20,000 in 2019. Figure 3 summarizes their work status as of late May 2020 based on responses to the following question: "Currently (this week) what is your work status?" Response options were "Working on my business premises," "Working from home," and other options that figure 3 groups under "Not working." Nearly 42 percent of our respondents report working from home. Adjusting for those not working, the survey results say that 62 percent of labor services were supplied from home as of late May (67 percent on an earnings-weighted basis).[13] In an independently conducted survey of persons who were employed pre-COVID, Brynjolfsson and others (2020) find that half were working from home as of late May and 10 percent had been recently laid off or furloughed. Adjusting for those not working, their results say that 56 percent of labor services were supplied from home as of late May. In another independent survey, Bick, Blandin, and Mertens (2020) find that 35 percent of persons employed in May 2020 report working entirely from home and another 14 percent report working from home on some days. All three surveys confirm that COVID-19 caused a massive shift to working from home.[14]

Anecdotal accounts and economic reasoning suggest that much of this shift will persist. For example, Horwitz (2020) reports that Facebook will move to a "substantially remote workforce over the next decade" in response to the "dispersed structure that the coronavirus pandemic forced on it." Facebook foresees a gradual shift to working from home because it "will require new techniques and tools to compensate for the loss of in-person office interactions." Given its success in creating platforms and tools for remote interactivity, Facebook's efforts to develop better tools for remote interactions are likely to have an outsized impact on the overall extent of working from home.

A large, permanent shift to working from home would have powerful effects on the spatial distributions of jobs, labor supply, and worker spending, with profound implications for the future of cities. Motivated by these considerations, we posed two questions in the mid-May SBU to assess how firms expect COVID-19 to change the extent of working from home *after* the pandemic recedes. To get a prepandemic starting point, we

13. The calculation is $41.9/(100 - 32.6) = 62$ percent for the equal-weighted figure and $49.8/(100 - 25.9) = 67$ percent for the earnings-weighted figure.

14. The propensity to work from home in May 2020 rises sharply with earnings, according to Bick, Blandin, and Mertens (2020), Barrero, Bloom, and Davis (2020), and the data that underlie figure 3. Since our sample excludes persons who earned less than $20,000 in 2019, it is likely to somewhat overstate the share of all employees who worked from home.

Table 3. Working from Home before and after the COVID-19 Pandemic

Survey of Business Uncertainty questions:
—What percentage of your full-time employees worked from home in 2019?
—What percentage of your full-time employees will work from home after the coronavirus pandemic?
Survey response period: May 11–22, 2020.

	Employment-weighted mean share of employees who worked				
	Rarely or never	*One full day per week*	*Two to four full days per week*	*Five full days per week*	*Paid workdays at home as a percentage of all workdays*
Survey of Business Uncertainty (May 2020)					
worked from home in 2019	90.3% (1.11)	3.4% (0.52)	2.9% (0.41)	3.4% (0.56)	5.5% (0.70)
will work from home after the coronavirus pandemic	73.0% (1.97)	6.9% (0.64)	9.9% (0.94)	10.3% (1.23)	16.6% (1.41)
American Time Use Survey (2017–2018)					
worked from home in 2017–2018	89.8%	3.8%	3.8%	2.6%	5.2%

Sources: Bureau of Labor Statistics (BLS) American Time Use Survey (ATUS); Survey of Business Uncertainty; authors' calculations.

Notes: In computing the Survey of Business Uncertainty statistics, we weight each firm by its employment and further weight to match the one-digit industry distribution of payroll employment in the US economy. We drop firms with responses that don't sum to approximately 100 percent across the response options for a given question. We also drop firms that clearly misinterpreted the pre-COVID-19 question as asking about the situation during the pandemic. The resulting sample has 279 observations for the 2019 question and 280 observations for the post-pandemic question. ATUS data cover full-time workers. We compute the number of paid workdays at home as a percent of all workdays by converting the number of days at home to a fraction of the workweek (0.2 for 1 day, 0.5 for 2–4 days, 1 for 5 days) and multiplying by the share in each category.

asked, "What percentage of your full-time employees worked from home in 2019?" And, to gauge the post-pandemic situation, we asked, "What percentage of your full-time employees will work from home after the coronavirus pandemic?" For each question, we let firms sort their full-time employees into five categories, ranging from a share that works from home five full days per week to a share that rarely or never works from home.

Table 3 summarizes the employment-weighted survey responses by firms as well as worker responses to a similar question in the 2017–2018 American Time Use Survey (ATUS). The firm-side SBU and worker-side

ATUS yield quite similar pre-COVID-19 results. Both surveys say 90 percent of employees rarely or never worked from home, and a very small fraction worked from home five full days per week.[15] As reported in the rightmost column, about 5 to 6 percent of full workdays were performed at home before the pandemic hit. According to the SBU results, the anticipated share of full workdays at home is set to triple after the pandemic ends—rising from 5.5 percent to 16.6 percent of all workdays. Put differently, more than one-tenth of full workdays will shift from business premises to residences. The implied spatial shift in worker spending is greater yet, because the scope for working from home is strongly positively correlated with earnings (Dingel and Neiman 2020).

As reported in table 4, firms in every sector anticipate a large shift to working from home. Consider finance, insurance, professional services, and business services, industries that disproportionately employ well-paid office workers in city business districts. Firms in this sector anticipate that full workdays at home by full-time employees will rise from 10.7 percent of all workdays before the pandemic to 29.2 percent after the pandemic. These figures say that 21 percent of full workdays performed on business premises before COVID-19 will switch to working from home.[16] This statistic implies a huge, persistent shift in worker spending power away from central business districts to locations closer to residences.

I.F. Dispersion in Equity Returns across Firms

Tables 1–4 and figures 1–3 draw on data sources with short histories, which makes it hard to situate the evidence in a broad historical context. Thus, we turn to time series evidence on the dispersion of returns across the common equity securities of US-listed firms.[17] Specifically, we compute the interquartile range and the standard deviation of value-weighted returns across firms using closing market prices from the end of one month to

15. For SBU industry sectors that we can match to ATUS statistics, the two sources imply a similar pre-COVID incidence of working from home. For manufacturing, SBU data say 9 percent of employees worked at home at least one day a week before COVID-19, and the ATUS data say that 7.3 percent did so. For retail and wholesale trade, the corresponding figures are 4.1 percent and 4.0 percent.

16. Calculated as $100 \times (29.2 - 10.7)/(100 - 10.7)$.

17. We are hardly the first to use the dispersion in stock returns as a proxy for reallocative shocks. See, for example, Loungani, Rush, and Tave (1990), Brainard and Cutler (1993), and Davis, Loungani, and Mahidhara (1997). Unlike these earlier works, we consider dispersion across firms rather than industries.

Table 4. Working from Home before and after the COVID-19 Pandemic by Industry Sector

Survey questions:
— What percentage of your full-time employees worked from home in 2019?
— What percentage of your full-time employees will work from home after the coronavirus pandemic?
Survey response period: May 11–22, 2020.

	Full workdays at home as a percentage of all paid workdays	
	2019	*After the coronavirus pandemic*
Overall	5.5 (0.70)	16.6 (1.41)
Finance, insurance, professional services, and business services	10.7 (1.88)	29.2 (2.96)
Education, health, and other services except government	4.6 (1.62)	14.1 (3.69)
Manufacturing	6.8 (1.50)	11.5 (1.91)
Retail and wholesale trade	2.6 (1.00)	7.4 (2.27)
Construction, real estate, mining, and utilities	1.4 (0.44)	22.4 (4.97)

Source: Survey of Business Uncertainty; authors' calculations.

the end of the next. We consider return dispersion rather than the excess reallocation of equity value given the predominant role of discount rate variation in aggregate stock market moves (Shiller 1981; Campbell and Shiller 1988; Cochrane 2011). If discount rates on risky securities generally rose in reaction to the COVID-19 shock, an excess reallocation measure would obscure heterogeneity in the shock's impact on expected firm-level cash flows.[18] In contrast, this heterogeneity shows up in return dispersion measures if the discount rate variation itself is dominated by common factors.

Figure 4 displays the dispersion in monthly equity returns from January 1984 to April 2020. Three episodes stand out: the dot.com market bust in the early 2000s, the financial crisis of 2008–2009, and the market's reaction to the COVID-19 shock. The first two episodes involve high return dispersion for more than a year and multiple peaks. It remains to be seen whether the same pattern will play out this time. Nevertheless, figure 4 suggests that the COVID-19 shock triggered unusually large differences across

18. That discount rates rose in reaction to COVID-19 finds support in Gormsen and Koijen (2020).

Figure 4. Dispersion of Monthly Firm-Level Stock Returns, January 1984 to June 2020

Interquartile range of equity returns in the value-weighted return distribution

Return difference (percent)

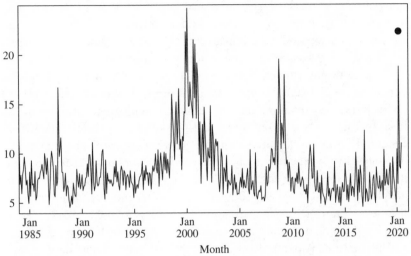

Standard deviation of equity returns in the value-weighted return distribution

Percentage return

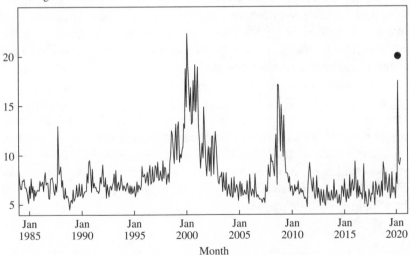

Source: Compustat Capital IQ Daily Security Files and CRSP, both via the Wharton Research Data Services.

Notes: Common equity securities traded on the NYSE, AMEX, and NASDAQ with share prices quoted in US dollars. Returns for month t computed as 100 times the log change of closing prices on the last trading days in months $t - 1$ and t with adjustments for dividends, share repurchases, stock splits, and reverse splits. The large dots reflect log changes from February 24 to March 21, 2020.

firms in shocks to their expected future cash flows. Online appendix C reports similar results for firm-level stock returns computed over four-month rather than one-month intervals. Thus, stock return data support the view that the COVID-19 shock had large reallocative effects among publicly traded firms. When we consider the one-month interval from February 24 to March 21, the impact of the COVID-19 shock on the dispersion in returns is greater yet, as shown by the large dots in figure 4.[19]

Several recent studies provide evidence on the sources of heterogeneity in the COVID-19 impact on listed firms. Hassan and others (2020) characterize and quantify the concerns that senior executives express in corporate earnings conference calls. As the pandemic spread from January to March, executives voiced growing concerns about negative demand shifts, rising uncertainty, supply chain disruptions, capacity curtailments, and employee welfare. Davis, Hansen, and Seminario-Amez (2020) and Ramelli and Wagner (2020) trace COVID-induced differences in firm-level returns to differences in their exposures to global supply chains, exports to China, food and drug regulation, energy regulation, and financial regulation. Papanikolaou and Schmidt (2020) report daily equity returns in 2020 for firms sorted by the share of employees able to work remotely. From February 14, 2020 to June 15, the cumulative return differential between the top and bottom quartiles is 19.4 percentage points, with the bulk of the return differential emerging by mid-March.[20] Pagano, Wagner, and Zechner (2020) also find much higher returns in the wake of COVID-19 at firms that are "resilient" to social distancing requirements, as measured by ability to perform jobs at home and without interactions in physical proximity. Resilient firms also enjoyed strong relative returns from 2014 to 2019, suggesting that the COVID-19 shock reinforced shifts in the economy that began before the pandemic. This reinforcing aspect of the shock may further raise unemployment and slow its decline, as argued in Davis (1987). Finally, Pagano, Wagner, and Zechner (2020) provide evidence that investors continue to price pandemic-related risks into firm-level equity prices as of May 2020, suggesting they assign material probabilities to future pandemics.

---

19. We chose February 24 because it is the first large daily move in the US stock market that next-day journalistic accounts attribute to the COVID-19 pandemic. See Baker and others (2020).

20. See the third chart at https://sites.google.com/site/lawrencedwschmidt/covid19, accessed on June 18, 2020. February 14 is the baseline date in this chart, and June 15 is the most recent available date.

II. Implications for the Economic Outlook

II.A. Reasons to Anticipate a Long Recovery

As of July 19, confirmed cases of COVID-19 exceeded 14 million worldwide, with roughly 603,000 persons thought to have died from the disease.[21] After slowly falling from mid-April to early June, weekly reported new cases in the United States rose rapidly and quickly surpassed earlier peaks.[22] Weekly (excess) deaths in the United States continued to fall until early July and then resumed an upward course.[23] As of mid-July 2020, more than four months after the pandemic struck the United States, there remained great uncertainty about how it will evolve and its longer-term economic effects. It appears that decisions at that time to relax restrictions on commercial activity contributed to a surge in new US cases, prompting some authorities to reimpose tight restrictions. Obviously, the future course of the pandemic and containment efforts will affect the recovery path. If pandemics with serious health effects become a recurring phenomenon, it will undercut growth for many years.

Under current tax and spending laws, the Congressional Budget Office (CBO 2020) projects (as of June 2020) that real GDP will not return to prepandemic levels until mid-2022 and that unemployment will remain above 6 percent through 2023–2024. The CBO is careful to note that these projections are subject to an unusually high degree of uncertainty. We anticipate a long recovery path even under an optimistic scenario, which we characterize as follows: the pandemic comes under control in the next few months, COVID-19 treatments continue to improve, an effective vaccine becomes available and widely deployed within six to twelve months, and the economy gradually comes back on line without further serious setbacks. We turn now to some reasons to expect a long recovery even in this optimistic scenario.

Voluntary and government-mandated efforts to contain the virus will curtail current and near-term aggregate demand through several channels. First, labor incomes and profits are still depressed and will remain so for some time. Second, economic uncertainty is extraordinarily elevated,

---

21. See the Johns Hopkins Coronavirus Resource Center at https://coronavirus.jhu.edu/map.html.

22. Centers for Disease Control and Prevention, "CDC COVID Data Tracker," https://www.cdc.gov/coronavirus/2019-ncov/cases-updates/cases-in-us.html.

23. Centers for Disease Control and Prevention, "Excess Deaths Associated with COVID-19," https://www.cdc.gov/nchs/nvss/vsrr/covid19/excess_deaths.htm.

which further depresses consumption expenditures and investment demand. Since uncertainties about the course of the pandemic and the stringency of social distancing measures may abate in the coming months (and will, hopefully), firms have strong incentives to defer investments that are costly to reverse. Third, temporary disruptions on the supply side of the economy can cause aggregate demand to fall more than one-for-one with the direct impact of the supply shock (Guerrieri and others 2020). Fourth, as we discuss momentarily, the COVID-19 shock has negative effects on the economy's near- and medium-term productive potential. That lowers expected future incomes, further depressing spending demands by forward-looking agents.

The overall fall in aggregate demand is massive. While policymakers have aggressively deployed fiscal and monetary tools to counter this fall, it seems unlikely that they will or can achieve a full offset. Thus, we expect demand-side forces to depress employment and output for at least the next few months. We also think it unlikely that fiscal stimulus will be as large in the next several months as it has been from March to July 2020. The tapering of fiscal stimulus is a source of falling aggregate demand in the coming months.

We now turn to supply-side considerations, with a focus on developments that influence the economy's future productive potential. First, the cash-flow crunch caused by the lockdown, uncertainty about the future course of the pandemic, concerns about reduced incomes in the near- and medium-term, and uncertainty about the outlook for growth and product demand have depressed capital investment in recent months and are likely to continue doing so for several months or more. Thus, the economy will carry a smaller stock of productive capital into the future as a consequence of the COVID-19 shock. In addition, pandemic-induced demand shifts and continuing concerns about infectious disease will undercut the production value of certain forms of capital such as large-scale entertainment venues, high-density retail facilities, and restaurants with closely seated patrons.

Second, universities, government labs, and commercial facilities have shuttered research projects that are not related to COVID-19. Schools have sent students home, and universities are making do with remote classes. Barrero, Bloom, and Wright (2017) and Bansal and others (2019) provide evidence that R&D investments are highly sensitive to uncertainty, because they are irreversible and riskier than investments in physical capital. Extraordinarily high levels of uncertainty in the wake of the COVID-19 shock may depress investments in these intangibles (Altig, Baker, and others 2020). Immigration and trade, facilitators of innovation, have also shriveled. We see these developments as lowering the trajectory of future productivity into 2021 and beyond.

The third reason we anticipate a slow recovery on the supply side leads us back to the pandemic-induced reallocation shock.

II.B. Creation Lags Destruction in the Response to Reallocation Shocks

Davis and Haltiwanger (2001) study the dynamic effects of oil price shocks in the 1970s and 1980s on job creation and destruction activity in the US manufacturing sector. They find sizable reallocative effects of oil price shocks spread out over several years. A key message is that the destruction side of reallocation precedes the creation side by one to two years. Employment and output are depressed in the interim. Reasons for the delayed creation response include the time needed to plan new enterprises and business activities, the time required to navigate regulatory hurdles and permitting processes to start or expand businesses, time to build in capital formation, uncertainties that lead to delays in making sunk investments, and search and matching frictions in forming new relationships with suppliers, employees, distributors, and customers.

To appreciate why creation responses can lag months and years behind destruction responses, consider the experience of the American auto industry in the wake of the 1973 oil price shock.[24] As Bresnahan and Ramey (1993) document, the shock increased the demand for small, fuel-efficient cars and simultaneously reduced the demand for larger cars. Capacity utilization and output fell in the wake of the oil price shock, even though a handful of plants equipped to produce small cars operated at peak capacity.

Several factors made it hard for the industry to respond rapidly to the increased demand for small, fuel-efficient cars. First, much of the physical capital in the US auto industry was dedicated to the production of larger rather than smaller cars. Second, US autoworkers had accumulated skills that were specialized in the production of particular models, and these tended to be larger vehicles. Third, many autoworkers laid off from large-car plants could not take up employment at small-car plants without a costly relocation. Fourth, the dealership network and sales force of the US auto industry had evolved under an era of thriving large-car sales,

---

24. This paragraph and the next borrow from Davis and Haltiwanger (2001).

and they were adapted to market and service larger cars. Fifth, the knowledge base and the research and design personnel at US auto companies were specialized in engineering larger cars. The development of smaller, more fuel-efficient cars required a reorientation of the knowledge base and the development of new skills by research and design personnel. Over time, US automakers adapted to the shift in demand for vehicle types, but much of the creation response involved the entry and expansion of new facilities in the United States built and operated by Japanese automakers (Mair, Florida, and Kenney 1988).

II.C. Intra-industry Reallocation

Perhaps because we often conceptualize the economy in terms of industries and regions, one might guess that pandemic-induced reallocation will mainly involve cross-industry and cross-region shifts. A large body of evidence suggests otherwise. Idiosyncratic, employer-specific factors dominate gross job creation and destruction, while employment shifts between industries and regions account for only a small share of job reallocation. For example, when Davis and Haltiwanger (1992) split the US manufacturing sector into some 450 four-digit Standard Industrial Classifications (SICs), between-industry shifts account for only 13 percent of annual excess job reallocation during the 1970s and 1980s. When they split manufacturing into roughly a thousand groups defined by the cross product of states and two-digit SICs, between-group shifts account for only 14 percent of excess job reallocation. This type of finding has been replicated many times across countries, sectors, and time periods.[25] Hence, we expect the bulk of the pandemic-induced reallocation response to occur within industries and regions.

The restaurant industry provides a salient example of intra-industry reallocation in the current crisis. A survey by the National Restaurant Association in late March finds that 3 percent of restaurant owners and operators had permanently closed in response to COVID-19, and another 11 percent expected to close permanently in the next 30 days (Taylor 2020). Applying these figures to the number of US restaurants yields more than 100,000 permanent restaurant closures in the near-term wake of the COVID-19 shock. At the same time, takeout and delivery-oriented chains have experienced a huge demand boom.

---

25. Davis and Haltiwanger (1999, table 5) review evidence from studies that span thirteen countries. Employment shifts between regions and industries account for less than 10 percent of excess job reallocation in half the studies and 10 to 20 percent in the rest.

Turning to another salient example, an unsettled economy and uncertain outlook favor large incumbents with deep pockets (Mims 2020). As Cutter and Thomas (2020) write:

> The biggest players in tech are hoovering up talent in the midst of the corona-virus pandemic.
>
> As some of Silicon Valley's most-promising startups lay off workers and others freeze hiring, established companies including Apple Inc., Alphabet Inc.'s Google and Amazon.com Inc. are pursuing software engineers, data scientists, product designers and others. Facebook Inc. says usage has spiked during the coronavirus crisis and it is committed to policing platforms ahead of the 2020 presidential election, so it will hire more than 10,000 people this year for critical roles on its product and engineering teams. The current moment may give well-capitalized tech companies a chance to poach skilled workers who until recently were gravitating to smaller upstarts, veteran technology recruiters say.

These remarks suggest that the pandemic will induce a reallocation from smaller, younger tech firms to larger, established ones. A similar dynamic may play out in other industries as incumbents with deep pockets attract workers concerned about job security.

A third example highlights the role of newfound concerns about face-to-face interactions. Before the pandemic, Medicare and Medicaid regulations largely precluded doctors, nurse practitioners, clinical psychologists, and licensed social workers from reimbursement for patient services pro-vided in virtual consultations. These regulations were cast aside during the pandemic, unleashing a flood of virtual consultations and surging interest in telemedicine.[26] In a recent article in *Medical Economics,* a publication aimed at health care professionals and business managers, Jackson (2020) remarks that telemedicine works "for most medication refills . . . urinary tract infections, colds and rashes, diabetes and hypertension follow-ups, lab results, post-op visits, birth control and fertility, and mental health." While a pandemic-induced shift to telemedicine may have little impact on the net demand for medical services, some physician practices and medical clinics will respond adroitly to the shift, and many will not. Horn (2020) offers an insightful glimpse into the commercial challenges presented by a partial shift to telemedicine. As his discussion suggests, there is high potential for a reallocation of customers, revenues, and workers across practices and clinics. A similar dynamic will play out in other professional, business, and

---

26. For a description of these regulatory changes, see the announcements by the Centers for Medicare and Medicaid Services at www.cms.gov/newsroom.

personal services: some businesses will respond deftly to newly intensified customer concerns about face-to-face interactions, and many will not.

A fourth example pertains to the grocery business and general retail. Concerns about face-to-face interactions have stimulated huge increases in the demand for online grocery shopping and delivery services. As of May 2020, online US grocery sales are up an estimated 450 percent from August 2019 and 24 percent from April 2020.[27] One-third of US households used online grocery shopping services in May 2020, more than double pre-pandemic projections for the month. Many large retailers, including Whole Foods, have hired new staff and reconfigured stores to meet the growing demand for online shopping. Walmart is testing new technology to autonomously select items from a storeroom, pack them, and prepare them for pickup or delivery. Amazon is experimenting with robot-powered fulfillment centers for online orders. These capacity expansions and investments in new technologies suggest that retailers see the pandemic as driving a persistent shift from traditional shopping modes to online shopping. Amazon, Walmart, and some other retailers are well positioned to respond to this shift. Many other retailers are not. So a large shift in shopping modes also means a reallocation of jobs and workers across firms. This process is already well under way, as indicated by a wave of recent bankruptcies and massive downsizings at J. C. Penney (general merchandise), J. Crew (apparel), Neiman Marcus (luxury retailer), Pier 1 (imported household goods), Stage Stores (department stores), and Victoria's Secret (lingerie) (Kapner 2020a, 2020b).

There are also well-documented examples of major structural transformations in the past that took the form of intra-industry reallocation. Foster, Haltiwanger, and Krizan (2006) attribute large productivity gains in the US retail sector in the 1990s mainly to a reallocation from small retail outlets to larger, more productive stores operated by national chains. Walmart, Target, Home Depot, Staples, Barnes and Noble, and Best Buy played significant roles in this process, expanding at the expense of rivals. Later, the rise of online shopping brought another major reallocation. In this regard, it's worth recalling that Amazon began as an online bookseller, eventually displacing rival booksellers who shifted online too little or too late. The coronavirus pandemic is accelerating the shift to online shopping.

As a final point about intra-industry reallocation, the long expansion that preceded the COVID-19 shock probably delayed the exit and contraction of marginal businesses, factories, and product lines that were sliding

---

27. This and other factual claims in this paragraph are based on Lee (2020).

toward obsolescence in any event. By depressing demand now and for at least several months, the COVID-19 shock triggered a recession that will likely involve some cleansing dynamics, as in the model of Caballero and Hammour (1994).

II.D. Potential for Transformative Shifts

Jones and others (2008) document the emergence of 335 new infectious diseases in human populations from 1940 to 2004, with a rising incidence over time even after efforts to control for reporting bias. Urbanization, long-distance travel, and cross-border commuting create the potential for new disease outbreaks to spread rapidly and become global pandemics. If major pandemics become a recurring phenomenon, we may see population shifts away from densely populated cities. Even if those shifts are largely confined to retirees and the well-off, it would involve a large reallocation of business, jobs, workers, and capital. Persistent concerns about disease transmission will also provide strong impetus for new products and new efforts to allay customer concerns about infection risks. Driverless taxis that automatically disinfect interior spaces after each passenger trip are but one possibility among many.

The capacity for large-scale, necessity-driven experiments to drive major shifts in workplace organization is well captured by Morgan Stanley's CEO James Gorman on a mid-April earnings call: "If you'd said three months ago that 90 percent of our employees will be working from home and the firm would be functioning fine, I'd say that is a test I'm not prepared to take because the downside of being wrong on that is massive" (Mattioli and Putzier 2020). In addition to Morgan Stanley and Facebook, Twitter, OpenText, Shopify, Snap (a messaging company), Skift (a business media company), and Discovery (parent of TV channels TLC and Food Network) have also indicated they plan large, permanent increases in working from home (Horwitz 2020; Mattioli and Putzier 2020). According to a survey of 500 hiring decisionmakers fielded in April 2020, 62 percent of respondents say working from home will increase in their organizations "as a result of their experiences during COVID-19."[28] Fifty-six percent of respondents say working remotely has exceeded their expectations, as compared to 9 percent that say it has fallen short. Barrero, Bloom, and Davis (2020) find similar results.

---

28. See the Upwork 2020 Future Workforce Report (slides), www.slideshare.net/upwork/2020-future-workforce-report/1. The survey covers most major industry sectors; 43 percent of respondents are from companies with more than 1,000 employees.

Shiva (2020) argues that countries around the world need large investments to upgrade public health systems and health care capacity: hospitals, treatment capabilities, protective gear for frontline health care workers, greatly enhanced testing capabilities, vaccine stocks, and stockpiles of masks and equipment to control and monitor infection risks. In the wake of the COVID-19 pandemic and its enormous economic toll, arguments for greater investments in public health systems and health care capacity will have broad appeal.

III. Messages for Policy

III.A. Many Lost Jobs Are Gone for Good

Many jobs lost since early March will return as the pandemic recedes and lockdowns ease. Many others are gone for good, as implied by our projections for the permanent layoff share of recent job losses. Broadly speaking, we anticipate permanent job losses in three overlapping categories: those due to COVID-induced demand shifts, jobs formerly at marginal firms that don't survive the pandemic and lockdown, and jobs lost due to the spatial and intra-industry reallocation triggered by the pandemic and by post-pandemic concerns about the transmission of infectious diseases. Sections I and II considered multiple types of evidence, and a few historical experiences, to explain why we anticipate many permanent job losses in each category.

If we are correct that many lost jobs are gone for good, there are important implications for policy. First, policy efforts to preserve all pre-COVID jobs and employment relationships could prove quite costly. They are analogous to policies that prop up dying industries and failing firms. These policies are feasible, but the cost is high in terms of resource misallocation and taxpayer burden. Second, there are large benefits of policies and policy reforms that facilitate a speedy reallocation of jobs, workers, and capital to newly productive uses in the wake of the pandemic. Policies that deter or slow reallocation are likely to further lengthen the lag of creation behind destruction, slowing the overall recovery from the pandemic, the lockdown, and the pandemic-induced reallocation shock.

In the rest of the paper, we develop these themes in connection with specific policy interventions and legacy features of the US policy landscape. We focus on policies that directly impact the economy's reallocation response to the COVID-19 shock. Policies that facilitate productive reallocation can also ease supply constraints and complement the role of fiscal and monetary policy in stabilizing demand. In turn, aggregate demand stabilization and monetary policy actions that ensure the smooth functioning of the financial system help set the stage for a speedier reallocation of jobs, workers, and capital to their most efficient uses.

III.B. High Unemployment Benefits Encourage Layoffs, Discourage Work, and Delay Productive Reallocation

President Trump signed the Coronavirus Aid, Relief, and Economic Security (CARES) Act on March 27, 2020. As part of this relief bill, the federal government is supplementing unemployment insurance (UI) benefit levels by $600 per week through the end of July 2020.[29] Each UI recipient receives the extra $600 per week irrespective of previous earnings or their potential earnings on a new job. For most workers, the extra $600 pushes total unemployment benefits to levels that exceed their previous earnings.

The Council of Economic Advisers estimates that, with the $600 weekly supplement, 64 percent of workers receive more income from unemployment benefits than from working. Industries like hospitality and retail have an even greater share of workers for whom unemployment benefits exceed earnings.[30] Ganong, Noel, and Vavra (2020) estimate that, under the CARES Act, the median replacement rate for unemployment benefit recipients is 134 percent. They also estimate that two-thirds of eligible workers receive benefits that exceed lost earnings, and that one-fifth receive benefits that are at least twice as high as lost earnings.

These generous unemployment benefits are not lost on employers. "When Equinox had to start furloughing some employees at its chain of upscale fitness clubs, Executive Chairman Harvey Spevak had a surprising message to stakeholders. 'We believe most will be better off receiving government assistance during our closure.'" This passage is from Thomas and Cutter (2020), who also write: "Equinox joins a number of companies, including Macy's . . . and [furniture maker] Steelcase, . . . that are citing the federal government's beefed-up unemployment benefits as they furlough or lay off staff amid the coronavirus pandemic. The stimulus package is changing the calculus for some employers, which can now cut payroll costs without feeling they are abandoning their employees." Thomas and Cutter also report that some workers in essential businesses who would receive

29. The Federal Pandemic Unemployment Compensation provision of the CARES Act also expanded UI eligibility to independent contractors, gig workers, self-employed persons, and to persons who are "unable or unavailable to work because of certain health or economic consequences of the COVID-19 pandemic," extended the duration of unemployment benefits by up to thirteen weeks, and relaxed job search requirements. See the US Department of Labor at https://www.dol.gov/coronavirus/unemployment-insurance, accessed on April 28, 2020.

30. This and the previous sentence reflect personal communications with CEA staff.

more income while unemployed are asking to be laid off. These remarks suggest that federal supplemental unemployment benefits have boosted layoffs and unemployment benefit claims during the pandemic.

The extra $600 per week in supplemental benefits also discourages unemployed persons from returning to work. Even at replacement rates in the historical range of 40–50 percent of prior earnings, unemployment benefits discourage job search by recipients; see, for example, the studies by Katz and Meyer (1990) and Krueger and Mueller (2010). Evidence has already emerged that today's much higher replacement rates discourage a return to work. Huffman (2020) and Kullgren (2020), for example, offer anecdotal evidence from the restaurant industry. The problem worsens as the economy reopens and employers seek to recall laid-off employees or hire new ones. On May 15, 2020, the House passed the Heroes Act, which would extend the supplemental $600 per week through January 2021 (with a phaseout through March 2021) and disregard the value of supplemental benefits in assessing eligibility for other means-tested federal assistance programs (Weidinger 2020). If enacted, these provisions in the Heroes Act would further discourage a return to work and slow the economy's response to the reallocative aspects of the COVID-19 shock.

Prang (2020) supplies an interesting example of how the $600 supplemental benefit affected a cleaning company that employed thirty workers before the pandemic. The owner received a $250,000 loan under the Paycheck Protection Program. The loan is forgivable if the company reopens within eight weeks and rehires its former employees. The owner thinks it will take more than eight weeks to reopen and that it is "unclear if his workers would want to stay at the firm over the next couple of months because many of them stand to make more from the country's expanded unemployment benefits. [The owner] estimated he would have to raise the pay of certain employees by up to 40% to compete with collecting unemployment." Many owners will confront similar challenges as they seek to reopen their businesses.

III.C. Linking Firm Aid to Employee Retention Deters Productive Reallocation

The CARES Act also created the Paycheck Protection Program (PPP), an emergency lending facility that extends loans to small businesses on favorable terms. Congress allocated $349 billion to the PPP in the CARES Act and added $321 billion about a month later, bringing the total to $670 billion (Boggs 2020). As Letteiri and Lyons (2020) explain, the PPP has two main goals: "1) help small businesses cover their near-term operating expenses during the worst of the crisis, and 2) provide a strong incentive for employers to retain their employees." Initially, PPP loans were forgivable in an amount up to the borrower's expenditures on payroll, rent, utilities, and mortgage interest in the eight weeks after loan receipt, *if* the borrower maintains its pre-crisis level of full-time equivalent employees. Otherwise, the amount forgiven falls in proportion to the head count reduction. In addition, payroll expenses must account for at least 75 percent of the forgiven amount. Thus, the loan becomes a grant if covered operating costs exceed the loan amount and the borrower maintains head count. Congress modified the PPP in June, relaxing the circumstances under which loans are forgivable.

If there is social value to business continuity that exceeds the private value captured by owners, employees, suppliers, and customers, then taxpayer subsidies that encourage the operation of temporarily unprofitable businesses might create positive social value. We say "might" because these subsidies involve other costs, including the deadweight cost of taxation and the misallocation and misuse of funds. In this regard, we note that PPP loan recipients to date include US congressional members, politically connected firms, top law and lobbying firms, and firms that allegedly defrauded student borrowers or sold fake coronavirus treatments (Podkul and McCaffrey 2020; Weaver and others 2020; Vielkind 2020). The US government watchdog agency recently expressed concerns about the potential for fraud and misuse of PPP funds (GAO 2020).

We make no effort to analyze the full range of benefits and costs of the PPP or to assess its implementation. Our modest aim is to highlight the program's potential for harmful effects on static efficiency and reallocation incentives in the wake of the COVID-19 shock. Given the program's design, an eligible firm has financial incentives to tap the PPP to fund current operations, even when its output has negative social value and its workers and other inputs would be more efficiently deployed elsewhere.[31]

Consider, for example, a restaurant that can generate $5,000 per week in revenues at a cost of $8,000 per week for payroll and $2,000 for food

---

31. Our example reflects the PPP as designed in the CARES Act. On June 3, 2020, Congress passed the Paycheck Protection Program Flexibility Act, which relaxed employee retention requirements, extended the period over which borrowers can accrue operating expenses for loan forgiveness, and lowered the amount firms must spend on payroll to qualify for loan forgiveness. See Lyons (2020) for a useful summary. We see these reforms as a belated, partial recognition of problems inherent in the design of the PPP.

and utilities. The short-run profit maximizing decision for the restaurant owner is to shut down during the crisis, saving $5,000 a week. That privately sensible decision frees up the employees to take other jobs or, if not working, to devote more time to valuable activities at home such as caring for children and monitoring their studies while schools are closed. That same owner with a PPP loan of $64,000 will find it profitable to stay open. The forgivable loan covers labor costs during the eight-week period, leaving net profits of $3,000 per week for the restaurant owner. In this example, the PPP-induced loss in social value is $5,000 per week in (net of subsidy) operating losses plus the value of employee time in alternative uses.

The PPP also creates incentives to delay socially valuable reallocation responses to the COVID-19 shock. To see this point, return to the example and suppose the owner anticipates the restaurant will remain unprofitable even after the pandemic recedes. This scenario is a plausible one, because the fall in demand for dine-in restaurants will persist, as we discussed above. Even in these circumstances, the PPP gives the restaurant owner a financial incentive to continue operating as long as forgivable loans are available to turn an unprofitable business into a privately profitable one. In other words, the PPP creates incentives to keep workers engaged in businesses that will not succeed beyond the duration of government subsidies and to postpone their redeployment to businesses with better outlooks.

There are other ways to channel liquidity support to viable, cash-strapped businesses during the crisis. Delinking financial assistance from employee retention would reduce the incentive to inefficiently deploy labor. Assistance in the form of low-interest loans without forgiveness provisions would discourage firms with poor prospects from applying for assistance. That way, taxpayer-backed programs to provide liquidity support for businesses could be directed to firms with better survival prospects. Modifying the PPP in these respects would also facilitate a speedier reallocation of inputs away from businesses with poor future prospects in the wake of the COVID-19 shock to existing and new businesses with better prospects.

The PPP is not the only current program that uses taxpayer funds to underwrite employee retention without regard for the employer's commercial outlook. The US Treasury struck an agreement with ten major US airlines to provide $25 billion in subsidies in exchange for barring layoffs and furloughs before October (Sider 2020a). According to Transportation Security Administration data, passenger counts at US airports were, relative to a year earlier, down 93 percent on March 31, 2020, down 94 percent on

April 30, and down 87 percent on June 30.[32] Airline executives say that "it will likely take years to get back to travelling as usual" (Sider 2020b). As of early July, United Airlines is considering laying off 36,000 employees, nearly half its workforce, after employee-retention subsidies end (Cameron and Sider 2020). Other major US airlines also plan to cut employment this fall. Boeing plans to cut 13,000 jobs in the United States in view of the collapse in air travel, and its suppliers have announced additional job cuts (Cameron 2020). In circumstances like these, employee-retention subsidies delay the redeployment of workers and other productive inputs to more efficient uses during the crisis and afterward.

III.D. Occupational Licensing Restrictions

Certain legacy features of the US policy landscape will also, unless reformed, inhibit the economy's response to the reallocative nature of the COVID-19 shock. Online appendix C discusses the role of land-use restrictions in this regard. In the main text, we discuss the role of occupational licensing and regulatory barriers to business formation and expansion.

The share of American workers who must hold a license to do their jobs rose from less than 5 percent in the 1950s to more than 25 percent by 2008 (Kleiner and Krueger 2013). About one-third of the growth in occupational licensing since the 1960s reflects changes in the mix of jobs (US Department of the Treasury 2015). The other two-thirds reflects a greater prevalence of licensing requirements within occupations. Carpenter and others (2012) provide an illuminating description of state licensure requirements in 102 low- and moderate-income occupations. They document onerous licensing requirements for barbers, manicurists, tree trimmers, funeral attendants, massage therapists, auctioneers, sign language interpreters, and hundreds of other jobs.[33] Government-mandated restrictions on who can work in what jobs impede responses to reallocative shocks.

Most occupational licenses are at the state level, and cross-state reciprocity is limited. Thus, licensing raises entry barriers in many jobs *and* inhibits worker mobility across states. Carpenter and others (2012), US Department of the Treasury (2015), Johnson and Kleiner (2017), Kleiner and Xu (2020), and Hermansen (2019) provide evidence that licensing reduces job-to-job mobility among workers, lowers occupational entry rates, reduces interstate mobility rates of workers in affected occupations,

---

32. See "TSA checkpoint travel numbers for 2019 and 2020," TSA www.tsa.gov/coronavirus/passenger-throughput, accessed July 15, 2020.

33. These examples are drawn from table 1 in Carpenter and others (2012).

and lowers inward worker migration in states with more extensive and stricter licensing regulations. For a fuller set of references to studies of occupational licensing effects, see Farronato and others (2020).

Occupational licensing restrictions have recently presented themselves in a particularly pointed manner, as observed in a recent *Wall Street Journal* editorial:

> Last month [New York Governor] Cuomo allowed medical personnel licensed anywhere in the country to practice in the state without a New York license. The Governor also expanded "scope-of-practice" rules to allow nurse practitioners, physician assistants and nurse anesthetists to perform jobs they've been trained to do without supervision from a higher-trained professional. . . . Washington, Colorado and Massachusetts are relaxing licensing for out-of-state medical professionals. (*Wall Street Journal* 2020)

Relaxing restrictions of this sort are thus one route to facilitating a helpful response to the pandemic *and* the necessary post-pandemic reallocation of resources. The US Department of the Treasury (2015) and Thierer and Mitchell (2020) provide several proposals for reforming occupational licensing practices in the United States. The state of Florida recently passed sweeping reforms that eliminate licensure requirements in some occupations, relax requirements and fees in many others, and expand options for licensing reciprocity with other states (*Tampa Dispatch* 2020). These reforms make it easier for Florida's workers and businesses to adjust to the COVID-19 shock and other reallocation shocks.

III.E. Regulatory Barriers to Business Formation and Expansion

The strength of the recovery in coming months and years will depend partly on how successfully the economy responds to the reallocative aspects of the COVID-19 shock. There are reasons for concern in this regard. Available evidence suggests the US economy responds more sluggishly to reallocation shocks now than decades earlier and that regulatory barriers to business entry and expansion are important reasons for the increased sluggishness.

Decker and others (2018) present evidence that plant-level employment growth became less responsive to plant-level total factor productivity (TFP) shocks after the 1980s in the US manufacturing sector. Among plants operated by young firms in high-tech manufacturing, the fall in responsiveness began after the 1990s. Plant-level investment rates also became less responsive to TFP shocks after the 1990s. Moreover, the intra-industry dispersion of labor productivity has drifted upward since at least the mid-1990s. Decker and others (2018) also find that firm-level employment growth has become less sensitive to labor productivity shocks in the US nonfarm private sector since the mid-1990s and that the intra-industry dispersion of labor productivity has risen since the mid-1990s. All of these findings point to greater sluggishness in responding to firm-level and establishment-level shocks.

Gutiérrez and Philippon (2019) find that the elasticity of market entry with respect to Tobin's q has declined since the late 1990s. They attribute this development mainly to rising entry costs driven by regulations and lobbying. Their evidence points to greater sluggishness at the level of markets in the US economy. It is complementary to the plant-level and firm-level evidence in Decker and others (2018).

Davis (2017) presents evidence that the US regulatory and tax systems grew enormously in scale, scope, and complexity in recent decades. He argues that regulatory burdens and complexity tend to fall more heavily on younger firms and incumbent businesses that expand into new markets. A vast, complex regulatory landscape creates large costs of learning the relevant regulations, developing compliance systems, and establishing relationships with regulators. Young businesses have had less time to develop the knowledge and internal processes required for compliance. Partly for this reason, complex regulatory systems favor incumbents while disadvantaging entrepreneurship and young businesses. Compared to smaller, newer, and would-be competitors, larger and incumbent firms have greater capacity and incentive to lobby for legislative exemptions, administrative waivers, and favorable regulatory treatment. Similar remarks apply to the US business tax code, which is also vast and complex.

We conclude with remarks on one class of regulations that is especially pertinent in light of the COVID-19 shock: certificate of need (CON) laws in the health care sector. As described by Mitchell (2020), these laws "limit the ability of healthcare professionals to open new facilities, expand existing ones, or offer new services. . . . [They] cover dozens of technologies and services . . . and are not intended to evaluate a provider's competency or safety record. Instead, [the CON process] is intended to evaluate the provider's claim that the service is actually needed. . . . Incumbent providers are invited to challenge the applications of their would-be competitors. Even if a CON is granted, applicants can expect the process to take months or years." In light of this description, the potential for CON laws to deter entry, reduce health care capacity, and inhibit the health care sector's responsiveness to reallocation shocks is obvious.

The number of US states with CON laws went from zero before 1964 to twenty-three in 1970 and forty-nine in 1980 (Mitchell and Koopman 2016).

Since then, many states have repealed CON laws, and they are currently in effect in thirty-five states and the District of Columbia (Mitchell and Koopman 2016). The adoption and repeal of CON laws at different times in different states is quite useful for research into their effects. According to Mitchell's (2020) timely summary of research in this area, CON laws are associated with fewer hospitals per capita, fewer hospital beds per capita, fewer ambulatory surgery centers per capita, fewer hospice care facilities, fewer dialysis clinics, fewer hospitals offering MRI, CT, and PET scans, and longer driving distances to obtain care.

This evidence suggests that CON laws will hamper the health care sector's response to demand shifts driven by the COVID-19 shock and make it harder and costlier to strengthen health care capacity in the United States. Mitchell, Amez-Droz, and Parsons (2020) offer several suggestions for phasing out or otherwise reforming CON laws.

ACKNOWLEDGMENTS　　We thank Katharine Abraham (our discussant), Dave Altig, Joseph Beaulieu, Jason Cummins, Marianna Kudlyak, Eddie Lazear, Brent Meyer, Adam Milsap, Giuseppe Moscarini, Jim Stock (the editor), participants at the summer meeting of the *Brookings Papers on Economic Activity*, and seminar participants at CBO, IGIER, and the IMF for helpful comments. We thank Emil Mihaylov for outstanding research assistance and Akhtar Muhammad and Till von Wachter for supplying data on the temporary layoff share of new unemployment claims in California. We gratefully acknowledge financial support from the Federal Reserve Bank of Atlanta, the Sloan Foundation, Stanford University, and the University of Chicago Booth School of Business.

References

Altig, David, Scott Baker, Jose Maria Barrero, Nick Bloom, Phil Bunn, Scarlet Chen, and others. 2020. "Economic Uncertainty before and during the COVID-19 Pandemic." *Journal of Public Economics,* 191, November, article no. 104274.

Altig, David, Jose Maria Barrero, Nick Bloom, Steven J. Davis, Brent Meyer, and Nick Parker. 2020. "Surveying Business Uncertainty." Working Paper 25956. Cambridge, Mass.: National Bureau of Economic Research. Forthcoming, *Journal of Econometrics.*

Bachmann, Rüdiger, and Steffen Elstner. 2015. "Firm Optimism and Pessimism." *European Economic Review* 79 (C): 297–325.

Baker, Scott, Nicholas Bloom, Steven J. Davis, Kyle Kost, Marco Sammon, and Tasaneeya Viratyosin. 2020. "The Unprecedented Stock Market Reaction to COVID-19." *Review of Asset Pricing Studies* 10, no. 4: 742–58.

Bansal, Ravi, Mariano Max Croce, Wenxi Liao, and Samuel Rosen. 2019. "Uncertainty-Induced Reallocations and Growth." Working Paper 26248. Cambridge, Mass.: National Bureau of Economic Research.

Barrero, Jose Maria. 2020. "The Micro and Macro of Managerial Beliefs." Working Paper 19-010. Stanford, Calif.: Stanford Institute for Economic Policy Research.

Barrero, Jose Maria, Nick Bloom, and Steven J. Davis. 2020. "Why Working from Home Will Stick." Working Paper. https://static1.squarespace.com/static/5e2ea3a8097ed30c779bd707/t/5f9f46f0c73af0034ba5447e/1604273911084/Why+WFH+Will+Stick+30+October+2020.pdf.

Barrero, Jose Maria, Nicholas Bloom, and Ian Wright. 2017. "Short and Long Run Uncertainty." Working Paper 23676. Cambridge, Mass.: National Bureau of Economic Research.

Bender, Ruth, and Matthew Dalton. 2020. "Coronavirus Pandemic Compels Historic Labor Shift." *Wall Street Journal*, March 29.

Bick, Alexander, Adam Blandin, and Karel Mertens. 2020. "Work from Home after the COVID-19 Outbreak." Working Paper 2017. Federal Reserve Bank of Dallas.

Bloom, Nicholas, Philip Bunn, Scarlet Chen, Paul Mizen, Pawel Smietanka, Greg Thwaites, and Garry Young. 2018. "Brexit and Uncertainty: Insights from the Decision Maker Panel." *Fiscal Studies* 39, no. 4: 555–80.

Bloom, Nicholas, Steven J. Davis, Lucia Foster, Brian Lucking, Scott Ohlmacher, and Itay Saporta Ecksten. 2017. "Business-Level Expectations and Uncertainty." Stanford, Calif.: Stanford Institute for Economic Policy Research.

Boggs, Justin. 2020. "Congress Approves Replenishing the Paycheck Protection Program." Denver Channel 7, April 23. https://www.thedenverchannel.com/news/coronavirus/congress-approves-replenishing-the-paycheck-protection-program.

Brainard, S. Lael, and David M. Cutler. 1993. "Sectoral Shifts and Cyclical Unemployment Reconsidered." *Quarterly Journal of Economics* 108, no. 1: 219–43.

Bresnahan, Timothy F., and Valery A. Ramey. 1993. "Segment Shifts and Capacity Utilization in the U.S. Automobile Industry." *American Economic Review* 83, no. 2: 213–18.

Brynjolfsson, Eric, John J. Horton, Adam Ozimek, Daniel Rock, Garima Sharma, and Hong-Yi TuYe. 2020. "COVID-19 and Remote Work: An Early Look at U.S. Data." Working Paper 27344. Cambridge, Mass.: National Bureau of Economic Research.

Bureau of Economic Analysis (BEA). 2020. "Gross Domestic Product, Second Quarter 2020 (Advance Estimate) and Annual Update." Blog post, July 30, BEA Wire. https://www.bea.gov/news/blog/2020-07-30/gross-domestic-product-second-quarter-2020-advance-estimate-and-annual-update.

Caballero, Ricardo, and Mohammed Hammour. 1994. "The Cleansing Effect of Recessions." *American Economic Review* 84, no. 5: 1350–68.

Cajner, Tomaz, Leland D. Crane, Ryan A. Decker, John Grigsby, Adrian Hamins-Puertolas, Erik Hurst, Christopher Kurz, and Aju Yildirmaz. 2020. "The US Labor Market during the Beginning of the Pandemic Recession." In the present volume of *Brookings Papers on Economic Activity.*

Cameron, Doug. 2020. "Boeing Details Plans for Mass Job Cuts." *Wall Street Journal,* May 27. https://www.wsj.com/articles/boeing-to-start-voluntary-layoffs-will-shed-an-initial-2-500-workers-11590558072?mod=searchresults&page=1&pos=1.

Cameron, Doug, and Alison Sider. 2020. "United Airlines Warns It May Furlough 36,000 Staff." *Wall Street Journal,* July 8.

Campbell, John Y., and Robert J. Shiller. 1988. "The Dividend-Price Ratio and Expectations of Future Dividends and Discount Factors." *Review of Financial Studies* 1, no. 3: 195–228.

Carpenter, Dick M., Lisa Knepper, Angela C. Erickson, and John K. Ross. 2012. *License to Work: A National Study of Burdens from Occupational Licensing.* Arlington, Va.: Institute for Social Justice.

Chen, Cheng, Tatsuro Senga, Chang Sun, and Hongyong Zhang. 2019. "Uncertainty, Imperfect Information and Learning in the International Market." Working Paper. http://tatsuro-senga.net/uploads/3/5/4/0/35400463/paper_lfrome_j19.pdf.

Cochrane, John. 2011. "Presidential Address: Discount Rates." *Journal of Finance* 68, no. 4: 1047–108.

Congressional Budget Office (CBO). 2020. "An Update to the Economic Outlook: 2020 to 2030." Washington. https://www.cbo.gov/publication/56442.

Cutter, Chip, and Patrick Thomas. 2020. "Looking for a Job? Big Tech Is Still Hiring." *Wall Street Journal,* April 14. https://www.wsj.com/articles/looking-for-a-job-big-tech-is-still-hiring-11586712423.

Davis, Steven J. 1987. "Fluctuations in the Pace of Labor Reallocation." *Carnegie-Rochester Conference Series on Public Policy* 27:335–402.

Davis, Steven J. 2017. "Regulatory Complexity and Policy Uncertainty: Head-winds of Our Own Making." Working Paper. Chicago: University of Chicago, Becker Friedman Institute.

Davis, Steven J., Jason Faberman, and John Haltiwanger. 2006. "The Flow Approach to Labor Markets: New Data Sources and Micro-Macro Links." *Journal of Economic Perspectives* 20, no. 3: 3–26.

Davis, Steven J., and John Haltiwanger. 1992. "Gross Job Creation, Gross Job Destruction, and Employment Reallocation." *Quarterly Journal of Economics* 107, no. 3: 819–63.

Davis, Steven J., and John Haltiwanger. 1999. "Gross Job Flows." In *Handbook of Labor Economics,* vol. 3B, edited by Orley Ashenfelter and David Card. Amsterdam: North-Holland.

Davis, Steven J., and John Haltiwanger. 2001. "Sectoral Job Creation and Destruction Responses to Oil Price Changes." *Journal of Monetary Economics* 48, no. 3: 465–512.

Davis, Steven J., Stephen Hansen, and Cristhian Seminario-Amez. 2020. "Firm-Level Risk Exposures and Stock Returns in the Wake of COVID-19." Working Paper 27867. Cambridge, Mass.: National Bureau of Economic Research.

Davis, Steven J., Prakash Loungani, and Ramamohan Mahidhara. 1997. "Regional Labor Fluctuations: Oil Shocks, Military Spending, and Other Driving Forces." International Finance Discussion Papers 578. Washington: Board of Governors of the Federal Reserve System.

Decker, Ryan A., John C. Haltiwanger, Ron S. Jarmin, and Javier Miranda. 2018. "Changing Business Dynamism and Productivity: Shocks vs. Responsiveness." Working Paper 24236. Cambridge, Mass.: National Bureau of Economic Research.

Dingel, Jonathan I., and Brent Neiman. 2020. "How Many Jobs Can Be Done at Home?" Working Paper 26948. Cambridge, Mass.: National Bureau of Economic Research. https://www.nber.org/papers/w26948.

Farronato, Chiara, Andrey Fradkin, Bradley J. Larsen, and Erik Brynjolfsson. 2020. "Consumer Protection in an Online World: An Analysis of Occupational Licensing." Working Paper 26601. Cambridge, Mass.: National Bureau of Economic Research. https://www.nber.org/papers/w26601.

Foster, Lucia, John Haltiwanger, and C. J. Krizan. 2006. "Market Selection, Reallocation, and Restructuring in the U.S. Retail Sector in the 1990s." *Review of Economics and Statistics* 88, no. 4: 748–58.

Fujita, Shigeru, and Giuseppe Moscarini. 2017. "Recalls and Unemployment." *American Economic Review* 107, no. 12: 3875–916.

Ganong, Peter, Pascal Noel, and Joseph Vavra. 2020. "Unemployment Insurance Replacement Rates during the Pandemic." Working Paper 27216. Cambridge, Mass.: National Bureau of Economic Research.

Gormsen, Niels J., and Ralph S. Koijen. 2020. "Coronavirus: Impact on Stock Prices and Growth Expectations." Working Paper. Cambridge, Mass.: National Bureau of Economic Research. https://www.nber.org/papers/w27387.

Government Accountability Office (GAO). 2020. "COVID-19: Opportunities to Improve Federal Response and Recovery Efforts." Washington. https://www.gao.gov/products/gao-20-625.

Guerrieri, Veronica, Guido Lorenzoni, Ludwig Straub, and Ivan Werning. 2020. "Macroeconomic Implications of COVID-19: Can Negative Supply Shocks Cause Demand Shortages?" Working Paper 26918. Cambridge, Mass.: National Bureau of Economic Research.

Guiso, Luigi, and Giuseppe Parigi. 1999. "Investment and Demand Uncertainty." *Quarterly Journal of Economics* 114, no. 1: 185–227.

Gutiérrez, Germán, and Thomas Philippon. 2019. "The Failure of Free Entry." Working Paper 26001. Cambridge, Mass.: National Bureau of Economic Research.

Hassan, Tarek A., Stephan Hollander, Laurence van Lent, and Ahmed Tahoun. 2020. "Firm-Level Exposure to Epidemic Diseases: COVID-19, SARS, and H1N1." Working Paper 26971. Cambridge, Mass.: National Bureau of Economic Research.

Hermansen, Mikkel. 2019. "Occupational Licensing and Job Mobility in the United States." Working Paper No. 1585. Washington: OECD Economics Department.

Horn, Daniel. 2020. "The Pandemic Could Put Your Doctor Out of Business." *Washington Post,* April 24. https://www.washingtonpost.com/outlook/2020/04/24/pandemic-could-put-your-doctor-out-business/?arc404=true.

Horwitz, Jeff. 2020. "Facebook to Shift Permanently toward More Remote Work after Coronavirus." *Wall Street Journal,* May 21. https://www.wsj.com/articles/facebook-to-shift-permanently-toward-more-remote-work-after-coronavirus-11590081300?mod=article_inline.

Huffman, Kurt. 2020. "Our Restaurants Can't Reopen till August." *Wall Street Journal,* August 21. https://www.wsj.com/articles/our-restaurants-cant-reopen-until-august-11587504885?mod=opinion_lead_pos7.

Jackson, Nancy Mann. 2020. "Coronavirus Offers Opportunity for Physicians to Try Telemedicine." *Medical Economics,* March 18. https://www.medicaleconomics.com/view/coronavirus-offers-opportunity-physicians-try-telemedicine.

Johnson, Janna E., and Morris M. Kleiner. 2017. "Is Occupational Licensing a Barrier to Interstate Migration?" Working Paper 24107. Cambridge, Mass.: National Bureau of Economic Research.

Jones, Karen E., Nikkita G. Patel, Marc A. Levy, Adam Storeygard, Deborah Balk, John L. Gittelman, and Peter Daszak. 2008. "Global Trends in Emerging Infectious Diseases." *Nature* 451:990–93.

Kapner, Suzanne. 2020a. "J. C. Penney to Close Nearly 30% of Its Stores." *Wall Street Journal,* May 18. https://www.wsj.com/articles/j-c-penney-to-close-nearly-30-of-its-stores-11589824977?mod=searchresults&page=1&pos=7.

Kapner, Suzanne. 2020b. "Coronavirus Widens the Retail Divide." *Wall Street Journal,* May 21. https://www.wsj.com/articles/coronavirus-widens-retail-divide-leaving-macys-and-victorias-secret-behind-11590058503?mod=searchresults&page=1&pos=6.

Katz, Lawrence F., and Bruce D. Meyer. 1990. "The Impact of the Potential Duration of Unemployment Benefits on the Duration of Unemployment." *Journal of Public Economics* 41, no. 1: 45–72.

Kleiner, Morris M., and Alan B. Krueger. 2013. "Analyzing the Extent and Influence of Occupational Licensing on the Labor Market." *Journal of Labor Economics* 31, no. 2: S173–S202.

Kleiner, Morris M., and Ming Xu. 2020. *Occupational Licensing and Labor Market Fluidity*. Federal Reserve Bank of Minneapolis. https://www.minneapolisfed. org/research/staff-reports/occupational-licensing-and-labor-market-fluidity.

Krueger, Alan B., and Andreas Mueller. 2010. "Job Search and Unemployment Insurance: New Evidence from Time Use Data." *Journal of Public Economics* 94, nos. 3–4: 546–72.

Kullgren, Ian. 2020. "Restaurants' Bailout Problem: Unemployment Pays More." *Politico*, April 20. https://www.politico.com/news/2020/04/20/restaurant-bailout-unemployment-coronavirus-197326.

Lazear, Edward P., and James R. Spletzer. 2012. "Hiring, Churn, and the Business Cycle." *American Economic Review* 102, no. 3: 575–79.

Lee, Dave. 2020. "US Online Grocery Shopping Jumps as Chains Rush to Add Capacity." *Financial Times*, June 1.

Letteiri, John, and Catherine Lyons. 2020. "Understanding the Paycheck Protection Program." Blog post, Economic Innovation Group, March 26. https://eig.org/ news/understanding-the-paycheck-protection-program.

Loungani, Prakash, Mark Rush, and William Tave. 1990. "Stock Market Dispersion and Unemployment." *Journal of Monetary Economics* 25, no. 3: 367–88.

Lyons, Catherine. 2020. "Congress Improves the Paycheck Protection Program." Economic Innovation Group, June 4. https://eig.org/news/congress-improves-the-paycheck-protection-program.

Mair, Andrew, Richard Florida, and Martin Kenney. 1988. "The New Economic Geography of Automobile Production: Japanese Transplants in North America." *Economic Geography* 64, no. 4: 352–73.

Massenot, Baptiste, and Yuri Pettinicchi. 2018. "Can Firms See into the Future? Survey Evidence from Germany." *Journal of Economic Behavior and Organization* 145:66–79.

Mattioli, Dana, and Konrad Putzier. 2020. "When It's Time to Go Back to the Office, Will It Still Be There?" *Wall Street Journal*, May 16. https://www. wsj.com/articles/when-its-time-to-go-back-to-the-office-will-it-still-be-there-11589601618?mod=article_inline.

Mims, Christopher. 2020. "Not Even a Pandemic Can Slow Down the Biggest Tech Giants." *Wall Street Journal*, May 23. https://www.wsj.com/articles/ not-even-a-pandemic-can-slow-down-the-biggest-tech-giants-11590206412? mod=searchresults&page=1&pos=2.

Mitchell, Matthew D. 2020. "First, Do No Harm: Three Ways That Policymakers Can Make It Easier for Healthcare." Special Edition Policy Brief. Arlington, Va.: George Mason University, Mercatus Center.

Mitchell, Matthew D., Alise Amez-Droz, and Anna K. Parsons. 2020. "Phasing Out Certificate-of-Need Laws: A Menu of Options." Policy Brief. Arlington, Va.: George Mason University, Mercatus Center.

Mitchell, Matthew D., and Christopher Koopman. 2016. "40 Years of Certificate-of-Need Laws Across America." Arlington, Va.: George Mason University, Mercatus Center.

Morath, Eric. 2020. "The Job Market's Long Road Back." *Wall Street Journal,* May 23. https://www.wsj.com/articles/the-job-markets-long-road-back-11590206400?mod=searchresults&page=1&pos=9.

Pagano, Marco, Christian Wagner, and Joseph Zechner. 2020. "Disaster Resilience and Asset Prices." Discussion Paper DP14773. London: Centre for Economic Policy Research. https://ssrn.com/abstract=3612841.

Papanikolaou, Dimitris, and Lawrence D. W. Schmidt. 2020. "Working Remotely and the Supply-Side Impact of COVID-19." Working Paper 27330. Cambridge, Mass.: National Bureau of Economic Research.

Podkul, Cezary, and Orla McCaffrey. 2020. "Firms with Troubled Pasts Got Millions of Dollars in PPP Small-Business Aid." *Wall Street Journal,* July 18. https://www.wsj.com/articles/firms-with-troubled-pasts-got-millions-of-dollars-in-ppp-small-business-aid-11595064602?mod=searchresults&page=1&pos=4.

Prang, Allison. 2020. "Small Businesses Need Money—But First They Need the U.S. to Reopen." *Wall Street Journal,* April 17. https://www.wsj.com/articles/small-businesses-need-moneybut-now-isnt-a-good-time-11587128400.

Ramelli, Stefano, and Alexander F. Wagner. 2020. "Feverish Stock Price Reactions to COVID-19." Research Paper 20-12. Zurich: Swiss Finance Institute.

Shiller, Robert J. 1981. "Do Stock Prices Move Too Much to Be Justified by Subsequent Changes in Dividends?" *American Economic Review* 71, no. 3: 421–36.

Shiva, Mehdi. 2020. "We Need a Better Head Start for the Next Pandemic." *VOX CEPR,* April 26.

Sider, Alison. 2020a. "Airlines Have the Cash. Now They Need the Passengers." *Wall Street Journal,* April 15. https://www.wsj.com/articles/airlines-have-the-cash-now-they-need-passengers-11586981976?mod=searchresults&page=1&pos=9.

Sider, Alison. 2020b. "U.S. Airlines Brace for Slow Recovery as Coronavirus Losses Mount." *Wall Street Journal,* May 2. https://www.wsj.com/articles/u-s-airlines-brace-for-slow-recovery-as-coronavirus-losses-mount-11588429480?mod=searchresults&page=1&pos=18.

Tampa Dispatch. 2020. "Occupational Licensure in Florida: Gov. Desantis Signs 'The Occupational Freedom and Opportunity Act.'" July 3. http://www.tampadispatch.com/occupation-licensure-in-florida-gov-desantis-signs-the-occupational-freedom-and-opportunity-act/.

Tanaka, Mari, Nicholas Bloom, Joel M. David, and Maiko Koga. 2020. "Firm Performance and Macro Forecast Accuracy." *Journal of Monetary Economics* 114:26–41.

Taylor, Kate. 2020. "3 Million out of Work, $25 Billion Lost, 8 Figures Reveal How the Coronavirus Pandemic Is Devastating Restaurants across America." *Business Insider,* March 31. https://www.businessinsider.com/how-coronavirus-devastating-restaurants-across-us-2020-3.

Thierer, Adam, and Trace Mitchell. 2020. "Occupational Licensing Reform and the Right to Earn a Living: A Blueprint for Action." Policy Brief. Arlington, Va.: George Mason University, Mercatus Center.

Thomas, Patrick, and Chip Cutter. 2020. "Companies Cite New Government Benefit in Cutting Workers." *Wall Street Journal,* April 7. https://www.wsj.com/articles/companies-cite-new-government-benefits-in-cutting-workers-11586264075.

US Department of the Treasury. 2015. *Occupational Licensing: A Framework for Policy Makers.* Washington: Council of Economic Advisers, Department of the Treasury, and the Department of Labor.

Vielkind, Jimmy. 2020. "Top New York Lobbying Firms Took PPP Loans." *Wall Street Journal,* July 19.

Wall Street Journal. 2020. "Doctors without State Borders: Governors Are Easing Rules on Caregivers, and It's Long Overdue." April 12. https://www.wsj.com/articles/doctors-without-state-borders-11586556847?mod=opinion_lead_pos1.

Weaver, Courtney, Sujeet Indap, Fan Lei, and Laura Noonan. 2020. "Luxury Fashion and Law Firms among U.S. Bailout Recipients." *Financial Times,* July 7. https://www.ft.com/content/67aec12a-e744-4bcb-ba91-7e7887e5363e.

Weidinger, Matt. 2020. *Extended: A Review of the Current and Proposed Duration of "Pandemic" Unemployment Benefits.* Washington: American Enterprise Institute.

Comments and Discussion

KATHARINE ABRAHAM   Barrero, Bloom, and Davis raise an issue that is central to setting and evaluating the labor market policy response to the COVID-19 crisis. At the risk of stating things somewhat more baldly than the authors actually do, the paper's argument can be summarized as follows: (1) the large negative shock to demand initially experienced by many businesses as a result of the COVID-19 crisis was accompanied by significant positive shocks to demand at other businesses; (2) the COVID-19 crisis can be expected to cause significant permanent restructuring; and (3) policy should support needed reallocation rather than emphasizing the preservation of existing employment relationships. My comments are organized around these three main parts of the paper's argument.

GROSS HIRING IN THE IMMEDIATE WAKE OF THE COVID-19 CRISIS In the face of health concerns related to the COVID-19 crisis, US employment fell sharply between mid-February and mid-April. Over that period, statistics published by the Bureau of Labor Statistics show a drop in total payroll employment of more than 22 million jobs, almost all in the private sector and with the bulk of the drop occurring between mid-March and mid-April. Although the news about employment during this period was grim, even as employment plummeted, many companies continued to hire.

The paper reports data on hiring from a special module on the Survey of Business Uncertainty (SBU) and from the ongoing Job Openings and Labor Turnover Survey (JOLTS). In the SBU, counting both actual staffing changes from the beginning of March through mid-April and further changes anticipated over the following four weeks, respondents expected three hires for every ten layoffs. The JOLTS data (as revised with the release of May data) show 4.6 private sector hires for every ten private

372

Figure 1. Private Sector Layoffs and Estimated Hiring to Fill New Positions, January 2001–April 2020

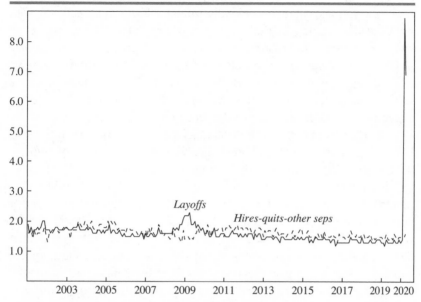

Source: Bureau of Labor Statistics, Series Report tool.
Note: Data are seasonally adjusted rates.

sector layoffs during March and April. While there was substantial gross hiring during these months, this does not establish that the economy was experiencing a surge of reallocation.

Reallocation occurs when employment declines at some businesses while increasing at others. In a dynamic economy, reallocation is an ongoing process. Because many hires replace workers who quit or left for reasons such as retirement, a firm may be hiring but not growing. In addition, to assess the effect that the COVID-19 crisis may have had on reallocation during March and April, hiring to fill new positions should be compared to its historical level.

The JOLTS provides historical information on hires but does not separately identify hires to fill new positions. To the extent that employers typically replace workers who leave voluntarily, however, hires minus quits minus other non-layoff separations may give a reasonable approximation. Using JOLTS data for the private sector, figure 1 plots both the layoff rate and hires minus quits minus other separations, also expressed as a rate. As can be seen in the figure, the layoff rate and this rough approximation for hiring to fill new positions generally are of similar magnitude. During the 2001 and 2007–2009 recessions, layoffs exceeded estimated hiring for new positions, but in most months estimated hiring to fill new positions has exceeded layoffs. The initial impact of the COVID-19 crisis was an enormous increase in layoffs during March and April; the rough estimate of hiring to fill new positions changed very little during those months. Put differently, although COVID-19 clearly caused an enormous negative shock to aggregate demand, the available data, albeit imperfect, do not suggest any *immediate* pickup in the pace of reallocation.

EXPECTED PERMANENT RESTRUCTURING AS A RESULT OF THE COVID-19 CRISIS
Even if the crisis did not lead immediately to significant shifts of employment to growing businesses, the more important question is whether and to what extent it will cause such restructuring to occur in subsequent months. The paper argues that COVID-19-related health concerns together with the positive experiences many businesses now have had with remote working can be expected to lead to sizable and persistent shifts in consumer demand and the organization of work activity. These changes, the argument continues, imply significant reallocation of employment across businesses over and above the sort of reallocation that normally occurs during and after recessions as weaker businesses fail and are replaced.

The authors, in the paper and its online appendix, present a collage of anecdotal evidence in support of this hypothesis. They make particular note of the responses to an SBU module in which respondents were asked, "What percentage of your full-time employees worked from home in 2019?" and "What percentage of your employees will work from home after the coronavirus pandemic?" Taken at face value, the answers suggest a tripling in days worked from home, from 5.5 percent of workdays in 2019 (consistent with data from other sources) to 16.6 percent of workdays following the pandemic. Based on these estimates, the authors speculate that significant permanent shifts in the locus of demand away from large central cities to other locations are likely, with correspondingly significant reallocations across businesses.

While this is a possible scenario, there is enormous uncertainty about how work arrangements will change in the post-pandemic world. In the weeks immediately following the crisis, many businesses were pleasantly surprised by how productive their employees were able to be while working from home. History provides good reasons to suspect, however, that for many enterprises working from home will not prove to be a sustainable model and at least some businesses with employees currently working remotely have found that productivity suffers without in-person contact

(Streitfeld 2020; Cutter 2020). Interestingly, the authors cite reports that Facebook plans to move to a substantially remote workforce over the coming decade, but the company also just leased all of the office space in a large, midtown Manhattan building, "cementing New York City as a growing global technology hub and reaffirming a major corporation's commitment to an office-centric urban culture despite the pandemic" (Haag 2020). I would add that increases in days worked at home do not necessarily imply a corresponding need to reallocate labor across businesses. For example, if workers never come into city offices, nearby shops and restaurants clearly will suffer, but if workers cut back from five days a week to four days a week in the office, it is less obvious what the impact will be.

To quantify the amount of reallocation that can be anticipated in the aftermath of the crisis, the authors turn again to the SBU. Each month, SBU respondents are asked to forecast their firm's employment and sales one year out. These forecasts can be used to construct measures of anticipated excess reallocation over the following year. Compared to the values for the period from January 2016 through January 2020, anticipated year-ahead excess reallocation jumped up sharply in the three months from April through June 2020.

Should we believe these numbers? The authors note that estimates of anticipated excess reallocation from past SBU responses, first collected in the fall of 2016, have been predictive of actual reallocation, but respondents' forecasts of their companies' future employment and sales seem likely to have been more accurate during years of steady economic growth than in the current unsettled situation. There also are reasons to be cautious in general about placing too much confidence in the SBU. Only about 350 sample responses are obtained each month and, based on available survey documentation, the typical effective monthly response rate appears to be in the vicinity of 10 percent.[1] Further, although the survey sample is constructed so that its industry and geographic distributions broadly match those of the US economy, small businesses are underrepresented. With respect specifically to growth in the pace of anticipated excess reallocation, because small firms have a higher baseline level of reallocation in normal times (Davis and Haltiwanger 1992), this could make the post-pandemic

---

1. According to Altig and others (2020), about 42 percent of businesses contacted to participate in the SBU agree to participate. Of those, about 62 percent complete at least one survey, and responses are obtained each month from about 43 percent of active panel members. Taking the product of the response rates at each stage yields an estimated overall response rate of about 11 percent.

jump in projected reallocation look proportionally larger than would be the case had small firms been represented in proportion to their share of employment.

A final point about respondents' expectations regarding future employment and sales is that it is difficult to disentangle effects that are specific to COVID-19 and its longer-term impacts on the structure of economic activity from the effects of the sharp decline in aggregate demand that has occurred. Respondents' expectations regarding the policy response to the crisis also may have affected their responses. There has been considerable uncertainty on this score; the index of economic policy uncertainty based on text analyses of US newspaper articles produced by Scott R. Baker, Nick Bloom, and Steven J. Davis, for example, spiked to unprecedented levels in March and April.[2] If variation in respondents' expectations about the government's policy response contributed to variation in forecasts regarding future employment, that in itself could have raised the measure of anticipated excess reallocation.

POLICY RESPONSE TO THE COVID-19 CRISIS   The government's response will have an important effect on the evolution of employment over the coming year and beyond. The authors argue both against what they view as overly generous unemployment benefits and against existing policies that subsidize employment, on the grounds that such policies will impede needed reallocation.

CARES Act Unemployment Benefit Provisions. In addition to expanding unemployment insurance coverage to the self-employed and others who ordinarily would not qualify for benefits, the CARES Act, passed at the end of March, added $600 per week to all claimants' benefits. Ganong, Noel, and Vavra (2020) have estimated that two-thirds of unemployment insurance beneficiaries are receiving payments that exceed their lost earnings, though they acknowledge that these calculations do not account for health insurance and other benefits lost when a person is out of work. Barrero, Bloom, and Davis express concern about these more generous unemployment payments, arguing that they encourage layoffs, discourage work, and delay productive reallocation.

In the present context, I am much less concerned about unemployment benefits being too generous than the authors seem to be. A body of research from the 2007–2009 recession suggests that, when unemployment is high, unemployment benefits have relatively little effect on job finding rates

2. Economic Policy Uncertainty, https://www.policyuncertainty.com/about.html, accessed June 22, 2020.

(Rothstein 2011; Farber and Valletta 2015). With unemployment currently in the double digits, there are far more job seekers than available jobs. Even if unemployment benefits are generous, workers who are offered a job will know that, if they turn it down, they may have a hard time obtaining a comparable offer in the future. There undoubtedly are people who, for health reasons, are reluctant to return to work under current conditions, but early analyses have found no evidence that the higher benefits payable under the CARES Act have raised unemployment (Altonji and others 2020; Bartik and others 2020; Dube 2020; Marinescu, Skandalis, and Zhao 2020). The more serious problem, in my view, is that without federal action too many adversely affected workers will be unable to sustain themselves and their families.

Still, I find it uncomfortable to defend paying unemployment recipients more while out of work than they had been earning before they became unemployed. The very low wages earned by a substantial share of the workforce are a serious problem, but this is not something that sensibly can be addressed through the unemployment insurance system. Indeed, continuing to pay benefits that so easily can be criticized as unfair to those who have continued to work could be counterproductive, leading to an erosion of support for needed benefits in any form. If it could be implemented, increasing replacement rates would be far preferable to adding a flat $600 per week (or other amount) to everyone's benefits. Unfortunately, given the limitations of many of the state computer systems used to administer unemployment insurance benefits, this does not appear to be a feasible option.

CARES Act Paycheck Protection Program. The second set of CARES Act provisions that the authors criticize are those that make support for struggling businesses contingent on their maintaining employment. The original Paycheck Protection Program (PPP) provided loans to cover operating expenses that could be fully forgiven if employment as of June 30, 2020 was as large as employment in a defined earlier base period. That date was later changed to December 31, 2020.

The authors are concerned that the PPP subsidies encourage firms to remain in business even when they otherwise would be losing money. In the current crisis, however, at least some of the business closures that would occur absent employment subsidies will be inefficient. In a simplified world in which labor is the only input, employment separations due to business closures are *privately* efficient when workers' marginal products are less than their compensation. They are *socially* efficient only when workers' marginal products are less than the shadow value of their time minus an adjustment to account for the cost of setting up a similar firm post-crisis in cases where that is likely to occur (Blanchard, Philippon, and Pisani-Ferry 2020). Things are more complicated when firms' production technologies include inputs in addition to labor, but the basic logic continues to hold.

The question, of course, is whether the businesses that would fail without government assistance have positive social value (i.e., worker marginal products that exceed the shadow value of the workers' time minus the adjustment reflecting the cost of later restarting the firm). There are reasons to think both that the shadow value of time for unemployed workers generally is low and that, in many cases, there will be significant costs associated with allowing businesses to fail, only to restart similar businesses at a later point in time.

With regard to the shadow value of time, the authors point to the productive things that unemployed individuals could do with the extra time they have at home. Past research suggests, however, that the unemployed spend twice as much of their extra time sleeping or watching television as they spend in productive home activities (Krueger and Mueller 2012). Further, focusing just on the potential value of home production ignores the serious adverse effects that becoming unemployed all too often has on mental health (Stutzer and Frey 2010) and long-term well-being (Davis and von Wachter 2011). And because the creation of new jobs will lag the destruction of old jobs, adding to an already large pool of unemployed may simply lead to unproductive job search.

In addition, although there undoubtedly will be some reallocation due to patterns of consumption that have permanently changed, if large numbers of businesses are allowed to fail because their current revenues fall short of their current expenses, costs later will be incurred to replace many of them with similar businesses. All of this suggests that, in many cases, the social value of continued operations may be positive even though the private value is not.

The authors do not argue entirely against extending assistance to businesses. Rather, they argue that employee retention should not be subsidized irrespective of the employer's longer-term outlook. Put that way, it is hard to disagree with the authors' position. The problem is that, given the considerable uncertainty about where we are headed, at this point it is hard to assess the longer-term outlook for many businesses. The paper does suggest that "assistance in the form of low-interest loans without forgiveness provisions would discourage firms with poor prospects from applying for assistance," but that approach also would mean firms that are losing money today and do not expect to make excess profits in the future would have an incentive to close, even in cases where their social value is positive.

CONCLUDING THOUGHTS The authors of this provocative paper undoubtedly are correct that the COVID-19 crisis will lead to economic restructuring. At this point, though, there is considerable uncertainty about the extent and nature of the resource reallocation this will involve.

There are multiple goals for policy in response to the crisis—protecting adversely affected individuals who find themselves out of work through no fault of their own; preserving otherwise viable employment relationships temporarily affected by the crisis; and creating an environment in which needed reallocation occurs in the medium to long run. Although they are careful with their language, the emphasis in the paper is strongly on the need to facilitate reallocation. In my view, that is not in fact the dominant concern at the present time.

REFERENCES FOR THE ABRAHAM COMMENT

Altig, David, Jose Maria Barrero, Nicholas Bloom, Steven J. Davis, Brent H. Meyer, and Nicholas Parker. 2020. "Surveying Business Uncertainty." Working Paper 25956. Cambridge, Mass.: National Bureau of Economic Research. https://www.nber.org/papers/w25956.

Altonji, Joseph, Zara Contractor, Lucas Finamor, Ryan Haygood, Ilse Lindenlaub, Costas Meghir, Cormac O'Dea, Dana Scott, Liana Wang, and Ebonya Washington. 2020. "Employment Effects of Unemployment Insurance Generosity During the Pandemic." Working Paper. https://tobin.yale.edu/sites/default/files/files/C-19%20Articles/CARES-UI_identification_vF(1).pdf.

Bartik, Alexander W., Marianne Bertrand, Feng Lin, Jesse Rothstein, and Matthew Unrath. 2020. "Measuring the Labor Market at the Onset of the COVID-19 Crisis." In the present volume of *Brookings Papers on Economic Activity*.

Blanchard, Olivier, Thomas Philippon, and Jean Pisani-Ferry. 2020. "A New Policy Toolkit Is Needed as Countries Exit COVID-19 Lockdowns." Policy Brief 20-8. Washington: Peterson Institute for International Economics.

Cutter, Chip. 2020. "Companies Start to Think Remote Work Isn't So Great After All." *Wall Street Journal*, July 24.

Davis, Steven J., and John C. Haltiwanger. 1992. "Gross Job Creation, Gross Job Destruction and Employment Reallocation." *Quarterly Journal of Economics* 107, no. 3: 819–63.

Davis, Steven J., and Till von Wachter. 2011. "Recessions and the Cost of Job Loss." *Brookings Papers on Economic Activity*, Fall, 1–72.

Dube, Arindrajit. 2020. "The Impact of the Federal Pandemic Unemployment Compensation on Employment: Evidence from the Household Pulse Survey." Working Paper. https://www.dropbox.com/s/q0kcoix35jxt1u4/UI_Employment_HPS.pdf?dl=0.

Farber, Henry S., and Robert G. Valletta. 2015. "Do Extended Unemployment Benefits Lengthen Unemployment Spells? Evidence from Recent Cycles in the U.S. Labor Market." *Journal of Human Resources* 50, no. 4: 873–909.

Ganong, Peter, Pascal Noel, and Joseph Vavra. 2020. "US Unemployment Insurance Replacement Rates during the Pandemic." Working Paper 27216. Cambridge, Mass.: National Bureau of Economic Research. https://www.nber.org/papers/w27216.

Haag, Matthew. 2020. "Facebook Bets Big on Future of N.Y.C., and Offices, with New Lease." *New York Times*, August 3.

Krueger, Alan, and Andreas Mueller. 2012. "The Lot of the Unemployed: A Time Use Perspective." *Journal of the European Economic Association* 10, no. 4: 765–94.

Marinescu, Ioana, Daphne Skandalis, and Daniel Zhao. 2020. "Job Search, Job Posting and Unemployment Insurance during the COVID-19 Crisis." Working Paper. https://papers.ssrn.com/sol3/papers.cfm?abstract_id=3664265.

Rothstein, Jesse. 2011. "Unemployment and Job Search in the Great Recession." *Brookings Papers on Economic Activity*, Fall, 143–213.

Streitfeld, David. 2020. "The Long Unhappy History of Working from Home." *New York Times*, July 29.

Stutzer, Alois, and Bruno S. Frey. 2010. "Recent Advances in the Economics of Individual Subjective Well-Being." *Social Research* 77, no. 2: 679–714.

GENERAL DISCUSSION Olivier Blanchard emphasized the need to differentiate between temporary and permanent shocks. Temporary shocks warrant different consideration than permanent shocks. Blanchard speculated that since it seems that most elements of this current crisis are temporary in nature (i.e., can be fully resolved once a vaccine is made available), then why would policymakers let workers become unemployed and firms go bankrupt, especially if the goal is for most of these workers and firms to go back to normal after the shock. Blanchard argued that a reallocation argument seems weak in the context of a temporary shock. And even though it is a stronger argument in the context of a permanent shock, Blanchard still had doubts about the idea of allowing for high unemployment for the sake of reallocation.

Şebnem Kalemli-Özcan raised the issue of the potential for a liquidity shortfall and the bankruptcies that may result. Kalemli-Özcan pointed out that this is a significant issue in nearly twenty European countries, even among firms in those countries that, at the end of 2019, were deemed financially viable firms but may go bankrupt because of the liquidity shortfall. Kalemli-Özcan wondered what the authors' thoughts were on this issue of liquidity, especially as it becomes harder to disentangle from solvency issues. Kalemli-Özcan concluded by asking what role recent US policies, especially those targeted to small firms (e.g., the Paycheck Protection Program), will play in this area.

Daron Acemoglu wanted to draw a distinction between efficient and inefficient reallocation. He raised the possibility that we could witness a significant amount of reallocation that is actually quite inefficient: for example, jobs could be permanently destroyed because of a demand shortage, in which case the efficient thing would be for that reallocation not to happen. Acemoglu encouraged the authors not only to document the reallocation shock as it appears in the data but also to explore whether it is an efficient or inefficient (i.e., due to inefficient business closings and separations) reallocation.

John Van Reenen, building on Acemoglu's point about efficient versus inefficient reallocation, stated that policymakers need to balance protection and reallocation. Acknowledging economists' support for and belief in reallocation, Van Reenen pointed out that the last decade or so of research has highlighted that reallocation is a long-term, costly process, and it sometimes has the effect of reallocating certain workers to long periods of inactivity. In light of this research, Van Reenen suggested that it is crucial for policymakers to find the right balance between reallocation in the medium and long run, with some degree of protection for workers in the shorter run. Van Reenen said that his sense was that the authors were perhaps putting too much emphasis on reallocation as we emerge from the lockdown period and encouraged them to think more about the optimal degree of protection.

Gerald Cohen asked if the authors had tried to leverage the SBU panel data to explore the impact on productivity from these efficiency gains. In particular, Cohen was interested in learning why SBU capital spending plans have not meaningfully dropped below historic levels.

Steven Davis thanked all of the participants for their helpful comments. Davis began by claiming he believes that despite how it may appear on the surface, the views expressed in the paper are much closer to those of Katharine Abraham than some may think. One area in which he does acknowledge disagreement is when it comes to subsidizing employee retention irrespective of the employer's long-term commercial outlook.

Responding to Kalemli-Özcan's point on liquidity, Davis explained that the paper explicitly comes down in favor of liquidity support for businesses.

Regarding Daron Acemoglu's comment about efficient versus inefficient reallocation, Davis acknowledges that point and suggested that their section on economic persistence mechanisms precisely speaks to that issue.

Davis continued that the United States has, for better or worse, undertaken a massive social and economic experiment where millions of households have moved much of their consumption online (e.g., trying online delivery shopping for almost all goods) for the past three months. As a result, Davis argued that there has been a lot of learning by doing, on both the customer and the business sides, which reflects associated investments and complementary inputs; importantly, those investments alter what is efficient going forward.

Davis pointed out that a similar phenomenon has been going on with working from home, speculating that there may be even larger changes in this area because of the extent of learning by doing and experimentation. Davis highlighted that while there is more evidence coming out about working from home, preliminary results suggest that most businesses have been positively surprised by how well it has worked now that it has actually been tried at scale.[1] Davis claimed that both of these trends (i.e., the shift to online consumption and working from home) have provided information that we didn't have back in February, and this new information has implications for what efficient resource allocation is as well.

Davis claimed that yet another example can be found with business travel. Due to the decline in travel, many businesses have been forced to shift what previously would be in-person meetings to virtual meetings with customers and clients out of necessity. According to Davis, some of them have learned that this works very well; this experience will also change whether it is efficient for them to do otherwise.

Davis also pointed out that in the paper they briefly summarize several recent studies that look at the heterogeneity in stock returns among individual firms in the wake of the pandemic. An important result from these studies is how favorably the pandemic shock has affected many firms that are well positioned to take advantage of the shift to working from home—either because they are suppliers of complementary services or because they are now relatively more efficient than other firms in conducting their business. For example, Davis highlighted Zoom Video, which has seen a nearly $50 billion gain in market cap.[2] Davis speculates that these sorts of effects suggest there is an expectation of a lot more virtual meetings going

---

1. See Jose Maria Barrero, Nicholas Bloom, and Steven J. Davis, "Why Working from Home Will Stick" (Chicago: Becker Friedman Institute, University of Chicago, December 2020), https://bfi.uchicago.edu/working-paper/why-working-from-home-will-stick/.

2. "Prospering in the Pandemic: The Top 100 Companies," *Financial Times*, June 18, 2020, https://www.ft.com/content/844ed28c-8074-4856-bde0-20f3bf4cd8f0.

forward. With all of this preliminary experience and evidence, Davis concludes that, in terms of efficiency, we do have some pretty suggestive evidence that much of the reallocation that the paper talks about is, in fact, efficient, and not only probably will happen but probably should happen.

Regarding the sample size, Davis admitted that it is a small sample and suggested that they obviously would love to be able to use sampling frames like the Bureau of Labor Statistics (BLS) or US Census Bureau. However, Davis did not believe their sample size is as concerning as others have suggested. One reason for this is because they routinely adjust recruitment contact rates to achieve a balanced sample. As a result, Davis believes they have a sample that meets their desires with respect to firm size, firm industry, and state. Davis also pointed out that they do ex post sample reweighting to match the industry distribution of activity in data sources that cover the universe of employer businesses.

Davis also mentioned that he and his coauthors are taking other steps to address sampling concerns. For example, Davis pointed out that, among other projects, he works with a team at the Census Bureau on a survey that has an SBU-like design but would be fielded by the Census Bureau and will hopefully be rolled out soon with large-scale repeated samples, drawing on the census sampling frame and utilizing other benefits that the census has to offer when it comes to survey design and administration.[3] So, Davis wanted people to think of the SBU as a pilot. Davis also said that he would be more than happy if BLS wanted to get involved in this type of survey as well. And he remarked that the SBU design has already been imitated in other countries around the world, most notably in the United Kingdom.[4] Davis concluded by mentioning that we also want to take the SBU micro data inside the Census Bureau, where they can then take the standard approach to ex post construction of sampling weights and get better versions of the sample statistics that come out of the SBU.

Jose Maria Barrero responded to Olivier Blanchard's inquiry about the existence of firms that are hiring some workers and laying off others at the same time by stating that this rarely occurs in the data, with the overwhelming majority of firms exhibiting either gross hires or gross layoffs.

---

3. See also Nicholas Bloom and others, "Business-Level Expectations and Uncertainty," working paper 28259 (Cambridge, Mass.: National Bureau of Economic Research, 2020), which analyzes data based on SBU-like questions fielded to US manufacturing plants.

4. See the UK Decision Maker Panel, https://decisionmakerpanel.co.uk; and Nicholas Bloom and others, "The Impact of COVID-19 on Businesses' Expectations: Evidence from the Decision Maker Panel," *Bank of England Quarterly Bulletin,* 2020:Q3.

DAVID BAQAEE
University of California, Los Angeles

EMMANUEL FARHI
Harvard University

MICHAEL MINA
Harvard University

JAMES H. STOCK
Harvard University

Policies for a Second Wave

ABSTRACT   In the spring of 2020, the initial surge of COVID-19 infections and deaths was flattened using a combination of economic shutdowns and noneconomic non-pharmaceutical interventions (NPIs). The possibility of a second wave of infections and deaths raises the question of what interventions can be used to significantly reduce deaths while supporting, not preventing, economic recovery. We use a five-age epidemiological model combined with sixty-six-sector economic accounting to examine policies to avert and to respond to a second wave. We find that a second round of economic shutdowns alone are neither sufficient nor necessary to avert or quell a second wave. In contrast, noneconomic NPIs, such as wearing masks and personal distancing, increasing testing and quarantine, reintroducing restrictions on social and recreational gatherings, and enhancing protections for the elderly together can mitigate a second wave while leaving room for an economic recovery.

eginning the third week of March 2020, much of the US economy shut down in response to the rapidly spreading novel coronavirus and rising death rates from COVID-19. The shutdown triggered the sharpest and deepest recession in the postwar period, with just under 30 million new claims for unemployment insurance filed in the six weeks starting March 15. The economic shutdown, combined with other non-pharmaceutical interventions (NPIs), slowed and then reversed the national weekly death rate and brought estimates of the effective reproductive number of the epidemic

Conflict of Interest Disclosure: The authors did not receive financial support from any firm or person for this paper or from any firm or person with a financial or political interest in this paper. They are currently not officers, directors, or board members of any organization with an interest in this paper. No outside party had the right to review this paper before circulation. The views expressed in this paper are those of the authors and do not necessarily reflect those of Harvard University or the University of California, Los Angeles.

385

to one or less in nearly all states.[1] With the epidemic seemingly under control, state authorities, urged on by a White House eager to resume normal economic activity, began relaxing both economic and noneconomic restrictions. Some of the least hard-hit states started reopening in late April or early May, while others waited until late May or June. As of the date of this conference (June 25), however, the weekly number of confirmed cases is rising nationally, especially outside the Northeast, raising the specter of a second wave of deaths. If countered by a second round of economic shutdowns, short-term unemployment could become long-term and firms could close, dimming prospects for a robust post-COVID-19 recovery.

This paper examines policy options for avoiding or mitigating a second wave of deaths and economic shutdowns. To do so, we use a combined epidemiological-economic model that permits considerable granularity in NPIs. We distinguish between economic NPIs, which directly constrain economic activity (such as closing certain sectors), and noneconomic NPIs, which do not (such as wearing masks and personal distancing).

Our main finding is that a second wave can be avoided or, if it starts, turned around through the use of noneconomic NPIs, avoiding the need for a second round of economic shutdowns. Effective noneconomic NPIs include personal distancing and the wearing of masks; limits on sizes of group activities, especially indoors; increased testing and quarantine; and enhancing protections for the elderly. There is strong evidence that much of the decline in economic activity was the result of self-protective behavior by individuals, not government shutdown orders, so simply reversing those orders will not by itself revive the economy. By using noneconomic NPIs, not only can shutdown orders be avoided but, at least as importantly, a declining trend in deaths will reassure workers that it is safe to return to the workplace and consumers that it is safe to return to shops and restaurants.

Strengthening noneconomic NPIs requires a combination of government guidance and financial support, compliance by firms and retail establishments, and public acceptance and adoption. Like others, we find that increased testing and quarantine can be particularly effective in reducing the circulating pool of contagious individuals. But increased testing requires wider availability of tests, faster turnaround, and reduced test costs. Similarly, additional protections for the elderly, such as regular

---

1. See, for example, the estimates on R_t COVID-19, https://rt.live/.

testing of staff and residents in nursing homes—who to date account for
an estimated 41 percent of COVID-19 deaths (Kaiser Family Foundation 2020)—require more than just guidelines and mandates to ensure
that long-term care facilities have the institutional capacity to test and to
handle the resulting staffing fluctuations. Wearing masks and maintaining personal distancing requires leadership and education at all levels of
government and, at the level of the individual, a desire not to be the reason
someone else gets sick. Each of these NPIs is imperfect but together they
can reduce the probability of transmission sufficiently to make room for
people to return to working, shopping, and eating out, even if a second
wave reemerges.

Our main findings are illustrated in figure 1, which shows our baseline
second wave scenario, and in figure 2, which examines the effectiveness of
tackling the second wave by an economic lockdown versus tackling it using
noneconomic NPIs while keeping the economy largely open. Each figure
shows simulated weekly US deaths, actual deaths (through June 25), and
the monthly unemployment rate. The bands represent statistical estimation
uncertainty. Figure 1 (bottom) shows quarterly GDP, although for brevity
GDP is not shown in subsequent figures. The simulation period begins on
June 1 (vertical dashed line). As described in section VI, in this second
wave scenario noneconomic restrictions such as social distancing, wearing
masks, religious gatherings, and limits on group sizes at social and sports
events are relaxed to be roughly halfway between their restrictive values
of mid-May and their prepandemic values of February 2020. In reality,
during the shutdown and reopening, economic activity is determined by
a complex interaction between policymakers regulating business openings
and individuals choosing to shop and work; we model this by a decision
maker ("governor") who expands or contracts economic activity in response
to economic conditions and deaths using a rule based on guidance from the
Centers for Disease Control and Prevention (CDC). In response to rising
deaths, in the second wave scenario in figure 1 the governor recloses some
businesses, and the unemployment rate rises to the mid-teens early in the
fall, leading to a W-shaped recession. By the end of the year, there will
have been 482,000 deaths, and GDP remains roughly 5 percent below its
peak in 2019:Q4.

The top panel of figure 2 examines whether the governor-cum-citizens
could avoid this scenario through a second economic lockdown with severity
comparable to April. In short, no: simply closing businesses, unaccompa-
nied by noneconomic NPIs, reduces year-end deaths to 410,000 but does

Figure 1. Second Wave from Relaxed Social Distancing and Early Reopening: Weekly Deaths, the Unemployment Rate, and GDP

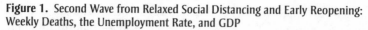

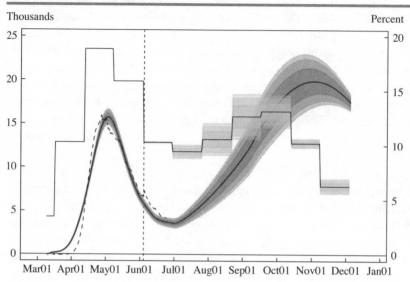

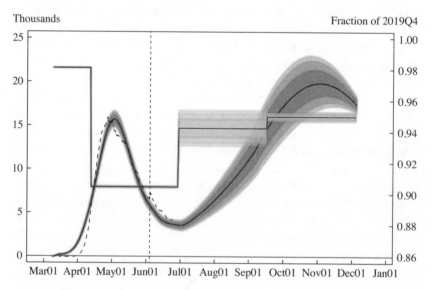

Source: Authors' calculations.

Notes: Each chart shows the level of weekly COVID-19 deaths, actual (dashed) and simulated. The top panel shows the unemployment rate (measured by hours lost) and the bottom panel shows the level of quarterly GDP, indexed to February 2020 = 1. Bands denote +/− 1, 1.65, and 1.96 standard deviations arising from sampling uncertainty for the estimated parameters. The population-wide IFR is 0.7 percent. Total deaths on January 1: 482,000. Simulation begins on June 1 (vertical dashed line).

Figure 2. Responding to the Second Wave: Deaths and Unemployment Rates

By closing businesses

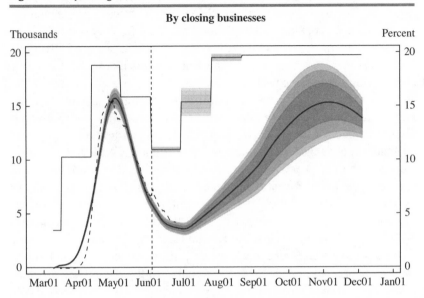

By emphasizing noneconomic measures

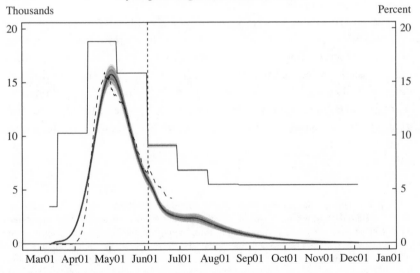

Source: Authors' calculations.

Notes: Both panels show weekly deaths and the monthly unemployment rate. Total deaths on January 1: 410,000 (top) and 147,000 (bottom). Bands denote +/− 1, 1.65, and 1.96 standard deviations arising from sampling uncertainty for the estimated parameters.

not prevent the second wave, at the cost of a vast increase in the unemployment rate. The main reason for this finding is that (as discussed in section II), among workers, contacts at the workplace account for only one-half of all their contacts; in our second wave scenario, the main driver of infections is contacts in nonwork activities, where protections like social distancing and wearing masks have been relaxed.

In contrast, as shown in the bottom panel of figure 2, noneconomic NPIs—including wearing masks, social distancing, limits on social group sizes, protections for the elderly, an achievably higher level of testing, and quarantine—combined with judicious use of economic NPIs like requiring workers who can work from home to continue to do so, eliminate the second wave. In this scenario, the decline in deaths allows the economy to return to near-normal levels of employment. Our modeling suggests that a second wave can be reversed through the adoption of noneconomic NPIs without needing to close either schools or the economy.

Relative to the fast reopening in figure 1, the smart reopening in figure 2 (bottom panel) saves 335,000 lives. Relative to the second shutdown in figure 2 (top panel), the smart reopening increases GDP in the second half of 2020 by \$115 billion and reduces the year-end unemployment rate by 14 percentage points.[2]

RELATED LITERATURE Our model combines epidemiological and economic components at a level of granularity that allows us to consider NPIs that vary by age (such as school closings) and across economic sectors (such as reopenings staggered by sector). The epidemiological component is an age-based susceptible-infected-recovered (SIR) model with five age bins, mortality rates that vary by age, and exposed and quarantined components, which we combine with a sixty-six-sector economic model.

---

2. Subsequent to the conference, as of the time of this writing (July 17), the national death rate started to rise again, led by states that reopened early without requiring noneconomic NPIs. Currently orders to wear masks and to limit large-group gatherings are being resisted by the public and some officials in some states, and in some cases are being litigated. The second wave/shutdown scenario in figure 2 (top panel) therefore currently appears to be the most likely of these three. The smart reopening simulation in figure 2 (bottom panel) would in particular have required earlier and more widespread wearing of masks, more testing, and more restrictions on high-risk noneconomic activity (bars, crowded beaches, mass events) than actually occurred, and currently actual deaths are on track to surpass, by the end of July, the year-end death total in the smart reopening simulation. Of course, the value of these noneconomic NPIs does not expire, and politicians and the public still could choose to transition to a low-death, high-economic-activity path like that in figure 2 (bottom panel).

There is a rapidly growing literature that merges epidemiological and economic modeling to undertake policy analysis for the pandemic.[3] Although most of the models in the literature are highly stylized, they provide useful qualitative guidance.

Broadly speaking, this literature provides six main lessons. First, for a virus with a high fatality rate like SARS-CoV-2, the optimal policy is to take aggressive action early to drive prevalence nearly to zero (Alvarez, Argente, and Lippi 2020; Jones, Philippon, and Venkateswaran 2020; Farboodi, Jarosch, and Shimer 2020); doing so not only decreases the costs from deaths but also provides an environment in which endogenously self-protecting individuals choose to return to economic activity. Second, testing combined with quarantine has high value and reduces the need for a severe economic lockdown (Alvarez, Argente, and Lippi 2020; Berger, Herkenhoff, and Mongey 2020; Eichenbaum, Rebelo, and Trabant 2020b). Third, because deaths are highest among the elderly, focusing resources on protecting older workers or the most vulnerable can provide large benefits (Acemoglu and others 2020; Rampini 2020). Fourth, noneconomic NPIs such as masks and social distancing can reduce both economic costs and deaths (Bodenstein, Corsetti, and Guerrieri 2020; Farboodi, Jarosch, and Shimer 2020). Fifth, nuanced economic NPIs, for example, with sectoral or age variation, can facilitate a quicker reopening (Azzimonti and others 2020; Favero, Ichino, and Rustichini 2020; Glover and others 2020). Sixth, a common theme through these papers is that individual self-protective behavior both anticipates and reduces the effect of regulatory interventions like lockdowns, although because of the contagion and other externalities, individual response alone is typically less than socially optimal.

Our modeling underscores many of these conclusions. Additionally, we are able to examine the interactions among various NPIs in a setting that is carefully calibrated to epidemiological parameters and to current US conditions, allowing direct comparisons of the various NPIs.

3. See Acemoglu and others (2020), Alvarez, Argente, and Lippi (2020), Atkeson (2020a, 2020b), Aum, Lee, and Shin (2020), Azzimonti and others (2020), Baqaee and Farhi (2020a, 2020b), Berger, Herkenhoff, and Mongey (2020), Bodenstein, Corsetti, and Guerrieri (2020), Budish (2020), Eichenbaum, Rebelo, and Trabant (2020a, 2020b), Farboodi, Jarosch, and Shimer (2020), Favero, Ichino, and Rustichini (2020), Glover and others (2020), Guerrieri and others (2020), Jones, Philippon, and Venkateswaran (2020), Krueger, Uhlig, and Xie (2020), Lin and Meissner (2020), Ludvigson, Ma, and Ng (2020), Morris and others (2020), Moser and Yared (2020), Mulligan (2020), Rampini (2020), Rio-Chanona and others (2020), and Stock (2020).

Additional pertinent literature estimates the extent to which the economic contraction starting in March was an endogenous response to the virus or a direct causal consequence of government strictures. This question is a topic of papers in this volume by Bartik and others (2020) and by Gupta, Simon, and Wing (2020), so we refer the reader to their discussion of this literature.

CAVEATS Our results require three important caveats. First, while our sixty-six-sector model provides considerable granularity, some of the highest-risk economic activities, such as nightclubs and attendance at indoor professional sports, are subsectors within our sixty-six sectors. Because we do not model those highest-contact activities directly, we exclude them from our general conclusion that the economy can be reopened safely by relying on noneconomic NPIs. Prudence suggests that this tail of highest-risk activities, which account for a small fraction of economic activity, should remain closed, perhaps until there is a vaccine. Second, our national model misses the regional heterogeneity of the pandemic. Third, although we have taken pains to include the best available estimates for calibrating the model, much about the pandemic remains uncertain, and the confidence bands in the simulation figures understate actual considerable uncertainty (this uncertainty is explored in the online appendix).

I. The Model

We use an age-based SIR model with exposed and quarantined compartments and with age-specific contact rates. An age-based approach matters for four reasons. First, death rates vary sharply by age. Second, workplace shutdowns affect working-age members of the population. Third, different industries have different age structures of workers, so reopening policies that differentially affect different industries could have consequences for death rates as a result of the death-age gradient. Fourth, some policies affect different ages differently, such as closing and reopening schools and only allowing workers of a certain age to return to their workplace.

I.A. Age-Based SEIQRD Model

The model simplifies Towers and Feng (2012) and follows Hay and others (2020), adding a quarantined compartment. We consider five age groups: ages 0–19, 20–44, 45–64, 65–74, and 75+. The epidemiological state variables are S (susceptible), E (exposed), I (infected), Q (quarantined), R (recovered), and D (dead). The state variables are all five-dimensional vectors, with each element an age group, so for example I_2 is the number of infected who are ages 20–44. The unit of time is daily. We assume that the recovered are immune until a vaccine or effective treatment becomes available.[4]

Let S_a (etc.) denote the ath element of S (ath age group). The SEIQRD model is:

(1) $$dS_a = -\beta S_a \sum{}_b \rho_{ab} C_{ab} \left(\frac{I_b}{N_b} \right)$$

(2) $$dE_a = -dS_a - \sigma E_a$$

(3) $$dI_a = \sigma E_a - \gamma I_a - \delta_a I_a - \chi I_a$$

(4) $$dQ_a = \chi I_a - \gamma Q_a - \delta_a Q_a$$

(5) $$dR_a = \gamma I_a + \gamma Q_a$$

(6) $$dD_a = \delta_a I_a + \delta_a Q_a$$

The total number of individuals of age a is $N_a = S_a + E_a + I_a + Q_a + R_a$.

The parameters of the model are the adult transmission rate β, the recovery rate γ, the latency rate σ, the age-dependent death rate δ_a, the quarantine rate χ, the 5×5 contact matrix C (with element C_{ab}), and age-dependent transmission factors ρ_{ab}. The adult transmission rate β reflects the probability of an adult becoming infected from a close contact with an infected adult. The factors ρ_{ab} allow for transmission rates involving children to differ from the adult-adult rate; ρ_{ab} is normalized to be 1 for adult-adult contacts. Transmission can be mitigated by protective measures such as masks. As discussed below, we model those protective measures separately and accordingly define β to be the transmission rate without mitigation, so that β is determined by the biology of the disease and preexisting social customs (e.g., hand shaking). The latency rate σ and the recovery rate γ are biological characteristics of the disease. The death

---

4. The assumption of subsequent immunity among the recovered is a matter of ongoing scientific investigation. A working hypothesis based on the related coronaviruses causing MERS and SARS is that immunity could decay but last for one to three years. Because our simulations run through the end of 2020, our assumption is that the recovered are immune through that period.

rate δ_a varies by age. The parameter χ is the removal rate into quarantine, the value of which depends on quarantine policy. Calibration and estimation of the model is discussed in section IV.

The contact matrix C is the mean number of contacts among different age groups in the population. Thus, according to equations (1) and (2), a susceptible adult of age a who comes into contact with an adult of age b has an instantaneous infection probability of β times the probability that the age-b adult is infected. The total instantaneous probability of infection is the sum over the expected transmission by contacts of different ages if those contacts are infected, times the probability that the contacted individual is infected.

In the model, an infected individual is placed into quarantine with some probability, at which point they no longer can infect others. In practice, identifying the infected individual requires testing, contact tracing, or both. In addition, in the United States, quarantine is imperfect and amounts to encouragement to self-isolate. The model abstracts from these complexities.

Other than the quarantine rate χ, the parameters in the model represent preexisting conditions at the start of the epidemic. Policy and self-protective behavior can be thought of as either changing the values of these parameters or, alternatively, introducing additional parameters in the model. For example, the probability of transmission from a contact is reduced substantially if both individuals are wearing masks. In addition, lockdown orders and self-limiting behavior can reduce the number and ages of contacts, that is, alter the elements of the contact matrix. Our modeling of such NPIs, both self-protective and mandated, is discussed in section III.

In a model without quarantine and with transmission rates and death rates that depend on age, the initial reproduction number R_0 is

$$(7) \qquad\qquad R_0 = \beta\,\text{maxRe}\left[\text{eval}\left(\tilde{C}\cdot\Gamma\right)\right],$$

where $\text{maxRe}[\text{eval}(.)]$ denotes the maximum of the real part of the eigenvalues of the matrix argument, $\tilde{C}$ is the normalized contact matrix with elements $\tilde{C}_{ab} = \left(\dfrac{C_{ab}N_a}{N_b}\right)$, $\Gamma_{ab} = \rho_{ab}/(\gamma + \delta_b)$, and $\cdot$ is the element-wise product.[5] Equation (7) generalizes the familiar expression for R_0 in a scalar

---

5. Equation (7) is derived using the next-generation matrix method; see Towers and Feng (2012) and van den Driessche (2017).

SIR model ($R_0 = \beta/(\gamma + \delta)$) to age-based contacts with age-dependent transmission and death rates.[6]

I.B. Sector- and Activity-Based Contact Matrices

The contact matrix C represents the expected number of contacts in a day between individuals in different age bins. We distinguish between contacts made in three activities: at home, at work (on the work site), and other. Other includes both contacts made as a consumer engaging in economic activity, such as shopping, air travel, or dining at a restaurant, and in noneconomic activities, such as free recreation and social events. In a given day, an individual can be in one, two, or all three of these three states.

The expected number of contacts made in a day is the sum of the contacts made at home conditional on being at home, plus those made at work conditional on being at work, plus those made while engaged in other activities conditional on doing other activities, times the respective probabilities of being in those three states. To differentiate between work in different sectors, which among other things differs by the degree of personal proximity and numbers of contacts at the workplace, we further distinguish work contacts by sector. Accordingly, the expected number of contacts at work is the weighted average of the expected number of contacts, conditional on working in sector i, times the probability of working in sector i. Thus,

$$(8) \qquad C_{ab} = p_a^{home} C_{ab}^{home} + p_a^{other} C_{ab}^{other} + \sum_{sectors\, i} p_{a,i}^{work} C_{ab,i}^{work},$$

where C_{ab}^{home} is the (a, b) element of the contact matrix conditional on being at home, p_a^{home} is the probability of an age-a individual being at home, similarly for other, $C_{ab,i}^{work}$ is the (a, b) element of the contact matrix conditional on being at work in sector i, and $p_{a,i}^{work}$ is the probability of an age-a individual working in sector i, that is, the employment share of sector i as a fraction of the population. That is, let $L_{a,i}$ be the number of workers of age a employed in sector i; then,

$$(9) \qquad p_{a,i}^{work} = \frac{L_{a,i}}{N_a}.$$

---

6. The parameter β differs in the scalar and age-based settings, where β in the scalar model is the transmission rate β in the age-based model times the expected number of contacts.

The disaggregation of the contact matrices in equation (8) distinguishes between different types of contacts. A server in a restaurant has contact with a customer in his or her capacity as a worker (work contact matrix for restaurants), while customers will have contact with the server in their capacity as consumers engaged in an other activity. Similarly, a home health aide providing services to an elderly person at the client's home will be in contact with the elderly person as part of work, while the elderly client will be making that contact at home.

I.C. Employment, Unemployment, and Output

Employment by age, by sector, and total (L) are respectively sums over sectors, ages, and overall. Let the subscript • denote summation over that index. Then,

$$(10) \qquad L_{a,\bullet} = \sum_{sectors\,i} L_{a,i}, \; L_{\bullet,i} = \sum_{ages\,a} L_{a,i}, \text{ and } L = \sum_a L_{a,\bullet} = \sum_i L_{\bullet,i}.$$

The departure of output from its full-employment level is estimated using Hulten's (1978) theorem, which says that the elasticity of real GDP to the total hours worked in a given sector is given by the total labor income in this sector, Ψ_i, as a share of nominal GDP:

$$(11) \qquad\qquad d \ln Y = \sum_{sectors\,i} \Psi_i d \ln L_{\bullet,i}.$$

We discuss this approximation further in section VI.C.

In the counterfactual simulations, labor supply is constrained in two ways. First, if schools are closed, a fraction of workers will not have other child-care options so will be unable to return to work. Second, the virus reduces labor supply because some workers are temporarily quarantined and some have died.

II. Data Sources

We briefly summarize the data used to calibrate the model and historical NPIs, with details provided in the online appendix.

II.A. Economic Data

Employment by age and industry are estimated using the 2017 American Community Survey.

An important NPI is reducing workplace density by having workers work at home. Using data from the Real-Time Population Survey, Bick,

Blandin, and Mertens (2020) estimate that 35.2 percent of the workforce worked entirely from home in May 2020, up from 8.2 percent in February. We use the fraction of workers working from home from their Real-Time Population Survey to estimate the fraction of workers working from home in February and at the end of May. We construct a daily time series of the national fraction working from home by interpolating and extrapolating these points using the national Google workplace visit mobility index.[7] This aggregate time series is apportioned to the sector level using Dingel and Neiman's (2020) estimates of the (prepandemic) fraction of workers in an occupation who can work from home, reported to the sixty-six input-output sectors classification using a crosswalk.

Mongey, Pilossoph, and Weinberg (2020) construct an index of high personal proximity (HPP) by occupation, which measures an occupation as HPP if it is above the median value of proximity as measured by within-arm's-length interactions by occupation. This occupational index was cross-walked to the sixty-six sectors.

Daily sectoral shocks to labor shares by industry are estimated from hours reductions reported in the February–June monthly establishment survey (tables B1, broken down to the sectoral level proportionally to the sectoral employment changes reported in table B2).[8] These provide the estimates of the sectoral shocks to hours for the establishment survey reference weeks. Between the reference weeks, the sectoral shocks were linearly interpolated, and extrapolated after the June reference week, using the Google workplace visit mobility index.

Data on workers' child-care obligations are from Dingel, Patterson, and Vavra (2020).

II.B. Contact Matrices and Epidemiological Data

The contact matrices are estimated using POLYMOD contact survey data.[9] Conditional contact matrices for home, work, and other were computed by sampling contact matrices from the POLYMOD survey data and then reweighting them to match US demographics on these three activities.

7. Google COVID-19 Community Mobility Reports, https://www.google.com/covid19/mobility/.
8. Establishment survey data can be found at the Bureau of Labor Statistics, "Labor Force Statistics from the Current Population Survey," https://www.bls.gov/cps/.
9. POLYMOD Social Contact Data, https://doi.org/10.5281/zenodo.1157934), version 1.1 (2017).

We used the age distribution of workers by industry and Mongey, Pilossoph, and Weinberg's (2020) personal proximity index, cross-walked to the sector level (HPP_i), to construct industry-specific conditional contact matrices, $C_{ab,i}^{work}$ as the product of HPP_i times the overall conditional mean contact matrix, with all sectoral matrices scaled so that the weighted mean equals the overall mean work contact matrix.[10]

The probabilities p^{other} in equation (8) are estimated from the POLYMOD contact data (normalized for US demographics). The probability p^{home} is nearly 1 in the POLYMOD diaries (i.e., nearly everyone spends part of their day at home) and is set to 1 for all simulations.

Daily death data, which are used to estimate selected model parameters, are from the Johns Hopkins COVID-19 GitHub repository.[11]

II.C. Calibration of Historical NPIs

We use an index of nonwork Google mobility data and school closing data to estimate the historical pattern of reduction in nonwork, nonhome (other) activities and thus other contacts. We refer to these generally as historical NPIs, some of which are a consequence of government decisions (e.g., closing schools) and some of which represent voluntary self-protection. We construct a Google mobility index (GMI) using three Google mobility measures at the daily level (national averages): retail and recreation, transit stations, and grocery and pharmacies. These three measures are averaged, normalized so that 1 represents the mean of the final two weeks of February 2020, and smoothed (centered seven-day moving average). Dates of school closings are taken from Kaiser Family Foundation (2020), aggregated to the national level using population weighting. Section IV explains the use of these data to create time-varying contact matrices.

II.D. Epidemiological Parameters

We reviewed twenty papers with medical estimates of incubation periods and duration of the disease once symptomatic (see the online appendix). These papers provided twenty-three estimates of the incubation

---

10. As an alternative, we sampled from the POLYMOD contact diary data to compute the conditional distribution (element-wise) for at-work contacts and sampled from the 15th, 50th, and 85th percentiles to construct low, median, and high conditional contact matrices, then assigned an industry to one of these three groups based on its HPP value. This approach yielded similar contact matrices by sector to the first approach and behaved similarly in simulations.

11. JHU CSSE COVID-19 Dataset, https://github.com/CSSEGISandData/COVID-19/tree/master/csse_covid_19_data.

(the latency) period and sixteen estimates of the period from becoming symptomatic to being recovered (the recovery period). For the latency period, we used the mean value from the three peer-reviewed studies with estimates, which yields a latency period of 4.87 days and a value of $\sigma = 1/4.87$ (continuous-time, daily time scale). For the recovery period, the studies have very long estimates, from 17.5 to 28.3 days, which appear to reflect sample selection in the studies which tend to consider the most severe (and longest-lasting) cases. Estimates of the recovery period used in the epidemiological literature are shorter, and we use Kissler and others' (2020) estimate of an infectious period of five days. As a sensitivity check, we also consider an infectious period of nine days; as shown in the online appendix, our simulation results are not sensitive to this change so the analysis in the text uses the five-day recovery period.

Salje and others (2020) and Verity and others (2020) provide estimates of the infection-fatality ratio (IFR) by age. Ferguson and others (2020) adjust Verity and others' (2020) IFRs to account for nonuniform attack rates across ages. Salje and others (2020) use data from France and the *Diamond Princess* cruise ship; they have lower IFRs at the youngest ages and slightly higher IFRs at the older ages than Ferguson and others (2020). We adopt the more recent IFR profile from Salje and others (2020), scaled proportionately to match a specified overall (population-wide) IFR.[12] The overall IFR is not known because of insufficient random population testing. We therefore adopt a range of estimates of the population IFR from 0.4 percent to 1.1 percent; the age-specific IFR is then obtained using Salje and others' (2020) IFR age profile. The population-wide IFR is weakly identified in our model. For our main results we use a population-wide IFR of 0.7 percent and report sensitivity analysis in the online appendix.

Boast, Munro, and Goldstein (2020) and Vogel and Couzin-Frankel (2020) provide largely nonquantitative surveys of the sparse literature concerning transmissibility of the virus in contacts involving children. To calibrate the parameters ρ_{ab} involving children, we reviewed nine studies on this topic posted between February 21 and May 1. These studies point to a lower transmission rate for contacts involving children, although the estimates vary widely. Of the seven studies that estimate a transmission rate from children to adults, our mean estimate, weighted by study relevance, is $\rho_{1b} = 0.44$, $b > 1$. Of the four studies that estimate transmission

---

12. Specifically, our vector of age-IFRs in percentages is $c(0.001, 0.020, 0.28, 1.35, 7.18)$, where c is set to yield the indicated population IFR (0.6 percent in our base case).

rates from adults to children, our weighted mean estimate is $\rho_{a1} = 0.27$, $a > 1$. We are unaware of estimates of child-child transmission rates so, lacking data, we set ρ_{11} to the average, $\rho_{11} = (\rho_{1b} + \rho_{a1})/2$. These estimates are highly uncertain and some of the simulation results are sensitive to their values; that sensitivity is discussed further in the text and in more detail in the online appendix.

III. GDP-to-Risk Index

One reopening question is whether sectors should be reopened differentially based on either their contribution to the economy or their contribution to risk of contagion. The expressions for R_0 in equation (7) and for output in equation (11) lead directly to an index of contributions of GDP per increment to R_0. Specifically, consider a marginal addition of one more worker of age a returning to the work site in sector i. Then the ratio of the marginal contribution to output, relative to the marginal contribution to R_0, is

$$(12) \qquad \frac{d \ln Y / dL_{a,i}}{dR_0 / dL_{a,i}} \propto \frac{\Psi_i / L_i}{\beta d \max \mathrm{Re}\left[eval\left(\tilde{C} \cdot \Gamma \right) \right] / dL_{a,i}} \equiv \theta_i$$

where the numerator does not depend on a because the output expression (11) does not differentiate worker productivity by age.

The derivative in the denominator in equation (12) depends on the contact matrix; however, as is shown in the online appendix, because of the way that $L_{a,i}$ enters C, this dependence on the full contact matrix is numerically small. Thus, while in principle θ_i varies as employment and the other components of the contact matrix vary, in practice this variation in θ_i is small so that the path of θ_i is well approximated by its prepandemic full-employment value. For the simulations that examine sequential industry reopening, we therefore used equation (12) with the derivatives of $\max \mathrm{Re}[eval(\tilde{C})]$ numerically evaluated at the baseline values of the contact matrix.

Some algebra for a single-age SIR model provides an interpretation of this index in terms of deaths. It is shown in the online appendix that the effective case reproduction rate, $R^{eff} = R_0(S/N)$, can be written as

$$(13) \qquad R^{eff} = 1 + \frac{1}{\gamma + \bar{\delta}} \frac{d \ln D}{dt} = 1 + \frac{1}{\gamma + \bar{\delta}} \frac{\ddot{D}}{\dot{D}},$$

where $\dot{D} = dD/dt$ and $\ddot{D} = d^2D/dt^2$. At the start of the epidemic, when $S/N = 1$, combining expressions (12) and (13) shows that

$$(14) \qquad\qquad \theta_i = \left(\gamma + \overline{\delta}\right)\frac{d \ln Y/dL_i}{d\left(\ddot{D}/\dot{D}\right)/dL_{a,i}},$$

where $\overline{\delta}$ is the population-wide death rate; the subscript a is dropped because equation (13) holds for a single-age SIR. Thus, in a single-age version of the model, θ_i is proportional to the ratio of the marginal growth of GDP to the marginal growth of the daily death rate from adding a worker to sector i.

It is tempting to translate θ into a GDP increment per death for a marginal reopening of a sector; however, the alternative formulation in equation (14) shows that such a calculation depends on the state of the pandemic because the denominator is the contribution to the growth rate of daily deaths. If daily deaths are increasing, adding a worker to a sector is costly because it increases the already-exponential growth rate of deaths. The more negative the growth rate of deaths, the smaller the contribution of the additional worker to the total number of deaths. This is a key insight, that the marginal cost of reopening is contained and can be kept small by a combination of sectoral prioritization and, especially, ensuring that noneconomic NPIs are in place to keep $R^{\mathit{eff}} < 1$ during the reopening.

Standardized and Winsorized values of θ are listed in the table in online appendix A for the sixty-six NAICS code private sectors in our model.[13] We refer to this Winsorized/standardized index as the GDP-to-risk index. The highest GDP-to-risk sectors tend to be white-collar industries such as legal services, insurance, and computer design, along with some high-value moderate-risk production sectors such as oil and gas extraction and truck transportation. Moderate GDP-to-risk industries include paper products, forestry and fishing, and utilities. Low GDP-to-risk industries tend to have many low-paid employees who are exposed to high levels of personal

---

13. The value of θ as defined in equation (12) depends on epidemiological parameters. To a good approximation, standardization eliminates this dependence, except for the ρ_{ab} factors for transmission involving children—the matrix $\Gamma \approx \rho/(\gamma + \overline{\delta})$, where the matrix ρ has elements ρ_{ab}. There are three outlier sectors (legal, management, and finance and investments) which have very high GDP-to-risk measures. It is numerically convenient to Winsorize to handle these outliers, although the conclusions are not sensitive to the Winsorization.

contacts at work, including residential care facilities, food services and drinking places, social assistants, gambling and recreational industries, transit and ground passenger transportation, and educational services.

IV. Calibration of Historical NPIs and Estimation

The historical paths of contact reduction and self-protective measures, which we collectively refer to as historical NPIs, combine calibration using historical daily data and estimation of a small number of parameters to capture the time paths of self-protective measures, such as wearing masks, on which there are limited or no data. Altogether, the model has five free parameters to be estimated: the initial infection rate I_0 as of February 21, the transmission rate β, and three parameters describing the path of NPIs from March 10 through the end of the estimation sample. The model-implied time-varying estimate of R_0 closely tracks a nonparametric estimate of R_0.

IV.A. Time-Varying Historical Contact Matrices and NPIs

The NPIs that were implemented between the second week of March and mid-May include closing schools, personal distancing, prohibiting operation of many businesses and making changes in the workplace to reduce transmission in others, orders against large gatherings, issuing stay-at-home orders in some localities; wearing masks and gloves, and urging self-isolation among those believed to have come in close contact with an infected individual. These NPIs are a mixture of policy interventions and voluntary measures taken by individuals protecting themselves and their families from infection.

These NPIs enter the model in two ways. The first is through the reduction of contacts; for example, working from home or being furloughed or laid off eliminates a worker's contacts at the workplace. The second is through reducing the probability of transmission (β), conditional on having contact with an infected individual; personal distancing and wearing masks falls in this second category. Our approach to producing time-varying contact matrices and β is a mixture of calibration when we have directly relevant data (for example, dates of school closures, mobility measures of nonwork trips, and measures of the number of employed workers and the fraction of those workers working from home) and estimation of the effect of NPIs for which we do not have data, such as personal distancing and the use of masks.

We introduce these NPIs by modifying equation (8) to allow for time-varying contacts and mitigation:

$$(15) \quad C_{ab,t} = [0.8 + 0.2\phi_t] p_a^{home} C_{ab}^{home} + \phi_t \lambda_{ab,t}^{other} p_a^{other} C_{ab}^{other}$$

$$+ \phi_t \sum_{sectors\,i} s_{it} (1 - \lambda_{wfh,t}) p_{a,i}^{work} C_{ab,i}^{work}.$$

As in equation (8), the total contacts made by someone of age a meeting someone of age b at time t is the sum of the contacts made at home, in other activities, and at work. The conditional contact matrices C_{ab}^{home}, C_{ab}^{other}, and $C_{ab,i}^{work}$ and the probabilities p_a^{home}, p_a^{other}, and $p_{a,i}^{work}$ in equation (15) refer to prepandemic contacts and population weights in equation (8). The remaining factors $\lambda_{ab,t}^{other}$, $\lambda_{wfh,t}$, and s_{it} represent measured reductions in contacts, and the factor ϕ_t captures NPIs that have the effect of reducing transmission conditional on a contact (e.g., masks).

We briefly describe these factors and motivate the structure of equation (15), starting with the second term, contacts made during other activities. The expected number of contacts made by a meeting b is $\lambda_{ab,t}^{other} p_a^{other} C_{ab}^{other}$. Attending school is an other activity, so for age < 20 we model school closings by letting $\lambda_{ab,t}^{other}$ be linear in the national average fraction of students with schools open on day t, with $\lambda_{ab,t}^{other} = 1$ if all schools are open and $\lambda_{ab,t}^{other} = 0.3$ if all are closed (accounting for nonschool other contacts). For contacts made by adults, we set $\lambda_{ab,t}^{other}$ to the Google mobility index for other activities described in section III.

The factor ϕ_t represents the reduction in the transmission probability, relative to the unmitigated transmission rate $\beta\rho_{ab}$, resulting from self-protective NPIs, such as personal distancing, hand hygiene, and wearing a mask. Guidance concerning and use of these protective measures evolved over the course of the pandemic. Early in the pandemic, public health guidance stressed hand washing and disinfecting surfaces. Until April 3, the CDC recommended that healthy people wear masks only when taking care of someone ill with COVID-19. On April 3, the CDC changed that guidance to recommend the use of cloth face coverings, and masks were adopted gradually through April into May.[14] For example, New York implemented a mandatory mask order on April 15, Bay Area counties did so on April 22, Illinois on May 1, Massachusetts on May 6. As of early July many states still did not require masks although some businesses in those

---

14. IHME, "COVID-19 Projections," https://covid19.healthdata.org/united-states-of-america?view=mask-use&tab=trend, accessed December 2020.

states did. There is now considerable evidence that personal distancing and the use of masks are effective in reducing transmission of the virus.[15] Although there are data on mandatory personal distancing measures by state (Kaiser Family Foundation 2020), we are aware of only limited data on the actual mask usage.[16] Lacking such data, we estimate the aggregate effect of those measures through the scalar risk reduction factor φ_t, parameterized using a flexible functional form, specifically, the first two terms in a type-II cosine expansion, constrained so that $0 \leq \varphi_t \leq 1$:

$$(16) \qquad \phi_t = \Phi \left\{ \begin{array}{l} f_0 + f_1 \cos[\pi(t - s_0 + 1/2)/(T - T_0)] \\ + f_2 \cos[2\pi(t - s_0 + 1/2)/(T - T_0)] \end{array} \right\}$$

where Φ is the cumulative normal distribution. We set the start date of the NPIs, s_0, to be March 10, three days before the declaration of the national emergency, reflecting the short period between the first reported COVID-19 death in the United States on February 29 and the start of the lockdown. The date T denotes the end of the estimation sample. This parameterization introduces three coefficients to be estimated, $f_0, f_1,$ and f_2.

The second term in equation (15) parameterizes contacts made at home. Most but not all contacts at home involve household members. Using the American Time Use Survey, Dorèlien, Ramen, and Swanson (2020) estimate that 85 percent of contacts made at home or in the yard involve household members; however, their total home contacts are fewer than in our contact matrices, especially for children under age 15, for whom they impute contacts. We therefore make a modest adjustment of their estimate and assume that 80 percent of contacts are among household members. Contacts among household members are modeled as unmitigated, with the remaining 20 percent of at-home contacts that are with nonhousehold members mitigated by the factor φ_t.

---

15. The effect of masks on COVID-19 transmission has been reviewed by Howard and others (2020), who, following Tian and others (2020), suggest that masks reduce the probability of transmission by the factor $(1 - ep_m)^2$, where e is the efficacy of trapping viral particles inside the mask and p_m is the percentage of the population wearing the mask. Chu and others (2020) conducted a meta-analysis of 172 studies (including studies on SARS and MERS) on personal distancing, masks, and eye protection; their overall adjusted estimate is that the use of masks by both parties has a risk reduction factor of 0.15 (0.07 to 0.34); however, they found no randomized mask trials and do not rate the certainty of the effect as high.

16. The COVID Impact Survey (at https://www.covid-impact.org/, accessed July 17) reports results for surveys at two points in time, late April and early June, and indicates an increase in mask usage over that period.

Figure 3. Illustrative Contact Matrices: Baseline, Estimated for April 15, and Counterfactual

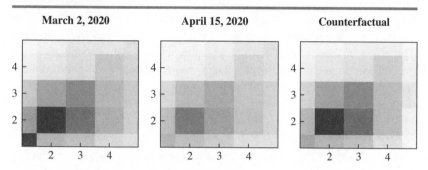

Source: Authors' calculations using POLYMOD data.

Notes: The (*a,b*) element is the number of contacts made by individual age *a* (y axis) of individuals of age *b* (x axis) in a day, for age bins 0–19, 20–44, 45–64, 65–74, and 75+. Darkest indicates eight to nine contacts, lightest indicates less than .2 contacts. From the left, the matrices are the baseline prepandemic contact matrix, the estimated contact matrix as of April 15 (accounting for working at home, layoffs, no school, reduced travel, but not accounting for masks or other transmission-reducing factors), and contacts under a hypothetical in which there is no school, all workers under age 64 return to work, workers 65+ work from home (or not at all), and visits to the elderly are reduced by 75 percent relative to baseline.

The final term in equation (15) parameterizes contacts at work. For workers in sector *i*, the baseline contacts are reduced by the fraction s_{it} of workers continuing to work,

$$(17) \qquad\qquad s_{it} = L_{\bullet,i,t} / L_{\bullet,i,t_0},$$

where $L_{\bullet,i,t}$ is the all-ages labor force in industry *i* at date *t* and t_0 is the final week in February 2020. Of those still working, a fraction $\lambda_{wfh,t}$ work from home, leaving the fraction $s_{it}(1 - \lambda_{wfh,t})$ of sector *i* workers remaining in the workplace. We set s_{it} and $\lambda_{wfh,t}$ equal to, respectively, the daily sectoral shock to the labor share and the time series on the fraction of workers working from home by sector, both of which are described in section II.A. These reduced contacts are then multiplied by the noncontact risk reduction factor φ_t in equation (16).

Figure 3 illustrates three different contact matrices. The first (left) is the baseline prepandemic contact matrix estimated for Monday, March 2. The second (center) is the calibrated contact matrix for Wednesday, April 15, in the midst of the lockdown, constructed using equation (15) with $\varphi_t = 1$, so that the matrix represents only the reduced contacts from school closings, layoffs, working from home, and reduced other activities, not from additional (unmeasured but estimated) protective precautions.

The third matrix is a counterfactual matrix for a scenario considered below, in which workers age 65+ work from home or not at all, other workers return to their workplace, there is no school, and visits to the elderly (including by home health and nursing home workers) are reduced by 75 percent. The effect of these counterfactual adjustments is to reduce contacts in the top row and final column (the oldest age groups), reduce child-child contacts (youngest age group), and for contacts among middle age groups to be similar to baseline levels.

IV.B. Estimation Results

After the calibration described in section IV.A, the SEIQRD model has five free parameters: the initial infection rate I_0, the unrestricted adult transmission rate β, and the three parameters determining φ_t, f_0, f_1, and f_2. These parameters were estimated by nonlinear least squares, fit to the daily seven-day moving average of national COVID-19 deaths from the Johns Hopkins real-time database, using an estimation sample from March 15 to June 12, 2020.[17] The mid-March start of the estimation period is motivated by the evidence of undercounting of COVID-19 deaths, especially early in the epidemic; see, for example, the *New York Times* estimates by Katz, Lu, and Sanger-Katz (2020). This systematic undercounting of deaths provides an important caveat on the parameter estimates; in particular, the initial infection rate could be higher than we estimate.

Table 1 provides estimates of these parameters and their standard errors for selected values of the overall population IFR. Standard errors are reported below the estimates, with the caveat that we are not aware of applicable distribution theory to justify the standard errors given the nonstationary, highly serially correlated data. The final column reports the root-mean-square error (units are thousands of deaths). The only parameter that is independently interpretable outside of the model is the initial number of infections on February 21, I_0, which we estimate to be 3,635 (SE = 370) using our base case population IFR of 0.7 percent.

One overall summary of the fit of the estimated model is the time path of the model-implied effective case reproduction rate, $R^{eff} = R_0(S/N)$. This is plotted in figure 4 over the estimation period (through June 12). The figure also shows a nonparametric estimate computed directly from actual daily

---

17. Daily deaths have a weekly "seasonal" pattern reflecting weekend effects in reporting. Using the seven-day trailing change in actual and model-predicted deaths smooths over this substantively unimportant noise.

Table 1. Estimated Parameter Values

IFR	$\hat{I}_0$	$\hat{\beta}$	$\hat{f}_0$	$\hat{f}_1$	$\hat{f}_2$	RMSE
0.005	4.932	0.051	0.012	0.832	0.804	1.195
	(0.485)	(0.001)	(0.003)	(0.040)	(0.039)	
0.007	3.635	0.050	0.005	0.854	0.821	1.200
	(0.371)	(0.001)	(0.004)	(0.035)	(0.041)	
0.009	2.932	0.0500	0.006	0.879	0.826	1.215
	(0.317)	(0.001)	(0.005)	(0.039)	(0.047)	

Source: Authors' calculations.

Notes: The parameters I_0 and β are, respectively, the initial number of infections on February 21 (in thousands) and the adult transmission rate. The coefficients f_0, f_1, and f_2 parameterize the scaling factor φ_t. Given the infection-fatality ratio (IFR) in the first column and the other model parameters given in the text, the parameters in the table are estimated using data on the seven-day moving average of deaths (in thousands) from March 15 through June 12. Nonlinear least squares standard errors are given in parentheses.

Figure 4. Model-Implied and Nonparametric Estimates of $R^{\textit{eff}}$

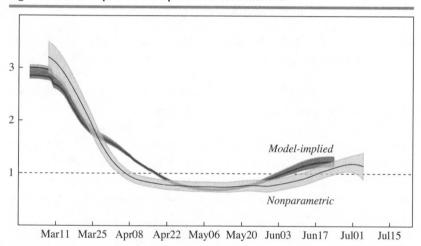

Source: Authors' calculations.

Notes: Ninety-five percent confidence bands shown. The model-implied estimate (dark gray) is computed from the estimated model, for population IFRs = 0.4–1.1 percent. The nonparametric estimate (light gray) is computed using equation (13) with the change in deaths estimated over seven days and daily deaths averaged over the week, using a local quadratic smoother. Nonparametric estimate is shifted by fourteen days to approximate the lag from infections to deaths.

deaths using equation (13).[18] Given the nonstandard serial correlation in the data, neither set of confidence intervals would be expected to have the usual 95 percent frequentist coverage. The model-based and nonparametric estimates are quite similar. Both estimate that, early in the pandemic, the initial R_0 was approximately 3.2, which is within the range of other estimates. With the self-protective measures and government-ordered shutdowns, the effective R dropped sharply through March into April and was estimated to be below 1 from mid-April through mid-May. Subsequently, with the reopening and the increased mobility, the model-based effective R rose slightly above 1, although the nonparametric estimate remained just below 1. The estimated values of R^{eff} are plotted for IFRs ranging from 0.4 percent to 1.1 percent; they are nearly the same, indicating that the IFR is not separately identified in the model as discussed by Atkeson (2020b).

V. Control Rules and Simulation Design

Decision making in the coronavirus epidemic has occurred at all levels of society: consumers decide if they feel it is safe to dine out or travel; workers weigh concerns about the safety of returning to work; local officials decide on when to apply for and how to implement reopening; state officials issue closure orders, mandate noneconomic NPIs, and permit reopenings; and federal agencies attempt to provide guidance. We combine these multiple decision makers, private and public, into a single representative decision maker who is averse to both deaths and unemployment. For convenience, we refer to this decision maker as a governor who has primary authority over decisions to shut down and to reopen, but the term "governor" stands in for the actual, more complex, decentralized decision-making process.

V.A. Control Rules

We model reopening decisions as reacting to recent developments with the twin aims of controlling deaths and reopening the economy in mind. In so doing, we treat the governor as following the CDC and White House

---

18. The growth rate of daily deaths in equation (13) is estimated by the average seven-day change in deaths divided by the seven-day average daily death rate, smoothed using a local quadratic smoother. The nonparametric estimates assume the SIR model. For an alternative estimator of R that does require information on disease-specific dynamics but does not assume a SIR structure, see Cori and others (2013).

reopening guidelines (White House, CDC, and FDA 2020), which advises reopening the economy if there is a downward trajectory of symptoms and cases for fourteen days, along with having adequate medical capacity and health care worker testing. Because of changes in test availability, confirmed cases are a poor measure of total infections, so we use deaths instead of infections but otherwise follow the spirit of the CDC guidelines.

Specifically, we consider a governor who will restrict activity when deaths are rising or high, relax those restrictions when deaths are falling or low, tend to reopen when the unemployment rate is high, and tend to reopen when the cumulative unemployment gap is high. This final tendency reflects increasing pressures on budgets—personal, business, and public—from each additional week of high unemployment and low incomes on top of previous months.

In the jargon of control theory, this amounts to the governor following a proportional-integral-derivative (PID) control rule, in which the feedback depends on current deaths, the fourteen-day change in deaths (declining death rate), the current unemployment rate, and the integral of the unemployment rate. Accordingly, we suppose that the governor follows the linear PID controller,

$$(18) \qquad u_t = \kappa_0 + \kappa_{up} U_{t-1} + \kappa_{ui} \int_{t_0}^{t-1} U_s \, ds + \kappa_{dp} D_{t-1} + \kappa_{dd} \dot{D}_{t-1},$$

where U_t is the unemployment rate ($= 1 - L_t/L_{t0}$), where t_0 is the end of February 2020) and $\dot{D}$ is the death rate. The CDC recommends tracking not the instantaneous derivative of infections (or D) but the change over fourteen days, and deaths are noisy, suggesting some smoothing of D. Similarly, U is unobserved and at best can be estimated with a lag, even using new and continuing claims for unemployment insurance and nonstandard real-time data. For the various terms on the right-hand side of equation (18) we therefore use, in order, the fourteen-day average of the unemployment rate, the cumulative daily unemployment rate since March 7, deaths over the previous two days (these are observed without noise in our model), and the fourteen-day change in the two-day death rate.

The governor decides whether workplaces can reopen and, if so, whether to stagger the reopening across industries using the GDP-to-risk index. Specifically, we consider a sequence of sectoral reopenings as determined by the PID controller, shifted by the GDP-to-risk index:

$$(19) \qquad s_{it} = s_{it_R} + \Phi(u_t + \kappa_\theta \theta_i)(1 - s_{it_R}),$$

where s_{it} is the workforce in sector i at date t as a fraction of its February value (see equation [17]), t_R is the initial date of the reopening, and Φ is the cumulative Gaussian distribution, which is used to ensure that the controller takes on a value between 0 and 1 (so sectoral relative employment satisfies $s_{it_R} \leq s_{it} \leq 1$). The industry shifter $\kappa_\theta \theta_i$ preferences industry i based on its GDP-to-risk index.

Reopening the economy requires not just working but shopping, which is an other activity. In the historical period, the factor $\lambda_{ab,t}^{other}$ for $a > 2$ is set to equal the Google mobility index for other activities. We model this factor as increasing to 1 proportionately to GDP from its value on t_R as the economy reopens, so that full employment corresponds to $\lambda_{ab,t}^{other} = 1$ for $a > 2$.

V.B. *Noneconomic NPIs*

Noneconomic NPIs are either under the control of the governor (e.g., reopening schools) or are decisions made by individuals that are influenced by the governor (e.g., attending church). Instead of specifying policy rules for these other NPIs, we examine different scenarios in which the governor behaves according to equations (18) and (19) concerning sectoral reopening. For example, one set of choices entails opening up schools, but with protections (which the governor and school districts can mandate); in the context of equation (15), opening schools corresponds to setting $\lambda_{ab,t}^{other} = 1$ for ages < 20, and protective measures at schools correspond to setting $\varphi_t < 1$ for contacts made at school. For adults, we allow for relaxation of protective measures (masks, personal distancing) according to three reopening phases. For age 75+, we consider scenarios in which they are subject to additional restrictions on visits and greater use of protection than in the general population. These stand in for regular testing of nursing home employees, requiring visiting families to gather outside and to wear masks, and so forth.

VI. Simulation Results

All the simulations have the same structure: the governor controls economic reopening according to the control rule in equation (18), given a specified path of noneconomic NPIs. This structure allows us to quantify the interaction between economic and noneconomic NPIs. In our second wave baseline (figure 1), the governor is pro-reopening so exercises a fast reopening. As an alternative, we consider a slower governor who is more willing to shut down the economy a second time.

The environment in which the governor makes these decisions is specified in terms of NPIs, which differ in each scenario. Some of these, like school reopening, are directly under the governor's control, while others, like masks and personal distancing, are individual decisions that can be influenced by state, federal, and local recommendations and education. The baseline is the fast-reopening second wave scenario in figure 1; each scenario is defined by departures from that baseline. All simulations begin on June 1, which approximates the middle of actual state reopenings. Georgia was the first state to reopen most consumer-facing businesses on April 24, while reopening for some of the hardest-hit regions (for example, Massachusetts, Michigan, and New York City) occurred mainly in June.

The multiple public and private reopening road maps (Gottlieb and others 2020; White House, CDC, and FDA 2020; National Governors Association 2020; Conference Board 2020; Romer 2020) generally reopen in phases, where transition to the next phase is determined by public health gating criteria. We follow this framework and relax (or reimpose) non-economic NPIs in three phases. In the reopening baseline, phase I reopening occurs on May 18, phase II reopening occurs on June 8, phase III reopening occurs on July 1. Nursing homes lag by one phase and enter phase III on September 15. These phases are modeled as (1) an increase, in three equal steps, in the number of other and nonhousehold home contacts from before the lockdown to prepandemic conditions, and (2) a relaxation of personal protective measures (masks, personal distancing) from their mid-May values to a value that is higher but still represents considerable reduction in transmission rates, given a contact, relative to unrestricted conditions. In the second wave baseline, the self-protective factor φ rises from its late-May empirical estimate of 0.26 to 0.67. As a calibration using the formula in footnote 12, a factor of 0.67 corresponds to one-quarter of the population using masks that are 75 percent effective for all nonhousehold contacts. In the reopening baseline, workers working at home return to the workplace during phases I–III. The roadmaps and actual reopenings typically prioritize safer sectors, so in our second wave baseline we use equation (19) with $\kappa_\theta = 1$. If primary and elementary schools reopen, they do so on August 24.

In all scenarios, we assume that workplace safety measures remain in place throughout the simulation period at their estimated late-May level, specifically, the within-workplace transmission factor β is reduced by a factor of 0.26. As calibration using the formula in footnote 12, this corresponds to 65 percent of workers wearing a 75 percent effective mask when in contact with workers or customers, although in practice workplace safety measures would vary by sector.

Each scenario also specifies an effective quarantine rate. The effective quarantine rate is the fraction of infected individuals who, at some point during their infection, enter quarantine. The rate that is achieved in practice reflects a combination of identifying the infected through testing or contact tracing, government policy concerning those who test positive, and individual compliance. Currently, the CDC website advises individuals who test positive or who are symptomatic to self-isolate "as much as possible."[19] We assume a current quarantine rate of 5 percent which, for example, corresponds to 10 percent of the infected restricting their contacts by half. We consider alternatives of higher quarantine rates later in the summer, which in turn hinges on testing and contact tracing becoming more widely available.

All simulations reported here are for a population-wide IFR of 0.7 percent; sensitivity analysis is provided in the online appendix. Uncertainty spreads in the simulation plots are two standard error bands based on the estimation uncertainty for I_0 and β in table 1. All simulations end on January 1, 2021. Details for all scenarios are available in the online appendix, as are sensitivity results for these scenarios that vary the population-wide IFR and epidemiological parameters.

Figure 5 shows total deaths and the share of recovered individuals by age for the baseline second wave scenario in figure 1. Of the 482,000 deaths by January 1, 56 percent are age 75 or older. By January 1, nearly one-quarter of the population has been infected, with those age 20–44 having the highest recovered rate (31 percent) because of their higher rates of contact. Because of the high rate of recovered individuals, the value of R^{eff} in this simulation is just over 1 by January 1.

Results for mortality by age and GDP are given in the online appendix.

VI.A. Economic NPIs

The first economic NPI, shutting down the economy while holding constant the other assumptions of the second wave baseline, is modeled by the slow governor's response, holding constant the other assumptions of the second wave baseline, and is shown in the top panel of figure 2.

---

19. "What to Do If You Are Sick," Centers for Disease Control and Prevention, https://www.cdc.gov/coronavirus/2019-ncov/if-you-are-sick/steps-when-sick.html?CDC_AA_refVal=https%3A%2F%2Fwww.cdc.gov%2Fcoronavirus%2F2019-ncov%2Fif-you-are-sick%2Fcaring-for-yourself-at-home.html, accessed June 19, 2020.

Figure 5. Deaths and Share of Recovered by Age for the Second Wave Scenario
in Figure 1

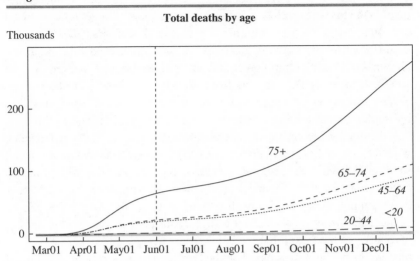

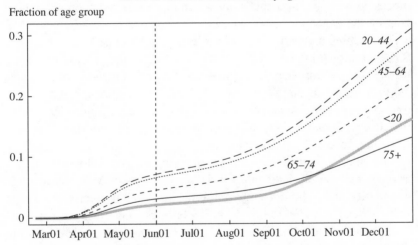

Source: Authors' calculations.

As discussed in the introduction, the second shutdown reduces but does not eliminate the second wave of deaths, while producing rates of unemployment in the mid-teens. Here, we consider the effects of three more-nuanced economic NPIs: relying more heavily on the GDP-to-risk index, so that high-risk, low-value sectors are reopened last and closed first; requiring all workers to work from home; and an age-based policy that requires all workers who are age 65+ to work from home if they can or not to work at all.

The top panel of figure 6 departs from the second wave baseline by implementing a more aggressive sectoral reopening than in figure 1, specifically by increasing κ_θ in equation (19) to $\kappa_\theta = 2$. As it happens, whether one makes more aggressive use of the GDP-to-risk index has a small effect: when the sectoral reopening exploits the GDP-to-risk index, deaths are reduced by 800 and second-half GDP is increased by 0.2 percent (the unemployment rate is very slightly lower under the nuanced reopening because the lower deaths permit a slightly faster reopening). This finding is robust: we have explored the gains from stronger or weaker phasing of reopenings or shutdowns based on the GDP-to-risk index, both Winsorized (used here) and not; while using this index reduces deaths, the gains are modest at best and, in scenarios in which deaths are being brought under control, the benefits of a staged sectoral reopening are nearly negligible. The remaining simulations therefore retain the baseline value of $\kappa_\theta = 1$. Some intuition for the limited benefit of a staged sectoral reopening is that, for the average worker, only half their contacts occur at work, and because workplaces are generally regulated, it is easier to implement and enforce transmission reduction measures at work than in noneconomic other activities such as church or parties; thus the potential gains from staged sectoral reopening are small to begin with.

This finding of small benefits to staggering the sectoral reopening has an important caveat: although our sixty-six sectors provide considerable granularity and exhibit a large variation in the GDP-to-risk index, the sectoral detail does not isolate those few businesses in the highest-risk tail of the contact distribution. For example, NAICS code 722 (food services and drinking places) includes establishments ranging from catering companies to nightclubs. Contacts among customers and workers at high-contact/high transmissibility activities such as nightclubs are in principle in the POLYMOD contact database, so these very high-contact economic activities are in both the workplace and consumption (other activity) components of the model. That said, judgment strongly suggests that such high-contact economic activity would appropriately be treated differently than broad-based reopening: keeping closed the highest-contact economic activities

Figure 6. Economic Non-pharmaceutical Interventions

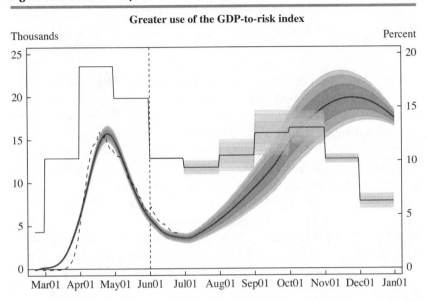

Greater use of the GDP-to-risk index

Thousands   Percent

Full working from home

Thousands   Percent

Source: Authors' calculations.

Notes: Baseline is the fast reopening second wave scenario in figure 1. Total deaths by January 1: 482,000 (top) and 383,000 (bottom). Bands denote +/− 1, 1.65, and 1.96 standard deviations arising from sampling uncertainty for the estimated parameters.

could be a justifiable NPI in a cost-benefit sense, perhaps indefinitely until a vaccine is available. These very high-contact activities are a small fraction of economic activity, for example, admissions to movie theaters, sports, and other live entertainment comprised less than 0.6 percent of personal consumption expenditures in 2019.

The bottom panel of figure 6 modifies the second wave baseline by requiring those workers who are able to work from home to continue to do so as businesses reopen. By reducing workplace contacts, this policy reduces deaths by January 1 from 482,000 to 383,000. This reduction in deaths allows the governor to implement a less severe second wave shutdown, so the unemployment rate is lower (by approximately 1 percentage point) during the fall than without the work-from-home order.[20]

Figure 7 (top panel) considers an age-based policy, in which only workers over age 65 are required to work from home, if they are able, or not at all. The effect of this NPI on employment and contagion varies by sector, depending on the age distribution of workers, personal proximity in the workplace, and the extent to which that sector admits working from home. This policy reduces total deaths from 482,000 to 466,000. The year-end unemployment rate is slightly higher under this scenario than the second wave baseline because of the laid-off age 65+ workers.

The bottom panel of figure 7 considers the combined effects of an economic lockdown with these three economic NPIs layered on: leaning more heavily on phasing by sector, requiring working from home, and laying off workers age 65+ who are not able to work from home. These instruments are complementary, and between them they reduce deaths by 171,000. Yet, this full arsenal of economic NPIs neither prevents nor quells the second wave, just limits its damage, and they are accompanied by very high unemployment rates.

Compared to the full shutdown, the three more-nuanced economic NPIs have the virtue of both reducing deaths and supporting overall employment. That said, the main conclusion from these simulations is that the full economic shutdown in figure 2 (top panel), even if combined with the additional economic measures in figures 6 and 7, is not potent enough, by itself, to stop the second wave.

---

20. We note that there are plausibly effects on productivity from working at home, although a priori the overall sign is unclear. Workers save time commuting; however, they could have distractions such as child care. Bloom and others (2015) find that workers who work from home are more productive; however, that is a pre-COVID-19 study, so there is plausibly selection in those results. See Mas and Pallais (2020) for a review. These potential productivity effects are not included in our calculations.

Figure 7. Economic Non-pharmaceutical Interventions

No on-site workers age 65+ and aggressive sectoral, work-from-home

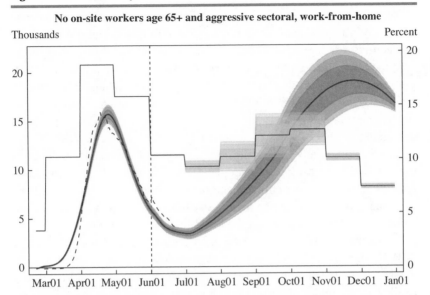

No age 65+ combined with economic shutdown

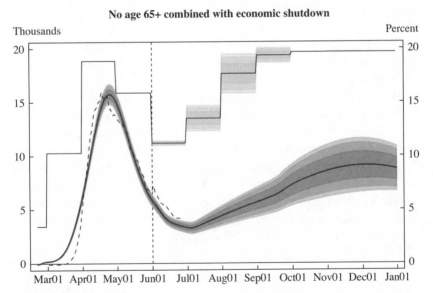

Source: Authors' calculations.

Notes: Baseline is the fast reopening second wave scenario in figure 1. Total deaths by January 1: 466,000 (top) and 311,000 (bottom). Bands denote +/− 1, 1.65, and 1.96 standard deviations arising from sampling uncertainty for the estimated parameters.

VI.B. Noneconomic NPIs

We now turn to four noneconomic NPIs that could mitigate the second wave: not allowing schools to reopen in the fall; undertaking enhanced protections for age 75+, especially the most vulnerable in long-term care facilities; increasing the quarantine rate, which would entail directing resources toward increased testing and contact tracing; and revoking phase III noneconomic relaxation, such as returning to prohibitions on large group gatherings and enhanced mask wearing and personal distancing.

The option of not reopening elementary and secondary schools in the fall is shown in figure 8 (top panel). Not sending children to school reduces contacts among children and between children and their teachers, so reduces the spread of the virus. As discussed in section II, however, contacts involving children are believed to entail lower risk of spreading the virus than contacts among adults, so deaths by January 1 only fall by 26,000. Moreover, if schools are closed, then some workers will be constrained in their labor supply because they must provide child care; as a result, the unemployment rate remains elevated through the fall at just over 10 percent. In addition, closing schools has the undesirable effect of retarding schoolchildren's education, especially for those least able to learn in an online environment. So not reopening schools alone imposes considerable economic and noneconomic costs while not solving the problem of the second wave.

Because COVID-19 mortality rates increase sharply with age, one possible policy is to devote additional resources focused on protecting the elderly. Current CDC guidelines for nursing homes recommend virus testing for all residents and staff but do not specify testing frequency.[21] The CDC also recommends that visitors wear cloth masks and restrict their visit to their relative's room. The Centers for Medicare and Medicaid Services guidelines for reopening long-term care facilities recommend weekly testing of staff, providing staff with personal protective equipment, and delaying outside visitors until the state enters federal phase III reopening.[22] In theory, these are strong and protective steps; however,

---

21. "Testing Guidelines for Nursing Homes," Centers for Disease Control and Prevention, https://www.cdc.gov/coronavirus/2019-ncov/hcp/nursing-homes-testing.html, accessed June 20, 2020.

22. "Nursing Home Reopening Recommendations for State and Local Officials," Centers for Medicare and Medicaid Services, https://www.cms.gov/medicareprovider-enrollment-and-certificationsurveycertificationgeninfopolicy-and-memos-states-and/nursing-home-reopening-recommendations-state-and-local-officials, accessed May 18, 2020.

Figure 8. Noneconomic Non-pharmaceutical Interventions

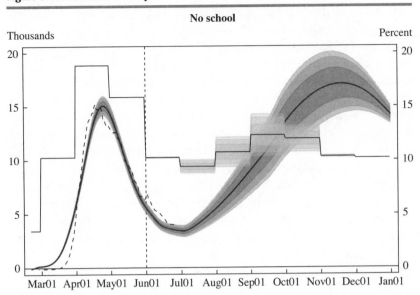

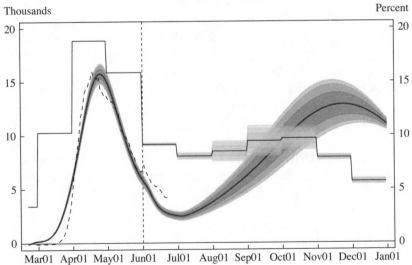

Source: Authors' calculations.
Notes: Baseline is the fast reopening second wave scenario in figure 1. Total deaths by January 1: 456,000 (top) and 355,000 (bottom). Bands denote +/− 1, 1.65, and 1.96 standard deviations arising from sampling uncertainty for the estimated parameters.

it is unclear how the testing and additional staff needed to implement these guidelines will be paid for and whether nursing homes have the institutional capacity to implement these measures.

Figure 8 (bottom panel) examines the effects of enhanced protections for the elderly, modeled as requiring nursing homes to maintain their restrictions on visitors and transmission mitigation measures of late May (the details of how these requirements are met could change in practice, for example, by more staff testing as tests become more available than they were in May). The reduction in deaths is large, by 127,000, about one-third of projected cases under the baseline from July 1 through January 1. This significant saving in life is consistent with the conclusions in Acemoglu and others (2020), although their estimated gains are even larger because they start from a much higher baseline number of deaths. The reduced number of deaths provides room for the governor to be less restrictive and, while under this policy the economy still has a *W*-shaped recession, the second dip is less severe.

The roadmaps generally stress the importance of widespread testing and quarantine. During the spring and summer of 2020, however, testing was notable mainly because of its absence. In some cases, test results were so delayed as to render testing useless for public health purposes. Our enhanced quarantine scenario has a 10 percent effective quarantine rate, that is, 10 percent of infected individuals are sent into perfect quarantine at some point during their infection.[23] Without legally enforceable quarantine, even a 10 percent effective quarantine rate evidently would require a significant increase in testing with fast turnaround, combined with incentives to quarantine. That testing need not be random but instead could be focused on populations who are both at a highest risk of getting the virus and are most likely to spread it.

The effect of a 10 percent quarantine rate (up from 5 percent in the baseline) is shown in the top panel of figure 9; the bottom panel shows results for a 15 percent quarantine rate. Increasing the quarantine rate to 10 percent

---

23. We consider this effective quarantine rate as ambitious but achievable. Current estimates of the asymptomatic rate vary from less than 40 percent to approximately 80 percent. Yang, Gui, and Xiong (2020) estimate a 42 percent asymptomatic rate for a sample of Wuhan residents. Data in Guðbjartsson and others (2020) suggest a comparable asymptomatic rate in Icelandic testing, and Poletti and others (2020) suggest a 70 percent asymptomatic rate among those younger than 60. As a calibration, suppose that 40 percent of the infected (a high fraction of the symptomatic) get tested, get their results back while they are still infectious, and are advised to self-isolate, that half of those comply, and that those who comply reduce their contacts by 50 percent. This results in a 10 percent effective quarantine rate.

Figure 9. Noneconomic Non-pharmaceutical Interventions

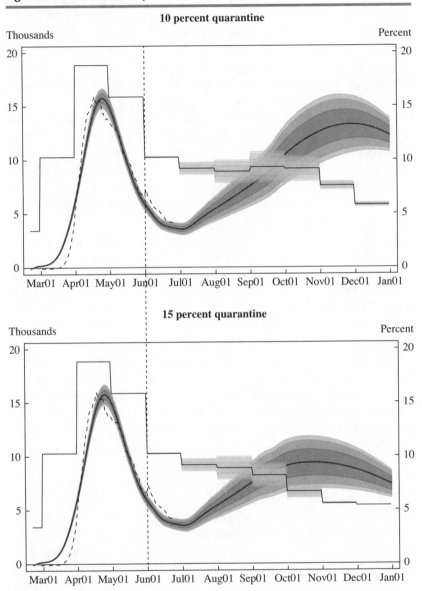

10 percent quarantine

15 percent quarantine

Source: Authors' calculations.

Notes: Baseline is the fast reopening second wave scenario in figure 1. Total deaths by January 1: 384,000 (top) and 331,000 (bottom). Bands denote +/− 1, 1.65, and 1.96 standard deviations arising from sampling uncertainty for the estimated parameters.

reduced fatalities from 482,000 to 384,000 and increasing the quarantine rate to 15 percent nearly flattens the death curve and reduced total deaths to 331,000. With increased testing and quarantine, the governor can pause the economic reopening but does not need a second economic shutdown.

These scenarios all have phased-in lifting of restrictions on noneconomic activities, such as basketball games, large group gatherings, and religious services, as well as partial relaxation of personal protections such as wearing masks. An option available to the governor is to revoke the phase II and III noneconomic reopenings and to call for increased wearing of masks and personal distancing. We therefore consider a case in which the governor reverts to phase I for noneconomic gatherings (church, social, etc.) on July 20, upon seeing the reversal of the previously declining trend in deaths. Recall that phase I noneconomic restrictions are less restrictive than our empirical estimates for mid-May.

Figure 10 (top panel) considers this reversal of noneconomic NPIs. Unlike the imposition of strict economic NPIs or economic shutdowns, this policy brings R^{eff} below 1 and deaths decline: the second wave is kept small and brief. Year-end deaths total only 188,000, and the economy is near full employment.

The final two cases combine some of these noneconomic NPIs. Figure 10 (bottom panel) considers the combined effect of returning to phase I social distancing, enhanced protections for the elderly, and 10 percent quarantine. The combined effect is to reduce year-end deaths to 155,000 with nearly full employment. Figure 2 (bottom panel), discussed in the introduction, additionally requires workers who can to continue to work from home; the result is a further reduction in deaths to 147,000 and nearly full employment throughout the fourth quarter.

VI.C. Cost per Life

A standard approach in the economics literature on the pandemic is to view NPIs through the lens of cost per life saved. There are technical reasons to object to this calculation: standard estimates of the value of life refer to marginal consumption losses whereas the current losses are nonmarginal, and the true cost of a shutdown-induced recession depends on the path of recovery which is highly uncertain.[24] More importantly, the preceding simulations underscore that the value-of-life framing is too narrow for many of these calculations, in which the NPI reduces lives lost *and* improves economic outcomes.

---

24. See Hall, Jones, and Klenow (2020) for a discussion.

Figure 10. Noneconomic Non-pharmaceutical Interventions: Strong Personal Distancing

With 10 percent quarantine

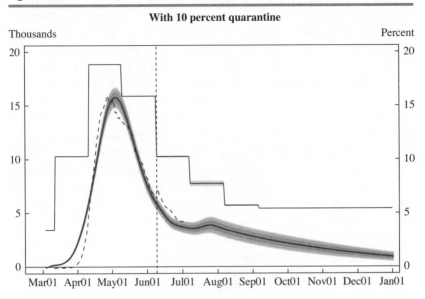

With enhanced protections for age 75+

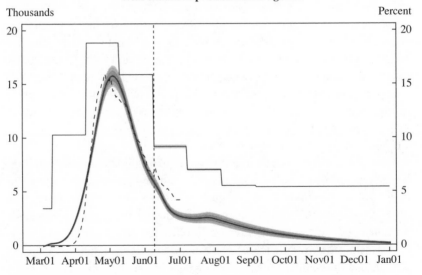

Source: Authors' calculations.

Notes: Baseline is the fast reopening second wave scenario in figure 1. Total deaths by January 1: 188,000 (top) and 155,000 (bottom). Bands denote +/− 1, 1.65, and 1.96 standard deviations arising from sampling uncertainty for the estimated parameters.

With these caveats, one component of a cost-benefit analysis of economic NPIs is the economic cost, measured by lost output, relative to lives saved. The paths of the fast and slow governors allow us to compute the value of lost output per death averted as a result of a slow reopening (or aggressive closing), relative to the fast governor, over the period of the simulation, holding constant all other NPIs.[25] These values vary substantially across NPI scenarios. If an economic lockdown is the only tool used, that is, the scenario in figure 1 versus figure 2 (top panel), the cost per death averted is $11 million. In scenarios with other NPIs, the cost per death averted tends to increase because the other NPIs are reducing deaths, so the marginal value of the lockdown measured in terms of deaths is diminished. For example, if an economic lockdown is layered on top of the reversal in noneconomic NPIs in figure 10 (top panel), the cost per death averted is $24 million. These values exceed typical US government estimates; for example, the US Environmental Protection Agency (2010, appendix B) recommends using $9.1 million (2019 dollars) per death averted.

VI.D. Nonlinear Input-Output Calculations

Our counterfactual GDP estimates use the approximation in equation (11) known as Hulten's (1978) theorem. Hulten's theorem is an equilibrium first-order approximation for small shocks. Given that the sectoral reductions in hours associated with lockdowns are very large, it is natural to question the validity of this approximation. As shown by Baqaee and Farhi (2019, 2020a, 2020b), the quality of the approximation depends on the size of the sectoral shocks and how sectoral labor income shares vary with the shocks, which in turn depends on the elasticities of substitution in consumption and in production. When all the elasticities are equal to one, the economy is Cobb-Douglas, the sectoral labor shares are constant, and Hulten's theorem applies globally and not only as a first-order approximation. However, if the elasticities are less than one, so that there are complementarities, then the quality of the approximation can quickly deteriorate when the shocks get large. This is potentially important given that the empirical literature typically finds that inter-sectoral elasticities are significantly below one.

To gauge the importance of these nonlinearities for our calculations, we consider the counterfactual sectoral reductions in hours in 2020:Q3 in the economic lockdown scenario of figure 2 (top panel). We explore different values within the plausible set of inter-sectoral elasticities (σ, θ, e, η),

---

25. This calculation misses differences in lives saved and costs incurred in 2021, outside the simulation window.

where σ is the elasticity of substitution in consumption, θ is the elasticity of substitution across intermediates in production, e is the elasticity of substitution between value added and intermediates in production, and η is the elasticity of substitution between capital and labor in production. We consider low elasticities given the short horizons involved. When $(\sigma, \theta, e, \eta) = (1, 1, 1, 1)$, so that Hulten's theorem applies globally, the reduction in real GDP is 7.3 percent. When $(\sigma, \theta, e, \eta) = (0.95, 0.001, 0.7, 0.5)$, the reduction in real GDP is 7.9 percent. When $(\sigma, \theta, e, \eta) = (0.7, 0.001, 0.3, 0.2)$, the reduction in real GDP is 9.5 percent. Finally, when $(\sigma, \theta, e, \eta) = (0.5, 0.001, 0.3, 0.2)$, the reduction in real GDP is 10.1 percent. Hence, empirically plausible complementarities in consumption and in production can amplify real GDP losses, relative to what we have reported, by somewhere between 10 and 40 percent.

VII. Discussion

The modeling presented here goes beyond what is in the literature by incorporating an age-based SEIQRD model into a sectoral economic model with multiple, explicitly specified NPIs, calibrated and estimated to current US conditions using the most recently available data. Still, multiple caveats are in order. One is that the situation differs by state, with Northeastern states seeing a sharp decline in infections and deaths in May through July 2020, but other parts of the United States seeing expansions in infections and deaths. The national modeling here abstracts from these differences. In addition, there is considerable uncertainty over some key epidemiological parameters, such as the infection-fatality ratio. Additional simulation results in the online appendix explore the sensitivity of the modeling results to some of the key epidemiological parameters. Although numerical values differ—for example, under all control scenarios deaths are higher if a higher value of the IFR is assumed—the conclusions from section VI are robust.

For convenience, we have called the decision maker in the model the governor. This is a simplification of a complex decision-making environment in which federal guidelines, state requirements and guidelines, local implementation, and individual decisions combine to influence the spread of the virus. There is a compelling body of work that much of the decline in economic activity in March and April was not directly caused by government intervention but instead was an endogenous self-protective response by consumers and, similarly, that official reopenings had limited if any direct causal effect on spending (Bartik and others 2020; Gupta, Simon, and Wing 2020). If so, one might think of consumers as more akin to our slow governor. Under this interpretation, our results align with the reduced-form evidence that the key to reviving the economy is providing a setting in which consumers and workers are comfortable returning to economic activity, that is, in which deaths are low and declining.

Our governor in these simulations used a backward-looking PID control rule based on the CDC suggested guidelines. This differs from most of the recent economic modeling surveyed in the introduction, which investigates optimal control rules. These approaches are complementary: optimal control provides insights about how economic decisions could optimally be made; the approach here asks how various NPIs can reduce or eliminate the need for adhering to lockdowns within the context of existing economic reopening or closing plans. One issue that has not been addressed in the economics literature using optimal control is the large amount of parameter and model uncertainty, which is ignored under standard optimal control rules but is reflected in the uncertainty bands in our figures and in the online appendix. Addressing this uncertainty could be done using the tools of robust control, but that has not yet been done in combined economics-epidemiological models.[26]

The main conclusion from the simulations in section VI is that aggressive use of noneconomic NPIs can lead to a reduction in deaths and a strong economic reopening. If a second wave emerges, a second round of economic shutdowns would be both costly and ineffective, compared to noneconomic NPIs. A key noneconomic NPI is returning to phase I–level restrictions on noneconomic social activities, combined with widespread adoption of measures to reduce transmission such as masks and personal distancing. When combined with other measures, such as ramped-up testing and quarantine and enhanced protection of the elderly, especially in nursing homes, these noneconomic NPIs can provide a powerful force to control a second wave and, based on our modeling, make room for bringing the large majority of those currently not working back to work.

ACKNOWLEDGMENTS   We thank Veronica De Falco, Michael Droste, Adriano Fernandes, Kathryn Holston, Stephanie Kestelman, Ed Kong, Danila Maroz, Chika Okafor, and Lingdi Xu for research assistance; Caroline Buckee, Jason Furman, James Hay, Abigail Wozniak, and Jan Eberly for discussions; and Daron Acemoglu and David Romer for comments. This research was supported by NSF RAPID Grant SES-2032493.

26. See, however, Morris and others (2020) for an example within an epidemiology-only model.

References

Acemoglu, Daron, Victor Chernozhukov, Iván Werning, and Michael D. Whinston. 2020. "Optimally Targeted Lockdowns in a Multi-Group SIR Model." Working Paper 27102. Cambridge, Mass.: National Bureau of Economic Research.

Alvarez, Fernando E., David Argente, and Francesco Lippi. 2020. "A Simple Planning Problem for COVID-19 Lockdown." Working Paper 26981. Cambridge, Mass.: National Bureau of Economic Research.

Atkeson, Andrew. 2020a. "What Will Be the Economic Impact of COVID-19 in the US? Rough Estimates of Disease Scenarios." Working Paper 26867. Cambridge, Mass.: National Bureau of Economic Research.

Atkeson, Andrew. 2020b. "How Deadly Is COVID-19? Understanding the Difficulties with Estimation of Its Fatality Rate." Working Paper 26965. Cambridge, Mass.: National Bureau of Economic Research.

Aum, Sangin, Sang Yoon (Tim) Lee, and Yongseok Shin. 2020. "Inequality of Fear and Self-Quarantine: Is There a Trade-Off between GDP and Public Health?" Working Paper 27100. Cambridge, Mass.: National Bureau of Economic Research.

Azzimonti, Maria, Allesandra Fogli, Fabrizio Perri, and Mark Ponder. 2020. "Social Distance Policies in ECON-EPI Networks." Working Paper. http://marina-azzimonti.com/wp-content/uploads/2020/07/Draft_july18.pdf.

Baqaee, David, and Emmanuel Farhi. 2019. "The Macroeconomic Impact of Microeconomic Shocks: Beyond Hulten's Theorem." *Econometrica* 87, no. 4: 1155–203.

Baqaee, David, and Emmanuel Farhi. 2020a. "Nonlinear Production Networks with an Application to the COVID-19 Crisis." Working Paper 27281. Cambridge, Mass.: National Bureau of Economic Research.

Baqaee, David, and Emmanuel Farhi. 2020b. "Supply and Demand in Disaggregated Keynesian Economics with an Application to the COVID-19 Crisis." Working Paper 27152. Cambridge, Mass.: National Bureau of Economic Research.

Bartik, Alexander W., Marianne Bertrand, Feng Lin, Jesse Rothstein, and Matthew Unrath. 2020. "Measuring the Labor Market at the Onset of the COVID-19 Crisis." In the present volume of *Brookings Papers on Economic Activity*.

Berger, David, Kyle Herkenhoff, and Simon Mongey. 2020. "An SEIR Infectious Disease Model with Testing and Conditional Quarantine." Working Paper 2020-25. Chicago: University of Chicago, Becker Friedman Institute for Economics.

Bick, Alexander, Adam Blandin, and Karel Mertens. 2020. "Work from Home after the COVID-19 Outbreak." Working Paper 2017. Federal Reserve Bank of Dallas. https://www.dallasfed.org/research/papers/2020/wp2017.

Bloom, Nicholas, James Liang, John Roberts, and Zhichun Jenny Ying. 2015. "Does Working from Home Work? Evidence from a Chinese Experiment." *Quarterly Journal of Economics* 130, no. 1: 165–218.

Boast, Alison, Alasdair Munro, and Henry Goldstein. 2020. "An Evidence Summary of Paediatric COVID-19 Literature." Blog post, September 26, Don't Forget the Bubbles. http://doi.org/10.31440/DFTB.24063.

Bodenstein, Martin, Giancarlo Corsetti, and Luca Guerrieri. 2020. "Social Distancing and Supply Disruptions in a Pandemic." Finance and Economics Discussion Series 2020-031. Washington: Board of Governors of the Federal Reserve System.

Budish, Eric B. 2020. "$R < 1$ as an Economic Constraint: Can We 'Expand the Frontier' in the Fight against Covid-19?" Working Paper 2020-31. Chicago: University of Chicago, Booth School of Business.

Chu, Derek K., Elie A. Akl, Stephanie Duda, Karla Solo, Sally Yaacoub, Holger J. Schünemann, and others. 2020. "Physical Distancing, Face Masks, and Eye Protection to Prevent Person-to-Person Transmission of SARS-CoV-2 and COVID-19: A Systematic Review and Meta-Analysis." *Lancet* 394, no. 10242: 1949–2020.

Conference Board. 2020. "A Realistic Blueprint for Reopening the Economy by Sector while Ramping Up Testing." Solutions Brief. Arlington, Va.: Committee for Economic Development of the Conference Board. https://www.ced.org/ 2020-solutions-briefs/a-realistic-blueprint-for-reopening-the-economy-by-sector-while-ramping-up.

Cori, Anne, Neil M. Ferguson, Christophe Fraser, and Simon Cauchemez. 2013. "A New Framework and Software to Estimate Time-Varying Reproduction Numbers during Epidemics." *American Journal of Epidemiology* 178, no. 9: 1505–12.

Dingel, Jonathan I., and Brent Neiman. 2020. "How Many Jobs Can Be Done at Home?" *Journal of Public Economics* 189, article no. 104235.

Dingel, Jonathan I., Christina Patterson, and Joseph Vavra. 2020. "Childcare Obligations Will Constrain Many Workers When Reopening the US Economy." Working Paper 2020-46. Chicago: University of Chicago, Becker Friedman Institute for Economics.

Dorèlien, Audrey M., Aparna Ramen, and Isabella Swanson. 2020. "Analyzing the Demographic, Spatial, and Temporal Factors Influencing Social Contact Patterns in the U.S. and Implications for Infectious Disease Spread." Working Paper 2020-05. Minneapolis: Minnesota Population Center, University of Minnesota. https://assets.ipums.org/_files/mpc/wp2020-05.pdf.

Eichenbaum, Martin S., Sergio T. Rebelo, and Mathias Trabandt. 2020a. "The Macroeconomics of Epidemics." Working Paper 26882. Cambridge, Mass.: National Bureau of Economic Research.

Eichenbaum, Martin S., Sergio T. Rebelo, and Mathias Trabandt. 2020b. "Epidemics in the Neoclassical and New Keynesian Models." Working Paper w27430. Cambridge, Mass.: National Bureau of Economic Research.

Farboodi, Maryam, Gregor Jarosch, and Robert Shimer. 2020. "Internal and External Effects of Personal Distancing in a Pandemic." Working Paper 27059. Cambridge, Mass.: National Bureau of Economic Research.

Favero, Carlo A., Andrea Ichino, and Aldo Rustichini. 2020. "Restarting the Economy while Saving Lives under COVID-19." Discussion Paper DP14664. London: Centre for Economic Policy Research.

Ferguson, Neil M., Daniel Laydon, Gemma Nedjati-Gilani, Natsuko Imai, Kylie Ainslie, Marc Baguelin, and others. 2020. *Report 9: Impact of Non-pharmaceutical*

Interventions (NPIs) to Reduce COVID-19 Mortality and Healthcare Demand.
London: Imperial College COVID-19 Response Team.

Glover, Andrew, Jonathan Heathcote, Dirk Krueger, and José-Víctor Ríos-Rull.
2020. "Health versus Wealth: On the Distributional Effects of Controlling
a Pandemic." Working Paper 27046. Cambridge, Mass.: National Bureau of
Economic Research.

Gottlieb, Scott, Caitlin Rivers, Mark McClellan, Lauren Silvis, and Crystal Watson.
2020. *National Coronavirus Response: A Road Map to Reopening.* Washington:
American Enterprise Institute. https://www.aei.org/research-products/report/
national-coronavirus-response-a-road-map-to-reopening/.

Guðbjartsson, Daniel F., Agnar Helgason, Hakon Jonsson, Olafur T. Magnusson,
Pall Melsted, Gudmundur L. Norddahl, and others. 2020. "Spread of SARS-
CoV-2 in the Icelandic Population." *New England Journal of Medicine* 382,
no. 24: 2302–15.

Guerrieri, Veronica, Guido Lorenzoni, Ludwig Straub, and Iván Werning. 2020.
"Macroeconomic Implications of COVID-19: Can Negative Supply Shocks
Cause Demand Shortages?" Working Paper 26918. Cambridge, Mass.: National
Bureau of Economic Research.

Gupta, Sumedha, Kosali Simon, and Coady Wing. 2020. "Mandated and Voluntary
Social Distancing during the COVID-19 Epidemic." In the present volume of
Brookings Papers on Economic Activity.

Hall, Robert E., Charles I. Jones, and Peter J. Klenow. 2020. "Trading off
Consumption and COVID-19 Deaths." Federal Reserve Bank of Minneapolis
Quarterly Review 42, no. 1: 2–13.

Hay, James A., David J. Haw, William P. Hanage, C. Jessica E. Metcalf, and
Michael J. Mina. 2020. "Implications of the Age Profile of the Novel Coronavirus." Manuscript, Harvard University.

Howard, Jeremy, Austin Huang, Zhiyuan Li, Zeynep Tufekci, Vladimir
Zdimal, Helene-Mari van der Westhuizen, and others. 2020. "Face Masks
against COVID-19: An Evidence Review." Preprints. https://www.preprints.org/
manuscript/202004.0203/v2.

Hulten, Charles R. 1978. "Growth Accounting with Intermediate Inputs." *Review
of Economic Studies* 45 no. 3: 511–18.

Jones, Callum J., Thomas Philippon, and Venky Venkateswaran. 2020. "Optimal
Mitigation Policies in a Pandemic: Social Distancing and Working from Home."
Working Paper 26984. Cambridge, Mass.: National Bureau of Economic
Research.

Kaiser Family Foundation. 2020. "State Data and Policy Actions to Address
Coronavirus." Issue Brief. San Francisco: Kaiser Family Foundation. Accessed
June 21. https://www.kff.org/health-costs/issue-brief/state-data-and-policy-
actions-to-address-coronavirus/.

Katz, Josh, Denise Lu, and Margot Sanger-Katz. 2020. "The Toll Since Coronavirus Struck: 266,000 More Deaths than Normal." *New York Times*, May 6
(accessed July 10, 2020). https://www.nytimes.com/interactive/2020/05/05/us/
coronavirus-death-toll-us.html.

Kissler, Stephen M., Christine Tedijanto, Edward Goldstein, Yonatan H. Grad, and Marc Lipsitch. 2020. "Projecting the Transmission Dynamics of SARS-CoV-2 through the Postpandemic Period." *Science* 368, no. 6493: 860–68.

Krueger, Dirk, Harald Uhlig, and Taojun Xie. 2020. "Macroeconomic Dynamics and Reallocation in an Epidemic: Evaluating the 'Swedish Solution.'" Working Paper 27047. Cambridge, Mass.: National Bureau of Economic Research.

Lin, Zhixian, and Christopher M. Meissner. 2020. "Health vs. Wealth? Public Health Policies and the Economy during COVID-19." Working Paper 27099. Cambridge, Mass.: National Bureau of Economic Research.

Ludvigson, Sydney C., Sai Ma, and Serena Ng. 2020. "COVID-19 and the Macroeconomic Effects of Costly Disasters." Working Paper 26987. Cambridge, Mass.: National Bureau of Economic Research.

Mas, Alexandre, and Amanda Pallais. 2020. "Alternative Work Arrangements." *Annual Review of Economics* 12, no. 1: 631–58.

Mongey, Simon, Laura Pilossoph, and Alex Weinberg. 2020. "Which Workers Bear the Burden of Social Distancing Policies?" Working Paper 27085. Cambridge, Mass.: National Bureau of Economic Research.

Morris, Dylan H., Fernando W. Rossine, Joshua B. Plotkin, and Simon A. Levin. 2020. "Optimal, Near-Optimal, and Robust Epidemic Control." ArXiv:2004. 02209. Ithaca, N.Y.: Cornell University.

Moser, Christian A., and Pierre Yared. 2020. "Pandemic Lockdown: The Role of Government Commitment." Working Paper 27062. Cambridge, Mass.: National Bureau of Economic Research.

Mulligan, Casey B. 2020. "Economic Activity and the Value of Medical Innovation during a Pandemic." Working Paper 27060. Cambridge, Mass.: National Bureau of Economic Research.

National Governors Association. 2020. "Roadmap to Recovery: A Public Health Guide for Governors." Washington: Author. https://www.nga.org/center/publications/health/roadmap-to-recovery/.

Poletti, Piero, Marcello Tirani, Danilo Cereda, Filippo Trentini, Giorgio Guzzetta, Giuliana Sabatino, and others. 2020. "Probability of Symptoms and Critical Disease after SARS-CoV-2 Infection. ArXiv:2006.08471. Ithaca, N.Y.: Cornell University.

Rampini, Adriano A. 2020. "Sequential Lifting of COVID-19 Interventions with Population Heterogeneity." Working Paper 27063. Cambridge, Mass.: National Bureau of Economic Research.

Rio-Chanona, R. Maria del, Penny Mealy, Anton Pichler, François Lafond, and J. Doyne Farmer. 2020. "Supply and Demand Shocks in the COVID-19 Pandemic: An Industry and Occupation Perspective." *Oxford Review of Economic Policy* 36, suppl. 1: S94–137.

Romer, Paul. 2020. "Roadmap to Responsibly Reopen America." https://roadmap.paulromer.net/.

Salje, Henrik, Cécile Tran Kiem, Noémie Lefrancq, Noémie Courtejoie, Paolo Bosetti, Juliette Paireau, and others. 2020. "Estimating the Burden of SARS-CoV-2 in France." *Science* 369, no. 6500: 208–11. https://science.sciencemag.org/content/early/2020/05/12/science.abc3517/tab-pdf.

Stock, James H. 2020. "Data Gaps and the Policy Response to the Novel Coronavirus." Working Paper 26902. Cambridge, Mass.: National Bureau of Economic Research.

Tian, Liang, Xuefei Li, Fei Qi, Qian-Yuan Tang, Viola Tang, Jiang Liu, and others. 2020. "Calibrated Intervention and Containment of the COVID-19 Pandemic." ArXiv:2003.07353. Ithaca, N.Y.: Cornell University. https://arxiv.org/pdf/2003.07353.pdf.

Towers, Sherry, and Zhilan Feng. 2012. "Social Contact Patterns and Control Strategies for Influenza in the Elderly." *Mathematical Biosciences* 240, no. 2: 241–49.

US Environmental Protection Agency. 2010. *Guidelines for Preparing Economic Analyses.* https://www.epa.gov/sites/production/files/2017-09/documents/ee-0568-22.pdf.

van den Driessche, Pauline. 2017. "Reproduction Numbers of Infectious Disease Models." *Infectious Disease Modelling* 2, no. 3: 288–303.

Verity, Robert, Lucy C. Okell, Ilaria Dorigatti, Peter Winskill, Charles Whittaker, Natsuko Imai, and others. 2020. "Estimates of the Severity of COVID-19 Disease." MedRxiv. https://www.medrxiv.org/content/10.1101/2020.03.09.20033357v1.

Vogel, Gretchen, and Jennifer Couzin-Frankel. 2020. "Should Schools Reopen? Kids' Role in Pandemic Still a Mystery." *Science*, May 4. https://www.sciencemag.org/news/2020/05/should-schools-reopen-kids-role-pandemic-still-mystery.

White House, Centers for Disease Control and Prevention, and Food and Drug Administration. 2020. "Testing Blueprint: Opening Up America Again." Washington: Authors. https://www.whitehouse.gov/wp-content/uploads/2020/04/Testing-Blueprint.pdf.

Yang, Rongrong, Xien Gui, and Yong Xiong. 2020. "Comparison of Clinical Characteristics of Patients with Asymptomatic vs Symptomatic Coronavirus Disease 2019 in Wuhan, China." *JAMA Network Open* 3, no 5.

Comments and Discussion

COMMENT BY

DARON ACEMOGLU
It is painful in the extreme to see that the extraordinary talents of Emmanuel Farhi, which are amply reflected in this paper, have since been lost to our profession. Emmanuel Farhi was a brilliant mind and a kind and generous person who illuminated, inspired, and influenced all of us and still had so much to contribute to our profession and the policy world. It is with a heavy heart that I am completing this comment on what is probably one of his last papers. He will be missed by our profession and of course by his many loving friends and collaborators among us.

As this comment is going to press, COVID-19 cases in the United States have already exceeded 25 million, deaths have surpassed 421,000, and the second wave that started in the fall has turned out to be much worse than most people expected. Any guidance for policy (if anybody were to listen) would be welcome in these troubling times. The paper by Baqaee, Farhi, Mina, and Stock is a timely and important contribution, providing exactly this type of guidance.

The authors develop an extended SEIR (susceptible, exposed, infected, and recovered) model that features five age groups arrayed in sixty-six sectors and contact matrices that depend on age and sector. The model is expertly calibrated, and the authors use it to evaluate various reopening scenarios.

The bottom line of the paper is simple and powerful: smart reopening policies can save both lives and the economy. The authors also give guidelines on what smart reopening should be. The most important lesson from this careful analysis is that economic measures, such as lockdowns, are neither necessary nor sufficient to control the pandemic. Instead, noneconomic nonpharmacological interventions, including personal distancing, face masks, and limits on large gatherings, can be very effective while

432

allowing the economy to return to some normalcy. The authors additionally (in my opinion very rightly) stress the importance of protecting the most vulnerable, in particular the elderly.

There is no doubt in my mind that if policymakers listened to and engaged with the authors, the United States would benefit significantly (though I am not optimistic about policymakers doing so, unfortunately). My very positive assessment notwithstanding, it is useful to place this paper in a broader context and point out areas for improvement, mostly for future research by the authors as well as other scholars.

BROADER CONTEXT How does the paper relate to the prior body of work? Two literatures should be distinguished in answering this question. The first is the voluminous literature in epidemiology using SIR (susceptible, infectious, and recovered) models, and especially the subbranch that focuses on COVID-19. A well-known example is the early work by Ferguson and others (2020). These works are very detailed in terms of heterogeneities in the population and infection dynamics, though less satisfactory when it comes to cost of lockdowns (because they do not model economic interactions). The authors of the current paper break new ground relative to these works by introducing a richer modeling of the economic aspects—for example, by recognizing differences across sectors in social contacts and costs of lockdown.

The second literature starts with more parsimonious models of infection dynamics, like the original SIR model of Kermack and McKendrick (1927), and aims to derive general lessons about how epidemics come to an end, how damaging they are, and how to deal with them. Early COVID-19 works in economics, starting with Atkeson (2020) and Alvarez, Argente, and Lippi (2020), have contributed to this literature. My own work in this area (Acemoglu and others forthcoming), which is related to this paper by Baqaee and his colleagues, is also in this genre. It can be viewed as a special case of the current paper, since it focuses on an SIR model with three age groups and no sectoral structure (rather than five age groups and sixty-six sectors). There is only one sense in which our work is not a special case, which I discuss next.

THE ISSUE OF OPTIMAL POLICY Our paper (Acemoglu and others forthcoming) considers optimal policy, while Baqaee and his colleagues eschew this focus and introduce a type of feedback rule that may be followed by governors as a function of COVID-19 cases and unemployment in their states (though the authors also note that these feedback rules may stand for other constraints on policy). They then discuss general strategies for reopening (including noneconomic and nonpharmacological interventions as well as guidelines on the speed of economic reopening) that have to be evaluated taking the policy feedbacks from the governors as given.

I believe that focusing on optimal policy helps us clarify the trade-offs. This is a particularly relevant issue for me, since I have spent much of my career studying problems of political economy, which are instances where actual policy choices have little to do with optimal policies. And unless we understand the political incentives and constraints facing collective choices, we would reach misleading conclusions and develop a faulty understanding of the situation.

I have not faltered in my commitment to political economy, but in this case there is an important benefit from characterizing optimal policy. This is for three reasons. First, the problem of controlling an infection is a complex one, and thus focusing on constrained solutions without understanding what would work best could lead to incomplete or even incorrect inferences. The possibility of a second wave illustrates this issue clearly. Ferguson and others (2020) saliently mentioned the likelihood of a second wave. But what is not clear from their analysis is whether this is inevitable because anything that would prevent a second wave would be more costly or whether a second wave would represent a policy failure. Without understanding the answer to this question, it is difficult to know how to approach and prevent a second wave.

Second, as our analysis in Acemoglu and others (forthcoming) highlights, the form of optimal policies differs greatly depending on the preferences of policymakers in terms of economic losses versus lives lost. In such situations, providing a transparent menu of choices is often most informative, and optimal policy analysis achieves this aim. This is what our work does by making use of "Pareto" frontiers between the two major objectives: saving lives and saving the economy.

Third, our paper also establishes that the form of optimal policy is simple, hence ameliorating concerns that it may be too complex to implement. In particular, we show that significant gains—of the order of one-third reduction in economic costs for the same cost in terms of lives lost or vice versa—can be achieved by simply having a differential lockdown on the more vulnerable, 65 and older age group versus the rest of the population.

Can Baqaee and his colleagues' choice of focusing on general reopening strategies while imposing a specific policy feedback by governors be justified? One way to do that would be to argue that governors will indeed follow such a feedback rule and that optimal policy that cannot be "implemented" via incentive-compatible choices of governors is irrelevant.

I believe this argument has merit, but I am not entirely convinced by it. If the authors' paper has a powerful message on the form of optimal policy, this could change governors' responses, especially if optimal policy is proven to be simple and significantly superior to those that would follow from the feedback rules of governors.

A second justification for Baqaee and his colleagues' focus on constrained, suboptimal policies may be that, as they rightly note, there is a tremendous amount of parameter uncertainty, thus imposing some specific values on transmission rates, mortality rates, contact rates, and individual social distancing; then computing optimal policies may not be very informative. This point is valid and important. However, the same parameter uncertainty also makes nonoptimal policy analysis similarly fragile, and one way to deal with it is to systematically investigate the robustness of optimal policies (or other analysis) to changes in parameters or parameter instability. There are other options, as well, that can be fruitfully pursued in future work. For example, instead of deterministic optimal control, one could investigate robust control, which would take parameter uncertainty and instability explicitly into account (Zhou and Doyle 1998; Hansen and Sargent 2008).

CONCEPTUAL LESSONS Another issue worth discussing is whether the framework the authors build generates new qualitative perspectives. To be sure, this is a high bar, partly because the authors' main aim is to carry out a detailed quantitative analysis (and they do this quite well). Nevertheless, I believe it is fair to ask this question because they are part of an emerging literature marrying economics and epidemiology, and the main fruits of this endeavor should not just be quantitative estimates in some specific instances, but also new conceptual lessons.

Fortunately, there are two ways in which the authors provide such lessons. I will next point out how more can be done in each case.

First, in investigating which sectors should be open first, the authors propose a powerful measure to focus on: GDP-to-risk ratio, defined as how any policy variation (e.g., opening one of the sectors) will have an impact on GDP relative to its effect on the basic reproduction rate of the virus (the so-called R_0), which measures how many new infections one more infected individual will generate. The GDP-to-risk ratio is a useful measure, but it could be further developed. First, additional illustrations of whether ranking sectors according to GDP-to-risk ratio does better than alternatives would have been useful. Second, and more fundamentally, a more systematic analysis of what this measure captures would also be useful to undertake in future work.

In essence, the GDP-to-risk ratio is not a sufficient statistic. One way of seeing this is as follows. The basic reproduction rate, R_0, is the largest eigenvalue of the (linearized) dynamical system defined by the model.[1] The largest eigenvalue is informative about the speed of convergence of the dynamical system induced by the multigroup SIR model considered by the authors (e.g., Draief and Massoulié 2009, theorem 8.2). Yet it does not provide sufficient information about the mixing properties of the dynamical system. These mixing properties, which loosely speaking capture how quickly the infection jumps from one part of society to another, are critical for the spread of the virus. To see this we can consider a simple example. Suppose the multigroup setting approximates what is called an "island model" in the context of social and economic networks (Jackson 2010), whereby an individual on an island has a very high probability of interacting with others from the same island, and a small probability of interaction with those from other islands. Suppose, for the sake of this example, that each one of the n groups has approximately the same overall contact rate, but some groups have higher rates of contact with other islands. In this setup, increasing infection in any one of the n groups will lead to the same change in R_0 (or in the largest eigenvalue). Nevertheless, confirming that R_0 does not contain all the relevant information, the consequences of infection in a group that has higher interactions with the rest are worse. The second largest and other eigenvalues are informative about this type of mixing between different groups or islands. This example illustrates how just relying on R_0 or the largest eigenvalue is not sufficient for understanding the dynamics of the infection. Along these lines, one could either develop a more comprehensive measure than the GDP-to-risk ratio or investigate in the context of the quantitative exercise how much we are missing by focusing on the GDP-to-risk ratio.

A second way in which the analysis can be pushed further is by evaluating whether all of the heterogeneity is critical, or if one could have reached the correct conclusions with a stripped-down model. This would be particularly important for future work, which will likely build on the current paper's insights regarding which simplifications are justified when other related aspects of the questions are being explored. For example, what happens if the authors used three age groups and a single sector as in Acemoglu and others (forthcoming) instead of five age groups and sixty-six sectors? In what ways would this simplification lead to quantitatively or qualitatively

---

1. More precisely, it is the largest eigenvalue of the next-generation Jacobian matrices. See Diekmann, Heesterbeek, and Metz (1990).

different conclusions? A discussion of these issues would have helped future work in the area by conceptually clarifying which dimensions of heterogeneity matter more and for what reason.

Let me again give a brief discussion of this issue by drawing on Acemoglu and others (forthcoming). In that paper, the main (qualitative) conclusion is that "semi-targeted" policy that involves a different lockdown on the 65 and older age group can significantly improve either economic outcomes or public health outcomes or both. For example, in our baseline parameterization, a move from uniform policies to semi-targeted policies can reduce economic damages by one-third without any more lives lost. Additional targeting within the younger groups has very few benefits. This has a good economic reason. The 65 and older age group is the most vulnerable to the virus, with a case fatality rate of about sixty times those between the ages of 20 and 50. To save lives, this group needs to be protected from the infection, and because different groups interact frequently and even strict lockdowns are not perfect, just locking down this older group is not sufficient. Semi-targeted optimal policy, instead, also imposes a relatively lengthy lockdown on other age groups in order to reduce their infections and the transmission of infection to the older group. This explains why finer targeting is not very effective: it can trade off infections among those in their fifties against infections of those younger than 50, but this has little mortality benefit, and both groups will transmit the virus to those older than 65. Hence, it is approximately optimal to use a semi-targeted policy that applies a strict lockdown (a "protective custody" so to speak) on the 65 and older group and, simultaneously, moderates the spread of the infection among the rest of the population. A slower growth of infections among the younger groups is critical to ensure that the virus does not spread to those over 65 (e.g., because of interactions within households, in nursing homes, or in the context of other inevitable interactions).

It would be interesting to investigate more systematically to what extent these conclusions remain true when there are more age groups and also sectoral differences. This is particularly important, in my opinion, because new work in the emerging epidemiology-economics intersection is most promising if it simultaneously provides general qualitative lessons and realistic quantitative evaluations. The current paper is an excellent example of the latter, but attempting to draw out some of the general lessons would enrich it and improve the evaluation of the quantitative contributions.

CHOICES The authors should be commended for their state-of-the-art careful parameterization that captures the most salient aspects of the

COVID-19 outbreak and its economic costs. It is for this reason that it has the potential to have an impact on the policy debate.

One place where the paper, and I hope future papers in this area, can improve their exposition is in justifying and motivating their authors' choices. For example, the model is very detailed in terms of its sectoral structure and fairly granular when it comes to age groups. It also engages with the education sector, which is of course a key for a broad reopening of the economy, since parents of school-age children cannot be fully reintegrated into the labor market when their children stay at home.

Four choices of the authors deserve more discussion. First, while the model incorporates 66 sectors, it does not model the input-output linkages between sectors and approximates the contribution of each sector by a Hulten-like first-order approximation (Hulten 1978), ignoring any complementarities between sectors that may become important when some open up while others remain largely closed. These choices may or may not be important, and it would be useful for the authors to explore these issues (or at the very least do more to justify these choices). For instance, a sector that has very low contact may appear as a good candidate for early reopening, but if it has critical inputs from a high-contact sector, this might change the relevant calculus. Or keeping certain sectors, such as retail, closed might significantly reduce the marginal contribution of other sectors, such as wholesale. The framework here is already detailed and flexible enough to explore these issues.

Second, and perhaps more important from a policy angle, the paper does not model infections within nursing homes, where about 40 percent of the US COVID-19 deaths have so far occurred (Chidambaram, Garfield, and Neuman 2020). This may be because doing so may have required some important extensions of the framework. Nursing homes are not only places where residents are highly vulnerable, but they also lead to the fast spread of the virus. This may require the introduction of the more heterogeneous network structure. Though this is clearly beyond the scope of the current paper, I would like to flag it as an important area for future research.

Third, the paper takes the contact matrix from the POLYMOD data set (Mossong and others 2008). One issue with these data is that they suggest fairly low contact rates for older individuals. This has major implications. For example, if we take these contact rates to be much lower than for other groups, then even without lockdowns the more vulnerable, older individuals would become infected at a much lower rate. This would then reduce the need for strict lockdowns on this group. However, low infection rates for the older group appears counterfactual (certainly given the very high infection rates in nursing homes, which as I have already mentioned seem to suggest greater, not lower, infection rates for the subpopulation). There are good reasons for conjecturing whether POLYMOD may be missing important context for the elderly within families or in other contexts. Indeed, the more recent (and highly systematically collected) BBC Pandemic Data, which we used in Acemoglu and others (forthcoming), has significantly higher contact rates for the elderly. Given the importance of this issue, more discussion and more robustness checks would be useful.

Finally, as I mentioned already, I agree with the authors' emphasis on the importance of noneconomic, nonpharmacological policies. Face masks appear to be critical for reducing infection on the basis of existing evidence and research on the trajectories of droplets (Chu and others 2020; Greenhalgh and others 2020). The paper and the authors should be commended on emphasizing and highlighting the major economic and public health benefits obtainable from noneconomic, nonpharmacological policies. More variations and robustness checks on this issue, especially a more detailed discussion of whether face masks can reduce transmissions in various different sectors of the economy, could have been useful.

OTHER ISSUES I would like to end this discussion with a brief mention of several issues that clearly lie beyond the scope of the current paper, but may be worth speculating on briefly.

There is every possibility that this pandemic may turn out to be what James Robinson and I called a critical juncture in our book *Why Nations Fail* (Acemoglu and Robinson 2012): an episode where existing institutions and social arrangements prove to be inadequate and thus it paves the way for major changes. We argued that, during such periods, small details matter and the direction of change is generally difficult to ascertain. If so, as important as dealing with the fallout from the current pandemic will be to prepare for what types of economic, political, and social changes will come. Though clearly not the focus of the current paper, pandemic-fueled social change is something the economics profession should start thinking about and may have useful ideas to contribute to.

Second, the economic costs of the pandemic have been lessened by digital technologies and automation that have enabled many sectors to function during lockdown. But it is also likely that the pandemic will give an additional boost to digital technologies and platforms as well as to efforts to further automate the economy. My recent work with

Pascual Restrepo (Acemoglu and Restrepo 2020a, 2020b) highlights the possible costs of investing too much in automation at the expense of other technologies and formulates the argument that we may have invested too much in the automation applications of artificial intelligence and not enough in the uses of this new technological platform to increase human tasks and productivity. If so, the current pandemic will exacerbate these trends, with potential costs in terms of future jobs and income inequality.

Finally, the current episode may have already increased the power of tech companies, and to the extent that there were already concerns about economic concentration and the rising social power of these companies (Zuboff 2019), this is another area we need to think about.

CONCLUSION Overall, this paper is a very important contribution to both the policy debate on how to deal with the COVID-19 pandemic and to the emerging epidemiology-economics literature. Many papers will build on it, and I dearly hope that it will influence the policy debate.

Before Emmanuel Fahri's untimely death, the last sentence of this commentary was already written and it read: Given the enormity of the challenges we are facing, which go beyond containing the epidemic and its economic fallout, it is encouraging to see the best minds in our profession turn their energy to this area.

All I can add is that it is devastating for all of us that our profession will no longer benefit from one of its best and most inspiring leaders.

REFERENCES FOR THE ACEMOGLU COMMENT

Acemoglu, Daron, Victor Chernozhukov, Iván Werning, and Michael D. Whinston. Forthcoming. "Optimal Targeted Lockdowns in a Multi-Group SIR Model." *American Economic Review: Insights.*

Acemoglu, Daron, and Pascual Restrepo. 2020a. "Robots and Jobs: Evidence from US Labor Markets." *Journal of Political Economy* 128, no. 6: 2188–244.

Acemoglu, Daron, and Pascual Restrepo. 2020b. "The Wrong Kind of AI? Artificial Intelligence and the Future of Labour Demand." *Cambridge Journal of Regions, Economy and Society* 13, no. 1: 25–35.

Acemoglu, Daron, and James A. Robinson. 2012. *Why Nations Fail: The Origins of Power, Prosperity, and Poverty.* New York: Crown Business.

Alvarez, Fernando E., David Argente, and Francesco Lippi. 2020. "A Simple Planning Problem for Covid-19 Lockdown." Working Paper 26981. Cambridge, Mass.: National Bureau of Economic Research. https://www.nber.org/papers/w26981.

Atkeson, Andrew. 2020. "What Will Be the Economic Impact of Covid-19 in the US? Rough Estimates of Disease Scenarios." Working Paper 26867. Cambridge, Mass.: National Bureau of Economic Research. https://www.nber.org/papers/w26867.

Chidambaram, Priya, Rachel Garfield, and Tricia Neuman. 2020. "COVID-19 Has Claimed the Lives of 100,000 Long-Term Care Residents and Staff." Blog post, November 25, Kaiser Family Foundation Policy Watch. https://www.kff.org/policy-watch/covid-19-has-claimed-the-lives-of-100000-long-term-care-residents-and-staff/.

Chu, Derek K., Elie A. Akl, Stephanie Duda, Karla Solo, Sally Yaacoub, Holger J. Schünemann, and others. 2020. "Physical Distancing, Face Masks, and Eye Protection to Prevent Person-to-Person Transmission of SARS-CoV-2 and COVID-19: A Systematic Review and Meta-Analysis." *Lancet* 394, no. 10242: 1949–2020.

Diekmann, Odo, Johan Andre Peter Heesterbeek, and Johan A. J. Metz. 1990. "On the Definition and the Computation of the Basic Reproduction Ratio R_0 in Models for Infectious Diseases in Heterogeneous Populations." *Journal of Mathematical Biology* 28, no. 4: 365–82.

Draief, Moez, and Laurent Massoulié. 2009. *Epidemics and Rumours in Complex Networks*. Cambridge: Cambridge University Press.

Ferguson, Neil M., Daniel Laydon, Gemma Nedjati-Gilani, Natsuko Imai, Kylie Ainslie, Marc Baguelin and others. 2020. *Report 9: Impact of Non-Pharmaceutical Interventions (NPIs) to Reduce COVID-19 Mortality and Healthcare Demand*. London: Imperial College COVID-19 Response Team.

Greenhalgh, Trisha, Manuel B. Schmid, Thomas Czypionka, Dirk Bassler, and Laurence Gruer. 2020. "Face Masks for the Public during the Covid-19 Crisis." *British Medical Journal* 369, m1435. doi: 10.1136/bmj.m1435.

Hansen, Lars Peter, and Thomas J. Sargent. 2008. *Robustness*. Princeton, N.J.: Princeton University Press.

Hulten, Charles R. 1978. "Growth Accounting with Intermediate Inputs." *Review of Economic Studies* 45, no. 3: 511–18.

Jackson, Matthew O. 2010. *Social and Economic Networks*. Princeton, N.J.: Princeton University Press.

Kermack, William Ogilvy, and Anderson G. McKendrick. 1927. "A Contribution to the Mathematical Theory of Epidemics." *Proceedings of the Royal Society of London A: Mathematical, Physical and Engineering Sciences* 115, no. 772: 700–21.

Mossong, J., N. Hens, M. Jit, P. Beutels, K. Auranen, R. Mikolajczyk, and others. 2008. "Social Contacts and Mixing Patterns Relevant to the Spread of Infectious Diseases." *PLoS Med* 5, no. 3: e74.

Zhou, Kemin, and John C. Doyle. 1998. *Essentials of Robust Control*. Upper Saddle River, N.J.: Prentice Hall.

Zuboff, Shoshana. 2019. *The Age of Surveillance Capitalism: The Fight for a Human Future at the New Frontier of Power*. New York: Profile Books.

GENERAL DISCUSSION   Justin Wolfers highlighted the paper's need for published standard errors. He noted that the exponential behavior of an epidemic should create a tremendous bias toward conservative parameter estimates.

Alan Auerbach expressed appreciation for the paper and subsequent discussion. He suggested that the paper should consider the broader feasibility of the interventions it proposes. He noted that current outbreaks are in some cases being driven by skepticism or exhaustion with social distancing and face masks. He highlighted that the practical sustainability of a policy will have an effect on the trade-offs the paper is studying. He observed that some of the policies the paper deems less attractive may in fact be more feasible than the policies it recommends.

Thomas Philippon complimented the paper and discussion. He then observed that what determines a policy's effectiveness is how behaviors change in response to the policy relative to the behavior in the absence of the policy. He highlighted the paper's proposed policy to isolate older-age cohorts and pointed out that as relatively high-risk and low-contact groups, compelling them to self-isolate creates a behavioral difference that is relatively small compared to the behavioral difference in young people—a low-risk, high-contact group—caused by limiting their social behavior. He supposed that even if the goal is ultimately to protect the old, it would be preferable to prevent young people from going to bars rather than locking down old people.

Austan Goolsbee highlighted the fact that data from China suggest a very high danger of cross-infection in the home.[1] He noted that in the United States there is a profound prevalence of COVID-19 risk factors outside of age, like obesity and other medical conditions. He suggested that this riskiness, combined with infections driven by home contact, may make targeted lockdowns unrealistic. He also suggested that using the Current Population Survey to create a matrix of spousal employment sectors would improve the model of at-home contacts.

Jim Stock responded to Philippon by explaining that the isolation driven by targeted lockdowns of the elderly is a less important behavioral determinant than changes to nursing home administration and capacity. He responded to Daron Acemoglu's strong recommendation that the paper

1. Qin-Long Jing and others, "Household Secondary Attack Rate of COVID-19 and Associated Determinants in Guangzhou, China: A Retrospective Cohort Study," *The Lancet* 20, no. 10 (2020): 1141–50, https://www.thelancet.com/journals/laninf/article/ PIIS1473-3099(20)30471-0/fulltext.

adopt an optimal control framework by explaining that he and his coauthors have considered such a framework at length but have ultimately decided that there is a real value to modeling people complying with CDC guidelines in circumstances as complex as this pandemic.

Emmanuel Farhi added that in the interest of simplifying the paper's models, he and his coauthors have made a number of assumptions that mitigate the economic impact of lockdowns, as discussed briefly in the paper. He stated that they could easily have worsened the economic outlook of lockdowns by incorporating more realistic assumptions, like complementarities and Keynesian spillovers, among other things.

Farhi also highlighted that the overall message of the paper is simple: contacts in the workplace largely do not drive infections, so what will prevent a second wave are policies that reduce contacts in settings outside the home or workplace. He noted that the primary outstanding question is how effectively that goal can be achieved, and what behavioral changes will be induced versus driven by policy itself. He states that this message is very simple and is explored fairly robustly in the paper.

SESSION SIX
Federal Reserve Programs

MARKUS BRUNNERMEIER
Princeton University

ARVIND KRISHNAMURTHY
Stanford University

Corporate Debt Overhang and Credit Policy

ABSTRACT   Many business sectors and households face an unprecedented loss of income in the current COVID-19 recession, triggering financial distress, separations, and bankruptcy. Rather than stimulating demand, government policy's main aim should be to provide insurance to firms and workers to avoid undue scarring that will hamper a recovery once the pandemic is past. We develop a corporate finance framework to guide interventions in credit markets to avoid such scarring. We emphasize three main results. First, policy should inject liquidity into small and medium-sized firms that are liquidity constrained and for which social costs of bankruptcy are high. Second, large firms for whom solvency is the dominant issue require a more nuanced approach. Debt overhang creates a distortion, leading these firms to fire workers, forgo expenditures that maintain enterprise value, and delay filing for a Chapter 11 bankruptcy longer than is socially efficient. Government resources toward reducing the legal and financial costs of bankruptcy are unambiguously beneficial. Policies that reduce funding costs are only socially desirable if the pandemic is expected to be short-lived and if bankruptcy costs are high. Last, transfers necessary to avoid bankruptcy allow borrowers to continue paying their mortgages or credit card bills and ultimately benefit owners of assets such as real estate or credit card receivables. Taxes to fund transfers should be raised from these asset owners.

Conflict of Interest Disclosure: The authors did not receive financial support from any firm or person for this paper or from any firm or person with a financial or political interest in this paper. Arvind Krishnamurthy is an academic consultant to the Federal Reserve Bank of San Francisco and the European Central Bank, and he is currently not an officer, director, or board member of any organization with an interest in this paper. Markus Brunnermeier sits on advisory boards for Deutsche Bundesbank, CBO, IMF, and Luohan Academy, an open research institute initiated by the Alibaba Group. No outside party had the right to review this paper before circulation. The views expressed in this paper are those of the authors and do not necessarily reflect those of Princeton University or Stanford University.

447

The recession of 2020 is unlike that of 2008. Although both the ongoing COVID-19 collapse and the global financial crisis have led to significant economic destruction and hardship, the nature of the collapse differs in fundamental ways. The recession in 2008 was preceded by an excessive buildup in housing and was triggered by the collapse in real estate prices. This resulted in losses to financial intermediaries, which reduced credit supply, and impaired household balance sheets, which reduced aggregate demand. Effective government credit policy worked to repair intermediary and household balance sheets, relaxing constraints, thus stimulating investment, spending, and hiring. As in most recessions, the 2008 recovery process involved creative destruction, dissolving some matches and forming others. In 2020, the pandemic has induced an economic pause of unknown length in what was otherwise a sound economy. With some exceptions, the January 2020 blueprint for the economy would still be applicable if a vaccine were to be discovered tomorrow. However, in this pause many business sectors and workers face an unprecedented loss of income. Coupled with their high debt burdens, many firms may not be able to service their debts and face financial distress. Separations between firms and workers, upstream and downstream firms, as well as corporate and personal bankruptcies, threaten to scar the economy long past the end of the pause. Even if the pandemic fades, the January 2020 blueprint may not be implementable because of these separations. Effective policy in this event does not stimulate current economic activity but instead provides insurance to avoid scarring and output losses once the pandemic is past.[1]

This paper analyzes the extent to which credit policy can reduce the scarring due to high debts and financial distress in firms. High debts lead firms to shift their focus to meeting debt obligations rather than pursuing new investment projects, keeping their workers, or maintaining their existing capital stock. High debts also push some firms into bankruptcy, which may result in excessive liquidation. It is critical to have a clear view of bankruptcy costs as well as the nature of the financial friction facing a firm in order to assess credit policy.

We distinguish between two cases: a large corporation that is run by a management team in the interest of outside equity shareholders and for

---

1. The typical recession calls for some reallocation of capital and labor from existing matches to new matches. This reallocation need is also likely present in the current recession as technology may change the nature of work; see Barrero, Bloom, and Davis (2020). Our perspective in this paper is that the COVID-19 collapse is atypical in that there is less of a need for reallocation and breaking matches.

which a Chapter 11 bankruptcy filing is the likely outcome, and a small owner-run enterprise facing liquidity constraints where a Chapter 7 liquidation is the likely bankruptcy outcome.[2] These two cases, the first of solvency concerns and the second of liquidity concerns, span the main macroeconomic concerns created by high levels of debt.

In the first case, high debt induces solvency problems and debt overhang à la Myers (1977). Having faced the negative COVID-19 shock, existing equity holders tend to delay restructuring, avoid issuing equity, cut back on maintenance investment, and lay off workers in order to meet their debt obligations. These socially harmful actions enable existing equity holders to stave off bankruptcy. A Chapter 11 filing allows the firm to restructure its debt, but it does so by wiping out existing equity holders and transferring control to creditors. Restructuring eliminates the debt overhang problem but can incur costs of bankruptcy.[3] Policies that reduce these costs are unambiguously beneficial. On the other hand, policies that subsidize continuation may or may not be beneficial. In a case where the social costs of bankruptcy are low or the recession is expected to last a considerable period, optimal policy does not subsidize credit. This is because doing so enables equity holders to delay a restructuring. Instead policy should induce restructuring to eliminate the debt overhang problem. We argue that currently in the United States, this is the relevant scenario for policy to consider for many large firms.

In the case of small firms, the second case, optimal policy subsidizes lending to firms. Chapter 11 restructuring is typically not a possibility for this firm, and the social cost of liquidation of the firm under Chapter 7 is high. In addition, the owners of these firms are likely cash-constrained and unable to inject equity into the firm. Thus, the most significant problem for small firms is that even solvent but temporarily illiquid firms may find it difficult to survive past the recession. For these reasons credit policy can have a significant positive impact. For small and medium-sized enterprises (SMEs) in 2020 one can draw similarities to high marginal propensity to consume (MPC) households that were underwater in 2008, and the policy

2. Chapter 7 of the US bankruptcy code governs the process of liquidation of a firm in bankruptcy. Firms also have the choice to file under Chapter 11 of the code, which governs the process of reorganization of a firm. In this case, a firm adopts a reorganization plan that must be approved by creditors. If a reorganization plan is not approved, then the firm is typically liquidated. See, for example, White (1989) on the corporate bankruptcy decision.

3. Restructuring of debt often also happens out of court, against the threat of entering formal bankruptcy proceedings. See Gertner and Scharfstein (1991) and Donaldson and others (2020).

Figure 1. Credit Terms for Small and Large Firms

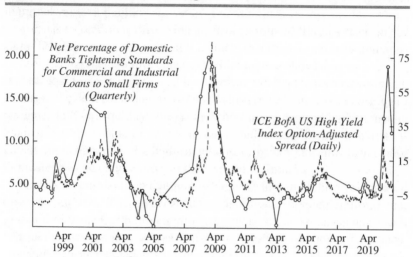

Source: Federal Reserve.

goal of providing liquidity to these sectors remains the same (although the design and execution problems differ).[4]

Figure 1 illustrates the differential financial conditions faced by large and small firms. We plot the credit spread on publicly traded high-yield bonds, based on the Intercontinental Exchange Bank of America Index, and the net percentage of domestic banks tightening credit standards on loans to small firms, from the Federal Reserve's senior loan officer survey. The data begin in April 1997 and run through October 2020. While these two measures have tracked each other well historically, they diverge in the current recession. Credit conditions faced by the small firm sector are almost as tight as they were in the 2008 recession, while credit conditions in the corporate bond market are far looser.

In section I, we review additional asset market data on large and small firms to shed light on the nature of the two cases outlined before

---

4. Household liquidity constraints (Mian and Sufi 2009; Dynan 2012) were a key financial drag in the recovery from the 2008 recession. Government credit policies such as the Home Affordable Modification Program (HAMP), the Home Affordable Refinance Program (HARP), and mortgage-backed security quantitative easing all worked via easing these liquidity constraints (Eberly and Krishnamurthy 2014; DiMaggio, Kermani, and Palmer 2020).

turning in section II to an analysis of the corporate financing problems facing these firms.

We draw a few conclusions from the asset market data. First, the dramatic market reaction to the pandemic in March 2020 had little to do with the corporate finance issues outlined above. Instead, there was a dislocation in asset markets in March 2020 driven by reduced asset market liquidity and risk-bearing capacity similar to 2008. The dramatic movements in Treasury bond prices and investment-grade corporate bonds in particular underscore these observations. The Federal Reserve's interventions in March, which drew from the 2008 playbook of injecting liquidity and risk-bearing capacity into capital markets, have effectively restored market function. Moreover, while market expectations in March may have reflected a chance of the type of financial intermediary instability spiral of the 2008 financial crisis, this risk had largely faded by mid-April. There are too little data to say anything definitive, but our conjecture is that the Fed's actions on March 23 and April 9 indicated to investors that the Fed stood ready to defuse this sort of spiral and eliminated tail risk in markets. Second, the risk premium for bearing macroeconomic risk, as of early June 2020, was near the levels that it was in January 2020. We reach this conclusion principally from examining stock market valuations, which are sensitive to this risk premium.

Third, while macroeconomic risk premia are low, risk in the cross-section of firms is elevated. Corporate bond spreads in June 2020 are higher across the board. This higher spread reflects market expectations of higher default due to a combination of higher cash-flow risks and higher existing debt burdens. The corporate finance debt concerns are evident in the cross-section. The COVID-19 recession affects firms differentially. Firms with business models that are sensitive to the pandemic, particularly the retail and energy sectors, have high corporate bond spreads. Firms with high preexisting debt, which has been true of high-yield firms, have seen much higher spreads. These facts are drawn from data on the publicly traded firm sector. We have limited data on the SME sector as of this writing, but the forces at work in the large firm sector are likely even more pressing for SMEs, as indicated by figure 1. We proceed under this hypothesis.

Section II of the paper discusses the Federal Reserve's credit policy actions in the context of corporate finance models. We note at the outset that, absent corporate financing frictions, there is no role for credit policy. The operating decisions of a firm are influenced only by the path of the Fed's policy rate. For example, take a technology giant that is flush with cash and whose behavior approximates a hypothetical Modigliani-Miller firm.

The operating decisions of this firm are based on comparing the risk-adjusted return on an expenditure to the return on holding cash. Federal Reserve purchases of this firm's corporate bonds, driving down its bond yield, will have minimal impact on its operating decisions.

We present a model of a large public or private equity–backed firm that faces a solvency problem, as in the first case mentioned above. The firm has high existing debt, and decisions are made by management to maximize equity holders' value. The high debt induces a debt overhang problem à la Myers (1977) for this firm that results in underinvestment, a macroeconomic cost. Can the Federal Reserve credit policy alleviate this problem? An investment-grade corporate bond quantitative easing (QE) likely has small beneficial effects. Purchasing investment-grade corporate bonds may drive down investment-grade yields for portfolio balance reasons, as in Vayanos and Vila (forthcoming), but since investment-grade firms are not the firms that suffer debt overhang, this policy will have limited real effect. A high-yield corporate bond QE may have a more significant impact. But the effects here are nuanced.

The debt overhang problem arises in cases where debt cannot be restructured. If renegotiation is costless, the debt overhang problem disappears and economic efficiency is obtained. Chapter 11 of the bankruptcy code is a mechanism to coordinate creditor claims and restructure debt in a manner that is consistent with preserving the viability of the firm.

The decision to file for a Chapter 11 bankruptcy rests with the equity holders of the firm. As in Leland (1994), the equity holders will continue to service the firm's debts as long as the option value of retaining control of the firm exceeds the debt service payment. That is, the equity holders will prioritize using earnings to make debt payments as long as their call option on the firm enterprise has high value. A key point is that the private decision to file for bankruptcy is based on an option valuation trade-off and not a consideration of the deadweight cost of bankruptcy.

In this context, reducing refinancing costs for a high-yield firm allows the equity holders to delay a Chapter 11 filing. If the deadweight costs of bankruptcy are low, then the delay is socially inefficient. The firm operating under debt overhang distorts spending decisions in a manner that is socially costly. Likewise, if the recession is expected to last a long time, it is better to induce resolution quickly than to delay and incur the bankruptcy costs at a later date. Uncertainty over the length of the pandemic also affects optimal policy. As bankruptcy incurs irreversible social costs, the decision of policy to induce bankruptcy and resolution is a real option. During times of large uncertainty, optimal policy may involve waiting before triggering bankruptcy. The key insight of our large firm model is that credit policy needs to balance the benefits of delay against the cost of inducing resolution.

We next consider a model of an entrepreneurial firm which is owner operated and subject to financing frictions, as in our second case above. We assume that the owner has limited personal assets, and what they have is tied up in the business. We also assume that the firm's borrowing capacity is a fraction of its capital. These two assumptions lead to a liquidity constraint that affects the firm's operating decisions. We also assume that the enterprise has significantly higher value if run and owned by this owner. That is, the social costs of bankruptcy are high for this firm.

The model is most applicable to SMEs. For example, consider a small auto parts supplier with an owner who is also the firm's principal employee. The firm has loans from a bank that are in part guaranteed by the owner against personal assets. Facing a temporary decrease in demand for automobiles and auto parts, this firm is unable to service its debts. The owner has pledged all of their personal assets to the firm previously and has no spare liquidity. As a result the firm files for bankruptcy. Typically, such a firm will enter a Chapter 7 liquidation, and in this case the owner may additionally file for personal bankruptcy. Even if the health crisis abates, this firm and its owner will only gradually scale back up to their pre-pandemic levels. Any loans required for restarting the business will require security of the owner's assets—which will be depleted as a result of the bankruptcy. This is where the liquidation scarring concern is most evident in the firm sector.

Effective government credit programs funnel liquidity to this entrepreneurial firm. This liquidity allows the firm to undertake expenditures that maintain its enterprise value as well as help stave off a socially costly bankruptcy. Programs such as the Main Street Lending Program (MSLP), the Paycheck Protection Program (PPP), as well as forbearance by banks, encouraged by the Federal Reserve, benefit these firms by easing liquidity constraints.[5] On the other hand, we argue that the MSLP would work better if it offered a lending subsidy that drove down the program's lending rate near zero. Doing so would allow borrowers to economize on scarce liquidity and would more closely resemble an insurance payment. The

---

5. The analogy of 2020 SME liquidity problems and 2008 household liquidity problems fails when it comes to capital market policy inventions. The structure of the mortgage market means that mortgage-backed security QE delivers liquidity benefits to households. No similar pipes exist via capital markets to SMEs.

current MSLP design requires that banks own a share of any MSLP loan. But as banks will only lend if the loan has positive net present value, this share requirement prevents passing on a lending subsidy. We also argue that the MSLP's leverage rules, restricting eligibility to low-leverage borrowers, excludes the firms with the greatest drag due to debt. Since the inception of the MSLP, the Federal Reserve has modified the program progressively in a manner that recognizes some of the issues we raise.

The Small Business Reorganization Act enacted by Congress in 2019 reduces the costs of small and medium-sized enterprises (SMEs) from filing for Chapter 11. This change in law can potentially be a game changer in terms of reducing scarring in the SME sector. However, there are concerns regarding the extent that SMEs will avail of this provision. Under the law, the business is required to propose a reorganization plan within 90 days of filing, which may prove challenging. Firms also have to obtain debtor-in-possession (DIP) financing to continue operating. Traditional DIP financiers focus on large firms. Repurposing the MSLP program to provide DIP loans will help the Chapter 11 process for SMEs and mitigate scarring.

We finally turn to household insurance. The government has insured workers against unemployment via both unemployment insurance and the PPP. In a counterfactual absent unemployment support for these workers, household budgets would have been squeezed to the point that they would be unable to cover fixed obligations such as rents, mortgage payments, or auto loan payments and would either fall delinquent or be forced into bankruptcy. Government insurance has aimed to forestall this outcome. While we do not review the efficacy of worker insurance programs in this paper, we draw out implications for these programs for financial asset prices. For example, currently the prices of securities backed by credit card receivables reflect relatively low expected rates of default.

In an Arrow-Debreu world, the insurance provided by the government's facilities would be unnecessary because it would have been arranged ex ante between private parties. Contracts would be written to reduce obligations such as interest, rent, and mortgage payments, in the event of a pandemic. Workers in pandemic-affected industries would receive insurance payments to cover their loss of income. The deadweight costs of separations and bankruptcies would thus be avoided via ex ante contracting. A useful way of seeing current government policy is that it has aimed, with varying degrees of success, to add contingency ex post to contracts and avoid deadweight costs.

Filling in the contingency ex post, even if done with surgical precision, is to a large extent a transfer to holders of capital assets. The holders of debt to SMEs gain when the government offers the SME a loan to avoid default. The owners of credit card asset-backed securities gain when unemployment insurance provides households with resources to repay credit card debt. The lender in a mortgage or owner of an apartment building receives payment because the household receives insurance from the government.

With this in mind, consider the question of where the government should source the resources used to fill in the contingency. The Coronavirus Aid, Relief, and Economic Security (CARES) Act costs in excess of $2 trillion which must be repaid at some point. In an Arrow-Debreu ex ante allocation, the equity owners of SMEs as well as households would purchase insurance in advance against the pandemic event. For example, debt contracts may be indexed such that debt principal is written down by 25 percent in the event of a pandemic.[6] By filling in the contingency ex post, the government transfers 25 percent to the borrower, who then makes this payment to the lender. The lender gains 25 percent relative to the no-government-action counterfactual and the borrower has received insurance for free that would otherwise have cost a negligible amount.[7] If the government aimed to replicate the Arrow-Debreu allocation via its ex post actions while apportioning losses to borrowers and lenders in a manner consistent with the Arrow-Debreu allocation, then it should raise taxes in such a manner that the bulk of the resources comes from lenders, that is, asset owners rather than workers.

To summarize, the principal lessons of our analysis are:

1. If the social cost of bankruptcy is low, then policy should not aim to subsidize credit to firms, which induces inefficient firm continuation, but instead induce firms to restructure their debts. As a result, we suggest that the government consider putting in place lending programs to firms in a Chapter 11 bankruptcy. Such a policy lowers effective bankruptcy costs and incentivizes debt restructuring to reduce liquidation.

---

6. A number of scholars have signed on to a March 24, 2020, letter drafted by Jonathan Berk (2020) in favor of COVID-19 policies that do not bail out large corporations, as such policies are a bailout of the investors of these corporations. They argue instead for policies that provide insurance to the workers at these corporations. Our argument is related to but distinct from this point. We argue that ex post insurance to the corporate sector may be beneficial depending on the social costs of bankruptcy, but the incidence of the tax burden should align with the incidence of the benefits of the bailout (i.e., the investors).

7. If the ex ante likelihood of a pandemic is p, the debt would carry an extra interest cost of $p \times 25$ percent. The premium would compensate lenders for the loss of 25 percent that they would suffer in the event of the pandemic. For small p, which was likely the assessed probability before 2020, this premium is low.

2. If bankruptcy costs are high, as with SMEs, we additionally recommend providing subsidized credit to enable firm continuation. For credit programs addressing smaller firms, we suggest the Federal Reserve consider relaxing its credit eligibility rules as well as aiming to introduce an explicit subsidy into its lending programs.

3. Many government programs in this pandemic recession should be seen as implementing part of an Arrow-Debreu insurance arrangement ex post.

4. The insurance perspective also indicates where government resources should be sourced. We argue that the high government debt that is incurred in the present recession should be met with higher future taxes on current asset owners.

I. Assessing Financial Market Conditions

This section reviews data from financial markets to assess where we are currently. We conclude that, as of early June, there is a low risk premium for aggregate risk. However, the recession has increased dispersion in risk in the cross-section of firms. There was a significant dislocation in asset markets in mid-March that has some similarities to the events of 2008, but it appears that this dislocation has faded, in part due to the Federal Reserve's actions.

I.A. Equity Markets Reflect Low Risk Premia

We consider the valuation of the S&P 500 via the Gordon growth formula:

$$P = \frac{D_1}{r} + \frac{D_2}{r^2} + \cdots,$$

where D is dividends and r is the gross discount rate. The dividend yield on the S&P 500 has been around 2 percent for the last few years. Suppose that corporate earnings and dividends dip for the next two years and then revert to prepandemic levels. To get an idea of the extent of the dip, note that the S&P 500 dividend futures contract traded on the Chicago Mercantile Exchange for December 2021 was 29 percent lower on June 1 compared to January 2 (it was 38 percent lower on March 23 than on January 2). Suppose that dividends are lower by 30 percent for the next two years, with nothing else changed about growth prospects or discount rates. Then we would expect that the valuation of the market would fall

Figure 2. S&P 500 and Real Ten-Year Interest Rate

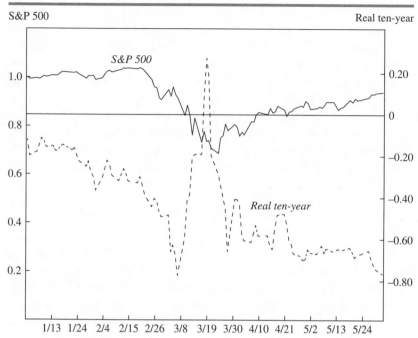

Source: Bloomberg.

by about 1.2 percent (= 2 × 0.3 × 2 percent). If dividends were low for five years, as may occur in "swoosh" recovery, the valuation of the market would fall by 3 percent. As these computations show, the valuation of the market is relatively insensitive to whether we have a shape like a U, a V, or a swoosh. Of course, these alternative scenarios can have a large impact on the path of the unemployment rate. That is, the stock market is not the job market.

Figure 2 graphs the S&P 500 stock market index and the real ten-year interest rate, measured as the ten-year nominal swap rate minus the ten-year inflation swap rate. The stock market movements are most informative about longer-term movements in dividend growth rates and risky discount rates:

$$P = \frac{D_1}{r} + \frac{D_2}{r^2} + \frac{1}{r^3} \times \frac{D_3}{r - g},$$

reflected in the last term in this valuation equation. If dividends fell by 30 percent for the next two years and then rose back to prepandemic levels, then to account for the roughly 6 percent fall in the stock market from January 2 to June 1, we need $r - g$ to rise by about 0.1 percent. Since the riskless rate has fallen by about 0.6 percent over this period, this computation indicates that either the risk premium has risen by 0.7 percent only or the growth rate of dividends has fallen by 0.7 percent. These are both small numbers relative to historic fluctuations in discount rates.

We conclude that aggregate market risk premia have not increased appreciably from the start of this year to the present (June 2020). This is in stark contrast to 2008, where risk premia on a variety of assets rose sharply in fall 2008 and remained elevated well into 2009.

I.B. Financial Crisis Risk in 2020 Is Low Compared to 2008, as of Now

Figure 3 graphs five-year credit default swap (CDS) rates for Goldman Sachs, Citigroup, and Bank of America. The movements in these rates in 2008 are an order of magnitude larger than the movements in 2020. In 2008, the US economy suffered a financial crisis as has been documented extensively in the literature. Risk-bearing capacity across the financial intermediary sector was reduced, leading to high risk premia in a variety of asset markets.

At this point, as of June 2020, the United States is not suffering a financial crisis. The relatively small shift in the equity market risk premium is also a reflection of this observation. There is a significant branch of research in asset pricing which constructs mechanisms whereby small changes in dividends are amplified via endogenous shifts in the risk aversion of the marginal holder of risky assets, leading to large changes in equity prices. For example, in intermediary asset pricing theories, losses on intermediary held assets lead to endogenous reductions in the risk-bearing capacity of the intermediary sector which then raises the discount rate on intermediary held assets, leading to further reductions in asset prices, and so on (Brunnermeier and Pedersen 2009; He and Krishnamurthy 2013). This type of theory is useful to understand movements in asset prices in 2008. But at present, this type of amplification mechanism is not present. Asset price movements can be understood through the simple neoclassical lens of forecasting changes in future cash flows.

However, we note that the disabling of this amplification mechanism is likely the result of the expectations of Federal Reserve policy actions. We turn to this topic next.

Figure 3. Five-Year CDS Rates on Select Banks, 2008 versus 2020

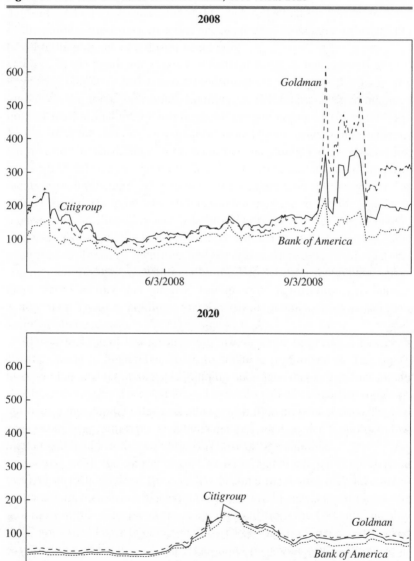

Source: Bloomberg.

Figure 4. Treasury, Corporate, and Stock Returns

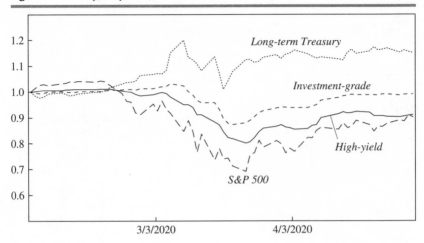

Sources: Bloomberg; Barclays indexes.

I.C. The March 2020 Dislocation and the Federal Reserve

There was a dislocation in asset markets in March 2020. This is apparent in the unusual movements in the ten-year real rate in figure 2. Figure 4 zooms in on this period. We plot the total return indexes for long-term Treasury bonds, investment-grade corporate bonds, high-yield corporate bonds, and the S&P 500. The first three of these are Barclays bond indexes. We normalize the indexes to one on February 3 and trace the index return through April 30.

At their low in mid-March, investment-grade corporate bonds were down about 13 percent relative to February 3. High-yield bonds were down 20 percent, and the S&P 500 was down 31 percent. While this ordering is in keeping with valuation norms, the beta on the investment-grade bond is much too high and is another indicator of a dislocation in valuations. Haddad, Moreira, and Muir (2020) make this point rigorously by comparing the beta-adjusted relative returns on these asset classes in 2020 versus 2008. Haddad, Moreira, and Muir (2020) show that the bond yields on a company's investment-grade bonds rise substantially relative to its CDS.[8] They argue that the behavior of asset prices in this period reflects

8. See also D'Amico, Kurakula, and Lee (2020) and Nozawa and Qiu (2020) for analysis of this episode.

fire sales and reduced risk-bearing capacity. Bond funds, fearing down-grades of investment-grade bonds, sell down their portfolios of bonds. Corporate bond dealers, because of balance sheet constraints and fears of further sales in anticipation of further downgrades, do not step in to absorb these sales and prices fall sharply.

Treasury bonds also fell in value in mid-March, reflecting market illiquidity problems in the Treasury market. This is surprising and in contrast to the typical flight-to-safety pattern in crises. Duffie (2020) analyzes the Treasury market in this period and concludes that the volume of sales in the market overwhelmed the dealer-intermediation infrastructure, leading to large swings in Treasury bond prices. Less-liquid Treasury bonds (so-called off-the-run securities) see the largest price declines.

The Federal Reserve's actions on March 23 and April 9, which drew from the 2008 playbook of liquidity provision and expansion of risk-bearing capacity, eased the dislocations.[9] The Fed's security lending programs and targeted purchases of the less-liquid segment of the Treasury market eased the liquidity issues in the Treasury market. Treasury prices rose substantially after this intervention.

The Federal Reserve's commitment to purchase investment grade corporate bonds on March 23, which was then expanded on April 9 to include fallen angels (high-yield bonds that were formerly investment grade), substantially reduced risk premia in corporate bonds. As Haddad, Moreira, and Muir (2020) note, the easing of the corporate bond disloca-tion stemmed from an announcement of future promised purchases, not current purchases. That is, what appears important in these interventions is the commitment of the Fed to inject its risk-bearing capacity in the market, if needed. The April 9 announcement in particular appears to have sub-stantially reduced risk premia across the board in asset markets. It is too soon—as of this writing in June—to definitively characterize the impact of the April 9 announcement on market expectations. Our conjecture is that the Fed's announcement has been viewed by the market as a "whatever it takes" moment. That is, the commitment to act aggressively in the high-yield bond market has been taken as a signal of the Fed's willingness to defuse future episodes of financial instability in the broad credit market. This commitment has removed a bad equilibrium and reduced market tail risk. If our conjecture is correct, then the Fed does not currently need to

---

9. The Federal Reserve's *Financial Stability Report May 2020* provides more details and analysis of this episode.

Figure 5. Credit Spread Histogram, January and March

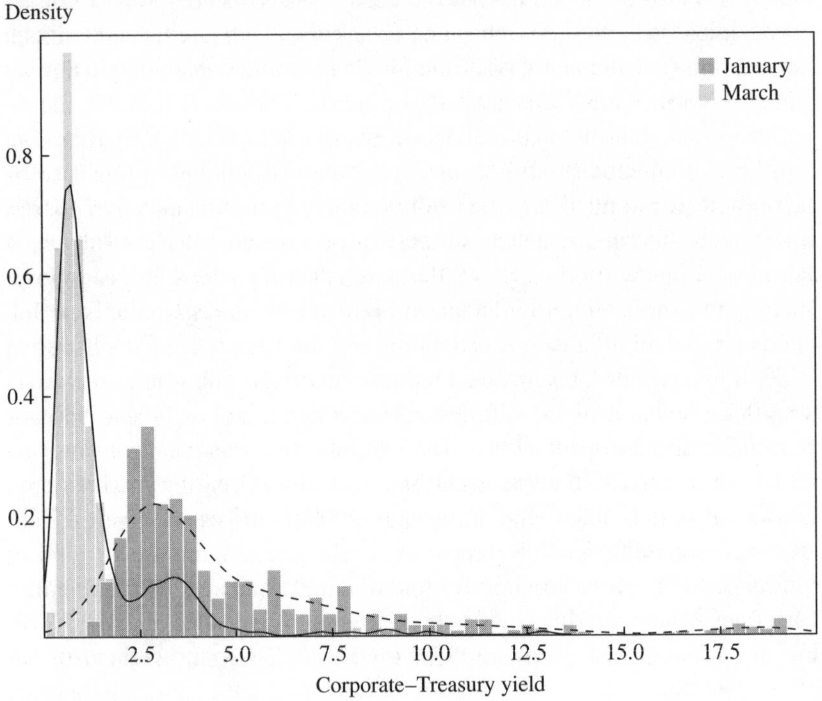

Density

Corporate–Treasury yield

Source: TRACE.

make good on its promise and activate the corporate bond purchase program at this point in time. The important aspect of the Fed's announcements has been the signal of its willingness to act if dislocations arise, and reinforcing this commitment is all that is needed at present.

I.D. Increased Cross-Sectional Firm Risk

Figure 5 measures dispersion in credit risk in the cross-section. We use bond price data from the Trade Reporting and Compliance Engine (TRACE) and compute the yield spread, relative to Treasuries, on bullet bonds with approximately five-year maturities. We compute this at the company level and plot the density of these spreads across companies. The January histogram (darker) corresponds to dates from January 20 to January 31, while the March histogram (lighter) corresponds to dates from March 16 to March 31. Clearly there is an increase both in the mean spread and the right tail of spreads.

Figure 6. Industry Average Credit Spreads

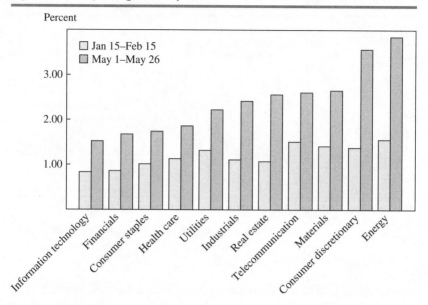

Source: S&P 500 bond indexes.

In figure 6, we consider dispersion at the industry level. We plot credit spreads on firm debts of roughly seven-year maturity. We plot these spreads pre-COVID-19, averaging observations from January 15, 2020, to February 15, 2020. We also plot these spreads in the present recession, averaging spreads from May 1, 2020, to May 26, 2020. We can see from the figure that spreads have increased across the board, indicating that investors' perception of repayment risks (i.e., cash flow risk relative to debt liabilities) has risen. Additionally, spreads in the energy sector, which has been facing reduced oil demand, and the consumer discretionary sector, where retail has been falling, have been particularly affected. The figure indicates a rise in expected cash flow risk at the firm level. We noted earlier that aggregate risk premia appear low, thus the correct way to think about these data are that they reflect a risk in idiosyncratic firm risk.

Figure 7 plots corporate bond spreads for investment-grade and high-yield bond issuers, to provide a sense of the changes in risk in the cross-section. There is a substantial increase in default risk across both classes of bonds. High-yield spreads in particular have roughly doubled since the start of the year.

Figure 7. High-Yield and Investment-Grade Corporate Bond Spreads

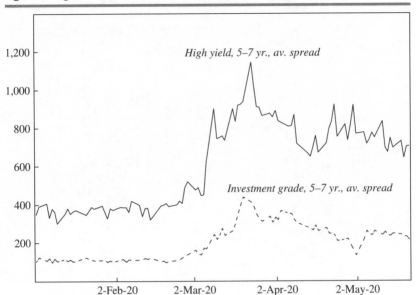

Source: JPMorgan.

The corporate sector enters this recession with higher debt burdens, making it more vulnerable to a downturn. Figure 8 plots the net debt (debt minus holdings of cash) of high-yield (HY) and investment-grade (IG) firms relative to earnings before interest, taxes, depreciation, and amortization (EBITDA). We fix the set of high-yield and investment-grade firms as of 2016. These net debt series are shown with solid lines. Debt burdens have increased for both types of firms, with a greater rise in the high-yield sector. With dashed lines, we plot the interest coverage ratio (EBITDA to interest expense) for both types of firms. There has been an erosion in this measure particularly for investment-grade firms. The Federal Reserve's *Financial Stability Report May 2020* offers further details on the buildup of leverage in the corporate sector.

The expansion in corporate leverage in the high-yield sector has led to increases in corporate default risk, as indicated by the rise in spreads. However, bankruptcies are just beginning to hit the economy. Bloomberg tracks large corporate filings. Figure 9 gives a count of the number of filings per month. Filings, as of June 2020, were approaching the levels of the 2008 financial crisis.

Figure 8. Corporate Leverage, 2010–2020, for High-Yield and Investment-Grade Firms as of 2016

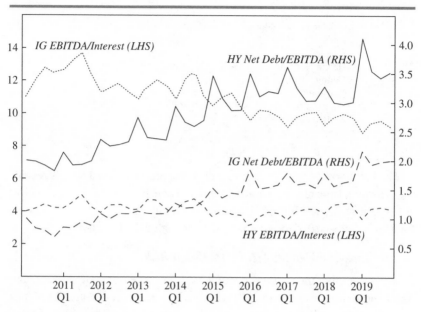

Sources: Compustat; Mergent.

Figure 9. Bankruptcy Filings Monthly Count, January 2007 to June 2020

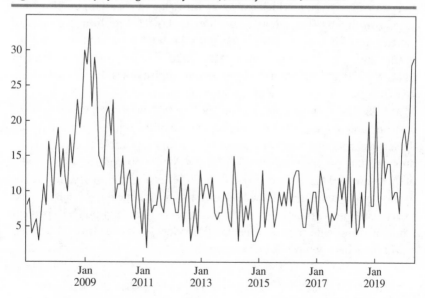

Source: Bloomberg BCY.

Table 1. Corporate Bankruptcy Filings as of June 1, 2020

Sector	%	$ billion
Consumer discretionary	40.82	52.25
Energy	16.33	20.90
Financials	10.2	13.06
Health care	9.18	11.75
Communications	5.1	6.53
Consumer staples	4.08	5.22
Industrials	4.08	5.22
Technology	4.08	5.22

Source: Bloomberg.

The breakdown of filings across industries, provided in table 1, is revealing. The bulk of bankruptcy filings are in the consumer discretionary sector, consistent with the high-profile filings by many large department stores. Energy is a close second, driven by the substantial fall in energy prices.

I.E. Small and Medium-Sized Firm Credit Risk

We expect that the patterns documented for large firms are present, and likely more pressing, for small firms. That is, we expect that credit risk has grown substantially since the start of the pandemic and that dispersion in the cross-section of firms has also widened. However, we have limited up-to-date information on small and medium-sized business credit risk.

Data from PayNet, which tracks credit risk in firms with employment largely in the 1–49 range and revenues under $2.5 million, indicate an increase in loan delinquencies.[10] PayNet's 31–90 day small business delinquency index was 2.39 percent in May 2020, compared to 1.6 percent in January 2020 and a high of 3.39 percent in August 2009. Bartik and others (2020) conducted a survey of 5,800 small businesses during the week of March 28, 2020. They report that the median firm has one to two months of cash on hand to meet expenses, giving a sense of the liquidity crunch facing these firms, absent a government credit program. Table 3 of the paper presents data on the cross-section of firms. While on average 44.6 percent of their sampled firms were closed (largely reflecting temporary closure) as of the sample date, there is wide dispersion in this measure. Banking and finance and professional services report closure rates of around 20 percent while arts and entertainment, personal services, and tourism and lodging report rates between 60 and 87 percent.

---

10. See Small Business Delinquency Index, PayNet, https://sbinsights.paynetonline.com/loan-performance/.

I.F.   Household Credit Risk and Government Insurance

Figure 10 (top panel) plots the return on three household credit assets: auto loans, credit cards, and mortgages. We track the return on an index, as compiled by JPMorgan, on asset-backed securities linked to these underlying loans. We normalize the value of the index to be one on January 2, 2020, and track the index value relative to this date. We see that all of these assets suffered losses in March but currently (as of June 1) reflect valuations that are at least as high as the start of the year. In the case of mortgage-backed securities, this is likely due to a mix of the Federal Reserve's decision to purchase mortgage-backed securities and the Federal Housing Finance Agency's (FHFA) decision to allow households to defer payments at no penalty. In the case of credit cards and auto loans, an important factor is likely the expansion of unemployment benefits and the stimulus checks in the CARES act. Baker and others (2020) observe that about one-third of the 2020 stimulus checks have been spent toward financial payments such as credit card, rent, and mortgage payments. In addition, spending is depressed due to the lockdown, resulting in high liquid asset holdings by households (Cox and others 2020). Thus government insurance to households has maintained the value of these financial securities.

Figure 10 (bottom panel) graphs the yield spread, relative to Treasury bonds, on a credit card asset-backed securities index. The underlying bond maturity of this index is roughly one and a half years. We note that the pre-COVID-19 recession spreads are around 30 basis points, indicating relatively low default probabilities and losses given default. These spreads rose in March substantially but were down to 77 basis points by the end of May. Risk has clearly risen, but the increase in risk is still modest relative to the dramatic increase in unemployment rates. Government insurance to households has likely played an important role in the behavior of this spread.

II. Government Credit Policy

This section discusses the government's credit policies enacted in the COVID-19 crisis. We begin by reviewing these policies. Then we lay out two corporate financing models, one of a hypothetical large firm facing solvency issues and a debt overhang problem, and one of a hypothetical entrepreneurial firm facing liquidity constraints. We use these models to discuss the merit of the credit programs. Our models capture many but not all salient corporate financing considerations. As a result, we do not attempt to discuss all aspects of the design of the government's credit programs.

Figure 10. Asset-Backed Securities Cumulative Returns and Credit Card ABS Spreads

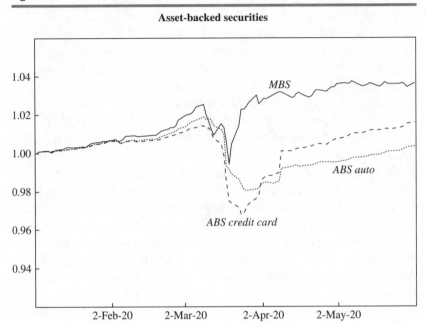

Asset-backed securities

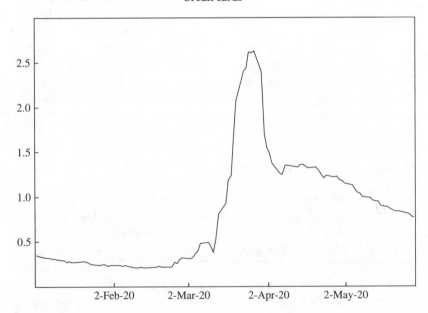

Credit cards

Sources: JPMorgan; Bloomberg.

II.A. Government Programs

Table 2 lists the government programs that address credit markets. These programs cover the bulk of the firm sector in the United States. The Primary Market Corporate Credit Facility (PMCCF) was introduced on March 23. It has the Federal Reserve purchasing corporate bonds in the primary markets. The Secondary Market Corporate Credit Facility (SMCCF) has the Federal Reserve purchasing corporate bonds in the secondary market. These two programs are designed for large corporations that finance themselves in public debt markets and had ratings of at least BBB-/Baa3 on March 22, 2020; that is, the firm universe is comprised of investment-grade corporations and fallen angels. The Commercial Paper Funding Facility (CPFF) addresses short-term public borrowing. There is overlap among the firms eligible for these facilities. To give a sense of the magnitudes involved, we compute the universe of firms eligible for the SMCCF and show the results in table 2. The SMCCF covers firms with total revenues of $14.3 trillion and equity market capitalization of $24.7 trillion.

The Federal Reserve's Main Street Lending Program (MSLP) addresses credit in medium-sized firms with fewer than 15,000 employees or up to $5 billion in annual revenue. By our count, the total revenues across the universe of MSLP firms that fall into this category is $23.8 trillion. However, the MSLP imposes credit limits that restrict borrowers to a maximum debt ranging from four times to six times their 2019 EBITDA. The MSLP also requires that borrowers have been in "sound financial condition" before the COVID-19 recession. We have not factored these restrictions into the computation.

Finally the Paycheck Protection Program (PPP), run by the Small Business Administration, addresses credit problems in the small firm sector. The mean revenue of a firm eligible for the program is $2 million, and the universe of eligible firms totals $11.8 trillion.

II.B. Solvency Problems and Corporate Debt Overhang

In this section, we develop a model to analyze how credit easing policies can have a beneficial impact on firms. The model in this section is applicable to a large corporation run by professional management, with publicly traded equity, the holders of which are the formal owners of the corporation. The model is also applicable to a private equity–backed large firm, where the management team runs the firm in the interest of the private equity holders. These private equity–backed firms are among those with high leverage, typically funded in the leveraged loan market.

Table 2. Lending Programs and Targets

Federal Reserve facility	No. of private firms	No. of public firms	Total no. of firms	Variable	Units	Aggregate	Mean	p10	p25	p50	p75	p90
1 Primary Market Corporate Credit Facility (PMCCF)[a]	71	463	534	Assets[b]	$US bn	38,293	79.8	4.8	8.8	22.7	58.7	162.3
				Market Cap.[c]	$US bn	22,370	48.4	2.8	5.2	15.0	43.4	107.7
				Revenue[d,d]	$US bn	11,760	23.4	1.3	3.5	8.6	21.1	60.1
2 Secondary Market Corporate Credit Facility (SMCCF)[a]	707	1,019	1,726	Assets[b]	$US bn	42,427	39.7	1.2	2.6	6.8	23.3	70.5
				Market Cap.[c]	$US bn	24,728	24.3	0.3	1.2	3.8	15.1	52.1
				Revenue[d]	$US bn	14,313	11.2	0.3	0.9	2.8	8.7	22.4
3 Commercial Paper Funding Facility (CPFF)[a]	12	72	84	Assets[b]	$US bn	9,418	122.3	13.2	23.7	62.1	152.2	294.0
				Market Cap.[c]	$US bn	12,455	173.0	20.6	29.7	66.7	191.7	351.0
				Revenue[d]	$US bn	4,512	56.4	4.1	11.6	28.0	65.9	146.3
4 Paycheck Protection Program Liquidity Facility (PPPLF)[e]	—	—	5,976,761	Payroll[f]	$US mm	2,711,537	0.5	—	—	—	—	—
				Employment[g]	—	60,556,080	10	—	—	—	—	—
				Receipts[h]	$US mm	11,816,839	2.0	—	—	—	—	—
5 Main Street Lending Program[e]	—	—	5,996,386	Payroll[f]	$US mm	5,034,489	0.8	—	—	—	—	—
				Employment[g]	—	99,073,784	16.5	—	—	—	—	—
				Receipts[h]	$US mm	23,801,346	4.0	—	—	—	—	—
Main Street Priority Loan Facility (MSPLF)												
Main Street New Loan Facility (MSNLF)												
Main Street Expanded Loan Facility (MSELF)												

Source: Capital IQ and 2017 (latest) Statistics of US Businesses (SUSB), US Census Bureau annual data set.

a. Assets, market capitalization, and revenue statistics are calculated mainly on public firm data; private firm disclosure of these figures is scant.

b. Asset figures are latest annual.

c. Market capitalization figures are latest available.

d. Revenue figures are latest annual.

e. Since Statistics of US Businesses (SUSB) only provides aggregate figures across firms by employee-size bucket, the mean is computed by first computing the mean for each employee-size bucket and taking the weighted average of these means, weighting by the number of firms in each employee-size bucket.

f. Payroll figures are annual.

g. Measured in number of people per firm.

h. Receipts are defined as annual operating revenue for goods produced or services provided. Receipts are taken from the 2012 SUSB, latest SUSB that reports firm receipts; receipts are only recorded for years ending in 2 or 7, and final figures on 2017 receipts have not yet been made available.

In section II.F we consider a model of entrepreneurial finance applicable to a small firm.

The model has two dates, $t = 1$ and $t = 2$. We denote the gross riskless interest rate as r. A firm needs cash to maintain an ongoing relationship that will generate some surplus in the future, at $t = 2$. The spending needed is ϵ, which we take to be near zero to keep the algebra simple. If the firm spends, then future surplus is ϵR, with $R > r$. Think of the spending as a decision to retain a worker or maintain facilities, and the assumption we make is that at the margin this spending is positive net present value.

If the firm does not spend, its assets at $t = 2$ will have a stochastic value of $\tilde{A}$. We assume that the firm has current debt outstanding of D. The probability that $\tilde{A} < D$ is denoted with ϕ_B; that is, ϕ_B is the default probability. In addition, we denote $\overline{A} = E[A | \tilde{A} > D]$ and $\underline{A} = E[A | \tilde{A} < D]$. This firm is subject to a classic debt overhang problem, as discussed in Myers (1977).

Suppose that the firm issues a corporate bond to undertake this spending. Investors charge the firm a gross interest rate of $\gamma \geq r$ to purchase the bond. If the firm issues the bond and spends, the value of the firm's equity is:

$$V_E = \frac{1}{r}(1 - \phi_B)\big(\overline{A} - D + \epsilon(R - \gamma)\big).$$

Assume that the management of the firm takes actions to maximize the value of equity. That is, either implicit or explicit schemes align the manager's incentives with those of the shareholders. Then clearly the spending is undertaken as long as $R > \gamma$.

In order to raise the funds, the firm issues a bond with the face value of $\gamma \epsilon$. We assume the new bond issue is pari passu with the existing debt. The zero-profit condition for investors is:

$$(1 - \phi_B)\gamma\epsilon + \phi_B \frac{\gamma\epsilon}{D + \gamma\epsilon}(\underline{A} + \epsilon R) - \epsilon r = 0,$$

or, taking ϵ to zero, rewritten as:

$$\gamma = \frac{r}{(1 - \phi_B) + \phi_B \frac{A}{D}}.$$

Note that $\gamma - r$ is the credit spread on the firm's bonds. A firm with no default risk ($\phi_B = 0$) has a zero credit spread.

The firm undertakes the spending as long as:

$$R > \frac{r}{(1 - \phi_B) + \phi_B \, A\!\!\Big/\!\!D}.$$

Debt overhang distorts this investment decision by raising the right-hand side of this expression leading firms to forgo investments that increase the entire firm value.

In the present recession, the corporate sector has been affected heterogeneously. Firms with high existing debts (low $E[A]/D$) and low profits face significantly more default risk and higher spreads. For these firms, spending decisions will not be aligned with efficiency. Firms will choose enterprise value–reducing actions, such as laying off employees, selling assets piecemeal, and forgoing maintenance investments in this case.

Debt overhang also gives rise to an incentive to pay out firm earnings as dividends. Suppose a firm has ϵ of earnings today. The shareholder can take these earnings as dividends today to receive ϵ. Alternatively, the earnings can be used to undertake investment in which case equity value rises by $\dfrac{\epsilon R(1 - \phi_B)}{r}$. Thus the firm will choose to pay out a dividend as long as:

$$\frac{1}{1 - \phi_B} > \frac{R}{r}.$$

As solvency concerns rise and the distribution of firm leverage shifts higher, as indicated in our empirical analysis, debt overhang will lead firms to prioritize payouts to shareholders over real operating expenditures. DeMarzo and He (2016) develop a dynamic model of debt overhang where a leverage ratchet effect arises: as solvency falls, firms continue to issue debt at higher spreads and use the proceeds to pay dividends and forgo positive surplus real investments.

II.C. Federal Reserve Corporate Bond Purchases

Can the Federal Reserve's actions ameliorate the debt overhang issue? By reducing r, the Fed reduces the corporate borrowing rate and boosts spending. This is a standard channel that is independent of the debt over-hang concerned outlined above.

More salient to this overhang problem is the Federal Reserve's corpo-rate bond purchase program. We first note that credit easing via Fed bond purchases only works if there is an underlying debt overhang problem. A Fed-induced credit subsidy to a firm like Apple that has a large cash hoard in excess of its outstanding debt will have a limited impact on Apple's real decisions. If it is optimal for Apple to downsize in the face of reduced demand for its product, Apple will do so, and credit easing will have no impact on its operating decision. This section clarifies the domain where credit easing programs can deliver economic benefits.

There are two ways of looking at the Federal Reserve's corporate bond purchase program. First, by purchasing investment-grade corporate bonds, as in the SMCCF or PMCCF, the Fed reduces the refinancing rate on existing debt. If a fraction of debt is due at any time, then reducing the refinancing rate reduces the debt burdens gradually and the debt overhang problem is somewhat reduced. However, note that this effect is likely small. Replacing debt paying 5 percent with debt paying 4 percent reduces D on the order of 1 percent per year of debt maturity. This is a flow reduction in debt accumulation, whereas the debt overhang problem is at heart a problem of high stock.

Second, by purchasing (or committing to purchase) corporate bonds the Federal Reserve takes bond risk onto its balance sheet and effectively increases the market's risk-bearing capacity and hence reduces the market price of credit risk (Vayanos and Vila forthcoming). To be more precise:

$$\phi_B = p_B \eta_B,$$

where p_B is the true (physical) probability of default and $\eta_B > 1$ is a market's risk price for bearing credit risk as in standard models of corporate bond pricing (Duffie and Singleton 1999). Then, the Federal Reserve's bond purchase programs reduce η_B and hence reduce the debt overhang problem. Note that this analysis clarifies a limit on the effectiveness of bond pur-chase programs. For firms with low p_B, the benefits will be small simply because a firm with a low credit spread cannot have its spread driven down further.

We reach three main conclusions from this analysis. First, bond pur-chase policies produce the most bang for the buck when targeted toward high default-risk firms. If the Federal Reserve's objective is to reduce the drag from debt overhang, then the Fed should target high-yield rather than investment-grade bonds. However, the Fed's corporate bond facilities target investment-grade firms and fallen angels.

Second, the policy works best in an environment where risk premia are large. If risk premia are low, as they currently (June) appear to be, then bond purchases will not have much effect. That is, while the Federal Reserve's interventions were valuable in mid-March when markets were dislocated, they are not an effective policy in an environment where markets are operating more smoothly. Krishnamurthy and Vissing-Jorgensen (2011) make this point in the context of the Fed's quantitative easing strategy in the global financial crisis. The first round of quantitative easing was more effective than subsequent rounds.

Third, any policy that subsidizes debt and allows firms to finance current operations via debt inevitably increases a future debt overhang problem. Dynamically, the longer the recession lasts, the more the distribution of firm leverage shifts toward higher values, worsening the aggregate debt overhang problem and worsening the aggregate underinvestment distortion.

II.D. The Chapter 11 Bankruptcy Option

The debt overhang problem is solved by renegotiating or restructuring existing debt. A version of the Coase theorem applies: if both equity and debt holders could renegotiate, then all positive net present value investments will be undertaken. The assumption of the debt overhang analysis is that the debt is sufficiently dispersed that it is not possible to achieve this negotiation.

The bankruptcy code offers Chapter 11 as a mechanism to deal with the drag from high debt and restructure existing debts. Upon a Chapter 11 filing, an automatic stay on payments to pre-bankruptcy debts comes into immediate effect, and current management becomes the debtor in possession controlling the firm. The firm's equity holders lose control and as part of the Chapter 11 restructuring also substantially reduce their claims on the firm's future cash flows. The firm can continue operations while the bankruptcy process determines whether the firm should remain a going concern or be liquidated. In an environment where high debt is the only drag on firm viability, the bankruptcy process allows for creditors to renegotiate their claims, allowing the firm to exit bankruptcy as a viable business. Typically, some creditors receive equity interests in the new post–Chapter 11 firm. For a fuller description of the bankruptcy process, see White (1989).

It is crucial to note that the decision to file for Chapter 11 rests with the equity holders. As in the analysis of Leland (1994), the equity holders control the firm and own an option on the firm's underlying assets. The coupon payments on debt are the option premia that the equity holders pay to retain their option. In the Leland analysis, the equity holder is a deep-pocketed investor whose opportunity cost of cash is r, the riskless discount rate. Then the equity holder weighs the cost of giving up cash at opportunity cost r to making a coupon payment and retaining control of the firm. When $E[A] - D$ is high, and the firm's solvency is not in question, the equity holder finds it optimal to make the option payment, and as in the analysis above, the investment decision is not distorted. As $E[A] - D$ falls, debt overhang begins to distort investment. For some value where $E[A] = \underline{D} < D$, the equity holder's option is sufficiently out of the money that it becomes optimal to not make the debt payment and trigger bankruptcy. If the underlying asset volatility is higher, as is the case currently, the default threshold $\underline{D}$ is lower for standard option valuation logic. If the cost of cash for the equity holder r is higher, then the default threshold $\underline{D}$ is higher.

Next consider the bankruptcy decision from a social perspective. There are two social costs associated with bankruptcy: inefficient liquidation of economically viable firms and inefficient continuation of firms whose business models may be permanently unprofitable. In an economic pause like the COVID-19 crisis, the first concern is likely to be much more significant than the second.

Consider a case where the inefficient liquidation problem is small and the social costs of bankruptcy are likewise small. That is, consider a case where, if the firm defaults, the creditors of the firm take control as its new owners, they retain the management of the firm, and they operate the firm efficiently, with no debt overhang distortion. In this case, the socially optimal decision is to have the firm file for Chapter 11 as soon as debt overhang leads to underinvestment.

The effects of the bond purchase program interact with a firm's decision to file for a Chapter 11 reorganization. Because the decision to file for a Chapter 11 is privately costly to shareholders—their claims are substantially reduced in value—bankruptcy is only triggered when the existing shareholders deem it too costly to retain control of the firm. If the social costs of bankruptcy are low for large firms, the equity holders may not undertake positive net present value investments and allow value to erode for longer than is efficient, hoping for a recovery. Lower corporate borrowing rates, as induced by the Federal Reserve's bond purchase program, increase this incentive.[11] There is a delicate balance that policy has to maneuver here. Facilitating firm continuation erodes firm value but avoids another cost, which is the deadweight cost of bankruptcy.

We conclude that if deadweight costs of bankruptcy are low, then reducing refinancing costs for a financially distressed firm and enabling the equity holders to delay a Chapter 11 filing is socially inefficient. The firm operating under debt overhang distorts spending decisions in a manner that is socially costly. Likewise, if the recession is expected to last a long period, it is better to induce resolution quickly than to delay and incur the bankruptcy costs at a later date. Uncertainty over the length of the pandemic also affects optimal policy. As bankruptcy incurs irreversible social costs, the decision of policy to induce bankruptcy and resolution is a real option. During times of large uncertainty, optimal policy may involve waiting before triggering bankruptcy.[12] Balancing these considerations provides an answer to the question, How long is too long?

II.E. The Costs of Bankruptcy and a Policy Proposal

Optimal policy depends on assessing the social costs of bankruptcy. The literature has documented costs associated with both financial distress and bankruptcy. There is considerable evidence that firms in distress, but pre-bankruptcy, take actions to erode firm value. This is the conclusion of Asquith, Gertner, and Scharfstein (1994), studying a sample of financially distressed firms who had issued junk bonds. Andrade and Kaplan (1998) document losses of around 10 percent of firm value via these actions of firms in financial distress. In terms of our model analysis, this evidence indicates that firms suffering debt overhang take actions that erode value in order for equity holders to retain their option on the firm's assets.

A Chapter 11 bankruptcy incurs costs that can reduce firm value. Administrative costs of bankruptcy stem from the fees paid to lawyers,

---

11. DeMarzo and He's (2016) dynamic debt overhang model indicates a further cost of subsidizing firm continuation. In their model, subsidizing the borrowing rate of a high debt firm will lead the firm to borrow and use the proceeds to pay dividends rather than undertake real expenditures such as retaining employees. As a result, the enterprise value of the firm can erode faster when debt is subsidized. Their analysis indicates the importance of placing restrictions on financial payouts (dividends or share repurchases) when accessing a government credit facility. The Federal Reserve's MSLP facility does impose such a restriction.

12. Stein (2020) proposes that the government should act as a venture capitalist, offering financing in stages to deal with these uncertainty concerns. This viewpoint aligns with the option logic we have outlined.

accountants, and so on. Bris, Welch, and Zhu (2006) provide median estimates of around 1.9 percent of firm value but also report heterogeneity in these estimates, with the estimates for the third quartile of 6.7 percent. Indirect costs of bankruptcy include possible reductions in value due to asset fire sales and conflicts among stakeholders leading to inefficient operating decisions. Davydenko, Strebulaev, and Zhao (2012) document median costs incurred both in distress and during bankruptcy of around 22.1 percent of firm value.

A Chapter 11 bankruptcy can also have effects on other stakeholders of a firm that enter as social costs. Banks and trade creditors will suffer direct losses on any loans to the firm. We return to this issue in section III in the context of bank capital levels. Additionally, employees may find long-term compensation contracts renegotiated in bankruptcy (Benmelech, Bergman, and Enriquez 2012) and thus suffer losses. Finally, other firms in the industry may suffer reductions in debt capacity if the bankrupt firm's assets are sold in a fire sale in a bankruptcy, thereby reducing industrywide collateral values (Shleifer and Vishny 1992).

At present, given the Chapter 11 filings we have witnessed (in retail, energy, and transportation), the bankruptcy process seems to be working smoothly. But it is worth flagging potential concerns that may lead to higher bankruptcy costs. First, as argued by Skeel (2020), the infrastructure of the bankruptcy process may be stretched in a recession where many firms file for Chapter 11. At this point, filings have proceeded at a pace that is in keeping with historical norms, as indicated by the data in table 1. But if the economic crisis persists and worsens, it is likely that we will see a wave of Chapter 11 filings. In this case, the process may lead to increased errors of the two types noted in section II.D. That is, the deadweight costs of bankruptcy may rise. Skeel (2020) offers proposals to reduce these types of costs. The Bankruptcy and COVID-19 Working Group, a large group of bankruptcy scholars, also offers suggestions to ready the infrastructure of the bankruptcy system in preparation for a large wave of bankruptcies.[13]

Second, under Chapter 11 the firm's operations are continued via debtor-in-possession (DIP) financing from a specialized lender. Although currently there is capacity among DIP lenders, a wave of bankruptcies can

---

13. Large Corporate Committee of Bankruptcy Scholars, Letter to Congress, May 7, 2020, https://www.dropbox.com/s/sf2daqrh8lr52we/Large%20Corporate%20Committee%20of %20Bankruptcy%20Scholars%20Letter%20to%20Congress%205.7.20.pdf?dl=0.

also overwhelm the financial infrastructure of bankruptcy.[14] In an environment of economic uncertainty and scarce DIP financing, the bankruptcy process may lead DIP financiers to require an elevated return on their capital. DIP financiers are often the senior creditor of a firm, who may act to liquidate assets to ensure repayment of their claims even if such actions destroy the value of the firm as an ongoing enterprise. Thus, scarce DIP financing could lead to an elevated cost of borrowing in bankruptcy, eroding enterprise value and leading to socially inefficient liquidations. Both of these create another deadweight cost of bankruptcy.

The preceding discussion indicates that Chapter 11 provides ex post debt contingency but incurs costs. It should be apparent that any government policy that reduces these costs and facilitates the contingency will yield benefits. Moreover, these benefits do not depend on what constitutes "too long" (unlike the case of reducing the corporate bond yields of distressed firms) since the policy reduces the social costs of bankruptcy. That is, the policy is unambiguously beneficial. Furthermore, there is an interaction between policies at work: if the government spends resources reducing the social costs of bankruptcy, it can spend fewer resources on reducing the financing costs of distressed firms.

DeMarzo, Krishnamurthy, and Rauh (2020) offer one proposal to this end. Their proposal involves subsidizing the Chapter 11 restructuring process. In particular, they propose a debtor-in-possession financing facility (DIPFF) under which the government would offer DIP financing at an interest rate equal to the Federal Reserve discount rate.[15] The macro benefits of such a proposal are twofold. First, this policy targets the lending subsidy to a firm operating without debt overhang and therefore avoids some of the erosion of value concerns raised in section II.D. Second, by subsidizing DIP financing Chapter 7 liquidation becomes less attractive relative to reorganization, and hence the government incentivizes restructuring of

---

14. Ganz and Smith (2020) present computations suggesting that the worry regarding scarcity of DIP financing is currently not an issue. They estimate that DIP financing needs in this recession will be around $80 billion, which lenders will be able to provide with little difficulty. Skeel (2020) argues that while this may be true for large firms, medium-sized firms may still find it difficult to obtain DIP financing. Furthermore, Eckbo, Li, and Wang (2019) document that DIP lenders charge rates well in excess of risk-adjusted returns on their DIP loans, likely due to their monopoly position with the borrower. These high interest rates will lead to scarring.

15. The rate on this loan, set at the discount rate, is subsidized in part to induce firms to restructure debts under Chapter 11 and so that the bankruptcy court recognizes that a reorganization under the DIPFF maximizes the enterprise value of the firm.

debt.[16] There are also benefits that accrue pre-bankruptcy. As Donaldson and others (2020) show, pre-bankruptcy restructurings become more likely when the bankruptcy process has lower costs. Additionally, since a DIP financing policy is debtor-friendly, it reduces the delay in Chapter 11 filings by equity holders.

Under the DeMarzo, Krishnamurthy, and Rauh (2020) proposal, firms that obtain financing from the DIP facility would be restricted from restructuring some contracts that lead to negative spillovers of bankruptcy, such as labor contracts, pension obligations, and trade credit. DIP financing is senior to all other pre-bankruptcy unsecured claims. Moreover, the loan can be structured so that it is nearly default-free. They propose that DIPFF loans be fully collateralized by the firm when the firm has sufficient unencumbered collateral. If the firm's collateral is already fully encumbered, then the facility could not lend unless the bankruptcy court allows the DIPFF loan to be a priming lien, ensuring that the DIPFF loan is senior or equal to liens already attached to the firm's collateral as necessary to ensure that the DIPFF loan is fully secured. Financing would be structured to cover only anticipated operating costs over the term. The goal of the program would be to supply ample capital for firms at a subsidized rate to survive the pause period. At the conclusion of the term, many firms would hopefully return to economic viability, repaying DIP financing and emerging from bankruptcy. Alternatively, those firms facing longer-term challenges post-crisis would continue through normal bankruptcy proceedings.[17]

II.F. Liquidity Constraints in Small Firms

We next consider the corporate financing considerations of a small owner-managed firm. The owner is essential to the operation of the firm

---

16. The bankruptcy process in general has two aims: first, to close businesses that are economically not viable, allowing resources to flow to more productive uses, and second, to restructure the debts of firms that are economically viable to ensure that they are financially viable. Our perspective is that in the COVID-19 recession, relative to the typical recession, the primary policy concern should be that economically viable firms will be liquidated due to financial distress. The principal beneficial role of bankruptcy is restructuring, and policies that enable debt restructuring are beneficial.

17. One potential issue with the DIPFF is that current legislation under Dodd-Frank and the CARES Act places a high bar on government lending to an insolvent firm, even if the underlying loan is nearly default-free, as under the DIPFF proposal. DeMarzo, Krishnamurthy, and Rauh (2020) describe an alternative implementation that deals with this concern and is related to the "good bank/bad bank" model for resolving financial institutions' bankruptcy. In their proposal, a firm that enters financial distress can opt in to a prescribed bankruptcy lending facility. The rules under the bankruptcy lending facility are that a distressed firm is

and is the equity owner of the firm. There is no separation between ownership and control of this firm, unlike the case of the large firm analyzed in
section II.B. Thus one key difference relative to the prior model is that we
assume that if the owner files for bankruptcy, there is zero residual value of
the enterprise, so that the social costs of bankruptcy are high.

The owner also cannot raise outside equity, either because of adverse
selection or moral hazard concerns. Thus, the second key difference relative
to the prior model is that the owner has no outside cash, or alternatively,
the opportunity cost of cash is ∞ rather than r.

In practice firms are distributed in a manner that mixes the considerations raised in section II.B and those we outline in this section.

We first describe the steady-state valuation of this firm. Suppose that the
owner-manager of the firm has personal assets of A and runs a firm with
scale K and earnings in steady state of RK. The firm has debt of D at a gross
interest rate of $\gamma > r$, which is secured by the capital of K. This capital can
be liquidated to give proceeds of θK in the event of firm default. The firm
takes on debt of $D \leq \theta K$ and its budget constraint is

$$K = A + D.$$

Suppose the firm borrows as much as possible and runs at full scale, then

$$K = \frac{A}{1 - \theta}$$

In a steady-state where the firm is able to run at this scale forever, the
(private) value of the firm to the owner-manager is

$$V_E = A \frac{R}{r(1 - \theta)},$$

where r is the gross discount rate.

---

split into a subordinate and a parent. The assets of the enterprise are transferred to the subordinate. Additionally, certain contracts such as labor contracts, pension obligations, trade
credit, and collateralized debt are moved to the subordinate. This latter stipulation reduces
some of the negative spillovers of bankruptcy. The parent enters bankruptcy retaining all
other firm liabilities, which are restructured under the Chapter 11 process to ensure firm
viability. The only asset of the parent firm is the equity of the subordinate. As a result of this
restructuring, the subordinate is a solvent entity and the position of the stakeholders in
the parent company is unaltered. DeMarzo, Krishnamurthy, and Rauh (2020) propose that
the government lend to the subordinate firm under the facility at a subsidized rate.

Consider next what happens in bankruptcy to this firm. Suppose that in this recession the firm's cash flows are uncertain and may fall below R. In particular the cash flows are R_1 with corresponding CDF $F(R_1)$. If $R_1 < \gamma D$, the firm is unable to make its debt payment of γD and will default and be liquidated under Chapter 7 (as is typically the case for small firms). Note that our assumption that the owner-manager has no outside resources here plays an important role. In the more general case where the cost of cash for the owner-manager is high (above r) but finite, the intuition that this firm will default for a wider set of outcomes still carries over.

The owner-manager's assets post-liquidation are $A' = 0$, and the bank receives the capital of the firm that is liquidated to receive θK. The firm would be better operated in the hands of the owner-manager, but since $A' = 0$, the owner manager cannot restart the firm in a manner that generates the previous value of $V_E = A\dfrac{R}{r(1-\theta)}$.

Thus, in this model, the firm cannot restart, and the deadweight social cost of bankruptcy is equal to the loss of $V_E - \theta K$. In the event that a vaccine is discovered, in order for the economy to restart and scale back to its prepandemic levels, firms such as this will need to operate again. However, if $A' = 0$, the owner-manager will not have the resources to restart the firm. While our model is stark, it illustrates the economic challenge in a restart. The aggregate pool of SME owner assets (capital) is a key factor in a restart. This is less of a concern for the large firm sector because equity capital comes from a widely diversified set of investors and not just the owner-managers of the firms.

Consider next the owner-manager's operating decisions in this recession. We show that the value of liquidity for this firm is high and the owner-manager will use any available resources to avoid liquidation. Suppose that the firm can lay off workers to reduce costs today by ϵ and hence raise R_1 by ϵ. Assume that this action reduces its post-recession revenues for one period so that R_2 falls by ϵ, but $R_t = R$ for $t > 2$. Then this action reduces the probability of bankruptcy by $f(\gamma D)\epsilon$ resulting in a gain to the owner-manager of just under $V_E f(\gamma D)\epsilon$, which is the present value of avoiding the deadweight cost of bankruptcy. The cost of this action is the lost revenue at $t = 2$ with present value of loss of $\dfrac{\epsilon}{r}(1 - F(\gamma D))$. The key point to note here is that the gain is in terms of a stock while the cost is in terms of a flow. The marginal value of liquidity for this firm is on the order of the stock valuation and is likely high, well above the interest rate r.

The operating decisions of this firm will be taken based on this high marginal value of liquidity.

We have noted that dispersion in firm risk in SMEs has risen in the COVID-19 recession. As a result it is likely that there is a substantial mass of firms facing the liquidity constraints highlighted above.

The liquidity constraint faced by this firm will lead to underinvestment, just as in the debt overhang model of the firm of section II.B. As the firm's revenues fall, the liquidity constraint tightens, and the firm will hit a point where it will be unable to service its debts and have to file for bankruptcy. Given our assumption of a high social cost of bankruptcy, this firm is also liquidated too quickly relative to the societal optimum.

A second consideration that looms large for this small firm is increased idiosyncratic risk. The owner-manager is a nondiversified equity owner of this firm. Faced with higher idiosyncratic risk, the owner-manager will take defensive actions such as conserving cash and laying off workers. Note this consideration applies even for a firm that is not facing an impending liquidity default. Thus while aggregate risk premia appear low, idiosyncratic risk looms large in this recession and can have a negative impact on the operations of small firms.

II.G. Government Policy for SMEs

The government has designed two facilities that are relevant to the model of the firm described here, the Main Street Lending Program (MSLP) and the Small Business Administration's Paycheck Protection Program.

The MSLP is designed for medium-sized firms with up to 15,000 employees or up to $5 billion in revenues, and with a maximum debt-to-EBITDA ratio of four times or six times, depending on the facility. These firms reflect a mix of the considerations of the entrepreneurial model and the large firm model. The Small Business Reorganization Act enacted by Congress in 2019 reduces the costs of small and medium-sized business filing for Chapter 11 so that many of these firms will file for Chapter 11 in the event of bankruptcy. Thus, some of the same considerations that we discuss in the context of the debt overhang model apply here. Subsidizing lending to these firms has to balance the consideration of keeping firms alive while eroding value against facilitating a restructuring under Chapter 11. One valuable design feature of the MSLP relative to the bond purchase program is that the Federal Reserve's eligibility criterion explicitly rules out the use of MSLP loans to pay dividends, which as noted earlier is a source of leakage in any corporate bond QE problem.

Skeel (2020) expresses concerns that while the Small Business Reorganization Act of 2019 enables small and medium-sized firms to file for Chapter 11, practical challenges remain. Under the law, the small business is required to propose a reorganization plan within 90 days of filing. It also has to obtain DIP financing to continue operating, while traditional DIP financiers focus on large firms, a concern that can be addressed with credit policy. Expanding the MSLP, in line with the DIPFF proposal, to provide DIP loans will help the Chapter 11 process for SMEs and mitigate scarring.

The MSLP is structured in a manner to minimize credit risk to the government. If the economy primarily faced capital market liquidity problems, as in 2008, such a design may be warranted. Indeed, many of the government's lending facilities in 2008 made money. However, the financing problems of 2020 involve significant solvency issues, so that some losses should be expected on government lending. The eligibility restrictions under MSLP thus work against the effectiveness of the program. We have noted that the MSLP imposes a restriction on leverage. The MSLP also requires that a bank coinvest with the Federal Reserve at a loan rate equal to the London Inter-Bank Offered Rate (LIBOR) plus 3 percent. This skin-in-the-game constraint helps to ensure that banks screen borrowers in a manner that will ensure they be repaid. However, this same consideration implies that the eligible borrowers are likely financially healthy and unlikely to be the ones facing the greatest debt distortion.

Liquidity constraints, as in the model in section II.F, among some of these firms add a further consideration. Reducing payments today has high benefits when there are liquidity constraints. Thus, if the bank's existing loan can be refinanced into a rate lower than γ, the liquidity need of $R_1 - \gamma D$ is reduced. In Brunnermeier and Krishnamurthy (2020) we argue that for firms with liquidity constraints the Federal Reserve should expect to lose money on its lending program. We propose that bank loans to liquidity-constrained firms under the MSLP be eligible collateral at the discount window at an advantaged rate of X percent below the primary credit discount window rate. By doing so, the bank's zero profit condition is shifted down, and the facility can make loans at a rate of LIBOR + 3 − X percent. Given that LIBOR is currently between 0.25 percent and 0.5 percent, setting X near 3.25 percent will ensure that the refinancing rate is near zero, thus alleviating the firm's liquidity problem.[18] Liquidity constraints also

18. An alternative proposal, similar in spirit, is for the government to provide a large fee to banks that originate MSLP loans. If the fee is structured correctly, banks can be induced to make the loan at a low rate. See English and Liang (2020) for an analysis of structuring alternatives for the MSLP program.

call for longer repayment schedules. The MSLP currently requires a repayment of one-third of principal in each of year two through four. Even if the pandemic is past by year one, any restart of a liquidity-constrained firm will track growth in its own earnings relative to debt repayment. The relatively short repayment schedule of the MSLP will lead to a slower restart.

The PPP, run by the Small Business Administration, is designed explicitly as a subsidy program with incentives to retain workers and with eligibility criteria that rule out using funds for dividends. The PPP-eligible firms also most closely match the model in section II.F. Although there have been implementation challenges in the PPP rollout, the subsidy aspect aligns well with our analysis. The Federal Reserve currently allows PPP loans to be pledged as collateral under its Paycheck Program Liquidity Facility (PPPLF) at a rate of 0.35 percent, which is 10 basis points above the primary credit discount window rate. An additional subsidy to this program can be introduced by the Federal Reserve were it to reduce the PPPLF rate below the primary credit rate.

III. Conclusion

So far, 2020 is not 2008. The policy lessons of 2008 carry over imperfectly to 2020. In 2008, liquidity and capital problems in banks and asset markets were front and center. The Federal Reserve's facilities provided liquidity and risk-bearing capacity to banks and markets, in line with Bagehot's principles, and stemmed the crisis. In 2020, solvency and liquidity problems in the firm sector are front and center. Our paper analyzes how credit programs should be designed in light of the corporate financing frictions faced by the firm sector. For a liquidity-constrained firm, such as a small firm, the priority should be to provide subsidized credit to ensure the firm remains a viable enterprise once the pandemic is past. Large firms for whom solvency is an issue require a more nuanced approach. Saving every firm is not the right strategy. Optimal policy needs to weigh the benefits of subsidizing the continuation of distressed firms against the benefits of resolving these firms in a Chapter 11 bankruptcy. For a long-duration downturn, which is the current projection of the Federal Reserve, inducing resolution among some firms is optimal. Reducing the costs of a bankruptcy, on the other hand, is unambiguously beneficial.

While 2020 is not 2008, economic conditions could yet deteriorate and trigger a financial crisis like the one in 2008. If there is a second wave, or a slower than expected recovery of economic activity from the current wave, then defaults and delinquencies will begin to occur both in the household and corporate sector. The losses on loans to these sectors will reduce capital levels in the financial sector. For sufficiently large losses, the economic crisis may become a financial crisis. There is no need to wait for that crisis to happen to act. We should think about the lessons learned from 2008 and implement policies now that benefit from the 2008 experience. The Federal Reserve should consider preemptive actions such as barring capital distributions by banks and triggering the countercyclical capital buffer to encourage equity issuance, while equity markets remain buoyant, to shore up bank capital levels.

ACKNOWLEDGMENTS   We thank our discussant, Ben Bernanke, and the editor, Janice Eberly, for their detailed feedback. We also thank Joseph Abadi, Peter DeMarzo, Jason Donaldson, Darrell Duffie, Zhiguo He, Ravi Jagannathan, Tyler Muir, Giorgia Piacentino, Ricardo Reis, and David Smith for comments and Lunyang Huang, Xu Lu, and Ulysses Velasquez for research assistance.

References

Andrade, Gregor, and Steven N. Kaplan. 1998. "How Costly Is Financial (Not Economic) Distress? Evidence from Highly Leveraged Transactions That Became Distressed." *Journal of Finance* 53, no. 5: 1443–93.

Asquith, Paul, Robert Gertner, and David Scharfstein. 1994. "Anatomy of Financial Distress: An Examination of Junk-Bond Issuers." *Quarterly Journal of Economics* 109, no. 3: 625–58.

Baker, Scott R., Robert A. Farrokhnia, Steffen Meyer, Michaela Pagel, and Constantine Yannelis. 2020. "Income, Liquidity, and the Consumption Response to the 2020 Economic Stimulus Payments." Working Paper 27097. Cambridge, Mass.: National Bureau of Economic Research.

Barrero, Jose Maria, Nicholas Bloom, and Steven J. Davis. 2020. "COVID-19 Is Also a Reallocation Shock." In the present volume of *Brookings Papers on Economic Activity*.

Bartik, Alexander, Marianne Bertrand, Zoe Cullen, Edward L. Glaeser, Michael Luca, and Christopher Stanton. 2020. "How Are Small Businesses Adjusting to COVID-19? Early Evidence from a Survey." *Proceedings of the National Academy of Sciences* 117, no. 30: 17656–66.

Benmelech, Efraim, Nittai K. Bergman, and Ricardo J. Enriquez. 2012. "Negotiating with Labor under Financial Distress." *Review of Corporate Finance Studies* 1, no. 1: 28–67.

Berk, Jonathan. 2020. "Economics, Law and Finance Professors from Major Universities Write to Congress: 'Bail Out People Before Large Corporations.'" *ProMarket*, March 24. https://promarket.org/2020/03/24/economics-and-finance-professors-from-major-universities-write-to-congress-bail-out-people-before-large-corporations/.

Bris, Arturo, Ivo Welch, and Ning Zhu. 2006. "The Costs of Bankruptcy: Chapter 7 Liquidation versus Chapter 11 Reorganization." *Journal of Finance* 61, no. 3: 1253–303.

Brunnermeier, Markus K., and Arvind Krishnamurthy. 2020. "COVID-19 SME Evergreening Proposal: Inverted Economics." https://scholar.princeton.edu/sites/default/files/markus/files/covid_sme_evergreening.pdf.

Brunnermeier, Markus K., and Lasse Heje Pedersen. 2009. "Market Liquidity and Funding Liquidity." *Review of Financial Studies* 22, no. 6: 2201–38.

Cox, Natalie, Peter Ganong, Pascal Noel, Joseph Vavra, Arlene Wong, Diana Farrell, and Fiona Greig. 2020. "Initial Impacts of the Pandemic on Consumer Behavior: Evidence from Linked Income, Spending, and Savings Data." In the present volume of *Brookings Papers on Economic Activity*.

D'Amico, Stefania, Vamsidhar Kurakula, and Stephen Lee. 2020. "Impacts of the Fed Corporate Credit Facilities through the Lenses of ETFs and CDX." Working Paper WP 2020-14. Chicago: Federal Reserve Bank of Chicago.

Davydenko, Sergei A., Ilya A. Strebulaev, and Xiaofei Zhao. 2012. "A Market-Based Study of the Cost of Default." *Review of Financial Studies* 25, no. 10: 2959–99.

DeMarzo, Peter, and Zhiguo He. 2016. "Leverage Dynamics without Commitment." Working Paper w22799. Cambridge, Mass.: National Bureau of Economic Research.

DeMarzo, Peter, Arvind Krishnamurthy, and Joshua Rauh. 2020. "Debtor-in-Possession Financing Facility." Proposal. https://docs.google.com/document/d/16enr-19otREaL5LDxEJqpDsNKvmNoJa_msbq8AAqKkU/edit.

DiMaggio, Marco, Amir Kermani, and Christopher J. Palmer. 2020. "How Quantitative Easing Works: Evidence on the Refinancing Channel." *Review of Economic Studies* 87, no. 3: 1498–528.

Donaldson, Jason Roderick, Edward R. Morrison, Giorgia Piacentino, and Xiaobo Yu. 2020. "Restructuring vs. Bankruptcy." Working Paper 630. New York: Columbia Center for Law and Economic Studies.

Duffie, Darrell. 2020. "Still the World's Safe Haven? Redesigning the U.S. Treasury Market after the COVID-19 Crisis." Working Paper 62. Washington: Hutchins Center on Fiscal and Monetary Policy at Brookings.

Duffie, Darrell, and Kenneth J. Singleton. 1999. "Modeling Term Structures of Defaultable Bonds." *Review of Financial Studies* 12, no. 4: 687–720.

Dynan, Karen. 2012. "Is a Household Debt Overhang Holding Back Consumption?" *Brookings Papers on Economic Activity*, Spring, 299–334.

Eberly, Janice, and Arvind Krishnamurthy. 2014. "Efficient Credit Policies in a Housing Debt Crisis." *Brookings Papers on Economic Activity*, Fall, 73–136.

Eckbo, B. Espen, Kai Li, and Wei Wang. 2019. "Rent Extraction by Super-Priority Lenders." Working Paper 3384389. Hanover, N.H.: Tuck School of Business at Dartmouth.

English, William B., and J. Nellie Liang. 2020. "Designing the Main Street Lending Program: Challenges and Options." Working Paper 64. Washington: Hutchins Center on Fiscal and Monetary Policy at Brookings.

Federal Reserve System Board of Governors. 2020. *Financial Stability Report May 2020*. Washington: Author.

Ganz, Elliott, and David Smith. 2020. "It's Not Time for a Government Bankruptcy Facility." *RealClear Markets*, June 15. https://www.realclearmarkets.com/articles/2020/06/15/its_not_time_for_a_government_bankruptcy_facility_496152.html#:~:text=As%20businesses%20deplete%20their%20cash,facility%20to%20finance%20bankrupt%20companies.

Gertner, Robert, and David Scharfstein. 1991. "A Theory of Workouts and the Effects of Reorganization Law." *Journal of Finance* 46, no. 4: 1189–222.

Haddad, Valentin, Alan Moreira, and Tyler Muir. 2020. "When Selling Becomes Viral: Disruptions in Debt Markets in the COVID-19 Crisis and the Fed's Response." Working Paper 27168. Cambridge, Mass.: National Bureau of Economic Research.

He, Zhiguo, and Arvind Krishnamurthy. 2013. "Intermediary Asset Pricing." *American Economic Review* 103, no. 2: 732–70.

Krishnamurthy, Arvind, and Annette Vissing-Jorgensen. 2011. "The Effects of Quantitative Easing on Interest Rates: Channels and Implications for Policy." *Brookings Papers on Economic Activity*, Fall, 215–87.

Leland, Hayne. 1994. "Corporate Debt Value, Bond Covenants, and Optimal Capital Structure." *Journal of Finance* 49, no. 4: 1213–52.

Mian, Atif, and Amir Sufi. 2009. "The Consequences of Mortgage Credit Expansion: Evidence from the U.S. Mortgage Default Crisis." *Quarterly Journal of Economics* 124, no. 4: 1449–96.

Myers, Stewart C. 1977. "Determinants of Corporate Borrowing." *Journal of Financial Economics* 5, no. 2: 147–75.

Nozawa, Yoshio, and Yancheng Qiu. 2020. "The Corporate Bond Market Reaction to the COVID-19 Crisis." Working Paper. https://papers.ssrn.com/sol3/papers.cfm?abstract_id=3579346.

Shleifer, Andrei, and Robert W. Vishny. 1992. "Liquidation Values and Debt Capacity: A Market Equilibrium Approach." *Journal of Finance* 47, no. 4: 1343–66.

Skeel, David. 2020. *Bankruptcy and the Coronavirus.* Washington: Brookings Institute. https://www.brookings.edu/wp-content/uploads/2020/04/ES-4.21.2020-DSkeel-2.pdf.

Stein, Jeremy C. 2020. "An Evaluation of the Fed-Treasury Credit Programs." Webinar, Bendheim Center for Finance, May 11. https://bcf.princeton.edu/event-directory/covid19_15/.

Vayanos, Dimitri, and Jean-Luc Vila. Forthcoming. "A Preferred-Habitat Model of the Term Structure of Interest Rates." *Econometrica.*

White, Michelle J. 1989. "The Corporate Bankruptcy Decision." *Journal of Economic Perspectives* 3, no. 2: 129–51.

Comments and Discussion

COMMENT BY
BEN S. BERNANKE Brunnermeier and Krishnamurthy have provided an insightful analysis of federal credit policies during the pandemic crisis, especially those implemented by the Federal Reserve. Policymakers, responding to an unexpected crisis under great time pressure, have mostly focused on the operational details of their programs. It is very useful to have first-rate financial economists like Brunnermeier and Krishnamurthy think through the rationale and design of credit policies from first principles.

Their paper is actually broader than their title suggests, in that the authors consider a variety of actual and potential interventions besides emergency lending to corporations, including the Federal Reserve's response to the financial market crisis in March 2020 and strategies for supporting smaller firms. In that spirit, I will discuss this paper in the broader context of the full range of recent Federal Reserve financial and credit-market interventions. (I exclude monetary policy actions.) In particular, building on measures taken during the 2007–2009 global financial crisis (GFC), the Federal Reserve in the current episode has gone well beyond classic lender-of-last-resort doctrine by becoming a market maker of last resort and providing a credit-market backstop for nonfinancial borrowers. These responses are appropriate and constructive given the exigencies of the current situation, and I commend Federal Reserve Chair Jay Powell and colleagues for their rapid and proactive response. Still, we have a lot to learn about these new types of interventions, including how well they work and how they may change the roles and the capacity of the Fed and other central banks in the future.

FEDERAL RESERVE NONMONETARY INTERVENTIONS: BEYOND BAGEHOT The Federal Reserve and other central banks have three broad responsibilities: (1) conducting monetary policy to meet macroeconomic objectives, which

489

in the era of the effective lower bound includes managing not only the short-term policy interest rate but also tools like forward guidance and quantitative easing; (2) regulating and supervising the financial system; and (3) maintaining broad financial stability. Historically, central banks fulfilled this third responsibility largely by serving as a *lender of last resort to the financial system*, in the sense of Bagehot (1873). Banks and similar institutions engage in maturity transformation, borrowing short and lending long, which makes them subject to runs when short-term funding providers lose confidence. Left unchecked, runs may result in asset fire sales, credit contraction, and, possibly, failures of even fundamentally solvent institutions. By standing ready to lend liberally against collateral to solvent institutions—the Bagehot doctrine—central banks can help end panics, or at least buy time for government or the banks themselves to find solutions.

The Federal Reserve was created by the US Congress in 1913, a time when banks dominated credit markets, primarily to serve as a lender of last resort to the banking system. The Fed's normal lending powers were accordingly restricted to banks. In the GFC, the Fed faced a mismatch between its authorities and the needs of the financial system. Some of the most severe liquidity problems occurred at nonbank financial institutions ("shadow banks"), which by the time of the crisis had become a large part of the US credit system. However, by invoking emergency lending powers granted by Section 13(3) of the Federal Reserve Act and by using other authorities, such as the ability to execute currency swaps with foreign central banks, the Fed provided liquidity (directly or indirectly) to a wide range of financial institutions.

Although the pandemic crisis is not centered in the financial system, at least not so far, the severity of the shock and the attendant uncertainty has created financial strains. The Federal Reserve has accordingly replicated most of the GFC playbook to provide liquidity to financial institutions. It has introduced more favorable terms on the discount window, a standing facility that provides loans to banks and thrifts. In addition, it has resurrected the GFC-era Primary Dealer Credit Facility, which lends to major broker-dealers, a facility that encourages banks to provide liquidity to money market mutual funds, and currency swaps that allow fourteen foreign central banks to supply dollars to institutions in their own jurisdictions. All of these programs were used successfully during the GFC. In this current episode, the Fed has also created a facility that lends to banks against small-business loans issued under the Small Business Administration's Paycheck Protection Program (PPP).

However, the Federal Reserve's nonmonetary interventions in the current crisis go beyond the traditional lender-of-last-resort function in two principal ways. These nontraditional interventions also have precedents in the Fed's response to the GFC, but, reflecting the special features of the coronavirus crisis, in scope and scale they have gone substantially beyond the policies of a dozen years ago.

First, in the pandemic crisis the Federal Reserve has actively served as *market maker of last resort*, standing ready to buy securities in key markets when limits on capital, liquidity, or risk tolerance have inhibited normal market making or arbitrage by private actors. Most notably, in March 2020, the economic uncertainty created by the onset of the pandemic led investors to shed longer-term securities, including Treasury securities, in a rush to deleverage and build liquidity. Constrained by capital requirements, risk limits, and other factors, the dealers who normally serve as market makers could not absorb this sudden increase in supply, leading to intense bouts of illiquidity and volatility (Duffie 2020). Serving as market maker of last resort, the Federal Reserve calmed markets by buying large quantities of Treasury securities and securities backed by residential and commercial mortgages. Additionally, the Fed set up a repurchase agreement (repo) facility that allowed foreign official institutions to borrow against their Treasury holdings, thereby making it unnecessary to sell their securities to raise cash.[1]

Market making of last resort could also describe the Federal Reserve's efforts, dating to September 2019, to stabilize repo markets. The spikes in repo rates and the associated funding shortages that began that month should, in theory, have been arbitraged by banks and other liquidity suppliers, but once again capital rules and other constraints prevented that. The Fed engaged in large term-repo operations that provided needed liquidity to that market and led to calmer conditions. Those efforts continue.

Second, with the approval of Congress and financial support from the Treasury, the Federal Reserve has become the *lender of last resort to nonfinancial borrowers*, backstopping key credit markets. Some of the programs in this category were again reprised from the GFC era, notably the Commercial Paper Funding Facility (CPFF) and the Term Asset-Backed Securities Loan Facility (TALF). But other programs were without precedent, at least in the United States—buying corporate bonds and lending directly (on a longer-term basis) to corporations; lending to states, cities,

---

1. This is known as the FIMA repo facility, for foreign and international monetary authorities.

and counties; and lending (through banks) to medium-size nonfinancial businesses (the Main Street Lending Program).

Like the authors, I interpret this backstopping of private credit markets serving nonfinancial borrowers as a form of after-the-fact insurance. The onset of the pandemic posed very large, and largely undiversifiable, risks for lenders and investors, which—at least initially—appear to have exceeded the risk-bearing capacity of private funding providers. The Federal Reserve's backstopping of these credit markets, with the fiscal support of the Congress and the Treasury, aimed to resuscitate private lending by signaling that the government was prepared to cap creditors' losses and by eliminating "run-like" equilibria in which no one lends for fear that no one else will lend. Because of their signaling aspect, backstop programs of this type may need only to be announced to be successful, with no actual loans required. However, if private lending does not resume, then the backstop program stands ready to provide credit to nonfinancial borrowers.

Table 1, drawn from the Federal Reserve's H.4.1 report as of the day of the conference (June 25, 2020), gives a sense of the relative sizes of the three types of interventions.[2] The top portion of the table shows Fed liquidity injections without Treasury participation, measured as changes from the Fed's holdings from a year earlier. The bottom of the table shows Fed lending programs backed by Treasury capital as authorized by the Coronavirus Aid, Relief, and Economic Security (CARES) Act. In the bottom portion of the table, the left column is net lending by program and the right column shows announced commitments of Treasury capital to each program.

Assigning these programs to my tripartite classification, I interpret the first three lines of the table (Federal Reserve purchases of Treasury bonds and mortgage-backed securities, and repo operations, including FIMA repo operations) as market-making operations of last resort. These interventions are very large, totaling more than $2.5 trillion. The remaining lines in the top of the table—central bank swaps, primary credit (the discount window), the Primary Dealer Credit Facility, and lending to banks to finance PPP loans—I count as traditional lender-of-last-resort activities aimed at providing liquidity to financial institutions. I also count the money market facility in the bottom of the table as a traditional lender-of-last-

---

2. Updates of the H.4.1 report on which this table is based are available weekly at www. federalreserve.gov. For a regularly updated summary of usage of Federal Reserve lending programs provided by the Yale Program on Financial Stability, see https://som.yale.edu/blog/use-of-federal-reserve-programs-06112020.

Table 1. Federal Reserve Interventions

	Change from June 26, 2019	
US Treasury securities	2,073,175	
Mortgage-backed securities	389,459	
Repurchase agreements	73,129	
Central bank liquidity swaps	276,679	
Primary credit	7,101	
Primary dealer credit facility	3,980	
Paycheck Protection Program	59,374	
	Net lending	*Treasury contribution*
Money market facility	21,389	1,500
Commercial paper facility	4,252	10,000
Corporate credit facilities	8,710	37,500
Main Street facility	0	37,500
Municipal facility	1,200	17,500
Term asset-backed securities facility	0	10,000

Source: H.4.1, June 25, 2020.
Note: Figures are in millions of US dollars.

resort facility, even though it is Treasury backed, because it was intended to forestall what looked to be nascent runs on money market mutual funds. These activities add up to just under $375 billion, with the currency swaps accounting for the bulk.

In contrast, credit-backstop loans to the nonfinancial sector—the remaining items in the table—are small, totaling only about $14 billion. This low usage reflects in part that several of these programs are just in the process of taking applications as I write but also that, as discussed, credit-backstop programs can succeed without actually making loans if they reassure private lenders and thereby restore normal activity in markets.

EVALUATING THE THREE TYPES OF INTERVENTIONS I turn now to a brief assessment and discussion of the Federal Reserve's interventions in the pandemic crisis. I will also relate these interventions more directly to the Brunnermeier and Krishnamurthy paper.

Unlike the GFC, the current crisis did not begin in the financial sector, and—at least so far—financial institutions remain well capitalized and liquid. As can be seen in table 1, traditional lender-of-last-resort activity as reflected in borrowing from the discount window (primary credit) and the Primary Dealer Facility has thus been relatively low. During the GFC, to reduce the stigma of borrowing from the discount window, the Fed created a facility that auctioned discount window credit (the Term Auction Facility).[3] It is indicative of the lack of concern about the banking system that, in this episode, the Fed has seen no need to reinstate that facility, even though the discount window likely remains at least somewhat stigmatized.

The Federal Reserve's money market facility, which through banks indirectly provides liquidity to money market mutual funds, has recorded some take-up, helping to reduce pressure on the funds and to limit the risk of runs. Quantitatively, though, the Fed's most important traditional lender-of-last-resort operation this time has been its currency swaps with foreign central banks. Globally, many banks both borrow and lend in US dollars, including branches of foreign banking organizations doing business in the United States but also foreign banks operating in dollar markets elsewhere. Early this year many foreign banks faced a shortage of dollars, both because they lost dollar deposits but also because many customers, concerned about their own cash flows, drew down their dollar-denominated credit lines (Cetorelli, Goldberg, and Ravazzolo 2020). As in the GFC, Fed currency swaps provided foreign central banks with dollars to on-lend to their own commercial banks, significantly reducing this pressure and mitigating spillovers into US markets. As Brunnermeier and Krishnamurthy discuss, while traditional lender-of-last-resort activities were central to the response to the GFC, they have been relatively less important in the current crisis.

The Federal Reserve's market-maker-of-last-resort interventions have also succeeded so far. The authors document that the equity risk premium spiked during the deleveraging crisis in March, then normalized following the Fed's aggressive purchases of Treasury bonds and mortgage-backed securities. Since both the origins of the problem and the Fed's interventions were in fixed-income markets rather than the stock market, it is instructive to look at indicators of the behavior of bond markets. Figure 1 shows two such indicators: (1) the Federal Reserve Bank of St. Louis's Financial Stress Index, which aggregates 18 variables but is dominated by interest rates and interest rate spreads, and (2) the Gilchrist-Zakrajšek (GZ) excess bond premium, a measure of the premium that investors demand (with default risk held constant) to hold corporate bonds.[4] These measures also

---

3. Borrowers from the Term Auction Facility paid what was effectively a market rate rather than the Federal Reserve's discount rate, which may be one reason that it was not stigmatized.

4. The financial stress index is available at https://fred.stlouisfed.org/series/STLFSI2. For a discussion of the GZ excess bond premium, its forecasting properties, and a link to current data see Favara and others (2016).

Figure 1. Financial Market Conditions, 2000–2020

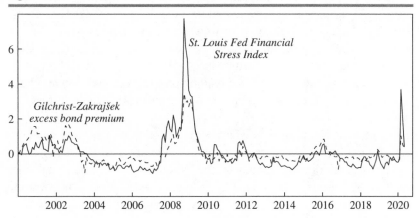

St. Louis Fed Financial
Stress Index

Gilchrist-Zakrajšek
excess bond premium

Sources: Favara and others (2016); Federal Reserve Bank of St. Louis.

show a sharp deterioration in financial conditions in March 2020, though not as severe as in late 2008. Conditions improved significantly after the Fed began large-scale securities purchases. However, according to the bond-based indicators in figure 1, the stress had not entirely reversed by May, in mild contrast to Brunnermeier and Krishnamurthy's finding using the equity risk premium.

The credit-market backstops for nonfinancial borrowers are the most novel interventions and get the most attention in the paper. Like the authors, I focus on two potential recipients of Federal Reserve–Treasury credit: large corporations, with access to stock and bond markets, and smaller businesses, without such access.

As the authors point out, the Federal Reserve's announcement of facilities to buy corporate bonds on the secondary market and to make loans directly to corporations substantially improved the functioning of investment-grade bond markets, even before any actual purchases. The authors see the effects of Fed corporate-bond purchases as analogous to the effects of quantitative easing, but because there can be no portfolio balance effects without actual purchases, this comparison seems inappropriate. A closer analogy is to the Outright Monetary Transactions (OMT) program of the European Central Bank (ECB), which was announced after Mario Draghi's "whatever it takes" promise in July 2012. Under the OMT, the ECB stood ready to buy the sovereign debt of troubled members of the eurozone, subject to some conditions. The announcement signaled that the ECB was willing to intervene to cap losses, and thereby it ruled out bad equilibria in which expectations of default became self-confirming. This signal was sufficient to calm sovereign debt markets—and lowered yields by several percentage points in some cases—without the ECB having to purchase any securities at all. By the same token, the Fed's primary and secondary corporate lending programs did not actually have to extend credit to succeed; it only had to convince private investors that it would lend if necessary.

An interesting question is whether the restoration of normal functioning of corporate credit markets should be the only goal of federal credit policy for large firms. The authors' modeling shows why additional steps may not be necessary. Assuming that the bankruptcy process is operating reasonably well (courts are not too overcrowded and debtor-in-possession, or DIP, financing is available), a Chapter 11 filing allows a troubled firm to reorganize its finances, without damage to its underlying productive capacity. And while bankruptcies do have costs, so does the failure to reorganize a nonviable firm. Accordingly, the authors argue, the best public policy may be to strengthen the bankruptcy process (by ensuring DIP financing is available, for example) and to allow financially stressed large firms to move quickly through Chapter 11.

The authors' basic point is an important one. Early in this crisis, when there was some hope that the pandemic would pass quickly, many saw the goal of policy as "freezing" the economy in its initial state, until safe reopening could occur. Now that the effects of the pandemic seem likely to be longer lasting, policymakers must recognize that not only financial reorganization but also the reallocation of capital and labor from sectors most hurt by the virus to other parts of the economy is likely to become increasingly necessary. That said, I still worry that, without further interventions, too many large firms (from a social perspective) will go bankrupt in the next year or two. First, for most large firms, bankruptcy is not as frictionless as simple models assume. Besides creating direct legal and administrative costs, which will increase if the courts are overwhelmed, bankruptcy may depreciate organizational capital and intangible assets, such as brand names. It also puts into limbo, at least for a time, explicit or implicit contracts with workers, suppliers, and customers (for example, warranties), imposing costs on those counterparties and possibly leading to the breakup of valuable matches. Second, under normal circumstances, the inability to service debt is usually a strong signal about a firm's ability to make profits in the longer run. In the current situation, however, that may or may not be true, depending in large part on the evolution of the pandemic. And while the pandemic and recession may go on for a while, it is certainly possible that better insight will be available relatively soon about the economy's prospects, and in particular about the long-run viability of some major industries, such as brick-and-mortar retail, leisure and hospitality, and tourism. For these reasons, quick recourse to Chapter 11 may not be the best alternative in many cases.

Policy approaches have been suggested that could reduce inefficient bankruptcies in the near term while still responding to market forces in the longer run. For example, in preliminary work, Stein and others (2020) have argued that the government should finance large corporations in need of support by taking a subordinated position (for example, preferred stock plus warrants) rather than by purchasing senior debt. This approach puts less pressure on firms to reorganize in the short run but gives the taxpayer more upside if the firm ultimately proves viable. Metrick (2020) proposes that the government should subsidize business interruption insurance for businesses hit by the pandemic. These insurance policies would be "stapled" to private loans or bonds and would pay the creditor if the pandemic intensifies, as measured by official government shutdowns or predetermined biomedical indicators. Metrick's proposal separates undiversifiable pandemic risk from ordinary business risk, with the government bearing the costs only of the undiversifiable pandemic risk. Especially if such policies were time limited, they could mitigate pandemic-induced bankruptcies in the short run without protecting firms that are nonviable, due to public health concerns or other reasons, in the longer run.

What about small and medium-size enterprises (SMEs), which typically do not have access to public debt markets? Here I agree with the authors that premature bankruptcy—which in most cases closes firms, rather than reorganizing them—can be very costly. The costs extend beyond the direct losses to the owner/entrepreneur, employees, and customers to encompass the broader reduction in aggregate demand and possibly permanent scarring effects, including the erosion of laid-off workers' skills and efficiency losses from greater market concentration. In contrast to their conclusions about larger firms, the authors recommend that credit to SMEs be subsidized—reflecting credit-market imperfections and externalities. This conclusion seems right to me, and their approach has been apparent in the subsidized PPP, for example.

The Federal Reserve is attempting to support SMEs with its Main Street Lending Program (MSLP), in which banks do the underwriting and the Federal Reserve takes a 95 percent share in the resulting loans. Since most SMEs do not have access to public markets, unlike larger firms benefiting from the corporate facilities, the simple announcement of the MSLP cannot by itself solve the problem of restoring normal credit flows to this group of borrowers. The program will accordingly be judged in large part by the amount of lending it does.

Will the MSLP work? As I write, the program has just opened, so conclusions are premature. However, the terms of the program have already been eased several times, and concerns remain that the program will not be sufficiently attractive to banks or borrowers. English and Liang (2020) make this case in a recent paper, suggesting amendments that could lead to greater use of the facility, at some increase in expected costs to the Treasury. Their conclusions seem quite consistent with those of the authors: smaller firms without access to public markets need more help, including subsidies or grants.

A funding-for-lending program, such as the ECB's successful targeted long-term refinancing operations, is an alternative that could be run in parallel with the MSLP. In a funding-for-lending program, the Federal Reserve and the Treasury could provide funds at a very low rate to banks to finance marginal loans made to qualifying borrowers. This approach makes the subsidy explicit and eliminates the need for the Fed to impose, effectively, a second set of underwriting standards and loan terms for loans made under the program.

CONCLUSION The pandemic crisis presents new challenges for economic policymakers. The Federal Reserve has responded creatively, going beyond its traditional lender-of-last-resort role (and expanding its GFC tool kit) to serve as a market maker of last resort and as a backstop for credit markets serving nonfinancial borrowers. Though public health policies are by far the most important for the economy and financial system in this episode, the Federal Reserve (alone and in collaboration with the Treasury) is helping the US and global economies weather this storm. Brunnermeier and Krishnamurthy provide a useful framework to help us better understand the rationales for these new policies and how they might be improved.

REFERENCES FOR THE BERNANKE COMMENT

Bagehot, Walter. 1873. *Lombard Street: A Description of the Money Market.* London: Henry S. King.

Cetorelli, Nicola, Linda S. Goldberg, and Fabiola Ravazzolo. 2020. "How Fed Swap Lines Supported the U.S. Corporate Credit Market amid COVID-19 Strains." Blog post, June 12, Liberty Street Economics, Federal Reserve Bank of New York. https://libertystreeteconomics.newyorkfed.org/2020/06/how-fed-swap-lines-supported-the-us-corporate-credit-market-amid-covid-19-strains.html.

Duffie, Darrell. 2020. "Still the World's Safe Haven? Redesigning the U.S. Treasury Market after the COVID-19 Crisis." Working Paper 62. Washington: Hutchins Center on Fiscal and Monetary Policy at Brookings. https://www. brookings.edu/wp-content/uploads/2020/05/WP62_Duffie_v2.pdf.

English, William, and J. Nellie Liang. 2020. "Designing the Main Street Lending Program: Challenges and Options." Working Paper 64. Washington: Hutchins Center on Fiscal and Monetary Policy at Brookings. https://www.brookings. edu/wp-content/uploads/2020/06/WP64_Liang-English_FINAL.pdf.

Favara, Giovanni, Simon Gilchrist, Kurt F. Lewis, and Egon Zakrajšek. 2016. "Updating the Recession Risk and the Excess Bond Premium." FEDS Notes. Washington: Board of Governors of the Federal Reserve System. https://doi.org/ 10.17016/2380-7172.1836.

Metrick, Andrew. 2020. "Proposal for Dual-Trigger Insurance + Loan (DTIL) Program." Mimeo, Yale University, June 9.

Stein, Jeremy, Sam Hanson, Adi Sunderam, and Eric Zwick. 2020. "An Evaluation of the Fed Treasury Credit Programs." Webinar, Bendheim Center for Finance, Princeton University, May 11. https://bcf.princeton.edu/event-directory/ covid19_15/.

GENERAL DISCUSSION   Nellie Liang began the discussion by noting that this paper has an interesting insight about the importance of trying to help small and medium-sized enterprises (SMEs) avoid high-cost failures. Liang pointed out that the restructuring costs of an SME failure may not be about the size of the firm but instead whether the firm's owner has pledged all of their personal assets to the business. Liang mentioned the Main Street Lending Program, set up by the Federal Reserve and the Treasury, which lends to firms with lower debt burdens, but measures SMEs by the number of employees of the firm. She asked the authors if they had any thoughts on better indicators to use to identify the firms for which extensions of credit would be most helpful.

Wendy Edelberg brought up the importance of who is taking the losses from bankruptcies of small versus large firms. She noted that losses will have to be taken by someone in both cases. For large firms, the losses could be taken by the equity holders and debt holders. For small firms, Edelberg was surprised that the authors suggested that owners would not be able to absorb any losses.

Raghuram Rajan suggested that any thinking about the costs of bankruptcy must account for the unusual circumstances. He commented that many otherwise viable firms will accumulate a lot of debt because they have temporarily shut down. Given this, Rajan proposed that current debt holders would want to restructure quickly. He asked why Brunnermeier and Krishnamurthy do not believe that debt restructuring and bankruptcy will not operate more efficiently now than in normal circumstances. If the market did not become more efficient, Rajan wondered whether making out-of-court restructuring faster and easier would be worth a lot more effort.

Şebnem Kalemli-Özcan said that while it is true that not a lot is known about the financing of SMEs in the United States, there is a lot more known about it in Europe. In Europe, the largest form of financing for these firms is bank loans, not corporate bonds. She argued that this fact implies that it is vital to save all SMEs by closing the credit shortfall. She acknowledged that there is still the question of how long support to SMEs should last. The wage bill of SMEs is equal to 13 percent of United States GDP, she noted, so policy must make the decision whether to save them all at a large expense or find a way to separate solvent firms with liquidity problems from insolvent firms.[1] She wondered what the authors' views were on this option.

Janice Eberly brought up the similarities between the issues in this discussion and the earlier discussion about labor reallocation and zombie firms, mentioning the importance of whether this is a short-run or long-run shock and wondering how much flexibility can be built into policy to account for that uncertainty. Eberly suggested that the authors should respond to Ben Bernanke's points about alternative policies to their proposed debtor-in-possession financing facility.

Markus Brunnermeier began his response to the discussion by thanking discussant Ben Bernanke for providing an outline of the classification of the recent Federal Reserve credit policies. Brunnermeier agreed that Federal Reserve policies played a big role in solving the market liquidity problems in March 2020. He and Krishnamurthy think of the Federal Reserve backstop as insurance, decreasing the chance of problems stemming from multiple equilibria.

Brunnermeier pointed out two uncertainties that are important for the analysis. First, because the future path of the economy is uncertain, there is some value to keeping firms alive. Second, the eventual length of the pandemic itself carries uncertainty. Because of these uncertainties, there is a difference in the incentives for equity owners and planners. Equity owners want to avoid the costs of bankruptcy and maintain their call options on their equity. He argued that the desire of equity owners to keep the firm

---

1. Thomas Drechsel and Şebnem Kalemli-Özcan, "Are Standard Macro Policies Enough to Deal with the Economic Fallout from a Global Pandemic?," policy brief 25, Economics for Inclusive Prosperity, March 2020, https://econfip.org/policy-brief/are-standard-macro-policies-enough-to-deal-with-the-economic-fallout-from-a-global-pandemic/.

alive can distort investment behavior, including worker retention. Instead of keeping their workers, owners may focus their resources on paying off debt and restructuring.

Brunnermeier highlighted that one of the main messages of the paper is that there are two classes of firms, each with a different set of costs to restructuring. For SMEs, these costs are very, very high. However, for larger firms, where management is done by equity holders, Chapter 11 bankruptcy is essentially just replacing one set of equity holders with another set of equity holders. In this second case, the distortions from shortsighted investments are much bigger than the legal costs of bankruptcy.

In regard to Jeremy Stein and others' proposal, Brunnermeier said that it is a very interesting way to maintain flexibility with so much uncertainty about the future.[2] He worried that pricing the warrants in Stein and others' plan would be very challenging. He suggested that taxing firms more heavily later on, effectively making the government an equity owner, would be an easy way to implement the program. It would retain flexibility and also have some future payoff to the government.

Responding to Liang, Brunnermeier acknowledged that, in this paper, size is a proxy for firm type. The important distinction between large firms and SMEs is whether the owner can inject equity into the firm or not. This is what will determine the ease of restructuring. He added that one way to measure this in the data would be to observe the financial resources of the main equity holders to see if they have the wealth to inject equity.

Brunnermeier agreed with Edelberg that who takes the losses is a big question. Citing Chapter 11 bankruptcy and the oil firm example from this paper, he described a process in which a firm filing bankruptcy gets a new name and nothing else in the firm really changes. In this case, the equity holders of the firm would be wiped out and debt would be restructured, but the management would be the same. Brunnermeier said that he and Krishnamurthy found that the cheapest way to get more efficient outcomes for this type of firm is to find ways to reduce the costs of restructuring.

Returning to Kalemli-Özcan's point about Europe, Brunnermeier said that he sees value in learning from Europe, in particular from the European Central Bank's targeted longer-term refinancing operations program, which allows banks to borrow at very low, negative interest rates. He referenced

2. Jeremy Stein, Sam Hanson, Adi Sunderam, and Eric Zwick, "An Evaluation of the Fed Treasury Credit Programs" [webinar], Bendheim Center for Finance, Princeton University, May 11, 2020, https://bcf.princeton.edu/event-directory/covid19_15/.

an earlier proposal that is in the paper for the Federal Reserve to create a similar program to help SMEs get funding and to give banks a strong incentive to participate. Brunnermeier urged that this program should be complemented with use of the countercyclical capital buffer. He said that it is important to have a big enough equity stake as rates would be negative if banks pass along the funding. It is also very easy to issue equity at this time with equity prices being very high. He said that it is important to capitalize on this possibility.

Arvind Krishnamurthy responded to Rajan's comment, saying that a finding of the paper is that the benefits of credit subsidies in today's circumstances are ambiguous. However, he noted that the paper finds that subsidizing and reducing bankruptcy costs is unambiguously beneficial. Krishnamurthy said that if policymakers are deciding where to spend a dollar, he and Brunnermeier believe that the marginal value of the dollar is highest if it is put toward reducing bankruptcy costs. Therefore, he suggested, that would be the place to spend. Krishnamurthy concluded by thanking the commenters and thanking Bernanke for his discussion.